Education of
Exceptional Learners

Education of
Exceptional Learners

THIRD EDITION

FRANK M. HEWETT
University of California, Los Angeles

WITH

STEVEN R. FORNESS
University of California, Los Angeles

Allyn and Bacon, Inc.   BOSTON   LONDON   SYDNEY   TORONTO

To Mike and Julie
and to Rejeana

Illustrations by Steve McAdam

Copyright © 1984, 1977, 1974 by Allyn and Bacon, Inc., 7 Wells Avenue, Newton, Massachusetts 02159.

Library of Congress Cataloging in Publication Data

Hewett, Frank M.
    Education of exceptional learners.

    Bibliography: p.
    Includes index.
    1. Exceptional children—Education.   I. Forness,
Stephen R.   II. Title.
LC3965.H47   1983   371.9   83-15531
ISBN 0-205-08102-9

Series Editor: Jeffery W. Johnston

Printed in the United States of America

10 9 8 7 6 5 4 3 2 1   88 87 86 85 84 83

Contents

Preface   ix

Part One   BACKGROUND DIMENSIONS   1

1 **Historical Origins**   3

Survival   4

Superstition   6

Science   8

Service   11

Helen Keller and Anne Sullivan   22

The Development of Institutional and Public School Programs for
   Exceptional Learners   23

President Kennedy's Commitment to Exceptional Learners   25

Public Law 94–142   26

Summary   29

2 **The Exceptional Learner**   33

What Are the Kinds of Uniqueness that Matter?   34

Who Are Exceptional Learners?   39

What Types of Services Has Special Education Traditionally Provided
   for Exceptional Learners?   54

Summary   58

3 **Flexibility and Social Uniqueness**   61

Flexibility   61

Sociality   62

Intelligence   63

Individualization   64

Flexibility Uniqueness:–Visually Handicapped Individuals   66

v

Flexibility Uniqueness:–Deaf and Hard-of-Hearing
Individuals   71

Flexibility Uniqueness:–Deaf-Blind Individuals   75

Flexibility Uniqueness:–Orthopedically and Other Health Impaired
Individuals   78

Social Uniqueness:–Emotionally Disturbed Individuals   84

Social Uniqueness:–Speech-Impaired Individuals   95

Social Uniqueness:–Economically Disadvantaged and/or Culturally
Different Individuals   99

Summary   104

4   **Intellectual Uniqueness**   109

Individuals with Learning Disabilities   109

Mentally Retarded Individuals: An Overview   120

Mildly Mentally Retarded Individuals   123

Severely Mentally Retarded Individuals   130

Profoundly Mentally Retarded Individuals   137

Gifted Individuals   139

Summary   144

Part Two   DIMENSIONS OF DIFFERENCE   147

5   **Flexibility Characteristics of Exceptional Learners**   149

Visually Handicapped Individuals   150

Hearing-Impaired Individuals   152

Orthopedic and Other Health Impairments   153

Emotionally Disturbed Individuals   155

Speech-Handicapped Individuals   156

Disadvantaged Individuals   157

Individuals with Learning Disabilities   158

Mentally Retarded Individuals   160

Gifted Individuals   162

Early Identification   162

Early Intervention   165

Summary   165

6   Social Characteristics of Exceptional Learners   171

Visually Handicapped Individuals   171
Hearing-Handicapped Individuals   173
Orthopedic and Other Health Impairments   175
Emotionally Disturbed Individuals   176
Speech-Handicapped Individuals   177
Disadvantaged Individuals   178
Individuals with Learning Disabilities   182
Mentally Retarded Individuals   183
Gifted Individuals   188
The Exceptional Learner and the Family   191
Summary   194

7   Intellectual Characteristics of Exceptional Learners   199

Intelligence Testing   199
Visually Handicapped Individuals   205
Hearing-Handicapped Individuals   206
Orthopedic and Other Health Impairments   209
Emotionally Disturbed Individuals   209
Speech-Handicapped Individuals   211
Disadvantaged Individuals   211
Individuals with Learning Disabilities   212
Mentally Retarded Individuals   213
Gifted Individuals   217
Intellectual Assessment of Infants   218
Infant Intervention Programs   221
Preschool Intervention Programs   223
Summary   228

8   Individualization of Exceptional Learners   231

Sex Education and the Exceptional Learner   231
Marriage and Child Bearing   233
Career Development   235
Visually Handicapped Individuals   239
Hearing-Handicapped Individuals   240

Orthopedic and Other Health Impairments   241

Emotionally Disturbed Individuals   242

Speech-Handicapped Individuals   243

Disadvantaged Individuals   244

Individuals with Learning Disabilities   246

Mentally Retarded Individuals   247

Gifted Individuals   252

Summary   252

Part Three   EDUCATIONAL DIMENSIONS   255

9 The Learning Triangle   257

Curriculum   257

Conditions   258

Consequences   259

Flexibility Curriculum   262

Social Curriculum   273

Conditions   283

Consequences   286

Summary   296

10 Making Special Education Work   299

Zero Reject   300

Nondiscriminatory Testing and Classification   303

Individualized and Appropriate Education   309

Least Restrictive Placement   315

Due Process and Parent Participation   322

Model for Implementing Public Law 94–142   328

Summary and Conclusion   337

References   339

Author Index   403

Categorical Index   413

Subject Index   415

Preface

The concept of exceptional *learner* has guided us in the third edition of *Education of Exceptional Learners* as it did in the first two editions. Our charge has been to emphasize the potential for change and growth for every exceptional individual, not the restrictions and limits imposed by handicapping conditions. For many exceptional individuals, this latter emphasis has been closely associated with the traditional labelling and categorization process. Over the past two decades, the stigma and negative implications of labels given to exceptional individuals and the categories into which they have been placed have been soundly criticized. Yet we still use labels and categories today and depend on their usefulness in communication, legislation, and program planning as we have always done.

In the first two editions of *Education of Exceptional Learners*, the authors spoke of taking a "transitional journey" away from labels and categories and of moving toward a noncategorical approach to special education. This may have appeared an admirable goal at the time, but it was probably unrealistic. It is our feeling today that we can live with labels and categories, and that the real challenge is not to eliminate them but to *unify* them. That is probably what we came closest to accomplishing in the previous two editions with the concept of exceptional learner and hope we have further accomplished in this edition.

Our framework for unification is the same as in previous editions: flexibility, sociality, intelligence, and individualization. However, we have incorporated this framework from the beginning of our discussion of exceptional learners. Flexibility uniqueness concerns the visually handicapped, deaf and hard-of-hearing, deaf-blind, and orthopedically and other health impaired. Social uniqueness refers to the emotionally disturbed, speech impaired, and economically disadvantaged and/or culturally different. Intellectual uniqueness focuses on the learning disabled, mentally retarded, and gifted.

The third edition of *Education of Exceptional Learners* has been shortened and streamlined. Part One, *Background Dimensions*, begins with a look at historical attitudes, events, and individuals that relate to the development of the field of special education. Chapters 2, 3, and 4 introduce the exceptional learner. Part Two, *Dimensions of Difference*, includes all exceptional learners for a discussion of flexibility, sociality, intelligence, and individualization (chapters 5, 6, 7, and 8). Part Three, *Educational Dimensions*, concludes the text with chapter 9 on special education curriculum and chapter 10, which is devoted to mainstreaming and major issues related to Public Law 94–142.

As in previous editions, the authors are grateful to a number of colleagues for their assistance. Carol Reynard, David McGee, Trisha Mettam, and Steve Funderburk, M.D., were particularly helpful in this regard. Thanks also to Grace Sheldrick of Wordsworth Associates for her help.

F.M.H.
S.R.F.

PART ONE

BACKGROUND DIMENSIONS

CHAPTER 1

Historical Origins

This text is about exceptional learners and special education. The term *exceptional* refers to physical, social, and intellectual uniqueness; the term *learners* refers to individuals who are waiting to be taught; and the term *special education* refers to adaptations of typical teaching approaches made to accommodate the uniqueness of the exceptional learner. In the chapters that follow, we discuss exceptional learners and their unique learning characteristics. We also discuss special educational approaches used with them. Finally, we deal with the field of special education, its rapid development, and its issues and concerns.

Unfortunately, the term *special education* only recently acquired widespread relevance for the exceptional learner. The same can be said for the term *learner*. For a long time before exceptional individuals were provided with the opportunities for an education or were truly considered candidates for learning, they were subjected to abuse and neglect. Much of this chapter is about that abuse and neglect. Fortunately, however, examples of acceptance and caring and attempts to understand and help the exceptional learner have always existed, albeit infrequently. This frequency has increased markedly over the past two hundred years and remarkably in the United States during the past two decades. It is hoped that a review of the attitudes toward and treatment of the exceptional learner over the past three thousand years will provide a meaningful background for discussion of current knowledge about exceptional learners and the field of special education that has developed to serve them.

In chapters 2 and 3, we identify a number of categories into which exceptional learners have been typically placed, depending on their particular uniqueness. However, such categorization is a fairly recent practice. Throughout most of history, perhaps the only categories that mattered were the *weak*, the *odd*, and the *poor*. In addition, children received little special attention or consideration separate from adults. Most physically defective infants and children died early in life, either from infanticide (being put to death) or from an inability to cope with the rigors of the environment. Children who were peculiar in their behavior were treated no differently than adults who were peculiar. As we shall see, children have only recently become individuals in their own right—physically, socially, and emotionally. Most of this chapter concerns the plight of individuals subjected to environmental demands for survival and adaptation and judged, accepted, or rejected by others, regardless of age or size.

This discussion deals with four critical aspects of the plight of the handicapped throughout history: *survival*, or the threat of harsh treatment or annihilation by the physical and social environments; *superstition*, or the wide range of beliefs related to the appearance and behavior of the handicapped; *science*, or attempts to understand and approach exceptionality in a natural, lawful, and objective manner; and *service*, or the provision of humane treatment, care, education, and social acceptance.

Survival

The Treatment of Handicapped Children in Early History

In the earliest primitive societies, physical abnormalities were not common beyond infancy because most tribes permitted the killing of a newborn if sickly or if the mother died during the birth process. Infants born under unlucky circumstances might also be killed. The ancient Egyptians were unique in forbidding infanticide. Parents guilty of this crime were required to hold the dead child in their arms for three days and nights (Durant, 1966).

During the Greek and Roman period, infanticide was a common practice. Ruthless eugenics was practiced in the Greek state of Sparta. Every child was vulnerable to a father's right of infanticide and to the judgment of a state council. Infants who appeared defective were thrown from a cliff on Mount Taygetus and left to die on the jagged rocks below. In Athens, infants who were of doubtful parentage or weak or deformed were left in large earthenware vessels near a temple where they would either perish from exposure or animal attack or be rescued for adoption by passersby.

The Roman practice of infanticide permitted the father to expose to death any deformed or female child. Eight days after birth, the child formally became a member of the most basic Roman institution, the patriarchal family, by means of a solemn ceremony. The father, however, continued to have the power of life and death over his children and could sell them into slavery. Abandonment of children was a widespread practice; Seneca records that professional beggars often collected such children, deliberately maimed them, and then used them to solicit alms from charitable passersby (Barclay, 1959). If this practice was truly profitable, it suggests that a compassionate attitude toward deformity must have existed among some of the Roman populace. History suggests that at least four Roman rulers were mentally ill: Nero, Commodus, Elegabulus, and Caligula (Wallin, 1955). Commodus was known to gather crippled individuals together periodically and use them for target practice with a bow and arrow (Durant, 1944).

Aristotle in 355 B.C. wrote, "Men that are deaf are also speechless; that is, they can make vocal sounds, but they cannot speak." He later stated, "Let it be a law that nothing imperfect should be brought up." It appears that the "imperfection" of the deaf and this latter pronouncement led to the destruction of many deaf children by the Spartans, Athenians, and Romans (Moores, 1978).

The Middle Ages brought war, poverty, and barbarism. Although the mentally ill were considered possessed by evil spirits, widespread torture and mass execution of "witches" and

Figure 1-1.

"sorceresses" did not appear for some time (Durant, 1950). During the sixteenth and seventeenth centuries, many mentally ill individuals wandered through the countryside seeking shelter
in stables and pigsties. They were mocked and beaten and, if apprehended, were placed with
murderers and other criminals in chains; the criminal served his term and was released, but some
of the mentally sick were never set free.

The Industrial Revolution brought many children into factories as unskilled laborers. There
were no safeguards for their welfare or lives, and work demands were often extreme. Discipline
in the factories was maintained by blows and kicks. Many children were deformed as a result of
heavy labor or accidents, and some even killed themselves (Durant & Durant, 1965). The Ulster
Institution for the Deaf and Dumb in Belfast recorded that "a little mute in his eighth year, a day
scholar, was unfortunately killed at one of the factories before he could have known the revealed
will of God" (Pritchard, 1963, p. 7).

As we shall see, threats to survival began to decrease late in the eighteenth century. But
first, let us consider an aspect of history that often bore directly on the survival of the
handicapped—superstition.

Superstition

How Did Stone Age Cavemen Practice Psychiatry?

The earliest "psychiatry" was practiced by Stone Age cavemen some half-million years ago. In cases of mental illness associated with severe headaches or convulsive disorders, a crude operation called *trephining* was often performed. A circular area of the skull was chipped away with a stone instrument, thus permitting the escape of the evil spirit that was thought to be responsible. Since it appears that some patients survived such treatment, the operation may have been successful and actually relieved a certain amount of pressure on the brain (Coleman, 1972).

Early Beliefs About the Causes of Mental Illness

The primitive world was filled with concern for good and evil spirits. In some cases, physically sound individuals who became deranged and behaved differently from members of their community were thought to possess supernatural power. If they were possessed by a good spirit, then they were naturally admired and revered; even if the spirit was considered evil, the individual might be indulged in order to appease the spirit and prevent its revenge. This indulgence and reverence lasted only until the notion was conceived of driving out evil spirits through ceremonial rites conducted by individuals of high station, such as priests (Zilboorg & Henry, 1941).

The writings of many ancient peoples reveal a belief that mental disorders were the results of demonic possession. Among the ancient Hebrews, such disorders were thought to represent the wrath and punishment of God. The primary treatment consisted of exorcism, an attempt to drive the spirit from the possessed through prayer, incantations, noisemaking, purgatives, flogging, or starving (Coleman, 1972).

The Babylonian world was filled with hostile demons who might hide in crannies or slip through doors and pounce on their victims in the form of illness or madness when the sacred protection of the gods was absent. Giants, dwarfs, and cripples sometimes were considered able to turn "the evil eye" on their enemies, who often tried to protect themselves with magic amulets, talismans, and charms. Early Babylonian writings were largely devoted to describing magic formulas for eliminating demons and avoiding evil (Durant, 1954).

The Greeks believed that mental illness was caused by the gods taking away the mind. Treatment of the mentally ill was attempted at the Aesculapian temples, where religious ceremonies were conducted calling on the gods to appear and produce a miraculous cure (Zilboorg & Henry, 1941). All sickness was considered the result of possession by an alien spirit, and ceremonies of purification were considered essential. From time to time, homes, temples, camps, and even entire cities were "purified" by water, smoke, or fire (Durant, 1966). Also among the Greeks, blindness was traditionally considered divine punishment for sin and, as with other ancient peoples, it was regarded as the worst possible affliction. The belief that blindness is a divine punishment for sin, particularly sexual transgression, was not restricted to ancient times; indeed, it can be traced through history to modern times.

During the Middle Ages, the rise of deep religious convictions throughout the world produced some increase in humanitarian care for the retarded, mentally ill, and physically handicapped. But the causes of deviant behavior were increasingly linked to the influence of Satan and extreme measures, such as flogging, starvation, and torture, were often used to punish the "devil" residing in a deranged individual. This particularly affected the mentally ill. Hostility to science grew intense; psychiatry became the study of the ways and means of the devil and his cohorts.

The Malleus Maleficarum

In 1484, Pope Innocent VIII appointed two Dominican brothers, Johann Sprenger and Heinrich Kramer, as "Inquisitors of Heretical Depravities." Their charge was to investigate all persons considered heretics, without regard to rank or high estate. To bolster their position, the priests authored a text on witchcraft, *Malleus Maleficarum* (The Witches' Hammer), which declared that anyone who did not believe in witches was either in honest error or polluted with heresy. The text described various types of witches and how they might be identified, and presented legal procedures for examining and sentencing witches. Published sometime between 1487 and 1489, the book went through nineteen editions during the next three hundred years. It served as the keynote of the law for more than two centuries, and otherwise enlightened individuals endorsed its doctrine.

Although not all who were accused of heresy under the provisions of this text were mentally ill, hundreds of thousands of deranged individuals were accused of being witches, sorceresses, or bewitched. There were few arguments that could hold up against the book. Individuals were viewed as responsible for their actions. If they succumbed to an illness that perverted their perception, imagination, and intellectual functions, they did so of their own free will.

The tradition of the *Malleus Maleficarum* did not die easily or quietly. The Puritans carried it into the Commonwealth of Massachusetts and, although the last witch in Germany was beheaded in 1775 and the last in Switzerland in 1782, as late as the twentieth century (1928) a Reverend Montagne Summers, who translated the *Malleus Maleficarum*, supported its doctrine.

> There can be no doubt that had this most excellent tribunal continued to enjoy its full
> prerogative and the full exercise of its salutary powers, the world at large would be in
> a far happier and far more orderly position today (Zilboorg & Henry, 1941, p. 154).*

During the eighteenth century, the mentally ill were increasingly regarded as "sick." However, demonic possession continued to be an explanation for disturbed behavior by some.

This seven-year-old girl, the offspring of an aristocratic family whose father remarried after an unhappy first matrimony, offended her "noble and God-fearing" stepmother by her peculiar behavior.

Worst of all, she would not join in the prayers and was panic stricken when taken to the black-robed preacher in the dark and gloomy chapel. She avoided contact with the people by hiding in closets

*Reprinted from A HISTORY OF MEDICAL PSYCHOLOGY by Gregory Zilboorg & George W. Henry. By permission of W. W. Norton & Company, Inc. Copyright 1941 by W. W. Norton & Company, Inc. Copyright renewed 1968 by Margaret Stone Zilboorg and George W. Henry.

or running away from home. The local physician had nothing to offer beyond declaring that she might be insane.

She was placed in the custody of a minister known for his rigid orthodoxy. The minister, who saw in her ways the machination of a "baneful and infernal" power, used a number of would-be therapeutic devices. He laid her on a bench and beat her with a cat-o-nine-tails. He locked her in a dark pantry. He subjected her to a period of starvation. He clothed her in a frock of burlap. Under these circumstances, the child did not last long. She died after a few months, and everybody felt relieved. The minister was amply rewarded for his efforts by her parents. (Kanner, 1962, p. 98)

Throughout history, there have been people who viewed mental illness as a disease and not the result of possession by demons. However, their voices were rarely heard by the majority before the last two hundred years. Let us now consider the rise of a scientific approach to exceptionality.

Science

Challengers of Superstitious Beliefs About Mental Illness

During the fourth and fifth centuries B.C., Hippocrates challenged the belief that illness was the result of the anger of the gods. He also dismissed the notion that epilepsy, considered "the sacred disease," was divinely caused. According to Hippocrates:

> It thus appears to me to be in no way more divine, nor more sacred than other diseases, but has a natural cause from which it originates like other affliction. . . . If you cut open the head, you will find the brain humid, full of sweat, and smelling badly. And in this way you may see that it is not a god which injures the body but disease. (Zilboorg & Henry, 1941, pp. 43–44)*

In 1584, Reginald Scot wrote a book entitled *Discovery of Witchcraft* that condemned the practice of torturing and burning individuals suspected of being witches. In it, he daringly denied the existence of demons and evil spirits as causes of deranged behavior.

> You must know that the effects of sickness on men, and still more on women, are almost unbelievable. Some of these persons imagine, confess, and maintain that they are witches and are capable of performing extraordinary miracles through the arts of witchcraft; others, due to the same mental disorders, imagine strange and impossible things. (Castiglioni, 1946, p. 253)

King James of England, however, personally condemned Scot's position and prolonged the influence of demonology by ordering the book seized and burned. Unfortunately, as a result, Scot's work had little effect (Coleman, 1972).

Concern with Measuring Intelligence

In the sixteenth and early seventeenth centuries, attempts were made to describe mental retardation and mental illness from a more psychological point of view. In Fitz-Herbert's *New Nature Brevium*, a mental retardate is defined as follows:

> And he who shall be said to be a sot (i.e., simpleton) and idiot from his birth is such a person who cannot account or remember 20 pence, nor can tell who was his father or mother, now how old he is, etc. so as it may appear that he hath no understanding or reason of what shall be for his profit nor what for his loss. But if he hath understanding, that he know and understand his letters, and do read by teaching or information of another man, then it seemeth he is not a sot nor a natural idiot. (Hilliard, 1965, pp. 2–3).

The quest for measurement devices to identify and classify individuals according to intellectual potential began seriously at the close of the nineteenth century. Alfred Binet and Theodore Simon were commissioned in 1904 by the French Ministry of Education to develop a test to determine if a child suspected of mental retardation should be transferred to a special class. The label "mentally deficient" would be applied when a child who demonstrated limited intelligence was unable to profit from regular-class instruction.

In 1916, Lewis Terman translated and revised the Binet-Simon test and restandardized it on American children. The overall impact of the Terman adaptation was revolutionary. The I.Q.

Figure 1-2.
Alfred Binet, 1857–1911.

score began to be accepted as a precise and valid indication of an individual's intelligence. In addition, thousands of children never before considered retarded but who fell below the normal range were "discovered." Chapters 7 and 10 deal with the controversial history of the I.Q. test in the United States.

The Influence of Science on Mental Retardation in the Twentieth Century

A scientifically oriented eugenics movement in the early part of this century led to an increase in negative attitudes toward the retarded. In the United States, Goddard and Dugdale traced the descendants of the Juke and Kalikak families, in which there were identifiable mentally defective individuals, and revealed that a large number of their ancestors had been criminals, prostitutes, and paupers.

In 1903, the American Breeders Association was formed, and a Committee on Eugenics was appointed in 1908. This committee included an impressive group of American scientists—David Starr Jordan, Alexander Graham Bell, and Luther Burbank (Sarason & Sarason 1969)—who were convinced that defects in the central nervous system that caused mental retardation were transmitted from one generation to the next. They studied the "best practical means for cutting off the defective germ-plasm in the American population." Segregation and sterilization were considered the two most acceptable; although the Committee ruled out infanticide or euthanasia, they went on record as admiring the ancient Greek state of Sparta for "her courage in so rigorously applying so practical a system of selection."

Fernald (1904) was an outspoken opponent of allowing the mentally retarded to move freely in society. In an address to the National Conference of Charities and Corrections in 1904, he stated his reasons:

> The adult males become the town loafers and incapables, the irresponsible pests of the neighborhood, petty thieves, purposeless destroyers of property, incendiaries and very frequently violators of women and little girls. It is well known that feebleminded women and girls are very liable to become sources of unspeakable debauchery and licentiousness which pollutes the whole life of the young boys and youth of the community.

Despite this ominous opinion, Fernald was to find himself proven wrong over the next decade as he studied the adjustment patterns of retarded adults paroled from institutions. The above statement simply could not be justified. The individuals studied did not prove to be immoral or a threat to others.

In the 1920s and 1930s, the field of medicine began investigation of brain injury at birth, Down's Syndrome (then known as mongolism), and endocrine disorders as they related to mental retardation. The Great Depression and World War II delayed progess in all areas of special education, but by the late 1940s demanding parents, enthusiastic professionals, and federal, state, and private funding gave new impetus to progress in the area of mental retardation. Scientific investigations of mental retardation increased significantly in the 1960s due to federal mandates set in motion by President John F. Kennedy. Scientific advances in the field of genetics also led to a reduction of birth defects involving all types of handicapping conditions.

Sigmund Freud and the Uniqueness of Childhood

The work of Sigmund Freud had a significant effect on the fields of child development and special education in the twentieth century. In addition to his theories of personality development, which influenced child rearing practices, psychotherapeutic approaches with emotionally disturbed individuals, and special education practices, Freud helped to establish children as uniqe persons in their own right and not miniature versions of adults. Childhood interactions and relationships with others were seen as critical in determining adult adjustment.

It is surprising how long it took for children to be recognized as unique and for the experiences of childhood to be related to success or a lack of it in later life. The nineteenth century saw rapid changes in the reduction of physical abuse, exploitation, and neglect of children, but an understanding of the psychology of childhood and a concern for the effects of early experiences on personality development was slow to emerge. The nineteenth century yielded increased respect for the physical and social rights of children; respect for their psychological and emotional rights increased in the twentieth century, with Freud making a major contribution.

The disadvantaged status of children is strikingly illustrated by the medical treatment afforded them as late as the early part of this century. During the nineteenth century, there were no pediatricians, and physicians in general refused to treat children leaving this to mothers or relatives. There were high death rates among children from birth to five years of age, and some families had ten to twelve pregnancies in an effort to insure that half of the children born would survive. By 1900, there were only 50 pediatricians in the entire United States. A further illustration of how children were perceived is seen in the fact that the Society for the Prevention of Cruelty to Animals was founded in 1866, eight years before the founding of the Society for Prevention of Cruelty to Children. (Alexander, 1980)

Service

Early Examples of Humane Treatment of Exceptional Learners

As mentioned earlier, if an individual in primitive times was thought to be possessed by a spirit, he or she might be admired, revered, and indulged. It appears that in ancient China a tradition of kindness and understanding existed toward the mentally ill (Zilboorg & Henry, 1941). Furthermore, contrary to the belief of some people in the West, the ideal of individual human worth first emerged in the Orient, not in the Middle East. In ancient China, it was not uncommon to find blind scholars, soothsayers, storytellers, and musicians. Confucious, for example, was tutored in music by a blind musician (Kirtley, 1975).

In Rome, there were a limited number of blind musicians, poets, lawyers, and scholars. Cicero was tutored in philosophy and geometry by a blind scholar. History records that the

Roman army administered aid to its blinded veterans and that the Egyptians provided the blind with gainful employment so that they could lead independent lives. The Egyptians also provided a twelve-year course of study in a university for some blind individuals.

In the first century A.D. Aretaeus was perhaps two thousand years ahead of his time when, in describing various disturbed mental states, he paid particular attention to what patients thought and felt. In the second century A.D., Soranus also considered the thoughts and feelings of the mentally ill important. He attacked those who placed patients in darkness, deprived them of food and water, and treated them as "ferocious beasts." His methods of treatment are handed down to us in detail:

> Maniacs must be placed in a moderately lighted room which is of moderate tempera-
> ture and where tranquility is not disturbed by any noise. No paintings should adorn
> the walls. . . . Much tact and discretion should be employed in directing attention to
> their faults; sometimes misbehavior should be overlooked or met with indulgence; at
> other times it requires a slightly better reprimand and an explanation of the
> advantages derived from proper conduct. (Zilboorg & Henry, 1941, pp. 81–82)*

The Arab world had inherited predominantly Greek scientific thought; in the eleventh century, Avicenna stands as one of the rare enlightened individuals of this era who approached mental illness in a rational and remarkably creative manner. The case below shows his unique treatment of a mental patient.

A certain prince . . . was afflicted with melancholia, and suffered from the delusion that he was a cow . . . he would low like a cow, causing annoyance to everyone . . . crying, "Kill me so that a good stew may be made of my flesh." Finally . . . he would eat nothing . . . Avicenna was persuaded to take the case. First of all he sent a message to the patient bidding him be of good cheer because the butcher was coming to slaughter him, whereat . . . the sick man rejoiced. Some time afterwards, Avicenna holding a knife in his hand, entered the sickroom saying, "Where is this cow that I may kill it?" The patient lowed like a cow to indicate where he was. By Avicenna's orders he was laid on the ground, bound hand and foot. Avicenna then felt him all over and said, "He is too lean and not ready to be killed; he must be fattened." Then they offered him suitable food of which he now partook eagerly, and gradually he gained strength, got rid of his delusion, and was completely cured. (Browne, 1921, pp. 88–89)

Although exploitation cannot be considered service, the well-to-do Romans began the practice of accepting "natural fools" or imbeciles into their homes, where they functioned as buffoons or objects of amusement at social gatherings (Wallin, 1955). During the Middle Ages, some mental defectives gained prestige as court fools or jesters. They were even exalted as

*Reprinted from A HISTORY OF MEDICAL PSYCHOLOGY by Gregory Zilboorg & George W. Henry. By permission of W. W. Norton & Company, Inc. Copyright 1941 by W. W. Norton & Company, Inc. Copyright renewed 1968 by Margaret Stone Zilboorg and George W. Henry.

Figure 1–3.

"heavenly infants" or "infants of the good God" who enjoyed the special favor of the Almighty and whose jabberings were regarded as heavenly communication.

Japan, in the Middle Ages, trained the blind in music, literature, religion, acupuncture, and massage. The blind acquired a virtual monopoly in the latter vocation. In Belgium in the fifteenth century, a shrine was established at Gheel where pilgrims from every part of the civilized world came to receive treatment for mental illness. Many of the pilgrims remained in Gheel and lived with the inhabitants, who came to consider it a natural thing to accept them into their community and homes (Coleman, 1972).

During the sixteenth century, Suleiman the Magnificent searched the Turkish empire for gifted Christian youth to provide them with education in the Moslem faith and in war, art, science, and philosophy. Within a generation after the start of this program for the gifted, the Ottoman empire became a great power in art, science, culture, and war and even attempted to conquer all of Europe (Sumption & Luecking, 1960).

The Development of Approaches for Teaching the Blind and Deaf

During the sixteenth and seventeenth centuries, the role of the humanitarian teacher or special educator was established. In 1651, Harsdorffer in Germany produced wax tablets on which the blind could write, and Bernouilli in Switzerland invented a frame for guiding a pencil on paper. In the eighteenth century, Valentine Huay introduced embossed print for use by the blind. Dedicated to proving that the blind could and should be educated, he opened a school in France. In a 1747 paper entitled "Letter on the Blind for the Use of Those Who See," Diderot stated that our ideas of right and wrong are not derived from God but from our sensory experience. He also suggested that the blind might be taught to read by touch (Durant & Durant, 1965).

Louis Braille was the most important figure in the history of work for the blind (Kirtley, 1975). Before he was four years old, Braille accidentally blinded himself in one eye while playing with an awl. The sight of the other eye was soon lost as well. Ten years later, Braille began to develop a revolutionary system of reading and writing for the blind. This method was based on a discovery of Charles Barbier, a veteran of the Napoleonic wars. Barbier had devised a system of "nightwriting" for the exchange of secret intelligence by the military in war zones at night. Messages were "read" through the sense of touch rather than vision. Braille recognized the immense potential of Barbier's technique and by 1834 had refined it for practical use. By the end of the century, the Braille system had become the universally accepted means of written communication for the blind. There had been earlier attempts to develop embossed printing materials for the blind, but these had involved raised Roman lettering. The Braille system, which used point stimuli, was successful because the fingers can discriminate such stimuli far more readily than they can discern the line properties of ordinary letters (Zilboorg & Henry, 1941).

Ponce de Leon is credited for being the first teacher of the deaf (Moores, 1978). He was a Benedictine monk who tutored deaf children of Spanish nobility during the 1500s. As would be

Figure 1-4.
Samuel Gridley Howe, 1801–1876.

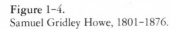

the case over the next several hundred years, the handicapped children of the wealthy and powerful were the first to receive special education. Eventually, the wealthy and powerful would step forward in support of special education for the masses. President John F. Kennedy, who had a retarded sister, is a case in point.

The 1600s saw development in communication techniques for the deaf. Bonet published a system of teaching based on finger spelling, which was elaborated by Pereira in the following century. Pereira also is credited with devising the lipreading method. In 1760, Abbe de l'Epee opened the first public school for handicapped children who were deaf and poor, the National Institute for Deaf-Mutes in Paris. Abbe de l'Epee was convinced that speech was not necessary in educating the deaf. In Germany, however, Samuel Heinicke believed that precise thought was possible only if speech were present and stressed that the deaf must develop language. The controversy surrounding the relation of speech and language to intelligence and to the education of the deaf still exists, as we shall see.

Samuel Gridley Howe was one of the first physicians in the United States to develop a keen interest in the education of blind and deaf children (Kanner, 1960). His phenomenal success with one of his pupils, Laura Bridgmen, a deaf-blind-mute, earned him international fame. Anne Sullivan, who later became the teacher of Helen Keller, also was his pupil. Gallaudet College for the Deaf in Washington, D.C., is the only college for the deaf in the world. It was named after Thomas Hopkins Gallaudet, a pioneer in education for the deaf. Gallaudet's interest in the problems of the deaf began in 1812 when he became acquainted with a deaf child and attempted to teach her.

Figure 1-5.
Thomas Hopkins Gallaudet, 1787-1815.

A statue of Gallaudet stands today in front of Gallaudet College. It is the work of the sculptor, Daniel Chester French, who also carved the marble statue of Abraham Lincoln that dominates the interior of the Lincoln Memorial in Washington, D.C. French became so intrigued with the communication methods used by deaf individuals while working on the Gallaudet statue that he carved Lincoln's hands making the manual signs for Lincoln's initials. The left hand is a closed fist for the letter *A* and the right hand has the thumb and index finger forming an *L*.

Individuals Responsible for Reforms in the Treatment of the Mentally Ill

We come now to an event that had far-reaching effects on the treatment of the handicapped. The French Revolution awakened the sense of an individual's social responsibility and, even more importantly, the sense of the community's responsibility toward its members, including children. French medical men were among the first to reflect this awakening. Phillipe Pinel was to have a profound effect on the treatment of the mentally ill, and he is recognized as the father of modern psychiatry.

To the revolutionaries, Pinel appeared a "madman" engaged in the liberation of animals when he sought and received permission to remove the chains of the mentally ill in the Bicetre.

Figure 1-6.
Phillipe Pinel, 1745–1826.

He reorganized the administration, retrained the personnel of the hospital, and collected perhaps the earliest psychiatric case histories. Pinel was driven by the conviction that "the mentally sick, far from being guilty people deserving of punishment, are sick people whose miserable state deserves all the consideration that is due to suffering humanity. One should try with the most simple methods to restore their reason." He classified mental diseases simply as mania, melancholia, dementia, and idiocy, and was opposed to bloodletting, ducking patients in water, and the use of drugs (Zilboorg & Henry, 1941, pp. 323–324).

While Pinel's reform was taking place in France, William Tuke established the York Retreat in England where mental patients lived, worked, and rested in a kindly, religious atmosphere. In the United States, Benjamin Rush assumed direction of the Pennsylvania Hospital, where he brought about more humane treatment of the mentally ill and wrote the first comprehensive volume on psychiatry in this country (Coleman, 1972).

Given impetus by Pinel in the previous century, reform in the treatment of the mentally ill was widespread. In France, Ferrus introduced a revolutionary procedure at the Bicetre when he selected patients capable of working and assigned them to a large farm containing a dairy, animals, and workshops. But he considered nonrestraint for mental patients, in general, impractical and idealistic. The issue of restraint for the mentally ill was widely debated throughout Europe and America in the 1830s. In the United States, Isaac Ray stated that although nonrestraint might be successful with Europeans, who traditionally are accustomed to obeying orders, it would not work with Americans, whose belief in liberty would cause them to assert themselves if they were not physically restrained.

Figure 1–7.
Dorothea Dix, 1802–1887.

One of the most spirited voices for reform in the United States was that of Dorothea Dix, a retired school teacher described as having "staggering grit." Her mission was to have hospitals built for the mentally ill. Between 1841 and 1881, she established thirty-two modern mental hospitals (Zilboorg & Henry, 1941).

The Wild Boy

The onset of the nineteenth century provided a landmark in the field of special education with the emergence (in 1799) of a wild boy of eleven or twelve years of age from a forest in southern France. He was animal-like in appearance and behavior, naked, dirty, scarred, and unable to speak, and he selected food by smell. He had apparently been abandoned in the forest at the age of three or four and had managed to survive until his capture. He drew immediate widespread attention across the country, partly because of the philosophical position of Rousseau in the eighteenth century that natural man living unfettered by societal demands and contamination might develop a peaceful disposition and acquire the status of a "noble savage." Did the wild boy exhibit any of the peacefulness and nobility that Rousseau described? Unfortunately, he did not, but this philosophical interest was only part of the reason for the boy's notoriety.

Throughout the years, there has been a great deal of interest in wolf or feral children believed to have been abandoned to the forest or jungle by their families at an early age, yet who survived to live among wild animals who some say actually raised them as their own (Dennis, 1951). A so-called ape boy appeared in Africa near Lake Tanganyika (*People*, Feb. 9, 1976). A tiny boy, covered with thick body hair and apparently about four years old, was found climbing the trees with a band of apes. He was caught, and it was believed he was one of the survivors of a tribe that had been massacred. The boy was placed in a mental hospital for adults for three years and then taken to a Catholic orphanage where he was named John for John the Baptist who lived in the bush. At age seven, he was three feet tall, sturdily built, and given to scratching himself constantly and stuffing bananas into his mouth. He was frequently very destructive, hurling objects and kicking and attacking small animals. John's coordination was poor, but he did learn to rattle a small box, twist a piece of grass, and hold a ball. The thick body hair disappeared and the boy showed signs of responding to adults by hurling himself up on their laps and breaking into a smile.

When news of the wild boy's capture reached Paris, it immediately aroused the interest of Abbe Sicard, director of the Institute for Deaf-Mutes. He was a widely renowned teacher of the deaf who had established his reputation by teaching so-called unteachable deaf and retarded children by means of his special language training. Sicard persuaded Napoleon's brother, Lucien Bonaparte, the Minister of the Interior, to have the boy placed under his supervision in hopes of further enhancing his reputation as a "miracle worker." However, because of the boy's "utterly uncivilized behavior" and lack of response to his approaches, Sicard must have decided that he could never train this brutish creature. He had better not test his reputation on an obviously impossible case" (Shattuck, 1980, p. 29).

As a result, a team of high-ranking physicians and scientists was appointed to examine the boy and present a report to the government. Phillipe Pinel, the father of modern psychiatry mentioned earlier, wrote the report that concluded the wild boy's behavior placed him "lower than all animals, both wild and domestic" and established him as an "incurable idiot." Training by Sicard or anyone was out of the question, and the boy was to be put away like the rest of those who were hopelessly retarded.

Into this atmosphere of pessimism and rejection stepped an ambitious young French physician who had been appointed medical advisor to the Institute for Deaf-Mutes, Jean-Marc-Gaspard Itard. In 1800, he requested and was granted government support to develop and implement a training program for the wild boy, a truly remarkable accomplishment in view of the fact he was challenging the most authoritative professional opinions of his time.

How Did Itard and Pinel Differ in Explaining Mental Development?

To understand what Shattuck (1980) has called Itard's "wager" that he could train the wild boy, we must review the setting of the times and the leading theories regarding intellectual development. The French Revolution had established the belief in the individuality and dignity of every human being and the right and potential of all people—the "nobodies" as well as the "somebodies"—to rise above any obstacle. Itard was reflecting that belief in his optimism. He was also reflecting the belief that environmental experience—education and training—could alter the seemingly unalterable. This was the essence of the so-called sensationalist theory of intellectual development. The mind was a blank tablet or *tabula rasa* waiting to receive all of its impressions from sensory experience. The wild boy simply had a mind that was literally blank due to his isolation. Itard's job was to write on it through sensory impressions. However, others such as

Figure 1–8.
Jean Marc Gaspard Itard, 1775–1838.

Pinel subscribed to the nativist theory, which maintained that the individual is born with innate ideas and potentials that gradually unfold as the mind develops. The wild boy was without the capacity for higher mental development. This theory was given some credence by the fact the boy had a scar on his throat, the probable result of an attempt to kill him when he was abandoned in the forest. The nativists reasoned that the abandonment and attempt to kill the boy was the result of his obvious mental defectiveness.

Itard's Training Program

Itard and the boy were both given apartments at the Institute for Deaf-Mutes and Itard began an intensive five-year period of training designed to normalize the boy, whom he came to call Victor, to the fullest extent possible. Itard employed the services of the wife of a groundskeeper for the institute, Madame Guerin, who fed and cared for Victor like a foster mother.

In the first nine months of training, the boy developed normal habits of sleeping, eating, and personal hygiene. He also became more sensitive to touch, taste, and smell and displayed affection for and dependence on his governess. Even though speech was not attained, he learned to voice certain monosyllables, such as *lait* ("milk") and *O Dieu*, and finally acquired the vowel sounds as well as the sounds of *d* and *l*. Victor also learned to place objects together in proper order, such as arranging the letters of the alphabet to spell *lait*.

Victor maintained his celebrity status among French citizenry and at one point he and Itard were invited to a luncheon at the Chateau of Madame Racamier, a beautiful and wealthy leader of French society who had a reputation for entertaining anybody who was anybody. According to Shattuck, the elegant Parisian elite invited to the luncheon were ready to meet the "noble savage in person" or a "dangerous animal." Itard was nervous and before long he had cause to be. After quickly devouring all the food on his plate, Victor scooped up handfuls of pastries being served, stuffed them in his pocket, ran quickly outside, took off all his clothes, and climbed a nearby tree. According to an eyewitness account, "The women, motivated as much by distaste as by a respect for decorum, kept to the rear, while the men set about recapturing the child of the woods." Victor was finally taken, but he was not invited back to Madame Racamier's. Unfortunately, the wild boy "was not ready for high society." (Shattuck, 1980, p. 88)

Based on the progress Itard had made with Victor during the first year, Sicard wrote a letter to the government urging continued support, thus reversing his earlier position that Victor was unteachable. Even Pinel, who made the original diagnosis of "incurable idiot," changed his position somewhat. Thus, buoyed by this support and his teaching success with Victor, Itard launched into four more years of training. First, greater attention was given to development of the senses. By blindfolding Victor so that hearing would not be distracted by sight, Itard taught him to distinguish gross differences in sounds, such as that between a drum and a bell. Gradually he taught him to respond to the varying tones of his teacher's voice.

After much work, Victor was able to identify various written words visually without understanding their meaning and to distinguish colors. The sense of touch was developed by teaching the boy to distinguish between chestnuts and acorns hidden in a bag. He also learned to select certain block letters by touch alone. Victor's sense of taste was likewise developed, and he learned to differentiate between sweet and tart.

The Results Prove Disappointing

Itard expected mental development rapidly to follow increased sensory development. Victor was trained to connect an object with its name and use. He also learned to distinguish between action verbs written on a blackboard and later was able to carry out the action indicated. Itard keenly wished to teach Victor to speak, but despite painstaking training, the boy did not progress beyond the utterance of a few monosyllables and remained essentially mute. This failure to develop speech and language was a bitter disappointment to Itard.

Despite this failure, Itard hoped Victor's mental development would rapidly progress with the onset of puberty. But the major effect of this period was to bring out wild and uncontrollable elements in the boy. He became violent and eventually unmanageable, and Itard's experiment ended with Victor's being given over to the care of his governess, with whom he resided in a small house near the Institute for Deaf Mutes. Unfortunately, his functioning deteriorated and, although he had been called Victor by all during his years with Itard, he began to be referred to simply as "the savage." Victor received kindly care from Madame Guerin until he died at forty in 1829.

Itard was bitterly disappointed over his failure to make Victor normal. He was forced to admit reluctantly that the boy was indeed mentally retarded, although not hopeless as Pinel had diagnosed. Despite his disappointment, Itard was praised by the French Academy of Science in its 1806 report:

> The Academy acknowledges that it was impossible for the institutor to put in his lessons, exercises, and experiments more intelligence, sagacity, patience, courage; and that if it has not obtained a greater success, it must be attributed not to any lack of zeal or talent, but to the imperfection of the organs of the subject upon which he worked. (Davies & Ecob, 1959, p. 12)

History was to add its commendation to Itard's work, for he was among the first to show that even a seriously retarded individual can be helped to improve his or her level of functioning through appropriate training. Itard was also perhaps the first educator to apply a completely individualized and clinical method (patterned after a medical approach) to the study, observation, and education of a pupil (Wallin, 1955). Itard's dedication, ingenuity, persistence, and optimism were to remain as a legacy for the special educator from the beginning of the nineteenth century to the present. The French director, François Truffaut, has made a moving and detailed film depicting Itard's work with Victor entitled *L'Enfant Sauvage* or *The Wild Child*.*

Seguin's Contributions to the Mentally Retarded

Itard's accomplishments were instrumental in stimulating the instruction of the retarded at both the Bicetre and the Salpetriere hospitals in the 1830s, when it was firmly established that the

*_____
The Wild Child, 1970, black and white, 85 minutes. Available from United Artists, UA/Sixteen, 729 Seventh Avenue, New York, New York 10019.

retarded could learn and improve (Doll, 1962). Itard's work influenced the contributions of Edouard Seguin, who reflected the most significant thinking of previous generations and who consolidated and built a unique educational system. Seguin has been described as "perhaps the greatest teacher ever to address his attention to the mentally deficient" (Doll, 1962). He was Itard's protégé, and his concept of education was the promotion of the harmonious physical, intellectual, and moral development of the child.

Seguin established the first successful school specifically for training the feeble-minded in Paris in 1837, where he continued his pioneering efforts on their behalf for the next ten years. In 1846, Seguin published his classic textbook, *Idiocy and Its Treatment by the Physiological Method*. It elicited immediate recognition from the French Academy of Science and a letter from Pope Pius IX thanking Seguin for the service he was rendering to humanity. In the 1890s, Maria Montessori translated the book, and Seguin's techniques and materials became the basis for the so-called Montessori method.

In 1848, Seguin, who was unhappy with the French government, emigrated to the United States at the urging of such individuals as Samuel Howe, who considered his particular method of teaching a way to help severely retarded individuals achieve normal functioning. Seguin assisted in setting up the first educationally oriented state residential facility for the retarded in the United States. Hopes were high that residential schools offering a strong training emphasis would literally cure the retarded.

By the end of the nineteenth century, however, hopes that training would normalize the retarded had faded. Despite important and significant contributions that made a difference in the lives of the retarded, Seguin's methods did not produce the sought-after miracle, and the view of residential schools as training institutions gave way to one of custodial facilities for children and adults who were hopelessly dependent (Dunn, 1973b).

Helen Keller and Anne Sullivan

The beginning of the nineteenth century was particularly noteworthy in the field of special education because of the teacher-pupil relationship between Itard and Victor and the development of training procedures aimed at educating the seemingly uneducable. A striking parallel to the experience of Itard and Victor occurred in the latter part of the same century in the teacher-pupil relationship between Anne Sullivan and Helen Keller and the training program that made such a remarkable difference in the life of a young deaf and blind child. Helen Keller was born a normal child in 1880, but nineteen months later she was stricken with a still undiagnosed illness that left her deaf and blind and led to muteness.

Anne Sullivan, who was visually handicapped herself, served as Helen's tutor when the child attained school age. By the end of her first month of teaching, Anne Sullivan had achieved a breakthrough; while Anne was pumping water over the child's hands and finger-spelling the word *water*, Helen revealed that she had made the association between the physical and symbolic experiences. From that moment on, Helen's progress was remarkable. She quickly learned the names of objects and events in her environment, and by the age of ten began oral speech when she learned to say aloud, "I—am—not—dumb—now." The story of the astonishing results of Anne Sullivan's work with Helen received widespread publicity.

Helen Keller went on to graduate cum laude from Radcliffe College and to write a number of books, several of which provide us with vivid, moving accounts of her life with Anne Sullivan (Keller, 1955). The stage play and later motion picture, *The Miracle Worker,** depict Anne Sullivan's dedicated efforts to teach Helen Keller.

The Development of Institutional and Public School Programs for Exceptional Learners

Between 1818 and 1894, residential institutions for the mentally retarded and other exceptional children had appeared in the United States. By 1890, state responsibility for the care of the retarded was generally accepted, and supplementary private agencies appeared. Institutional segregation on either a temporary or permanent basis was seen as most effective, but the special-class movement in the community, first to gain impetus in Germany, was being considered in America as well. Educational theory reflected developmental concepts and concern with the child's total personality, and the importance of individualized instruction was recognized. The profoundly retarded were considered in need of lifetime custodial care, but the less severely retarded were seen as candidates for some level of gainful employment.

The first special class for mentally retarded children living outside an institution was developed in Germany as early as 1860. In the United States, special classes for the retarded were held in Cleveland in 1875 and again in 1893. By 1905, classes had been initiated in Chicago, New York, Providence, Springfield, Philadelphia, Boston, and Portland, Maine (Doll, 1962). By 1911, there were public school classes for the retarded in ninety-nine American cities, and by 1922 some 23,000 children were enrolled across the country.

The early public school programs for the retarded in the United States often included a mixture of problem children, and the optimism and dedication of the teachers was not always matched by adequate preparation and experience. An example of this occurred in 1918 in the Cleveland, Ohio, public schools.

"About 14 of the most serious cases of imbecility in the most congested quarters of the city were gathered together and a superior, conscientious teacher placed in charge. The good folk responsible for this inauguration were united in their belief that the pupils would soon become as normal children, once they were properly taught. The teacher heroically attacked the problem, but before the close of the school year, all were aware that their experiment was doomed to failure. At the close of the term, the class was disbanded—the imbeciles returned to their homes, probably not much the worse for their 'schooling,' but the poor teacher

*The Miracle Worker, 1962, black and white, 107 minutes. Available from United Artists, UA/Sixteen, 729 Seventh Avenue, New York, New York 10019.

suffered a mental collapse which necessitated a
sojourn at our Capital State Hospital" (Steinbeck as
cited in Goldstein, 1957).

Special programs for the retarded declined during the Great Depression of the 1930s, but after World War II they increased rapidly: in 1948, there were 87,000 special programs for the retarded; in 1958, 213,000; and in 1963, 390,000 (Farber, 1968).

The date of initiation of special classes for those other than the retarded in the United States is presented in Table 1-1.

In the 1920s and 1930s, efforts were made to place retarded individuals in colonies, on parole in foster homes, or on leave. Such efforts gained momentum in the 1960s and were widespread in the 1970s. In the 1970s and 1980s, the group home became popular. Such a home generally includes six retarded or disturbed young adults who live with two supervisors (often a young married couple). The adults work during the day at a sheltered workshop or other jobs and return home to share in responsibilities associated with cleaning, cooking, and managing their residence.

Out of the tragedies of war has come a positive contribution to the cause of the handicapped due to the compulsory military physical examination and the return of injured and disabled veterans to their homes after the wars (Cruickshank, 1967). The physical screenings revealed tens of thousands of men who were physically impaired, yet who had led normal lives. This discovery tended to contribute to greater understanding and acceptance of handicapping conditions. Disabled veterans who previously had been accepted in their communities tended to be viewed as normal when they returned, even though they had suffered physical impairment. Successful motion pictures depicting the adjustment facing physically impaired veterans ap-

Table 1-1
Years in which special classes for the exceptional were first instituted

Deaf	1869	Boston
Unruly or truant boys	1874	New York City
Blind	1896 (or 1899)	Chicago
Orthopedically handicapped	1899 (or 1900)	Chicago
Speech defective	1908	New York
Pre-tuberculosis or malnourished	1908	Providence
Epileptics	1909	Baltimore
Partially sighted	1913	Roxbury (Mass.)
Hard of hearing	1920	Lynn (Mass.)

Source: From Wallin, J.E., *Education of mentally handicapped children.* New York: Harper & Row, 1955. Reprinted by permission. (p. 18)

peared following World War II (*The Best Years of Our Lives*) and the Viet Nam conflict (*Coming Home*).

President Kennedy's Commitment to Exceptional Learners

The 1950s began a significant era in special education in the United States when a series of federal legislative provisions established grants for research and training of personnel in education of the handicapped. In 1961, President John F. Kennedy boldly committed the country's resources to the cause of handicapped individuals in general and to the mentally retarded in particular:

> The manner in which our Nation cares for its citizens and conserves its manpower resources is more than an index to its concern for the less fortunate. It is a key to its future. Both wisdom and humanity dictate a deep interest in the physically handicapped, the mentally ill, and the mentally retarded. Yet, although we have made considerable progress in the treatment of physical handicaps, although we have attacked on a broad front the problems of mental illness, although we have made great strides in the battle against disease, we as a nation have for too long postponed

Figure 1-9.
John Fitzgerald Kennedy, 1917–1963.

an intensive search for solutions to the problems of the mentally retarded. That failure should be corrected. (President's Committee on Mental Retardation, 1962)

President Kennedy's mandate established a President's Committee on Mental Retardation made up of leading professionals in a variety of fields related to special education. The Committee surveyed the national scene with regard to the problems of the mentally retarded and the need for increased services. Its recommendations, as well as the impetus of the surging special education movement, were reflected in Public Law 88–164, which allocated federal funds for training professional personnel to work with the handicapped and for supporting research and demonstration projects in special education. In 1967, a Bureau of Education for the Handicapped was established in the United States Office of Education to administer research, educational, and training programs supported by the federal government across the country. This bureau has since been renamed the Office of Special Education and Rehabilitative Services.

As early as 1851, Howe had stressed that blind children should be educated in regular schools because of the social advantages of such a setting. He was advocating *mainstreaming*, or exposing the exceptional learner to an educational experience as close to that of the nonhandicapped as possible. It was 1900 before a special class for the blind was established in the Chicago public schools. The 1970s saw the principle of mainstreaming firmly established for all handicapped individuals. Indeed, it became one of the cornerstones of Public Law 94–142, the Education for All the Handicapped Act of 1975.

Public Law 94–142

Public Law 94–142 is a landmark piece of federal legislation designed to guarantee that all handicapped individuals from ages three to twenty-one in the United States receive a free and appropriate education. Historically, the principle that education should be available and free to all in the United States goes back to 1840, when Rhode Island adopted a compulsory education law; Massachusetts followed in 1852. After the Civil War, this principle was put into practice across the nation (Pulliam, 1968). The only problem was that it was put into practice selectively. For some children, a free school education was provided on a *mandatory* basis, for others it was provided on a *permissive* basis. Unfortunately for most exceptional learners, a free public school education was a permissive issue, not a mandatory one. It would have been nice to provide such an education for the handicapped, but states were not required to do so.

Education as a Privilege

What we see reflected here is the long-standing concept of education as a privilege, not a right. If any child failed to measure up to the specification of a local code for physical appearance, ability, or behavior, he or she could be excluded without question. The privileged status of education is

Figure 1-10.

vividly illustrated by a 1919 court decision regarding the rights of the school to exclude children (*Beattie* v. *State Board of Education*, 1919). Students could be expelled if they displayed continuous disorderly conduct or had:

> ...a depressing and nauseating effect on the teachers and school children. The rights of a child of school age to attend the schools of the state could not be insisted upon, when its presence therein is harmful to the best interest of the school.

Education as a Right

Education as a privilege rather than a right continued to exist until the civil rights movement of the 1950s. During that memorable decade, when the constitutional rights of minority individuals were established by court decisions, the seeds for legislation guaranteeing the rights of the handicapped were also sown. However, it would take more than two decades for fruition. Perhaps the most celebrated court decision regarding education as a right came in 1954 as the result of *Brown* v. *Board of Education*. The foundation for Public Law 94–142 was presented in the court's decision:

> In these days, it is doubtful that any child may reasonably be expected to succeed in life if he is denied the opportunity of an education. Such an opportunity, where the state has undertaken to provide it, is a right which must be available to all on equal terms.

The constitutional foundations for the Brown decision and Public Law 94–142 are found in the Fourteenth Amendment, which declares that no state may deny to any person within its jurisdiction the equal protection of the laws. In addition, both the Fifth and Fourteenth Amendments provide that a person shall not be deprived of life, liberty, or property without due process of law. It was argued that denying an education to any citizen was tantamount to denying an opportunity for that citizen to develop the skills necessary for acquiring property (Turnbull & Turnbull, 1978).

In addition to a provision for free education for all the handicapped, Public Law 94–142 specifies that all testing and assessment procedures employed by the school be nondiscriminatory and not penalize anyone because of background or nature or mode of communication. The law also states that the education must be "individualized" and "appropriate," for unless the educational opportunity is meaningful and significant to the child it is tantamount to no education at all (Turnbull & Turnbull, 1978). In this regard, the law requires that an Individualized Education Program (IEP) be written for each child. The IEP is discussed in some detail in chapter 10.

Another provision of Public Law 94–142 is that handicapped individuals be integrated or mainstreamed into regular education programs "to the maximum extent possible." The practice of placing handicapped children in separate, isolated classes has generated controversy for many years. In the early part of the nineteenth century, when the first special class for the retarded opened in Providence, Rhode Island, a newspaper columnist composed a sarcastic editorial entitled "The Fool Class," implying that the supporters and teachers for the class were as retarded as the children they were attempting to educate (Kanner, 1964). Binet and Simon (1905) challenged special class placement in the early part of this century: "To be a member of a special class can never be a mark of distinction, and such as do not merit it, must be spared the record" (p. 82).

The law further specifies that should the handicapped individual's parents or the handicapped individual be dissatisfied with the educational program provided by the school they have the right to challenge the school in a fair hearing. This involves a legal proceeding in which both the school and the advocates for the handicapped individual present their cases before a panel of experts who then rule on the matter. This is an example of the constitutional provision for due process stated in both the Fifth and Fourteenth Amendments.

Among the court cases that had nothing to do with the handicapped, but yet had a bearing on the principle of due process being put into Public Law 94–142, was one involving a woman identified as a problem drinker in Wisconsin (*Wisconsin* v. *Constantineau*, 1971). During the day, the woman would make a nuisance of herself by pestering the neighbors and disturbing the peace. Finally, the police posted her name in liquor stores in the area with explicit instructions that she was not to be sold any alcoholic beverages because of her drinking problem. The woman regained enough lucidity to go to court and challenge the public posting of her name and problem as unconstitutional stigmatization. She won. The court ruled that such a public announcement was serious enough to require that prior notice be given the woman and a hearing held before any posting of information could take place. Due process before labeling was thus established as a constitutional right.

Although we can sympathize with the Wisconsin woman whose constitutional rights of due process were violated, when we consider the thousands of exceptional learners who have had such labels as "mentally retarded" or "emotionally disturbed" entered into their school records with no prior notice, the severity of her problem appears to diminish considerably. Being called "someone with a drinking problem" is bad enough, but being called "retarded" is likely to result in a much more negative stigmatization and have far more serious, long-term effects.

Finally, Public Law 94–142 guarantees parents active participation in the formulation of the educational program and requires their signatures on the Individualized Education Program. Parent participation with respect to gaining the rights of handicapped children to a free and appropriate education was clearly visible long before the passage of the law. Parent organizations, particularly for the mentally retarded, went to the courts to challenge exclusion of the handicapped from a free public school education. In 1971, parents in the Pennsylvania Association for Retarded Children (PARC) sued the commonwealth of Pennsylvania, seeking a free and appropriate education for the handicapped, and won, as did parents in the Maryland Association for Retarded Children (MARC) against the state of Maryland in 1974. There are numerous other examples of litigation brought by groups and individuals to gain a free and appropriate education for the handicapped.

Public law 94–142 came about because of the long-standing educational neglect of many handicapped individuals in the United States. Its provisions directly address this neglect and other grievances. In chapter 10, we discuss the law in detail and present issues and problems related to its implementation.

Summary

In this first chapter, we have examined some of the beliefs, attitudes, individuals, and events that have been responsible for the treatment of the exceptional learner throughout much of history.

Survival

Perhaps the primary problem faced by the exceptional, particularly those with physical handicaps, was merely staying alive. The harshness of nature eliminated the weak in primitive times; the practice of exposure and infanticide during the Greek and Roman periods further threatened their existence. War, poverty, barbarism, and disease continued to take their toll through the Middle Ages. In some ways, just being a child was a handicapping condition. As late as the eighteenth century, exploitation and neglect contributed to the death before the age of ten of more than half the children born in London.

Superstition

The survival of the exceptional learner has been continuously threatened by human fascination with and fear of the unexplained, whether in the natural world or in human behavior. In ancient times, both good and evil spirits were viewed as causing deranged behavior, and reverence, worship, or appeasement resulted. With civilization came elaborate demonological beliefs and the development of rites of exorcism for protection against evil spirits. Despite the objective, naturalistic position of Hippocrates regarding the source of deviant behavior, the metaphysical dominated Greek thought.

Much of the Middle Ages was an era of darkness and demonology, partly due to the polarization by early Christians of the good and evil components of human nature. Some mentally retarded individuals were viewed as enjoying the favor of God, but the mentally ill were uniformly considered possessed by Satan and were targets for cruel and inhumane treatment. In the fifteenth century, a mass persecution of "witches" began, and many whose beliefs and behavior violated church, state, and community expectations were executed. Just as Hippocrates spoke out against demonology in his time, others continued to challenge the irrational beliefs of their times; unfortunately, their voices were not clearly heard until the end of the eighteenth century.

Science

While superstitious beliefs reigned supreme, attempts at a lawful explanation of natural events and human behavior through observation, study, and experimentation were stifled. Thus, whatever beginning level of scientific thought had been developed by the Greeks and Romans was quickly overshadowed by the superstition of the Middle Ages. Even though physical illness gradually was recognized as the result of natural causes, mental illness continued to be viewed as the result of possession by demons and evil spirits. It was not until the late eighteenth and early nineteenth centuries that psychiatry emerged as separate from medicine and the role of psychological factors in mental illness was recognized. Itard's scientific documentation of his work with Victor was the beginning of special educational procedures based on observation and study that were to have far-reaching effects. The early twentieth century saw scientific approaches applied to the development of personality by Freud, measurement of individual differences by Binet, and the beginnings of the investigation of genetic and biochemical factors in mental retardation.

Service

The concepts of humane treatment and service for exceptional learners have had widespread meaning only for the past two hundred years. Prior to that time, there were isolated instances of acceptance, kindly care, and education, but in general service was the exception rather than the rule. The seventeenth century saw the beginning of the development of special instructional techniques for the blind and deaf and attempts to describe mental retardation and mental illness from psychological and educational points of view. But the greatest impetus for respect and concern for the rights of all human beings, including the handicapped, came in the eighteenth century as a result of the French Revolution. Pinel struck off the chains of the mentally ill in France, and others followed in Europe and the United States. Schools for the blind and deaf appeared. In the early nineteenth century, Itard and Seguin developed techniques for teaching exceptional individuals heretofore never considered "learners."

Seguin brought his enthusiasm and optimism in this regard to the United States and helped launch a program to educate rather than institutionalize the mentally retarded. However, the alarmist eugenics movement and the notion of fixed intelligence, which appeared at the beginning of the twentieth century, had a negative effect on the program. But commitment to the welfare and education of exceptional learners was underway in the United States. Special schools and classes were developed beginning in the mid-1800s. Delayed somewhat by World Wars I and II and the Great Depression, this development reached an all-time high, as did commitment to special education training and research, with the mandates of President John F. Kennedy in the 1960s. The 1970s gave us Public Law 94–142, and almost two centuries of good intentions toward the rights of the exceptional learner finally became federal law.

As we look back, it is apparent that handicapped individuals' chances for survival, the enlightened understanding of their problems, the scientific contributions to their welfare and development, and the range of services available to help them develop and use their potential exist in greater measure today than ever before. We have recaptured some of Itard's and Seguin's enthusiasm and optimism regarding the roles that education and training can play in improving the functioning level of the handicapped, particularly the retarded. Our present level of optimism does not naïvely assume that the mentally retarded can be cured through training procedures, but we are firmly convinced that special education can make an important difference in their lives and in the lives of all handicapped children. Such optimism is reflected in the philosophy of this book—that all exceptional children are, first and foremost, learners, ready at all times to learn something and only secondarily handicapped by conditions that limit learning. With this historical journey behind us, we turn to the present. Chapter 2 presents a general introduction to the exceptional learner, and chapters 3 and 4 consider more specifically nine types of exceptionality.

The Exceptional Learner

Children are unique. If we survey a busy playground, we see a spectacle of this uniqueness. In a dodge ball game, some children move more quickly and with better coordination than others. Some children are surrounded by admiring friends whereas others sit alone at some distance. The differences we observe on the playground are more obvious than those we might see inside the classroom. Notice Mike squinting at the chalkboard as his teacher writes down an assignment. See how the teacher makes certain that Mark hears her directions. She has him sitting at the front of the room so he can hear her more clearly.

Todd's hand goes up when the teacher asks a question. As he starts to answer, several children giggle. Todd's speech is immature, and he speaks with a lisp. One of the gigglers is Dora. She starts talking to Jennifer beside her. The teacher looks annoyed.

> "If I have to remind you, Dora, one more time not to speak to your neighbor, you will stay in during recess."

The assignment is storywriting. Bill has been selected as paper monitor because of his consistently good behavior. The teacher nods approvingly as she sees him take charge and make sure that each row gets the proper supply. He is the brightest pupil in the class. What a delight!

The teacher walks around the room looking down at the children's papers as they commence their story-writing efforts. Susan is staring blankly out the window. The teacher shakes her head. Daydreaming again. After she gets Susan started, she looks down at Matthew's paper. The handwriting is almost illegible, and as usual there is at least one word reversal. This time *on* appears as *no*. Poor Matthew; he seems bright enough, but he has great difficulty with reading and spelling.

Then there is Paul. He is doing no better than Matthew academically, but he seems definitely on the slow side in most areas. The teacher returns to the front of the classroom. Yes, her children are unique, some more than others and some in ways that matter more when it comes to learning successfully.

What Are the Kinds of
Uniqueness that Matter?

The field of special education is concerned with children who are unique in ways that matter when it comes to learning in school and functioning successfully elsewhere. The children we have just described were unique in some of these same ways but perhaps not to the degree that would result in their being identified for special education services. The uniqueness we are talking about can be conceived of as falling along a series of dimensions: vision, hearing, movement, communication, perceptual-motor, social-emotional, and intelligence.

—   vision   +

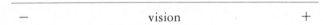

The dimension of vision is critical with respect to instruction in the classroom and free, independent movement through the environment. We all vary visually. Some of us have excellent vision that enables us to see farther and more clearly than most. Many of us fall around the midpoint of the vision dimension. As we begin to

Figure 2–1.

fall toward the problem end, we may wear corrective lenses. When we get to the point where a stimulus a person with normal vision can see at two hundred feet must be brought to within twenty feet before we can see it, we are legally blind and close to the extreme end of the visual deficit range. Visually handicapped individuals fall at varying points within this range, and special education adapts the educational program to compensate for their deficits.

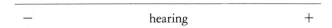

—   hearing   +

Another dimension very critical to learning, particularly the development of language, is hearing. Some of us have acute hearing, able to detect sounds many do not notice. Again, most of us fall near the middle on the hearing dimension. As we begin to experience difficulty hearing, we may need varying degrees of amplification provided by a hearing aid. When we are unable to detect useful sounds, we fall far down the problem range and must rely on lipreading, signing, and other methods for communication. Some severely handicapped individuals have extreme problems on both the dimensions of vision and hearing and are called deaf-blind.

Figure 2-2.

— movement +

Gifted athletes may function far up in the positive range on the movement dimension, but most of us are likely at midpoint. This movement dimension is critical to individuals who are orthopedically impaired and chronically ill. As movement due to a crippling condition such as cerebral palsy limits us, we may need braces or a wheelchair. Also, if our vitality is limited due to a chronic illness, we will need special consideration. Some children are almost completely immobilized and must be taught in beds or on mats.

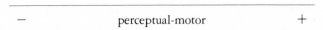

— perceptual-motor +

The perceptual-motor dimension is concerned with how accurately we see and hear stimuli in our environment. Most of us who have no problem with vision or hearing have no difficulty recognizing and writing the word *girl* or hearing the difference between the spoken words *sap* and *sat*. But for some, the word *girl* may be

Figure 2–3.

perceived and written as *gril* and the two spoken words perceived as identical. This is a frequent problem for children with learning disabilities. Some individuals seriously afflicted along this dimension may perceive everything visually as upside-down and backwards. There is no problem with them *seeing* things; the problem is how the visual area in the brain organizes or perceives what is seen.

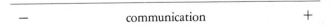

—   communication   +

The communication dimension is important for many exceptional learners. The hearing-handicapped have a particularly unique problem here. If you have never heard any spoken language, imagine how difficult it would be to learn the meaning of concepts such as *space* or *abstract*. Some of us function very well along this dimension, speaking clearly and distinctly, using an adequate vocabulary, and readily understanding the meaning of the words used by others. But some individuals have difficulty making themselves understood. This may involve a slight stutter or articulation problem, or muteness at the extreme position in the problem range.

Figure 2–4.

—   social-emotional   +

The social-emotional dimension is vague and more difficult to define than the
other dimensions. It has to do with how well we get along in our day-to-day living,
particularly how well we relate to others. Some of us are real winners. We are loved,
respected, sought out, and happy. Others manage to get by, and still others experience serious problems. Emotional disturbance is not quantifiable as are blindness
and deafness. Some children display problem behavior in some situations and not in
others. And the same problem behavior called "disturbed" by one individual might be
called "assertive" or "independent" by another. The autistic child probably occupies
the most extreme position in the problem range along this dimension.

—   intelligence   +

We come now to a dimension along which both the positive and problem ranges
are of concern to the field of special education. Individuals who lack normal intelligence and those who have a superior intellect are all considered exceptional learners.

Figure 2–5.

In times past, I.Q. tests were viewed as a completely valid means for determining where an individual might fall along this dimension, but no longer. In chapters 7 and 10, we discuss the serious social and legal problems that have arisen around this practice, particularly as it has related to designating someone as mentally retarded.

These are seven critical dimensions related to successful learning in school and successful adaptation elsewhere. *We all vary on each dimension, but as we vary to a degree that adaptation of the regular school program becomes necessary as does special consideration elsewhere, we become exceptional.* It is important at this point to present the specific types of exceptional learners dealt with in this text.

Who Are Exceptional Learners?

Visually handicapped individuals

Deaf and hard-of-hearing individuals

Figure 2-6.

Figure 2–7.

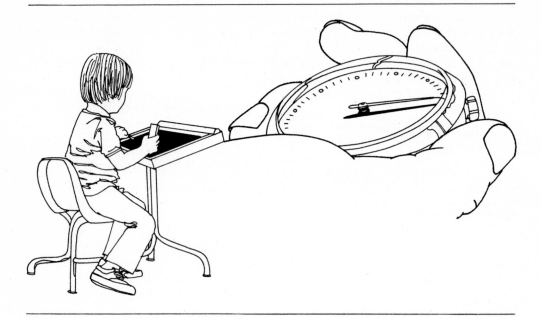

Deaf-blind individuals

Orthopedically and other health impaired
individuals

Emotionally disturbed individuals

Speech impaired individuals

Economically disadvantaged and/or culturally
different individuals

Individuals with learning disabilities

Mentally retarded individuals

Gifted individuals

Although most of these exceptional learners do have a primary problem on one of the seven
dimensions, many fall toward the problem end on more than one dimension, and some fall
toward the problem end on all seven. One type of exceptional learner who clearly does not fall on
any single dimension is the economically disadvantaged and/or culturally different individual. In
our discussion of such individuals, we use the term *disadvantaged*, but our actual reference is to
individuals who live in poverty or who have culturally different backgrounds that may create
problems when they attend middle-class oriented, American public schools.

Visually impaired individuals are also only partly described by placing them on the dimension of vision. Along the dimension of hearing, they may have developed an acute sensitivity to sound cues that will greatly aid them in mobility; hence, they are superior in functioning. Along the dimension of communication, they may have had to develop alternate ways of reading and writing. The perceptual-motor functioning of the visually impaired has been studied, and it has been found that despite the inability to see such objects as a tree or mountain, they can "get the idea" through auditory and tactual sensations.

We can discuss every type of exceptional learner from this cross-dimension perspective:

Exceptional Learner	Primary Dimension(s)	Possible Related Dimensions
Visually handicapped	vision	hearing, movement, perceptual-motor, communication, social-emotional
Deaf and hard-of-hearing	hearing	vision, movement, perceptual-motor, communication, social-emotional
Orthopedically and other Health impaired	movement	perceptual-motor, communication, social-emotional, intelligence
Emotionally disturbed	social-emotional	movement, perceptual-motor, communication
Speech impaired	communication	social-emotional
Disadvantaged	none	vision, hearing, movement, perceptual-motor, communication, social-emotional
Learning-disabled	perceptual-motor, communication	movement, social-emotional
Mentally retarded	intelligence	vision, hearing, movement, perceptual-motor, communication, social-emotional
Gifted	intelligence	vision, hearing, movement, perceptual-motor, communication, social-emotional

It is interesting to note that the related dimensions for the mentally retarded and the gifted are identical. However, each would fall in an opposite range on each dimension. One purpose of this text is to emphasize the overlapping relationships among characteristics of many exceptional learners and to unify them. In Part Two, we orient our entire discussion with reference to this unification.

We mentioned earlier that placement of an individual along the dimension of intelligence had, in the past, relied heavily on the use of an I.Q. test. What approaches do we use to decide where an individual falls along the other six dimensions? Basically, for both the dimension of intelligence and the other six we rely on *informal* and *formal* observation.

Informal Observation

When the teacher in the classroom described at the opening of this chapter was surveying her children and puzzling over their uniqueness, she was engaging in informal observation related to deciding who might or might not have a problem on one or more of the dimensions. Parents do the same thing as they watch their sons and daughters emerge from infancy into childhood and beyond.

One of the first questions new parents ask or certainly consider when they first observe their newborn is, Is our baby normal? Most parents will continue to ask that question as the child grows and matures. Some severe problems may be discernible at birth, whereas others may not become apparent until a later time. Visual or movement problems may be more readily identified at an earlier age than is a problem in hearing. Hearing problems become particularly noticeable when we expect a child to begin to speak in the second and third years of life. Parents are not the only ones engaged in ongoing informal observations. Relatives, neighbors, friends, and other people may observe that a child is late in walking or speaking, poorly coordinated, slow to learn new things, unusually irritable, active, passive, or withdrawn.

Throughout early life and into the school years, parents, teachers, and others who informally

Figure 2–8.

observe how children are functioning along the seven dimensions may seek a more thorough and accurate picture of a possible problem through formal observation.

Formal Observation

Formal observation is usually conducted by a physician or other specialist trained to know when and how children should be functioning along the seven dimensions. Problems related to vision, hearing, and movement may be identified and diagnosed, and a treatment program implemented. Speech specialists can study children's speech and language patterns and provide therapy. Psychologists can administer a standardized intelligence test. They may also use tests to study possible perceptual-motor problems or emotional conflicts.

Even though teachers primarily engage in informal observation, they can administer individual and group tests to obtain a more formal picture of a child's functioning in academic

Figure 2–9.

subjects. Finally, psychologists, parents, teachers, and others can formally observe children's behavior by keeping records of the types of problems that occur, their frequency, and factors possibly related to their occurrence. Such formal observations help pinpoint behavior problems, lead to the development of special educational approaches to alleviate them, and provide a means for evaluating whether or not such approaches are effective.

Accounting for Our Uniqueness

So far we have defined the term *exceptional learner* by relating it to an individual's functioning level on one or more of seven dimensions—vision, hearing, movement, perceptual-motor, communication, social-emotional, and intelligence. We have discussed how such levels of functioning are identified through informal and formal observation. The next logical question is, What determines where exceptional learners fall on each of the seven dimensions? The same question also might be asked in relation to all nonexceptional learners. In other words, what accounts for the differences found among us all with respect to how we see, hear, move, perceive, communicate, relate, and think? Is it simply a matter of our not being able to do any differently than we do, or is there some other explanation?

Consider the following statements:

"I never have been any good with numbers and know I can't do anything about it."

"I would like to learn to ski, but I know my poor coordination would make it impossible."

Figure 2-10.

"I understand Frank's father never finished the sixth grade. No wonder Frank is so far behind in reading."

"The school psychologist says Vernon has specific developmental dyslexia. So that's why he hasn't made any progress in my classroom this year."

"Billy is legally blind and keeps bumping into things. I know he can't do anything about it so I keep him sitting at his desk all day."

"Poor Fred. I've had both his older brothers and sisters in my class, and I know he's retarded just like they were."

"Too bad Phil is confined to a wheelchair and can never take part in any sports."

"They say Roger is autistic and you know autistic children never learn to talk."

"Oh, I always dress and undress Margaret. She simply never could learn to do it herself."

"Gary ride a bicycle? You must be kidding. How can someone who is blind do that?"

What do these statements have in common? They all relate to assumptions that a basic capacity to learn is missing; that efforts to teach math, skiing, reading, mobility, sports, speech, and self-care skills are *automatically* doomed to failure because the individuals described are defective.

We were introduced to the notion of "cannot" versus "has not learned," "defective" versus "untaught," in the last chapter with respect to Itard's work with Victor. You may recall Victor was found living in the forest as a "wild child" apparently having been abandoned eight or nine years earlier. Pinel, a psychiatrist of the times, considered Victor to be clearly defective. The physician Itard, on the other hand, considered him simply lacking in experience or untaught. Let us return to 1799 and through the exercise of literary license imagine that we are listening to a conversation between Pinel and Itard regarding the boy's future.

ITARD: What is your opinion of the young savage, Dr. Pinel?

PINEL: It is obvious. He is a hopeless idiot, abandoned by his family and left to die in the forest because he was clearly defective. He is deaf, you know. When I slammed the door behind him he did not react in the slightest.

ITARD: But when I cracked an acorn behind him, he reacted instantly. It was a sound familiar to him. He has not heard slamming doors before.

PINEL: Probably pure chance. Just why are you so interested in this idiot, Dr. Itard? Come to our institution, the Bicetre, and I will show you other hopeless idiots like him. Your young savage, however, is more helpless and more like an animal than most of them.

ITARD: But he has never had the opportunity to learn human ways. The inmates of the Bicetre have lived in the world of humans and yet did not learn. The savage has known only the world of animals for most of his life.

PINEL: No matter. He, like them, lacks the capacity for learning human ways.

ITARD: But what if the savage is simply untaught and behaves as he does because of lack of experience in the human world?

PINEL: Dr. Itard, are you suggesting that this idiot can be taught?

ITARD: It is possible that given the proper training he could learn to live in a human world and acquire human ways, such as caring for himself, developing skills, reading, writing, and speaking.

PINEL: Reading, writing, speaking! Perhaps you will come to the Bicetre and make scholars out of all the hopeless idiots there.

ITARD: No, they are different. Don't you see? With the savage we do not know if he lacks capacity because he has never had the opportunity to learn.

PINEL: You propose to train him then?

ITARD: I have been thinking a great deal about the savage. Perhaps by impinging on his primitive, undeveloped senses through rigorous training, we could provide the opportunity to learn that he has never had.

PINEL: I doubt if anything you might do will make any difference.

ITARD: I would like to petition the authorities for permission to develop a special training program for him here in the School for Deaf-Mutes.

PINEL: Dr. Itard, I admire your optimism, but you will see. The savage is defective. His lack of capacity will thwart your every effort to train him.

ITARD: Perhaps my training will reveal that he has the capacity for learning human ways after all.

PINEL: We shall see, Dr. Itard.

ITARD: Yes, Dr. Pinel, we shall see.

Defective or Untaught

As history records, both Pinel and Itard were partly right. Pinel's conviction that Victor was *defective* was borne out by the fact that the boy did not acquire spoken language and higher levels of other intellectual skills. However, Itard's belief that Victor was simply *untaught* was certainly supported by the remarkable changes he brought about in Victor's behavior during his five-year special education program. Pinel was wrong in believing Itard could not make an important difference in Victor's functioning level. Itard was wrong in believing he would completely normalize the boy. Thus, whereas we all may have limitations with respect to what, how, how much, or how well we learn imposed on us by our basic capacities, there is no one who cannot be taught to improve his or her functioning level. That is a recurring theme throughout this text.

Certainly, we all have basic limitations but these should not eliminate us as learners. Number-haters can learn to do math, clumsy people to ski, dyslexics to read, blind individuals to move independently through the environment and even to ride bicycles, those confined to wheelchairs to play basketball and other sports, autistic children to talk, and the retarded to dress and care for themselves.

What we are emphasizing here and in the title of this text is that everyone is, first and foremost, a learner waiting to be taught and only secondarily handicapped. *Everyone is a learner.* The term *learner* is exciting and dynamic; it is optimistic. It overshadows the negative and sidetracking aspects of the term *defective*. It suggests change. It directs us to look at what children can do, not at what some ominous label suggests they cannot do. Teachers can teach learners, even though they may have second thoughts about being able to teach brain damaged, retarded, physically handicapped, or autistic children.

If we use the term *defective* to explain why a given exceptional learner functions at a particular point on a particular dimension, we are strongly suggesting that not much can be done to improve things. If we use the term *untaught* to explain it, we are strongly suggesting that a lot can be done. Here, we run into a dilemma with our learner orientation. No one can dispute that clear limitations exist with respect to visual or auditory potential or capacity among many exceptional learners. They cannot learn *not* to be blind or deaf. But we can dispute the certainty with which we establish the limits of this capacity. Formal observation methods may tell us a child can see or hear at precisely a particular level—*and be wrong*. An intelligence test may assign and I.Q. score to an exceptional learner that results in the diagnosis of mental retardation—*and be wrong*. We are apt to be more accurate in our formal observations of exceptional learners who have the most severe problems.

By maintaining a learner orientation, we can resist efforts to place any exceptional learner along any dimension with any sense of absolute certainty. This does not reflect a refusal to recognize that definite limitations do exist among exceptional learners. We are simply assuming a healthy "let's wait and see" or "keep an open mind" attitude whenever possible.

No matter how far in the problem range on any dimension an individual may fall, every exceptional learner is at all times ready to learn something. The most skilled special educators are constantly on the lookout for those "somethings." We are not talking about the blind suddenly gaining sight or the orthopedically handicapped suddenly walking. We are talking about "some-things," some small, some big. A multihandicapped boy of twelve, immobilized in bed, learned to move his fingers—a most significant "something" along the movement dimension. The term *completely immobilized* no longer accurately described him. A ten-year-old girl with Downs Syndrome, a condition associated with mental retardation, learned to read at a primary level. The term *uneducable* certainly no longer applied to her. Both children were aided immeasurably by people in their environment who maintained an unfailing learner orientation toward them.

Capacity and Experience

Now that we have established all individuals as learners, let us examine the factors responsible for differences among them. We can describe these factors as:

capacity

range of experience

nature of experience

functioning level

Capacity.   At birth, we all arrive with certain inherited characteristics or capacities: sex, hair color, physique, and potential for height and weight. Our intellectual capacity is also partly determined by inheritance. Our capacities for receiving and perceiving sensory stimuli and eliciting motor and verbal responses are also largely fixed at birth, although injury and illness or medical and other interventions may alter these throughout an individual's lifetime. Thus, there is a blueprint at birth that, except for identical twins, makes us unique. And although certain limits are established by this blueprint, experience will play a major role in determining whether our capacities are maximized or minimized.

Range and Nature of Experience.   Following birth, we are exposed to warmth and coldness, hunger and satiation, wetness and dryness, being held and cuddled and lying alone. We gradually make out visual stimuli and hear sounds. The range of experiences that will make up our lifetime is underway. No matter what our capacity pluses or minuses, our range of experience from birth onward will be critical in determining the level of functioning we attain.

One of the authors recalls seeing a picture and reading a newspaper account about a fifteen-year-old boy and his father who had bicycled 150 miles in two days. What made this accomplishment remarkable was the fact that the boy was blind, had epilepsy, and had been partially paralyzed. His father blew a whistle while they were riding to guide his son along the right-of-way and out of danger. The story revealed that the parents had been told by a neurologist when the boy was two years old that he would be little more than a vegetable because his capacity-based problems were so severe. Refusing to accept this, the parents placed their son in an intensive physical therapy program and provided

Figure 2-11.

him with as normal a range of experience as possible. As a result of the therapy, the paralysis was overcome, and medication brought the epileptic seizures under control. The boy was planning to enter a regular high school program and was described as having an excellent attitude about his handicap and a strong determination to be self-sufficient. How different the outcome of the story might have been if the "vegetable" prognosis had been accepted and the parents had considered the boy totally lacking in the capacity to attain self-sufficiency. The parents' determination to maximize their son's range of experience through training and stimulation and their conviction that he could learn to participate in many normal activities of childhood and adolescence made the difference.

In addition to the presence or absence of experiences, there are also pleasant, neutral, and unpleasant experiences or mixtures of all three. That is, in terms of experience, range refers to quantitative aspects and nature to qualitative aspects. Air trapped in an infant's stomach

Figure 2–12.

following feeding makes that aspect of eating unpleasant, but the warm, satisfied glow experienced once the air is removed is most pleasant. It is not long after birth that pleasantness and unpleasantness become a part of daily life. Some children are less fortunate than others, having many unpleasant experiences with routines imposed on them (e.g., weaning, toilet training) and having conflicts with key individuals in their lives. Others find life a generally pleasant business despite its ups and downs. Children born with a handicapping condition may suffer in terms of both the range and nature of experience. Overprotection may lead to a narrow range of experience, and parental guilt and anxiety and peer rejection may cause the child much unpleasantness.

Functioning Level.   As the children arrive at 9:00 A.M. and file through the classroom door, what does the teacher see? Does she see their capacity for learning and success in school? No. Does she see their previous range of experience? No. Does she see their previous nature of experience? No. What the teacher is confronted with every day is the result of the *complex interaction of capacity and the range and nature of experience*; in other words, each child's individual functioning level. For some children, capacity factors (e.g., birth defects) may primarily determine how they function in school. For others, a limited range of experience (e.g., isolated from the environment by anxious parents) may be of primary importance. For still others, the nature of previous experience (e.g., child abuse) may have had the greatest effect on the children's functioning level. But whether capacity or experience factors primarily determined a child's functioning level, what teachers have to work with always reflects the interaction of both. And although teachers can do nothing about capacity or the range or nature of the child's previous experience, we can accept the child's present level of functioning and do a great deal about the range and nature of future experiences. That is really what teaching is all about.

How Do Capacity and Experience Interact?

Along with the many other individual differences displayed by infants shortly after birth are differences in temperament. A visitor to a maternity ward nursery may be struck by these differences. Some infants are active, intense, and responsive, whereas others appear passive, lethargic, and unresponsive. Thomas, Chess, and Birch (1969) studied temperamental uniqueness in infants and young children. They identified several patterns of temperament, one of which was called "difficult." Difficult children (or "mother killers" as they were called informally) had irregularity of biological functions (sleeping, eating, eliminating), negative reactions to new stimuli, slowness in adapting to change, high frequency of negative moods, and predominance of intense reactions.

Two children, a boy and girl who were considered difficult in terms of temperament, were studied by Thomas, Chess, and Birch. They both displayed most of the problems listed above. The two were very similar during infancy, but nature of experience was going to affect their early years. The girl's father was impatient and angry with his daughter. He spent little time with her and was often punitive in response to her problem behavior. The girl's mother exhibited concern for the child and was more understanding and permissive but quite inconsistent. The one area in which there was consistency between the two sets of parents related to regard for rules of safety. The boy's

Figure 2–13.

parents were seen as unusually tolerant and consistent. His problems with adjustment were accepted in a calm manner. When friction arose between the boy and his siblings, it was dealt with good-humoredly. The parents waited out his negative moods without getting angry themselves. They were very permissive but set safety limits and consistently pointed out to their son the needs and rights of his peers when he was playing.

At the age of five and one-half years, these two children, who had been so similar in early life, were remarkably dissimilar in their behavior. The boy had experienced initial difficulties in nursery school, but these had disappeared, and he was now an accepted and constructive member of his class and had a group of friends. He also functioned

smoothly in most areas of his daily life. The girl had developed a number of symptoms of increasing severity. She was given to explosive anger, negativism, fear of the dark, encopresis (lack of bowel control), thumb-sucking, excessive demands for toys and sweets, poor peer relationships, and lying. The authors comment, however, that there were no problem behaviors in the one area where her parents had been consistent—safety rules.

The boy had achieved a somewhat marginal but adaptive functioning level as a result of the consistent and patient nature of experience provided by his parents, who understood and accepted their son's uniqueness and gave him support. The girl had steadily developed a behavior disorder as the result of the inconsistent and rejecting nature of experiences provided by her parents. No one can say that, had the boy been raised by the girl's parents and the girl by the boy's parents, the boy would have developed the behavior disorders and the girl would be making a satisfactory adjustment. Sex itself is a capacity-given, and perhaps both families would have reacted differently to a child of the opposite sex.

This longitudinal example of two children's dramatic differences in functioning level at five and one-half years, contrasted to their similarity in functioning during the first two years, underscores the contributions of range and nature of experience to functioning level. Had the girl been an "easy child" from birth, her behavioral outcome would probably have been very different. It was her unique capacity from birth in interaction with her parents' expectations, attitudes, and child-rearing practices that made the difference.

Throughout this text, we stress the importance of the interaction of capacity and range and nature of experience in discussing other types of exceptional learners. We will see that children

Figure 2-14.

born blind or crippled do not have a completely predestined future with respect to functioning level simply because of their capacity-based handicap at birth. Optimism, patience, acceptance, consistency, encouragement for independence, and exposure to a wide range of experiences on the part of the parents can result in a far different functioning level in childhood than hopelessness, impatience, rejection, inconsistency, and overprotection.

Defining an Exceptional Learner

Now that we have focused on the interactions of capacity and experience as the determiners of a child's functioning level at any given time, let us define the exceptional learner:

> An exceptional learner is an individual who, because of uniqueness in sensory, physical, neurological, temperamental, or intellectual capacity and/or in the nature or range of previous experience, requires an adaptation of the regular school program in order to maximize his or her functioning level.

All children traditionally labeled as *exceptional* fall under this definition. The use of the term *uniqueness in* rather than *limitations in* allows us to include the gifted learner in this definition.

How Many Exceptional Learners Are There?

The figures in Table 2-1 reflect the percentages of school-age children falling into traditional special education categories and reported as being served by the schools in 1981–82. These

Table 2-1
Percent of Exceptional Learners in School-Age Population
Reported As Served in 1981–1982*

Exceptional Learner	*Percentage of School-Age Population*
Visually handicapped	0.07
Deaf and hard of hearing	0.19
Orthopedic and health impaired	0.34
Multihandicapped	0.18
Seriously emotionally disturbed	0.85
Speech handicapped	2.83
Learning disabled	4.04
Mentally retarded	1.96
Total	10.46

*Represents data published by U. S. Department of Education (1983); data published in Education of the Handicapped: *The Independent Bi-Weekly News Service on Federal Legislation, Programs and Funding for Special Education*, Volume 9, 1983; and data published in Edgar, E., and Hayden, A., "Who are the children special education should serve and how many children are there?" Presented at American Association of Mental Deficiency, Boston, June 1982.

percentages suggest that approximately 10.5 percent of children from ages three to twenty-one have been identified by the schools as possible candidates for special education services. Does this mean that the incidence or prevalence of handicapped individuals in this age group in the United States is precisely 10.5 percent? By no means. The difficulties in making accurate population estimates is discussed in detail in chapter 10. However, consideration of a few of these difficulties merits our concern at this point in the text.

To begin with, since many exceptional learners have more than one handicapping condition, how do we account for these in specifying percentages? Suppose a child is mentally retarded, has a speech handicap, and also manifests a severe emotional disturbance? Which is the primary handicap for this child? Do we only count the primary handicap, or are all three to be counted separately? Or do we consider such a child multihandicapped? If so, how many handicapping conditions of what degree of severity constitute the criteria for placement in the multihandi-capped category?

Variations in definitions of emotional disturbance also confound the issue. A child rated "disturbed" by one teacher might be seen merely as "strong-willed" or "pensive" by another. Also, such disorders are often transient and disappear over time, as do speech handicaps. Thus, we are not always dealing with stable handicapping conditions. Geographic differences also present problems. The mildly retarded are found in greater numbers in the inner city as compared with the suburbs, while the reverse is true for the gifted. Finally, separate estimates at preschool, elementary school, and high school levels may be more meaningful since needs for special education services may vary among levels (Dunn, 1973a).

Not all of the children included in the 10.5 percent figure require special education services that take them out of the regular classroom. This is particularly true of children with speech handicaps who usually remain full-time in regular classes and receive speech therapy on a scheduled basis during the week. Those with orthopedic handicaps may also be in regular-class programs, provided physical facilities are furnished to meet their special needs. In addition, as we shall see, many other exceptional learners previously considered full-time special education students are being viewed differently and provided experience in regular-class programs when appropriate.

What Types of Services Has Special Education Traditionally Provided for Exceptional Learners?

The types of special education programs available for exceptional learners can be structured along a continuum that ranges from integration to segregation. This continuum has been described in various models that have appeared in the special education literature (Deno, 1970; Dunn, 1973). It begins with full-time placement of exceptional learners in the regular classroom and ends with their total isolation and home instruction.

Full-Time Placement in a Regular Classroom.   Despite the existence of the special class, special education has never removed all exceptional learners from the regular-class program. Regular teachers often react to the announcement that mildly retarded, disturbed, and learning-disabled children are going to be integrated into their classrooms with a remark such as, "So what else is new? I've always had children with learning and behavior problems in my classroom."

Placement of exceptional learners on a full-time basis in a regular classroom usually involves providing the teacher with a wider range of individualized instructional materials so that, particularly during academic lessons, these children will have work appropriate for their functioning levels. Speech-handicapped children are usually full-time students in regular classrooms and seldom need such materials. However, for the mildly retarded and for children with behavior disorders or learning disabilities, remedial programs that stress fundamentals and have high interest levels are necessary. Some visually handicapped learners who work well independently with Brailled texts (copies of regular texts), Braille-written texts (specifically prepared for the blind), or talking books also can be full-time students, as can the partially hearing whose hearing loss can be compensated for with a hearing aid. Many crippled children could be full-time students in regular classrooms if doors were widened for wheelchairs and ramps and lifts were available in place of stairs.

Full-Time Placement in a Regular Classroom with Special Education Consultation.   In this option, the child is a full-time student in the regular classroom, but instead of merely providing the regular teacher with materials and equipment, a special education consultant works directly with the teacher in selecting materials and teaching strategies. The consultant also may give diagnostic tests and tutor and counsel students, as well as consult with parents. Such consultants are usually experienced regular classroom teachers with advanced training in special education.

Full-Time Placement in a Regular Classroom with Special Education Tutoring.   Here the child is still enrolled in the regular classroom as a full-time student. However, the focus of the special educator is on direct service to children, rather than on consultation with the teacher. This approach traditionally has been called the itinerant teacher plan. On a scheduled basis, the special educator works individually with children in whichever area they need help. In the case of the speech-handicapped, the teacher is a speech therapist. For the blind or deaf, the teacher is a specialist who aids in Braille instruction or language training. This plan can be used in rural areas where schools are far apart and too small to have full-time special educators as staff members.

Full-Time Placement in a Regular Classroom with the Use of a Resource Room.   Gradually, we are moving toward more involvement of the exceptional learner with special education in this option. Although a full-time student in a regular classroom, the child participates in scheduled lessons in a separate classroom or resource room. Here, small-group instruction may be provided by a special educator who, in contrast to those in the earlier options, has a special classroom facility in which to offer services. The resource room teacher also acts as a consultant (as in the earlier plans) and must work closely with the regular teacher.

One major advantage of the resource room is that children with similar learning problems receive group instruction, allowing more efficient use of the teacher's time and also helping the children learn how to work in a group setting.

Learning how to pay attention and participate in a lesson presented by the teacher from the front of the room to the entire class is often difficult for exceptional learners enrolled in regular classrooms. The resource room teacher can help the children develop group-learning skills, repeat directions as often as needed, and answer questions with less delay. Resource rooms can serve many types of exceptional learners, particularly those with learning disabilities and other learning and behavior disorders.

Part-Time Placement in a Regular Classroom and Part-Time Placement in a Special Class. Here we shift the child's actual class assignment to a special classroom. In the earlier options, the child was considered a member of a regular classroom who received outside assistance. Here the child is a member of a special class who participates during scheduled activities in a regular classroom. When possible, these will be academic work periods. However, since many exceptional learners need individualized attention in academic areas, they more often participate in regular classroom activities involving music, art, and physical education.

Full-Time Placement in a Special Class. The special self-contained class has traditionally been the most frequently used placement option for the exceptional learner. In general, there are ten to twelve students with a teacher and sometimes a teacher's aide. The class and its students are assigned a label. The educable mentally retarded child goes to a class for the mentally retarded. Children in special classes are isolated from other children in the school except during recess, lunch, after-school activities, and other all-school functions. Usually only one type of exceptional learner is included in a special class, but in rural areas where the number of such children is small, separate classes for each type are not possible. Hence, a special education teacher might have to work with visually and hearing-handicapped children, as well as with the mentally retarded and children with learning disabilities or behavior disorders. Needless to say, considerable demands are made on a teacher working with children with such diverse problems.

The special class has come under attack in recent years, and the mainstreaming movement is a direct result of criticism of and disenchantment with practices of isolation and segregation in special education.

Part-Time Placement in a Special Day School and Part-Time Placement in a Regular Classroom. Special education programs are expensive, and not every school can afford a class for each type of exceptional learner. As a result, some special programs may be centralized in a single school, and children from a wide geographical area brought in daily by buses. The special day school usually is the student's primary placement. As is the case when a child is in a special class part time and in a regular classroom part time, his or her degree of participation in the regular program varies. Isolation from neighborhood classmates is one of the drawbacks of taking children from their home school to a special day school.

Full-Time Placement in a Special Day School. This option is similar to the previous one except that the special day school is totally separate from any regular school. Such schools usually serve only one type of exceptional learner. Their advantage is that the entire physical plant can be specially designed to accommodate the child. Special swimming pools, wide halls and doors, easy access to the building from the school bus, and special gymnasium and playground equipment are often features of day schools for the crippled and multihandicapped. Thus, costly facilities that are not possible to duplicate throughout a district may greatly enhance the exceptional learner's experiences in school. Such advantages may well outweigh the disadvantages of being separated from neighborhood peers and travelling a long time by bus.

Full-Time Placement in a Residential School.   Historically, the oldest plan for caring for and educating exceptional learners is the boarding or residential school. The blind, deaf, and mentally retarded were the first to be provided with such facilities during the first half of the nineteenth century. The residential school traditionally became the children's home, and they spent time with their families during vacation or on weekends, depending on the distances involved between the school and their family homes. Placement of exceptional learners in residential schools has been a continuing source of controversy, particularly recently. However, there are both advantages and disadvantages related to such placement.

To begin with, a twenty-four-hour school can provide an intensive and comprehensive program, compared to a day school or special class where the child is enrolled for only six hours a day. For the deaf, such a total program may be of great value in the area of language development. Other exceptional learners may profit from the specialized educational, vocational, and recreational services available and, particularly at the secondary level, from the greater number of teachers offering special subjects. Children living in rural areas where local schools offer limited special education may receive a far better education in a residential school. In the Soviet Union, where a large percentage of the population still resides in rural areas, the residential school is the only special education plan for exceptional learners.

The major disadvantage of the residential school is that it removes children from their homes and families. It also denies them contact with nonhandicapped children, although some residential schools do enroll students in nearby public schools during the day. Other disadvantages of this placement include the stigma of going to the "deaf school," and the geographic isolation of many residential schools that makes it difficult to attract the most qualified teachers.

The residential school concept discussed here primarily applies to the deaf and blind. Institutions for the severely retarded and disturbed provide educational programs but also offer the custodial care and medical treatment necessary for these children. The rationale for applying the residential school concept to the delinquent and socially maladjusted includes protection of society and corrective treatment, as well as educational responsibility.

Hospital Instruction.   When children are confined to a hospital for long periods of time because they are ill or convalescing from surgery, local or county school systems may send a teacher to the hospital to provide bedside instruction. In addition, crippled and chronically ill children who reside much of the time in convalescent homes or sanitariums may also be provided with instruction by a visiting teacher.

Home Instruction.   When a child is home full time and even denied contact with children with similar handicapping conditions, he or she is the most isolated of all handicapped children. School districts have traditionally sent visiting teachers to the home to work with such children three times a week for one- or two-hour tutoring sessions. Children requiring home instruction may be the chronically ill, who are bedridden and who will never be able to attend school; those from regular schools who are recovering from an illness or injury or convalescing from surgery; or those excluded from school because no program is available to meet their needs. Children may be excluded because of behavior disorders that the school is unable to control, but with the increase in special education programs for these children, exclusion is becoming more of an emergency measure than a permanent one.

Recent technological advances have brought telephone and television instruction to children confined at home. The teaching-by-telephone technique allows a teacher to call a group of children on the telephone and conduct a lesson while they are all on the same line.

A sophisticated telephonic system has been developed for the Los Angeles Unified School District by Pacific Telephone Company. At Widney High School for the Physically Handicapped, there is a Teleclass Department that has ten consoles. Each console has nineteen outgoing lines and one for incoming calls. Students may be connected to the consoles so they can hear one another's voices and hold group discussions. Teachers are able to prevent students from hearing each other while they speak with them in private; they can also divide the class so that small groups can hold separate discussions. The class periods follow the Widney bell schedule, and teachers offer required courses for grades seven through twelve, as well as electives. Parents must come to school to pick up textbooks and instruction sheets. Homework is sent by mail to the school and returned to the student once it is graded.

Until recent years, special education services for exceptional learners primarily were provided by means of the special class. However, with more consultation and assistance currently available for regular teachers, placement in a regular classroom on at least a part-time basis is becoming increasingly common. The resource room plan has also emerged as a usable and effective replacement for the self-contained special class.

Summary

The field of special education is concerned with learners who are unique along seven critical dimensions related to learning in school and functioning elsewhere. Although many of us are unique in one way or another along one or more of these dimensions, it is not until we reach a certain level of uniqueness—negative or positive—that special adaptations need to be made for us to learn and function in an optimal manner. The dimensions are *vision*, *hearing*, *movement*, *perceptual-motor*, *communication*, *social-emotional*, and *intelligence*. Once we establish an individual's uniqueness on a given dimension through either informal or formal observation, we often assign a label:

Visually handicapped

Deaf and hard-of-hearing

Deaf-Blind

Orthopedically and other health impaired

Emotionally disturbed

Speech impaired

Learning disabled

Mentally retarded

In addition, in this text we consider a type of exceptional learner not traditionally considered handicapped or exceptional—the economically disadvantaged and/or culturally different.

Whereas some of these labels reflect uniqueness on a single dimension, many reflect uniqueness on more than one. For example, the deaf or hard-of-hearing individual has problems not only on the dimension of hearing, but also on the dimension of communication.

Uniqueness in vision, hearing, movement, communication, and intelligence may relate to inborn or birth-related characteristics or *capacity*. Social-emotional uniqueness may relate primarily to *range* and *nature* of *experience*. The interaction between capacity and experience is responsible for the actual *functioning level* of any exceptional learner. Whatever the movement potential or capacity of such a learner, if we restrict opportunities for movement experiences and associate movement with negative and fear-producing stimuli, we will markedly affect the movement functioning level we see at any time. You can substitute any of the above capacity-related characteristics (e.g., vision, hearing) and the same will be true. If we focus primarily on the capacity limitations associated with functioning level (e.g., intelligence) we may consider the exceptional individual "defective." However, if we focus more on limitations in range and nature of experience, such an individual becomes "untaught." The term *exceptional learner* used throughout the text establishes our position that no matter what the limitation imposed by capacity, all exceptional individuals are at all times untaught and ready to learn something. The field of special education is concerned with those somethings they are ready to learn.

Special education services in the past were much more restrictive than they are today. Now, rather than isolate exceptional learners, efforts are made to keep them involved at least part time in a regular education program.

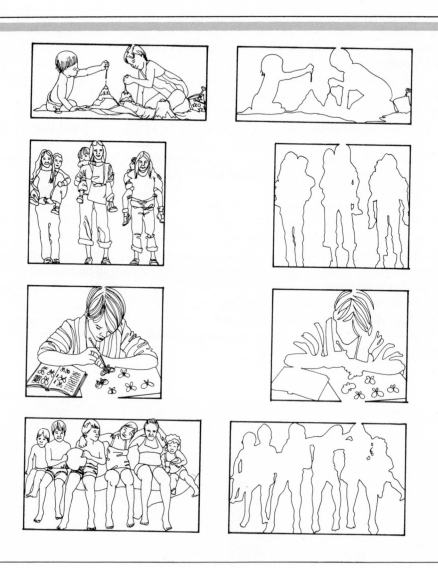

CHAPTER 3

Flexibility and Social Uniqueness

In our discussion of exceptional learners in the previous chapters, we spoke of uniqueness. In this chapter and the next, we discuss this uniqueness within a framework suggested by Simpson (1950), an evolutionary psychologist who wrote about the uniqueness of human beings in nature. According to Simpson, when compared to all other species, the human being is unique because of four interrelated concepts: (1) flexibility, (2) sociality,* (3) intelligence, and (4) individualization.

Flexibility

Flexibility refers to the unusual human attribute of adapting to a changing environment. People can adapt to geographic regions with wide extremes in climate, such as the North Pole or the African jungle. In fact, wherever they are they can adjust and modify their behavior even when conditions vary across time or increase in complexity. The concept of flexibility as we use it includes the following dimensions discussed in chapter 2: vision, hearing, movement, and perceptual-motor. We broaden the dimensions somewhat and define flexibility as follows:

1. looking, listening, and other sensory experiences

2. perceiving environmental stimuli

3. physical movement

4. active and independent participation

5. learning knowledge and acquiring skills related to successful adaptation to the environment.

*Simpson actually uses the term *socialization*, but we use *sociality* as did Martin and Stendler (1959).

Figure 3-1.

Sociality

Sociality refers to the unique human attributes of needing and interacting with each other. Human beings are biologically helpless at birth. Without the care and protection of others, human life would be over almost as soon as it begins. Initially, the infant is concerned with the attention of others and with having others meet his or her needs. Before long, the concern is for other persons themselves, communicating effectively with them, and for social living, quite apart from any biological necessity. Including the communication and social-emotional dimensions presented earlier, we define sociality as follows:

1. communicating effectively with others

2. seeking social interactions

3. establishing harmonious relationships with others.

Intelligence

Whatever intelligence is, human beings possess it in an amount, if not in kind, superior to all other forms of life. The dimension of intelligence was discussed earlier with the uniqueness of exceptional learners. Among definitions of intelligence are the following:

1. competence in learning new things

2. the grasping of broad and subtle facts, particularly abstract facts

3. ability to see relationships and plan for the future

4. memory and the ability to profit from past experience

5. ability to use symbols, especially verbal symbols.

Individualization

Simpson's final unique attribute refers to the multiple possibilities for human beings to attain an almost unlimited variation in their growth and development and to achieve career and vocational goals. The concept of individualization relates to the outcome of an individual's development along all seven of the dimensions previously discussed: vision, hearing, movement, perceptual-motor, communication, social-emotional, and intelligence.

Figure 3–2.

Figure 3–3.

Although capacity factors will play a part in determining our eventual attainment along these dimensions, range and nature of experience will also be critical. Consider the young school-age boy and girl and what may be ahead for them as they grow and mature and enter adult life. Consider the many influences and opportunities or lack of opportunities that will gradually shape their future development. Our definition of individualization includes the following:

1. possibilities for marriage and family life

2. possibilities for vocational and career development

3. possibilities for adult functioning level.

In the following discussion of exceptional learners, we use the concepts of flexibility, sociality, intelligence, and individualization. Our rationale for selecting these is presented in the following statement regarding exceptional learners:

> If all human beings can be viewed as truly unique in nature because of flexibility, sociality, intelligence, and individualization, then individuals can be considered truly unique or exceptional in relation to other human beings as they demonstrate greater or lesser competence with respect to these same four concepts.

In this chapter and the next, we use three of these concepts—flexibility, sociality, and intelligence—as headings under which we group nine types of exceptional learners. Individuali-

Figure 3–4.

zation, or the status of exceptional learners in later life, is discussed in chapter 8. Our grouping of exceptional learners by category under a particular concept is far from exact. The dimensions of flexibility, sociality, and intelligence all overlap. However, we have attempted to select the particular concept that appears most relevant to the uniqueness of each type of exceptional learner and discuss them categorically as follows:

FLEXIBILITY UNIQUENESS

Visually handicapped individuals

Deaf and hard-of-hearing individuals

Deaf-Blind individuals

Orthopedically and other health impaired individuals

SOCIAL UNIQUENESS

Emotionally disturbed individuals

Speech impaired individuals

Economically disadvantaged and/or culturally
different individuals

INTELLECTUAL UNIQUENESS

Individuals with learning disabilities

Mentally retarded individuals

Gifted individuals

Flexibility Uniqueness: Visually Handicapped Individuals

Perhaps no other handicapping condition evokes as marked an emotional response as blindness. Blindness has historically been considered the most severe of all handicapping conditions. In the past, pity for the blind child led to early establishment of custodial institutions. Although pity may be a positive attitude with respect to their general welfare, it can deprive blind and other individuals of the range and nature of experience necessary to maximize their functioning levels and to aid them in achieving self-sufficiency. A reduction of pity for the blind and an increase in the expectation that they can become self-sufficient have been viewed as significant phenomena of the twentieth century (Lowenfeld, 1973). Despite its severity, blindness does not preclude learning in school or economic independence, provided modifications and adaptations are made for blind individuals.

Definition and Classification

Public Law 94–142 defines a visual handicap as follows:

> "Visually handicapped" means a visual impairment which, even with correction, adversely affects a child's educational performance. The term includes both partially seeing and blind children.

Traditionally, the visually handicapped child who was considered blind was placed in classes where Braille was the primary medium of instruction. Those considered partially sighted attended classes where large print was used. However, since many children considered legally blind were found to be able to read large print, the dichotomy between the two types of visually handicapped children has tended to disappear and both are educated more and more in single programs.

The most frequent definition of blindness used by agencies and states to determine eligibility for aid is based on visual acuity and field of vision. Children are considered blind if they meet either of two criteria. In terms of visual acuity, the child is blind if corrected vision in the better eye is 20/200 or less. This ratio refers to distance and states that the child can see at a distance of twenty feet what a person with normal vision can see at two hundred feet. The child may also be considered blind if the widest diameter of his or her visual field subtends an angle no greater than twenty degrees, even though visual acuity in that narrow field may be better than 20/200. If the corrected vision in the better eye is 20/70, that is, the child can see at twenty feet what the individual with normal vision can see at seventy feet, he or she is considered partially seeing.

Several limitations in these legal definitions of visual impairment concern the special educator (Scholl, 1975). To begin with, they are based on measures of distance vision obtained by having the child attempt to read block letters on a wall chart (e.g., Snellen chart) some twenty feet away. Since most school tasks (such as reading) require near vision, a measure of near rather than distance vision is more relevant to the child's actual functioning level in the classroom. A special Snellen chart held fourteen inches from the child allows measurement of near vision and provides more useful information for the teacher.

According to the American Academy of Ophthalmology and Otolaryngology and the International Council of Ophthalmology, it is useful to classify visual handicaps in terms of visual performance (Jan, Freeman, & Scott, 1977). It has been proposed that visually impaired individuals be grouped functionally as follows:

1. Normal or near-normal vision indicates the ability to perform all visual tasks adequately without special aids.

2. Low vision indicates that, without special aids, a person is unable to perform tasks that normally require detailed vision.

3. Blindness means that, without increased reliance on other senses, a person is unable to perform tasks that normally require gross vision.

Incidence

As a group, the visually handicapped constitute the smallest group of exceptional learners, next to the multihandicapped. The United States Office of Special Education cites an incidence of 0.07 percent. In addition, one-half of the legally blind persons in the United States are age sixty-five or older. The group under twenty years of age accounts for only 10 percent of the legally blind.

In the school-age population, an estimated one in five hundred children has a visual problem that warrants some intervention, but the majority probably only require corrective lenses. However, since visual screening procedures are not widespread, many children with visual difficulties are never identified. It is also not known how many such children become school failures or drop out of school early because visual problems limit their academic achievement (Scholl, 1975).

Causes

The major causes of blindness and visual impairment include heredity, infectious diseases, oxygen poisoning, accidents and injuries, and tumors. Factors related to heredity (e.g., cataracts, optic nerve atrophy, and albinism) are the most frequent causes of blindness and remain fairly constant in their appearance across age groups. Infectious diseases and poisonings, however, have varied as causes of blindness across age groups because of their relationship to two critical events.

Rubella epidemics constitute the first of these events. Rubella is known to have caused major increases in visual impairment, and epidemics used to occur almost once a decade. Rubella is a virus disease that is often difficult to diagnose. Approximately 20 percent of women of childbearing age have had it and have developed an immunity. However, if the disease is contracted during the first three months of pregnancy or sometime later, the virus may kill or cripple by crossing the placental barrier and attacking the fetus. The virus is capable of killing growing cells and attacks tissues of the eyes, ears, and other organs. The development of a rubella vaccine has led to a marked decrease in the occurrence of the disease in expectant mothers. The last rubella epidemic in the United States was in 1964, and it reportedly affected some thirty thousand infants. Of those who survived, almost 50 percent had visual defects (Montgomery, 1979).

The second critical event related to the blinding of thousands of children between 1938 and 1955 was the development of the incubator and the use of an enriched oxygen mixture to save the lives of premature infants. Such use often resulted in a destructive disease, retrolental fibroplasia, that defied efforts to discover its source for more than a decade.

Identification and Diagnosis

Identification of children who are born blind is almost always made by parents within the first year of life. Children with lesser visual impairments may not be singled out until elementary school when vision becomes important in the performance of school work. The National Society for the Prevention of Blindness considers these ten behavioral signs as possible indicators of visual defects (National Society for the Prevention of Blindness, 1965):

1. Attempting to brush away blurs, rubbing eyes excessively, frowning.

2. Shutting or covering one eye, tilting head or thrusting it forward when looking at near or distant objects.

3. Difficulty in reading or in other work requiring close use of eyes.

4. Blinking more than usual, crying often, irritability when doing close work.

5. Stumbling or tripping over small objects.

6. Holding books or small objects close to eyes.

7. Inability to participate in games requiring distance vision.

8. Excessive sensitivity to light.

9. Red-rimmed, encrusted, or swollen eyelids; recurring sties; inflamed or watery eyes; crossed eyes.

10. Complaints of not seeing well; of dizziness, headaches, or nausea following close eye work; of blurred or double vision.

Treatment and Educational Provisions

Any child consistently manifesting one or more of these signs should be referred to the school nurse, who may then refer the child to an eye doctor for intensive examination. An *ophthalmologist* is a medical doctor who specializes in the diagnosis and treatment of defects and diseases of the eye. He or she can perform surgery and also prescribe other types of treatment, including medication and glasses. Another eye specialist who can examine a child having visual difficulty is the *optometrist*, who is a licensed, nonmedical practitioner. He or she measures refractive errors and eye muscle disturbances and prescribes glasses, prisms, or exercises for the eye.

It was once believed that partially seeing children actually damaged their eyes by using them, and in the 1930s "sight saving" classes for such children were common. This belief no longer exists, and the partially sighted are encouraged to use their eyes by an increasing emphasis on the use of magnification (Jan, Freeman, & Scott, 1977). Glasses with lenses of various strengths help improve vision, as do simple hand magnifiers.

A closed-circuit television reader has been developed to aid partially sighted students. A camera with a zoom lens photographs part of a page of print and projects a magnified image onto a television screen. The student moves the book while reading so the appropriate portion of the page is magnified. The size of the magnified print can be controlled, and some models feature either white print on a black background or vice versa.

A number of devices have been developed to aid the blind in reading. A recent technological advance resulted in the development of the Optacon, a portable electronic device that includes a camera for converting print to vibrating letter images. This is accomplished by a photo-chemical-to-mechanical energy conversion process. The visually handicapped individual slides a small probe with photocells across the printed page with one hand, and reads the letters through a finger on the other hand that is placed on a receiver plate. The actual letter forms are "felt" as electronic impulses on the surface of the finger. Although a major problem exists with respect to reading speed, the Optacon has reduced dependence on sighted readers and the transcription of special materials from print into Braille.

The partially seeing child also may be given reading material printed in large type (letters approximately one-eighth inch high). However, such print reduces reading speed, and many children with visual problems prefer to hold books in regular print close to their eyes or use some form of magnification. Under ideal reading conditions, reading speed and comprehension using regular print were found to be equal to large print, with no difference in terms of fatigue (Sykes, 1972).

Some educators of the visually impaired feel that the student who cannot read regular print, even with a magnifying aid, should develop skills in the use of Braille or an electronic reading

A desk-top machine that can actually "read" printed material aloud to blind persons has been developed. The machine, a two-foot cube about the size of a desk-top photocopier, "speaks" in a deliberate, expressionless voice. To operate it, an open book or other printed material is placed on a glass-topped scanning device. The machine studies the material line by line and reads it aloud at about 200 words a minute. This speed is the equivalent of recorded aids, such as Talking Books or tape recordings.

The machine can recognize letters printed in virtually any typeface. In a television demonstration, the device read aloud Lincoln's Gettysburg Address. The reading was clear and distinct and in a sing-song voice with what sounded like a slight Scandinavian accent.

---

device. They recommend that large print be limited to reference material, dictionaries, mathematics, and maps (Corrigan, 1977).

Both the partially sighted and the blind may profit from a "talking calculator." Once basic mathematical skills are mastered, the calculator can be used as any electronic calculator with the exception that numerical entries are read aloud to the student through an earplug. The Cranmer abacus is a specially designed abacus with raised markings and a backing that holds the beads in position. It also is a popular mathematical aid for the visually impaired. Braille rulers, protractors, and compasses are also available.

Despite technological advances that facilitate the reading and number work of the visually impaired, Braille will probably continue to be of great importance for years to come. Braille was first introduced in the United States in 1860, but the Standard English Braille system was not adopted until 1932. Braille is a far from efficient system, but it does provide the exceptional learner who is blind with a means of reading and writing. It consists of a six-dot cell that provides for sixty-three different characters. Twenty-six combinations of dots are used for alphabet letters; the remaining thirty-seven represent punctuation signs and contractions that allow for shortening or abbreviating words. In some ways, Braille is a system of shorthand since each word is not spelled out letter-for-letter. As a result, blind children have difficulty with spelling because of the frequent abbreviations used in the Braille system. In addition to a Braille code for reading and writing, there are codes for music, mathematics, computer sciences, and chemistry.

As a means of reading, Braille has many disadvantages. Books and periodicals printed in Braille are very bulky and take up a great deal of storage space. For example, a single Braille edition of the *Reader's Digest* consists of four volumes, eleven by thirteen and one-half inches, each approximately one inch thick. Braille also is a slow method of reading; a good Braille reader can read only about as fast as a sighted person can read printed material aloud. A professionally published book in Braille can cost twelve times as much as the book in print. As a result, individual texts and materials often have to be transcribed by hand by teachers and volunteers. Transcription into Braille can also be done by computers, but again the cost is high.

Tape recordings are very important tools for learning. The ready availability of compact cassette recorders make them particularly popular. Again, teachers or volunteers can transcribe reading material from both standard texts and books for leisure reading.

Two writing approaches are in use. One involves the Perkins Braille writer, a typewriter-like device that produces the configurations of Braille letters in raised dots, which the student can feel immediately to check for accuracy. The other method involves the use of a standard typewriter. Once the student has mastered standard typing skills, class work can be typed and given directly to the individual's regular classroom teacher. This direct communication, which eliminates the translation of work prepared on a Braille writer into standard English, provides a more personal level of participation in the regular-class program.

Teachers of visually impaired children often serve as resource teachers in the public school. That is, they are available to work with students to help them acquire basic reading, mathematical, and written language skills by providing the necessary technical aids, Braille materials, or equipment. They also help the visually impaired student master orientation and mobility skills. We discuss the importance of these skills in chapter 6. Once the blind individual is integrated into a regular-class program, the special education teacher serves as a tutor and resource teacher continuing basic skill development and aiding with homework assignments on a scheduled basis.

From this brief introduction to the visually impaired, we move to a discussion of hearing-impaired individuals, after which we discuss more severely handicapped individuals—the deaf-blind.

Flexibility Uniqueness:
Deaf and Hard-of-Hearing Individuals

One of the most significant experiences of developing human life is the hearing of spoken language. Things have names; they can be described; you can talk about past, present, and future events; you can learn rules; and you can learn how others feel about you. Language plays a critical part in the socialization of the individual and in the educational process. Partial or total lack of access to language experience presents serious problems. In this section, we discuss individuals who are denied such access to varying degrees.

Definition and Classification

Public Law 94–142 divides hearing-handicapped individuals into two categories: the deaf and the hard-of-hearing. According to the law:

> "Deaf" means a hearing impairment which is so severe that the child is impaired in processing linguistic information through hearing, with or without amplification, which adversely affects educational performance.

> "Hard of hearing" means a hearing impairment, whether permanent or fluctuating, which adversely affects a child's educational performance but which is not included under the definition of "deaf" in this section.

The child who suffers a hearing loss after he or she has developed speech and language is more fortunate than the child who is born deaf or with a hearing impairment. Helen Keller actually experienced nineteen months of normal development of hearing, speech, and language before she became deaf. This brief period of normalcy undoubtedly contributed greatly to her remarkable achievements in developing speech and language skills after the still undiagnosed illness that left her both blind and deaf. Generally, the later the hearing loss occurs, the less serious its effect on oral communication, since maintenance of speech and language is much less difficult than its acquisition (Avery, 1975).

Hearing is usually measured in terms of decibels (dB), a logarithmic unit of sound intensity above an arbitrary reference point. This reference point is established as the average level at which normal-hearing young adults, using both ears, can detect the faintest sound of which they are capable (Davis, 1970). The average whisper requires about 20 dB of sound intensity and moderate conversation about 60 dB; 130 dB of sound begins to produce discomfort for the listener.

In terms of simple definitions, a deaf person cannot hear below 70 dB of intensity and cannot understand speech by means of the ear alone or with the use of a hearing aid. The hard-of-hearing person requires 35 to 69 dB of intensity and, although it may be difficult, can understand speech through the ear alone with or without a hearing aid. Moores (1978) designates four levels of deafness:

Level 1 (requires 35 to 54 dB intensity). Individuals in this category usually do not require special education services but may need special speech and hearing assistance.

Level 2 (requires 55 to 69 dB intensity). Persons at this level occasionally require special education services and do require special speech, hearing, and language assistance.

Level 3 (requires 70 to 89 dB intensity). At this level the individual will routinely require special education services and special speech, hearing, and language assistance.

Level 4 (requires 90 or greater dB intensity). Individuals at this level require the same assistance as those at Level 3.

Incidence

Hearing impairment exists in many degrees of severity. As a result, incidence estimates can be misleading if only the most severe hearing handicaps are considered. Many children with hearing problems go unnoticed, although their difficulties may interfere with their learning in school. The United States Office of Special Education estimate for the deaf and hard-of-hearing is approximately 0.19 percent, but estimates as high as 5 percent have been reported when milder hearing losses are considered (Myklebust, 1964; Silverman & Lane, 1970). Of this 5 percent, probably only 1 to 1½ percent require some form of special education intervention; the remaining 3½ to 4 percent primarily need prompt medical assistance so that their condition is remedied and further hearing loss prevented. Children in this latter group may also profit from educational assistance, ranging from special seating in the regular classroom to part-time tutoring in communication skills (McConnell, 1973).

Causes

For almost half of the hearing handicapped population, the causes of hearing loss are unknown. Among the most common presently identified causes of childhood deafness are: heredity, maternal rubella, meningitis, prematurity, and mother-child blood incompatability (Moores, 1978). In a study of 41,109 students enrolled in programs for the deaf during the 1970–71 school year (Ries, 1973), approximately 14 percent of the cases were attributed to maternal rubella. Heredity accounted for 7½ percent, prematurity for slightly more than 5 percent, meningitis for just under 5 percent, and mother-child blood incompatability for about 1 percent (down from 3½ percent due to preventative techniques).

Mother-child blood incompatability occurs when the mother and fetus have different Rh blood group factors or when the mother has blood group O and the fetus has blood group A or B. Mixing of fetal and maternal blood is common at birth. Thus, in subsequent pregnancies, the mother's system produces antibodies that destroy fetal red blood cells, thereby reducing the oxygen supply to the fetus. Routine blood tests for prospective parents and in-utero blood transfusions can prevent these effects.

Maternal rubella was not associated with hearing loss until World War II. However, rubella epidemics, such as those during 1958–59 and 1964–65, established the disease as the major nongenetic cause of deafness among school-age children during the 1960s and into the 1970s. The development of the rubella vaccine has led to a marked decrease in the occurrence of the disease. However, the fact that some mothers do not seek immunization and the additional fact that the vaccine's period of effectiveness has not been precisely determined have raised questions about the possibilities of future rubella epidemics (Harris, 1979). Recently, sexually transmitted diseases, such as herpes simplex, cytomegalovirus, B-strep, and *Chlamydia Trachomotis*, have come to be viewed as the most likely causes of the increasing prevalence of deafness in children (Vernon & Rabush, 1981).

In addition to hereditary and disease causes of deafness, hearing loss may occur today through frequent exposure to very high-intensity noise associated with occupational and other environments. Major hearing problems may not be caused by such sounds, but certain toys, such as cap guns and toy rockets, can produce noise levels sufficient to damage hearing (McConnell, 1973). Rock and roll music has also been shown to be played in public places at intensity levels above the damage-risk levels (Lipscomb, 1969).

Identification and Diagnosis

In identifying hearing-handicapped children, teacher referrals and parent requests for evaluation locate some children who need help. But the majority may not be detected because they hear conversational speech and learn to talk at an average age. A loss of thirty or forty decibels often goes unnoticed, and the deviant behavior that develops may be attributed to low intelligence or emotional problems.

One recommendation has been to conduct a periodic group screening test of all school children (Lipscomb, 1969). For children who appear to have a hearing loss on a screening test, an individual evaluation is recommended. This test is usually conducted by an *audiologist* under the supervision of an *otologist*, a physician who can determine the exact nature of the hearing difficulty and, if necessary, administer or prescribe treatment. This specialist may discover wax in the child's ear, infected adenoids or tonsils, or some other abnormality that can be corrected. The audiologist and otologist also can determine the type of hearing aid that will improve the child's hearing.

Treatment and Educational Provisions

For more than 200 years, a controversy has existed among those concerned with teaching language skills to deaf children: to what degree, if any, should manual communication be taught along with lipreading and speech? Manual communication consists of both finger spelling and signing. Finger spelling means literally that—a series of twenty-six hand configurations representing the letters of the alphabet. A person communicating through finger spelling holds his or her hand in front of the chest and spells each word, letter by letter, with hand configurations. In the American manual alphabet, a closed fist with thumb extended and fingers facing the receiver stands for the letter *A*, a closed fist with thumb placed under the three middle fingers stands for the letter *M*. Individuals proficient in finger spelling can present words at a rate somewhat faster than the rate of an accomplished typist (Moores, 1978).

Signing, a second manual communication approach, uses word signs instead of a literal letter-by-letter spelling of a word. Each sign has three elements: (1) the position of the hands, (2) the configuration of the hands, and (3) the movement of the hands to different positions. For example, the sign for *good* consists of the left hand's being held in front of the chest spelling the letter *B* (fingers extended with thumb crossing palm). The right hand, also in the *B* position, is touched to the lips and then brought down so that the back of it rests against the palm of the left hand.

There has been a long-standing controversy over the best method of teaching language skills to hearing-impaired children. The controversy is whether to include finger spelling and/or signing in the language training process. Strict oralists prohibit gestures and signs and teach only lipreading and speech. The so-called Rochester method combines finger spelling and oral training, whereas the Total Communication method consists of oral training, finger spelling, and the use of signs.

One approach to exploring whether manual communication methods interfere with the development of speech and lipreading is to compare deaf children reared by deaf parents who used manual communication with those reared by hearing parents who did not. The children of deaf parents would be exposed to manual communication from an early age; children of hearing parents most likely would not. The results of several studies comparing such children reveal that those with hearing parents have more preschool experience and tutoring and come from families on higher socioeconomic levels; yet, the children of deaf parents exhibit consistent educational, social, and communicative superiority. Moores (1978) reflects on these studies: "One only can speculate on the attainment of deaf children of hearing parents if, in addition to familial, social, educational, and economic advantages, they had benefited from some form of early systematic communication with their parents" (p. 180).

Lowell (1981) thinks the results of such studies should be qualified because deaf parents, besides using manual communication, have a better understanding of all aspects of deafness than do hearing parents and are able to do a better job with their children, regardless of the method of communication. The Total Communication method (oral training plus finger spelling plus the use of signs) is probably the method used most widely today. In addition to the evidence provided by studies of deaf children reared by deaf parents, there are other factors contributing to the increased use of Total Communication: (1) the recognition that a language of signs is a true language; (2) the recognition that purely manual or oral methods have limitations for the profoundly deaf; (3) the increasing militancy of deaf adults who had strict oral training but who have come to recognize the advantages of Total Communication; and (4) the increased interest in sign language by hearing people.

Education for deaf children is provided in residential schools, day schools, and special classes in public schools. Approximately 40 percent of deaf children in educational programs go to residential schools that are operated privately or publicly. The remainder are enrolled in public or private day schools or public day classes. In public school special classes, about five to ten children are assigned to work with a special teacher. The decision as to whether a deaf child should be placed in a day school or residential school program cannot be made on the basis of which is the most effective educational setting; it must consider what is most beneficial for a particular child in a particular community (Kirk, 1972). If adequate resources are available at home, such children are probably best placed in a day school or class. As we stressed earlier, since the normal-hearing child benefits from a great deal of incidental learning *before* entering school, educating parents of preschool deaf children to provide simple but necessary learning experiences before school entrance is very important.

The John Tracy Clinic in Los Angeles has one of the oldest and best known programs for training parents and guardians to work with preschool deaf children and deaf-blind individuals of any age. In addition, a four-year nursery school program for deaf children is run at the Clinic. Much of the parent training is through correspondence courses. One such course deals with the deaf baby; another, the deaf preschooler; and a third, deaf-blind preschoolers. There is no charge for the correspondence courses, and the Clinic has requests for them from many countries. As part of the courses, parents report on an on-going basis to the Tracy Clinic about their child and the progress being made during their training. The Clinic then prepares individual letters responding to concerns expressed by the parent.

Children with hearing handicaps are at a serious disadvantage in learning to communicate and understand human language. As we have seen, this disadvantage is our primary concern in defining a hearing handicap and planning treatment and educational programs for children who are deaf or partially hearing. This concern is expressed continuously throughout the text as we examine more closely the psychological and educational characteristics of the hearing handicapped.

Flexibility Uniqueness: Deaf-Blind Individuals

The individual born with severe or total impairment in both the senses of hearing and sight is destined to experience serious sensory isolation. Despite such isolation, there is no deaf-blind child who cannot be considered a learner.

Definition

According to Public Law 94–142:

> "deaf-blind" means concomitant hearing and visual impairment, the combination of
> which causes such severe communication and other developmental problems that
> they cannot be accommodated in special education programs solely for deaf or blind
> children.

McInnes and Treffry (1977) stress that the so-called deaf-blind child is not a deaf child who
cannot see, a blind child who cannot hear, or a retarded child with visual and auditory problems.
He or she is a child with a multiplicity of problems. They suggest the term *multisensory
deprivation* as a more accurate description than deaf-blindness and define the condition as
follows:

> The deaf-blind child is one whose combination of visual and auditory impairment
> results in multi-sensory deprivation, which renders inadequate the traditional ap-
> proaches to child rearing used to alleviate the handicaps of blindness, deafness, or
> retardation. (p. 338)

Causes

As is the case with severe visual or auditory impairments, the common causes of deaf-blindness
are premature birth and infectious diseases such as rubella and meningitis. As stated earlier, these
diseases are far less frequent today due to medical advances.

Identification and Diagnosis

The deaf-blind child will be identified by a physician, the parents, or in very rare cases a special
educator in programs for the blind, deaf, or retarded. One problem associated with identification
is that an initial handicap of blindness *or* deafness *or* retardation will be identified, the child
treated accordingly, and a significant period of time allowed to pass before another evaluation
reveals any further handicaps. Another problem arises when the child is identified as having a
major handicap, such as deafness, with an additional handicap. There is treatment of the major
handicap, but no effort to uncover and treat the problems of sensory *integration* that are involved
(McInnes & Treffry, 1977).

Treating the deaf-blind child as blind may result in the child's becoming a functionally
retarded deaf child with gradually developing severe behavior disorders; treating him or her as
deaf with a visual impairment may result in the child's becoming a functionally retarded blind
child who also develops severe behavior problems. The term *functionally retarded* means that
"without any knowledge of the child's true intellectual potential, what we see is retarded
behavior." This retarded behavior is not the result of the effects of blindness *or* deafness. Rather,

it reflects the great difficulty the child has in integrating environmental information into a meaningful whole.

As soon as there is reason to believe an infant or young child is deaf-blind (or one or the other), an in-depth evaluation should take place immediately. The evaluation should be conducted by an interdisciplinary team including an ophthalmologist, otologist, audiologist, neurologist, pediatrician, psychologist, and geneticist. These team members must understand the interrelatedness of their specialties and communicate to the parents that they are not being bounced back and forth among a number of professionals but participating in a concerted effort to evaluate the child's problems.

Regardless of the findings of the evaluation, the evaluative process is not over. This process must be ongoing because the child's developmental status may change over time. It is one thing if vision and hearing loss have been present since birth but quite another if the child was either blind or deaf at birth and developed the other impairment sometime later. Also, the impairments may change in degree of severity over time, and these changes must be recognized as quickly as possible if the child is to benefit.

Treatment and Educational Provisions

In addition to the professionals concerned with evaluating the deaf-blind child, others stand ready to assist in developing and implementing an intervention program. The social worker, physical therapist, and special educator may all participate in this process. Communication becomes the central goal in the intervention program. The physical, developmental, and social handicaps of the deaf-blind child are so severe that their combination seems to bring all environmental interaction to a halt. The most significant early intervener is the child's mother or other caretaker who must learn to establish communication with the child. Such communication may use whatever residual vision or hearing the child possesses or involve tactual stimulation of various types (e.g., raising the baby's arms, stroking the arms, shaking the crib). This stimulation will eventually become a form of language; the baby learns that one stimulus means the mother is present, another that it is time to eat, and so on.

From these early efforts at communication with the environment, a highly individualized educational program must be developed. One such program includes seven areas of focus: (1) social and emotional development, (2) living skills, (3) orientation and mobility, (4) language development, (5) cognitive development, (6) perceptual development, and (7) gross and fine motor development (McInnes & Treffry, 1977). These broad goals translate into countless hours of building block training and are simultaneous rather than consecutive in emphasis. For example, social and emotional development is a concern in every experience undertaken by the child.

From what is known of the learning potential of deaf-blind individuals, there is no excuse for neglecting them, considering them profoundly retarded, or confining them to the forgotten wards of custodial institutions. The specialized curriculum used with deaf-blind individuals is discussed further in Part II of this text.

Flexibility Uniqueness: Orthopedically and Other Health Impaired Individuals

Orthopedically handicapped individuals are also highly visible, and their movement and speech problems and use of wheelchairs and braces may evoke a variety of emotional responses in others, such as pity, fear, guilt, or embarrassment. One of the most unfortunate persistent myths regarding exceptional individuals is that a crippled body and a crippled mind invariably go together. Although mental retardation may occur in relation to such orthopedic impairments as cerebral palsy, there is no one-to-one correspondence.

Individuals with other health impairments, such as asthma or a heart condition, may be indistinguishable from normal children intellectually, but their lowered vitality, inability to participate in strenuous school activities, and frequent absences may greatly interfere with their education.

Definition

According to Public Law 94–142:

> "Orthopedically impaired" means: A severe orthopedic impairment which adversely affects a child's educational performance. The term includes impairments caused by congenital anomaly (e.g., clubfoot, absence of some member, etc.), impairments caused by disease (e.g., poliomyelitis, bone tuberculosis, etc.), and impairments from other causes (e.g., cerebral palsy, amputation, and fractures or burns which cause contractures).

The law then defines other health impairments as follows:

> "Other health impaired" means limited strength, vitality, or alertness due to chronic or acute health problems such as a heart condition, tuberculosis, rheumatic fever, nephritis, asthma, sickle cell anemia, hemophilia, epilepsy, lead poisoning, leukemia, or diabetes which adversely affects a child's educational performance.

As seen in these definitions, we are talking about a very diverse group of individuals. And within each type of disability condition there is further diversity. Thus, we can only refer to "children with cerebral palsy" or "children with asthma" and make general statements with a limited degree of certainty. Each individual will be unique, as is the case with all exceptional learners. In an effort to cut across the diversity presented by individuals with orthopedic and other health impairments, Pless and Douglas (1971), suggest considering the following questions in describing individual cases:

1. Type of disability
    a. Does the impairment affect the individual motorically?
    b. Does the impairment involve sensory problems such as restricted vision or hearing?
    c. Does the impairment constitute a disfigurement which is visible to others?

One of the authors is reminded of a college student with cerebral palsy who asked for an appointment. Sitting on the edge of his chair, staring intently at the author, he slowly and deliberately struggled to make his speech intelligible, saying, "Inside this crippled body, there is a good brain, and I intend to go on with my education and use it." Such determi-nation certainly reflected the positive interaction of capacity and experience in this young man's past. The educational problems he faced were the result of mobility limitation in getting to school, walking, climbing stairs, and writing rather than intellectual factors.

2. **Duration of disability**
   a. Is the impairment permanent?
   b. Is the impairment of indefinite duration?
   c. Is the impairment only temporary?

3. **Severity of disability**
   a. Does the impairment severely interfere with the individual's educational opportunities?
   b. Does the impairment only moderately interfere with the individual's educational opportunities?
   c. Does the impairment only mildly interfere with the individual's educational opportunities?

Referring to these questions for each orthopedically or other health-impaired individual gives us a functional description of the effects of the impairment. The United States Office of Special Education cites an incidence estimate of 0.34 percent for orthopedic and other health impairments. We cannot discuss each of these impairments, but we have selected those that affect a sizeable number of children.

Orthopedic Impairments

Among the conditions that affect the individual motorically are cerebral palsy, spina bifida, muscular dystrophy, limb deficiency, Legg-Calve-Perthes disease, osteogenesis imperfecta, juvenile rheumatoid arthritis, and physical trauma.

Cerebral Palsy (CP).   Bobath and Bobath (1975) have defined cerebral palsy as the general category of motor handicaps that involve an impairment of the coordination of muscle action with an inability to maintain normal postures and balance and to perform normal movements and skills. There are more children with cerebral palsy in special education programs than children with any other orthopedic impairment.

There are four types of cerebral palsy:

1. Spasticity—muscle tightens from increased muscle tone (seen in about 50% of cases).

2. Athetosis—uncontrollable, involuntary, rhythmic movements (seen in about 25% of cases).

3. Ataxia—muscular incoordination related to balance (seen in about 10% of cases).

4. Mixed condition—various combinations of the first three types.

In addition, the particular limit(s) involved and the degree of severity of the paralysis is also categorized: *mono*—one limb; *para*—both legs; *hemi*—both limbs on the same side of the body; *di*—all four extremities with greater involvement in the legs; and *quad*—all four extremities. These terms serve as prefixes for the terms *plegia* (total paralysis) and *paresis* (partial paralysis). This categorization is also used to describe paralysis occurring as the result of injury or disease.

Cerebral palsy is caused by events before, during, or after birth that lead to an injury to the brain. There is a greater risk of cerebral palsy for children born prematurely, born during a difficult labor, who experience anoxia during birth (lack of sufficient oxygen), and who sustain head injuries during their early years.

Spina Bifida.   Spina bifida is a congenital defect resulting in a portion of the spinal cords not being covered by the vertebrae. In the most severe state, the spinal cord and its membranes protrude and are not covered with skin. A less severe form involves spinal nerve roots and spinal fluid protruding through the bony protection of the spine with the protrusion covered by skin.

The effects of this spinal cord defect range from minor sensory and motor handicaps to paraplegia and loss of bladder and bowel control. Another effect may be hydrocephaly (swelling of the head) due to excessive fluid in the cranial cavity.

Muscular Dystrophy.   One childhood form of muscular dystrophy, called pseudohypertrophia is inherited, progressive, and terminal. The disease weakens muscles, resulting in crippling as the affected muscles supporting the skeleton contract and cease functioning. Walking becomes increasingly difficult, and confinement to a wheelchair is eventually necessary.

Limb Deficiency.   In the 1960s, a large number of babies whose mothers had taken thalido-mide during pregnancy were born with malformed or missing limbs. Thalidomide was a tranquilizer prescribed for many pregnant women in Europe. In addition to a condition present at birth, limb deficiency can result from amputation.

Legg-Caelve-Perthes Disease.   This disease affects the head of the femur or bone that fits into the hip socket and hampers the ability to walk. The cause of this disease is unknown, but it may be genetic or it may occur as a result of an injury to the upper leg or hip. Treatment usually involves wearing a brace, and recovery occurs in some 80 percent of cases.

Osteogenesis Imperfecta.   This disease appears to be congenital and is also known as "brittle bones." It renders bone growth defective in both length and thickness, and dwarfism and deafness may occur.

Juvenile Rheumatoid Arthritis.   Arthritis results in the deterioration of the lining of the joints and can be both painful and deforming. Afflicted individuals may develop fevers, rashes, and morning stiffness. Children who contract arthritis may have problems in school because it is painful for them to sit for long periods of time and difficult for them to write.

According to figures released by the U.S. Department of Health, Education and Welfare in 1975, some one million children are victims of physical abuse or neglect every year. Of those children, at least one in five hundred dies as the result of mistreatment. A large percentage of physically abused children suffer brain damage, which often results in orthopedic impairment (Soeffing, 1975). The National Center of Child Abuse and Neglect has stated, "If you had a communicable disease that struck as great a number of children, you'd say you had an epidemic on your hands."

Because statistics on child maltreatment have never been collected on a nationwide basis, there is no way of telling if child-abuse cases are on the rise. Some experts have estimated that the incidence of child abuse may actually be higher, given the unreported cases of children who are beaten, burned, sexually molested, sustain serious physical injuries that go untreated, and are inadequately clothed or fed. In dealing with this problem and problems associated with drug and alcohol abuse, an ecological or total environmental approach must be taken by the school and other agencies and professionals concerned with the welfare of children. In 1974, the Council for Exceptional Children adopted a resolution recognizing abused and neglected children as "exceptional" children.

In addition to these diseases causing orthopedic impairment, we would have added poliomyelitis in the recent past. However, the effectiveness of the polio vaccine and its administration on a routine basis to most children in their early years has all but eliminated polio as a cause of orthopedic problems.

Traumatic Conditions.   Car accidents are responsible for the largest number of impairments due to physical trauma. Accidents at home, including accidental poisoning and burns, may lead to skin disfigurement, blindness, deafness, orthopedic impairment, neurological damage including seizures, mental retardation, and emotional disturbance.

Educational Provisions

A number of school programs exist for children with orthopedic impairments; the type of program depends on the extent of the handicap. Home instruction may be provided if the child has normal or near-normal intelligence and is severely physically disabled. Home-to-school telephone units in which several children are connected simultaneously with a teacher, or in which one child is connected to a regular classroom, are also established instructional media for physically impaired children. Hospital schools offer short-term diagnostic and treatment periods during which special education is provided; long-term care is available in institutions for the mentally retarded, where totally dependent children with all degrees of physical handicaps may reside on a twenty-four-hour basis. Perhaps the most common type of educational facility is the special day school or class. Here, children with mild or moderate physical handicaps and normal or near-normal intelligence receive their schooling. However, the majority of children who have mild handicaps and normal intelligence are generally found in regular public school classrooms, where slight modifications in school buildings and classrooms can be made to accommodate their physical impairments.

Orthopedic impairments often restrict children to special education programs because of the physical facilities necessary to accommodate them. Once they can maneuver successfully in the school environment, children with orthopedic problems may equal or excel their nonhandicapped peers in learning. Fortunately, as medical science learns more about the causes of orthopedic impairments, much can be done in terms of prevention and treatment.

Other Health Impairments

As was the case with sources of orthopedic impairments, there are many more diseases and problems leading to health impairments than can be covered in this section. Therefore, we have chosen to discuss seizure disorders, cystic fibrosis, sickle-cell anemia, cardiac conditions, juvenile diabetes mellitus, hemophilia, cancer and asthma.

Seizure Disorders.   Epilepsy has had considerable historical significance. The essence of the definition of epilepsy comes from the Greek word, *epilepsia*, which means "a taking hold of, a something seizing the subject as though that something were outside himself." This definition dramatically describes the most pronounced feature of epilepsy, a disturbance in the electrochemical activity of the discharging cells of the brain, which results in a seizure.

Generalized seizure disorders include grand mal and petit mal seizures. Witnessing a grand mal epileptic seizure may be upsetting to an individual who has never seen one. A number of individuals afflicted with epilepsy experience a warning (called an aura) of an impending seizure. An aura may be olfactory, visual, or auditory in nature. The aura may precede the seizure by an instant, or it may allow sufficient time for some safety precautions to be taken, such as the removal of sharp or hard objects. During the actual seizure, the child may exhibit a rolling and jerking of the eyes, rapid pulse movements, changing facial color, teeth gnashing, and laborious breathing. He or she may utter a shrill cry, begin spasmodic movements and convulsions of the body, and slump or fall to the floor. This may be followed by drowsiness, headache, or nausea. Unconsciousness may be prolonged, but seldom for more than half an hour. Approximately two-thirds of the cases of epilepsy take this form. During the actual seizure, little can be done to help the child. If in a precarious position, the child may be gradually eased to the floor, using the bodily rhythms rather than holding on tightly. Placing something soft like a coat or blanket under the child's head may prevent discomfort; the head should also be turned to one side to ease the discharge of saliva.

A less serious form of epilepsy is the petit mal seizure, in which there is mental confusion, a blocking of consciousness, perhaps accompanied by vacant staring, twitching eyelids, a nodding head, and a sigh or gasp. Such a seizure can take place during a pause in conversation or during an activity such as bicycle riding or playing. Some petit mal seizures last only a few seconds and resemble daydreaming or lack of attention. Others last for two to three minutes, during which the child unconsciously makes sucking noises, moves his or her hands aimlessly but with force, or walks around in a daze. Following such a seizure, the child characteristically has no recollection of what has happened.

Partial-psychomotor seizure disorders are characterized by a momentary loss of consciousness accompanied by some type of repetitive behavior that is inappropriate to the situation. Such seizures are usually followed by a brief period of amnesia or loss of memory. One type of partial-psychomotor seizure, called a Jacksonian seizure, begins with a twitch or numbness in one part of the body, spreads throughout the body, and sometimes results in unconsciousness. Miscellaneous-febrile seizures are associated with high fevers and usually occur in young children.

Cystic Fibrosis.   This disease is found primarily among whites and is the result of an inborn error of metabolism that affects the body's ability to produce saliva, perspiration, and mucus. The lungs are affected by a sticky mucus that clogs air passages, leads to difficulty fighting infection, blocks the pancreas and intestines, and interferes with digestion. If the disease is diagnosed early, treatment (e.g., antibiotics, modifying diet, breathing exercises) may extend life into adulthood.

Sickle-Cell Anemia.   In this hereditary disorder, the shape of red blood cells is changed into a crescent or "sickle" that prevents the cell from passing normally through the blood vessels. During a "crisis" situation, the blood and oxygen supply are abruptly cut off in various parts of the body, causing severe pain, swelling of the joints, fatigue, and fever. These blockages may damage the joints or heart or cause neurological impairment. This disease is often fatal by the age of twenty. Some live to forty if treated by blood transfusions, but the pain experienced during a crisis situation is intense and cannot always be relieved by drugs.

Cardiac Conditions.   In the past, cardiac problems in children were usually related to rheumatic fever and subsequent heart disease. However, the broadened interest in heart disease and medical advances has shown that there are many more children born with heart defects than those who acquire them from a disease such as rheumatic fever. Today, surgical technology often can correct congenital heart defects, enabling affected children to lead more normal lives. However, physical activity may have to be severely restricted, and studies have shown that such restriction is negatively perceived by children with cardiac problems who resent being singled out and made to feel "different" (Wrightstone, Justman, & Moskowitz, 1953).

Juvenile Diabetes Mellitus.   This disease is often a hereditary metabolic disorder involving failure of the pancreas to produce enough insulin and maintain a proper balance between sugars and starches and the body's energy needs. The symptoms of too little insulin are gradual onset of fatigue, drinking large amounts of water, excessive hunger, deep breathing, and warm, dry skin. If untreated, it can lead to a diabetic coma, lowered resistance to infection, decreased circulation of blood in the lower extremities, decreased vitality, loss of weight, and eye damage (Newman, 1971). When the body is exposed to too much insulin, the child may experience a rapid onset of headaches, nausea, vomiting, palpitations, irritability, shallow breathing, and cold, moist skin.

Hemophilia.   This disease involves a genetic blood disorder in which there is poor clotting ability. As a result, minor cuts and bruises can be very hazardous. However, more important than external bleeding is bleeding that occurs within the body. A simple bump can cause bleeding in the joints and surrounding tissue. Such bleeding leads to temporary immobility and pain and can cause permanent disability from degeneration of the joints. Hemophilia was once primarily treated by blood transfusions, but today treatment usually involves injecting the clotting factor missing from the composition of the blood.

Cancer.   When cancer strikes children it may involve tumors in the eyes, brain, bones, or kidneys. The most common form of cancer in children is leukemia. Treatment may consist of radiation, chemotherapy (drugs), and surgery. Both the disease and the treatment generate side effects, such as emotional problems, fatigue, extreme weight loss or gain, nausea, susceptibility to upper respiratory infection, headaches, and hair loss.

Asthma.   Asthma is usually caused by an allergic disorder and can affect practically every organ and tissue of the body. Asthmatic reactions, such as wheezing, labored breathing, gasping, and coughing, occur when a substance the individual is allergic to (antigen) enters the body and produces antibodies. This creates tissue sensitivity and a predisposition to an allergic reaction whenever the antigen is encountered.

Health impaired children are apt to appear in any regular or special classroom. Although teachers do not have to be medical specialists, they need to be aware of the most common health impairments of childhood that can cause lowered vitality, lack of alertness, and frequent absences.

In this section, we have surveyed orthopedic and health impairments that often require special educational services. We have tended to describe the impairments from a medical point of view in terms of symptomology and resulting type of handicap. Part II of the text deals with the social and psychological effects of such impairments on the individual and others.

This section has presented individuals who are particularly unique with respect to flexibility and who have problems in vision, hearing, movement, and vitality. They were introduced within a categorical framework covering definition and classification, incidence, causes, identification and diagnosis, and treatment and educational provisions. In chapter 5, we expand on the flexibility characteristics of these and all other exceptional learners. The remainder of this chapter is devoted to a discussion of exceptional learners who are particularly socially unique— the emotionally disturbed, speech impaired, and disadvantaged.

Social Uniqueness:
Emotionally Disturbed Individuals

Tommy is four and one-half years old. He has been outside playing with his friend, Bobby. Actually, he has had to go to the bathroom for some time, but he is so engrossed in teasing Bobby's cat that he has put off going home. Suddenly, the cat scratches him on his arm. The scratch begins bleeding and Tommy starts to cry. Bobby laughs uproariously and calls Tommy a "big baby." Tommy runs home in tears and goes in the kitchen where his mother is baking cookies. Hungry, he reaches for a cookie, only to be stopped by his mother and scolded because she is afraid he will spoil his dinner. Angry, hurt, and frustrated, he runs into the front room where he finds that his older brother has broken his toy electric robot. The brother is also watching television, but not Tommy's favorite program, which is on at this time. Tommy's brother tells him to "get lost" and refuses to change the program. At this moment, Tommy has had it. He throws himself on the floor, kicking and screaming and crying loudly. His tantrum brings his mother from the kitchen to try to calm him. But for a few moments Tommy is uncontrollable, out of contact with reality, and, if you will, evidencing psychotic-like behavior. Can we consider Tommy emotionally disturbed?

Mark is ten years old. His teacher is standing at the front of the room holding up a social studies text. She is reviewing several lesson summaries, which the class has done over the past four weeks. "Now turn to page 82," she says. Pages flip quickly as the children follow her directions. They sit waiting for further instructions. That is, all but Mark. Oh, he has turned to page 82 all right, but he quickly rips it out of his text, wads it up, and sends it sailing across the room toward his archenemy, "Good Citizen of the Week," Greg. The children gasp. The teacher's face reddens. Through her head passes a quick flash of Mark's classroom antics over the semester: tardiness, always out of his seat, teasing the younger children on the playground, and so on. But this has done it! Mark sticks his chin out defiantly and waits for the teacher's reaction. Is Mark emotionally disturbed?

Peter is five. He is sitting on the preschool rug rocking back and forth. The teacher approaches him holding out a ball. "Ball, Peter. Here let's play ball." But Peter's eyes do not move to look at the teacher. The rocking continues with Peter staring vacantly straight ahead. The teacher takes his hand. Peter resists. He emits a shrill scream and curls himself up on the rug still rocking. Peter does not speak; he never has. His parents report he never wanted to be picked up or hugged from birth. What about Peter? Is he emotionally disturbed?

What is emotional disturbance, and what qualifies a child to be called emotionally disturbed? This section deals with these questions.

Definition

Under Public Law 94–142, only "seriously emotionally disturbed" individuals are eligible for special education services.

"Seriously emotionally disturbed" is defined as follows:

(i)   The term means a condition exhibiting one or more of the following characteristics over a long period of time and to a marked degree, which adversely affects educational performance:

   (A) An inability to learn which cannot be explained by intellectual, sensory, or health factors;

   (B) An inability to build or maintain satisfactory interpersonal relationships with peers and teachers;

   (C) Inappropriate types of behavior or feelings under normal circumstances;

   (D) A general pervasive mood of unhappiness or depression; or

   (E) A tendency to develop physical symptoms or fears associated with personal or school problems.

(ii) The term includes children who are schizophrenic or autistic. The term does not include children who are socially maladjusted, unless it is determined that they are seriously emotionally disturbed.

By using the term *seriously*, it appears the framers of the law wanted to exclude mildly and moderately disturbed children. Why?

1. Exactly what constitutes mildly or moderately disturbed behavior exists largely in the eye of the beholder. Teachers and others differ with respect to their range of tolerance for problem behavior. One teacher's "aggressive" and "rude" Johnny Dixon may be another teacher's "all boy" and "independent" Johnny Dixon. One teacher's "withdrawn" and "timid" Mary Sue Taylor may be another teacher's "sweet" and "cooperative" Mary Sue Taylor.

2. Mildly and moderately disturbed behavior may be transient in nature, being observed in some children in the early grades but not later on.

3. Since we do not have a consensus as to what behaviors qualify as mildly or moderately disturbed, if teachers could identify anyone they wanted out of their classrooms as "disturbed," the floodgates might well open and special education could become an indiscriminate dumping ground for unwanted individuals.

When it comes to identifying schizophrenic and autistic children, there is much greater agreement among teachers and other professionals. One teacher's "self-stimulating" and "inaccessible" Philip Tompkins is likely to be another teacher's "self-stimulating" and "inaccessible" Philip Tompkins. But there are definite problems with the PL 94–142 definition in deciding when such a problem as "an inability to build or maintain satisfactory interpersonal relationships with peers and teachers" leaves the mild and moderate stage and becomes truly serious. There is also a contradiction in the definition, which initially includes children with interpersonal problems but later excludes children who are socially maladjusted.

One of the authors has attempted to define emotional disturbance as consisting of problem behaviors that are negative variants of six levels of learning competence: attention, response, order, exploratory, social, and mastery (Hewett & Taylor, 1980). These levels of competence are necessary for effective learning to take place. Their acquisition makes the normal learner normal; their nonacquisition makes the disturbed learner disturbed. The levels can be defined as follows:

Attention: the level of competence associated with receiving and perceiving sensory stimulation, coming to and sustaining attention and retention.

Response: the level of competence associated with motor responding, verbal language skills, and active participation.

Order: the level of competence associated with following directions and routines.

Exploratory: the level of competence associated with gaining an accurate and thorough knowledge of the environment through sensory-motor experiences.

Social: the level of competence associated with gaining the approval and avoiding the disapproval of others.

Mastery: the level of competence associated with self-help skills, academic skills, and vocational and career development.

Table 3–1 presents the six levels of learning competence as optimal. To the left and to the right of each level are behaviors that constitute negative variants, consisting of "too little" of the competence or "too much" of the competence. The problem behaviors have been drawn from several sources as well as the author's experience. Based on this framework, we define emotionally disturbed behaviors as consisting of *bipolar deviations from optimal behaviors required for learning* (too little or too much of a good thing).

In concluding this section on definition, let us return to the three boys described earlier. Were they emotionally disturbed?

>   *Tommy?* Probably not. Longitudinal studies (MacFarlane, Allen, & Honzik, 1955) have shown us that many normal children manifest disturbed behaviors during the course of growing up. But what separates them from children considered disturbed is: (1) the frequency of their disturbed behavior, (2) its degree of severity, (3) its duration, and (4) the number of disturbed behaviors found collectively in a single individual.

>   *Mark?* Depending on the range of tolerance for problem behavior of the teacher, he may or may not qualify. Also, the four conditions mentioned above in connection with Tommy would have to be considered before making the decision as to whether Mark was disturbed. According to Public Law 94–142, Mark may not be considered "seriously emotionally disturbed" and may "fall between the cracks" of the definition, as many mildly and moderately disturbed children are bound to do. Precise and consistent interpretation of the law's definition of emotional disturbance across states and school districts seems highly unlikely, and children like Mark may or may not be provided special education services as "seriously emotionally disturbed" based on individual circumstances.

>   *Peter?* No question. When the continuous frequency of his atypical behavior, its degree of severity, its duration, and the fact he manifests many problem behaviors are considered, he must be considered "seriously emotionally disturbed."

Classification

The Behavior Problem Checklist (BPC) (Quay & Peterson, 1975) is a classification approach based on a sampling of the many behaviors of children that can be considered deviant. This checklist consists of statements concerning fifty-five problem behaviors. These behaviors were selected after examination of more than 400 case folders from the files of a child guidance clinic (Peterson, 1961). The checklist was submitted to a large number of elementary and secondary teachers who used it to rate each of their pupils. These ratings were then subjected to a factor analysis to determine if there were any underlying unitary dimensions along which groups of items could be placed. Three such dimensions emerged, and the items were found to describe problems labeled "conduct problems," "personality problems," and "inadequacy-immaturity." Examples of the characteristics associated with each of these dimensions are as follows:

>   *Conduct problem:* restlessness, attention seeking, disruptiveness, rowdiness, dislike for

Table 3-1
Common characteristics of disturbed children viewed as negative variants of six levels of learning competence

too little	optimal	too much
disturbances in sensory perception (sed); excessive daydreaming (ii); poor memory (a); short attention span (ii); in a world all his own (ii)	ATTENTION — selective attention (a)	fixation on particular stimuli (a)
immobilization (a); sluggishness (ii); passivity (ii); drowsiness (ii); clumsy (a); depression (pp)	RESPONSE (MOTOR) — hyperactive (cp); restlessness (cp)	self-stimulation (sed)
failure to develop speech (sed); failure to use language for communication (sed)	RESPONSE (VERBAL) — extremely talkative (a)	uses profanity (cp); verbally abusive (a)
self-injurious (sed); lawlessness (a); destructiveness (cp); disruptiveness (cp); attention seeking (cp); irresponsibility (cp); disobedience (cp)	ORDER — overly conforming (a)	resistance to change (sed); compulsive (a)
bizarre or stereotyped behavior (sed); bizarre interests (sed); anxious (pp); preoccupation (pp); doesn't know how to have fun (pp); behaves like adult (pp); shyness (pp)	EXPLORATORY — plunges into activities (a)	tries to do everything at once (a)

preoccupation with inanimate objects (a)	social withdrawal (pp)		
	alienates others (a)		inability to function alone (a)
extreme self-isolation (sed)	aloofness (pp)	hypersensitivity (pp)	
	prefers younger playmates (ii)		
	acts bossy (cp)	jealousy (cp)	
inability to relate to people (sed)	secretiveness (pp)	overly dependent (a)	
	fighting (cp)		
	temper tantrums (cp)		

SOCIAL

blunted, uneven, or fragmented intellectual development (sed)	lacks self-care skills (a)		overintellectualizing (a)
	lacks basic school skills (a)		
	laziness in school (ii)		
	dislike for school (cp)	preoccupation with academics (a)	
	lacks vocational skills (a)		

MASTERY

cp–conduct problem (Quay, 1969)
ii–inadequacy-immaturity (Quay, 1969)
pp–personality problem (Quay, 1969)
sed–severely emotionally disturbed (Eisenberg & Kanner, 1956)
a–authors' examples

school, jealousy, fighting, irresponsibility, disobedience, hyperactivity, destructiveness, cursing, hot-tempered, negativism

Personality problem: doesn't know how to have fun, behaves like an adult, easily embarrassed, feelings of inferiority, cries easily, social withdrawal, easily flustered, secretiveness, hypersensitivity, anxiety, depression, aloofness

Inadequacy-immaturity: preoccupation, "in a world of one's own," short attention span, laziness in school, excessive daydreaming, passivity, suggestibility, sluggishness, drowsiness

The BPC can be completed by a rater in ten minutes and takes only five minutes to score. Over the past decade, it has been used in educational, mental health, medical, and correctional settings, as well as for research. Parents, teachers, mental health professionals and paraprofessionals, and parole and correctional staff have served as raters.

One advantage of the BPC is that it permits a reliable classification of children with behavior disorders that is based on descriptions of observable behavior. A disadvantage is that many children have characteristics found in all three groupings and are not "pure" conduct problems, personality problems, or inadequacy-immaturity problems. However, this type of approach toward classification does open up possibilities for continuing research related to matching types of children to optimal educational plans (Quay, 1969).

At the present time, two types of severe emotional disturbance or psychosis are thought to exist (Werry, 1979):

Schizophrenic disorders: evidenced by a regression or arrest in development after a period of relatively healthy development. In addition, schizophrenic children have some useful language and are able to relate at some level to others. (Onset 5–12 years of age.)

Early infantile autism: evidenced by two primary symptoms—extreme self-isolation and an obsessive insistence on sameness. A secondary symptom consists of speech and language disorders, which range from mutism to echolalia (repeating what others say rather than initiating spontaneous speech). (Onset 0–2-1/2 years of age.)

Whether schizophrenic disorders and early infantile autism comprise separate homogeneous classes, or whether they are related causally or to the development of adult psychosis is unknown.

Identification and Diagnosis

In identifying disturbed children, the judgment of the classroom teacher is a common criterion. A casual observer in any classroom can usually select several children who appear out of step with their peers and the expectations of the teacher. However, the teacher who is familiar with the typical range of learning and behavioral differences found among children in a certain age group is in a better position to single out children with special problems. Significant correlations between teacher ratings of "disturbed" behavior and results of the individually administered California Test of Personality, designed to measure adjustment problems among children, have been found (Harth & Glavin, 1971). Earlier studies have revealed that teachers were surprisingly accurate in their designations of disturbed children when their selections were compared to those made by psychologists and psychiatrists (Bower, 1960; Bower, 1961).

Depending on the type of problem behavior the child exhibits and the orientation of the professionals involved in evaluating the child, a variety of diagnostic procedures may be used. Hyperactive children may be referred to a pediatrician or pediatric neurologist who may prescribe drug treatment for them. Children who appear seriously disturbed may be referred to a psychologist or psychiatrist for consultation. A psychologist may also administer projective personality tests, such as the Rorschach, aimed at getting children to reveal inner conflicts. Observational ratings of the type of problem behavior exhibited and its frequency of occurrence may be taken in the actual classroom setting by the teacher or an independent observer. All of these approaches are directed toward gaining a clearer understanding of the children's difficulties and eventually providing a more adequate and successful school experience for them.

The identification of psychotic children may be made early in life as their parents become aware of the serious discrepancy between their functioning levels and those of other children their age. Frequently, the first professional contact with a pediatrician or psychiatrist is the result of parental concern when the child fails to develop speech or exhibits unusual speech patterns.

Schizophrenic children usually have serious language problems and communicate poorly. They may demonstrate narrow interests and seek a sameness in the conditions of their environments, sometimes becoming totally preoccupied with one object, such as a particular toy. Their behavior may be bizarre, with rituals, angry outbursts, or reclusiveness evident. Although their thinking is illogical, they may have the potential for average or better intelligence.

Infantile autism is a more extreme condition than schizophrenia, although the autistic child may exhibit behavior similar to the schizophrenic. Two features that distinguish autism from schizophrenia are the age of onset (autism is usually present at birth whereas schizophrenia develops in early childhood) and the autistic individual's failure to develop typical schizophrenic symptoms, such as hallucinations and delusions in later life (Eisenberg & Kanner, 1956).

Incidence

Judging from the preceding discussion, it is not surprising that attempts to determine the incidence of emotional disturbance among school-age individuals are largely losing propositions. Percentages ranging from .01 to 25 percent have been reported (Hewett & Blake, 1973). This variance, as mentioned earlier, relates to differing ranges of tolerance for problem behaviors on both an individual and geographical basis and the fact that mild emotional disturbance may be quite transient in nature. The United States Office of Education uses a 0.85 percent incidence figure for "seriously emotionally disturbed" individuals.

Causes

What causes a child to become emotionally disturbed? As with learning disabilities (discussed in the next chapter), it often depends on your point of view. In this section, we examine six points of view.

Developmental. We have already established that essentially normal children, like Tommy, who was presented in the introduction, may on occasion exhibit serious problem behaviors. But their frequency of occurrence, degree of severity, duration, and clustering fall within limits that are acceptable to the child's environment and those within it. During the course of growing up, we are all exposed to stresses and strains, disappointments and frustrations, and pain and unpleasantness. As a result, at times we are tense and anxious, angry and sad, or fearful and depressed. But these times are overshadowed by the times we are relaxed, loving, happy, confident, and content.

Temperamental.   In chapter 2, we introduced the concept of temperament. Shortly after birth, we can identify differences among children with respect to such characteristics as activity level, regularity of basic bodily functions, and ease in adjusting to change. Fortunate children find themselves in families and environments that value or accept their unique temperamental characteristics and are patient, tolerant, and supportive. Unfortunately, this is not always the case. Children who are "wall climbers" can create havoc in a family of sedate "seat sitters." The negative nature of experience that may ensue can result in the child's developing emotional and behavioral problems. The same problem can occur between a child predisposed to a low activity level and family members who are always on the go and who are constantly impatient with their child's lethargic behavior.

Biological.   Evidence linking biological factors to the development of emotional disturbance is strongest in relation to schizophrenia and autism. There is no conclusive evidence linking such factors to the vast majority of mildly disturbed children (Kauffman, 1977). Schizophrenia appears to have a definite inherited component. If an identical twin has schizophrenia, some studies have reported that the chances are as high as 85 percent that the other twin will become schizophrenic (Meehl, 1969). This expectancy rate is four times higher than the rate for fraternal twins (Buss, 1966). Using a constitutional-predispositional explanation, schizophrenic children have been viewed as predisposed by heredity to develop the disorder; but some environmental stimulus, either physical or psychosocial, is required to activate it (Rosenthal, 1963). Studies of schizophrenic children have revealed evidence of irregularities in many biological processes, such as pulse, temperature control, sleep patterns, and respiratory and elimination functions (Ritvo, Ornitz, Tanguay, & Lee, 1970; Bender, 1968).

   Rimland has proposed that infantile autism is the result of neurological impairment, not experience (Rimland, 1969). He has cited as evidence: (1) most siblings of autistic children are normal; (2) autistic children are behaviorally unusual from birth; (3) in most reported cases of autism in identical twins, both twins are autistic; and (4) the symptomatology of autism is highly unique and specific. According to Rimland, infantile autism is the result of a neurological deficit in the reticular formation in the brainstem, which governs the integration of current perception with memory. The autistic child, therefore, is unable to relate current to past experience and to integrate and attach meaning to his or her sensations. The insistence on sameness, ritualistic behavior, and failure to establish relationships with people that are commonly observed with autistic children are seen as reflections of this inability to integrate experiences meaningfully.

Psychodynamic.   From a psychodynamic perspective, emotional disturbance results from the child's failure to withstand the psychological strain produced by critical adjustment periods during early childhood. These adjustment periods center around feeding, weaning, toilet training, or the development of sexual awareness. The theory underlying this perspective was originally set forth by Freud, but it has gone through continuous revision. Erikson (1963) represents a contemporary psychodynamic position that views emotional disturbance as resulting from conflicts with significant others during these critical adjustment periods. During the early feeding and weaning period, conflict may instill a basic mistrust of others. During the toilet-training period, shame and doubt may develop in the child if there is conflict with the mother over the training. Excessive orderliness or defiance are other characteristics that may result from such conflict. As children gain sexual awareness, boys may exhibit exaggerated masculinity and girls vindictiveness toward males as they seek to establish their unique identities. Excessive guilt may also be a by-product of conflicts during this period.

Although there are other critical adjustment periods of concern to the psychodynamic position as disturbed behaviors develop in later childhood, their roots are viewed as emanating from conflicts during these early childhood adjustment periods.

Behavioral.   Previous perspectives regarding possible causes of emotional disturbance generally focused on "in-child" issues—temperament, biological factors, and psychological conflicts. In contrast, the behavioral approach concentrates on "outside-child" issues, such as the relationship of agents and events in the child's environment to observable maladaptive behaviors. In this view, such behaviors are the result of reinforcement and punishment. By the same token, the behaviorists believe maladaptive behavior can be unlearned or replaced by adaptive behavior through training involving these same two consequences. Thus, questions related to type of temperament, biological characteristics, or history of adjustment during stressful periods in early childhood are replaced by the question: What is the child doing or not doing that needs to be changed?

Ecological.   The broadest, most all-encompassing explanation for the development of emotional disturbance is provided by the ecological approach. There is no side-taking with respect to the importance given "in-child" versus "outside-child" issues. The focus is on the child's *ecosystem* or the myriad of interactions that have occurred or are occurring between the child and all aspects of his or her environment. The home and family are components of the ecosystem, as are the school and teachers. Relatives, neighbors, television personalities, mail carriers, bus drivers, and playmates all contribute to the unique environmental interactions the child experiences. You do not speak of emotional disturbance within the child, you speak of discordance between the child and his or her ecosystem.

Treatment and Educational Provisions

What one considers the cause of disturbed behavior receives primary emphasis when it comes to treatment and education of the disturbed child. Thus, medication, psychotherapy, behavior modification, and ecological appraisal and intervention have been involved in efforts to help disturbed children.

Medication has been found useful for some emotionally disturbed individuals. Psychostimulant drugs have been found to increase the teachability and manageability of from 50 to 80 percent of hyperactive children studied (Schain & Reynard, 1975; Safer & Allen, 1976). Vitamins have been used in the treatment of children considered schizophrenic or autistic. Rimland (1969) conducted a national study on the effects of vitamins C and B₃ on autistic children and reported that 80 percent of the children demonstrated anywhere from "slight" to "striking" improvement.

Psychotherapy or some form of counseling may be recommended for disturbed children. However, follow-up studies comparing disturbed children who received therapy with those who did not found two-thirds to three-quarters of both groups improved over time (Lewis, 1965). Intensive psychotherapeutic treatment on a twenty-four hour basis has been provided severely disturbed children. Although its effects have not been systematically studied, one of its proponents, Bettelheim (1967), claims a cure rate of 42 percent and an improvement rate of 38 percent. This claim, however, has been considered dubious due to a lack of objective criteria for both diagnosis and improvement (Wing, 1968).

The application of behavior modification approaches to the treatment of the severely disturbed began in the 1960s and is currently being used by many practitioners. Unlike psychotherapy, behavior therapy very specifically defines its treatment, techniques, and goals. The therapist concentrates on observable behavior and assumes an active role, reinforcing adaptive behaviors that the child displays and ignoring or punishing maladaptive behaviors immediately after their occurrence.

Behavior modification techniques have also been used with mildly disturbed children in public school programs. In the main, the techniques have been successful in increasing attention and reducing problem behavior. However, such behavioral improvement has not always been accompanied by academic improvement (O'Leary & Drabman, 1971). Many children with behavior problems are not referred for special education in the public school. Those who are referred out have exceeded the school's or teacher's ranges of tolerance. In the past, full-time, special day classes consisting of ten to twelve "disturbed" children provided the usual special education setting; today such children often participate part-time in regular classroom programs. In place of a full-time, self-contained classroom, a resource room can provide part-time remedial assistance. However, there will always be some children who will need full-time special education in a separate setting.

Several investigators have used the behavioral approach to stop self-destructive behavior displayed by some severely disturbed as well as some severely retarded children. This behavior may involve severe biting of the shoulder or other body parts, banging the head on the sharp corner of a table, or smashing the nose with fist or knee. With some children, the threat to their safety or life is so great that they have to be tied down in bed. In one study, a painful electric shock was administered when children given to self-destructive behavior moved to harm themselves (Lovaas & Simmons, 1969). The results of this technique were quite dramatic. After only a few electric shocks, the self-destructive behavior was effectively terminated. However, problems of generalization occurred with some children. The shock terminated the self-destructive behavior in a specific setting with specific individuals, but the effect did not carry over to other settings and individuals.

Educational programs for severely emotionally disturbed children usually focus on individual or small-group activities. Speech and language training are often the primary concerns, along with self-care and social skills. In the past, severely disturbed children were placed in residential institutions or hospital schools and seldom in public school programs. However, in recent years more public schools have included autistic and other severely disturbed children in their day programs.

An ecological approach to the problems presented by disturbed children is found in Project Re-ED (Hobbs, 1975). Begun in the early 1960s, this project conceptualized disturbed children as needing to be "re-educated" rather than "treated" and set up twenty-four-hour group homes where children attended school, worked, played, and lived with special educators.

A typical Re-ED unit consists of eight children and three key adults—two teacher-counselors and one liaison counselor. The teacher-counselors operate the daily program. One is assigned as a classroom teacher to conduct a daily school program until early afternoon. After school, the other teacher-counselor takes over and leads recreation activities and group discussions into the early evening. A dorm counselor then takes over for the night.

While the teacher-counselors operate the daily program, the liaison counselor examines and explores each of the eight children's ecosystems. The home schools are visited and conferences held with the home teachers. The children's families are counseled. The support of various agencies in the community, which may be critical in terms of the future adjustment of the child (e.g., YMCA, church, mental health clinics), is enlisted and plans made to optimize the chances for the child's successful return. In general, children enrolled in Re-ED programs stay for approximately six months. When it appears that they are ready to leave and that the ecosystem is ready to receive them, they are discharged. The advantage of the Re-ED model is that it can subsume all other traditional approaches. Concern for the physical well-being of the child, opportunities for emotional support and counseling, and behavioral shaping are all present in the Re-ED program.

Mild emotional disturbance is particularly difficult to define, although each of us can specify the kind of problem behavior that would lead us to apply the label to a child. We would be more in agreement regarding severe disturbance such as autism. The flexibility, social, and intellectual uniqueness of disturbed children is discussed in Part II.

Social Uniqueness:
Speech Impaired Individuals

Speech is the tool used to develop and express language. It begins with the birth cry and progresses through squealing, gurgling, babbling, and sound play (or imitation of sound patterns in the environment) into word use and understanding, and later into true speech. Speech and language are not synonymous, but speech necessarily involves language and, hence, language defects may be considered speech defects.

Definition and Classification

According to Public Law 94–142, speech impairment is defined as follows:

> "Speech impaired" means a communication disorder, such as stuttering, impaired articulation, a language impairment, or a voice impairment, which adversely affects a child's educational performance.

According to Eisenson (1980), speech is significantly defective "when the amount of distraction is sufficient to make it difficult to communicate with a normal listener." (pp. 173–174) Speech defects may be classified as:

1. Defects of articulation

2. Defects of voice

3. Stuttering

4. Delayed language development

5. Cleft palate speech

6. Cerebral-palsied speech

7. Speech defects associated with defective hearing

Disorders of articulation involve substitutions, omissions, distortions, and additions of sounds. Typical substitutions are *w* for *r* (as in "wight" for "right") or *th* for *s* (as in "yeth" for "yes"). Such errors are commonly found among young children with immature speech. If extensive, omissions tend to make a child's speech almost unintelligible, because consonants are often dropped from the beginning, middle, or endings of words. Distortions in speech reflect an attempt to approximate a correct sound, such as a "whistling" *s*. These are more readily corrected than are substitution problems. Omissions are the most difficult to correct. Additions appear in unintelligible speech and jargon and in the speech of deaf children who may say "sumber" for "summer" or add a vowel between other syllables as "on-a the table."

The hard-of-hearing child often has articulation problems. Depending on the severity and kind of hearing loss, there may be omissions and distortions of sounds in the high frequency range, omissions and indistinctness of word endings, and poor discrimination between voiced and voiceless sounds.

Voice defects are not found as often as articulation defects. They include problems in (1) vocal quality, (2) vocal pitch, and (3) vocal intensity. Defects in vocal quality appear in the production of sound and include breathiness, hoarseness, or huskiness. Resonance of sound may occur largely in the nasal cavity producing a nasal, twangy quality; outside the nasal cavity, it may produce "spring has cob," instead of "spring has come." Since the growing larynx may develop at a faster rate than the rest of the body, pitch may remain at a high level into adolescence. The intensity, loudness, or softness of the voice may reflect attention seeking, lack of control of vocal power, or immaturity and insecurity.

Stuttering has probably received more study than any other speech problem. It is generally considered a disorder of rhythm or fluency. However, young children are often disfluent in the early acquisition of language, and "normal" speakers also experience moments of disfluency. Therefore, it is not until the disfluencies occur with a frequency and severity that becomes noticeable to the listener and irritating to the speaker that the condition is called stuttering.

Delayed speech occurs when the child does not develop speech according to age level or develops only a partial understanding of language or vocal expression. The term *aphasia* has been used to denote loss of speech specifically associated with cerebral dysfunction. Aphasia among children has been termed *childhood aphasia* and *congenital* or *developmental aphasia*. Childhood aphasia usually refers to a language dysfunction associated with some form of central nervous system damage that resulted after language had begun to develop; congenital or developmental aphasia implies that damage to the central nervous system occurred prior to the development of language.

If the bone and tissue of the hard palate fails to fuse during the second and third months of pregnancy, the child will be born with a cleft in the roof of the mouth and sometimes in the lip. Some cleft palates can be remedied through surgery, making adequate speech possible. In cases where the condition cannot be corrected, the speech may be so defective that the person is judged mentally retarded by the layman. Typical characteristics of cleft palate speech are hypernasality, nasal emission, and misarticulation. Speech defects associated with cerebral palsy are clearly related to the neurological impairment associated with the condition.

Incidence

Determining the incidence of speech defects is at best an approximation because the reliability of judgments made that a given sample of speech is defective can always be questioned. According to Perkins (1977), a review of the literature suggests there are 12,500,000 school-age children with speech defects in the United States. Eisenson (1980), in recognizing the questionable accuracy of any incidence figures, considers an approximation of 5 percent of the school-age population a reasonable estimate. The United States Office of Special Education estimates that 2.83 percent of school-age children are speech handicapped.

Males at all age levels are found in greater numbers than girls within populations of children with defective speech (Milisen, 1957). Differences between the sexes are smallest for articulation problems not due to organic causes and highest for stuttering problems, where males outnumber females three or four to one (Eisenson & Ogilvie, 1977).

Causes

Some speech defects are definitely organic in origin. The child with a cleft palate will have articulatory and vocal difficulties directly related to the severity of the cleft. Early hearing impairment, if severe, can also account for these difficulties.

Many children who display no evidence of organic problems also have defects of articulation and voice. Some may have learned such defects by imitating an older sibling, playmate, or an adult. If speech defects found in children are not organic or imitative in origin, the presumed cause is psychogenic (due to psychological problems). Nature of experience, particularly as it relates to faulty parent-child relationships, then may be the source of many speech problems (Eisenson, 1980).

Faulty parent-child relationships have been viewed as one cause of stuttering. Some studies have found that parents of stutterers set unrealistic goals for their children and are overprotective and controlling. After reviewing a number of studies related to the cause of stuttering, Bloch and Goodstein (1971) concluded that a relationship between a particular personality pattern or severe maladjustment and the development of stuttering has not been established. These authors did acknowledge, however, that there is evidence that adult stutterers are "somewhat more anxious, somewhat less confident, and somewhat more socially withdrawn than nonstutterers (p. 30).

Identification and Diagnosis

Actual identification of the child with a speech handicap may originate in the school as a result of either a brief screening of every pupil enrolled or a teacher referral. Once the child is identified as having speech problems, he or she may be evaluated by one or more professionals concerned with various aspects of speech and language. Such an evaluation aims at assessing (1) variables outside the speech and language area that may relate to the problem, including hearing impairment, intellectual deficits, and behavior disorders; and (2) the ability of the child to produce and to comprehend the language of the culture. Formal tests provide normative data, but are limited because they sample only a limited number of responses. As a result, informal testing procedures by skilled clinicians have gained increasing popularity (Turton, 1975).

Articulation may be assessed by both spontaneous and imitative tests. In a spontaneous test, the child is shown pictures of familiar objects, events, or people and asked to name or describe them. An imitative test is one in which the examiner asks the child to repeat words, phrases, or sentences containing particular sounds with which he or she may have difficulty. Additional tests to determine the child's auditory discrimination or ability to hear differences in sounds and words or to determine intellectual ability may also be given.

Evaluation of a child who stutters generally includes tests to assess hearing sensitivity, intelligence, and school achievement, and an analysis of the sounds, syllables, and words that lend to disfluency. It is also important to learn the nature of the social situations that are most stressful for the child, such as being asked to recite in front of the class or talking on the telephone.

Voice problems are caused by actual physical abnormalities in the respiratory system or larynx, or they may result from excessive screaming. A physician can conduct a laryngoscopic examination to examine the larynx, although this is difficult to do with young children.

Treatment and Educational Provisions

The decision to place the preschool child who demonstrates an articulation disorder in a treatment program or to wait to see if the disorder is corrected as the child matures is a subject of a still ongoing controversy (Flower, Leach, Stone, & Yoder, 1967). It has been argued that the question is not whether intervention should take place but what type of intervention, since referral of a child for a speech evaluation in and of itself demonstrates that there is a significant problem (Turton, 1975). Formal speech therapy is only one type of intervention. An alternative is to work with the child's parents to help them understand the problem and to give them specific suggestions for aiding the child with articulation problems in the home. Another alternative is to have a speech therapist work with the teacher to initiate a speech stimulation program in preschool or kindergarten. Such a program might include auditory discrimination activities, as well as speech production exercises. Finally, the speech therapist may actually enroll the child in a formal speech therapy program on a group or individual basis.

A speech therapist who works in the schools often has a master's degree, and the majority have done graduate work beyond the bachelor's level. Many hold a state certificate, since thirty-two states have speech certification requirements. The speech therapist may serve both as an individual therapist with children and as a consultant to regular classroom teachers.

In the treatment of stuttering, the child's age, the extent of background information available, and the theoretical approach of the speech therapist are all factors to consider. As with the young child with an articulation problem, the young stutterer will probably receive more help indirectly, through guidance given to parents, than by direct treatment. It is only with older elementary children that direct therapy becomes the treatment of choice (Turton, 1975). The decision actually to undertake such therapy depends on the severity of the problem, the child's awareness of the problem, and the presence of secondary symptoms, such as emotional and behavioral problems.

The treatment approach with the child who stutters varies with the orientation of the therapist. The underlying emotional problem may be the primary focus of treatment, rather than the stuttering, if the therapist follows the psychodynamic approach. Or the stutterer may be dealt with directly by negative practice (e.g., consciously practicing stuttering to gain control over it) or by means of behavior modification.

The child with a voice problem enrolled in formal speech therapy may be given breathing exercises to improve voice quality and provided with models of good voice patterns to imitate. In voice therapy, considerable effort goes into helping the child recognize and attend to fine shades of difference in vocal quality.

The treatment of cleft lip and palate usually involves surgical intervention. In the case of cleft lip, the surgery may be done as soon after birth as possible. Early surgery is also important for cleft palate, to take advantage of normal growth and development processes. Mechanical closure of the cleft palate can be effected by prosthetic devices. These may be used during intervals between surgical procedures and during infancy, for feeding purposes and to prevent other health problems. Finally, in addition to surgical or prosthetic intervention, speech therapy may be necessary to help the child produce as many normal speech patterns as possible. Such therapy is very similar to that provided for children with articulation problems.

Because speech and language are so fundamental to the communication process, and because communication is so fundamental to learning and adapting to the demands of the environment, concern with speech and language problems ranks high on the priority list of the special educator.

Social Uniqueness: Economically Disadvantaged and/or Culturally Different Individuals

Poverty is one of the oldest and most widespread of all handicapping conditions. It has also constituted more of a problem for certain racial and ethnic groups than for others. Yet not all poor people are from ethnic minorities, and not all culturally different individuals are poor. That is why we have chosen to discuss economically disadvantaged and/or culturally different children. The children we are talking about may be exceptional learners because of poverty, culturally unique backgrounds, or a combination of the two. Since they are not a homogeneous population, it is difficult for us to generalize about them. In our discussion, we try to relate content to lower-class status or cultural difference where we can, but this is not always possible. For "poverty and ethnic minority status are so inextricably linked that the impact of each separately on the lives of poor people is difficult to determine" (Chan, 1975).

Economically disadvantaged and/or culturally different children have had a variety of euphemisms applied to them. They are said to live in the *ghetto*, *inner city*, or *disadvantaged community*. They are often labeled *deprived* and *disadvantaged* and their cultural patterns are viewed as *inferior*, *primitive*, or *deficient* (Rivers, Henderson, Jones, Ladner, & Williams, 1975).

The individuals we are describing have not traditionally been considered exceptional in a categorical sense, even though large numbers of them have been given labels such as mentally retarded. The concept of being poor and/or culturally different does not readily fit the notions of exceptionality based on medical or psychological approaches. Yet when we review the definition of an exceptional learner presented in chapter 2, uniqueness in range and nature of experience certainly qualifies children who are economically disadvantaged and/or culturally different for consideration. In addition, factors associated with poverty, such as poor nutrition, illness, and injury, may affect the capacity of such children.

We have chosen to include this group of children in this text because of a conviction that as rigid labeling and categorizing practices diminish, it will be the child—*any child* whose uniqueness makes modification of regular education necessary—who will be the concern of special education. We have also chosen a term to describe these children that hopefully avoids the connotation of inadequacy and inferiority conveyed by *socially disadvantaged* or *culturally deprived*. We are talking about children who are apt to have problems in the American school because of poverty and/or the fact that some come from backgrounds that are different from the backgrounds of white, middle-class children. Throughout the text, we use the abbreviated reference *disadvantaged* when describing economically disadvantaged and/or culturally different children. Our reference will be to poverty and/or difference as contributing to disadvantaged status, not to inadequacy or inferiority.

Definition and Classification

Disadvantaged children appear among all racial and ethnic groups. They often come from rural backgrounds, lack education and job skills, and frequently face discrimination in employment and housing. They are mainly blacks from the rural South, whites from southern Appalachia, and Puerto Ricans who have migrated to northern industrial cities. Also included are Hispanics and American Indians living in western and midwestern urban or isolated rural areas (Boger & Ambron, 1969).

The common denominator of poverty remains more important than race in the definition of disadvantaged (Chan, 1975). Studies reveal that whereas social class is often closely interwoven with race and ethnicity, family values and attitudes are determined more by social class than by race. For example, the child-rearing practices of middle-class blacks are more similar to those of middle-class whites than to those of lower-class blacks (Deutsch, 1973). Social class status also has been found to account for differences in achievement level among students as compared to race (Coleman, Campbell, Hobson, McPartland, Mood, Weinfeld, & York, 1966).

Causes

Although poverty may be the major determiner of disadvantage, its specific effects on the child that lead to educational problems have been viewed differently by researchers. Biomedical, cultural deficit, and cultural difference positions have emerged related to defining these effects. These positions, like the ones taken with reference to the emotionally disturbed child, reflect differing degrees of emphasis on capacity and experience as causal.

The Biomedical Position.   Inadequate health care and nutrition before and after birth and the effects of impoverished living conditions may greatly limit the ability of disadvantaged children to function successfully in school (Birch & Gussow, 1970).

Disadvantaged expectant mothers have been found to have poorer diets, and poorer health in general, be less likely to receive prenatal care, and be far more likely to give birth under substandard conditions. Such mothers encounter a higher incidence of pregnancy complications, which lead to an increased probability of physical, sensory, or neurological defects in their infants, who are also smaller than average at birth and have a higher mortality rate.

Severe malnutrition in infancy and chronic undernutrition from birth into the school years may result in basic information-processing deficits and account for the inattention, apathy, irritability, and lower energy levels often displayed by disadvantaged children in school (Birch, 1972). Malnutrition also makes these children more susceptible to illnesses that interrupt their education.

The impoverished and unsafe conditions of the slum environment also make the child more susceptible to injuries (Deutsch, 1973). Crowded streets and the absence of recreation areas increase the probability of accidents. Fires in tenement housing may result in serious burns. Children living in substandard housing also face increased chances of lead poisoning, caused by ingesting plaster and wood containing particles of lead-based paint, that can cause neurological impairment.

The Cultural Deficit Position.   In the 1960s, the limited range of experience of the disadvantaged child was viewed by many as the explanation for frequent school failure. This is the cultural deficit position, and it focuses on the disorganized and impoverished physical and family environment of the child. Such a limited environment is viewed as failing to provide the quality of sensory, social, and language stimulation necessary for normal cognitive development.

The Cultural Difference Position.   In more recent years, the cultural deficit position has been challenged by proponents of the cultural difference approach in explaining the learning problems of the disadvantaged in school. Cole and Bruner (1972) argue that the disadvantaged child possesses the same basic competence as a middle-class counterpart, but that the two express their competence in different ways. They give an example from Labov's influential work on an eight-year-old black child who is brought into a standard interview room for an assessment of his language competence. The interviewer is a neighborhood figure and black. Yet the child responds only in monosyllables, and is judged to be the victim of a cultural deficit. However, if the same interviewer were to drop in on the boy in his apartment and bring along one of his young friends so the three of them could have a "rap" session, things might go quite differently. Reclining on the floor, munching on potato chips the interviewer has brought, and starting to talk about clearly taboo subjects in black dialect, the previous monosyllabic interviewee becomes an excited participant in the conversation, demonstrating superior reasoning and debating skills.

Identification

Even though both identification and diagnosis are considered with reference to other exceptional learners, the concept of diagnosis, which implies formal medical and psychological assessment procedures leading to a specific categorical placement, is not truly relevant to the disadvantaged child. But researchers and those concerned with providing educational services for the disadvantaged have used a variety of criteria for identification. Economic, social, and academic characteristics frequently considered include low family income, welfare as primary income, ethnic minority-group status, deteriorated housing, urban or isolated rural living environments, poor overall school performance, poor reading skills, limited language skills, low scores on standardized intelligence and achievement tests, high school dropout rate, low college admission rate, and high unemployment (Robison, 1972).

Disadvantaged children also often exhibit certain psychological characteristics related to their school problems. Such children may give up easily and fail to display drives for achievement. They may express feelings of powerlessness and possess a poor self-concept. It has been suggested that the disadvantaged child has problems in delaying gratification and is more motivated to work for external rewards such as money than for internal rewards such as the satisfaction of acquiring knowledge and skill.

It is important to stress that in identifying and describing disadvantaged children, we are not talking about a homogeneous population (Allen, 1970). There are major differences among individuals who are disadvantaged, and certainly not all of the identification characteristics cited above apply to them all. This consideration is relevant to our discussion of the characteristics of all exceptional learners.

Because some of the characteristics of disadvantaged children are also found among children placed in traditional special education categories, disadvantaged children may readily acquire the label associated with these categories. Although the disadvantaged child does not typically display apparent neurological defects, he or she may be placed in a classroom for the retarded because of cognitive limitations caused by impoverished cultural and educational experiences (Frost & Hawkes, 1966). These limitations may be evident the first day the child arrives for school, when it becomes apparent that he or she lacks the readiness skills for successfully mastering the traditional school curriculum.

Educational Provisions

Educational approaches for aiding disadvantaged children have reflected differences in orientation toward their problems. In the 1960s, the cultural deficit orientation was widely supported. Young disadvantaged children were thought to need help to catch up as quickly as possible to their middle-class counterparts so they could enter school with an increased probability of success. The Head Start preschool intervention program was designed toward this end; it attempted to expose the disadvantaged child to an enriched environmental experience that would overcome previous deficits. The program, however, was disappointing because the children enrolled failed to sustain their acquired intellectual gains in later school years (Spicker, 1971).

The 1970s witnessed a shift in focus from the cultural deficit approach to one of cultural differences. The school, not the child, is viewed as needing to change. Modifications in traditional middle-class curricula and goals are being suggested in order to capitalize on the unique talent and skills the disadvantaged child already possesses when entering school. From the biomedical point of view, more efforts are being made to provide training for parents to improve conditions in the child's home and to deal with the family's health and financial needs.

Actual interventions and educational programs have been established for the disadvantaged from infancy to adulthood. One of the most intensive and successful infant intervention programs has been developed by Heber at the University of Wisconsin Infant Education Center in Milwaukee (Horowitz & Paden, 1973). Identified infants are placed in an enrichment program that continues through early childhood. Trained adults make daily home visits, from shortly after birth until the child is three months old. At that time, the infants begin to attend daily sessions at the Center, where they are exposed to a variety of stimulation experiences on a one-to-one basis. Their mothers receive training in home economics, child rearing, and job skills. Other home intervention programs have been directed toward modifying parent-child interactions. Objectives of these programs have ranged from helping the mother learn to actively teach her child to improving family stability (Passow, 1972).

Preschool education programs with the disadvantaged largely began with Project Head Start, created by the Economic Opportunity Act of 1964. Although follow-up evaluation of sustained intellectual gains was disappointing, a number of curriculum models emerged that provide for continuing development and implementation. Project Follow Through was launched in 1968 to reinforce in kindergarten through third grade the earlier gains made by children in Head Start. Special enrichment activities were added to the traditional school program by this project.

Since the disadvantaged adolescent often drops out of school at the secondary level, increased attention has been paid to adapting the secondary school curriculum. Work-study programs emphasize work skills and basic academic skills equally and provide vocational education and training, as well as actual work experience. However, it is important not to consider all disadvantaged individuals as candidates for semiskilled or unskilled work, but rather to provide each person the kind of educational opportunities that are meaningful individually.

Increasing the participation of disadvantaged youth in higher education has also been a national concern. Some school systems have initiated programs to identify disadvantaged ninth-graders with college potential. Begun by the United States Office of Education in 1965, Upward Bound provides an intensive residential summer education and counseling program designed to motivate disadvantaged young people to prepare for college. Colleges and universities also have modified admission criteria to increase the number of disadvantaged youth who attend college. Some colleges have open admission policies, set differential requirements, and substitute nominations or recommendations for test scores.

Bilingual instruction may be provided as a part of the modification of traditional educational programs for the disadvantaged child for whom English is not the home language. Although the practice has been to teach standard English to the child with nonstandard speech, such as a dialect, programs that take his or her natural language into account, rather than exclude it, have been developed. Courses and curriculum material dealing with the heritage and culture of various racial and ethnic groups are also becoming more available. These include instructional materials depicting multiethnic and multisocial class conditions and urban rather than suburban life.

Despite the many efforts to remedy the school problems of the disadvantaged, Birch and Gussow caution that such efforts will ultimately fail if the health and nutritional problems of poverty are not dealt with.

> Intervention at a single point must inevitably have a limited effect. Compensatory education may make up for a home in which the "cognitive environment" is restricted, but it cannot make up for a childhood spent with an empty belly. (Birch & Gussow, 1970, p. 267)

Bronfenbrenner (1974) also calls attention to the fact that intervention efforts with the disadvantaged must go beyond alteration of instructional approaches in the school and involve the family unit as well. He advocates intervention before the child's birth by providing parents with training in child care and nutrition and by helping them acquire adequate housing, economic security, and employment. After the child's birth, parents would assume the role of primary agent of intervention and would participate in school and neighborhood parent groups. This approach is essentially an application of the ecological strategy described in reference to the child with behavior disorders. It is relevant to most of our exceptional learners. For many of them, six hours of "something" in school may not be enough. More and more special educators and others concerned with the welfare and development of exceptional learners are looking to the other eighteen hours in the day and to ways of making those hours more positive and constructive in the child's life.

Rather than falling neatly into a medical or psychological disability category, the problems of the economically and/or culturally different child are diffuse and stem from a variety of capacity and experimental determiners. Although such children may be considered a new addition to the types of children traditionally considered exceptional, they have always been represented in large numbers in populations of many exceptional learners, such as the behavior disordered, mentally retarded, learning-disabled, speech handicapped, and chronically ill.

Summary

The uniqueness of the exceptional learner can be discussed within a framework describing the uniqueness of human beings in nature. When compared with all other species, human beings are superior in *flexibility* (accommodating to a changing physical environment), *sociability* (interacting and communicating with others), *intelligence* (using verbal symbols and learning more effectively), and *individualization* (possibilities for multiple outcomes in later life). Exceptional learners with flexibility uniqueness include the visually handicapped, hearing impaired, and orthopedically and other health impaired. Those with social uniqueness include the emotionally disturbed, speech impaired, and disadvantaged.

Flexibility Uniqueness

The visually handicapped comprise the next to the smallest group of exceptional learners. They are currently classified more on the basis of visual performance rather than by measures of visual acuity and field of vision. As with most handicapping conditions, both congenital and acquired causes account for the handicap, with the former more pronounced. Children with visual problems may be identified by parents early in life or by teachers who notice such signs as excessive rubbing of the eyes in the classroom. An *opthalmologist* is a medical specialist concerned with diagnosis and treatment of defects and diseases of the eye. An *optometrist* is a licensed, nonmedical practitioner who examines eye problems and prescribes glasses.

Even though many technological aids have been developed for use in the classroom by the visually handicapped, Braille continues to be of great importance. Visually handicapped learners are often integrated into regular classrooms and receive part-time help from special education teachers with respect to training in Braille and orientation and mobility skills.

Children who are deaf or hard-of-hearing are fortunate if they have developed some measure of speech and language before their hearing loss. Degree of hearing impairment is measured by the sound intensity necessary for the understanding of speech. The causes of hearing loss are unknown for almost one-half the hearing-handicapped population. Heredity, disease, prematurity, and mother-child blood incompatibility are known causes. Children with a suspected hearing problem may be screened by an *audiologist* under the supervision of an *otologist*, a medical specialist.

In teaching language skills to the hearing handicapped, a continuing controversy exists with respect to combining manual communication (finger spelling and signing) with the teaching of lipreading and speech. Approximately 40 percent of deaf children attend residential schools. The remainder are enrolled in public or private school programs. The child who is born with severe or total impairment in both the senses of hearing and sight (the deaf-blind) requires a program aimed at sensory integration, not one involving a combination of approaches for the blind and deaf.

The orthopedically and other health impaired may be victims of an unfortunate myth that a crippled body and a crippled mind inevitably go together. The list of orthopedic impairments (e.g., cerebral palsy) and other health impairments (e.g., epilepsy) is a long one. Because of this, special education programs for these exceptional learners are apt to be more varied than for others (from special school to school-to-home telephone teaching). For those with mild impairments, full-time placement in a regular classroom commonly occurs.

Social Uniqueness

Identifying emotionally disturbed children is complicated by the fact that teachers and others have their own criteria for judging what constitutes disturbed behavior. For this and other reasons, the federal definition of emotional disturbance is concerned with "seriously" disturbed behavior *only* because there is apt to be greater consensus when a child's behavior problems are extreme, as with schizophrenic disorders and early infantile autism. Various classification approaches have been developed to describe disturbed children's behaviors, the most useful of which have direct educational relevance to what teachers can do something about in the classroom.

Causes of emotional disturbance are varied. Many children exhibit disturbed behavior during the normal course of growing up. Temperamental differences among children account for some problem behavior. Biological factors also may be responsible, for if one identical twin has schizophrenia, there is a high probability the other twin will develop the disturbance. From a psychodynamic perspective, emotional disturbance results from stress experienced by children during critical adjustment periods, such as those associated with feeding, weaning, and toilet training. Behavioral explanations focus on "outside-child" issues and view problem behavior as resulting from reinforcement and punishment. The broadest explanation is ecological in nature, viewing disturbed individuals as "victims" of discordance in their ecosystems (the network of past and present events and relationships) rather than as emotionally disturbed themselves. Treatment and educational provisions for disturbed individuals emanate directly from these diverse causal explanations.

Individuals who are speech impaired are socially unique with respect to problems in communicating with others. Communication difficulties may result from defects in articulation, voice, stuttering, delayed language development, cleft palate speech, cerebral-palsied speech, and defects associated with defective hearing. Speech defects may result from organic problems (e.g., cleft palate) and faulty nature of experience, particularly with respect to parent-child relationships (e.g., stuttering). Speech problems are often identified in the classroom with subsequent examinations conducted by speech therapists and/or physicians. Most children with speech problems remain in regular classrooms full time, receiving speech therapy on a scheduled basis during the school week.

Disadvantaged children have not traditionally been considered exceptional, even though many have been given labels such as mentally retarded. We include them in the text, not because they are handicapped, but because they qualify as exceptional learners because their range and nature of previous experience may require special understanding and consideration if they are to succeed in the middle-class American school. Disadvantaged status may occur due to inadequate health care and nutrition before and after birth and the effects of impoverished living conditions. It may also relate to a cultural deficit or lack of sensory, social, and language stimulation necessary for normal cognitive development. Cultural differences may also be involved when the range and nature of the child's previous experience, although adequate, are markedly different from that of the typical child in the school. Efforts to adapt public school educational programs to meet the needs of the disadvantaged have taken all three of these considerations into account.

The exceptional learners discussed in this chapter have been considered to exhibit flexibility uniqueness (visually handicapped, deaf and hard-of-hearing, orthopedically and other health impaired) and social uniqueness (emotionally disturbed, speech impaired, and disadvantaged). In the next chapter, we examine those exceptional learners considered intellectually unique—the learning disabled, mentally retarded, and gifted.

CHAPTER 4

Intellectual Uniqueness

Our discussion of intellectual uniqueness includes individuals with learning disabilities, the mentally retarded, and the gifted. Although the learning disabled are considered to possess average or above average intelligence, they usually function well below their intellectual level in academic subjects. Thus, even though they do not have limited intelligence, they do have problems related to intellectual functioning level (i.e., achievement). These "disturbances in intellectual functioning" qualify them for inclusion as intellectually unique (Tarjan & Forness, 1979). The gifted are considered intellectually unique, although within the superior range of intelligence.

Individuals with Learning Disabilities

Jim is in the fourth grade and barely reading at middle first-grade level. He has normal intelligence, and as far as his doctor is concerned, he has no physical or neurological problems. What accounts for this discrepancy between Jim's reading level and the reading level of the majority of his classmates? His teacher notes that he sometimes reverses letters when he reads (e.g., "was" for "saw") or spells (e.g., "gril" for "girl") and that his handwriting is barely legible. Jim is somewhat shy and a bit of a loner in the class. Across the room from Jim sits Mark. Or rather, "sometimes" sits Mark. Mark is a wiggler and a mover, fidgeting at his desk, tapping his feet on the floor, seldom paying attention for more than a few seconds, and often out of his seat. Like Jim, he is behind in all of his subjects, but not as far. Mark actually is above average on intelligence and has no identifiable physical problems. What about Jim and Mark? Are they boys with learning disabilities? As we shall discover in this section, it is not easy to define exactly what constitutes a learning disability.

Definition

The first definition of a learning disability to gain wide acceptance was proposed by Kirk (1962):

A learning disability refers to a retardation, disorder, or delayed development in one or more of the processes of speech, language, reading, spelling, writing or arithmetic, resulting from a possible cerebral dysfunction and/or emotional or behavioral disturbance and not from mental retardation, sensory deprivation, or cultural or instructional factors. (p. 263)

In 1968, the National Advisory Committee on Handicapped Children in the United States Office of Education proposed the following definition of learning disabilities:

Children with special (specific) learning disabilities exhibit a disorder in one or more of the basic psychological processes involved in understanding or in using spoken or written language. These may be manifested in disorders of listening, thinking, talking, reading, writing, spelling, or arithmetic. They include conditions which have been referred to as perceptual handicaps, brain injury, minimal brain dysfunction, dyslexia, developmental aphasia, etc. They do not include learning problems which are due primarily to visual, hearing, or motor handicaps, to mental retardation, emotional disturbance, or to environmental disadvantage.

In 1975, Public Law 94–142, The Education for All the Handicapped Act, defined a learning disability as follows:

"Specific learning disability" means a disorder in one or more of the basic psychological processes involved in understanding or in using language, spoken or written, which may manifest itself in an imperfect ability to listen, speak, read, write, spell, or to do mathematical calculations. The term includes such conditions as perceptual handicaps, brain injury, minimal brain dysfunction, dyslexia, and developmental aphasia. The term does not include children who have learning problems which are primarily the result of visual, hearing, or motor handicaps, of mental retardation or of environmental, cultural, or economic disadvantage.

In his definition, Kirk (1962) proposed citing as acceptable causes of a learning disability *possible cerebral dysfunction and/or emotional disturbance* and excluded mental retardation, sensory deprivation, or cultural or instructional factors. The federal definition of 1968, however, did not include any references to causation and specifically excluded *emotional disturbance* as an acceptable cause.

Public Law 94–142 also omits any references to causation. But unlike the 1968 definition, it does not mention emotional disturbance as a necessary exclusion when considering causes of learning disabilities. However, a clarification did appear in the 1977 *Federal Register* to the effect that individuals whose learning problems were primarily the result of emotional disturbance could not be considered learning disabled (p. 65083).

The two most important things to consider when attempting to identify a child as learning disabled are *discrepancy* and *exclusion*.

Discrepancy: There is significant discrepancy between the child's actual intellectual ability and the level of academic functioning exhibited.

Exclusion: The child does not have any other primary handicapping condition(s) (underlying the learning problem), such as visual, hearing, or motor handicaps, mental retardation, emotional disturbance, or environmental, cultural, or economic disadvantage.

These two criteria offer only a "bare bones" reference for defining a learning disability, but they serve to introduce this type of exceptional learner. The concept and definition of a learning disability have grown out of many years of studying the puzzling nonretarded child who exhibits serious learning problems. Initially, a medical-neurological perspective was taken to explain such problems; more recently, a psychoeducational perspective has emerged. We explore both of these perspectives in the following section.

The Medical-Neurological Perspective: From Brain Injury to Minimal Brain Dysfunction

As early as 1896 (Morgan), physicians became interested in children with very severe reading problems. From a medical perspective, such children were "diagnosed" as suffering from "word blindness," and the notion that such problems may well have a neurological basis was established. This notion received further support from Hinshelwood in 1917, when he differentiated between adults who had lost the ability to read (acquired word blindness or *alexia*) and children who were unable or who had great difficulty learning to read (congenital word blindness or *dyslexia*). However, the concept of a learning disability is usually traced back to the 1930s and the work of Alfred Strauss, a neuropsychiatrist, and Heinz Werner, a psychologist. Although they worked with mentally retarded children, their descriptions of the behavior of brain-impaired individuals have greatly influenced our current concept of what constitutes a learning disability. Scientific interest in the behavior of brain-impaired persons commenced with the work of Goldstein, following World War I (Gelb & Goldstein, 1920), when returning veterans who had sustained head wounds were studied. It was found that such individuals were often distractible, hyperactive, and given to extreme mood swings and problems in visual and auditory perception.

Strauss and Werner identified two contrasting groups of mentally retarded children. One group was made up of children for whom there was no explanation for their retardation except that they had been "born that way." The other group consisted of children whose retardation was thought to be the result of a brain injury at some time during their lives. Although both groups of children were clearly retarded, the brain-injured group could be distinguished by their hyperactivity, perseveration (tendency to pursue a single task past the point when most individuals would stop), perceptual disorders, distractability, and emotional lability (frequent mood changes).

As the results of this work became more widely known, children—any children—who exhibited those behaviors found among Strauss and Werner's retarded, brain-damaged group were thought to be brain damaged. Thus, some considered the presence of the behaviors as proof of an existing brain injury, even when conclusive or suggestive evidence of a neurological problem was lacking. One did not have to be mentally retarded or evidence signs of neurological impairment; all one had to do was act like a member of Strauss and Werner's retarded, brain-damaged group to qualify for the label "brain damaged." Even though such a simplistic extrapolation may not be widespread today, the notion that such behaviors as hyperactivity, perceptual disorders, and distractability are evidence of actual, if subtle, brain damage has by no means disappeared in special education or related disciplines.

What has changed, however, are the labels used to describe so-called brain-injured children. The term *Strauss-Syndrome* was suggested by Stevens and Birch (1957) to designate children with behavioral abnormalities milder than those in Strauss's original studies. The terms *neurological disorder, neurologically handicapped,* and *psychoneurological learning disorder* were also coined (Myklebust, 1963). In 1966, a national task force (Clements, 1966) selected *minimal brain dysfunction* (MBD) as the most suitable designation. From the medical-neurological point of view, the most common term at the present time is *attention deficit disorder*, which is now used to specify the official medical diagnosis (Forness & Cantwell, 1982).

Hyperactivity.   The most frequent characteristic of children labeled MBD is hyperactivity. Although this appears to suggest an activity level significantly higher than that of nondesignated children, it is not an entirely accurate picture. What is hyperactive about a hyperactive child is the random, purposeless, and extraneous movement that is situationally inappropriate (Schworm, 1982).

Unfortunately, hyperactive has been used to cover all sorts of behavior problems, such as impulsivity, perceptual problems, short attention span, distractability, and immaturity. In order to differentiate normally active children who are labeled by intolerant observers, and those who are hyperactive due to mental retardation or emotional disturbance, from the MBD child, the term *neurologically hyperactive* has been suggested (Baren, Liebl, & Smith, 1978). For children whose hyperactivity is the result of food additives (Feingold, 1976), food allergies, or sugar stress, the term *medically hyperactive* has been used.

The question again is: What is a learning disability? Is the child labeled learning disabled the same as children labeled MBD or hyperactive? It depends on your point of view.

The Psychoeducational Perspective

A more behaviorally and educationally oriented approach to learning disabilities is provided by the psychoeducational perspective. The issue of whether hyperactivity or other problem behaviors are suggestive of brain dysfunction is simply sidestepped and focus is shifted to what the child can or cannot do in learning (Myers & Hammill, 1982).

Perceptual Disorders.   In chapter 1, we discussed the ambitious educational program Itard undertook with Victor, the wild boy. Central to the program was sensory motor training that included improving Victor's perception of both visual and auditory stimuli. We may see a drawing of a circle and a square side by side on a card perfectly well. There is nothing wrong with our vision. But when asked to draw the circle and square, we may reverse their position. The child who reads aloud the word *saw* as *was* is demonstrating a similar perceptual problem. Thus, we can pass a visual screening test with flying colors but still have problems during the process of seeing a certain stimulus and reacting to or perceiving it. Such problems are found among children considered learning disabled, but are not currently thought to represent the major difficulty underlying their learning problems (Forness, 1981a; Kavale, 1982).

Strauss was very interested in the perceptual problems of his brain-injured retardates. Over the years, such followers as Kephart (1971) and Barsch (1965, 1967) shifted the focus from concern with the source of perceptual disorders to the development of training approaches for correcting them. Others (Getman, 1965; Getman, Kane, Holgren, & McKee, 1968; Frostig & Horne, 1964) have also contributed perceptual training approaches that we will consider later.

Attention.   Studies done with children considered learning disabled have revealed that many have attentional disorders (Douglas, 1972; Sykes, et al., 1971, 1972). These disorders may involve problems in coming to attention or focusing, sustaining attention or vigilance, and decision making based on rapid or impulsive attending behavior (Keogh & Margolis, 1976; Krupski, 1981). The study of attention has become important because the type of attention problems a child has can suggest specific neurological or psychological learning processes that may be deficient (Samuels & Edwall, 1981). Problems relating to attention have been found to persist as the child matures even when other problems, such as awkwardness and clumsiness, have subsided (Alley & Deshler, 1979).

Memory and Information Processing.   Recent approaches to learning disability have also focused on certain problems in remembering or processing information (Forness, 1981a; Wong, 1979). Problems may occur not only because the child fails to receive adequate information in one or the other sensory modalities, but also because he or she fails to relate such information to an existing "information array" or previously learned material (Senf, 1976). Incoming information, whether letters, words, or numbers, is processed and remembered better when it can be related to such material. Poor learners may actually have a diminished capacity for storing information and cross-referencing it to sights, sounds, meanings, or even feelings that occur at the time the information is received. Before school, learning proceeds through the child's interaction with objects or events in the environment; school tasks require that the child actively generate his or her own cognitive associations (Torgeson, 1979). Children who may be slow in developing their own memory strategies, such as a silent rehearsal of material to be remembered, may be very inefficient learners when it comes to learning to read, spell, or do basic calculations.

Psycholinguistic or Oral Language Disorders.   Among the characteristics of a learning disability identified by Public Law 94–142 are problems "in using language" and an "imperfect ability to listen." Individuals may have difficulty expressing themselves and use sentences that are fragmented or more like expressions of younger children (expressive language disorder). Or children may have difficulty understanding what is said or shown to them (receptive language disorder). Some children may have inner language disorders and have difficulty thinking in an organized and accurate manner. Vellutino (1979) has suggested that subtle disorders in speech or language are actually one major cause of learning disabilities, particularly in reading. He has shown how visual-perceptual disorders may actually be a result of linguistic problems; for example, poor readers often reverse letters such as *b* and *d* but do *not* reverse similar visual symbols that have no linguistic meaning. Such children may correctly identify easily confusable words such as *was* and *saw*; their reversal errors only seem to occur when they are asked to *read* their words aloud. Vellutino feels that children who frequently use the wrong form of a verb or noun, or otherwise exhibit subtle difficulties in their spoken language, may develop reading disabilities. Support for his contention comes from other sources, including the facts that a majority of children referred to reading clinics often have a history of language or speech problems and that the majority of errors made by poor readers tend to be related to linguistic rather than visual-perceptual confusion (Forness, 1981a).

Written Language Disorders.   Public Law 94–142 also refers to "an imperfect ability to read, write, spell" or do "mathematical calculations" as characteristics associated with a learning disability. From the medical-neurological perspective, these disabilities are referred to as dyslexia (reading disability), dyscalculia, (mathematic disability), dysgraphia (spelling and written language disability), and strephosymbolia (reversing of letters in writing or reading, i.e., *on* for *no, was* for *saw*).

Again, the question is: What is a learning disability and how do we know if a given child is learning disabled? Here is a summary of what has been presented so far.

1.   A child has a learning disability if he or she has normal or above average intelligence and exhibits a significant discrepancy between intellectual ability and level of academic achievement.

2.   This discrepancy is not the result of physical or sensory handicaps, mental retardation, emotional disturbance, or environmental, cultural, or economic disadvantage.

3.   Once these two conditions are met, the specifics of a learning disability differ among children. Hyperactivity, perceptual and attentional disorders, problems in memory and information processing, and disorders of oral and written language may appear together, singly, or in various combinations. Which of these problems receive priority status when one or more appear together will relate directly to one's orientation regarding treatment or education (as discussed in a later section).

Causes

The actual cause of a learning disability is unknown. However, genetic, organic, biochemical developmental, and environmental causes have been postulated. The persistence of severe reading problems within succeeding generations of the same family has provided evidence of a possible genetic source (Lewitter, 1975). Complications during the birth process, such as anoxia (oxygen deficit), can cause neurological impairment, as can injuries to the head and certain diseases, such as measles and encephalitis, that produce an extremely high body temperature. The fact that some children with learning disabilities are aided by drugs has also led some to study possible biochemical causes (Baren, Liebl, & Smith, 1978).

Children with learning disabilities are often described as "immature." Consider the following description:

> The child is "charged with runabout compulsion . . . he lugs, tugs, dumps, pushes, and pounds with gross motor activity taking the lead over fine motor . . . his attention, like his body activity, is mercurial."

This description could very well fit some hyperactive seven- or eight-year-old who is identified as having a learning disability. The fact is, the quotation was written by Gesell and Ilg (1943) and describes their impression of the typical eighteen-month-old child. Gesell and Ilg also describe age two and one-half as a time when the child may evidence perseveration and find changes in routine upsetting. These are also characteristics associated with learning disabilities. Thus, another possible causal explanation is that learning-disabled children are behind schedule developmentally and will eventually mature (Hewett, 1973). Indeed, in the Soviet Union, where the equivalent field to special education is called *defectology*, a learning disability is referred to as "developmental backwardness" or "psychophysical infantalism." The Soviets take the position that such children will eventually mature and achieve normally (Hewett & Wilderson, 1974).

Finally, environmental causes of learning disabilities have been explored. Severe malnutrition at an early age can actually alter a child's learning capacity, as can an impoverished range of experience or lack of environmental stimulation (Cruickshank & Hallahan, 1973; Cravioto & DeLicardie, 1975). Emotional or behavioral problems may produce such learning disability characteristics as inattention and hyperactivity, and motivational deficits common among children who have experienced continual failure may do the same. Inadequate instruction in the early grades may create problems for the child that will be viewed later as indicators of a learning disability (Adelman, 1971).

The problem with using environmental disadvantages including malnutrition, early stimulus deprivation, or poor instruction as explanations for a learning disability is that they are excluded as primary causes by definition. Yet they may be primarily responsible for some behaviors associated with a learning disability and secondarily responsible for others. The same may be said for emotional disturbance, which we discussed earlier. We will not attempt a full-scale discussion of whether one can decide with any degree of certainty what caused what on a primary *or* secondary basis. The waters are very muddied in this respect. Until a more precise definition emerges and until we know more about underlying causes, they will continue to be muddied. Chances are, there are many roads to a learning disability—genetic, organic, biochemical, and environmental.

Identification and Diagnosis

The identification of a child suspected of having a learning disability usually begins when someone (e.g., classroom teacher, parent) becomes concerned with one or more problem behaviors. The problem behaviors or characteristics most often displayed by children with learning disabilities have been compiled over the years. In 1966, Clements reviewed over one hundred publications concerned with identifying children with learning disabilities. In 1974, Tarver and Hallahan conducted a similar review and confirmed Clements's earlier findings. The ten most cited characteristics, along with clarifications (Bryan & Bryan, 1978) and in order of frequency, are as follows:

1. Hyperactivity (motor behavior that is not demanded by the situation or the task involved and that is disruptive to the group or to the expectations of observers).

2. Perceptual-motor impairments (difficulty in coordinating a visual or auditory stimulus with a motoric act, such as copying letters of the alphabet).

3. Emotional lability (emotional outbursts that are not reasonably expected by observers

on the basis of knowledge concerning the situation or the immediate past history of the child).

4. General coordination deficits (clumsiness).

5. Disorders of attention, such as: distractibility (behavior that reflects the child's interest in things other than those on which he or she should be concentrating) and perseveration (behavior that reflects the child's inability to change the focus of attention, even when the reason for interest has changed).

6. Impulsivity (behavior that appears to reflect little thinking concerning its consequences).

7. Disorders of memory or thinking (difficulty in recalling material that should have been learned, or difficulty in understanding abstract concepts).

8. Specific learning disabilities (inability to learn or remember reading, writing, arithmetic, or spelling).

9. Difficulty in comprehending or remembering spoken language, deficits in articulation of speech or in expressing self verbally using appropriate grammar and vocabulary.

10. Equivocal neurological signs (neurological signs that are not clearly associated with particular neurological problems but that are clearly not within the normal range of functioning).

Since the evidence suggests that learning disabilities may have multiple causes, we approach the assessment of a suspected learning-disabled child from both medical-neurological and psychoeducational perspectives. In addition, we may go beyond formal diagnostic and test procedures and explore the child's total environment (Spache, 1981).

A medical-neurological assessment involves examining the child's developmental and family medical history, vision, hearing, physical-motor abilities, and neurological status. Problems during pregnancy or the child's birth are noted, as are family medical problems and illnesses and injuries sustained by the child. Tests of vision and hearing help determine if the child's problems may be due in part to sensory loss. A partial hearing loss may go unnoticed well into a child's school years and can result in any number of the problem behaviors noted earlier. The neurological examination may look for "soft" neurological signs. These signs are not clearly associated with a specific neurological disorder, but they definitely fall outside the normal range of functioning. For example, the child may exhibit problems of balance or coordination or difficulty in maintaining a left-right orientation. In some cases, an electroencephalogram (EEG), a recording of the electrical activity of the brain, may be included.

Psychoeducational assessment entails examining the child's school history and behavioral characteristics, and administering selected tests. School records provide information about the child's academic progress or lack of it, behavior in school, and teacher and peer relationships. A psychologist, psychiatrist, or social worker may interview the child in an effort to assess the child's self-concept and personal and social adjustment. The child's parents may also be interviewed. Of concern is the adequacy of the home environment and the relationship between the child and others in the family. Children who are unhappy at home, and who are neglected or abused by others, may exhibit many of the characteristics associated with learning disabilities. A similar look at the child's school environment is also in order. Children who are unhappy in school, and who experience continual frustration and failure, may exhibit many characteristics associated with learning disabilities. Does the child have friends? What about the teacher-child relationship? Are the teacher's instructional approaches appropriate for the child? A major mistake in diagnosing a child as learning disabled is assuming that a child has had a reasonable period of balanced instruction (both phonetic and whole-word approaches to teaching reading, for example) in the regular classroom (Forness, 1982a). If such is not the case, the disability may be in the classroom, not in the child.

In addition, the psychologist may administer tests to assess intelligence (e.g., Wechsler Intelligence Scale for Children Revised [WISC-R], Wechsler, 1974), visual perception (e.g., Developmental Test of Visual Perception, Frostig, 1964), auditory perception (e.g., Auditory Discrimination Test, Wepman, 1958), and language functioning (e.g., Illinois Test of Psycholinguistic Abilities [ITPA], Kirk, McCarthy, & Kirk, 1968). The particular profile of the child on the WISC-R may also be examined to determine if patterns exist that can further pinpoint the child's approach to learning (Kaufman, 1981), though this approach may not always be clinically sound (Kavale & Forness, in press).

This comprehensive approach to assessment can be used for any exceptional learner; the more information we have about the individual, the better we can understand the problem and plan a special education program. Since there are so many views of what constitutes a learning disability, assessment and identification remain difficult tasks (Ysseldyke, Algozzine, Richey & Graden, 1982).

Treatment and Educational Provisions

We have now defined learning disabilities, identified characteristics associated with them, and discussed typical assessment approaches. But this discussion is only a prologue to actually helping the child. What specifically does one do to aid a learning-disabled child? Again, we draw on the perspectives previously presented.

Medical-Neurological Perspectives.   The child viewed as suffering from minimal brain dysfunction (MBD) becomes a patient to be treated just like any other individual afflicted with a disease or injury. Quite logically, medication of some type would be sought to alleviate the child's symptoms. The symptom associated with MBD that is most commonly treated by medication is hyperactivity; the most widely prescribed drugs are psychostimulants (Stevens, 1980). More than any other drug, methylphenidate (Ritalin) is used because it results in fewer side effects than the second most commonly prescribed drug, dextroamphetamine (Dexedrine) (Krager & Safer, 1974). Side effects refer to changes in an individual's physiology or behavior not intended to be brought about by administration of a drug, such as loss of appetite, sleep problems, stomach distress, dizziness, trembling of the hands, coldness of arms and legs, and skin pallor (Grinspoon & Singer, 1973). These side effects may gradually diminish or disappear. However, long-term side effects, such as alteration of blood pressure or stunting of stature or growth, have not been adequately studied (Safer, Allan, & Barr, 1972; Safer & Allen, 1976).

There have been numerous studies concerning the effectiveness of psychostimulant drugs on the behavior of hyperactive children. Effectiveness is usually defined as increasing the child's teachability and manageability and reducing activity level. The most favorable studies place the effectiveness rate at 80 percent (Hoffman, Englehardt, Margolis, Polizos, Waizer, & Rosenfeld, 1974; Schain & Reynard, 1975). Others are more cautious, suggesting a 35 to 50 percent "dramatic" improvement rate, 30 to 40 percent "moderate" improvement rate, and no improvement at all among 15 to 20 percent (Safer & Allen, 1976).

In addition to the problems and unknowns associated with taking psychostimulant drugs, there is little evidence to suggest they actually enhance children's learning abilities. They do lead to improved behavioral ratings by parents and teachers, but not always to gains in academic achievement (Rie, Rie, Stewart, & Ambuel, 1976). The issue of dosage is critical. It has been found that the drug dosage that brings about the most improvement in behavior may exceed the dosage that optimizes the child's learning effectiveness (Sprague & Sleator, 1977). Thus, a reduced dosage may aid the child in learning whereas an increased dosage may foster behavioral improvement. Since the criteria for whether or not the drug is "working" usually consists of behavioral ratings by adults who live and work with the child, one can see how behavioral improvement is possibly attained at the expense of learning effectiveness. Determining the exact dosage for a given child should take into account both learning effectiveness *and* behavioral improvement.

Drugs currently in use do not appear to be addictive. Children on drug treatment for several years have shown no signs of withdrawal after missing a dose (O'Malley & Eisenberg, 1973). Some investigators, however, speculate that drug treatment continued into adolescence may lead to habitual drug use (Stewart, 1970). Another concern is that children may learn that their behavior is controlled by a drug, not by themselves (Whalen & Henker, 1976).

The final verdict regarding the efficacy of drug treatment with children with learning disabilities has not been reached. It has, in fact, been shown that behavioristic approaches often are just as effective as medication in helping a child control his or her behavior, when both are compared in controlled studies (Forness, 1975; Tarjan & Forness, 1979). Available evidence does suggest that stimulant drugs can have a positive effect on a child's classroom behavior and, in many cases, on learning (Kavale, 1982). But no matter how effective drugs are in helping the child become more manageable and teachable, we cannot always count on them to remediate the child's learning problems. Only a teacher who zeroes in on the child, motivates that child, and provides appropriate instruction can do that.

Other medical approaches to the problems of children with learning disabilities include megavitamin therapy (Cott, 1975) and diet management (Feingold, 1976; Wender, 1977). Despite encouragement in individual cases, the effectiveness of the latter approach in well-controlled studies is practically nil (Kavale & Forness, 1983). The term *neuroeducator* has been used to describe the role of the teacher trained to deal with children suspected of having a medical-neurological type of learning disability (Cruickshank, 1981). Such a teacher would apparently be well prepared to deal with specific medical or neurological deficits that are presumed to cause various learning disabilities and would be especially prepared to address such issues as which remedial techniques might be best for specific, neurologically based deficits, which children might benefit most from medication and, in general, how to integrate the educational program with medical or neurological treatment.

Psychoeducational Perspective.   From the psychoeducational perspective, the learning-disabled child needs to be trained in areas of weakness that are identified by assessment procedures. The child is not a "patient" but a "learner," waiting to be taught. A well-known, comprehensive environmental approach to the education of children with learning disabilities is found in the work of Cruickshank (Cruickshank, Bentzen, Ratzeberg, & Tannhauser, 1961). The approach emphasizes a distraction-free physical environment with children assigned to individual cubicles. It is intended to help the child compensate for problems in distractibility or inattention by reducing outside influences and heightening the intensity of the materials to be learned.

Related to this is the somewhat controversial area of perceptual-motor training, which is provided by the programs of both Kephart (1971) and Frostig (Frostig & Horne, 1964). The term *motor* is added to *perceptual* to indicate that any act of visual or auditory perception involves some degree of movement (e.g., moving the eyes or head). Kephart's program is concerned with five areas of perceptual-motor skill: balance, positive body image and differentiation, perceptual-motor match, ocular control, and form perception. The Frostig program is concerned with visual-perceptual skills in five areas: eye-motor coordination, figure-ground perception, constancy of shape, position in space, and spatial relationship.

Both of these programs assume that training in these preacademic areas will eventually facilitate academic progress, particularly in reading. But research studies have not confirmed this (Bryan & Bryan, 1975; Forness & Kavale, in press; Kavale, 1983). Children trained in perceptual-motor skills improve on tests designed to measure *perceptual-motor* proficiency. Children who participate in training activities related more directly to reading improve on tests designed to measure *reading* proficiency.

Multisensory training in which visual, auditory, and tactual senses are stimulated simultaneously has also been used with learning-disabled children. The approach is found in the reading and written language programs of Gillingham and Stillman (1960), Slingerland (1972), and Fernald (1943). Language-oriented programs have also been developed to aid children with learning disabilities. Kirk and Kirk (1971) have devised treatment exercises for children whose basic linguistic abilities are found to be deficient on the Illinois Test of Psycholinguistic Abilities (ITPA). These exercises are used to strengthen such abilities as auditory and visual perception, association, expression, memory, and closure (i.e., the ability to grasp automatically the whole of a visual pattern or verbal expression when only part of it is presented). Studies comparing groups of learning-disabled children trained by perceptual-motor exercises with groups trained by a multisensory approach, and these in turn with groups of children given language training, have not found one method superior to any other in facilitating academic progress over time (Belmont, Flegenheimer, & Birch, 1973; Kavale, 1981; Kavale & Glass, 1981; Kavale & Mattson, 1983; Silberberg, Iversen, & Goins, 1973).

More recently, however, interest has focused on teaching children with learning disabilities, as well as mentally retarded children and other types of exceptional learners, by helping them to monitor their own performance in learning situations and to be aware of their own approaches to cognitive tasks (Blackman & Goldstein, 1982; Feuerstein, Miller, Hoffman, Rand, Mintzker, & Jensen, 1981; Meichenbaum & Azarnow, 1978; Sabatino, Miller, & Schmidt, 1981). Known variously as metacognition, metamemory, or cognitive behavior modification strategies, these approaches are directed toward providing learning-disabled children with an awareness of how people learn or remember. Thus, children are taught how to slow themselves down before they read a word or give an answer, look carefully at all cues and alternative possibilities, consider their response carefully, and then respond. In remembering, they are taught to group information into small bits or clusters, rehearse these by saying them over and over to themselves, and even use mnemonic devices to aid in memory storage. It has been found that many learning-disabled youngsters improve dramatically when they are simply made aware of the most effective way to approach learning, but research is far from clear in this area (Gerber, 1983).

Children with learning disabilities have only recently been identified and studied. Definitions tell us that they have the potential to achieve in a normal manner but for some reason do not. They also tell us that no other handicapping condition can be the primary cause of the problem. About all that is left is some sort of minimal brain dysfunction as the source; although, the federal definition notwithstanding, emotional disturbance or other behavioral or motivational problems can produce many of the symptoms associated with learning disabilities.

Medical-neurological approaches consider drugs important in treatment. The definition of a learning disability also tells us the wide variety of problems children may have in areas of perception, movement, language, and academics. Psychoeducational approaches zero in on these problems, and diverse special education interventions have been developed. So far, the concept of a learning disability has remained ambiguous, and it is likely to remain so for some time.

Mentally Retarded Individuals: An Overview

The recommendations of President Kennedy's first Panel on Mental Retardation began a modern era of unprecedented progress in the lives of the mentally retarded. Perhaps nowhere have these changes been more dramatic than in the schools. The use of the courts and subsequent federal legislation to establish fundamental rights of the retarded to appropriate education and services; mainstreaming of the retarded out of institutional and special-class settings; emphasis on new behavioral and curricular approaches; and interest in early education and prevention have all been hallmarks in the field of mental retardation in the past two decades (Scheerenberger, 1983). Much of this effort tended to blur a precise distinction between mildly and severely retarded children. It is still useful to consider these groups separately, as long as one bears in mind that there are actually two *overlapping* groups of mentally retarded individuals (Tarjan & Forness, 1979). The first tend to be mildly retarded, with no discernible pathological signs, and often come from economically disadvantaged families; a second, smaller group (around 20 percent) usually with IQs below 50, come from all socioeconomic levels and have evident physical abnormalities. In this section, we consider some general aspects of mental retardation and then focus on the mildly retarded and the more severely retarded.

Definition

There have been a number of lingering difficulties over the years in defining mental retardation. Many medical, social, and psychological problems can cause an individual to be classified as retarded, and a number of different professionals are concerned with the diagnosis and treatment of mentally retarded children. The American Association of Mental Deficiency (AAMD) has, in fact, had to adopt as many as five different official definitions over the past twenty years. The most recent AAMD definition is that mental retardation refers to significantly subaverage intellectual functioning existing concurrently with deficits in adaptive behavior, and manifested during the developmental period (Grossman, 1983). Thus, a person must meet three criteria in order to be classified as mentally retarded.

1. *Subaverage intellectual functioning.* This is generally determined on an individual intelligence test by performance more than two standard deviations below the mean (e.g., IQ 70). However, the most recent AAMD definition cautions against the rigid use of IQ cut-off points and allows for more flexibility in diagnosing a person whose IQ is borderline. Thus, even a child with an IQ of 75 might be diagnosed as retarded if it can be shown that his or her deficits in adaptive behavior are due primarily to problems in reasoning and judgement. The emphasis is thus on the child's need for service and recognizes that IQ is not always a precise measure.

2. *Concurrent deficits in adaptive behavior.* During preschool years, adaptive behavior refers primarily to the development of sensory-motor, self-help, and communicative skills, such as sitting up, walking, dressing oneself, and talking. During school years, it refers basically to academic achievement, the ability to apply academic skills, and socialization. At the adult level, adaptation is generally defined by the person's social and economic adjustment. However, all three factors—maturation, learning, and social adjustment—are considered important at every age as indices of adaptive behavior and may determine an individual's need for special programs or services. MacMillan (1982) has stressed the problems, however, of measuring adaptive behavior without reference to the cultural environment of the individual.

3. *Manifestation during the developmental period.* Since it is a developmental disorder, mental retardation should not be the diagnosis if the impairment occurs during adult years or after the eighteenth year. This serves to distinguish mental retardation from other disorders, such as brain injury or emotional disturbance, that can develop in adulthood.

An important aspect of the definition is its emphasis on both intelligence and adaptation. A school-age child who performs below average on a test of intelligence but still manages to succeed even marginally in most other situations could not be strictly classified as retarded according to this definition. The assumption is that the child's adaptive behavior reflects a higher level of intellect than recorded by the test. A child who is unable to adapt to the regular classroom but who has measured intelligence in the normal range would not be considered retarded either. Impaired adaptive behavior, in this case, might be the result of some factor other than low intellectual ability, such as a behavior disorder. Thus, a system of checks and balances is established to avoid labeling children as mentally retarded on the basis of a single criterion. A public school version of the AAMD Adaptive Behavior Scale has been developed (Lambert & Nicoll, 1976); and adaptive behavior is often used as a screening measure for special education placement (Kazimour & Reschly, 1981; Windmiller, 1977), although not always consistently from state to state (Huberty, Kroller, & Ten Brink, 1980). The problems of defining and measuring social competence have been especially troublesome (Greenspan, 1979, 1980; Meyers, Nihira, & Zetlin, 1979). The questionable validity of intelligence test scores, especially with very young children or children from disadvantaged backgrounds, makes it essential that adaptive behavior be considered (Reschly, 1981).

It is also important to realize that, according to the AAMD definitions, a person might be classified as mentally retarded at one time in life but not at another. Children with low intelligence who do poorly in academic work would most likely be considered mentally retarded. As often happens, however, they may be able after graduation from high school to support themselves independently at an unskilled or semiskilled job, especially if they have had good vocational preparation. At that point, society would not necessarily consider them retarded. Surprisingly, IQ has been a relatively poor predictor of later community adjustment for retarded individuals (Bell, 1976; McCarver & Craig, 1974). Social competency, in fact, has been considered by some as the most important diagnostic criterion for mental retardation (Doll, 1953; Gunzburg, 1973). Thus, numerous changes occurring over time in a person's life situation often play an important part in determining whether he or she will be labeled mentally retarded. This is particularly true in cases where the level of retardation is mild and less likely the result of some central nervous system disorder. Environmental demands also play an important part in the development of adaptive behavior (Nihira, 1976, 1977; Nihira, Foster, Shellhaas, & Leland, 1974). Chapter 7 describes how social expectations often determine the nature of the problems of a retarded child.

Classification

Although there are several ways to classify retarded children, the method generally favored by educators is to classify such children by their expected level of educational progress. Retarded children are divided into three groups:

1. *Educable mentally retarded (EMR) children* (IQ 50 to 70 or 75) are, for the most part, normal in appearance but said to function at an intellectual level generally limited to learning only the most basic school skills in reading, spelling, writing, and numerical calculation. EMR children are usually not ready for such academic skills as reading and math in the first grade but can be expected eventually to attain anywhere from a second- to seventh-grade level in academic achievement. Most begin school in the regular classroom, but low achievement or adaptive behavior makes it necessary for many to receive special assistance or attend special classes.

2. *Trainable mentally retarded (TMR) children* (IQ 30 to 50) function at a level where formal academic learning is quite limited. Most can be expected to have physical or sensory impairments, and many tend to look different in terms of facial features or physical characteristics. Unlike EMR children, the developmental problems of TMR children emerge quite early in

infancy or preschool years. Usually placed in special classes or special schools, TMR children need training in self-care activities and language development; in many cases, they acquire only rudimentary academic skills.

3. *Profoundly mentally retarded children* (IQ below 30) are for the most part totally dependent on others for their existence, and many are institutionalized early in life. There is increasing concern for the quality of education and treatment of profoundly retarded individuals; behavior modification and environmental stimulation techniques are being used in as many cases as possible to enable them to achieve some level of independence within supervised environments.

This educational system of classification does not completely correspond to the AAMD system (Baumeister & Muma, 1975). Table 4–1 illustrates the overlapping of the two systems, as well as the expected levels of adaptive behavior and adult outcome. A serious caution regarding the interpretation of Table 4–1 is in order. These "levels" of mental retardation *should not* be considered *limits* of functioning; great variability is found within each level in terms of the academic progress, social adaptation, and eventual outcome for each individual.

The classification of "borderline mentally retarded" was at one time used to designate the IQ range of 70 to 85. Educators now categorize such children more appropriately as learning disabled, economically disadvantaged, or culturally different. Throughout the text, it is important to remember that certain referenced studies on mental retardation were based on children with IQs as high as 80 or 85 (MacMillan, Meyers, & Morrison, 1980). It should also be noted that the IQ ranges given in Table 4–1 are quite arbitrary and only a frame of reference. There is considerable overlap among classifications and a considerable variety of educational placements within each category.

Mildly Mentally Retarded Individuals

In this book, we use the terms *mildly retarded* and *severely retarded*, instead of *educable* and *trainable*, because they connote degrees of difference rather than clear-cut educational distinctions.

Incidence

The United States Department of Education has estimated the percentage of all school-age mentally retarded children at 2.3 percent, but statistics gathered during the 1981–82 school year indicate that only 1.96 percent of school-age children were actually identified at *all* levels of retardation. The number of retarded persons, however, is not the same at every age level. Figure 4–1 illustrates the incidence of retardation by age of persons identified as retarded; it is a smoothed-curve adaptation of epidemiological data reported in two sources (Gruenberg, 1964;

Table 4-1
AAMD Classification of mental retardation with special education categories

AAMD Level	IQ Range*	Special Education Category**	Expected adaptive behavior**	Adult outcome**
Profound	Below 25	*Profound.* Capable of some pre-school activities.	May eventually be able to feed self and to interact with others in simple play activities, but speech and toileting remain at a primitive level.	Will require continued custodial care.
Severe	25–39	*Trainable.* Capable of some skills at kindergarten level, such as recognizing words and basic number concepts.	May eventually be able to feed, toilet, and dress self adequately, carry on rudimentary conversation, and run errands or do simple household chores.	Will need to live in closely supervised environment.
Moderate	40–54	*Trainable or Educable.* Capable of first- or second-grade learning, such as reading simple sentences and basic addition and subtraction.	May eventually be able to feed, dress, and groom self adequately; carry on simple conversations; interact cooperatively with others; and be responsible for simple routines of daily living	Able to live independently but will need periodic supervision; can work in sheltered situations.
Mild	55–70	*Educable.* Capable of second- to seventh-grade learning, such as reading stories, communicating in writing, and handling simple financial transactions.	May eventually be responsible for all feeding and personal grooming activities; communicate effectively in everyday conversation; enjoy friendships and group social activities; and travel with ease in hometown.	Able to live independently, may marry or have children, and hold unskilled or semi-skilled jobs, but will need occasional assistance in all these areas.

*Note that these levels are determined using the Wechsler Intelligence Scales. IQ values for other individual intelligence scales may be slightly different.

**Again, the reader is reminded this should not be considered a "table of limitations." Considerable variability is found at each level and many children at the moderate or even severe levels of intelligence are capable of much higher levels of academic achievement and eventual social adaptation than suggested here.

Heber, 1970). Figure 4-1 shows a small percentage of children diagnosed as retarded before school age; these are usually mostly the severely retarded who are more easily identified and are indicated by the shaded area in the figure. Mildly retarded children, who comprise the largest percentage, are ordinarily not identified until after school entrance, when their intellectual differences are most obvious. As these persons leave school, their differences become less evident to society and the percentage of identified mildly retarded persons decreases. The number of mildly retarded children identified *before* school age is certainly less than 1 percent, but those identified *during* school years appears closer to the U.S. Office of Education estimate of between 1 and 2 percent.

The incidence of mild retardation also varies with socioeconomic class (MacMillan, 1982; Wyne & O'Connor, 1979). According to normal epidemiological distributions, the number of mildly mentally retarded should be around 15 per 1,000 school children; but the figure may range from below 10 per 1,000 in areas of high socioeconomic status to over 50 per 1,000 in poverty areas. The President's Committee on Mental Retardation (1970) termed some inner-city retarded children as "six-hour retarded" children since they were only identified as retarded for the six hours spent in school each day and not in other situations. When criteria of adaptive behavior by racial and ethnic subgroup are employed, incidence figures for school-age mildly retarded are somewhat closer to 1 percent (Kirk & Gallagher, 1979). Public agencies, such as schools, have been shown to label poor or ethnic minority children living in deteriorated housing far more

Figure 4-1.
Estimated Percentage of Mentally Retarded Persons by
Chronological Age

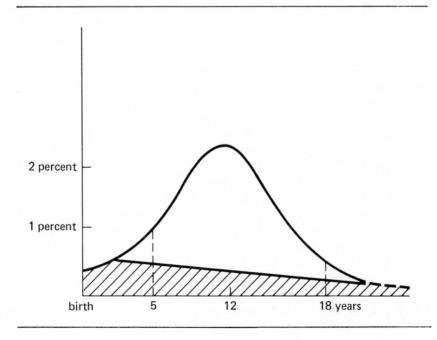

frequently than white children living in middle-class neighborhoods (Lei, Butler, Rowitz, & McAllister, 1974; Kirk, 1978; Patrick & Reschly, 1982). If a strict definition of mental retardation that employed precise measures of adaptive behavior and eventual social competence were used, the exact incidence of mild retardation would undoubtedly be less than 1 percent overall (Childs, 1982).

Causes

What causes mild retardation? In discussing etiology, it is important to remember that mental retardation is merely a symptom—not a disease. More than two hundred different diseases or other states of medical pathology are known to cause mental retardation, but in general they account for no more than 20 percent of all mentally retarded individuals, usually the severely retarded. For approximately 80 percent of mentally retarded persons, however, it is impossible to pinpoint precisely what caused the retardation. In most cases, these individuals have IQs over 50, are relatively normal in appearance, and come mostly from lower socioeconomic classes. Although controversy exists about whether these individuals are simply at the lower end of the polygenetically determined distribution of intelligence (Baroff, 1974; Jensen, 1972, 1979), it is clear that mild mental retardation most likely results from the complex interplay of familial, environmental, and social factors in which heredity tends to set limits on intellectual potential or capacity, whereas experience determines to what extent such potential will be fulfilled.

For example, a prime predictor of premature birth (a condition in which 10 to 20 percent of affected children may have mental retardation or physical handicaps) has been found to be the maternal grandfather's income (Drillien, 1964). Initially, it is difficult to see why a grandfather's income would have anything to do with mental retardation. However, his financial ability to provide good nutrition, health care, and a minimal amount of education for the child's mother during her formative years may ultimately be related to mental retardation in a variety of complex and subtle ways. The following factors, among others, have been found to relate to a child's intelligence: the socioeconomic status that the mother attains; the community in which she lives; her health and thus her ability to carry the fetus to term; her awareness of and willingness to seek child health services; the amount of cognitive stimulation she can provide for the child in infancy; her interest in preschool experiences of the child; and her reinforcement of the child's later school efforts (Hurley, 1969; MacMillan, 1982; Robinson & Robinson, 1976). In other words, the mother's upbringing tends to set the stage for the kind of resources the child will have from the very beginning of life.

With regard to etiology, there are probably four overlapping types of causes associated with mild retardation. The first type is familial, which includes the small percentage of each ethnic group that falls at the lower end of the polygenetic distribution of intelligence for their respective groups. As mentioned previously, there is controversy over the relative percentages of certain ethnic groups in the lower ranges of intelligence, but it should be understood that *every* racial and ethnic group is represented. The failure to recognize this inheritability factor may misplace the blame for some cases of retardation on inadequate home or school environments, resulting in unrealistic expectations for the child (Wyne & O'Connor, 1979).

The second type of cause is neurological, representing the upper end of the continuum of biomedical causation (discussed in the next section on severe retardation). It is possible in some cases to pinpoint a specific pathologic condition that may have caused some damage to the child's central nervous system, resulting in a mild level of retardation. Lead poisoning, either through prolonged exposure to industrial lead dust or ingestion of chipped lead paint, may be one such cause (Beattie, Moore, & Goldberg, 1975; Moore & Moore, 1977). Neurological causes are present in children who exhibit characteristics of the Strauss syndrome, discussed earlier; and it is likely that many such biomedical causes emanate from culturally related reproductive factors, such as family size, poor obstetrical care, and the like (Ramey, Stedman, Borders-Patterson, & Mengel, 1978; Mednick, 1977; Rosenzweig, 1981).

The third type of cause is nutritional. There is increasing documentation that chronic malnutrition, either in the mother or subsequently in the developing child, may be one of the more significant factors in eventual mental performance (Begab, 1974; Perkins, 1977; National Institute of Child Health and Human Development, 1976; Winnick, 1976). A lack of sufficient nutrients during critical periods of brain growth often results in mild retardation, but the exact processes are not clearly understood. There is also speculation that the malnourished mother may not have the energy needed to provide the proper upbringing for her child (Zeskind & Ramey, 1978).

The fourth cause is environmental. Children who lack sufficient environmental stimulation during critical periods of infancy and early childhood usually fail to develop at the normal rate. Children from low-income families or barren institutional settings often lack sufficient sensory stimulation, perceptual experience, adequate adult language models, and a variety of other experiences necessary for cognitive growth and development. The causal relationship between inadequate early range and nature of experience and later mental retardation is well documented. The relative success of early infant stimulation or early educational intervention programs, designed to provide experiences in home or preschool settings to prevent or ameliorate conditions possibly leading to eventual mild retardation will be discussed in chapter 7. The point needs to be made, however, that interventions must be sustained and intensive to assure a child's continued progress (Clarke & Clarke, 1977).

These four subgroups are not mutually exclusive. They are meant to illustrate the major capacity and experience factors that underly the very complex syndrome of mild retardation. It is also clear that socioeconomic variables or poverty have more than just a correlational relationship with mild retardation (Haywood, 1970). Particularly in the schools, there is evidence that socioeconomic status is a factor that sometimes biases both teachers (Smith & Greenberg, 1975) and school psychologists (Neer, Foster, Jones, & Reynolds, 1973) regarding the diagnosis of mental retardation. Although placement in classes for the retarded may be closely associated with factors of poverty or even ethnicity (Burke, 1975; Mercer, 1973b), clearly this is a complex issue for school personnel who must respond to the special needs of such children (Ashurst & Meyers, 1973; Meyers, MacMillan, & Yoshida, 1978).

Although subtle and as yet undiscovered biological factors may be the actual cause of mild retardation, the problem of a large percentage of the mildly retarded remains a nonmedical issue. As we shall see, there is considerable overlap in characteristics and in programs between the mildly retarded and children who are economically disadvantaged and culturally different. Unlike more severe mental retardation, where medical sciences become the primary (but not the only) focus, solutions for the problems of mild retardation remain with behavioral scientists in such disciplines as psychology, psychiatry, sociology, anthropology, and special education (Zigler,

1978). Preventive efforts are needed in which parents are taught to provide early environmental stimulation, adequate nutrition, and routine health maintenance for their infants (Ramey & Campbell, 1979). Adequate early preschool experience should be provided to overcome, at least in part, the social and educational deficits associated with mild mental retardation.

Identification

Mildly retarded children are usually not identified before reaching school age. Although a potentially mildly retarded child may have problems in communication, physical development, and socialization during the preschool years, differences tend to be moderate and may not cause undue concern until the child begins formal schooling. Up to this point, such children may have been able to function marginally at home or in their neighborhoods; however, school is a more complex social and academic environment that demands increasingly more of children over the years. A child with an IQ of 70 may not be ready to begin reading until he or she is eight years old and in the third grade, whereas nonretarded classmates will have been reading for some time.

Although early school identification is essential to prevent additional problems, the mildly retarded child frequently is not identified until he or she has spent one or more years in the regular classroom. Even though elementary teachers are increasingly prepared to identify mildly retarded children in the early grades, some children eventually classified as mildly mentally retarded may go unrecognized in regular classes, competing with normal peers until their learning problems become too severe or their frustration eventually becomes too obvious for the teacher to ignore. At that point, the teacher seeks help, and the child usually is referred for evaluation by a school psychologist or other members of a special education admissions team.

Traditionally, a child referred to such a team has been given a battery of tests by the school psychologist designed to explore functioning in areas of intelligence, achievement, and adaptation. On the basis of these measures, the school psychologist makes a decision as to the child's potential. However, controversy surrounding the use of IQ scores obtained from standardized tests as a basis for diagnosing mental retardation has altered this traditional approach in some states. (Some of the difficulties encountered when using such tests with exceptional learners were discussed earlier.) Other professionals, such as a pediatrician or the school nurse, may also be consulted; but usually, a team composed of the school psychologist, the teacher, the principal, a special educator, and the child's parents makes the final determination. If the child's inability is due primarily to low intelligence and not to other factors, and if he or she is not expected to make satisfactory progress in the regular grades, the child is then referred for some form of special education.

Treatment and Educational Provisions

Although the most common form of special education for mildly retarded children has been the special education classroom, this approach is rapidly being replaced by programs that include as much integration in regular classrooms as possible. When used, special classes are generally grouped according to the following levels: primary, elementary or intermediate, and secondary. Class enrollment is usually less than half that of the thirty or more children usually found in regular classrooms (twelve to eighteen pupils) depending on the range of ages and mental abilities. Preschool classes (ages three to six) are now available in increasing numbers and provide experiences for children to improve their school readiness, much as normal preschools do but at a somewhat slower pace.

Special education classes at the primary level (ages six to eight) provide experiences in oral language and speech development, sensorimotor development, self-awareness, group member-ship and social adjustment, self-care, safety, manipulation of materials, work habits, direction following, and reading readiness. Academic tasks are not generally emphasized except for beginning instruction in counting and recognition of letters or words. By the elementary level (ages eight to thirteen), mildly retarded children have begun to learn tool-skill subjects, such as reading, writing, spelling, and math. Instruction in reading and math (Mason, 1978; Vitello, 1976) often takes into account the particular perceptual and cognitive deficits of retarded children, which will be discussed in more detail in later chapters. Units in basic social studies and practical science are also taught, not only as academic subjects but also as activities in which tool-skill subjects can be applied and practiced.

The secondary program provides consolidation in the use of basic academic skills learned earlier, but with increasing emphasis on preparation for work and home living. Civic responsibil-ity, news media, use of leisure time, family life education, consumer education, finances, practical law, social roles, travel, and vocational choices are stressed. The mildly retarded adolescent typically has more opportunity for interaction with normal peers at the high school level because he or she may be integrated into regular classes in physical education, industrial arts, home economics, and fine arts. Toward the end of their formal school careers, mildly retarded youths are often assigned to a work-study program, a vocational training program run by an agency other than the school, or even a trial job on a part-time basis. The recent movement toward assessing the minimum competency of high school graduates has created special problems for mildly retarded students; only 6 percent passed a recent proficiency exam in one state (Safer, 1980).

Resource rooms for mildly retarded children, who spend most of their day in regular classrooms, and integration of special-class retarded children at least part-time into regular classes are now common approaches (Forness, 1979b; MacMillan & Semmel, 1977; Heron, 1978). Problems inherent in segregating mildly retarded children in special classes, where opportunities for educational progress and social contact with normal peers are limited, have been well documented. Several studies of special classes for the mildly retarded have suggested that many children in these classes were not classifiable as retarded when proper diagnostic criteria were applied (Mercer, 1973a; Garrison & Hammill, 1971). Research on existing classes for the mildly retarded suggests that these classes contain extremely heterogeneous populations and that care should be taken to individualize the classroom approach for each mildly retarded child (Algozzine, Whorton, & Reid, 1979; Forness, 1979b; Lombardi, 1975; Kaufman & Alberto, 1977). Mainstreaming of mildly retarded children into regular classes is an effective alternative in many cases (Corman & Gottlieb, 1978), and representative programs are presented in chapter 10. MacMillan has stressed, however, that special classes should remain an educational option for retarded children (MacMillan, 1982; MacMillan, Jones, & Myers, 1976).

Special education for mildly retarded children, whether in mainstreamed or special class-room environments, will continue to focus on (1) developing basic academic skills, (2) social competence, (3) personal adjustment, and (4) occupational adequacy. Approaches to education for the mildly retarded stress the need for two basic skills that cut across all curriculum areas: (1) thinking critically or being able to weigh the facts of a given situation together with their implications, and (2) acting independently or making a decision based on these facts and following it through (Goldstein, 1974; Payne, Polloway, Smith, & Payne, 1977). Thus, in order to become an independent adult, the mildly retarded youngster must be taught in a variety of settings and given experience in problem-solving methods that apply generically to a multitude of academic, personal, social, vocational, financial, and leisure situations.

Perhaps no other exceptional learner has experienced such rapid changes in both special and regular education as the mildly retarded. Whereas IQ scores were once interpreted as strict indicators of learning ability and special class placement was the only option for such children, we now look at individual children, not at scores or labels, and offer them a broad range of educational placement including assignment to regular classrooms, when appropriate, and even participation in community college programs (President's Committee on Mental Retardation, 1978). The psychosocial characteristics of the mildly retarded that have important implications for their education are examined in following chapters.

Severely Mentally Retarded Individuals

As mentioned, a large majority of mentally retarded persons are classified as mildly retarded. They are often indistinguishable in appearance from normal children but frequently have problems related to social conditions or experience. In this section, we discuss a second, smaller group of children who often look and behave quite differently from normal children and whose problems in adaptation are quite severe and related to capacity-based determiners. These children have been a major focus of research and development efforts in mental retardation in the past few years (Berkson & Landesman-Dwyer, 1977; Engel, 1977; Haywood, 1979; Meyers, 1978; Sontag, Smith, & Sailor, 1977).

Consider the case of Eddie, who is twelve years old. Eddie has Down's syndrome, a condition caused by the presence of an extra chromosome (Abroms & Bennett, 1983). His mother was almost forty when Eddie was born, and his condition was recognized almost immediately. Eddie looks different. He is short for his age and somewhat stocky; his head is smaller than normal and flattened slightly at the back. The bridge of his nose is flat, and his tongue is a bit large for his mouth, protruding slightly. The most striking feature is his eyes, which have an extra fold of skin at the corners giving him a mongoloid appearance.

Eddie has developed at less than half the rate of his two older, normal brothers. His speech is immature, often slurred, and difficult to understand. Physically, he has the coordination of a much younger child. Although he has been attending a special day school, Eddie is still unable to read or write, but he is able to count to five and to recognize a few letters of the alphabet. He is usually a likeable child and eager to please but subject to severe temper tantrums when frustrated. His brothers have often had to bear the brunt of caring for Eddie and, even as teenagers, had to interrupt their social activities to look after him when he wandered off in the neighborhood or was teased by the younger children. Although he now lives with his parents, with one brother in college and his father only a few years from retirement, his parents are becoming quite concerned about what will happen to Eddie.

There are other types of severely retarded children with different types of distinguishing features whose families have been faced with equally serious problems. The continuing traumatic impact on the family of a severely retarded child has been well documented. Unlike mild retardation, where other family members may also function at low levels of intelligence, it is more common for the severely retarded child to be the only family member affected.

Unlike solutions to the problem of mild retardation, the prevention of severe mental retardation rests primarily in the area of biomedical research and treatment. The capacity-based problems of children like Eddie do not necessarily preclude favorable results from school or environmental interventions, but they certainly reduce expectations for any substantial gains. The National Association for Retarded Citizens held a conference in 1976 on the severely and profoundly retarded, entitled "The 24-Hour Retarded Child." Although most severely retarded children do not require constant twenty-four-hour care and supervision, they do fall somewhere between the twenty-four-hour retarded child and the six-hour retarded child (the child considered retarded only during school time).

Definition and Incidence

In general, the definition of mental retardation given previously applies to both the mildly and severely retarded. The difference for educational purposes is primarily one of degree. The severely retarded child (IQ approximately 30 to 50) functions at a level one-third to one-half that of normal children and usually requires continuing supervision in self-care and social and economic adjustment. In school, some severely retarded children may be capable of rudimentary academic skills, perhaps limited to counting and recognizing a few words. Some may read at the first-grade level or even higher. Most will be able to talk or develop some language skills, and many can profit from systematic training in social awareness and occupational skills.

Nearly all severely retarded children are identified before reaching school age, and a significant number may have to be placed in supervised residential or institutional settings as they grow older or cannot be cared for by their families. Many at higher functioning levels may be able to achieve some measure of economic self-sufficiency, but this is often in a sheltered workshop, and most of these people may have continuing difficulties in social adjustment. The expectations for profoundly retarded children (IQ below 30) are obviously lower; some of the additional problems of these children are discussed later in this section.

Kirk and Gallagher (1979) estimate the number of school-age severely and profoundly retarded children at about ¼ to ½ percent (or 2 to 5 per 1,000 school children). A review of twenty-seven epidemiological studies of severely retarded children tends to confirm this figure (Abramowicz & Richardson, 1975). The number of children who actually need services may be somewhat larger (Meyers, 1978). Normal distributions of intelligence are derived from testing normal populations. A smaller bell-shaped curve or "hump," composed of the severely and profoundly retarded, actually overlaps the lower end of the normal curve Dingman & Tarjan, 1960). Actual prevalence data confirm this (Mercer, 1973b; Heber, 1970; Tarjan, Wright, Eyman, & Keeran, 1973). Given prevailing trends, it is clear that some 3 per 1,000 school children will need services. In marked contrast to mild retardation, most epidemiological studies indicate that the prevalence of severe mental retardation tends to remain relatively constant across all socioeconomic classes and ethnic groups and does not fluctuate greatly by age. Epidemiological data also confirm that more than half of all severely retarded children have another major handicap requiring additional services (Abramowicz & Richardson, 1975; Grossman, 1983).

Causes

Mental retardation is merely a symptom resulting from a bewildering array of diseases, conditions, and other biomedical disorders. Although there are more than 200 known causes of severe mental retardation, it is frequently impossible to determine the exact etiology of a given case. The most recent AAMD *Manual of Terminology and Classification in Mental Retardation* (Grossman, 1983) lists scores of possible syndromes under such headings as infections and intoxications, traumas or physical agents, disorders of metabolism or nutrition, postnatal brain diseases, cerebral malformations, chromosome abnormalities, gestational disorders, psychiatric disorders, and environmental influences. The *Manual* also contains categories for additional medical complications, including other genetic components, secondary cranial anomalies, sensory impairments, disorders of perception and expression, convulsive disorders, and motor dysfunctions. In giving some examples of the more common causes of severe mental retardation, it is convenient to discuss them under the headings of prenatal, perinatal, and postnatal periods.

Prenatal Causes.   Occurring before birth, these causes can be genetic or environmental. The most common example of a genetic cause, and indeed the one that may account for nearly a third of all cases of severe retardation, is the chromosomal disorder known as Down's syndrome. The study of human chromosomes has revealed that in Down's syndrome there are forty-seven chromosomes instead of the usual forty-six, and that chromosome pair number twenty-one is not a pair, but a triplet or "trisomy" condition. Rarer chromosomal variants, known as translocation or mosaicism, also result in Down's syndrome. As described in the case of Eddie, the syndrome results in relatively specific physical and mongoloid characteristics and severe retardation. However, there are recorded cases of Down's syndrome children who function within the mildly retarded or even the normal range of intelligence (Rynders, Spiker, & Horrobin, 1978).

Also typical of Eddie's case, Down's syndrome is closely associated with increasing maternal age at birth, although there is some speculation that Down's syndrome births may be increasing slightly in younger mothers (Zarfas & Wolf, 1979). For mothers younger than thirty-five, the incidence has been approximately 1 in 1,000 live births, but rises to 1 in 300 during the next five years and to 1 in 30 over age forty-five. In such high-risk mothers, detection can be made through a recently developed process known as *amniocentesis*, in which amniotic fluid surrounding the fetus is withdrawn through the membrane of the womb and subjected to chromosome study. Amniocentesis is complicated but involves relatively little risk to mother or unborn child. If chromosomal abnormalities are discovered, the mother can consider a therapeutic abortion.

Other genetic conditions can result in inborn errors of metabolism, such as phenylketonuria (PKU) in which the infant's system is unable to metabolize phenylalanine. If the child is fed a normal infant diet, certain injurious amino acids are released that cause brain damage. Most hospitals in the United States now have routine screening for PKU in newborn infants. If a low-phenylalanine diet is substituted quickly enough, the level of retardation will be slight or nonexistent (Johnson, Koch, Peterson, & Friedman, 1978); later in life, the diet may no longer be necessary. The condition is based on a recessive gene. Although the parent or carrier is typically not affected, when both parents are carriers the risk is 1 in 4 for each pregnancy.

Prenatal Environmental Causes.   These are hazards that can alter the intrauterine environment and cause fetal malformation. Maternal infections, such as rubella (German measles) or CMV (cytomegalia virus), a common virus similar to chicken pox (Melish & Hanshaw, 1973), can cross the placental barrier and attack the fetus, with few, if any, symptoms in the mother. It is essential that prospective mothers be vaccinated against such viruses. As with deafness, mother-fetus blood incompatability can also cause mental retardation. Ingested chemical agents have also been demonstrated to have harmful effects on fetal-cell metabolism. One well-known agent is thalidomide; more recently, alcohol has been accepted as a very frequent cause of mental retardation (if the mother is a chronic alcoholic) (Jones, Smith, Ulleland, & Streissguth, 1973). Nicotine and even aspirin can cause changes in fetal heart rate and activity levels. Although the exact influence of these agents on the developing fetus remains largely unknown, pregnant women are encouraged to avoid all such medication except under the careful supervision of their physicians.

Perinatal Factors.   These occur during delivery and have somewhat less impact as causes of mental retardation because problems predisposing an infant to birth difficulties are more likely to have arisen early in the gestation period. Thus, there has been renewed interest in genetic determinants, biochemical and cell-division disorders, and other prenatal hazards, but certainly not to the exclusion of perinatal problems and obstetrical procedures. Certain congenital malformations present at birth strongly suggest that prenatal factors were actually involved. Epidemiological studies suggest that mental retardation is often due to prenatal factors, whereas motoric disorders, such as cerebral palsy, are more often due to perinatal complications, including prematurity (Hagberg, 1979).

Prematurity, defined as a birthweight of less than five and one-half pounds (2,500 grams) or a gestation period of less than thirty-seven weeks, leaves the infant biologically vulnerable to postnatal hazards. Generally, the lower the birthweight, the greater the possibility of postnatal complications. Infants below three and one-half pounds are especially at risk. The majority of premature infants, however, do well developmentally if they receive comprehensive care. *Anoxia*, or lack of oxygen supply to the brain for a sustained period of time, can often result from problems arising during delivery, such as the child's head not emerging first or the umbilical cord's being wrapped around the neck. Other perinatal causes of brain damage may be related to prolonged or difficult labor and forceps delivery.

Recent concern for newborn infants who are small for their gestational age (SGA), though not necessarily premature, has begun to sensitize physicians to a variety of other obstetrical and developmental problems. There is also speculation that babies who did not survive to term in the past are now being saved through modern obstetric and neonatal medical advances, such as ultrasound scanning of the fetus and monitoring of fetal heartrate. These infants are surviving intact but with a variety of medical and developmental disorders that necessitate further care and special education.

Recently, there have been rather ominous findings that an increased incidence of birth defects has occurred in areas of the Southwest United States where uranium mining and milling have taken place. In Shiprock, New Mexico, for example, a study is underway to examine the hypothesis that prolonged exposure to uranium wastes leads to an excessive risk of birth disorders, including mental retardation. Preliminary studies by Dr. Alan Good-man of the University of New Mexico School of Medicine have already demonstrated that twice the number of birth defects one would ordinarily expect have occurred in each of the Four Corner states in areas associated with intensive uranium mining activity. If confirmed, these findings point to *regional* prenatal environmental causes leading to mental retardation.

Postnatal Causes.   These occur after birth and are associated with a number of childhood diseases, such as encephalitis or meningitis, in which sustained high fever—especially during the first two years of life—may result in damage to the developing brain. Other factors, such as asphyxia, a blow to the head, accidents with neurological complications, lead poisoning, or tumors can alter intellectual development and result in severe mental retardation.

This discussion of causation is far from exhaustive, and the reader is referred to excellent treatments of this complicated topic by Clarke and Clarke (1977), Crandall (1977), MacMillan (1982), Menolascino and Egger (1978), Robinson and Robinson (1976), and Sels and Bennett (1977).

Almost every cause of severe mental retardation discussed here can result in mild mental retardation. Many causes are on a continuum of causality. For example, we discussed malnutrition and sensory deprivation in the previous sections on mild mental retardation and learning disabilities. When causes are sustained and severe, they have been known to cause severe mental handicaps as well. For example, a recent study on the use of massive vitamin and mineral supplements with sixteen severely retarded children showed IQ gains averaging ten points or more in this group (Harrell, Capp, Davis, Peerless, & Ravitz, 1981). Although these results are quite tentative and have yet to be convincingly replicated, they suggest that some types of hereditary mental retardation may be caused in part by chemical nutritional deficiencies that hinder brain development. Many of the biomedical factors discussed here also cause other handicapping conditions mentioned elsewhere in this chapter.

Identification

Severely mentally retarded children are usually identified before reaching school age. The mongoloid characterisics of Down's syndrome, for example, usually can be identified at birth, as can a number of other cases of mental retardation involving abnormal physical appearance. Even when gross physical abnormalities are absent, retardation may be so marked that the child fails to develop normally during the first years of life. Children who are listless, fail to smile or babble, or are unable to sit up, walk, or talk within a normal length of time are all suspect.

A pediatrician is usually the first person concerned parents approach for advice. Most pediatricians are not experts in mental retardation and often refer parents to clinics or regional centers that specialize in developmental disabilities. In these centers, various professionals, such as pediatric neurologists, social workers, public health nurses, speech and hearing clinicians, and child psychologists and psychiatrists work together to evaluate the child.

The physician usually obtains a medical history. It includes genetic information on other family members, fertility history of the mother, experiences during pregnancy and delivery, significant medical episodes in the child's life, and the child's progress through developmental levels. Of particular interest is the child's score on the Newborn Scoring System, a brief scale widely used in delivery rooms to assess the newborn's vital signs immediately after birth (Apgar & James, 1962). An actual physical examination is done to assess the child's sensory, motor, physical, and general health status, with particular attention to neurological abnormalities.

The psychologist's assessment of the child's general intelligence is particularly critical. The most widely used scales for suspected retardation in infants are the Gesell Developmental Schedules (Gesell, 1940), Cattell Infant Intelligence Scale (Cattell, 1976), Bayley Scales of Infant Development (Bayley, 1969), and Denver Developmental Screening Test (Frankenburg & Dobbs, 1971). Most include items on motor, adaptive, perceptual, social, and language skills, but because each emphasizes somewhat different areas, the tests have to be carefully evaluated for certain children. Caution should be used in interpreting results; it is not uncommon for some infants who appear to be lagging in development to be considered normal at follow-up (Holden, 1972; Vanderveer & Schweid, 1974). From early childhood on, the psychologist uses standardized individual intelligence tests. The meaningfulness of IQs in the lower ranges may be problematic, but close correlations have been demonstrated between these measures and behavioral evaluations (Ross & Boroskin, 1972). Some tests ordinarily used to assess Piagetian levels of cognitive development in infants can also be used to evaluate elementary-aged severely and profoundly retarded children (Kahn, 1977). Also, the response of severely retarded children to behavior modification can be used as an additional measure of learning potential (Carter & Clark, 1973).

The psychologist or other professionals may also need to determine the child's social or adaptive levels through such instruments as the Vineland Social Maturity Scale (Doll, 1953), Cain-Levine Social Competency Scale (Cain, Levine, & Elzey, 1963) or the AAMD Adaptive Behavior Rating Scale (Meyers, Nihira, & Zetlin, 1979; Nihira, 1976; Nihira, Foster, Shellhaas, & Leland, 1974). Additional tests to assess perception and personality may also be administered by the psychologist and supplemented by clinical judgments. A psychiatrist may be called on to evaluate the child's personality or to establish a differential diagnosis between mental retardation and childhood schizophrenia. The social worker's task is to assess the emotional climate of the child's family and the family's response to the stress of having a handicapped child. The degree to which the child's basic health, nutritional, or training needs can be met in the home is usually assessed by a public health nurse, who may also be the first one to evaluate the child's growth and development during a home visit. A specialist in speech and hearing usually evaluates the child's receptive and expressive language and hearing, an especially critical area in mental retardation (Fristoe, 1977). The interdisciplinary team then meets to discuss their findings, arrive at a diagnosis, and make recommendations for treatment or education. This is now being done in many centers with a written, individual program plan developed by team members (Schacter, Rice, Cormier, Christensen, & James, 1978). Such plans are similar to the Individual Education Plan (IEP) that is a part of Public Law 94–142.

At this critical point, the parents must be informed of the diagnosis of mental retardation. A great deal has been written on this topic; interested readers should consult Wolfensberger and

Kurtz (1969) or Hutt and Gibby (1976). If the parents are informed shortly after the birth of their child, the news of the diagnosis may be more traumatic than for parents who bring their child for evaluation after some months or even years of suspecting that something was wrong. Most parents go through predictable stages of reaction, including shock, denial, searching for a cause, guilt, helplessness, rejection, and often profound grief. Parents need reassurance and counsel based on sound information about mental retardation and realistic plans for caring for their child (Spitalnik & Rosenstein, 1976; Townsend & Flanagan, 1976). There is evidence that physicians and other clinicians have a great deal of difficulty themselves imparting diagnostic information accurately and completely to parents (Lipton & Svarstad, 1977; Pueschel & Murphy, 1976; Yale Law School, 1978). Despite efforts of the most sensitive and knowledgeable professionals, it is not uncommon for parents to "hear," through a filter of shock and grief, only certain information about their child. Therefore, arrangements should be made for continuing contact. It is also important that parents not be overwhelmed with more information than they can handle or forced into decisions they may later regret. It may be a matter of years before some parents are able even tentatively to accept their child's condition; and some often "shop around" in vain for a diagnosis that meets their expectations. Family reactions to exceptional learners are dealt with in chapter 6.

Treatment and Educational Provisions

In most cases, the young severely retarded child can gain from systematic training in dressing, feeding, and toileting (Whitman & Scibak, 1979). Nursery schools or day care centers have been established in greater numbers to provide habit-training and language development programs for young children. Special cooperative approaches have also been developed wherein families are trained to assist in their retarded child's development (Balthazar, 1976; Barnard & Powell, 1972; Conner, Williamson, & Siepp, 1978; Latham & Hofmeister, 1973); and it is important that these programs assist in strengthening the parent-child bond (Lacoste, 1978; Stone & Chesney, 1978). With the aid of other professionals, such as specially trained public health nurses who visit the home and provide guidance in child care and management, parents can usually maintain the child at home through the preschool years.

Public education facilities are increasingly available for severely mentally retarded children of school age. Impressive progress has been made, much of it through the courts, in mandating public school programs for the severely retarded (Collings, 1973; Gilhool, 1973). Special education is typically provided for such children in special day schools. It is clear, however, that educational settings for severely retarded children can and should range from residential school placement up to and including integration into regular classroom settings, depending on the particular strengths and weaknesses of the individual child (Burton & Hirshoren, 1979; Frankel, Forness, Rowe, & Westlake, 1979; Guess & Noonan, 1982; Sontag, Certo, & Button, 1979; Meyen & Altman, 1976; Ziegler & Hambleton, 1976).

Emphasis should generally be on (1) language development, (2) self-help skills, (3) socialization, and (4) preparation for living and working in sheltered environments (Burton, 1976; Geiger, Brownsmith, & Forgnone, 1978; Lathey, 1978). School activities include practice in listening, following directions, communicating with others, reading or recognizing common signs and labels, counting, and telling time. Teaching techniques for applied reading skills often stress errorless training and modified phonics approaches (Nietupski, Williams, & York, 1979; Walsh & Lamberts, 1979). There has been recent emphasis on systematic training of TMR pupils in listening and story comprehension skills (Zetlin & Gallimore, 1980) and in use of nonverbal symbols (e.g., geometric forms, pictures) and sign language (Fristoe & Lloyd, 1979). Self-help activities include lessons in dressing, grooming, eating, care of personal belongings, toileting, and safety. Severely retarded children also engage in arts and crafts, motor and recreational activities, some vocational experiences, and practice in home living. Several excellent texts have emerged in recent years on the particular classroom approaches needed for working with severely retarded children (Bender & Valletutti, 1976; Haring & Brown, 1977; Snell, 1978; Sontag, 1977; Sailor & Wilcox, 1981).

Many severely mentally retarded persons can ultimately live at home or in community residential settings and work in sheltered workshops or other work situations where special supervision is available. With increasing emphasis as the child grows older, special education programs are generally geared to prepare the child to function optimally in such situations. The public school curriculum for the severely retarded has long been criticized for not emphasizing the practical arts and skills necessary for daily living (Hudson, 1960). This may reflect a public-school bias toward academic subjects. Indeed, a review of research on the effectiveness of these programs tends to confirm that many are not adequately preparing the severely retarded for life adjustment (Kirk, 1964; Sontag, Certo, & Button, 1979; Walls, Tseng, & Zarin, 1976). Trends toward instruction in simulated home or workshop settings should result in more realistic preparation for severely retarded youngsters (Martin, Rusch, & Heal, 1982).

Profoundly Mentally Retarded Individuals

The profoundly retarded—those who fall at the lower end of the severe category, as well as those severely retarded who have multihandicapping conditions—tend to present unique problems in medical and behavioral management (Switzky, Haywood, & Rotatori, 1982). These children generally have special needs for continuing supervision or custodial care. It has been suggested that their educational goals should emphasize skills that will maximize their happiness within the environment rather than unrealistic expectations for a future role in everyday society (Cleland, 1979; Rago & Cleland, 1978). Subgrouping such children according to their need for supervision has been attempted in order to provide more effective programming (Rago, 1977b); this subgrouping is often a critical factor in the retention of certain institutionalized retarded children in school programs (Peterson, 1977; Storm & Willis, 1978). The development of methods to increase basic socialization and communication among even profoundly retarded individuals is evident in research with this population (Meyers, 1978).

Most profoundly retarded persons may indeed have to be placed in residential facilities as they grow older, in many cases because of the debilitating effect the presence of a retarded child has on other family members (Allen, 1972; Farber, 1975). Only about 5 percent of all the mentally retarded are in residential institutions, because the trend is toward keeping more retarded individuals in community settings whenever possible (Conroy, 1977; President's Committee on Mental Retardation, 1976; Scheerenberger, 1982). The decision of where to place a retarded child is not an easy one. Placement of severely retarded individuals in foster homes or in small, community-based residential facilities has become a popular alternative to placement in large, depersonalized, and often dehumanizing state institutions (Baker, Seltzer, & Seltzer, 1979; Roos, 1978; Zigler & Balla, 1977). Institutionalization has become a controversial issue because of the bleak and often less than humane conditions of many state institutions (Blatt, Winschel, & Ensher, 1977; Burton, Burton, & Hirshoren, 1977). However, there is evidence that even large institutions can be humane places if enlightened and effective approaches are used in their operation (Balla, 1976; Eyman, Silverstein, McLain, & Miller, 1977; Singer, 1978; Throne, 1979). There are serious concerns about precipitous deinstitutionalization of individuals who may not be ready to face the problems of living in community settings (Scheerenberger & Felsenthal, 1977; Silva & Faflak, 1976; Turnbull & Turnbull, 1975).

Whatever the type of setting, decided efforts have been made to normalize the lives of the severely and profoundly retarded and to provide them, as much as possible, with the rights, decision making, and privileges allowed normal citizens (Wolfensberger, 1972). The Developmentally Disabled Assistance and Bill of Rights Act (HR 4005), signed into law in 1975 and amended in 1980, makes federal monies available for research and services to all developmentally disabled children and adults, including the severely and profoundly retarded. It also mandates a state protection and advocacy system to protect the rights of all citizens with developmental disabilities.

The term *developmental disability* refers to a severe chronic disability that is attributable to a mental and/or physical impairment, that is manifested before age twenty-two, that can be expected to continue indefinitely, and that results in substantial functional limitations in three or more of the following major areas of life activity: (1) self-care, (2) receptive and expressive language, (3) learning, (4) mobility, (5) self-direction, (6) capacity for independent living, and (7) economic self-sufficiency. The disability should also reflect the person's need for individualized, interdisciplinary care, treatment, or other lifelong or extended services (Feingold & Bank, 1978; Johnston & Magrab, 1976; Lubin, Jacobson, & Kiely, 1982). Disabilities attributed to mental retardation, cerebral palsy, epilepsy, and autism are included by definition in the Act. Other impairments that affect the individual in much the same manner as mental retardation, and require similar treatment and services are also included. Thus, children with severe intellectual, physical, and emotional handicaps have received increased attention on a national level; and increased treatment services have become available for them, as has an increased guarantee that their rights are protected (Stedman & Wiegerink, 1978).

It is clear that some of the issues regarding the severely retarded, as we have used this term, overlap those of the mildly retarded, as well as those of the profoundly retarded child. Care of severely retarded children involves treatment and education, medical prevention, and family management, which often require efforts of several professionals in addition to the special education teacher.

Gifted Individuals

We close this chapter on intellectual uniqueness with a discussion of an exceptional learner whose uniqueness contrasts with that of the other individuals we have discussed. The uniqueness of the gifted learner enhances rather than handicaps; it is a positive rather than a negative characteristic that facilitates rather than restricts.

Definition

Any attempt to define giftedness is culture bound (Gallagher, 1975). That is, it inevitably reflects talents and abilities that are highly valued by the culture. Among primitive peoples who depend on hunting for survival, the outstanding hunter is most highly valued. In a warring tribe, the bravest and most successful warrior achieves greatest prominence. Among the ancient Greeks, the orator and the artist were highly acclaimed, but not the inventor. The Romans valued the soldier and the politician but failed to recognize many other talents among their citizens or slaves (Flanagan, Dailey, Shaycroft, Gorham, Orr, & Goldberg, 1962).

Before 1900, giftedness was ascribed to child prodigies and other highly accomplished adults (Payne, 1974). However, with development of the standardized intelligence test, the operational definition for giftedness became a very high IQ score and superior achievement in academic areas. By the middle and late 1960s, society had begun to place increasing value on the importance of social sensitivity and leadership, creativity, and special talents, such as those associated with drama, art, and music. As a result, the definition of giftedness has gone beyond the IQ score and has been broadened to include various gifted types of talents and abilities (Getzels & Dillon, 1973; Payne, Kauffmann, Brown, & DeMott, 1974).

According to Gallagher (1975), "the ability to manipulate internally learned symbol systems is perhaps the *sine qua non* of giftedness" (p. 10). Such an ability allows gifted learners to learn on their own, to initiate rather than follow, to imagine, and to create. He considers gifted learners as those who by virtue of outstanding abilities are capable of high performance in academic areas, creative or productive thinking, leadership, visual and performing arts, and psychomotor functioning.

Incidence

The criterion most commonly used to determine a gifted learner has been the IQ score. Thus, when we ask the question How many gifted learners are there? we must first answer the question How many, at what level? Over the years, the range of IQ scores considered indicative of giftedness has varied from 115 to well over 150 (Laycock, 1979), with IQ 125 to 140 perhaps the most frequently used range.

It has been obvious from the earliest incidence studies concerned with giftedness that the majority of children with high IQ scores come from homes that reflect economic and cultural advantage. Gallagher (1959) found that 16 to 20 percent of the children in an "average" community obtained IQs higher than 115, whereas 45 to 60 percent of their counterparts in a "superior" community obtained the same. IQs greater than 130 were obtained by 2 to 4 percent of the average community children and 6 to 12 percent of the superior community children, respectively.

Depending on the breadth of the definition of giftedness, we can expect actual incidence estimates of the numbers of gifted learners to vary. If we use the IQ score as the defining criterion, then, based on the normal curve, a cutoff of 130 or 140 would lead to an estimate of 2 or 3 percent of the school-age population as gifted. However, broadening our definition to include talent in a range of domains, such as the visual and performing arts, we might expect at least 3 percent to be gifted. Some would even consider from 3 to 5 percent of the school population as gifted learners (Marland, 1972).

The most ambitious, systematic study of gifted learners was conducted by Terman (Terman & Oden, 1959). It began in the early 1920s; the participants were 1,528 California school children who obtained an IQ score of 140 or more on the original (1916) version of the Stanford-Binet Intelligence Test. It was Terman, himself, who brought the test to the United States and adopted it from the original devised by Alfred Binet and Theodore Simon of France. Despite some design and methodological shortcomings (Laycock, 1979), the study has provided us with the characteristics and accomplishments of the gifted from the early school years to the present. The last data collected was in 1972, when the participants' average age was 62 (Sears, 1977; Sears & Barbee, 1977).

Findings of the study are presented in Part II of the text. However, one conclusion was that gifted individuals are gifted in all areas including physical development and emotional stability. A persistent myth portrays gifted children as spindly bookworms and "undersized, sickly, hollow-chested, stoop-shouldered, clumsy, nervously tense, and bespectacled" (Terman & Oden, 1959, p. 8). The results of the study clearly laid this myth to rest, as physical superiority was the rule.

Causes

Over the course of history, giftedness has been viewed as resulting from abnormalities, motivational sources, qualitative superiority, and quantitative superiority (Anastasi, 1958). A common belief has linked high intelligence and psychosis. Although very high IQ children (e.g., above 180) may experience "special perplexities" and "puzzling difficulties" (Hollingworth, 1942) related to a lack of friends who can really converse with them, there is no evidence that high intelligence predisposes an individual to mental illness. Indeed, the Terman study clearly confirmed the mental health of the gifted group.

Sigmund Freud and other psychoanalysts believed that strong motivational rather than strong intellectual forces were the real determinants of giftedness. Certain defense mechanisms, such as sublimation and compensation, drive individuals with seemingly ordinary minds and talents to achieve gifted accomplishments. In classical Freudian terms, it is sublimated sexual energy that emerges as great music, poetry, and intellectual attainment. The role of motivation in helping each of us achieve our potential is well recognized, but this explanation is primarily of interest to those within the psychoanalytic school.

Genius has often been regarded with awe as if it represented "some superhuman power, divine inspiration, demonic intervention, witchcraft, or mystical experience" (Laycock, 1979, p. 61). That is, the gifted are qualitatively unlike other human beings, functioning on another plane or in a different world. Such a qualitative explanation has given way to the notion of quantitative superiority. The gifted and the average are simply at different points along the same line. The differences are due to degree and not to kind. In the Terman study, it was demonstrated that the gifted are very superior with respect to the same abilities ordinary individuals possess.

In the late 1800s, Galton took the position that talent and giftedness were almost exclusively determined by capacity. Since that time, the controversy over capacity versus experience as the prime determiner of intelligence in general and giftedness in particular has never been resolved. Jensen (1969) concluded that 70 to 85 percent of intelligence is determined by heredity. Earlier, Watson (1924) had claimed that although he respected the influence of heredity, environmental experience was the potent determiner of intellectual functioning. The nature and source of intelligence are discussed further in chapter 7. However, we do reiterate our position that interaction between capacity and experience is responsible for an individual's functioning level, including his or her intelligence.

Identification

When identification of gifted children is left to the classroom teacher, studies suggest that many children who are not gifted are selected and that many truly gifted children are overlooked. One study found that 31.4 percent of teachers' choices of gifted children were in error and that teachers missed more than half of those who had superior ability (Pegnato & Birch, 1959). Academic and social success with talent in areas such as drama or art tend to promote identification as gifted, whereas underachievement, shyness, and nonconformity can result in an individual's being excluded from consideration as gifted.

During the first two decades of this century, teacher nomination was the only method of identifying gifted children. Gallagher (1975) regards this method as limited because many children who have a high aptitude for reasoning and conceptualization are *not* performing well in school. Teachers would probably not have identified Albert Einstein, Thomas Edison, and Winston Churchill as gifted since they all had problems succeeding in school.

However, teacher observation and nomination was reported to be the major identification procedure by 93 percent of a large number of school districts with programs for the gifted (Marland, 1972). Group intelligence and achievement scores were used by 87 percent, grades and previously demonstrated accomplishments by 56 percent, individual intelligence test scores by 23 percent, and scores on tests of creativity by 14 percent. When a group of experts in the field was asked to recommend methods for identifying the gifted learner, 93 percent selected the individual intelligence test and 75 percent recommended teacher nomination.

Torrance (1969) has summarized a number of the characteristics of historical geniuses. Galileo Galilei's favorite pastime as a young boy was the construction of ingenious toy machines. He also was very talented in art, music, and poetry. Lord Byron was referred to as a "hot-headed little lad." When he was five years old, Byron cried out passionately in the middle of one act of *The Taming of the Shrew*, supporting one of the characters in an argument with another. From the age of five, he read while eating and in many other situations. Goethe began arranging and conducting plays in his puppet theater when he was six or seven years of age. At eight, he was writing poetry of a creative quality and at nine he built an altar and developed a mystical religion of his own. Galton, whose IQ has been estimated to be at the 200 level, was collecting and classifying insects and minerals when he was six. He was modest about his abilities; when put in classes with fourteen- and fifteen-year-olds at the age of six, he remarked that he thought it was sad that his classmates' education had been so much neglected.

Educational Provisions

Public support for the gifted in the United States has waxed and waned. One problem is that some perceive giving special attention to gifted children as favoring a few unfairly and leading to the creation of an elitist group. Another is that when special education funding is provided by the federal and state governments, exceptional learners who are handicapped are often given priority over the gifted. The latter was particularly puzzling to specialists in Soviet special education (defectology) when one of the authors visited with them. There is strong national commitment to the identification and education of gifted Russian children at as early an age as possible. The brightest may be identified at the preschool level and enter special schools in which the entire curriculum is presented in English.

In 1972, the Office of the Gifted and Talented was set up by the U. S. Commissioner of Education. This office is responsible for authorizing funds for model school programs, teacher training, research, and dissemination of information regarding the gifted. The level of funding has increased over the years, and one reason for this support may be that the term *gifted and talented* is used rather than gifted alone (Laycock, 1979). This term communicates a broader definition of giftedness and extends special programs to children who demonstrate general intellectual ability, specific academic ability, creative or productive thinking, leadership ability, talent for the visual and performing arts, and psychomotor ability. The IQ test alone does not make a particular child eligible for participation. There must be eivdence from at least two types of assessment.

However, it should be noted that the link between talent and intelligence is still open to question. Low correlates have been found between general intelligence and scientific, mathematical, and writing aptitudes (Vernon, Adamson, & Vernon, 1977). Generally, a distinction between high IQ and inventiveness is accepted, but it is also recognized that they are not completely separate (Laycock, 1979).

Educational Approaches

There have been three major approaches to the education of gifted individuals: acceleration, grouping, and enrichment (Laycock, 1979).

Acceleration.   Supporters for acceleration, that is, placing bright children at a grade level advanced for their ages but commensurate with their intellectual functioning levels, claim it is the simplest approach, that it keeps gifted children from being bored, and allows them to graduate earlier and begin their careers. Critics claim that academic acceleration is simplistic and that it ignores social and emotional development. The child may have little in common with older peers, may not be regarded as a legitimate classmate, or may be treated as "weird" because of his or her high visibility. The author recalls a very gifted twelve-year-old boy enrolled in an honors program at UCLA. He was small in stature and carried a brief case almost half his size. It was difficult to see how he could experience much of a degree of "socialness" with his college classmates. Undoubtedly, special provisions were made for social experiences with others who were physically similar and closer to his age.

Early admission to school and acceleration have been shown in the main to have positive effects on gifted children (Braga, 1969; Plowman & Rice, 1967; Laycock, 1979). Despite these findings, there is often strong opposition to acceleration by both parents and teachers. Gallagher (1975) concludes that parental opposition may stem from anxiety because the child is being moved swiftly out of the parental nest and may leave home sooner.

Grouping.   Gifted individuals also may be grouped together in small clusters within classrooms, in special classes, or in special schools. Grouping children by ability is a widespread practice in the United States, although it is often confined to certain subjects such as reading. Open or ungraded classrooms that include five or six grade levels and team teaching offer opportunities for grouping bright children without the social isolation inherent in acceleration. A review of the literature has revealed that grouping, like acceleration, is not harmful to children (Gallagher, 1975). However, it has been resisted by some who question the methods used to identify gifted children for special grouping or who consider it inappropriate to give attention to skillful pupils when the unskillful need help so desperately.

Values and ethics were explored in a curricular activity pursued during weekly hour sessions with a group of ten to sixteen gifted, fifth-grade children (Gallagher, 1975). The sessions involved discussions about an imaginary trip to Mars. The children took the roles of the adult members of the first expedition to this planet. The teacher maintained a neutral attitude and did not present his own opinions on their problems or eventual decisions.

The first problem that arose was a shortage of food. The spaceship had crashed and would take eleven months to repair before the expedition could return to Earth. The students finally agreed that what food was left would be distributed evenly and that no special rations should be given to anyone, regardless of rank. Next, the expedition was faced with the fact that one crew member was dying. Should he continue to receive food? The children reacted in various ways, but the majority favored giving the man food, since maybe the doctor was wrong and the man would actually live. The next crisis faced by the earthlings had to do with a crewman who, instead of working to repair the spaceship, chose to go off and paint pictures of the beautiful Martian landscapes. The children worked out a compromise. The crewman would be encouraged to paint during off-duty hours. He would be given repair work on the night shift to allow this. However, if he refused to cooperate, his painting materials would be confiscated. Another problem was the rights of the native Martians. One scientist discovered a deposit of the exact metal necessary to repair the spaceship, but it could only be obtained by violating the holy ground of the natives. The children pondered over this, but finally decided to take the metal—but only as much as was needed. Furthermore, they would return the metal plus payment for damages when they returned to Earth.

The issue of discussing values and ethics in school may be questioned by some. But this type of learning may simply never take place on a random basis. Curriculum related to attitudes and values presented by a competent and objective teacher may serve a very useful purpose with normal children as well as the gifted. The children in this program were enthusiastic participants and were stimulated by the opportunities for creative and divergent thinking provided by this special group experience.

Enrichment.   Enrichment experiences may be offered to gifted students within the regular school program and during outside activities. One program used the services of a substitute teacher with a doctorate in science (Sklarsky & Baxter, 1961). During a daily hour with a group of gifted children, the teacher conducted a project on "The Microbe and I." Numerous field trips were made to a large microbiology laboratory. The children carried out experiments on bacteria, yeast, and molds and wrote reports much as a scientist would. Guest speakers visited the classroom, and the children wrote final reports of the project at the end of the year. This project was extremely valuable to the children because they were required to invest long periods of time in planning and conducting their experiments and in writing and rewriting their reports. Some had never had to critically redo work in school because ordinarily they "breezed through" lessons.

In San Francisco, the resources of the California Academy of Science, the Steinhart Aquarium, and the Morrison Planetarium were made available to gifted fifth-grade students (Ryder, 1972). The children were trained by museum staff members to be guides for regular visitors. They were soon explaining the natural science exhibits with purpose and enthusiasm. Other field trips were provided, and parents were encouraged to participate in the program with weekend nature walks.

Not all cities have such rich resources, but comparable efforts have been made with gifted youth even in rural areas (Morris, 1957). One program offered a twice weekly seminar to high school students. The seminar included listening to records of poetry, reading books such as *Patterns of Culture* by Ruth Benedict and *Language and Thought in Action* by S. I. Hayakawa, and conducting discussions about the students' experiences. The students were very enthusiastic and felt the seminar gave them the opportunity to think aloud and develop thoughts orally, without fear of criticism, and to examine answers to questions rather than consider them either right or wrong.

In selecting educational provisions for gifted children, three objectives are important to consider. First, the range of talent and achievement that a teacher must face should be decreased. Second, reducing the time gifted students must spend in school during the first twenty years of their lives will make much better use of their potential. And third, programs must aim at matching the special talents of the student with the special talents of the instructional staff.

Summary

In this chapter, we have discussed exceptional learners who are intellectually unique: the learning disabled, mentally retarded, and the gifted. Individuals with learning disabilities have been defined by means of *discrepancy* and *exclusion*. In order for the label to be assigned, there must be a significant discrepancy between intellectual ability and the actual level of academic functioning. In addition, the cause for such a discrepancy cannot be associated with visual, hearing, or motor handicaps, retardation, emotional disturbance, or environmental, cultural, or economic disadvantage. Historically, the field of learning disabilities goes back to the work of Alfred Strauss and his studies of retarded children with and without suspected brain injury. As a result, one major perspective in the field views severe reading and language difficulties and hyperactivity as neurological problems. Another perspective focuses on disorders in the learning process related to perception, attention, memory, information processing, and language.

Although the exact cause of a learning disability is unknown, genetic, organic, developmental, and environmental explanations have been postulated. Thus, in assessing an individual with a possible learning disability, a thorough medical-neurological and psychoeducational evaluation is often undertaken. Treatment of hyperactivity often associated with a learning disability may involve the use of medication, particularly a psychostimulant such as Ritalin. Many children so treated experience a reduction in inappropriate activity level and behavior but not necessarily an improvement in academic learning. Educational programs for the learning disabled may provide training in perceptual-motor, linguistic, and academic areas and use cognitive behavior modification strategies.

In recent years, the criteria for assigning the label of *mental retardation* have been broadened. In addition to subaverage intellectual functioning (e.g., below IQ 75), an individual must exhibit deficits in adaptive behavior (e.g., self-help skills, socialization) and the retardation itself must be manifested during the developmental period or before age eighteen. Thus, an individual who performs below average on an IQ test but manages to adapt in most other situations could not strictly be considered retarded by this definition. Also, an individual might be considered retarded at one time in life but not in another, depending on societal expectations.

Classification of retarded learners is most meaningful when based on expectations for educational progress, which can be related (with caution) to IQ score. IQ 50 has been used as a cut-off between mild or *educable* retardation (above) and severe or *trainable* retardation (below). Severely retarded children are most apt to be identified before the school years, whereas the mildly retarded usually do not encounter serious problems until faced with the intellectual demands of school. Mental retardation is not a disease but a symptom that may be the result of numerous physical abnormalities as well as environmental causes.

In the past, mildly retarded children have traditionally been placed exclusively in segregated classes, but current trends often involve at least part-time placement in regular classrooms. Educational emphasis at the primary level is on the development of language, speech, motor, and social skills; at the elementary level, academic skills are introduced.

Severely retarded children receive training in language, self-help, and socialization skills usually in special schools or special classes, although part-time regular classroom integration may be appropriate for some. At the secondary level, preparation for work and independent living is stressed for the mildly retarded; for the severely retarded, the emphasis may be similar but focused toward home or residential living situations or sheltered workshops. In recent years, retarded learners have probably experienced a greater increase in opportunities for education and training than any other type of exceptional learner.

The gifted learner possesses a uniqueness that enhances rather than restricts functioning level. Although the definition of giftedness may reflect any highly respected or desirable skill or trait, it traditionally refers to intellectual functioning associated with an IQ of from 125 to 140 and higher. Terman, who adapted the IQ test (developed by Binet in France) for

American children, began a study of gifted children in the 1920s. Data collected in this study have provided us with much of what we know about the functioning level of gifted individuals.

Teacher observation and nomination are the primary means for identifying gifted children, although some gifted individuals who perform poorly in school are overlooked by teachers. Public support for special education programs for the gifted has been limited due to some concern that fostering intellectual elitism is undemocratic or that truly handicapped exceptional individuals deserve the bulk of available funding. The Office of the Gifted and Talented, established on the federal level in 1972, extends the notion of giftedness to include uniqueness in athletics and in the visual and performing arts.

Educational programs for the gifted have included acceleration (advancing the individual to a grade level commensurate with intellectual functioning level), grouping (setting up clusters of similarly gifted individuals in regular classrooms, special classes, or special schools), and enrichment (providing special intellectually stimulating experiences outside the regular school program).

This chapter concludes Part I and our introduction of the exceptional learner in a traditional framework. In Part II, we examine flexibility, social, and intellectual uniqueness in a much broader fashion. Each type of exceptional learner is no longer assigned to a single type of uniqueness; we are now concerned with a collective portrait of all exceptional learners' flexibility, social, and intellectual uniqueness. In addition, we discuss the individualization of exceptional learners as they mature and move into adult life.

PART TWO

DIMENSIONS OF DIFFERENCE

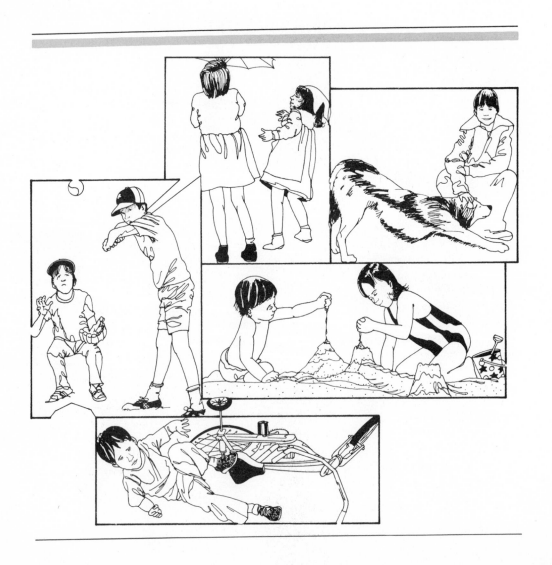

Flexibility Characteristics of Exceptional Learners

In this and the next three chapters, we examine exceptional learners across categories in contrast to the category-by-category discussion in Part I. Because of the stigmatization of labels and their tendency to call attention to what individuals cannot do rather than what they can do, there has been interest in the field of special education in developing a noncategorical approach. This interest is shared by the authors. However, as we stated in the Preface, it has become increasingly apparent that attempts to eliminate all references to exceptional learners by categories and labels are both unrealistic and naïve. The organization and implementation of legislative, public action, and educational programs for exceptional learners will always depend in part on categorical designations.

A realistic approach is to downplay the *defective* implications of categorical labels and emphasize the *untaught* and *learner* status of all exceptional individuals. We stated earlier that this is the authors' intent throughout this text. It is also realistic to attempt to *unify* the various categories of exceptional learners by examining how they are alike and/or different in relation to the same basic characteristics. Such unification is used in this part of the text using the basic characteristics introduced in Part I in our discussion of flexibility, social, and intellectual uniqueness. Chapters 5, 6, and 7 deal with each type of exceptional learner in relation to each type of uniqueness, rather than in relation to a single type of uniqueness. Within each chapter, exceptional learners are referred to by category and as we move from discussing one category to another we shall introduce the new category by means of bold-faced type. The discussion is expanded to individualization in chapter 8.

For purposes of organization, exceptional learners are presented in the following sequence: visually handicapped, deaf and hard-of-hearing, orthopedically and other health impaired, emotionally disturbed, speech handicapped, disadvantaged, learning disabled, mentally retarded, and gifted.

In this chapter, we discuss the flexibility uniqueness of each type of exceptional learner with regard to:

- looking, listening, and other sensory experiences

- perception of environmental stimuli

Figure 5-1.

- physical movement

- degree of active and independent participation

- acquisition of knowledge and skill related to successful adaptation to the environment.

The visually handicapped individual who is born blind or whose vision was lost during the early years must rely on the remaining senses of hearing, touch, and, to a lesser extent, taste and smell for knowledge of the environment and for clues for successful adaptation. Even though hearing alerts us to the distance and direction of an object that made a sound, it does not provide a concrete idea of the object itself. A large part of accurately knowing and successfully adapting to a changing environment is based on seeing. Among the visually handicapped, the most seriously disabled individual in terms of visual flexibility is the one who became blind before the age of five. Such an individual has no useful visual imagery (Blank, 1958; Schlaegel, 1953) or any real idea of color (Lowenfeld, 1971). Thus, dreams will largely reflect auditory, tactile, and kinesthetic experiences, and may include taste, smell, and temperature perceptions. Those who become blind after age seven may retain visual imagery in their dreams that is very similar to that of the sighted (Kirtley, 1975).

With so much dependence on the nonvisual senses, it has been postulated that blind persons are endowed with or develop hyperacute sensitivity of the senses of hearing, touch, taste, and smell. Lowenfeld concludes that research evidence does not support this notion (Lowenfeld, 1980). For example, one study found that, compared to sighted children, visually limited children (median age eight years) have no superior auditory discrimination skills, despite the fact that hearing constitutes their major sensory modality (Hare, Hammill, & Crandell, 1970). Likewise, no superiority has been demonstrated by the blind in either rote or logical memory. However, a Japanese study found that totally blind children made higher scores than did sighted youngsters (grades one through six) on the form, length, and size subtests of a tactual perception test for the blind. A conclusion drawn from this study suggests that the blind, who are so dependent on tactual exploration to learn about their world, become more efficient than the sighted in the manual analytic manipulation of objects (Rogow, 1975). Whatever superiority certain blind individuals display in any of these areas is the result of experience, increased attention to small cues, and greater reliance on such cues for information and guidance, not of unique endowment.

Despite the lack of visual imagery, blind individuals do develop concepts of form, space, and distance beyond those seemingly provided by touch and movement alone. With respect to form, Lowenfeld reports that the blind are able to reproduce all kinds of objects, both large and small, in modeling with clay and handwork, based on nonvisual observations and experiences (Lowenfeld, 1980). They can also recognize objects on the basis of these observations and experiences. This is viewed as evidence that the blind can unify separate, nonvisual perceptions into a total concept of an object.

Blind infants may manifest a delay in some areas of physical and motor development, and blind children tend to score lower on tests of gross motor performance, compared with normal and partially sighted youngsters. The visual impairment does not retard such development, but rather factors related to blindness: (1) any physical disabilities accompanying blindness; (2) lack of opportunities due to parental overprotection; (3) inability to learn skills by imitating others; (4) limited experiences in body movement; and (5) motivational problems.

In a study of ten infants born blind but otherwise normal, from birth to age two, a different pattern of gross motor development was observed for the blind infants, compared to that of sighted infants (Adelson & Fraiberg, 1974). During the first year, there was little difference except in the area of self-initiated mobility (e.g., reaching out toward an attractive sounding toy). Also, compared to sighted infants, blind infants were delayed in advancing from crawling to creeping to independent walking. This delay in achieving independent mobility was attributed to the absence of motivation ordinarily provided by vision, not to a lack of motor impetus.

Unlike the sighted infant who can rely on eye-hand coordination, the blind infant must use ear-hand coordination (reaching for an invisible distant object on sound cue alone). Ear-hand coordination, however, does not normally occur until late in the first year, for blind as well as sighted children. Until sound at a distance can provide an incentive, the blind child remains immobile, not reaching out or actively seeking what is heard. Only after the child has become practiced in reaching out on sound cues will creeping and walking begin (Adelson & Fraiberg, 1974). Deprived of visual "lures," many children who are born blind never learn to crawl and remain immobile until they begin to walk. Hence, from about the eighth to the fifteenth month, blind children may stay in one place, missing important learning experiences that are normally achieved during this period through encounters with the environment (Knight, 1972; McGuire & Meyers, 1971).

In a study of five- to seven-year-old blind and sighted children, it was found that blind children are limited in their acquisition of knowledge and skill as compared to sighted children (Kephart, Kephart, & Schwarz, 1974). Subjects were asked to construct verbally an imaginary boy or girl, the outer and inner structures of a house, a yard, neighborhood, street, and city. Results showed that blind youngsters had misinformation, fragmented concepts, and limited ability to differentiate information. For example, the blind subjects revealed less knowledge of general body parts, giving little information about facial features and frequently omitting fingers and ears. One explanation of these findings is that because blind children in the early years must rely on information from persons whose primary frame of reference is visual, they do not gain an adequate understanding of the physical world around them. Their deprivation of visual experience is not sufficiently compensated for by auditory and tactile information.

As blind children grow, physical activity becomes important because they lack both the motivation and opportunity for free, varied movement. Blind children cannot learn to run and play by imitating other children, and overprotection at home reinforces feelings of inadequacy and dependency. As a result of this deprivation, many blind young people lack vitality and physical stamina, have poor posture, and lack outlets for tension release (Resnick, 1973). Mobility difficulties cause the blind to miss many opportunities for developing both gross (catching a ball) and fine (picking up bits of paper from the floor) motor skills.

In chapter 2, to illustrate the efficiency in mobility that the blind can acquire, we cited the case of a fifteen-year-old blind boy who bicycled 150 miles in two days. The orientation and mobility skills of another unusually capable blind boy have been reported elsewhere (McCarty & Worchel, 1954). This young man successfully rode a bicycle over a course on which two movable obstacles had been placed. Riding as fast as he could, he was able to avoid the moving obstacles almost as well as when riding at slow speeds.

Mobility for the blind has been described as involving both mental orientation and physical locomotion (Lowenfeld, 1950). Moving through the environment, the blind individual must keep a "mental map" in mind and relate to it while walking toward a destination. Once experienced in a particular route, such an individual uses available clues for guidance, such as the audible traffic signal at a given corner, the change in ground level at a certain point, air current changes indicating open space, and all kinds of odor sensations. He or she also uses "muscular memory" to recognize when the top of the stairs or the wall or door of a familiar room has been reached. Time sense also helps blind persons trace their position on their mental maps. Obstacle perception is limited, however, when the blind individual must move in crowded or noisy places, or when rain or wind drown out or snow deadens the necessary perceptions.

The news media often report special aids developed for the blind that enable them to orient themselves more fully to the environment. A relief map of the entire campus of the University of Wisconsin, with each building represented in proportion to its size, has been useful for helping blind students become acquainted with their campus.

Many normal athletic activities can be engaged in safely by blind children. Technological aids, such as bases that "buzz" and large baseballs that "beep," enable blind individuals to play baseball. Many national tournaments in various sports are held regularly for the visually impaired. One middle-aged man participating in a learning-to-ski program for the blind was quoted as saying, "Sports have become a substitute way to learn self-worth." Overprotective parents significantly determine a visually handicapped child's performance in sports. One author concludes that, as far as motor performance is concerned, some neglect may be preferable to overprotection (Buell, 1950).

What effect does impaired hearing have on the flexibility of an individual? Like the visually impaired, individuals who lack effective functioning in one sense modality (hearing) do not develop totally compensatory abilities or special acuity in remaining modalities. Available empirical data do not indicate that deaf individuals possess a superiority over comparable hearing

Perhaps the most comprehensively researched area related to the mobility of the blind concerns the so-called obstacle sense. It has been observed that many totally blind individuals actually sense obstacles in their paths. This observation led to a continuing series of experiments begun in the 1930s. These studies have established the following facts: (1) individuals who are both deaf and blind do not possess and seem incapable of acquiring the obstacle sense and, in general, auditory stimulation is both a necessary and sufficient condition for the perception of obstacles (Worchel & Dallenbach, 1947); (2) a change in the pitch of a sound or echo is a necessary condition for the perception of obstacles; (3) blind subjects lacking the obstacle sense can develop it with practice (Worchel & Andies, 1950); and (4) blindfolded, normally sighted subjects, with practice, can develop the obstacle sense (Worchel & Mauney, 1951). The accumulated knowledge gained from these studies indicates that the obstacle sense is based on small, unrecognized auditory cues such as echoes. There appears to be nothing supersensory or mystical about the phenomenon.

individuals in visual acuity and perception. In addition, the visual system is less effective than the auditory system for receiving and comprehending spoken language. The effects of impaired hearing on flexibility become clearer when we consider the role of hearing in a child's exploration and adjustment in the environment. Myklebust has described hearing as nondirectional, as scanning the environment simultaneously in all directions (Myklebust, 1963). It is a necessary sense since we do not cease hearing even in sleep; its importance in self-preservation is obvious. When deafness occurs, the individual loses the basic sense for environmental contact and exploration and must use vision for both foreground and background scanning. Vision is not an efficient monitoring sense for the environment because the individual must look up from and leave what he or she is doing and thinking in order to maintain an awareness of what is happening. Because the experiences of noise, sounds, warnings, music, and voices are unavailable, gaining knowledge of the environment and many of its critical features is seriously restricted. An organization in Oregon, Dogs for the Deaf, has begun training dogs to "hear" for deaf individuals. A knock at the door, a telephone ring, the jangle of an alarm clock, the cry of a baby, or the buzzing of a fire alarm causes the dogs to spring into action and signal their owners.

When playing, deaf children often look up from their toys in order to scan the environment and assure themselves that changes going on around them are not threatening. Environmental change is critically important to deaf children because early in their lives startling and frightening experiences often occur that could not be predicted or monitored visually. Thus, vibrations felt through the floor may place the deaf child "on guard." Also, when an unfamiliar object is introduced into the environment, such a child may immediately move to explore it by touching, smelling, or even tasting it. Such behavioral consequences of deafness have important teaching implications. For example, eliminating unnecessary visual and vibrating sensations can create a more effective learning environment for deaf children (Myklebust, 1963).

Orthopedic and other health impairments may greatly limit exploration of the environment and the satisfaction of natural interests in moving, jumping, running, touching, holding, climbing, throwing, and catching. During the early years, children whose movement or vitality is

Gallaudet College, the world's only liberal arts college for the deaf, fields both basketball and football teams. In basketball, the players communicate with signs and are guided by the beat of a drum on the sidelines. The vibration of the drumbeat is felt through the floor. Gallaudet first fielded a football team in the 1890s. Their opponents were all hearing individuals who soon learned to read the signs the deaf players flashed to indicate their plays. To negate this, the Gallaudet players began standing close together in a circle so that their signs could not be seen by opposing team members. Before this, there were no huddles in football. But after playing Gallaudet, other teams began to stand in a huddle to call their plays. Soon it was a common practice among football teams across the country and became a permanent part of the game.

restricted may be denied the simple but meaningful experiences of crawling on the floor, tumbling on the grass, helping around the house, playing with intriguing toys, or playing games with their friends.

Such restrictions might lead one to believe that ordinary or extraordinary physical activities can never be entered into by individuals with orthopedic or health impairments. In recent years, it has become more and more apparent that such is not the case as the news media have covered some truly remarkable accomplishments. A young Vietnam veteran who lost his left leg was

Figure 5–2.

Dogs have been trained to help both visually and hearing-impaired individuals increase their flexibility. An intriguing example of how an animal can be trained to aid a severely orthopedically handicapped individual was provided by Tufts University in Massachusetts. A capuchin monkey had been given special training to assist a twenty-four-year-old quadriplegic man. The monkey could brush the young man's hair, place food in a microwave oven, and was pictured in a newspaper article placing a straw inserted in a bottled drink in the man's mouth.

shown training for a marathon run wearing an artificial limb he designed himself. An eight-year-old girl, born without the lower part of her right leg was pictured training for gymnastics and ballet with her artificial limb. Her beaming mother was quoted, "She can have as full and rich a life as any other kid. I've always told her 'Anything you want to try, try it!'"

A wheelchair tennis tournament was entered by thirty men and women with various orthopedic handicaps. The man voted the most valuable player of a national wheelchair basketball tournament averaged over twenty points a game, eight rebounds, and twelve steals. Seated in his modified wheelchair, he is faster than most people on their feet and rolls 100 yards in seventeen seconds and a mile in a little more than five minutes. An all-amputee, sky-diving team, made up of eight men who lost either an arm or leg due to disease, accident, or war injury and who call themselves The Bone Saw Gang, has totalled more than 12,000 jumps. Many were group jumps during which they formed a circle in midair during their descent. A seventeen-year-old girl afflicted with a seizure disorder was shown crossing the finish line of a three-month, 2000-mile run from Minneapolis to Washington, D.C. She said she wanted to "prove to other people who had epilepsy that they could do it too, if they tried." The flexibility of orthopedic and health-impaired individuals may be sharply curtailed, but when we read of such accomplishments we realize anew how the range and nature of experience may combine to challenge many previously held beliefs regarding limits for the handicapped. The individuals in these examples are *truly* exceptional learners.

Severely emotionally disturbed individuals have been studied with respect to deficits in reception and perception of sensory stimuli. Ornitz and Ritvo postulate that such children may suffer from an inability to maintain perceptual constancy; that is, they do not perceive identical experiences in the same way each time they occur (Ornitz & Ritvo, 1968). The behavior of autistic infants suggests they are getting too much or too little input from the environment; without constancy of input, such children may fail to distinguish between themselves and the outside world and to develop imitative behavior. These authors link perceptual inconstancy in the severely disturbed child to neurological impairment.

The perceptual distortions of young schizophrenics have been studied. (McGhie & Chapman, 1961). Such comments as "Everything seems to grip my attention although I'm not particularly interested in anything," "Colors seem brighter as if they were luminous," "I'm not sure things are solid until I touch them," and "If there are three or four people talking at one time I can't take it in," revealed the problems in sensation and perception experienced by these individuals. Severely disturbed children who close their eyes or stuff objects in their ears actually may be trying to protect themselves from disturbing stimuli.

Some disturbed children approach the activities and experiences of childhood at home, in the neighborhood, and in school with impulsive, uncontrolled behavior; others draw away, preferring to remain uninvolved, isolated, and withdrawn. In chapter 3, we discussed three types of behavioral characteristics of disturbed children: conduct problems, inadequacy-immaturity, and personality problems (Quay, Morse, & Cutler, 1966). All three characteristics lead to flexibility problems. The conduct-problem child is seen as aggressive, hostile, and contentious. Such a child moves through the environment freely and directly, participating in a wide range of experiences. But he or she often does so in a random, coercive, or even destructive manner, failing to profit or learn from experience and attempting to set the rules and limits, rather than abiding by those set by others. Toys are broken before being used creatively, interest span varies greatly, and participation in games is contingent on being able to dominate and having things done his or her own way.

The inadequacy-immaturity child exhibits sluggishness, laziness, lack of interest, preoccupation, and inattentiveness. Here, the problem may be one of holding back from new experiences and developing singular interests. The child often prefers to stay home and watch television for long periods rather than to seek out play activities with others. He or she also often engages in excessive fantasizing.

The personality-problem child has been described as demonstrating inferiority feelings, self-consciousness, lack of self-confidence, fearfulness, and depression. This child may view new experiences as threats, worry about his or her ability to perform as well as others, and be generally unhappy much of the time. Such withdrawal can greatly limit the number and kind of activities engaged in and can lead to distorted beliefs about the environment.

Autistic, schizophrenic, or psychotic children have extreme flexibility problems. Such children often retreat from reality and participation in everyday events and live in their own fantasy world. Instead of playing with appropriate toys and seeking the stimulation of others, they may sit and endlessly rock back and forth or crouch fearfully in a corner. Or they may engage in handflapping, whirling, and finger fluttering or exhibit excited reactions to spinning objects. This high degree of inflexibility denies them the involvement with sights, sounds, objects, and events that are essential for normal childhood development. A relatively high proportion (38 to 40 percent) of childhood schizophrenics engage in self-mutilative behaviors. A review of the literature on psychotic children suggests their behavior remains remarkably stable and relatively unaffected by environmental events or fatigue, thus making them most inflexible (Hingtgen & Bryson, 1972).

Individuals with speech handicaps not associated with observable organic defects may have motor problems in the use of appropriate rhythm, coordination, and the application of strength, although no single specific type of physical disability characterizes all speech-defective children (Belto, 1941). The performance of speech-impaired children is slightly below that of normal children on tests of motor proficiency, and children whose speech problems persist are inferior on such tests to those who outgrow their problems (Jenkins & Lohr, 1964). Although it is frequently impossible to find evidence of a specific neurological deficit, some evidence indicates

An inflexible child with an emotional disturbance particularly related to school participation is one with so-called "school phobia." Such a child is similar to the personality-problem child and may be in an acute panic state when in school (Levison, 1962). He or she might turn pale, begin to tremble, become immobilized, or feel a strong urge to run away. Psychosomatic symptoms, such as abdominal pain and dizziness, also can occur. These problems do not occur on days the child does not have to go to school. Much has been written about the faulty family relationships, particularly between mother and child, that appear basic to school phobia and again point to the overlap between flexibility and sociality.

that the development of motor abilities is less favorable for those with defective speech than for the population at large (Berry & Eisenson, 1956). Perhaps speech impairments limit children's range of experience by causing them to shy away from social situations and activities with other children due to self-consciousness. With this line of reasoning, flexibility and social uniqueness may interact to limit the development of motor proficiency.

The disadvantaged individual who lives in a large city often has a more limited range of experience than the child from a middle-class home in the suburbs. Narrow sidewalks, busy streets, back alleys, deserted buildings, and crowded, impoverished living quarters impose limits on what can be done and how it can be done. Crowded living conditions may have differential effects during the child's early life (Hunt, 1961). In infancy, being surrounded by a large number of individuals and exposed to a constant bombardment of sights and sounds may actually be advantageous. But during the second year, when a youngster typically begins to move about constantly, to throw objects, and "to get into everything," his or her freedom may be sharply curtailed because of these same crowded conditions. Poverty is more likely to be associated with such conditions than is racial or ethnic status.

The lower-class child has been credited with a number of adaptive strengths, such as being able "to negotiate the jungle of the slums" (Eisenberg, 1963–1964). Such children often have a realistic "know-how" and demonstrate responsible, adaptive behavior under difficult circumstances. They also appear to possess a high degree of self-reliance and a sense of autonomy and independence (Cuban, 1970).

A number of writers have described the physical, concrete style of some disadvantaged individuals as they move through and interact with the environment. Their motoric, "thing-oriented," and nonverbal style contrasts with the more abstract, symbolic, "idea-oriented," and verbal style of the middle-class child (Goldberg, 1963). Such a concrete approach to learning limits the child's flexibility and makes generalizations and transfer difficult (Eisenberg, 1963–1964). In addition to having a physical style, disadvantaged individuals may be more visually than auditorily oriented. They would rather look than listen. Since so much listening is associated with words spoken by others, the language problems of some disadvantaged individuals may in part reflect a nonauditory orientation.

The flexibility of the Pueblo Indian child is partly determined by cultural values, which often contrast markedly with those held by the teacher and school (Zintz, 1962). The Indian child is

Some disadvantaged children in the inner city may never have been more than a short distance away from their own neighborhoods and hence live in a "constricted world" (Goldberg, 1967). They may have a limited opportunity to explore the outside world, a lack of aesthetically pleasing surroundings, a scarcity of books, toys, puzzles, pencils, and paper, and a lack of guidance and encouragement in their use. Among the many deficits such children may bring with them to school is a limited understanding and knowledge of the physical, geographical, and geometric aspects of the environment.

oriented toward maintaining harmony with nature, rather than attaining mastery over it. He or she may not be totally committed to a scientific explanation of natural phenomena. A belief in myths and sorcery and a fear of the supernatural may greatly alter the types of experiences sought and the learning that results. In addition, such a child may be "present time" rather than "future time" oriented and not responsive to long-range tasks that hold promise for attaining eventual goals.

Individuals with learning disabilities may have problems accurately perceiving visual, auditory, and tactual stimuli, which can lead to frustration and misinterpretation. Unlike sensory defects, such as blindness and deafness, which preclude the individual's receiving visual and auditory stimuli, perceptual disorders refer to a lack of ability to recognize or decode such stimuli in an accurate manner. The child may copy geometric forms incorrectly and exhibit figure-ground confusion (difficulty in discriminating central figures from their background context). However, few generalizations can be made about problems in visual perception among children with learning disabilities. They are no more likely to have visual acuity problems than are normal children. The problems they exhibit in visual perception may be the result of difficulty in maintaining attention to visual stimuli and selecting the relevant from the irrelevant (Bryan & Bryan, 1975) or may occur only when applied to linguistic stimuli such as letters and words (Vellutino, 1979). Likewise, problems in auditory perception manifested by learning-disabled children may relate to difficulty in discriminating auditory content when it is embedded in irrelevant stimuli. Such problems may be a function of how a child uses and remembers the information, rather than a function of basic perception or discrimination of sounds. The child with a learning disability may be physically awkward or clumsy and have problems in hand-eye coordination.

Even though the problems of the child with a learning disability are often most visible and disruptive in the confines of the classroom, it is interesting to follow such a child to the playground, to his or her neighborhood, and into the house, and then to consider how flexible the child is in adapting to the larger environment. Hyperactivity, perhaps the most commonly recognized characteristic of children with learning disabilities, may go unnoticed in the world of running, jumping, tumbling, climbing, and playing. Outside the classroom, where demands for conformity and control are lessened, hyperactivity may not be maladaptive. In fact, a review of twenty-one experimental studies of attention deficits in learning-disabled children revealed that hyperactivity may be situationally specific, with higher levels of activity being exhibited in structured situations such as the classroom (Tarver & Hallahan, 1974).

Figure 5-3.

In describing such children, Cruickshank has included hyperactivity along with hyperdistractibility, disinhibition, and impulsivity under the general problem heading of distractibility (Cruickshank, 1967). He feels that the basic difficulty stems from the child's inability to refrain from reacting to extraneous external or internal stimuli. As a result, such a child is often a poor participant in games requiring prolonged concentration and attention; he or she is readily drawn away by distracting noise and activity or by irrelevant thoughts about past or future events. To such a child, a sign saying "wet paint" may be an open invitation for touching, and a knothole in a fence may be an irresistible spot for finger poking.

Empirical studies on attention deficits reveal that children with learning disabilities are deficient in their ability to maintain attention over prolonged periods of time (Krupski, 1981). In a study on ability to attend to visual signals, three subjects were required to press a lever in response to particular flashing lights and to refrain from pressing the lever when presented with other flashing lights. Results indicated that learning-disabled children tended to commit more impulsive errors and to respond less quickly when correct than did their nondisabled peers (Tarver & Hallahan, 1974).

Parents of children with learning disabilities often express concern with the child's tendency to "not concentrate for more than a few minutes at a time," "to jump from one thing to another," and "to mind everybody's business but his own" (Clements & Peters, 1962). Interviews with mothers of hyperactive children and mothers of normal children indicate that hyperactive youngsters exhibit a number of problems at home (Stewart, 1970). The ten most commonly reported symptoms of hyperactive subjects, together with the percentage exhibiting these symptoms, were overactivity (100 percent), failure to finish projects (84 percent), fidgeting (84 percent), inability to sit still at meals (81 percent), failure to stay with games (78 percent), wearing out toys and furniture (68 percent), talking too much (68 percent), failure to follow directions (62 percent), clumsiness (62 percent), and fighting with other children (59 percent).

The more severely retarded the child is, the more likely it is that there will be accompanying physical handicaps, since the possibility is greater that the same disease or organic factor that caused the retardation affected physical functioning as well. As mentioned earlier, it is not unusual for a mentally retarded child to have one or two other handicapping conditions.

In comparisons between the retarded and those with physical or sensory impairments (the blind and the deaf), flexibility problems have often been found to overlap (Bialer, 1970). The retarded have a very high incidence of problems in hearing (Keiser, Montague, Wold, Maune, & Pattison, 1981; Lloyd, 1976; Reynolds & Reynolds, 1979) and vision (Ellis, 1979). The presence of physical disabilities is also a highly prevalent problem (Hardman & Drew, 1977) and one of the primary factors determining whether or not a retarded child may have to be institutionalized (Eyman, O'Connor, Tarjan, & Justice, 1974).

Mentally retarded children have also been found to be less proficient in physical motor behavior than are normal children of the same chronological age; but in many cases, differences are not as marked in gross motor areas or when tasks are relatively simple (Cratty, 1974; Moon & Renzaglia, 1982; Rarick, Dobbins, & Brodhead, 1976). There is some speculation that delays in motor development may begin with the retarded infant's inability to use feedback effectively to regulate his or her posture (Molnar, 1978). Retarded children have also been found to respond more slowly on reaction-time tests (Baumeister, 1967), but such deficits may be due to the task situation (Brewer, 1978; Brewer & Nettelbeck, 1977). Attending to sustained tasks is often quite difficult for retarded children, especially in classroom situations (Forness, Guthrie, & MacMillan, 1981; Forness, Silverstein, & Guthrie, 1979; Krupski, 1979; Porges & Humphrey, 1977); but we will discuss in chapter 6 the possibility that social needs of retarded children can sometimes interfere with attending behavior.

One concept that relates to how well the mentally retarded child moves through and interacts with the environment is the notion of *rigidity*. Rigidity refers to the persistence of a response or behavior beyond the point where it is appropriate or correct. It was Lewin (1936) who first advanced the notion that retarded children are more "rigid" in their thought processes, and thus are more apt to persist at monotonous tasks for longer periods of time than normal children. In experiments on this concept, Kounin (1941) gave retarded and normal ten-year-olds the task of drawing simple cat figures and then drawing figures of bugs. Normal children drew cats up to a point, became bored, and then switched, but retarded children persisted and continued to draw cat figures long after the others had stopped. The retarded children were also given a deck of cards to be sorted, first by form and then by color. These children seemed to persist in sorting according to the first principle and could not shift as readily to the second. It was postulated that such inflexibility would affect the development of adequate intelligence in the retarded because it makes the occurrence of cognitive change more difficult.

The concept, however, was not entirely accurate. Later experimental studies (Green & Zigler, 1962; Zigler, 1963) in which retarded and nonretarded children were given similar satiation tasks did not verify the supposed presence of rigidity among the retarded. Some retarded children could make the necessary shifts in activity, and this seemed to depend more on their experience and background than on the fact that they were retarded. The difference seemed to be that all the retarded children in the earlier studies were institutionalized. Zigler (1966) suggested that retarded children living in institutions are more apt to have been deprived of social contact, and that persistence in tasks given by an adult may occur due to the child's high motivation to secure adult contact. Such children may have sensed that by continuing at the task, boring as it was, they could maintain the adult's presence; but if they changed the situation by shifting to another task, the session would be terminated and the adult would go away. Thus, in a situation where an adult assigns a task and directs the child to "keep doing it as long as you wish," the institutionalized, retarded child may often persist in an effort to maintain social contact and thus only appear to be rigid or inflexible. Retarded children living at home, on the other hand, may not have as much difficulty shifting from one activity to another, since they are not subject to the same degree of social deprivation. As noted throughout this text, certain presumed deficits of retarded children often reflect motivational and experiential differences, rather than mental retardation per se.

One study examined the phenomenon of helplessness in mildly retarded young adults, as measured by their responses in certain contrived situations, for example, being left alone in an office while the phone rang or being given a drawing assignment for which only unsharpened pencils were available (Floor & Rosen, 1975). It was found that retarded adults were indeed less flexible in coping with these everyday problems. Mentally retarded children also may not move as freely and openly through their environments, even in play activities (Wehman, 1977; Hopper & Wambold, 1978; Switsky, Ludwig, & Haywood, 1979; Li, 1981). These deficits, however, may not be totally inborn characteristics. When such children select the familiar (well-understood games, favorite toy, neighborhood play area) rather than the unfamiliar (games with new rules, complex toys or objects, play area with strangers or new hazards), they may be exhibiting a wariness of others, particularly of adults with whom they have had negative experiences in the past (Zigler, 1966). Or they may be exhibiting immature personality development (Cromwell, 1967), difficulty in relating language concepts to physical acts (Luria, 1963; Hermelin & O'Connor, 1963), lack of previous experience (Hunt, 1961), or limited ability to process incoming information (Spitz, 1979).

Because of lowered intelligence, retarded children have fewer options in relating to the physical world than do normal children; that is, they may not as readily consider all the alternatives in getting from one place to another, or they may not think as critically as do normal children about the consequences of certain physical acts. When normal children are confronted with a problem in relating to or interacting with their environment, they are more apt to come up with alternative solutions and try different approaches. Retarded children may perceive fewer

One should keep in mind, nonetheless, that even profoundly retarded persons living in institutions are reported to be surprisingly adept sometimes in certain areas of flexibility, for example, escaping from physical restraints (Cleland, 1973). Likewise, the flexibility of the most profoundly retarded persons can be markedly improved with careful training (Hasket & Hollar, 1978; Hobson & Duncan, 1979; Webb & Keller, 1979; Westling & Murden, 1978). Thus, it is hazardous to generalize about the capabilities of the retarded. As we review current knowledge, it appears that the flexibility of the retarded child, at least in some areas, may be determined less by capacity than by experience.

strategies and are much more apt to be thwarted by obstacles in their physical environments. They are therefore subject to greater frustrations because of this decreased flexibility.

As gifted individuals survey and move through the world about them, they learn rapidly and easily, show much curiosity, examine rather than display cursory interest, and appreciate many things of which other children are unaware. The Terman study collected data on the interests of gifted children in activities, games, and general play (Terman & Oden, 1959). Although there were some exceptions, the typical gifted child liked active games requiring much exercise and liked to play with tools and machinery. Thus, the belief that gifted children seek withdrawal from physical exertion and are preoccupied with books was not confirmed.

Interest in collecting appeared in twice as many of the gifted subjects as in those in the control group. These collections tended to be large and more often of a scientific nature. In terms of play interests, gifted boys tended to be more masculine than were unselected boys between eight and twelve years of age. After this age period, these was little difference between the groups. As adults at mid-life, more than four-fifths of the subjects reported an interest in two or more avocational pursuits, and more than one-half had three or more. Although no general population norms are available for comparison, the breadth and diversity of the gifted adults' interests is impressive.

The possibility of failure causes some gifted children to shun new experiences (Dunlap, 1967). If they are not wholly secure, such children may participate halfheartedly, seek excuses, or give up altogether. This may be a reflection of the gifted child's keen sensitivity to possible eventualities not typically found among the less gifted.

Early Identification

There has been concern recently with evaluating flexibility or the potential for flexibility as early as possible in an individual's life. Since some handicapping conditions are not clearly recognizable or are not developed at birth, there has been increasing interest in infants born *at risk*, that is, infants who might be considered possible or probable candidates for the development of a handicap that would interfere with their flexibility.

Three basic categories associated with risk have been identified: (1) infants and children with organically based physical or sensory conditions that will interfere with normal development (e.g., visual or auditory impairments); (2) infants and children born under conditions that are often associated with later developmental problems (e.g., prematurity); and (3) infants and children born into environments where social and economic conditions place them at risk (e.g., poverty) (Keogh & Kopp, 1978).

In the first category, the indicators of risk are present in the child at the time of diagnosis; in the latter two categories, risk is inferred in terms of probability, largely based on a child's membership in the particular category. In all three categories, "more predictive confidence can be placed in diagnostic decisions based on infants or young children in the extreme ends of the risk distribution than about those in the marginal or borderline areas" (Keogh & Kopp, 1976, p. 11).

Intervention programs for infants and young children from the first category, such as those with cerebral palsy or those with visual or auditory handicaps, may be based on a downward extension of rehabilitative approaches used with older individuals or on approaches developed specifically for infants. The focus in these programs is on remediation and compensation of sensory and motor impairments and on the development of sensory-motor skills that are presumed to foster cognitive growth. Enhancing the range and nature of experience of young handicapped children is considered of overriding importance. Enrichment programs may be appropriate for a variety of risk conditions (Friedlander, Sterritt, & Kirk, 1975).

The problems of infants and young children who fall in the other two categories cannot be approached quite as directly. In some cases, their membership in these categories will in no way interfere with later development. One study examined 243 children whose mothers had contracted rubella before they were born. Although this situation is associated with high risk, the

Figure 5-4.

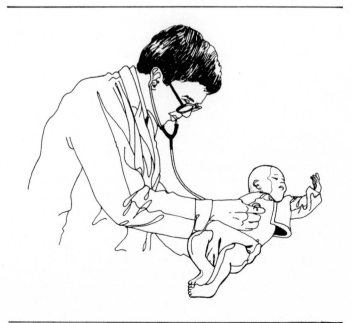

There is agreement in the research literature that prematurity may be associated with later mild intellectual deficit (Keogh & Kopp, 1978). But there is also evidence that many, even the majority of premature infants, develop normally and that by school age they cannot be distinguished from their peers. Thus, prematurity alone cannot be used as a predictor of later intellectual deficits, but conditions associated with it (e.g., low birthweight, pro-longed hospitalization, disruption of the mother-child relationship) may account for subsequent developmental problems (Parmelee & Haber, 1973). Anoxia or oxygen deprivation at birth also has not been found to be predictive of later developmental status. In a follow-up study of anoxic and normal babies, few differences were found between the two groups in later childhood (Corah, Anthony, Painter, Stern, & Thurston, 1965).

examinations revealed consequences ranging from no detectable physical handicaps to single handicaps in vision, hearing, or neurological or cardiac functioning, to various combinations of multiple handicaps (Chess, 1974). In terms of proportion of the sample, about one-fifth had no defects, one-fourth had physical defects in one area, one-fifth had defects in two areas, one-fifth had defects in three areas, and the remainder had defects in the four major areas of vision, hearing, and neurological and cardiac functioning.

A follow-up study of fifty-four of the children revealed several possible trends that may be important in planning intervention programs. First, a defect in one area can retard or interfere with development in another area, for example, a hearing impairment can affect language development. Second, a particular defect may be present in infancy but not identifiable until a later age when an anticipated higher level of functioning fails to emerge, such as fine motor coordination in a child with cerebral palsy. Third, as the child's cognitive capacity increases, the effect of the handicapping condition may be increasingly mitigated. Finally, the identical handicapping condition in two children may result in differing functioning levels because of individual differences in temperament and in parent-child or teacher-child interaction.

It has been found that one-half of a population of children genetically predisposed to the development of schizophrenia displayed no symptomatology after several years of follow-up (Rolf & Harig, 1974). For many, severe emotional disturbance has come to be viewed as an interactional phenomenon, with certain negative experiential factors and vulnerability (i.e., capacity) contributing to its precipitation.

The infant in category three—the one born into an environment involving both social and economic risk—has been studied increasingly over the past decade. Although there is clear evidence that the infant's environment is a powerful contributor to early risk and a continuing influence on early development, the exact nature of the interaction between biological conditions and environmental milieu is unclear (Sameroff & Chandler, 1975). However, there is no question that infants born "with signs of biological vulnerability (e.g., prematurity) have a higher probability of developmental problems if born into poverty rather than into more affluent families" (Keogh & Kopp, 1976, p. 17).

For early identification, multiple predictors of risk have been suggested (instead of single indicators) (Rosenblith, 1975; Parmelee, Kopp, & Sigman, 1976), and a cumulative risk index for assessment of infant status has been developed. This index combines prenatal, natal, and postnatal information in an additive fashion, taking into account biologic events and conditions and behavioral indicators. Specific measures include scales identifying obstetric and postnatal complications, postnatal neurological and behavioral measures, and data from examination at four months and nine months of age.

Despite problems with identification and prediction and questions about the continuity and stability of development, there has been a remarkable increase in intervention programs over the past ten years. They are based on the assumption that there are indeed recognizable conditions in infancy and early childhood that will lead to long-term negative consequences if not dealt with appropriately (Keogh & Kopp, 1976).

Early Intervention

Once identified, what can be done to reduce or eliminate the risk experienced by an individual? The optimal time for intervening in the life of a high-risk child is not known, although there is support for intervention in the first three years of life (Horowitz & Paden, 1973). Disadvantaged infants with low birth weights have been enrolled in a special sensory-motor stimulation program (Scarr-Salapatek & Williams, 1973). Two types of stimulation were offered during the first year: (1) sensory stimulation to provide varied tactile, visual, kinesthetic, and auditory stimulation experienced by normal newborns through human contact but denied the isolated premature infant, and (2) intellectual stimulation. The program involved both nursery and home stimulation. Thirty low-birthweight infants born consecutively over a one-year period were alternately assigned to experimental and control groups. The experimental group received visual, tactile, and kinesthetic stimulation during the six weeks they were kept in the hospital nursery. This stimulation was provided by bird mobiles, rocking, talking, and fondling by nurses. An effort was made to offer stimulation as similar as possible to that experienced by normal infants.

Weekly home visits were made to improve maternal care until the infants reached twelve months of age. Infants in the control group received standard pediatric care for low-birthweight infants, such as being placed in an isolated crib and fed and changed with a minimum of disturbance. At four weeks of age, there were indications of slight-to-significant differences in functioning levels in favor of the experimental group. By one year, Cattell IQ scores indicated a significantly higher developmental status for the experimental group; an average difference of nearly 10 IQ points separated the experimental group (mean = 95.3) from the control group (mean = 85.7).

Summary

We will unify our summary of flexibility uniqueness by discussing exceptional learners collectively under the main topics associated with flexibility.

Looking, listening, and other sensory experiences

The visually impaired or hearing-impaired individuals will rely on the remaining senses for adapting to and learning about the environment. Those whose loss of vision or hearing occurred in middle childhood will have advantages over those who were handicapped at birth. Since the visually impaired depend so much on hearing and touching, and the hearing-impaired on seeing, it was once thought that they were especially endowed with an innate superior auditory, tactual, or visual capacity. Such is not the case, for their superior sensory functioning level is the result of range of experience. The retarded often have accompanying physical impairments, particularly in the area of hearing, that interfere with their flexibility.

Looking, listening, and other sensory experiences are not just a matter of sensory capacity. They also depend on motivation and involvement. Emotionally disturbed children may see and hear perfectly well, but their lack of attention and interest and daydreaming may greatly interfere with their profitting from what we show or tell them. The same may be true for other exceptional learners.

Perception of environmental stimuli

Despite the loss of sight, visually impaired exceptional learners develop concepts of form, space, and distance. The development of these concepts appears to be the result of processes that go beyond experiences of touching and movement and involves a unification of separate, nonvisual perceptions into one total concept of an object.

It has been postulated that some severely emotionally disturbed individuals have difficulty maintaining perceptual constancy or perceiving identical experiences in the same way each time they occur. In addition, some visual or auditory experiences may be disturbing due to their perceived intensity or distortion.

Problems in seeing or hearing accurately lead to frustration and misinterpretation with some learning-disabled individuals. This is not a visual or auditory sensory problem but a perceptual problem that may be related to difficulty in paying attention, discriminating the relevant from the irrelevant, or memory.

Physical movement

Blind infants may be delayed in some areas of physical and motor development, but this delay is caused by a limited range of experience (sometimes the result of parental overprotection) rather than by the visual impairment itself. It may also reflect a lack of opportunity to imitate others or motivational problems. The physical movement of the blind is enhanced by the development of the so-called obstacle sense. By perceiving small, unrecognized auditory cues such as echoes, physical obstacles can be identified. This skill can be developed by the nonvisually handicapped if practiced blindfolded.

Physical movement for the orthopedically impaired will be restricted, depending on the nature and extent of the handicap, but wheel chairs (some driven by electric motors) permit mobility for some. Technological developments in the field of prostheses have also resulted in greater movement potential. The individual with a chronic health problem may have the full use of arms and legs, but lowered vitality may restrict the amount and type of physical activity.

Emotionally disturbed and learning-disabled children may display a great deal of physical movement, sometimes to their detriment. Hyperactivity can be a serious problem when it occurs during those times children should be devoting their energies to paying attention and following directions. Some severely disturbed individuals may move very little, even to the point of immobilization. It has been reported that the motor proficiency of some speech-impaired children may be poorer than that of children with no speech problems. In explaining such poor proficiency, as well as hyperactive behavior, some postulate subtle neurological problems; but faulty range and nature of experience can also account for them.

Disadvantaged youngsters may display more of a motoric or thing-oriented style than one related to passive looking or listening. Some learning-disabled and retarded children are somewhat awkward physically, particularly in activities requiring fine motor coordination. Despite their "bookworm" stereotype, gifted individuals are readily drawn to games and activities involving vigorous physical exertion.

Active and independent participation

One real surprise with respect to the flexibility uniqueness of exceptional learners is the extent of their active participation in a wide range of activities. In fact, this is one of the earliest and important considerations for parents and all those working with them. Overprotection, although motivated by concern for the welfare of the exceptional learner, can interfere greatly with the quality of life for any child, but it is particularly harmful for the exceptional individual. Once the blind develop orientation and mobility skills, they can travel in a largely unrestricted manner. They may also participate in many types of athletic activities. The hearing-impaired can also be active and independent participants relying on visual monitoring of the environment. Individuals with orthopedic impairments, including those confined to wheel chairs, compete in many types of athletic contests and have achieved impressive physical feats. Recent efforts to provide access for wheel chairs at street corners and in many buildings have helped increase the flexibility of many of these exceptional learners.

Emotionally disturbed individuals may have none of the physical obstacles to overcome as do the blind and orthopedically impaired, but they may withdraw from participation, be overly dependent on others, or participate in a random and impulsive manner. Self-consciousness may prevent the individual with a speech defect from entering into activities that call attention to his or her speech. Disadvantaged youngsters may excel in active and independent participation and display a high degree of self-reliance and autonomy dealing with difficult circumstances in their environments. The retarded may prefer to remain in familiar surroundings and engage in familiar activities. However, with support and guidance, their flexibility can be markedly improved.

Gifted individuals are likely to be active and independent participants and to ask questions readily and probe more deeply.

Learning knowledge and acquiring skills related to successful adaptation to the environment

The outcome of listening, looking, perceiving, moving, exploring, and participating is *learning*. Special education is devoted to maximizing this outcome for all exceptional learners.

The blind and the deaf will rely on opposite sensory modalities but will learn the same things and acquire knowledge and skills like the nonexceptional. The orthopedically handicapped and health impaired will do likewise, although they may be less physically active in the process. Disturbed individuals may, for a variety of reasons, learn in a fragmented fashion. Many, however, will be undistinguishable from the nonexceptional. With respect to flexibility, the same can be said for many individuals with speech defects or learning disabilities and the disadvantaged. We have learned that we can be fooled by setting rigid limits for flexibility expectations with respect to the mentally retarded. Finally, the gifted, by definition, may go well beyond the nonexceptional in learning knowledge and acquiring skill.

What accounts for the differences among exceptional learners in flexibility? For some, it clearly relates to sensory or physical factors. For others, it reflects motivation or opportunities for learning. Finally, for many exceptional learners, the interaction of sensory and physical factors, opportunity and motivation will determine their ultimate level of flexibility.

CHAPTER 6

Social Characteristics of Exceptional Learners

In addition to considering the flexibility characteristics of exceptional learners, special educators are concerned with the degree of success they experience interacting with others. In this chapter, we consider social uniqueness, and include a discussion of exceptional learners and their families. Primary concerns are:

- communicating effectively with others.

- seeking social interactions.

- establishing harmonious relationships with others.

The biological helplessness of early infancy initiates a dependence on other human beings and a lifetime relationship of giving and taking, obeying and challenging, pleasing and displeasing, accepting and rejecting. Children learn to fit into a society with rules, traditions, expectations, beliefs, and values determined by others. They are influenced by parents, siblings, neighbors, peers, teachers, television personalities, sports heroes, scout leaders, clergy, and politicians. Human beings are highly social creatures, forming close attachments and intimate involvements with significant others around them.

For visually handicapped individuals, the social consequences of their uniqueness may have a greater impact on their lives than the physiological or flexibility problem itself. For example, when visually handicapped individuals enter a room filled with normally sighted people, their hearing enables them to gain information and maintain communication, but they are seriously disadvantaged in many respects. People may not talk; they may move away or enter the room without being heard. Comments directed toward blind individuals may go unnoticed unless these individuals are addressed by name. Thus, the social world of the blind can be an uncertain and frustrating one.

> Much of the disability of blind and visually impaired people is occasioned by restrictions, overprotection, rejection, unrealistic expectations, and the ignorance of society. Thus, the blind or visually impaired individual is further handicapped by being excused from the usual developmental, educational, and vocational experiences and often being permitted to maintain unpleasant habits, poor posture, and a

Figure 6-1.

debilitating dependence. The fear occasioned in others by blindness is associated not only with the rejection of blind persons, but also often with a confining benevolence which cares for but also segregates them from sighted society. (Connor & Muldoon, 1973, p. 353)

It has been hypothesized that the fear of the blind in sighted persons, as mentioned by Connor and Muldoon, may result from their fear of becoming blind themselves. For example, when high school seniors were asked to rank five potential injuries according to severity of personal impact, four-fifths ranked blindness first (Gowman, 1957). Blindness was judged to be the worst handicap for college students by college faculty members (Newman, 1976).

Rejection of blind individuals also may be associated with limited knowledge about the visually handicapped. Teachers and administrators selected the visually handicapped as the least preferred for teaching (except aggressive delinquents) from among eight categories of exceptional children. As a group, educators apparently knew the least about the blind. Some special educators, however, tended to place the visually handicapped in a more favorable position than did educators in general (Murphy, 1960).

Bateman (1967) investigated sighted children's perceptions of blind children and found that those who had actually known blind children appraised their abilities more positively than those who had not. Such positive appraisals increased progressively from grades three through six with the number of blind children known, and urban children were found to be more positive in their appraisals than were rural children.

Contact alone, however, may not improve sighted children's attitudes toward their blind peers, as was found in a study concerned with the acceptance of blind children by their sighted classmates in social, academic, and physical activities (Jones, Lavine, & Shell, 1972). The blind children in the study all used Braille and were integrated into regular classrooms for at least half of the school day. The sighted subjects responded to a sociometric questionnaire asking them to list classmates they would most want to interact with or to avoid. The results indicated that blind youngsters were generally less accepted by their sighted peers. Blind children who were accepted tended to be personally congenial and free from annoying personality and behavior problems, whereas those rejected showed the opposite pattern. Interestingly, it was generally found that sighted children who listed the blind among their first three choices were themselves social isolates. The authors view the effects of acceptance by low-status sighted children on the social status of the blind as actually negative. They stress the importance of developing classroom programs in which blind children gain acceptance from all their sighted peers.

A number of false attitudes toward the blind and false attitudes adopted by the blind have been discussed by Cutsforth (1951). He does not believe the blind suffer because they yearn for sight, unless social pressure creates this attitude. The fear of being watched may create an emotional strain on the blind child, and this fear may persist well into later life. Cutsforth does not believe the blind have as normal a sexual development as sighted children, and he is critical of segregation of boys and girls in residential schools because normal sexual growth can only be fostered by normal social conditions.

The possibility that severe and prolonged visual impairment may lead to problems in adjustment emerged from one study with congenitally blind children (McGuire & Meyers, 1971). The authors concluded from their results that "to be congenitally blind puts the child in the high risk category for personality problems" (p. 139).

Behavioral studies have provided increasing evidence that blindness, uncomplicated by other capacity or experiential problems, does not cause psychological or developmental disturbances. However, as we saw with other exceptional learners, the chances for the occurrence of such disturbances are heightened by the effects of the child's blindness on range and nature of experience (particularly the mother-child relationship). (Lowenfeld, 1980).

The hearing-handicapped individual is often at a serious disadvantage when interacting with others. A loss of 30 to 45 decibels makes conversation difficult without amplification. The individual can communicate, however, by having sound amplified by a hearing aid and by getting close to the speaker. This level of hearing loss appears to affect basic awareness and monitoring, rather than socialization. A loss of 45 to 60 decibels clearly affects social interaction. Even though amplification makes conversation possible, the individual must give all sound equal attention, thus often limiting interaction to one person or a small group. There is a sense of detachment from others, and social relationships with those who have similar hearing problems may be preferred. When the hearing involves a 70 decibel loss, amplification is less satisfactory for maintaining social relationships. Reliance on visual and tactual senses becomes considerable. The individual may suffer from a poor sense of identity and find relationships with similarly impaired individuals more satisfying. Deafness is associated with a loss of 85 or more decibels. At this level, the hearing disability precludes the understanding of speech through the ear alone, with or

The personality adjustment of blind and partially seeing individuals has been studied through questionnaires, experimental reactions to stress, behavioral inventories, projective methods, and interview techniques. In one study of the adjustment of three groups of children—blind children in a day school program, blind children in residential school programs, and comparable sighted children—it was found that no basic differences emerged among the three groups (Cowen, Underberg, Verillo, & Benham, 1961). There were also no differences when the attitudes and levels of understand-

ing of their parents were compared. Better adjustment was associated with *greater visual disability*, and the findings suggest that partially seeing children may actually have greater adjustment problems than do the blind. This may be because partially seeing children must learn to adjust to two worlds—one of the sightless and one of the sighted, whereas the blind face a single adjustment to a nonvisual world. The confusion and frustration of the partially seeing may be related to a greater incidence of adjustment problems.

without the use of a hearing aid (Moores, 1978). Visual and tactual senses become mandatory for functioning in the environment, and the difficult task of interacting with others may preclude relationships with any but the profoundly deaf.

In recent years, there have been positive developments in increasing communication opportunities for deaf individuals. Access to teletypewriters and specially designed portable telephone equipment is more readily available. The presentation of Line 21 television captioning of selective programs has made media and information more accessible.

The adjustment of deaf adults was studied in New York state (Baroff, 1969). Deaf individuals were found capable of establishing effective personal contacts. Seventy-five percent of those interviewed claimed they had close friends, and a higher percentage reported being with others on a social basis at least once a week. Almost half reported having hearing as well as deaf friends; one-third of the deaf individuals interviewed, however, felt that hearing people had negative feelings toward them.

A part of self-identity depends on the knowledge that our own feelings and attitudes are similar to those of our peers. The inability of the deaf individual to profit from the many subtleties of language regarding sex roles and interpersonal relationships may create serious problems in this area (McConnell, 1973). The deaf may be somewhat self-centered because they lack understanding of the emotions of others that are communicated by language (Sanders, 1980). Deafness itself does not cause emotional problems or mental illness. The problem behaviors of the deaf are more similar to than different from those of hearing children (Reirich & Rothrock, 1972). If present from early childhood, however, deafness may create considerable stress and adversely affect personality development, as indicated by the fact that schizophrenia occurs in the deaf population almost two and one-half times as often as in the hearing population (Altshuler, 1967). Although it has been claimed that deaf individuals often exhibit paranoid-like thinking, there is no evidence that hospitalized psychotic individuals who are deaf display a preponderance of paranoid symptoms (Altshuler & Baroff, 1969).

In a review of investigations of the social maturity of deaf children, Myklebust concluded that they are often less mature than are hearing children (Myklebust, 1964). This appears to be the result of the higher levels of social competence required with advancing years, and deaf children's

The age of onset of deafness can have a marked effect on the ability to communicate and on social adjustment. If profound deafness occurs prenatally or before age two, the child may be extremely isolated and very dependent on visual and tactual senses. Serious problems in communication and identification can develop. If a child hears normally for the first two years of life, he or she has oral language advantages and manifests fewer detrimental psychological effects than the child who has never heard. The advantages are even greater if the child has hearing to age five or six. When hearing loss occurs during the school years, the child's language problems diminish, but friendships and identification with the majority group are difficult to maintain. Individuals who suffer hearing impairment during this period often become leaders in the deaf community. Once an individual reaches early adulthood, the onset of hearing loss may not alter the personality, but it may accentuate undesirable traits. In addition, social relations, including marital plans, educational goals, and vocational levels, can be seriously disrupted (Myklebust, 1964).

difficulty in attaining self-help and self-direction skills needed to meet these levels. According to Myklebust, deaf individuals may manifest 15 to 20 percent less social maturity than do hearing individuals by age twenty-one. This state of "emotional immaturity" is supported by others (Schlesinger & Meadow, 1972). However, the situation is not as clear-cut as a summary of literature might indicate. A number of factors, such as the questionable suitability of the research instrument used, may lead to an inaccurate assessment of the social maturity of deaf individuals (Moores, 1978).

Many social problems of orthopedically impaired individuals result from the impact of others' reactions to the handicap, the individual's interpretation of these reactions, and conflicts that arise between the child's aspiration level and his or her actual capacity. The visibility of a handicap has been shown to be related to rejection by others and, even though additional factors are involved, the presence of a visible handicap also appears to negatively effect the self-concept of an orthopedically impaired individual. These individuals may perceive themselves as different and not fitting in, and as a result they may withdraw from peer contacts. The teasing and criticism of others may also intensify a negative self-image. In general, there seems to be no significant difference between orthopedically impaired and normal individuals in terms of mental health; overall adjustment seems to be related more closely to the social impact of the impairment rather than the actual impairment itself (Lewandowski & Cruickshank, 1980).

The physical hazards associated with seizure disorders may be secondary to the emotional disturbances developed by afflicted individuals as the result of negative experiences in the home, school, and community (Livingston, 1966). The main antisocial characteristics that many individuals with seizure disorders exhibit are irritability, temper outbursts, and aggressiveness, along with moodiness and emotional changeability. Such problems can result from deprivation and maltreatment (Keating, 1961).

A study of 266 patients in the pediatric seizure clinic of a general hospital revealed that many children with epilepsy are terrified by the loss of control inherent in having seizures (Voeller & Rothenberg, 1973). The relationship between loss of control and incontinence (loss of bladder

The American Institute of Public Opinion surveyed adult attitudes toward epilepsy throughout the United States in 1949, 1954, 1959, and 1964 (Caveness & Merritt, 1965). When asked if they had knowledge of epilepsy, 92 to 95 percent of those sampled responded in the affirmative over the fifteen-year period. To the question, "Would you object to your child playing with epileptics?" 57 percent answered no in 1948; 68 percent in 1954; 67 percent in 1959; and 77 percent in 1964. When asked if they thought epilepsy was a form of insanity, 59 percent said no in 1949; 68 percent in 1954; 74 percent in 1959; and 79 percent in 1964. The question, "Should epileptics be employed?" was answered yes by 45 percent in 1949; 60 percent in 1954; 75 percent in 1959, and 82 percent in 1964.

control) aggravates this fear. For patients who had auras (an advanced sensory warning that a seizure is about to occur), the situation was less threatening because they could often place themselves in a safe position before the seizure occurred. Patients whose seizures were sudden and unpredictable often attempted to exert excessive control over others.

Health impairments (e.g., asthma, heart disease) may lead to both psychological and social difficulties. Studies have shown chronically ill children to be troublesome in school and socially isolated (Pless & Roghmann, 1971). As with orthopedic impairments, chronically ill children may have low self-esteem. Hospitalization and surgery can also affect social adjustment. Fifty children who underwent cardiac catheterization (a diagnostic surgical procedure for heart examination) were studied, and more than half of them later exhibited negative behavioral and emotional reactions (e.g., physical aggression, regression, and anxiety). The younger the child, the more likely the negative reaction (Aisenberg, Wolff, Rosenthal, & Nadas, 1973). Children with health impairments may come to realize how anxious their parents and others become when health problems occur and use these problems to gain attention and control.

If emotionally disturbed individuals are handicapped by disorganized and inflexible behavior in the environment at large, their problems increase substantially in the world of people. Of 133 boys and 39 girls of elementary school age who were referred to a special education program because of behavior and learning problems, poor social relations were the primary reason for the referral of 47 percent of the boys and 46 percent of the girls (Woody, 1964). The problem of getting along with others has frequently been found to be central to the school difficulties of children with behavior disorders (Bower, 1969; Rubin, Simson, & Betwee, 1966).

We can extend our discussion of the three types of children described in the last chapter to the area of sociality (Quay & Peterson, 1975). The conduct-problem child may be the "bully," relating to others through force and intimidation. Even though some measure of control and prestige over others may result, such a child may always operate on the fringe of the group. This type of a behavior disorder often reflects an early environmental experience of rejection by others and a lack of close and meaningful relationships. The inadequacy-immaturity child may have few interests in common with other children. In addition, such a child may not go out of his or her way to make friends and engage in play activities. This reticence to become involved with others may occur because of the child's fearfulness and anxiety due to previous failures in social situations.

Various forms of social deviancy (including schizophrenia and autism) have been viewed as related to delayed acquisition of role-taking skills, that is, the ability to take the perspective of another person. Such deficiencies in role-taking and communication skills seriously interfere with development of social competence. Individuals who are delayed in acquiring these skills tend to misread social expectations, misinterpret other people's intentions, and act in ways disrespectful of others' rights (Chandler, Greenspan, & Barenboim, 1974).

The personality-problem child may greatly fear competition, give and take, and unexpected adjustments involved in group interaction, and hence will avoid others at all costs. The child may find fantasy preferable to reality because of earlier negative social experiences. The psychotic, schizophrenic, or autistic child is likely to represent extremes in social maladjustment in relation to the inadequacy-immaturity and personality-problem child. From a review of analyses of spontaneous behavior of psychotic children, it has been found that generally such children are relatively inattentive to either adults or peers and that they engage in little constructive play (Hingtgen & Bryson, 1972). Evidence is not conclusive as to whether or not autistic children selectively avoid eye-to-eye or eye-to-face contact. It does appear, however, that autistic children look less at all objects in the environment, including adults, than do nonautistic counterparts. When they do look at adults, they do not exhibit the accompanying behavioral responses that indicate attention in normal children. In some cases, neurological factors may largely account for such behavior, although limited range and negative nature of experience may compound the problem. Without continual efforts on the part of others in the environment to initiate contact and involvement, detachment and self-preoccupation usually increase in severity over time as a result of isolation.

In a study comparing the role-taking ability of forty-five delinquent and forty-five nondelinquent boys, ages eleven to thirteen, a substantial portion of delinquent subjects demonstrated a marked developmental lag in the ability successfully to adopt roles or perspectives of others (Chandler, 1973). Differences between the two groups persisted despite controls for social class and intelligence. Institutionalized emotionally disturbed children also have been found to be significantly delayed in the acquisition of role-taking and communication skills compared to their nonhandicapped age-mates (Chandler, Greenspan, & Barenboim, 1974).

The individual with a speech handicap may be constantly frustrated in attempts to relate to other people and may react to such frustration with either aggression or withdrawal (Van Riper & Irwin, 1958). Although there is little evidence that children who stutter have a certain personality problem or are severely maladjusted, many display greater anxiety, oversensitivity, and shyness (Prins, 1972).

Investigations have been made of the attitudes of others toward speech-handicapped children. As a group, children with speech problems tend to be less well accepted by their peers than are children with normal speech (Woods & Carrow, 1959). However, in a study of the social status and perceived speaking competence of stuttering and nonstuttering boys in grades three

A number of studies have focused on the role of the parent in relation to a child's speech handicap. Parents of articulation-disordered children may be less well adjusted and have poorer attitudes toward child rearing than parents of normal-speaking children. In addition, the more adequate parental adjustment, the more likely the child will profit from speech therapy (Bryant, 1971). Parents of stutterers and nonstutterers do not seem to differ significantly in terms of adjustment, although parents of stutterers have been found to set more unrealistic goals for their children, show more concern for adequacy of speech, be overprotective and controlling, and often have feelings of rejection toward their children (Bloch & Goodstein, 1971; Yairi & Williams, 1971).

and six, it was found that stuttering boys do not expect to be and *in fact are not* rated differently from their normal-speaking age-mates on social position (Woods, 1974). They do, however, expect to be and actually are rated less favorably on speaking competence.

Speech clinicians' descriptive adjectives for adult male stutterers and elementary school-age boy stutterers were compared and many of the same adjectives were listed for both men and boys, indicating a fairly well-established stereotype for a stutterer, regardless of age (Woods & Williams, 1971). Most of these adjectives were judged as undesirable personality traits for males. Approximately 75 percent of the speech clinicians listed adjectives in the "nervous or fearful" category, and 64 percent listed adjectives related to "shy and insecure." It is interesting to note that only 31 percent of the clinicians listed adjectives that reflected "abnormalities in speech."

There may be significant differences in the social and emotional adjustments of children with communication disorders, depending on whether their problems are in speech or in language. Cantwell, Baker, and Mattison (1979) studied some one hundred children referred for speech and language problems. It is important to note that over 50 percent of these children had recognizable psychiatric disorders. These findings were confirmed in a subsequent study of some 600 children with speech and language problems. In addition, it has been found that a far higher incidence of psychiatric problems occurs in children with both speech and language disorders (58 percent) or with language disorders (73 percent) than in children who have only a speech disorder (38 percent). The possible interaction of language difficulties and emotional problems was also noted by these researchers, but the question of which is primary (i.e., do problems in language lead to problems in adjustment or vice versa) has not yet been answered.

The family life of the disadvantaged individual in the inner city has been described by Eisenberg as marked by a level of mutual aid and cooperativeness not typically found in the middle-class home (Eisenberg, 1963–64). He views lower-class children as enjoying each others' company more freely and fully than may be the case with self-oriented, middle-class children. In addition, there is a diffuseness in the family situation that, according to Eisenberg, lessens the occurrence of sibling rivalry or competition for mother's or father's love. Others have recognized this lessened rivalry and the lack of strain accompanying competition, in addition to an ease in separating from parents, as positive features of the lower-class home.

However, there may be a number of negative family conditions in the homes of lower-class children. Such children are less likely to have two parents with whom they can identify and from whom they can derive a sense of security (Crow, Murray, & Smythe, 1966). In teaching their children, lower-class mothers tend to use more negative criticism and coercive statements, whereas middle-class mothers give more praise and explanation (Hess & Shipman, 1968). In spite of the lower-class mother's good intentions, her teaching style may depress her child's motivation to engage in new tasks and therefore contribute to the child's slowness to learn in the classroom (Hess, 1970).

Eisenberg points out that the inner-city child may have collective rather than individualistic values (Eisenberg, 1963–64). The family may be oriented toward making advances through social group forces, not individual activity. This may be due to the feelings that "the odds are stacked against you" and "if we are going to get anywhere, all of us have to do it at one time." The home and neighborhood of the lower-class child are seen as maintaining a different reward system than that of the school (Goldberg, 1967). At home, physical prowess and physical aggression in the face of frustration may be rewarded, as may physical work done well. In school, most rewards are not related to the physical realm but to conceptualization, verbal response to frustration, and intellectual work done well.

These observations by Eisenberg and others essentially refer to lower-class status, rather than unique cultural influence. However, such influences may contribute to problems for the child who has to function in the larger society and the school. Compared with urban white children, rural Hispanic and urban Hispanic children tend to be less competitive, less rivalrous, less assertive, and more submissive and conforming (Kagan & Ender, 1975). There is some suggestion that this greater compliance is related to cultural factors, such as emphasis on obedience to parental authority, punishment of assertiveness, and inconsistent reinforcement. Degree of urbanization may also be a factor; regardless of ethnic group, urban children are more assertive than are rural youngsters (Kagan & Carlson, 1975).

In a long-term study of Hawaii's disadvantaged, the Hawaiian family was found to be an organized socialization system based on interdependence, shared work, and benevolent authoritarianism on the part of the parents (Gallimore, Boggs, & Jordan, 1974). As a consequence of these features, Hawaiian youth learn to approach their elders with respect, make requests in a subtle and indirect manner, and handle authority by group cooperation or by avoidance rather than by negotiation. Achievement is defined in terms of interdependence and increasing cooperative contributions to the family, rather than in terms of personal development and independence. Data compiled by the investigators indicate that these characteristics and values bring Hawaiian youth into conflict with the middle-class-oriented school and teacher. The conflicting culture-based behaviors and attitudes of Hawaiian pupils and teachers include achievement viewed as helping others versus personal accomplishments; working as a group versus doing individual work; and avoiding confrontation versus demanding direct negotiation. Other conflicts arise from the reluctance of Hawaiian students to ask for help and their view of verbal responding as "talking back" and showing disrespect for elders.

A similar culture conflict can be seen in the case of the American Indian. The values related to getting along with others that Pueblo Indian children bring to school may markedly contrast with the teacher's expectations. The traditional culture from which the children come supports anonymity and submissiveness rather than individuality and aggression. Many Indian children would rather follow traditional ways, maintain the status quo, and not engage in competition or any steady quest for success (Zintz, 1962). Erikson has written about the exasperation of white teachers working with Indian children in government schools when, at the start of a footrace, the runners hesitate and ask why they should run when it is already certain who is going to win (Erikson, 1963). For some American Indian students, to be singled out in praise is a source of shame; to look directly into the eyes of another may be an act of rudeness (Allen, 1973).

An economically disadvantaged background can interfere with the child's social and emotional well-being in the classroom. Socioeconomic status is at least partially responsible for friendship choices (Warden, 1968), and it has been found that both elementary and high school students tend to follow class lines in choosing friends (Neugarten, 1946). Among younger children, peer rejection appears linked to social class discrimination. In a review of studies on teacher ratings of pupil acceptability, it was concluded that school performance is a more consistent determiner of a favorable teacher rating than is social class; but it is also "highly probable" that lower-class poor achievers are viewed more negatively than are their middle-class counterparts (Goldberg, 1963).

Before closing this section on sociability and children who are economically disadvantaged and/or culturally different, we will briefly discuss problems that may arise in school achievement due to language and cultural differences. Some children come to school with little or no understanding of the English language, having been reared in a family in which another language

Figure 6–2.

Some behaviors considered normal and appropriate in the home can mark the disadvantaged child as "exceptional" in the classroom. The child's home and neighborhood environment may consider him or her anything but handicapped, different, or exceptional. However, a few blocks away is another environment called school. Here the child suddenly becomes a candidate for all sorts of labels and for placement into any number of categories, such as culturally deprived, socially maladjusted, or mentally retarded. In this environment, the disadvantaged child may get into serious problems with the teacher, fail to meet many of the school's expectations, and eventually be suspended or expelled.

Once back in the neighborhood environment, he or she ceases to be an exceptional individual in terms of school criteria.

Some children, particularly those from poverty areas, have been characterized as "six-hour retarded children." These children function within normal expectations at home and in the immediate neighborhood. Yet, when they walk through the classroom door to begin participation in a six-hour daily school program, they are viewed as mentally retarded. Once the school day is over, they leave their label of mentally retarded on the school premises and return to their home and neighborhood environment as normal children.

is constantly spoken. The Bilingual Education Act (BEA) was signed into law in 1968 and has provided funds for the development and implementation of bilingual educational programs. Bilingual education is instruction in *two* languages, with both the home language and English being used. The study of the history and culture associated with a child's home language is considered an important and integral part of such an education.

The goal of a bilingual program is to achieve a fifty-fifty time distribution with respect to usage of the two languages. This is easier at the nursery and kindergarten level than in later grades. Three typical approaches are: (1) split total time for a subject between the two languages; (2) allot some subjects to one language and some to the other; or (3) a combination of the first two, using one system for some subjects and one for other subjects. The teaching may be done by a single teacher proficient in both languages or a teacher and an aide, each of whom is very proficient in one language and teaches in that language. The advantage of the latter is that the language instruction is apt to be more authentic and lead to a better understanding of both cultures. In addition, such an arrangement may hold promise for a more interesting and varied program of learning activities.

Research has not established that children introduced to schooling bilingually go on to achieve academically and linguistically any better than do children introduced by means of their native language (Tucker, 1977). However, a study of Finnish students in Swedish-speaking schools found those who were proficient in their mother tongue enjoyed significantly greater success in subjects requiring conceptual thinking (e.g., biology, physics) than those who were not proficient—even though the subjects were taught in Swedish (Skutnabb-Kangas, Twokamaa, 1976).

Paulston (1977) suggests that the real value of bilingual instruction can be assessed best in terms of social adjustment, employment figures on leaving school, statistics on drug and alcohol abuse, suicide rates, and personality disorders rather than in terms of language and academic skills. For example, the general dropout rate for American Indian high school students in Chicago

Salisbury (1967) has presented a telling example of the dilemma that may face a young Eskimo child who speaks only his local dialect of Indian, Aleut, or Eskimo, or perhaps some halting English, and who is familiar only with his home culture when he is required by law to enter an English-speaking school.

He now enters a completely foreign setting—a Western classroom. His teacher is likely to be a Caucasian who knows little or nothing about his cultural background. He is taught to read the *Dick and Jane* series. Many things confuse him: Dick and Jane are two gussuck (Eskimo term for "white person," derived from the Russian Cossack) children who play together. Yet, he knows that boys and girls do not play together and do not share toys. They have a dog named Spot who comes indoors and does not work. They have a father who leaves for some mysterious place called "office" each day and never brings any food home with him. He drives a machine called an automobile on a hard-covered road called a street which has a policeman on each corner. These policemen always smile, wear funny clothing, and spend their time helping children across the street. Why do these children need this help? Dick and Jane's mother spends a lot of time in the kitchen cooking a strange food called "cookies" on a stove which has no flame in it, but the most bewildering part is yet to come. One day they drive out to the country, which is a place where Dick and Jane's grandparents are kept. They do not live with the family and they are so glad to see Dick and Jane that one is certain that they have been ostracized from the rest of the family for some terrible reason. The old people live on something called a "farm," which is a place where many strange animals are kept: a peculiar beast called a "cow," some odd-looking birds called "chickens," and a "horse," which looks like a deformed moose . . . (pp. 82–83).

So it is not surprising that 60 percent of the native youngsters never reach the eighth grade.

is 95 percent but in the city's bilingual-bicultural Little Big Horn High School the dropout rate is 11 percent.

Language and cultural differences are fortunately receiving much attention in the schools today. Hopefully, fewer and fewer children will be penalized because of their language and cultural backgrounds as bilingual and bicultural efforts continue.

Research on learning-disabled individuals suggests that parents, teachers, and peers alike often view them negatively (Bryan & Bryan, 1978). Parents have described their learning-disabled children as clinging but unable to receive affection, showing little control in both emotional and motoric expression, showing less consideration for others, and having trouble listening and expressing themselves. Teachers have been found to view learning-disabled children as behaviorally less desirable in the classroom than are nondisabled children. Results from teacher ratings of learning-disabled and control children suggest that teachers judge the former as less competent in following directions, comprehending class discussions, vocabulary, time concepts, and general coordination (Bryan & McGrady, 1972). They are rated lower on cooperation, paying attention, organizing themselves, coping with new situations, being socially acceptable, accepting responsibility, completing assignments, and being tactful. In one study, teachers were interviewed regarding their perceptions of learning-disabled and educable mentally retarded children (Keogh, Tchir, & Windeguth-Behn, 1974). Whereas the teachers tended to view retarded children primarily as educational problems, they viewed learning-disabled children as learning, behavioral, and personality problems.

When compared to nondisabled classmates of the same sex and race, learning-disabled children appear to be significantly less popular and more rejected by their peers, especially if the learning-disabled are both female and white (Bryan, 1974b). Peers of learning-disabled young-sters do not perceive them as hyperactive but do view them as worried and frightened, never having a good time, sad, not neat and clean, not very good looking, and as children to whom no one pays much attention (Bryan & Bryan, 1978). Recent research (Prillaman, 1980) has, in fact, suggested that learning-disabled children are most often social "isolates," that is, neither accepted nor rejected but simply ignored by the majority of their peers. There is some evidence that learning-disabled children are less able than their nonhandicapped peers to perceive subtle affective and nonverbal cues given by others (Bryan, Wheeler, Felcan, & Henek, 1976). This insensitivity may be one factor underlying their interpersonal difficulties with parents, teachers, and peers (Bryan & Bryan, 1975).

Observational analyses of classroom situations indicate that learning-disabled children's social life in the classroom differs from that of other children (Bryan, 1974a; Bryan & Wheeler, 1972; Forness & Esveldt, 1975). They receive less attention from the teacher during nonacademic activities and more negative and less positive teacher reinforcement than do their nondisabled counterparts. They also seem to be ignored more often when they attempt to initiate social interaction with the teacher or peers. Thus, learning-disabled children are likely to be rejected by or in conflict with parents, teachers, and peers.

Learning-disabled children's academic retardation may contribute to a lower self-concept. In a study on reading achievement and self-concept, learning-disabled children with reading retardation were found to view themselves more negatively than did similar learning-disabled children with normal reading achievement; the greater the underachievement, the poorer the self-concept (Black, 1974). There was also a significant decrease in self-concept as age and grade increased; older learning-disabled youngsters tended to view themselves more negatively than did similar younger children. These results have been viewed as supporting the hypothesis that learning and behavioral problems commonly associated with learning disabilities may function as both the cause of learning problems and as the result of frustration from repeated failure (Odom, Jenkins, Speltz, & Deklyen, 1982). As the child encounters more failure in school, his or her self-concept declines and frustration increases, hindering academic achievement and resulting in further failure. Because children's perception of their own adequacy is determined in part by the adequacy of their school performance, efforts should be made to remediate problems in self-concept as well as the learning problems.

The physical appearance of some mentally retarded individuals may serve as a cue to their retardation and lead to stigmatization, discrimination, and rejection (Aloia, 1975; Siperstein & Gottlieb, 1977). Abnormal features that lead to labeling a subject as retarded include eyes, teeth, facial expression, and hair style. In one study, cosmetic alterations were used to make retarded persons appear normal or less retarded without using medical, dental, or plastic surgical interventions (Shushan, 1974). Improvement in hair styling, wigs, eyeglass frames or sunglasses, necklines (change of collar or lapels), and facial expressions were found to reduce stigmatization. Normal, middle-class adults rated photographs of the subjects before and after cosmetic interventions. Cosmetic therapy significantly reduced noticeable deficits for both non-Down's syndrome and Down's syndrome subjects. Because social success is highly dependent on first impressions, which are often determined by physical attractiveness, cosmetic intervention for the mentally retarded may hold promise for increasing social acceptance. In addition, since satisfaction with one's body is strongly related to self-esteem, improved physical appearance and skill may contribute to the development of a more positive self-concept. For example, learning to ski has been found to positively effect the self-concept of severely retarded adolescents (Simpson & Meaney, 1979).

Most mildly retarded children may be relatively normal in appearance, and thus expected "to act their ages." Their mental ages, of course, may not match their appearance because they may have the cognitive capacity and social awareness of much younger children. Professionals who work with retarded persons for any length of time are quite adept at spotting immature behaviors, such as speech, gait or posture, and facial expressions, that characterize the retarded, whereas the general public can spot only some of these characteristics (Mulhern & Bullard, 1978).

The social conduct of retarded children has been shown to be closely related to their reasoning ability (Kahn, 1976; Stephens, 1974). A retarded adolescent may therefore exhibit behavior that appears at first to be antisocial, but that is often simply immature. Although the notion of "a child's mind in a grownup body" is simplistic and not always adequate to explain behavior, it should be kept in mind, particularly in relation to social situations. At the same time, we must not physically overprotect retarded persons. They should be allowed to dress appropriately for their chronological age (some parents dress retarded adults with clothing more appropriate for someone of their mental age), to take emotional and physical risks, and generally to lead as full and normal lives as possible.

In order to be effective in social interactions, an individual must be sensitive to the environmental requirements and responsive to appropriate ways of dealing with social demands. These are, of course, requisites for social competence for all of us; but there are a number of reasons that they become problematic for the retarded child. Because of maturational lag, the mentally retarded may be slower to incorporate values of right and wrong and to develop internal controls. As a result, they may frequently exhibit inappropriate or antisocial behavior. It has been shown that when the retarded child knows that someone is watching, his or her performance may improve (Zucker, 1978). An increased incidence of speech disorders often impedes retarded children's social interactions and may prevent them from obtaining reinforcement from others for their efforts in language.

Normal children's attitudes toward the retarded are even less favorable than are their attitudes toward other categories of exceptional children (Gottlieb & Gottlieb, 1977; Gottlieb & Switzky, 1982; Harasymiw & Horne, 1976; Jones, Gottfried, & Owens, 1966; Willey & McCandless, 1973). Retarded children are often rejected and ridiculed by their peers in school, which carries over into their neighborhood. For example, retarded children attending special classes were found to be as well known as other children on their block, but they were not played with as often (Meyerowitz, 1967). Even in experimental situations in which normal children were given opportunities to choose a partner for a game, retarded children were chosen significantly less often (Gottlieb & Davis, 1971). It is not clear how much this peer rejection depends on the retarded child's placement in special classes or in regular grades (Guskin, 1974, 1978; Guskin, Bartel, & MacMillan, 1975; MacMillan, Jones, & Aloia, 1974; Peterson, 1974). Retarded children in special classes may be seen by their peers as subject to a different standard of behavior and therefore treated with special consideration. On the other hand, retarded children in regular classes who are not formally labeled may not be excused as readily for low performance or immature behavior (Budoff & Siperstein, 1978, 1982; Siperstein, Budoff, & Bak, 1980).

What about the social and emotional adjustment of mentally retarded children? Do they exhibit more disturbances in getting along with others than normal children do? A study of 100 retarded individuals referred to a psychiatric clinic revealed that the symptoms of the retarded did not differ in kind from the referred nonretarded (Philips & Williams, 1975). No unique pattern of symptomology has been found (Russell & Forness, in press; Rutter, 1972). A higher incidence of emotional disturbances has been reported among the retarded than among the general population, especially among the more severely retarded (Russell & Tanguay, 1981; Szymanski & Tanguay, 1980; Wehman & McLaughlin, 1979). The retarded individual is subject to greater stresses, frustrations, and conflicts and consequently is more likely to develop behavioral disorders. Although there is some question that the retarded child inevitably develops a negative self-concept, it is clear that the stresses of daily living are greater for a person with fewer coping skills (Begab, Haywood & Garber, 1981; Lawrence & Winschel, 1973).

Retarded children—particularly the mildly retarded—tend to be overrepresented in lower socioeconomic classes and so have a great deal in common with disadvantaged children. This often means that they come from broken homes or homes in which parents, for a variety of reasons, are not always good adult models. The retarded child thus has fewer opportunities to learn social skills and modes of social interaction than the child whose parents are present and available. A personality structure peculiar to the socioculturally retarded child has been described as characterized by lower self-concept and higher manifest anxiety, particularly in school situations (Tymchuk, 1972).

Much has been written about the negative effects of placing retarded children in a regular classroom because of the possibility of rejection by other children. It has been suggested, however, that retarded children might actually prefer rejection in regular classes to segregation in a special class (Quay, 1963). There is some wisdom in this view, since the mildly retarded child in particular will be expected to live and compete in a world filled with normal peers. Indeed, on follow-up, retarded adults in the community continued to hold favorable views toward integration, even though they had quite accurate views of their own limitations (Gan, Tymchuk, & Nishihara, 1977). After being integrated into regular classes, or classes for nonretarded children, some mildly retarded children have been shown to behave more like their nonretarded peers than like retarded children left in special classes (Forness, Guthrie, & MacMillan, 1981; Gampel, Gottlieb, & Harrison, 1974). In one study, mildly retarded children in inner-city schools were rated *higher* than most of their nonretarded classmates on sociometric measure when integrated in regular classrooms (Bruininks, Rynders, & Gross, 1974). In another study, integration of severely retarded children into a high school setting did not adversely affect their self-concept (Nash & McQuisten, 1977).

Retarded children have been found to be extremely concerned about the effect special-class placement has on their friendships (Jones, 1972, 1974). One factor affecting a retarded child's placement in a special class may be whether or not he or she has been able to develop a friendship

Many behavioral patterns of the retarded stem from reactions by parents and siblings who may either tend to overprotect such children, thus preventing them from realizing their potential, or to reject them in subtle, often unconscious ways, thus lowering their feelings of self-worth (Cleveland & Miller, 1977; Farber, 1968; Farber, 1975; Wolfensberger, 1967). Likewise, it seems that the presence of a retarded child in the family affects the family as well. In one study, for example, mothers of handicapped children were actually observed as less happy, less relaxed, and less affectionate with their children compared to mothers of nonhandicapped children (Redner, 1980). Some families may have to remain at a level of growth and adaptation typical of families with very young children. Even though the retarded person grows older, the demands made on other family members continue to remain the same; and the family itself may not "develop" beyond a certain level. The family atmosphere can, however, have a marked influence on the outcome of a mentally retarded child's life. This is the case, for example, even with TMR children whose school performance is supposedly limited because their retardation is likely due to biomedical and not environmental factors. A study by Nihara, Mink, and Meyers (1981) demonstrated that several qualities in the home environment of TMR children were related to their eventual success in school settings. Even though severe mental retardation may be caused by capacity or biomedical factors, we continue to stress that range and nature of experience will always play a part in determining the eventual level of functioning.

with someone in the regular class (Mercer, 1971). From studies of residential settings, there is evidence that even profoundly retarded individuals are capable of developing rather intense friendships (MacAndrew & Edgerton, 1966; Landesman-Dwyer, Berkson, & Romer, 1979). The issue of peer relationships is a critical one since it has been shown that retarded children learn a great deal just by imitating nonretarded peers (Aloia, Beaver, & Pettus, 1978; Becker & Glidden, 1979; Hekkema & Freedman, 1978; Peck, Apolloni, Cooke, & Raver, 1978). Part of the problem of friendship for some retarded children may be their difficulty in "role-taking" or taking another person's perspective, and there has been new interest in developing role-taking skills among both retarded and nonretarded children (Blacher-Dixon & Simeonssen, 1978; Greenspan, 1979; Monson, Greenspan, & Simeonssen, 1979; Kitano & Chan, 1978). There has been speculation that the special class environment itself may affect friendship choices and how retarded children see themselves (Gresham, 1983; Morrison, 1981; Morrison, Forness, & MacMillan, 1983).

   The retarded child is further characterized by a motivation to interact with adults, a trait that actually depends more on past experience than on the fact of retardation. Research experiments on retarded children deprived of meaningful social contact, such as those in state hospitals or those from culturally deprived backgrounds, indicated that they were actually more interested in social contact with the adult experimenter than in the experimental task itself (Harter, 1967; Lustman & Zigler, 1982; Zigler, 1966; Zigler & Butterfield, 1968). In fact, the presence of an attending adult often decreased the child's performance on a task. Normal children, whose needs for social attention have usually been met, are free to complete the task at hand, but the same may not be true for retarded children. Whereas the normal child views such situations as an opportunity to solve a task or learn new information, the retarded child appears to use the task situation as an opportunity to meet needs for social attention and affection. Such personality differences may often lead the retarded child to see the classroom situation as social rather than cognitive, an important possibility for teachers to bear in mind (Balla & Zigler, 1979).

Retarded children have also been found to be outerdirected, to look to adults to interpret reality for them (Lawrence & Winschel, 1975). Their own judgment or cognitive ability naturally tends to be somewhat unreliable; therefore, they may look to others for answers rather than trust their own judgment. In one study, retarded and normal children made similar predictions about the outcome of an event; but when an adult experimenter made a counter suggestion, the retarded children changed their initial predictions more readily (Carlson & MacMillan, 1970). It has been shown that retarded persons are much more likely to answer yes to any question requiring a yes or no answer, primarily because of this tendency to acquiese (Sigelman, Budd, Spannel, & Schoenroch, 1981). Retarded persons may also defer to group pressure, even when they feel that their own perceptions are correct (Trippi, 1973; Zachofsky, Reardon, & O'Connor, 1973). Indeed, it has been shown that the amount of failure retarded children encounter may relate to whether they become outerdirected (Maguire, 1977).

Edgerton (1967) has described how many mildly retarded adults in the community tended to rely heavily on another adult in their lives for support and social adaptation. The adult "benefactor" was often a spouse, employer, or apartment manager. Very few of the retarded persons in Edgerton's study were in any way independent of their benefactor for assistance in their daily lives, although many became less dependent on their benefactors as time went on and as they gained more experience in fending for themselves (Edgerton & Bercovici, 1976).

This social motivation is complicated by the fact that retarded children are also wary of adults (Zigler, 1966; MacMillan, 1971). Their hesitancy arises from previous encounters in which adults may have reprimanded them or otherwise reacted unfavorably because of their failures or inadequacies. The paradox of wanting to interact and at the same time being hesitant to do so is one that can be overcome through initial acceptance and support. For example, one study showed that when an adult demonstrated acceptance of the child by first imitating the child's actions, severely retarded adolescents learned far more rapidly than under other conditions (Hallahan, Kauffman, Kneedler, Snell, & Richards, 1977). It has also been shown that the presence of a familiar adult leads to more vocalization and socialization among preschool retarded children than when the adult is absent (Berry & Marshall, 1978). Interestingly, it has also been found that the social conduct of some severely retarded persons is less influenced by adults around them than by notions of what a favorite television star might do in a given situation (Baran & Meyer, 1975).

Mentally retarded children appear to have particular problems in the area of speech, with a high percentage having disorders in articulation (Tarjan, Dingman, & Miller, 1960; Webb & Kinde, 1967). Speech disorders not only may impede children's social relationships but also may make it particularly difficult for them to make their needs known effectively. As might be expected, *delays* in language development also hamper the retarded child (Bricker & Bricker, 1977; Mahoney & Seeley, 1976). For example, it has been shown that when severely retarded children acted out simple sentences with toys, they could not seem to take active and passive verbs into account and always acted as if the first noun in the sentence was the actor (Dewart, 1979).

Influences on language development of the mentally retarded have been studied extensively, particularly in Down's syndrome children (Buckhalt, Rutherford, & Goldberg, 1978; Chesaldine & McConkey, 1979; Guttman & Rondal, 1979; Layton & Sharifi, 1978; Rohr & Burr, 1978), and it is clear that at least some of the language problems of retarded children are due to the interaction between their capacity and environmental experience. Retarded children with speech and language handicaps are likely to be less flexible in acquiring school skills (Campbell, Moffatt, & Brackett, 1978; Ross & Ross, 1979; Taylor, Thurlow, & Turnure, 1977) and in dealing with their social environments (Cooke, Cooke, & Appolloni, 1976) than are normal children, who can express a discomfort, pinpoint a dissatisfaction, or ask a question about something they do not understand.

Multihandicapping conditions can increase a child's social problems beyond those imposed by visual handicaps, hearing impairments, physical disabilities, or mental retardation. When a child possesses two or more of these handicaps, a marked deficiency in social development often results. Potential for effective social functioning decreases as the number of handicaps increases. In studies of mentally retarded individuals who had hearing *or* visual impairments, poor social relationships and generally maladaptive interpersonal behaviors, such as aggressiveness and antisocial tendencies, have been reported. One study compared a group of institutionalized retardates possessing both auditory *and* visual impairments with a matched control sample of retardates without sensory handicaps (Hutton, Talkington, & Altman, 1973). All subjects were rated by the ward staff on eighteen variables, including aggression, stereotyped behavior, disruption, running away, hyperactivity, and positive and negative peer and staff relationships. The major area in which multihandicapped subjects were rated significantly different from the control group was in interpersonal contacts and responsiveness to others. Multihandicapped subjects were described as significantly less responsive to staff or to peers, even when others initiated the contact. They were also markedly withdrawn.

Thus, multihandicapping conditions interfere greatly with the development of even basic social-response skills. A high priority in program planning for multihandicapped children should be efforts to develop responsiveness to others. It is interesting to note that some promising approaches toward developing socialization in profoundly or multihandicapped retarded persons seem to be derived from anthropological perspectives, which emphasize basic concepts such as territoriality and dominance hierarchies (Bailey, Tipton, & Taylor, 1977; Boe, 1977; Rago, 1977; Rago, Parker, & Cleland, 1978).

One of the several myths about gifted individuals pictures them sitting alone, far off from their peers, looking disdainfully through their horn-rimmed glasses at the other children's immature play antics, shrugging off taunts, and calmly reflecting on some aspect of Newtonian physics that they find far more satisfying than social interaction. This picture simply does not reflect what is known about the social behavior of gifted children. Their general social status among peers is high. The social popularity of high-IQ elementary school children in a midwestern town was investigated and it was found that they were chosen as friends far more often than were classmates falling in the average range of intelligence. (Gallagher, 1959). A positive relationship between IQ scores and popularity has also been shown in other studies (Miller, 1956; Grace & Booth, 1958).

Studies tend to provide evidence that the popularity of gifted individuals is not due to their high IQs. In addition, it has been found that the extent to which academic brilliance leads to social acceptance depends on such pertinent factors as athletic skill or amount of studiousness. The brilliant, studious student who is a nonathlete is less well accepted than is the gifted, socially

A moving example of a close, enduring social relationship between two severely retarded individuals has been provided by MacAndrew and Edgerton (1966) in a paper entitled, "On the Possibility of Friendship." Lennie and Ricky were in a large public institution for the retarded. Lennie was twenty-eight and Ricky thirty-three. Both men had IQs in the low to mid 30s and were multihandicapped; Ricky was blind and Lennie dutifully guided him throughout each day. In the morning, Lennie would describe the breakfast set before each of them in great detail and quickly slap the hand of any tablemate who tried to take advantage of Ricky's blindness by stealing some of his food. During the day, they sat on their "special" bench and talked endlessly about earlier experiences or events going on around them. Encroachers on the bench would be quickly dispatched as Ricky and Lennie would tip it over, set it right side up, and then sit down themselves. They often exchanged gifts including valentines they made for each other. These were kept under their pillows and were constantly shown off to staff members and fellow patients. Once Lennie went on a home visit and missed a barbeque held for the ward. Upon his return, he was presented with portions of everything served at the barbeque by Ricky who had saved them for him. The friendship of Lennie and Ricky had spanned ten years and prior to their meeting both had been described as withdrawn, suspicious, and fearful with no friends. Official ward notes repeatedly recorded "these two patients are inseparable" and as far as any staff member could recollect such an all-abiding friendship between two severely retarded individuals was unique in the institution.

outgoing athlete. On personality tests, gifted students were found to display more dominant, forceful, independent, and competitive types of behavior than average children (Gallagher, 1975).

Gifted individuals tend to be quite socially aware and sensitive (Strang, 1963). If academic achievement is not accorded prestige by their classmates, and if superior work on their part puts them in a visible, nonvalued position with other children, they may actually do poorer work in order to maintain acceptance. Also, Strang suggests that public praise by the teacher may actually decrease the learning efforts of gifted children, if they sense that it will be detrimental to their relations with classmates.

In terms of interest in play activities involving varying degrees of social participation and organization, the gifted individuals in the Terman study tended to prefer mildly social games, such as checkers and chess, that were less popular with average children because of the demands on intelligence. Also, since gifted children may be a year or two younger than their classmates, they may be at a disadvantage in strenuous competitive sports, such as football and basketball, and may not rate them as high among their social play interests. However, some gifted individuals mature earlier, develop well physically, and have better health, which would tend to reduce such a disadvantage.

The mental health of gifted individuals has been found consistently superior in relation to mental illness rates within the general population. Gallagher states that social and emotional problems can and do occur among gifted children (Gallagher, 1974). These problems stem from the same general sources as those found among disturbed children of average ability. However, since there is a tendency for the high-IQ child to come from a better family than the average-IQ child and to possess superior physical health, the probable occurrence of psychological problems is lessened.

The child with an IQ well over 155 may encounter serious social adjustment problems unique to his or her intellectual status. Terman and Oden found the highly gifted in their study to be poor social mixers and solitary children (Terman & Oden, 1947). The IQ range that is most adaptable in school is probably around 125 to 155 (Hollingworth, 1942). Within this range, enough peers with similar interests and abilities can be found to avoid intellectual isolation, and the gifted child is not so different that positions of leadership in various activities are denied him or her. Gifted individuals in this middle range often become social leaders.

According to Hollingworth (1942), who studied the child with an IQ above 180 (found about once in 1 million cases), such a child faces five general conduct problems. "He must find enough difficult and interesting work at school, suffer fools gladly, avoid becoming negativistic toward authority, avoid becoming hermitic, and avoid the formation of habits of extreme chicanery."

Compared to the home life of the average child, the family situation of the gifted child from an advantaged background is more intellectually stimulating. The family pattern is less autocratic, more reading occurs, and better books and magazines are available. Travel is undertaken more often, and overall the family demonstrates greater energy and stability. The cultural patterns of an advantaged family directly support education and achievement (Stouffer & Shea, 1959).

One type of gifted learner not included to any great degree in the Terman study is the culturally different gifted child. Recently, there has been increasing concern with identifying and planning for the talented child whose cultural background is far removed from that of the typical white, middle-class child. In evaluating the characteristics of gifted children from differing socioeconomic backgrounds, it was found that high socioeconomic status gifted learners spent more time reading during recreational hours and the lower status gifted were more interested in action and competitive team sports (Frierson, 1965). No major differences were found with respect to physical characteristics or personality. Gifted children from lower-class homes experience more family tension and tend to perform substantially lower than their predicted achievement levels (Karnes, Zehrback, Studley, & Wright, 1965).

The ethnic groups with the highest incidence of giftedness place a great emphasis on intellectual values and provide many opportunities for the development of skills and talents already present in the child. In general, it is not unusual to find gifted learners among black children (Gallagher, 1975). High-ability girls outnumber high-ability boys among blacks, whereas gifted boys outnumber gifted girls in the general population. Gallagher thinks that more gifted black girls are identified than boys because of differences in opportunities within the subculture for realizing intellectual potential. The National Achievement Scholarship Program for Negroes began with secondary schools nominating outstanding black students for competition for college scholarship funds. Sixty-two percent were girls. A follow-up of the more than 4,000 students revealed that all but 1 percent of the males and 3 percent of the females were functioning well at the completion of their freshman year.

It has become commonplace to equate the socially and economically disadvantaged child with weaknesses in verbal and semantic skills. However, Torrance points out strengths that often appear in much greater incidence among disadvantaged children as compared with the general population (Torrance, 1969). Originality, creative productivity in small groups, visual art adeptness, creativity in movement, dance, and other physical activities, high motivation for games, music, sports, and humor, and a language rich in imagery are some of the talents and interests distinguishing culturally different and disadvantaged children.

In the past, the portrait of the gifted child was that of a middle-class child from a successful and well-established family that mirrored the majority cultural values of the community. With the discovery of many children from different cultural backgrounds who have unique talents, we now face the necessity of altering the content, style, and environment of the school to take advantage of and to develop the special abilities of these children.

The Exceptional Learner and the Family

The anticipation an expectant mother and father share from the moment pregnancy is confirmed to the moment they see the newborn infant is often intense and filled with expectations of the child's physical beauty, potential, and future accomplishments. The father who arrives at the delivery room with a baseball bat and mitt, or who notifies his alma mater of a pending admission seventeen years hence, represents a somewhat amusing but most telling example of this anticipation.

If the much-anticipated child has a defect at birth or acquires a handicap during childhood or adolescence, these expectations are cruelly shattered and the parents are forced to deal with a reality for which they were not prepared. Ross has described the rewards of parenthood: establishing womanhood and manhood for the wife and husband, adding fulfillment to a marriage, and looking forward to events ranging from the child's first word or first birthday party to his or her later marriage and presentation of a first grandchild (Ross, 1975). Such potential rewards become uncertain, limited, or totally impossible when the child is in some way defective or deficient. In addition, the milestones of the child's life become difficult to chart since reference to normal children's development may have little relevance or meaning. Instead of a happy future with a successful son or daughter in adult life, the parents must often face the prospect of the child's total dependence on them throughout their lives and on some other caretaker after they die. Parenthood always involves some conflict and anxiety, but with a handicapped child all the normal adjustment demands are accentuated.

Sooner or later the parents of a handicapped child ask themselves, Why? Why did this happen to us? What did we do to deserve this? What really caused our child to be defective? This search for a plausible explanation is greatly complicated because actual causes for a number of handicapping conditions are unknown or are still being debated. Without a clear-cut medical explanation for the child's problem, the parents may imagine all sorts of reasons that they had a defective child.

A study was done with the parents of twenty infants who had been born with a variety of congenital malformations and ranged from one week to five years of age (Drotar, Baskiewicz, Irvin, Kennell, & Klaus, 1975). Interviews with these parents revealed reactions and feelings that have been found to be fairly typical of parents who must deal with the reality of a handicapped child. The first response of most of the parents was one of shock and disruption. This gradually gave way to denial or disbelief and a wish not to have to deal with the situation. Sadness occurred next, accompanied by an intense anxiety and a fear that the infant might die. In addition, many of the parents felt angry—angry at themselves, the infant, or the doctor or other members of the hospital staff. Gradually, most of the parents began to adapt to the situation. They displayed greater confidence in their abilities to be successful care-givers, effectively reorganized their family lives, and began to experience some measure of rewarding interaction with their babies.

Research studies vary with respect to the degree of disruption the birth of a handicapped child has on family life. Interviews with more than 400 rural Alabama families, each with a child with cerebral palsy, revealed that the majority felt the handicapped child had no serious adverse effect on the family (Dunlap & Hollinsworth, 1977). However, demands on time, money problems, physical demands, and discipline problems were cited as difficulties that were encountered. Barsch (1968) studied families with blind, deaf, Down's syndrome, cerebral palsied, or brain-injured children and found most to be well adjusted and similar in child-rearing practices among social class groups. As a result, Barsch rejects the stigmatization of parents of the handicapped as guilt-laden, anxious, overprotective, and rejecting. Other studies with parents of blind and deaf children have reported similar results (Jan, Freeman, & Scott, 1977; Freeman, Malkin, & Hastings, 1975).

However, the birth of a child who is mentally retarded or who manifests hyperactivity or behavior disorders early in life may have an adverse effect on the family. In a study comparing the personality traits and attitudes of mothers of mentally retarded children with mothers of chronically ill and mothers of healthy children, the mothers of the retarded appeared more depressed, enjoyed their children less, were more preoccupied with them, and had more difficulty handling their anger than did the others (Cummings, Bayley, & Rie, 1966). A related study (Cummings, 1976) compared fathers of children with the same handicaps and found those with retarded children were also more depressed and preoccupied with their children than were the other fathers. Studies of the divorce rate for families of the physically handicapped (Martin, 1975) and the sensory handicapped reveal no differences in relation to the general population. Approximately equal numbers of parents of blind and parents of deaf children report their marriages have either been strained or improved as a result of the birth of a blind or deaf child, with the majority citing a neutral effect (Jan, Freeman, & Scott, 1977).

Despite the gloomy picture regarding the effect of a retarded child on the family, some investigators have found very good adjustment in such families, including high cohesiveness (O'Connor & Stachowiak, 1971) and favorable attitudes toward the retarded family member by both parents and siblings (Schonell & Watts, 1956). Therefore, any generalization regarding the effects of a retarded or otherwise handicapped child on the parents' marriage is impossible. The effects will result from many factors, and it has been found that when divorce occurs the reason for it may have existed before the birth of the handicapped child (Walker, Tomas, & Russell, 1971).

Hyperactive children may cause feelings of frustration, anger, helplessness, or withdrawal on the part of their parents (Caplan, 1976). The child's apparent inability to control undesirable behavior even when punished, along with continual negative behavioral reports from the school and others, may place the marriage in jeopardy. However, studies of the disruptiveness of behavior-disordered children who were not necessarily hyperactive have not yielded isolated family patterns reliably different from normal groups (Jacob, 1975).

The specific effects of handicapped children on siblings has only partially been studied. One of the authors recalls an undergraduate student, whose identical twin had cerebral palsy, relating the rejection and insecurity she experienced growing up and the intense anger she felt because everything the family did revolved around the needs and desires of her sister. In a research study of thirty pairs of twins in which one member had cerebral palsy, very similar feelings and reactions were found among the nonhandicapped twins (Shere, 1956). In general, only a few siblings of blind or deaf children appear to be negatively affected (Freeman, Malkin, & Hastings, 1975). However, among the problems that do occur are not being able to express openly rivalry with a deaf or blind sibling and being forced to assume an unusually mature and understanding attitude at an early age (Jan, Freeman, & Scott, 1977). Older female siblings of deaf children are given significantly more child care and other home responsibilities and may enjoy fewer social activities than do their peers (Schwirian, 1976). The older female siblings of retarded children have been found to have behavior disorders and to exhibit tension, whereas male siblings who are not expected to share the burden of caring for a retarded brother or sister do not (Grossman, 1972).

The effects of gifted children on their families have not been systematically studied, but a number of clinical impressions have been described (Ginsberg & Harrison, 1977). The gifted child's continual questioning and constant chatter may frustrate parents and make them feel inadequate. Nongifted siblings are also apt to view themselves as inferior. Parents have been found to be better predictors of whether or not their children are gifted than are teachers (Ciha, Harris, Hoffman, & Potter, 1974). This may bring them into conflict with the school over the adequacy of the child's educational program.

Whereas most families of exceptional learners may not be severely disrupted and most parents may display a resilience after the initial shock and grief wears off, some do need help in learning to cope with their handicapped children. The most traditional method of aiding parents is individual or group therapy. Unfortunately, this approach may lead the parents to perceive themselves as the source of the problem and pay little attention to the role the child plays in family interactions (Stanhope & Bell, 1981). Parent education may be attempted by referring books, films, magazine articles, and training manuals or holding classes in which professionals discuss ways to increase parent effectiveness. Having parents observe others working with their children can be useful as can training the parents to work with the child in a clinic setting. Training programs can also be carried out in the home as parents observe and learn from trainers how to relate to, teach, manage, and motivate their children.

One project at a summer camp for retarded children aimed at training their older brothers and sisters as therapists (Weinrott, 1974). During a nine-week period, the siblings learned techniques of behavior management and practiced them with their retarded brothers and sisters; two months later, parents reported much improved sibling relationships.

What effect does an exceptional learner have on the family? There is no question that additional stress and pressure are brought to bear, particularly in the initial stages of learning to understand and relate to the child. Once this occurs, we cannot make any general statement regarding inevitable consequences. What we can do is respect the myriad of interactional factors that are involved as parents attempt to cope with each other and their handicapped and nonhandicapped children who, in turn, must cope with each other and their parents. Add the interactional effects of relatives, neighbors, friends, professionals, and societal attitudes and expectations and we may be surprised at the generally positive adjustment of families of exceptional learners.

Summary

In our summary of social characteristics, we further unify exceptional learners by discussing them collectively under the headings of communicating effectively with others, seeking social interactions, and establishing harmonious relationships with others.

Communicating Effectively With Others

When visually impaired individuals enter a room full of people, they may readily hear all that is being said but have difficulty responding to comments addressed to them if they are not spoken to by name. Hearing-impaired individuals relying on residual hearing or amplification may readily ascertain who is speaking to them but have to attend to all sounds, thus making it difficult to communicate with more than one person or a small group. If oral speech is limited, and others cannot communicate in signs, there will be a need for an interpreter. If lipreading is relied on, the speaker must be positioned so that lip movement can be easily perceived.

Speech difficulties cut across all categories of exceptional learners. The individual whose speech is immature, who exhibits an articulation disorder, or who stutters may experience continual frustration attempting to be understood accurately by others. Mentally retarded learners display a high percentage of articulation problems as well as delays in language development. Language delays or disorders also are prevalent among the learning disabled who may, in addition, fail to pay attention to what is being said to them. Some disadvantaged individuals may profit more from what is shown to them than from what is spoken. Because of their speech and language problems, retarded learners may be limited in readily expressing discomfort or pinpointing a dissatisfaction. They may also have difficulty formulating questions when they do not understand.

Such difficulty in formulating questions and verbal responding is not limited to the retarded. Individuals from varying cultural backgrounds may also display this difficulty, but for different reasons. Verbal responding may be viewed as "talking back" among some Hawaiian youth. Asking questions in a direct manner may constitute showing disrespect. Among some American Indians, direct eye contact may be considered rude. For some severely emotionally disturbed learners, noncommunication may be strictly elective; for others, confusion in language usage may create serious problems.

Effective communication involves more than the ability to produce speech. It involves accurate perception and understanding of the speech and language of others and a motivation to communicate with them. Again, capacity and range and nature of experience combine to explain differences in communication effectiveness among exceptional learners.

Seeking Social Interactions

Visually impaired learners may find their efforts to interact with others thwarted by the anxiety of the nonhandicapped, much of it related to their ignorance of visual impairment. The age of onset of deafness is a determiner as to whether hearing-impaired learners seek interaction with hearing individuals or largely with other hearing-impaired friends. The earlier the onset and to some degree the more severe the hearing loss, the more deaf individuals may seek each other's company. However, deaf adults do report an equal number of hearing-impaired and nonimpaired friends.

Individuals with highly visible physical handicaps may come to view themselves negatively and avoid social interaction. However, with the increased mobility of the ortho-pedically impaired, increased opportunities for interaction are occurring, which hopefully will reduce such negative self-perceptions. Increased enlightenment regarding the nature of such chronic health problems as epilepsy has also led to more social opportunities for the exceptional.

Disturbed children may seek social interactions but demand to dominate and bully others. Some may fear competition, failure, and rejection and avoid social contacts, and others may find the world of fantasy more fulfilling. Autistic children often seem unaware of those around them as well as disinterested in relating to them. Speech handicaps may also cause individuals to limit their involvement in social situations.

Social class lines are major determiners of friendship among elementary and secondary students, which may be particularly limiting for disadvantaged individuals. Although the child with a learning disability may seek attention from and involvement with others, studies reveal many such children are simply ignored. The mentally retarded child is often highly motivated to interact with and to please adults. However, this may create a dependence on the judgement of others and a willingness to alter a belief or expectation to coincide with someone else's perception. Retarded individuals living independently or semi-independent-ly in the community very often require the support of a benefactor, a nonretarded individual (e.g., apartment manager) to whom they can turn for guidance. Gifted individuals are highly social and enjoy high status in their social relationships.

Whether or not exceptional learners seek social interaction is partly determined by how they perceive their worth and status and how they believe others perceive them (and, in fact, how they are perceived by others). Such worth and status in both the exceptional learner's estimation and the estimation of others will reflect the interaction of capacity and range and nature of experience.

Establishing Harmonious Relationships With Others

One of the most important skills for developing harmonious relationships with others is to be able to put ourselves in someone else's shoes and see things from their perspective, not just our own (to *role take*). Role-taking skills may be difficult for some exceptional learners to acquire. For example, problems in understanding language may lead to a degree of self-centeredness in the hearing impaired and difficulty in understanding the emotions and feelings of others. Disturbed individuals are often also preoccupied with themselves and insensitive to others reactions or needs, as are the learning disabled who are often isolated.

Because of their immaturity, the retarded may be slow to incorporate values of right and wrong and to appreciate how their behavior is perceived by others and how others feel. This may be particularly true of the severely retarded.

Both physical and behavioral problems may distance exceptional learners from the nonexceptional. The physical appearance of some retarded individuals may cause them to stand out, sometimes in an unnecessary manner. It has been found that when the retarded dress in an age-appropriate manner, are well groomed, and take advantage of such aids as cosmetics, hair styling, wigs, and dark glasses, they are far less noticeable in social situations. Overall, the visually impaired do not evidence more behavioral or psychological problems, although the partially seeing may encounter adjustment problems dealing with both the sighted and nonsighted worlds. The hearing impaired may be socially immature and evidence more behavioral disturbances than do the blind. Chronically ill children have been found to manifest behavior problems such as aggression, regression, and withdrawal that interfere with positive relationships. Poor social relationships are often high on the list of the disturbed child's difficulties as the result of bullying, atypical interests, and insensitivity. Individuals with learning disabilities are often unpopular and may be viewed by their peers as fearful, detached, and unattractive. Disadvantaged learners may display "six-hour" behavior and learning problems because the conflicts they experience are school-based and are put behind them when school is over. Children with speech and language problems have been found to display disturbed behavior, particularly if they have both types of problems. Large numbers of retarded learners, particularly the more severe cases, have negative behavioral characteristics.

With most exceptional learners, the better others know them the more favorable the attitudes others display. This is particularly true of the visually impaired; the uneasiness some feel in the company of a blind individual will be lessened through knowledge of blindness and social experiences. The physical visibility of some orthopedic handicaps may cause exceptional learners to be teased and criticized, but as others get to know them, particularly their strengths and mutual interests, this may no longer occur. Even very severely retarded individuals form close relationships, but the retarded probably are perceived more unfavorably than other exceptional learners by the nonexceptional. This has a bearing on the acceptance mildly retarded children receive in regular classrooms. But even with some ridicule and rejection, retarded learners have shown an increase in appropriate behaviors by modeling on the nonretarded, something they have limited opportunities for in special classes.

In our discussion of exceptional learners and their families, a high percentage of harmonious family relationships was noted.

The range and nature of social experience may be the most critical factor in determining the eventual functioning level of exceptional learners. Despite obvious physical handicaps, those exceptional learners who are helped to communicate, to participate readily in social situations, and to learn the give and take of interpersonal relationships will develop more positive self-concepts and achieve much more happiness and success.

CHAPTER 7

Intellectual Characteristics of Exceptional Learners

Intelligence essentially refers to the unique characteristics of learning efficiency, problem-solving capacity, and language facility made possible by the relatively greater size and complexity of the human brain. Children profit from experience, attach labels to events and objects, learn to read, master number concepts, recall information in test situations, and develop extensive vocabularies. Some children demonstrate more intelligence than others; they "catch on" more quickly, generalize from one experience to another more efficiently, plan for the future more adequately, and develop academic skills more rapidly and extensively. In this chapter, we discuss intelligence testing and the intellectual characteristics of each group of exceptional learners. The chapter concludes with a discussion of infant testing and early intervention programs to enhance intellectual functioning.

Intelligence Testing

Before we discuss the intellectual functioning of exceptional learners, we must ask these questions: What is intelligence? and How is it measured? From the simple operational definition that intelligence is what an intelligence test measures, much has been theorized about the nature of intellectual ability. One of the earliest attempts to define and measure intelligence systematically was made in the 1880s by Francis Galton, a cousin of Charles Darwin. According to Galton, sensory-motor functioning was a valid measure of intellectual ability. His tests included tasks to measure sensory acuity and reaction time, and such things as counting the number of taps a person could make in thirty seconds. But the tests clearly failed to predict academic performance, and it was not until the work of Alfred Binet and Theodore Simon that a successful test for making such a prediction was developed (Achenbach, 1974).

In 1904, the French minister of public instruction assigned Binet and Simon the task of devising objective procedures for determining which children were incapable of profiting from regular instruction and needed special class placement. Thus, the whole notion of IQ testing had

Figure 7-1.

its genesis in the field of special education, a problem we discuss later. Binet and Simon were pragmatists concerned with developing a reliable and valid measure of a child's current functioning level, not a theory regarding intelligence and whether or not it was a fixed ability. They assumed that judgement and reasoning were the basic processes of higher intellectual functioning. They also wanted their test to distinguish between children whose intelligence was below normal for their ages and those whose poor school functioning was due to experiential determiners, such as a disadvantaged background, school absences, poor motivation, distractibility, and emotional instability.

Broader, more encompassing definitions of intelligence began to appear in the 1940s (Burton, 1967). Typical of these was Wechsler's definition:

> Intelligence, operationally defined, is the aggregate or general capacity of the individual to act purposefully, to think rationally, and to deal effectively with his environment. (Wechsler, 1958)

Jensen (1969, 1980) has admitted that intelligence is easier to measure than define; and Eysenck (1973) has suggested that, although we may think of intelligence as something that really exists "out there," it is nothing more than a concept existing in the minds of scientists that enables them to make generalizations and predictions about events. Other psychologists, such as Spearman (1927), Cronbach (1960), and Guilford (1967), have also attempted to define intelligence; but, only a general consensus exists, which includes such themes as capacity to learn, acquired knowledge, and adaptation to new situations.

In determining what behaviors are considered intelligent, the culture and society in which the individual lives become extremely important. An intelligence test is based on extensive sampling. First, a sample of the behaviors deemed intelligent by the society is selected (e.g., problem solving, abstract thinking) by the test constructor or psychologist. Next, a sample of possible test items is selected that will measure an individual's level of functioning in relation to these critical behaviors; for example, How many apples are two apples and six apples? or How are a cat and a dog alike? Once these items have been assembled in a test, complex sampling is undertaken; that is, the test is given to a large, representative group of individuals for whom the test is intended in order to standardize it and establish norms.

Binet and Simon assembled tasks or items for their test that they believed would measure a child's intellectual capacity and could be effectively and economically administered, such as short-term memory for digits, defining abstract words, finding missing parts from familiar figures, and the like. They then moved to the third stage and selected a large number of children from the school-age population as a standardization group. These collaborators were well aware of the potential relationship between test performance and socioeconomic status. They selected children from lower-class neighborhoods in establishing norms for their test in order not to penalize poor children by comparing them to standards based on more privileged children's performances (Achenbach, 1974). This practice was not followed in the later American translation and standardization of the test by Lewis Terman at Stanford University. Much of the controversy over the use of intelligence tests with the economically disadvantaged and/or culturally different might never have occurred if such children had made up the standardization group in the American translation.

After giving the test to this sample of children, Binet and Simon found that the ability to succeed on each task varied among children at each age level and between children at various levels. From this, they derived the notion of mental age (MA), which reflected the average score or level of intellectual functioning on Binet's test for a child of a given chronological age (CA). The intelligence quotient (IQ)—or the relationship between chronological age and mental age—was later conceived by Terman in his adaptation of the Binet test for American children.

In practice, the IQ signifies the relationship between a child's mental age and chronological age. Thus, an eight-year-old who scores as well on the test as the eight-year-olds in the standardization sample is assigned an IQ of 100. Another eight-year-old, whose score is identical to that of the average six-year-old in the sample, is given an IQ of 75.

Although there are statistical differences in calculating IQs on the two most widely used individual tests—the Revised Stanford-Binet Intelligence Scale (Terman & Merrill, 1973) and the Wechsler Intelligence Scale for Children-Revised (Wechsler, 1974)—the basic concept of relating MA to CA is similar. Administration methods for each test are somewhat different. In the WISC-R, the examiner presents items from ten or twelve areas of intellectual functioning to each child until the level in each area exceeds the child's capacity. Not only is a full-scale IQ obtained, but IQs also can be derived in both verbal and performance scales, for comparison purposes. In the Stanford-Binet, the examiner presents six items at each age level until the child can no longer do all six at any given age level. The Stanford-Binet IQ generally seems to be loaded more heavily with verbal or conceptual items, especially at older ages.

There is another sampling stage involved in obtaining an IQ score by means of an intelligence test, which is in addition to selecting a definition of intelligence, selecting specific test items, and selecting a sample of children to establish the test norms. When Binet and Simon actually gave the test to a child, they were sampling that child's intellectual functioning level on a given *day* at a given *time* in a given test *situation*. It is at this stage that caution and controversy enter into the practice of IQ testing.

The economically disadvantaged and/or culturally different child has perhaps suffered most from the practice of IQ testing, for several reasons (Bailey & Harbin, 1980). It should be pointed out, however, that other types of exceptional learners are also penalized. One reason is that IQ tests focus most often on language skills. Even though disadvantaged children may have the ability to answer questions on intelligence tests correctly, they may fail to do so because they have not been exposed to the material. When asked, "What is a gown?" such children may shake their heads because they have never heard the word before. When shown a picture of a window and asked to point to the "sill," a disadvantaged child may respond in a similar manner for the same reason. The question, "How are a baseball and an orange alike?" may be puzzling to a child who knows the color orange but has never seen or tasted the fruit. Similar experiential deficits can cause other exceptional learners to fail on test items.

In addition to range and nature of experience differences found among exceptional learners as compared with normal children, there are capacity differences (other than intellectual) that may interfere with a child's functioning level on an intelligence test. The child with a crippling condition or poor hand-eye coordination may recognize how a puzzle or manipulative task should be done but fail because he or she lacks the motor skills to perform it; or, such a child may be able

Figure 7-2.

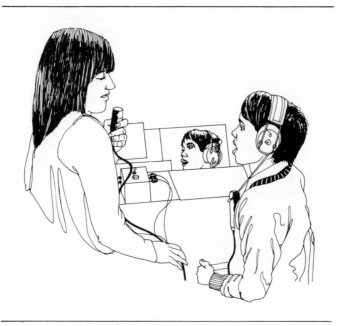

to succeed on the task if given enough time but still fail because the task is not completed within the time allotted. Thus, an intelligence test that samples a range and nature of experience unfamiliar to exceptional learners and requires capacity-based skills that are not intellectual and that such children may lack does not provide accurate information about their actual intelligence (Sattler, 1974; Sternberg & Detterman, 1979). A new intelligence test, the K-ABC, may avoid some problems just discussed because it includes children in special classes in its standardization and relies less on experience or language items (Kaufman & Kaufman, 1983).

Problems with Test Administration

The actual administration of the test to a given child, in a given place, with a given examiner also has cast doubts on the validity of the IQ scores of some exceptional learners. For example, a minority child or even an emotionally disturbed child may know the answer to a question but may automatically respond, "I don't know," in order to terminate the unpleasantness of performing in a strange and demanding situation as quickly as possible. This resistance may also be heightened by negative events in the child's recent experience, such as a fight on the school bus, lack of sleep, or an empty stomach. Fear, suspicion, or anger toward the adult authority figure giving the test can also take its toll, as can low motivation, anxiety, slower speed, and lack of experience in test taking (Oakland, 1980).

In addition, when a white, middle-class examiner tests a black, disadvantaged child, the examiner's enunciation may be unclear to the child, who in turn may use words incomprehensible to the examiner; words and phrases used by black, disadvantaged children may have special meanings, although superficially they appear awkward or incorrect. Experimental studies on using reinforcement in the test situation have also challenged the reliability and validity of intelligence tests. In one study, two groups of children took the same IQ test form under standard conditions (Edlund, 1972). A second form of the same test was also given to both groups, but one group was given immediate food rewards for correct responses. The rewarded children showed a mean gain of over thirteen points; the standard condition children gained one point. In another study, a group of mentally retarded adults were deceived into believing that the intelligence test results might be used either to better or worsen their future placement (Braginsky & Braginsky, 1971). This raised or lowered their scores accordingly by significant margins.

The issue that arises with respect to the intellectual assessment of both normal and exceptional learners centers around the constancy of the IQ score. Does intelligence as measured by the IQ test change over time? According to both Hunt (1961) and Bloom (1964), the notion of fixed intelligence can no longer be supported. Early experience has a crucial effect on cognitive development. The problem of assigning a fixed IQ score to a child may stem from the widely held assumption that intelligence and IQ are synonymous with innate ability. They are not. From our review of the importance of experience in determining how much knowledge and skill a child actually possesses and his or her functioning level in the test situation, we can respect the possible difference between an IQ score and basic intellectual capacity. In a group of middle-class children who were followed over a ten-year period, many were consistent in their IQ test performance and resultant scores; but some showed a steady, continuous increase, and some showed just the reverse (Sontag, Baker, & Nelson, 1958). Thus, intelligence as measured by an IQ test can and does change.

It should be readily apparent that IQ tests are fallible and that our misuse and misinterpretation of the tests in the past has done a disservice to many children. In the 1950s, one of the authors tested a fifteen-year-old boy who had been given an IQ test in the third grade, found to have an IQ of 70, and placed in a class for the mentally retarded where he remained for seven years with no retesting. The boy obtained an IQ of 115 on the test the author administered. He was not mentally retarded—far from it. He actually was above average in intelligence. The tragedy here was that in many respects he really was mentally retarded. He felt he was retarded; he expected others to consider him retarded; and he seldom tried very hard because he doubted his ability. He acted retarded because he had modeled children who were retarded and had been given school work for nearly seven years that was commensurate with teachers' expectations for retarded children.

The other author was involved in the early 1970s in retesting some half dozen children who had been placed in special classes in a small school district in California. Apparently, they had been placed in these classes because regular classroom teachers could not cope with their learning problems. Parents of these children contended that they had been placed in these classes on the basis of a single IQ score and because they all came from the "other" side of town. Some were minority children, but others were from poor white families. Their IQ scores were found to be mainly in the normal range. Their parents ultimately sued the school district in a class action law suit and won damages for the effects of the children's long-term placement in classes for the retarded.

Much evidence exists that many students have been misdiagnosed as mildly retarded and misplaced in classes for the retarded, and that such misdiagnosis and misplacement have resulted from overreliance on the IQ score in the decision-making process (Garrison & Hammill, 1971; Mercer, 1971; Rubin, Krus, & Balow, 1973). When used as a single criterion for diagnosis and placement, serious errors have occurred (Martin, 1980; Smith & Knoff, 1981).

Mercer (1973), for example, found an overrepresentation of minority individuals labeled as retardates in the public schools of a southern California community she studied intensively. Although whites made up over 80 percent of the population of the community, only 37 percent of those identified as retarded were white. But Hispanics, who comprised about 10 percent of the population, made up 45 percent of those labeled retarded in the schools. The population estimate for blacks was about 7 percent, but among those considered retarded in the schools, 16 percent were black. In another study surveying the composition of classes for the retarded in a large metropolitan school district, blacks made up 27 percent of the total school population but constituted 53 percent of the students in classes for the mildly retarded (Rivers, Henderson, Jones, Ladner, & Williams, 1975).

There is also evidence that professionals concerned with identifying, assessing, and placing the mildly retarded have moved away from a primary reliance on IQ scores (Ashurst & Meyers, 1973; Hannaford, Simon, & Ellis, 1975; Meyers, Sundstrom, & Yoshida, 1974). Psychologists and educators are beginning to view the student's actual functioning level as more important, and a number of children are no longer being placed in special classes who once might have been. Alternatives to evaluating exceptional children's levels and potential, such as task analysis and criterion-referenced tests, are also being used (Howell, Kaplan, & O'Connell, 1979; Newland, 1980; Sabatino & Miller, 1979; Wallace & Larsen, 1978). The observation and assessment of a child's actual *approach* to test items or classroom situations is becoming increasingly important (Forness, Guthrie, & Hall, 1976; Feurerstein, Miller, Rand, & Jensen, 1981; Hendrix, 1981; Miller & Davis, 1981; Poplin & Gray, 1980; Reid & Hresko, 1980). Finally, Mercer and Lewis (1975) have developed a System of Multicultural Pluralistic Assessment (SOMPA) that incorporates standard IQ tests and interview data, with both ethnic and other cultural norms, into a comprehensive index of a minority child's potential.

In 1979 in San Francisco, in what has become known as the "Larry P." case, a federal judge banned the use of IQ tests throughout the state of California for the purpose of deciding if minority children are mentally retarded. In 1980, however, a federal judge in the U.S. District Court in Chicago upheld their use for the same purpose, claiming that there was no clear-cut evidence that the tests were directly responsible for misassignment of black children to special education in Chicago's city schools. According to MacMillan and Meyers (1980) and Lambert (1981), the overrepresentation of minority children in special classes will not be substantially affected by either banning or upholding the use of IQ tests. They contend that the real villain is school failure on the part of the student, which necessitates withdrawal from the regular education program and placement in a special education class. It is likely that the IQ test controversy will continue for some time. Bearing the limitations in mind, let us now consider the intellectual functioning of exceptional learners.

Visually handicapped individuals do not differ markedly from children with normal vision in terms of intelligence. We are, of course, referring to children whose visual impairment is not accompanied by mental retardation or other major disabilities. The Stanford-Binet Intelligence Test adaptation for the blind, the Hayes-Binet test, was administered in the 1930s to nearly 2,400 pupils in seventeen residential schools for the blind. The mean IQ obtained was 98.8 (Hayes, 1941). Among the schools, the mean IQ ranged from 92 to 108.

Subsequent studies using the Hayes-Binet or the verbal portion of the Wechsler Intelligence Scale for Children have reported similar findings (Hayes, 1952). Children who are born blind or who suffer visual impairment during childhood years do not seem to differ in intellectual functioning from those who become blind at a later age. There also seems to be no correlation between general intelligence and the age at which sight was lost, and no difference between the two groups in functioning in various school subject areas. Even though there may be qualitative differences in the type of intellectual potential of those born blind compared with others who suffer blindness later in their lives, their mental functioning—as measured by standardized tests—does not reveal a difference (Lowenfeld, 1973).

The visually handicapped seem to be more limited than sighted individuals in learning abstract concepts. There is some indication that blind children retain experiences or facts and are able to conceptualize, but do both in a more concrete and less integrated fashion than do sighted children (Lowenfeld, 1980). It has also been reported that seeing children show significantly higher imagination in play, spontaneous fantasy, and dreams, whereas the visually handicapped demonstrate more concreteness and lack of flexibility (Singer & Steiner, 1966).

In terms of overall cognitive development, it has been hypothesized that visually handicapped individuals do not have a decreased ability to process information but do have limitations imposed by the sensory data available for such processing. In cases where sensory data are

An interesting finding emerges when we consider the mean IQs of partially seeing children. A group of 131 such children was evaluated according to severity of defect (Bateman, 1963). Those with a mild defect had a mean IQ of 95; those with a moderate defect, a mean IQ of 101; and those with a severe defect, a mean IQ of 106. Those results are in agreement with earlier findings that IQ scores *decrease* as degree of vision *increases* among visually

handicapped children selected for special education services (Hayes, 1941). This is possibly related to the confusing experience of being able to use some vision in learning, rather than relying on a totally compensatory approach as do the blind. It may also have something to do with the finding presented in the last chapter that partially seeing individuals are more apt to have emotional problems than are the blind.

---

seriously limited due to the nature and range of experience, visually handicapped children might fall behind sighted children in cognitive development (Bateman, 1967). The discovery of conservation—the idea that an object that changes in appearance can still be the same quantity (e.g., a cup of colored water in a test tube looks different from the same amount of water in a dish)—is thought to underlie acquisition of abstract quantity and number concepts. Findings of one study indicate that blind and sighted children achieve conservation at about the same age, suggesting that blind children are not deficient in the thinking processes important to learning conservation (Cromer, 1973). Later in this chapter, we discuss a program for blind infants that illustrates the importance of physical movement and manipulation in the cognitive development of the visually handicapped (Fraiberg, 1971).

In discussing intelligence in relation to hearing-handicapped individuals, we must first consider their problems in language development. Intelligence has been defined as the ability to carry on abstract thinking, and abstract thinking assumes the presence of language symbols. Language symbols are learned relatively easily by hearing children from birth, as they continually listen to people talk about objects, events, and feelings at the moment those experiences happen. The child with a hearing impairment cannot begin to listen and learn like this until his or her problem is detected and some measure initiated to compensate for it. In many cases, the deaf do not come in contact with language until age three or four, the point when most hearing children have mastered the skill (Davis & Silberman, 1978; Moores, 1978). This delayed start, plus the fact that no other sense or combination of senses can truly substitute for hearing, puts the child at a serious disadvantage in acquiring language. As a language-handicapped child grows and matures, a number of questions arise regarding his or her intelligence.

Among the questions regarding intelligence and deafness are the following: (1) Does a serious language handicap prevent the development of abstract intelligence? (2) Does abstract intelligence always rely on language or other symbols? (3) Does a lack of hearing preclude the development of a symbolic structure, which is considered the basis of abstract intelligence? (Levine, 1956). The ultimate answers to these questions are yet to be provided (Russell, Quigley, & Power, 1976), but it does not appear that restricted language development due to deafness has a generalized effect on intellectual functioning (Avery, 1967; Sanders, 1980). Rather, deafness appears to have a qualitative effect in such areas as memory and conceptualization (Myklebust, 1963, 1964). For example, it is difficult for deaf children to perform on test items measuring "same" and "different" because these terms are abstractions themselves (Pronovost et al., 1976).

Use of the Stanford-Binet Intelligence Test with deaf children has been questioned because of its language emphasis. Nonlanguage or performance tests, such as the Porteus Maze (Porteus, 1965), the Grace Arthur Performance Test (Arthur, 1947), the Goodenough Draw-A-Man Test (Goodenough & Harris, 1963), the Ontario School Ability Test (Amoss, 1936), and the Pintner-Patterson Non-Language Group Test (Pintner, Eisenson, & Stanton, 1945) have all been recommended. It has been found that the average IQ of deaf children on such tests approached 90, as compared to 100 for hearing individuals. This is also the case with the *performance* (as opposed to the verbal) IQ on the WISC-R (Brooks & Riggs, 1980; Hirshoren, Kavale, Hurley, & Hunt, 1977).

With regard to intelligence testing with deaf and partially hearing children, several basic considerations have emerged from research: (1) intelligence scores obtained at the preschool or early school level are more likely to be inaccurate for deaf than for hearing children; (2) a low IQ estimate is more apt to be wrong than a high IQ estimate; (3) there is a greater probability that psychologists who have not had experience working with deaf and hard-of-hearing children will commit testing errors; (4) tests with rigid time limits are probably less valid than tests that do not

Figure 7–3.

In a review of fifty years of research on the intelligence of the deaf and hard-of-hearing, it has been reported that no major relationship appears to exist between type of deafness and IQ, degree of hearing loss and IQ, or age of onset of deafness and IQ (Vernon, 1968). There also seems to be very little difference in intelligence between children taught orally and those taught by a combined method of spoken word and finger spelling. For partially hearing students, verbal intelligence measures reveal slightly but significantly lower scores as compared with hearing individuals. Nonlanguage tests show little, if any, difference between the two groups. (Wooden, 1963).

impose such limits; and (5) administration of group tests to deaf and hard-of-hearing children is a questionable procedure (Sachs, 1977; Vernon & Brown, 1964). Testing of deaf students often shows IQs well below the 90s; but when an interdisciplinary team examines a pupil's true potential, very few have been shown to be in this range (Pronovost et al., 1976).

Research on deaf individuals seems to suggest that deaf children do not differ significantly from hearing children in their thinking processes (Furth & Youniss, 1971). This conclusion provides strong support for Piaget's theory that language is not a basic element of logical thinking (Inhelder & Piaget, 1964). In more recent studies of deaf children and adolescents, additional evidence is provided that although such individuals may be unable to speak and communicate freely, they develop intellectually much like their hearing counterparts (Youniss, 1974; Altshuler, 1974). If trained to amplify residual hearing with hearing aids, the deaf can gain valuable speech understanding that assists their development in this area (Winthrow, 1981).

The effect of hearing handicaps on school learning, however, becomes dramatically apparent in the area of academic achievement. On the average, deaf children are at least three to four years below grade level; partially hearing children are from one-half to two years behind (McConnell, 1973; Trybus & Karchmer, 1977). Trybus and Karchmer (1977) found that half the students in special schools and classes for the deaf read below the mid-fourth-grade level. Only 10 percent of the eighteen-year-olds read at eighth-grade level or above. More than one fourth of all mainstreamed pupils in a recent survey could not be integrated into *any* academic subject (Libbey & Pronovost, 1980).

A nationwide testing program for hearing-impaired students revealed that, in general, the *multihandicapped* have even greater problems in academic achievement (Jensema, 1975). Most had at least one additional "educationally significant" handicap besides hearing impairment. As one might expect, mental retardation is the primary additional handicap. Mentally retarded, hearing-impaired children fell 1.3, 3.0, and 1.8 grade equivalents below the total hearing-impaired group on reading, spelling, and arithmetic, respectively. Those with visual, emotional, brain damage, cerebral palsy, learning disability, or orthopedic additional handicaps also had mean grade equivalents below those of the total hearing-impaired group. Only those who had cleft lip/palate as an additional handicap had mean grade equivalent scores *above* the total group in all areas. Assessments of deaf-blind children likewise indicate severe limitations in intellectual functioning, especially in the area of language (Bennett, Hughes, & Hughes, 1979; Diebold, Curtis, & DuBose, 1978). These findings suggest that education of children with multiple handicaps presents a challenge to educators that cannot be met unless the unique influence of each specific handicap is considered (Dollar & Brooks, 1980; Flathouse, 1979; Jensema, 1975; Pronovost et al. 1976).

Efforts to determine intellectual levels of orthopedically or other health-impaired individuals must consider capacity to participate in the testing situation as well as previous experience. Stephen and Hawks (1974) estimate that some 40 to 60 percent of the cerebral palsied may function in the mentally retarded range, but this may not be an entirely accurate picture. Children with cerebral palsy of the spastic type were carefully matched with normal controls in order to compare scores on verbal and performance items of the Stanford-Binet Intelligence Scale (Luszki, 1966). It was found that cerebral-palsied children did not differ in verbal ability but were inferior on performance items requiring visual-motor coordination. The best estimate seems to be, however, that anywhere from a third to a half of cerebral-palsied children may be in the mentally retarded range of intelligence (Lewandowski & Cruickshank, 1980). Excluding children with cerebral palsy, the measured intelligence of children in classes for the crippled in New York City was found to be similar to that of the general school population (Wrightstone, Justman, & Moskowitz, 1954). However, children with muscle weakness and other physical problems seem to be rated slightly lower by their teachers in academic achievement (Guerin, 1979). One must keep in mind that intellectually the crippled and chronically ill represent a very heterogeneous group of children (Lewandowski & Cruickshank, 1980; Newman, 1980).

Frequent absences, lack of stamina, and general discouragement accompanying other health impairments can have negative consequences on school achievement. Data from two independent epidemiological surveys on chronic illness and its consequences suggest that the achievement of chronically ill children is significantly lower than that of healthy children (Pless & Roghmann, 1971). There is some indication that the greater the severity of the condition, the greater the extent of underachievement, even after age and IQ have been taken into account.

In general, intelligence test scores are lower among emotionally disturbed children than among children without behavior disorders (Bower, 1960; DeMyer, Barton, & Norton, 1972). "Well-behaved" boys were found to score significantly higher than those with "behavioral problems" on the Verbal, Performance, and Full Scale IQ measures of the Wechsler Intelligence Scale for Children (Woody, 1968). Low intelligence was found to be predictive of poor educational outcome in socially maladjusted adolescents who were first identified in grade school (Feldhusen, Roeser, & Thurston, 1977). Another study, however, found that "problem" and "nonproblem" children had essentially the same mean scores on the Stanford-Binet (Vane, Weitzman, & Applebaum, 1966).

Because definitions of behavior disorders vary so markedly, it is difficult to make any conclusive statements about behavioral disturbance and intelligence. A review of studies on behavior-disordered children's performance on intelligence tests (Woody, 1969) suggests that few definitive diagnostic patterns (e.g., verbal versus nonverbal strengths and weaknesses) can be found. Gajar (1980) examined both learning-disabled and behavior-disordered children, however, and discovered that although both groups had WISC-R IQs in the low 90s, children with

Children afflicted with seizure disorders display a wide range of intelligence, from low borderline to high superiority, but their average level corresponds to the normal population (Lennox & Lennox, 1960). When the Wechsler Intelligence Scale for Children was administered to more than one hundred epileptic children, the mean IQ obtained was 99 (Bagley, 1970). Distribution of intelligence levels, however, was significantly skewed from normal, with a larger number of children falling into lower IQ ranges and a smaller number achieving higher levels. Since a teacher's questionnaire

relating to emotional adjustment of these children suggested that 40 percent had serious psychiatric problems, this unevenness of functioning may be explained on an experiential rather than a capacity basis. A review of studies of epileptic children show that lower IQs may sometimes be associated with age of onset and frequency of seizures but that deterioration of IQ over time is not always predictable (Von Isser, 1977). Likewise, it is not always clear that different types of seizures result in differing levels of intellectual functioning (Richardson, Koller, Katz, & McLaren, 1981).

learning disorders generally had a more uneven or "scattered" profile of abilities. It has also been shown that rewards and positive feedback do increase the performance of disturbed children on an IQ test (Jackson, Farley, Zimet, & Gottman, 1979). Recent interest has also focused on cognitive styles of children with behavior disorders and on how they process information and approach problem-solving situations (Knoblock, 1980).

Research related to the academic progress of disturbed children reveals consistent evidence that they do not perform in line with their intelligence (Forness, Bennett & Tose, 1983; Forness & Dvorak, 1982; Gajar, 1980; Woody, 1964, 1968). Bower (1960) found that children with behavior disorders functioned significantly below other children in their classrooms in reading and arithmetic. Differences were greater in arithmetic than in reading and increased in the higher grades. Whether behavior problems cause academic failure or vice versa, a vicious cycle can occur with any type of exceptional learner. School consultation programs for disturbed children are therefore frequently based on the assumption that intellectual limitations may lead to reduced ability to resolve conflict and hence to behavior problems (Berkovitz, 1980; Cowen, 1980).

With regard to language, autistic and psychotic children frequently manifest speech abnormalities, such as failure to develop speech, immediate or delayed echolalia (echoing or repeating back verbatim what someone says), or impaired communicative function (Baltaxe & Simmons, 1975; Simmons & Baltaxe, 1975). Some, however, do evidence adequate or normal speech development. Whereas mutism or echolalia in psychotic children can be relatively common, adequate or normal speech development is found in only a few cases. A psychotic individual's speech is generally characterized by low developmental level, lack of questions and informative statements, few personal pronouns, greater use of imperatives, limitations in verbal output, and more frequent idiosyncratic use of words (Baltaxe, 1977; Baltaxe & Simmons, 1980). These individuals often show little comprehension of speech, rarely use gestures to reinforce their speech, and display deviations in articulation, pitch, stress, rhythm, and inflection. Psychotic children's language difficulties have been variously attributed to a delay in normal development, disturbances in interpersonal relationships, and inadequate maternal speech models.

Psychotic or autistic children are often extremely difficult to test on standardized psychological tests because of their lack of cooperation or lack of attention to test materials. Some have attempted to portray these children as possessing innate intelligence that simply is not demonstrated during testing (Prior & Chen, 1975); but research review leads to the conclusion "that psychotic children who test retarded, for all practical purposes, are retarded" (Baker, 1979, p. 347). Psychotic children frequently have severe deficits in intellectual and perceptual areas; and the lower the child's IQ, the poorer the prognosis becomes (DeMyer et al., 1973; Hingtgen & Bryson, 1972). A large majority of psychotic children score at extremely low levels on intelligence tests, with few achieving an IQ above 90 (DeMyer et al., 1974; Forness, 1974; Goldberg & Soper, 1963). However, higher levels of functioning and large variations in scores have also been observed, with psychotic children frequently displaying extreme variability among subtests and autistic children performing higher on visual-motor than on verbal comprehension tasks.

Speech-handicapped individuals do not perform as well as non-speech-handicapped children on intelligence tests (Bloom & Lahey, 1978; Eisenson, 1980; Everhart, 1953; Hoffnung, 1981). This is not surprising since language proficiency is positively related to measured intelligence level. As discussed in chapter 5, many mentally retarded children have defective speech; however, we are *not* speaking of children whose primary problem is mental retardation when we discuss the intelligence of children with speech defects (Bricker & Bricker, 1977; Mahoney & Seeley, 1976).

Although not unanimous, research findings do suggest a relationship between speech and reading problems (Eisenson & Ogilvie, 1977). It has been found that as problems of articulation increase, reading skills decrease among first graders (Weaver, Furbee, & Everhart, 1960). In addition to the possibility, discussed in chapters 3 and 4, that both reading and speech problems have a common cause, such as neurological lesion of the language centers in the brain (Dalby, 1979), speech defects can contribute to reading problems. Because children with speech defects make errors in pronunciation or have poor rate and rhythm in their oral reading, they may not comprehend or interpret correctly what they have read. The anxiety and concern generated by a speech defect may also cause the child to avoid all forms of oral expression. These problems of children with speech and language disorders may thus be caused by a variety of factors other than low intelligence (Eisenson, 1980).

Disadvantaged individuals appear at first glance to function at lower intellectual levels, and we discussed in chapter 4 the overlap between poverty and mental retardation. Cronbach (1960) found the mean IQ of lower-class children in urban and rural areas to be 90, whereas middle-class children in these areas had a mean IQ of 115. In reviewing studies comparing IQ scores obtained by blacks and whites, it has been found that blacks tend to score from 12 to 15 points below the average for the white population (Jensen, 1980; Shuey, 1966). However, in this chapter and in chapter 4, we discussed the inequity of giving intelligence tests to children whose range and nature of previous experience may be markedly different from children with whom the tests were standardized. Therefore, when given such tests, economically disadvantaged and/or culturally different children do more poorly than nondisadvantaged ones. Simply making the test situation more familiar for a disadvantaged child can markedly increase his or her IQ (Zigler, Abelson, & Seitz, 1973). Factors related to the early prevention of conditions associated with low intelligence in this group are discussed later in this chapter.

Individuals with learning disabilities typically range from low average to average on individual intelligence tests (Benton, 1978; Vellutino, 1979). The discrepancy between their normal intelligence and their academic achievement, as measured by standardized achievement tests, thus becomes the benchmark of learning disabilities. As mentioned in chapter 4, approximately two years difference between a child's actual achievement level and the level of expected achievement, based on a child's age, IQ, and school experience, is considered necessary to diagnose a learning disability in most cases (except for very young children).

The difficulty with this concept of discrepancy is that IQ tests frequently measure some of the skills on which learning-disabled children by definition do not perform well, thus leading to considerable controversy about intellectual criteria used to define learning disabilities (Blank, 1978; Coles, 1978; Harber, 1980; Vellutino, 1978). Another problem has been that the standard margin for error on both IQ and reading tests may be large enough, in some cases, so that a significant *discrepancy* between achievement and intelligence does not exist, even though the obtained scores seem to indicate a difference (Elliott, 1981; Forness, Sinclair & Guthrie, 1983; Hoffman, 1980; McLeod, 1979; Shepard, 1980). Another problem is related to achievement tests themselves since it has been shown that up to two years difference can occur in a child's achievement scores, depending on which test was used to measure that child's reading (Jenkins & Pany, 1978). As a matter of fact, one study found that nearly two-fifths of the children placed in classes for the learning disabled actually did not meet the criterion of normal intellectual ability and thus did not belong there (Smith, Coleman, Dokecki, & Davis, 1977a). Wide variation in IQs is also found when learning-disabled children are retested after assignment to special classes (Martin, 1979). Rutter (1978) and Coles (1978) have both made the point that we may not be doing a very good job of distinguishing a learning-disabled child, who is bright enough but not performing well, from a slow-learning child, who is in the low-normal range of intelligence and doing poorly but still in line with his potential.

Another issue in the intellectual functioning of learning-disabled children is that of profiles of specific intellectual abilities. A great deal of effort and research seems to have gone into determining whether a typical or characteristic intellectual profile of a learning-disabled child actually exists (Keogh & Hall, 1974; Smith, Coleman, Dokecki, & Davis, 1977b; Stevenson, 1980; Swerdlik & Wilson, 1979; Vance & Singer, 1979; Vance, Wallbrown, & Blaha, 1978). The conclusions seem to be that a learning-disabled child's performance IQ on the WISC-R, which is derived from subtests on visual and motor proficiency, will likely be higher than his or her verbal IQ. This is not difficult to understand when one considers that such subtests as vocabulary, arithmetic, and other language-dependent skills comprise the verbal IQ on this intelligence test and are thus likely to reflect reading ability or school learning. Also, there does tend to be a profile of scores on specific verbal and performance subtests that is *sometimes* characteristic of learning-disabled children and that includes items measuring attention or memory factors. This is not always the case, however, nor is it clear that this profile of specific subtest scores always distinguishes learning-disabled children from other exceptional learners or even from nonhandi-capped children (Ackerman, Peters, & Dykman, 1971; Kavale & Forness, in press). There is the possibility that the more severely learning disabled a child is the more likely a characteristic profile of intellectual functioning will emerge (Blaha & Vance, 1979), or that means of testing intelligence other than the highly favored WISC-R might demonstrate such patterns (Hill, 1980).

Subtle impairments in linguistic functioning were mentioned in chapter 4 as a possible factor associated with learning disabilities, and it is becoming clear that undetected problems in both language and information processing may be characteristic of a large number of learning-disabled children (Hessler & Kitchen, 1980; Kirk & Kirk, 1971; Morrison, Giordani, & Nagy, 1977; Senf, 1976; Vellutino, 1979). The overlap between linguistic impairment and learning disabilities may in turn lead to problems in correctly identifying economically disadvantaged or culturally different children as learning disabled (Kavale, 1980; Tucker, 1980). The point has also been made that even a mentally retarded child can be diagnosed as learning disabled if his or her performance lags significantly behind his or her mental age (Cruickshank & Paul, 1980).

There continues, then, to be considerable concern about the diagnosis of learning disabilities because of the overlap between measures used to assess learning-disabled children's intellectual or academic functioning (Adelman, 1979; Ysseldyke & Algozzine, 1979). Considerable variability also exists in research criteria used to identify samples of learning-disabled students for study (Keogh, Major, Reid, Gandara, & Omori, 1978). This is perhaps why the learning disabled have been found in one study in Illinois to be the most frequently tested group of exceptional learners (Mardell-Czudnowski, 1980).

The mentally retarded individual has been described as "not able to keep pace intellectually in a world that places ever greater stress on intellectual accomplishments" (Robinson & Robinson, 1976, p. 540). The dimension of intelligence is perhaps the most crucial one in considering the traditional concept of mental retardation. Although in many respects the retarded child can be considered as functioning like a normal child at a younger age level, this view has unfortunately determined much of what is "special" about special education—that is, assigning retarded children essentially the same material in the same manner as normal children, but in lesser amounts and at a slower rate of learning (Baumeister, 1967). However, the research findings discussed here suggest something different. Mild or severe mental retardation is not necessarily a global, general disability; it may sometimes be task-specific, or related only to certain aspects of the learning situation. There is a tendency to think of mental retardation as a lack of *intelligent* behavior and to ascribe less intelligent behavior to a lack of *intelligence*. Intelligence, however, is not necessarily an all-encompassing, general commodity. It appears to depend on a host of variables that determine whether or not intelligent behavior is elicited from a retarded child.

For example, comparison of the rate at which learning progresses in both retarded and normal children suggests that the differences in learning to discriminate between two or more objects occur mainly in the early stages of a task or in learning how to learn (Ellis, Deacon, Harris, Poor, Angers Diorio Watkins, Boyd & Cavalier, 1982; Zeaman & House, 1963). Retarded children take longer at this stage, but once they have learned the relevant cues or characteristics of the task and overcome their tendency to attend to extraneous cues, they may learn almost as quickly as normal children. Retarded persons have been shown to require a longer inspection time before choosing correctly (Nettelbeck & Lally, 1979). Much of such children's attention to incorrect cues may be a function of attending to cues that were correct in previous tasks but are irrelevant to the present task (Fisher & Zeaman, 1973), or possibly limited ability to attend to several cues at once (Zeaman & House, 1979).

Such an attention theory suggests ways that discrimination tasks can be organized so that retarded children attend more effectively: (1) using an easy-to-hard sequence by initially reducing the number of significant cues that need to be attended to; (2) increasing the saliency of some cues by emphasizing colors, sizes, or shapes, particularly those the retarded child seems to prefer; (3) reinforcing attention to certain cues; and (4) having the child "label" objects before choosing. It has also been shown that having the child pick up and manipulate the objects to be chosen also improves performance (Richman, Adams, Nida, & Richman, 1978). Somewhat related to this area of research is the area of incidental learning (Denny, 1964, 1966; Mercer & Snell, 1977) in which it has been shown that retarded children are not able to apply all the skills learned in one situation as readily to new situations, where less important skills learned in one task now become a primary focus in a new task. It is interesting to note that many of the suggestions for improving performance in this area also apply to attending behavior and task structure, including the use of feedback on correct responses, insuring success in the early stages of learning, and teaching the same responses in a variety of contexts.

Retarded children may learn some types of tasks more easily than others. They tend to do better in associative tasks (learning pairs of items and then naming one item when shown its partner) than in learning a series of items (Baumeister, 1967). Some studies using such paired-associate tasks show the retarded performing at lower levels than much younger normal children of their mental age; others show no difference, even when retarded children are compared with their own age mates (Jensen, 1970). In serial-learning tasks (identifying which item comes next in a series of items), retarded children may not perform as well as normals but they have been shown to perform quite similarly to learning-disabled children (Swanson, 1977).

Retarded children have also been found to have serious deficiencies in regulating and organizing their behavior through language (Spitz, 1966, 1973, 1979). In many instances, providing retarded children with some form of verbal mediation or input organization has improved their learning. For example, reminding them to label certain cues before choosing, or giving them a word or phrase that associates a pair of items, has been found to enhance learning. Classroom lessons designed to give retarded children a verbal description of their actions have also been shown to improve their performance markedly (Bender, 1977). Elaboration of temporal or physical relationships through a phrase or sentence is not something that retarded children do spontaneously (Taylor & Turnure, 1979; Turnure & Thurlow, 1975). An examination of the development of thought processes in retarded children may provide clues to certain areas of their learning (Butterfield & Belmont, 1977; Klein & Safford, 1977). A longitudinal study of Piagetian reasoning, for example, confirms that formal operations—the ability to solve problems without recourse to concrete materials—may be lacking in mildly retarded persons (Stephens, 1974); reasoning abilities of retarded children are now being evaluated much more carefully (Bricker, Macke, & Levin, 1981; Goldstein & Goldstein, 1980; Woodward, 1979). Certain

Another area is motivation. Although it is impossible to review even briefly the extensive literature in this area, one example should illustrate its impact. A simple Piagetian task was presented to very young, normal children (Mehler & Bever, 1967). The task was composed of two rows of pellets, the shorter row containing the larger number of pellets. On being asked which row had "more," most children picked the longer row, since children at that age tend to be distracted by such extraneous considerations as length of the row. The experiment was then repeated with two rows of candies of a similar size and shape as the pellets. Not surprisingly, most children proceeded to pick the correct row. Although cognitive dimensions of the tasks were essentially the same, the results were quite dissimilar under a different motivational set. Children, therefore, appeared "retarded" under the first condition but not under the second. Such an experiment has rather grave implications not only for teaching but for intelligence testing as well, although there are many factors involved (Hunt, 1975). Other factors related to social motivation and its effect on learning in the mentally retarded were discussed in the last chapter and are just as critical here. Use of social reinforcement is an especially critical factor in retarded children's learning (Forness & MacMillan, 1972; MacMillan, 1971; Rotter, 1975).

prerequisites to this level of cognitive development, such as the ability to classify and reorganize items by certain criteria, may also be seriously deficient. It is clear that such a skill is quite complex and may depend, in part, on the phrasing of questions to elicit the correct response from retarded youngsters (Carlson & Michaelson, 1973) or on the mode of presentation (Litrownik, Franzini, Livingston, & Harvey, 1978).

Once the retarded child has learned a task, he or she is likely to remember it as readily as normal children over long periods of time, particularly if the task has been "overlearned" (Belmont, 1966; Butterfield & Belmont, 1977). When meaningful and familiar learning materials are used, the retarded can recall about as well as normals after intervals of one week and one month (Eisman, 1958). However, they often evidence difficulties in *short-term* memory (repeating back or using information within seconds after hearing it) (Ellis, 1963). Retarded children are at a disadvantage since they may not process information as quickly as normal children. Nor can they spontaneously use the rehearsal strategies that normals do, such as grouping information into clusters and silently repeating it for easier recall (Ellis, 1970). Training in which the retarded child is given specific practice in rehearsal techniques significantly improves memory ability (Glidden, 1979; Turnbull, 1974). It has also been demonstrated that memory variables are one of the most important predictors of reading in the mildly retarded (Blackman, Bilsky, Burger, & Mor, 1976; Das & Cummins, 1978) and are also related to adaptive behavior of severely retarded persons (Latham, 1978). Recent research has also focused on how little retarded children seem to know about their own memory strategies and how seldom they seem to use this information (Belmont, Ferretti & Mitchell, 1982; Borkowski & Cavanaugh, 1979; Campione & Brown, 1977; Eyde & Altman, 1978; Friedman, Krupski, Dawson, & Rosenberg, 1977). Systematic programs to help retarded children be aware of and learn to use a variety of "instrumental" learning strategies are meeting with considerable success (Borkowski & Konarski, 1981; Feurerstein, Rand, Hoffman, & Miller, 1980).

Figure 7–4.

It is difficult to generalize about the intelligence of retarded children because many of the subjects for such studies are institutionalized. Any comparison with normal children who may have had a wider range of experience, success in previous learning, and supportive environments tends to put even the noninstitutionalized retarded at a disadvantage. Because of their past experiences, many retarded children expect to fail a task even before they begin, which obviously affects their performance (Chan & Keogh, 1974; Gruen, Ottinger, & Ollendick, 1974; MacMillan & Keogh, 1971). Numerous other variables determine how a retarded child will use what "intelligence" he or she has (Bortner & Birch, 1970; MacMillan, 1971; Mercer & Snell, 1977; Zigler, 1966).

It is generally accepted that intelligence in children whose mental retardation is a clear symptom of some underlying organic pathology is generally less amenable to change through motivational or situational variables. These children tend to be different in the sense that their lowered performance is more likely the result of a limited neurological capacity. Biomedical research, however, has yet to demonstrate cause-and-effect relationships, except in a very generalized fashion. It is clear that there is wide variability in intelligence even among specific biomedical types of mentally retarded children (such as Down's syndrome children) (Connolly, 1978; Demaine & Silverstein, 1978; LaVeck & Brehm, 1978), and experience and training continue to account for much of this variability (Baumeister & MacLean, 1979; Throne, 1977).

Profound retardation produces obvious limitations on an individual's ability to learn and function independently. As we move up the dimension, we find that moderate and mild retardation are less a global disability and more task-specific, or related to certain aspects of the learning situation.

But there is a further issue relative to the mildly retarded, generally referred to as the *developmental versus difference* issue (Kamhi, 1981; Schoenbaum & Zinober, 1977; Zigler, 1969). Developmental theorists hold that the retarded child passes through essentially the same cognitive levels of development, but at a later age than normal. The difference between a retarded child and a normal child is not markedly dissimilar from the difference between a normal and a gifted child. It is a matter of the level each has attained. When matched with younger, nonretarded children of the same mental age but normal IQ, the retarded child will perform essentially the same on cognitive tasks, all other things being equal.

The difference theorists, on the other hand (Ellis, 1969), posit low IQ as something more than an indication of a retarded child's stage of mental development. They suggest further that it must be a measure of neurological integrity, rate-of-information processing, or some other measure of cognitive functioning. The central cognitive processes are said therefore to be somewhat different than those of a younger child of the same mental age, and these differences are viewed as relatively independent of the child's background or experience.

Both views have validity and exemplify the capacity versus experience relationship that, to an extent, characterizes all exceptional children. The developmental view is perhaps more consistent with the orientation of this text; it allows for more consideration of motivational and situational variables when dealing with the concept of mental retardation, and this is particularly critical in special education. The response of the child to teaching may actually be a more effective way of measuring his or her true potential (Budoff & Gottlieb, 1976; Hamilton & Budoff, 1974). Recent statements regarding research on the learning of the mentally retarded seem to suggest that retarded children be studied in more natural learning situations so that findings can be applied more readily to their education and treatment (Belmont & Butterfield, 1977; Brooks & Baumeister, 1977; Prehm, 1976; Scott, 1978).

Gifted individuals are increasingly considered a more heterogeneous population than they were in the past. The point is being made that gifted and talented students should be identified by criteria other than an IQ above 130 or some other arbitrary cutoff (Gallagher, 1975; Torrance, 1980; Whitmore, 1980). Renzulli (1980) argues that no single IQ cutoff point should be established, but that "gifted behavior" rather than "being gifted" should be the criterion for giftedness or exceptional talent. He goes on to stress that gifted behavior is defined by three criteria: (1) above average ability, (2) task commitment, and (3) creativity. Outstanding talent in "right brain" or creative enterprises is now being recognized as giftedness, not solely "left brain" skills or excellence in verbal fluency (Passow, 1981; Sisk, 1980). Thus, IQ scores are expected to play a decreasing role in the identification of giftedness. Achievement scores have, in some cases, been found to be more realistic measures of gifted accomplishment (Moore, Hahn, & Brentnall, 1978). Case study or case history approaches are also being used to identify the gifted or talented student, and they seem to be especially effective in identifying gifted minority pupils (Renzulli & Smith, 1977).

Another concern about intelligence in the gifted is that the range of giftedness, even as measured in the traditional way by an IQ above 130, is extremely broad (Pringle, 1970). If we consider that the gifted IQ range is 130 to 200 or more, then considering the gifted as a single category is as injudicious as treating a profoundly retarded, nonambulatory individual with an IQ of 5 the same as a mainstreamed child with an IQ of 68. When we add various other dimensions of giftedness, such as talent in the performing or creative arts or leadership, we see that the gifted are intellectually a very heterogeneous group (Zettel & Ballard, 1979). The intellectual prowess or accomplishments of the extremely gifted may be worlds apart from the gifted sixteen-year-old ballerina who, although only an average student, is sought after by every major ballet company in the country.

Children who display superior intelligence but do average or below-average work are referred to as *underachievers*. For teachers and parents, they are a puzzling and frustrating group (Gallagher, 1975; Whitmore, 1980). The psychological rather than the physical environment of the home seems more crucial. Parents of high-achieving children spend more time with their children and show a greater interest in education (McGillivray, 1964). Fathers of underachievers appear to show more hostility and rejection than fathers of high-achieving children. Mothers of underachievers scored high on authoritarianism with respect to their sons but low on authoritarianism with respect to their daughters (Pierce & Bowman, 1960). But another study found just the reverse for boys (Drews & Teahan, 1957). Low achievers have been found to feel less accepted by their families, more constricted in their actions, and generally more negativistic and defensive. The world seems an unfriendly and unsympathetic place to them, and they appear hesitant to accept the values of the family or of society.

The Terman study (Sears, 1977; Sears & Barbee, 1977) suggests that four major characteristics separate underachieving individuals from those who achieve effectively: lack of self-confidence, inability to persevere, lack of integration of goals, and presence of inferiority feelings. When early school records were examined, these same differences existed even at the preadolescent level.

The importance of early experience in determining the effective use of potential is clearly illustrated in certain case histories of gifted individuals here. Also, the importance of early recognition and intervention in relation to behavioral and personality difficulties of the gifted is underscored (Newland, 1976; Zettel & Ballard, 1979). Therefore, we will examine the problems of early assessment and intervention for all exceptional learners.

Intellectual Assessment of Infants

In general, tests of infant intelligence are uncertain measures of future potential (Lewis, 1976; Urginis & Hunt, 1975). One conclusion that has been reached is that mild mental retardation is probably not predictable in infancy (Holden, 1972). Such tests also have little value in measuring improvement in competence over time with children who have been given specific enrichment experiences. These measures may simply be too gross to reflect anything but major changes. It

The child with an IQ over 180 appears once in a million cases (Hollingworth, 1942). The unusual nature and character of such a child usually means that he or she will need special tutoring sessions with a skilled person who understands the problems the child faces, rather than mere adaptations of the school program. Historically, many of the most intelligent or creative individuals did not receive a formal education and were, instead, privately tutored (Goertzel & Goertzel, 1962).

John Stuart Mill wrote of how his father kept him out of school to avoid "contagion of vulgar modes of thought and feeling." He concluded that his isolated education had prepared him more to know than to do. Norbert Weiner started school at age seven, at which time he was placed in the third grade. By age nine, he was admitted to high school, by eleven he entered Harvard, and by eighteen, he had a Ph.D. in mathematics. Weiner's father, who tutored him at home, has been described as a perfectionist and a severe taskmaster. Weiner paid a great price for his accomplishments. Periodically he was mentally ill and given to general personal unhappiness. Louisa May Alcott's family firmly discouraged her writing, and one of her editors once told her she would never write anything with popular appeal. Albert Einstein did not have par-

ticularly happy school experiences. He was slow in developing verbal skills and did poorly in areas dependent on language; but he studied mathematics apart from school, tutored by his uncle. Thomas Edison's mother became outraged when the teacher called him muddled and confused, removed him from school, and tutored him at home. He responded well to this program and cultivated a creative engineering mind. Leo Tolstoy, Winston Churchill, Emile Zola, and Rodin all failed grades in school, and even Werner von Braun flunked ninth-grade algebra (National/State Leadership Training Institute on the Gifted and Talented, 1979).

Kirk and Gallagher (1979) raise several questions as a result of the educational careers of these eminent individuals. Is it necessary to segregate very superior children from their peers in order to develop their abilities? Is it possible to accomplish such an education in school? Are the achievements of these people the result of tutorial systems begun at an early age, uncontaminated by school curriculum and grade placement? To answer these questions, we would probably have to look separately at each individual, although it is difficult to see how genius could flourish in the confines of a lockstep traditional school program.

appears that each stage of infant and early childhood development consists of a set of relatively discrete abilities, with limited continuity between intelligence as defined at different stages. For infants without severe or multiple handicaps, the educational level of the parents or their socioeconomic status may be better predictors than infant intelligence test scores during the first one to two years of life (Keogh & Kopp, 1978). However, there are so many influences within low socioeconomic status, such as poor nutrition, inadequate care giving, or chaotic environment, that it is impossible to rely on this variable for explanation (Zigler, 1970).

It has been stated that although infant intelligence tests are not valid predictors of later intellectual potential, they do provide a measure of a given infant's intellectual functioning in relation to other infants of the same age. However, using such tests to screen random populations of infants to identify those who are mentally retarded may present serious problems (Cross, 1977; Mercer, Algozzine, & Trifiletti, 1979a, 1979b). For example, suppose a hypothetical test has been found to identify correctly 90 percent of infants known to be mentally retarded, while incorrectly classifying only 15 percent of normal infants as retarded. If we were to give the test to 1,000 infants, only fifty of whom were truly retarded, we would miss 10 percent, or five of the retarded

Figure 7-5.

children. This would not necessarily rule out the use of the test for screening. But when we consider the 15 percent of the remaining 950 normal infants—or 142 individuals who would be misidentified as probably or actually retarded—we can see how impractical and inappropriate the test would be for large-scale screening. Keogh and Becker (1973) have suggested that identifying children who do not need intervention may unnecessarily subject them to the stigma of labeling and its attendant problems.

Tests given young children may penalize the quiet, less sociable, young child and the mentally retarded (Honzik, 1976). They often fail to take into account the effects of a child's cultural environment. Even at an early age, cultural influences may cause a child to approach a test situation in a markedly different manner from that of a typical child in the standardization sample. In addition, standardized testing approaches ignore the possibility of the child's developing adaptive and coping mechanisms over time to compensate for apparent problems in early life (Escalona, 1972; Sameroff & Chandler, 1975). For this reason, Parmelee and his colleagues (Parmelee, Kopp, & Sigman, 1976; Sigman & Parmelee, 1979) have developed a "cumulative risk index" that combines a variety of measures, at birth and at intervals thereafter, that take into account both biomedical and performance indicators in an additive fashion. A similar suggestion has been made in regard to recording the cumulative total of skills and behaviors a child has acquired on infant tests over time as a measure of *effectiveness* of the intervention program (Sommers, McGregor, Lesh, & Reed, 1980).

Regardless of the possible capacity-based problems we identify in infancy, we are limited in

Researchers continue to search for a screening test than can be given to all infants and young children to determine those at risk and to provide direction for intervention efforts. The focus of intervention often stems from the *content* of assessment measures. Screening tests that are available, however, have high error rates; and assessment-diagnostic tests have only limited predictive validity for later development in life. Johnson and Kopp (1981) have analyzed some seventy-eight such tests developed since 1950. They found that fewer than one in five specified how test items were selected or why they were included. Many do not specify the training needed to administer the test nor do they provide complete procedures for administering each item. Most failed to measure such important areas as play skills, attention, memory, and social interaction.

predicting the ultimate effects of range and nature of experience during the early childhood years. Moreover, the bridge from assessment to intervention is an elusive one (Keogh & Kopp, 1978; Sigman, Cohen, & Forsythe, 1981), and thus relatively little is known for certain about evaluation of intervention efforts for exceptional infants.

Infant Intervention Programs

Very few states have mandated programs for handicapped children under age three (Cohen, Semmes, & Guralnick, 1979), although some programs for infant intervention have in fact been funded through public school sources (Swan, 1980). Some of the difficulties in determining which infants actually need intervention were discussed previously, but Hayden (1979) mentions other factors that make public acceptance and funding of infant intervention programs difficult. For example, there are several problems in estimating how many handicapped infants and young children actually exist. Child-find programs operated by public schools are often unable to identify such children because of funding problems. Others may be reluctant to identify such children because they are unprepared to serve them and do not wish to raise parents' hopes or appear to federal agencies as having a large, unserved population. Recent estimates suggest that only one in four handicapped children under age three are actually receiving appropriate services (Hayden, 1979), with current figures of children actually reported as served being considerably lower (Education of the Handicapped, 1981).

Intervention in infancy or even in early childhood is difficult. Twenty years ago, it was thought that specific problems or disorders early in life preordained a child to later difficulty. The truth is that we cannot really predict that such events as prematurity, obstetrical complications, temporary interruption in the brain's oxygen supply at birth, or other biomedical problems will *inevitably* lead to subsequent problems in any given child. Moreover, environmental events, such as inadequate child care, poor nutrition, or even child abuse, do not always result in a poor outcome.

Thus the "continuum of reproductive casualty" and the "continuum of caretaking casualty" are interactive and overlapping (Keogh & Pullis, 1980; Keogh & Kopp, 1978). A single event, occurring either within the infant or in his or her environment, is not always a sufficient reason to begin intervention. We must not only consider both capacity and experience determiners (stressed so often throughout this text), but timing is crucial, particularly in infant intervention. Sameroff and Chandler (1975) have shown how the effect of an isolated biomedical event at birth might be influenced or mediated for good or ill by the mother's perception of the child and that event. For example, it may not be prematurity itself that causes a problem but factors associated with prematurity, such as prolonged hospitalization, disruption of mother-child interaction, and the like (Friedman & Sigman, 1981). These in turn may affect the mother's care giving.

Related problems facing early interveners are a lack of an empirical basis for intervention and a limited understanding of child development. Many programs for infants seem to be based on teaching through enhancement of sensory, motor, or cognitive growth. The question has been raised, however, whether we actually "teach" infants at all (Johnson & Kopp, 1981; Langley, 1980). Too much active teaching and curriculum might preclude the self-directed activities of the child, which are so important in the first year of life, as he or she interacts with, or acts on, the environment and sets the stage for later learning. Longitudinal studies of at-risk infants also suggest that the special needs of children at two weeks of age might spontaneously resolve themselves by three months, whereas special-needs youngsters may appear who were not identified before (Kochanek, 1980). In far too many infant intervention programs, we may be rushing to intervene first and then reflecting too late on whether the intervention is appropriate (Greenspan, 1980; Keogh & Kopp, 1978).

Notwithstanding these cautions, countless infant intervention programs have been developed and studied (Horowitz & Paden, 1973; Levitt & Cohen, 1975; Keogh & Kopp, 1978). Effective programs seem to have some common characteristics. Generally, such programs involve the mother *directly* in the intervention. Concern has been raised that to do otherwise may seriously interfere with normal mother-child bonding (La coste, 1978; Stone & Chesney, 1978). Mothers are therefore strongly encouraged to believe that how they interact with their infants will make a difference in the infant's future. They are taught to be responsive to any behavioral indicators of distress when the infants are very young. Mothers are also trained to observe their infants in interaction with play materials and in social situations for signs of interest and surprise, boredom or frustration. They are encouraged to provide the infant with materials and interaction that produce interest and remove those that upset or produce boredom. Finally, mothers of handicapped infants are taught about the sequence of developing abilities and interests of children so that they can choose appropriate materials and activities.

Most of the studies done on intervention programs with high-risk infants have reported success in raising the level of performance of enrolled infants as compared with unenrolled control infants. The success of intervention programs appears directly correlated with the intensity of the program and the age at which it is begun. One of the most critical problems of early intervention efforts with infants is related to the effects of program withdrawal. In some cases, the infant's level of functioning abruptly declines, with the intervention appearing only to delay developmental problems. An important factor in such programs, then, is the establishment of formal links with the social agency or school program responsible for continuing the intervention (Karnes & Teska, 1975; Swan, 1980).

Preschool Intervention Programs

The national Project Head Start program and several other preschool programs have attempted to prepare the disadvantaged child for the culture of the middle-class school. These approaches have their genesis in the classic Iowa studies of the 1930s (Skeels, 1966) and the Illinois preschool study in the 1950s (Kirk, 1958), which demonstrated that enriching a child's environment was apt to provide dramatic changes in later school or life adjustment. Four preschool approaches are currently widely recognized and fairly well established.

Project Head Start was conceived within a traditional preschool framework and emphasizes providing appropriate early experiences that will form the foundation for further development (Miller & Dyer, 1975). Disadvantaged children are viewed as lacking confidence, experiences with the environment, and curiosity. The Head Start curriculum is not characterized by any particular content, but rather by its flexibility. Content areas found in many traditional preschool programs are included: learning to name common objects, learning such concepts as time and size, learning about foods, and learning to make sensory discriminations. Playground activities and equipment are directed toward developing gross-motor skills; small-muscle skills are developed through such activities as putting on wraps, tying shoes, using scissors or crayons, and manipulating toys. There is no formal grouping. In most cases, the children, not the teacher, decide what is to be learned, though the development of a more efficient use of language is stressed. The atmosphere is one of freedom within some established limits.

An interest in Montessori methods has been revived as programs in early education for disadvantaged children have increased (Montessori, 1964). Montessori characterized the environment of the disadvantaged child as lacking the order and structure of that of nondisadvantaged peers. She viewed this environmental disorganization as underlying children's handicaps in conceptualization and learning. In contrast to contemporary notions, Montessori emphasized that the disadvantaged child had an innate pride in achievement and was curious and highly motivated to learn. She believed all preschool children were capable of intense and prolonged periods of concentration. The Montessori curriculum materials fall into three categories: exercises for daily living, sensorial materials, and academic materials. The classroom is quiet and orderly. Exercises include button boards, tying boards, and activities designed to develop competence in housekeeping and personal care. Children start with these materials. Sensorial materials, such as containers with substances of differing odors or bells that make differing sounds, are introduced next. Finally, academic materials are introduced to teach mathematical concepts of size, weight, and volume. Ages range from three to five years in a Montessori preschool classroom, and children are encouraged to imitate older peers. Children are expected to work on an individual basis, and all tasks are carefully sequenced in small steps. The child, not the teacher, decides what to study; the teacher's task is to have the appropriate materials available at the proper time. The teacher is not a substitute mother but a resource to aid the child in the process of self-education.

The Demonstration and Research Center for Early Education (DARCEE) emphasizes the remediation of linguistic and conceptual deficiencies and the development of attitudes related to academic achievement (Gray, Klaus, Miller, & Forrester, 1966). There is major emphasis on involving parents. The skill development portion of the DARCEE curriculum focuses on effective listening, verbal communication, and expression of thought patterns. For each process, skills are organized from gross and simple to specific and complex and from concrete to abstract. DARCEE also attempts to develop a motivation to achieve, persistence in tasks, resistance to distraction, and delay of gratification. Children are placed in groups of five or six, based on ability. Teaching materials focus on sensory discrimination, such as stringing beads or counting cubes. Informal conversations between the teacher and children are encouraged. Reinforcement for correctness and persistence is provided frequently, and the classroom is kept quiet and orderly. The teacher is not viewed as a substitute mother but as a teacher.

The Bereiter-Engelmann program is remedial and emphasizes the acquisition of academic learning tools, that is, verbal and numerical symbols (Bereiter & Engelmann, 1966). The disadvantaged child is seen as coming from a background characterized by disorder, lack of discipline, and minimal reward for intellectual efforts. The children are considered unmotivated to learn, not readily responsive to adult social praise, and deficient in language. The curriculum is organized into three content areas: reading, language, and arithmetic. Reading instruction is largely phonetic, and arithmetic programs are based on counting operations, such as learning to count toward a number and then counting backwards. Language training is oriented toward structural and logical components of language. The program groups children by ability into three groups of about five children each. Group instruction includes patterned drill, during which the teacher calls out a question or answer, that is repeated in unison by the children. A rapid and repetitive pace is maintained, and drill in each of the academic areas lasts for twenty minutes, for a daily total of one hour of patterned drill. The atmosphere is business-like and task oriented. Toys are limited to form boards, puzzles, books, drawing materials, Cuisenaire rods, and the like. Inattentiveness is not allowed during patterned drill, and children are not permitted to leave the activity. In the Bereiter-Engelmann program, the teacher—not the child—decides the curriculum.

These four preschool programs were subjected to a four-year comparative study that continued until the children had completed the second grade (Miller & Dyer, 1975). The sample of children in the study totalled nearly 300; the majority were placed in the four experimental programs and less than 10 percent did not attend any type of preschool program. The experimental children were randomly assigned to programs typical of the Head Start, Montessori, DARCEE, or Bereiter-Engelmann approaches, and a variety of measures were taken over the four-year period. The findings of the study are briefly summarized:

1. The four preschool programs were observed to differ not only ideologically and educationally, but also in both teacher and child behaviors.

2. The programs had different effects on children, both immediately and over the four-year period.

3. Children in programs that were highly structured and emphasized language development (e.g., Bereiter-Engelmann) made the highest immediate gains in IQ and achievement. However, although children from all programs declined in IQ over the four years, children in the structured language program declined most.

4. After the four-year period, the program effects that were still detectable were in

The backgrounds of the experimental children in the Miller and Dyer study provide us with an interesting summary of the limitations imposed by range and nature of experience, which exist in the lives of some economically disadvantaged children. The typical child was four-years old and black. His or her family consisted of a mother, two or three siblings, and one or two others living in a four-room apartment. They all subsisted on a near poverty-level income or on welfare. Only two out of five of the children had fathers living at home.

Almost all of the families owned a television, two-thirds received a daily newspaper, and two-thirds had a telephone. Fewer than half owned an automobile. Almost none of the children had been in a lake, river, or ocean, although half had been in a swimming pool. Only one or two had ever visited a zoo, library, museum, farm, or airport or traveled on a boat, train, or plane. Fewer than half had been on a bus trip, and only slightly more had been out of town in a car. Only two out of five had ever had a birthday party, but nearly two-thirds had been to a birthday party and had had a birthday cake. Less than one-half had a pet. Although this study was completed some years ago, there is little reason to think that much has changed this typical picture of the economically disadvantaged youngster.

---

nonacademic areas, such as curiosity, persistence, independence, and confidence. These effects appeared to result from the prekindergarten intervention alone.

5. The most consistent and beneficial effects of the four kindergarten programs occurred for males.

These findings are similar to those of others who have examined the effects of preschool intervention to determine which characteristics are most effective (Bronfenbrenner, 1974; Karnes & Teska, 1975; Gotts, 1981; Haskins, Finklestein, & Stedman, 1978; Levitt & Cohen, 1975). The conclusions also seem to be true of "Follow-Through" programs that attempt to continue the gains made by these children as they move into the primary grades (Becker & Englemann, 1977). The controversy still continues, however, over just how long lasting the effects of such preschool interventions actually are (Hodges & Cooper, 1981). Clarke and Clarke (1977) have suggested that even four years of follow-through, added to one or two years of Head Start, "will be insufficient to make any great impact on the later lives of these children while they remain in poor homes, both economically and culturally disadvantaged" (Clarke & Clarke, 1977, p. 528). They go on to suggest that "while it is at last generally conceded that brief early intervention has effects that fade, it is less often appreciated that the effects of much longer early intervention that is not followed by similar stimulation will also fade" (p. 528).

A recent Cornell University study, however, reports encouraging results (Consortium for Longitudinal Studies, 1979; Darlington, Royce, Snipper, Murray, & Lazar, 1980). The Cornell group went back to a dozen researchers who had examined Head Start projects in the 1960s. They were able to contact nearly 1,600 representative subjects from these twelve studies who were now in upper elementary or high school grades. They compared children who had been in various Head Start programs with those who had served as controls. The findings on IQ replicated what had already been reported: large effects as a result of intervention that tapered down to smaller but still significant effects three or four years later and then disappeared. But an important contribution of the Cornell study is that it examined some "real world" concerns about the later special needs of a select group of these children. For those children who had to repeat one or more grades or had to be placed in special education, the combined rate of failure was 45 percent in the control group and only 24 percent for those who had preschool intervention. For those children who ultimately had to be assigned to special classes for the mentally retarded, emotionally disturbed, or learning disabled, the rate was 29 percent for the controls and 14 percent for the treatment group.

The contrast in this study between IQ measures and real world concerns, such as the need for services, raised a serious question about intelligence tests as outcome measures. This point has been raised elsewhere. Zigler and Trickett (1978) have suggested that IQ measures are relatively meaningless, for a variety of reasons, as evaluations of progress or effectiveness of interventions. The fact that psychologists are enamored of the standardization and reliability of IQ tests is no reason to consider gains in intelligence as the principal criterion for intervention. Zigler and Trickett contend, as we have mentioned elsewhere, that social competence is the only standard that society can justly impose as a measure of success for any individual.

Zigler and Trickett suggest that a social competence index be developed, and they demonstrate that research has already provided the beginnings of such an index. They mention several variables that should be included, such as measures of physical health and well-being, academic achievement, and motivational or emotional factors. These last factors might include effectance motivation, outerdirectedness, responsiveness to social reinforcement, learned helplessness, self-image, and the like. Others have pointed to teacher ratings (Mercer, Algozzine, & Trifiletti, 1979a, 1979b) or mothers' reports as effective measures of special needs. Zigler and Trickett are concerned that excessive reliance on IQ alone as an outcome criterion for Head Start very nearly caused this nation "to jettison the most popular and highly regarded program ever mounted for children in America" (Zigler & Trickett, 1978, p. 794).

More recently, early intervention has focused on more comprehensive and cumulative programs. For mildly handicapped youngsters, two well-known programs are the Milwaukee Project (Garber & Heber, 1977) and the Carolina Abecedarian Project (Ramey & Campbell, 1979a, 1979b). In both of these programs, mothers in low-income neighborhoods who had IQs in the 80s or below are randomly assigned to experimental and control groups when their infants are only a few months old. Teachers work with the infants and mothers from the very beginning on a one-to-one basis; but as the infants reach the end of their first year, they are gradually moved into a nursery school setting. As the toddlers reach the end of their second or third year, they are systematically transitioned into preschool classrooms. Focus is on both the cognitive language and social-emotional experiences of the child. The Abecedarian Project has not only developed a systematic curriculum but has also begun to consider more carefully the contributions of various components of its program. For example, nutritional supplements have been offered to its participants and attempts are being made to consider the differential effects these may have over and above environmental stimulation (Zeskind & Ramey, 1978). Both programs have shown rather dramatic results. The Milwaukee program had produced IQ differences of nearly 18 points between experimental and control children at age ten (Garber, 1980). As one measure, Abecedarian staff have calculated an "odds ratio," which suggests the likelihood that a child at age four would avoid a significant developmental delay is 6 to 1 in favor of the experimental group (Ramey & Campbell, 1979). Both projects are concerned with "tying in" their children closely to equally nurturing and supportive classroom environments in the later grades. It should be mentioned here, however, that the Milwaukee Project has been severely and perhaps justly criticized because of its investigators' failure to control for certain initial differences between experimental and control children and to demonstrate gains in areas other than IQ (Page & Grandon, 1981).

For more severely handicapped youngsters, two equally impressive programs are the one for blind infants at the University of Michigan (Fraiberg, 1971, 1977) and the Minnesota University Project EDGE for Down's syndrome youngsters (Rynders & Horrobin, 1975). In the first, Fraiberg and her colleagues taught mothers of blind infants to become "hand watchers." Painstaking observations had shown that failure in hand behavior, such as grasping and switching objects from hand to hand, led to delays in sensorimotor input and learning in blind infants. Thus, interveners taught mothers to "educate" their babies' hands to facilitate cognitive growth in the absence of vision. Assessment of specific deficits led directly to individual intervention to prevent developmental delays. The EDGE project (Expanding Developmental Growth through Education) emphasized direct instruction in language, which was begun at age two and one-half. Mothers were taught to read to their Down's syndrome youngsters for at least thirty minutes each day and to focus on other aspects of developing language. Mothers were given increasing responsibility for their child's total program over time, continuing as the children entered school programs. Impressive gains were shown in language and concept function in both these projects.

Another creative intervention program is the FEED program developed at the University of Indiana (Anastasiow, 1977). FEED, or Facilitative Environment Encouraging Development, does not deal directly with infants or even young children. Instead, this program focuses on seventh- and eighth-grade students from low-income neighborhoods who are likely to become parents themselves within a few years. The program attempts to teach these junior high pupils, *before* they become parents, about child growth and development and the importance of the quality of care provided during the first days and months of an infant's life. It includes lectures and discussions on care giving, nutrition, health care, and the like as well as practical experience in both normal and handicapped preschool settings and in pediatric wards of local hospitals. Extensive curriculum guides and materials have been provided to junior high school faculty in several cities across the country. Early results suggest that significant gains have been made in both the attitudes and knowledge of these young people in regard to care giving (Anastasiow, 1977). Plans are underway to follow up program participants to see if these preventative efforts pay off during actual parenthood, and emphasis on preparation for family life is expected to be a major part of prevention efforts in the future (Anastasiow, 1981).

It is clear that early intervention is becoming a part of public school programming. The spirit of Public Law 94–142 stresses intervention at birth. The letter of the law has led to mandated programs for children as young as three years, whenever possible; related legislation has led to mandates to include handicapped children as no less than 10 percent of each Head Start population (Cohen, Semmes, & Guralnick, 1979). Texts on early intervention with handicapped children are beginning to appear (Caldwell & Stedman, 1977; Neisworth et al., 1980; Tjossem, 1976). However, we often want to give broad-based intervention to all at-risk children or infants, believing that any intervention is better than none. A review of even a single area influencing at-risk outcome, such as maternal deprivation (Rutter, 1979), suggests that extremely heterogeneous factors are involved. The task ahead, as Keogh and Kopp (1978) have suggested, is to discover which child requires which interventions and when.

Before leaving this topic, it is important to note that *early* intervention has traditionally been regarded as much more effective and preferable than programs that begin at later stages of development. Actually, there is relatively little empirical support for the position that the critical period for intervention is *only* during the first years of life and that programs initiated beyond the preschool years have no lasting impact (Zigler, 1981). In fact, it has been shown that intervention programs for high-risk, lower-socioeconomic children and youth can have a significant effect on school achievement when initiated in the elementary years (Becker & Engleman, 1977) and even during high school (Rutter, Maugham, Mortimore, Ouston, and Smith, 1979). Even though we have discussed infant and preschool intervention for children from high-risk families in some detail, we should not ignore the potential of intervention at *any* point during the school years.

Summary

Exceptional learners vary across the entire dimension of intelligence, some limited or enhanced by capacity-based factors, some by range and nature of experience. Blindness does not appear to affect measured intelligence negatively, and compensation for visual deficits can be provided to a considerable extent by environmental experience. However, the partially seeing score consistently lower than the blind, and studies show that IQ scores decrease as degree of vision increases. The deaf individual may be limited in such areas as memory and conceptualization due to the restriction on language development imposed by severe hearing loss. On nonlanguage tests, the deaf child has been found to fall toward the lower limits of the average range of intelligence. Compared with hearing children on such tests, the hard-of-hearing child shows little, if any, difference. Orthopedically impaired individuals demonstrate normal verbal abilities on intelligence tests but inferior perform-ance on tasks requiring motor and coordination skills. Children with seizure disorders display a wide range of intellectual abilities, with a greater number falling in the lower range and a smaller number achieving higher levels.

Emotionally disturbed children tend to score lower on intelligence tests than do normals. Selective and often faulty experience may contribute to low functioning. Although speech-handicapped children have been found to score lower on intelligence tests than does the general population, this may be due to problems in language proficiency and/or disturbed interpersonal relationships. Disadvantaged children—both black and white—do not perform as well on intelligence tests as their middle-class counterparts. The role of experience must be considered critical in explaining this finding, and early intervention programs show rather dramatic effects if maintained over time. The learning disabled typically range from low average to average on intelligence tests. Despite continuing interest in unique patterns related to learning disabled children's functioning on such tests, there is no agreement that such a pattern actually exists.

Understanding the relationship between mental retardation and intelligence is much more complex than merely assuming that the retarded are "slow" or "stupid" or that they are invariably limited to functioning on a level commensurate with IQ alone. Rather than a global disability, mild and even severe retardation may be task-specific and related only to certain aspects of the learning situation. Learning to learn, using verbal mediation techniques to enhance short-term memory, and social motivational approaches must be considered. Under optimal conditions, such children may demonstrate increased intellectual functioning. The severely retarded child whose condition is the result of some organic factor tends to profit less from special motivational and instructional efforts. Some theorists view mental retardation as a developmental abnormality, with the retarded child's passing through the same cognitive levels of development as normals, but at a later age. Others believe that a low IQ reflects a qualitative difference in intellectual capacity that results from a neurological abnormality.

Gifted children represent extreme variability in intellectual functioning, with IQ, achievement, and indicators of special talent and commitment all seen as necessary in identification. The child with an IQ over 180 may require special tutoring sessions conducted by a skilled individual who understands the problems; the underachieving gifted child may need special help in bolstering self-concept.

With all exceptional learners, special care is needed in assessing infants, developing early infant intervention programs, and establishing preschool programs aimed at enhancing intellectual development in preparation for the school years.

CHAPTER 8

Individualization of Exceptional Learners

What happens as the exceptional learner matures and enters adult life? What is the range of outcomes considered possible for exceptional learners? The answers to these questions are discussed under the heading *individualization*—the unfolding on an individual basis of adult potential. We are specifically concerned with the following:

- possibilities for marriage and family life

- possibilites for career development

- possibilities for adult functioning level.

These outcomes in adult life are vitally important to all individuals—exceptional and nonexceptional. Although attainment of these outcomes will be more difficult for exceptional learners, a surprising number of options may be open to them. Range and nature of previous experience are particularly critical in this respect.

Sex Education and the Exceptional Learner

Before we consider the questions of marriage and family, we must consider an issue that has become increasingly important—sex education. Sex education for children and adolescents has never been a simple matter in American society. When introduced into the public school curriculum, it often ignites a controversy. Many parents object to outsiders introducing their children to a topic whose moral significance may vary according to family traditions, beliefs, or religious teachings. But whether it is taught in the home through discussion or the introduction of sex education materials, in the classroom with teacher-led discussion and presentations, or outside both the home and school with the sharing of information and misinformation by peers, sex is a subject that young people will learn about. Unfortunately, that learning may be more confusing and conflictual than necessary.

In the case of exceptional individuals, special assistance may be needed to help them

Figure 8-1.

understand, accept, and deal appropriately with the feelings and bodily changes they encounter in adolescence. Some may believe that a retarded individual will have a retarded sexual development or that physically handicapped individuals are incapable of normal sexual experiences. Such beliefs are not true. Just as normal girls between the ages of nine and seventeen begin to menstruate and boys from twelve to fifteen have spontaneous ejaculations while asleep, most retarded, physically disabled, and other exceptional learners have the same experiences. There is no fixed relationship between IQ and sex drive; there are normals and retarded individuals who have very little interest in sex and others who have strong sex drives (AAHPER, 1971).

At the start of our discussion, it is important to distinguish between sex and sexuality. Sex is only the genital part of sexuality. Sex may develop primarily with the onset of adolescence, but the development of sexuality begins shortly after birth. How severe or subtle the child's handicap may be is not as relevant as "participation in those experiences that are generic to the early sexual development of all human beings" (Craft & Craft, 1978, p. 16). Among the early phases of the development of sexuality are experiences of being held close and being fed, being tickled and played with, being hugged and teased by brothers and sisters, feeling pride following acquisition of toileting skills, having curiosity about all the parts of one's body, and developing an awareness of one's sexual identity (I'm a boy; you're a girl) (Perske & Perske, 1973).

Many normal children have complicated or negative early experiences related to sexuality. For many exceptional individuals, the problems may be more severe, particularly as adolescence approaches. Whereas parents of normal children may avoid dealing with discussions of sex, hoping the whole problem will take care of itself, some parents of exceptional children may avoid it hoping that sex simply will not be a part of their children's lives. Others may feel that providing knowledge about sex will raise false hopes and expectations on the part of their children (Diamond, 1974). Fears surrounding possible marriage and, more importantly, having offspring have also caused many professionals to question the advisability of sex education for the retarded (Craft & Craft, 1978).

In any case, the exceptional individual, like his or her normal counterpart, must be prepared for the bodily changes that will occur. Rather than detailed explanations, retarded girls may need simple, matter-of-fact statements informing them that one of these days they will have some bleeding, like other girls they know. They should be assured that it is "okay," that it won't hurt them, and that it will come back. It is not a sickness that will restrict activities but just a part of growing up, as is developing breasts like their mother, girl friends, or other females (Quinn, 1976). Likewise, boys need assurance that erections will occur automatically and periodically, and that they are completely normal and natural.

Sex education for the blind is complicated by the fact that they are denied the visual experiences of girls developing breasts, wearing miniskirts or see-through blouses, or boys displaying the hair on their chests. In addition, they cannot see how different people look when walking around unclothed or partially clothed at home. Some educators of the blind advocate overcoming the resistance to using touch in sex education for the blind, since this modality is so necessary to their learning. The use of dolls with male and female genitalia, originally produced for teaching medical students, has been effective in this regard (Bass, 1974).

Masturbation has long been a controversial subject, although it is becoming accepted as a normal part of the process of sexual maturation. It has been described by Bass (1974) as being as "innocently acquired" by boys as by girls and as occurring as frequently among the disabled as in the general population. A critical concern is that the child should learn that masturbation is appropriate at certain times and in certain places, just as one learns that urinating is done in the bathroom (Gordon, 1969). Distinguishing between private versus public situations may require special training with severely retarded or blind individuals. Excessive masturbation can occur among exceptional individuals as it can among the nonexceptional. It can be related to boredom or nervousness, and involving children in meaningful activities that occupy the major part of their time is often effective in dealing with the problem.

Sex education for the exceptional individual has become even more important because of the trend away from institutionalization and toward mainstreaming (Bass, 1974). In most respects, it is no different than sex education with the nonexceptional, and fortunately we have moved in the direction of viewing the exceptional learner primarily as a person with human needs and drives just like everybody else and only secondarily as handicapped.

Marriage and Child Bearing

Two issues that have received increased interest are the advisability of marriage for or between exceptional individuals and, if married, the advisability of having children. Many exceptional individuals enjoy successful marriages. The average deaf man holds a job, owns a home, marries the woman of his choice, and participates in the social life of the community (Telford & Sawrey, 1967). However, only 5 percent of some 10,000 married deaf individuals studied had hearing partners (Brill, 1961).

Sex or sexuality eduction for the retarded may begin as early as age four and deal with aspects of sexuality presented here—developing a healthy body image, toileting skills, an understanding of what it means to be a boy or girl, respect for others, and a positive self-image. Around ages seven to nine, emphasis is on social development, differences among people, understanding negative feelings, and basic facts related to human reproduction. At ages nine to thirteen, embryonic and fetal development may be presented along with social, emo-

tional, and physical development. Children at this age level should be able to recognize and verbalize physical differences between boys and girls and the bodily changes that occur during puberty. For individuals over fourteen, adult attitudes, dealing with authority, relating to the peer group, dating, premarital sexual relationships, veneral disease, smoking, alcohol, drugs, marriage, and family living should be topics considered. (Meyen & Carr, 1967). In addition, contraception may be discussed.

A thirty-year, follow-up study comparing child guidance clinic patients who had been labeled either antisocial or neurotic found that more neurotic men never married and that fewer neurotic women married before age twenty-one (Robins, 1966). In another study described in detail in a later section (Baller, Charles & Miller, 1967), 206 retarded graduates from public school classes in Nebraska were followed for thirty years. At the end of this period, more than half had married and their divorce rate was equal at that time to the general population. The majority of their children were making satisfactory progress in school without evidence of retardation. Most of these graduates had married nonretarded spouses. A striking finding was that although their mean IQ was 58 at the beginning of the study, on follow-up it had risen to 81. The individuals in this study were not severely retarded, a condition that would appear to eliminate the possibility of marriage entirely. However this is not always the case.

It is difficult to rule out marriage for any exceptional learner. Each case has to be reviewed on an individual basis. The matter of children is more complicated. Although blindness has obvious inconveniences for motherhood, it does not seem to interfere drastically with normal child care. One interview study of ten blind mothers reported that one month after arriving home from the hospital, the mothers assumed full responsibility for dressing their infants (Ware & Schwab, 1971). The mothers also changed soiled diapers, ironed and sorted clothing, fed the infants, and read from Braille books. Although much responsibility was given to older siblings, the mothers carried out the major responsibilities for child care.

Robinault cautions that "society at large is concerned and has some reason to be cautiously watchful of would-be parents who have problems which will require *prolonged social solutions*" (p. 135). Carriers of critically defective genes or individuals likely to create environments that are threatening to children must be carefully considered (Meyers, 1977; David, Smith, & Friedman, 1976). In addition, the offspring of retarded adults may eventually become a problem for someone else. There have been few valid long-term studies of children of psychotic parents, but there is enough data to suggest they are at risk for developing serious emotional problems of their own (Robinault, 1978). Babies born to alcoholic mothers often have physical defects, such as small heads and stunted bodies, and almost half are below normal in intelligence. "As for babies born to drug addicts, one needs no substantiating study—they are seen writhing with symptoms of drug withdrawal in every hospital nursery where they are born" (Robinault, 1978, p. 135).

Bill and Ida were originally classified as severely subnormal. Bill had spent most of his adult life in institutions, incapable of caring for his personal hygiene. He dressed in a slovenly manner and was described as evidencing a "hangdog" expression. Ida was the illegitimate child of a mental defective and had also spent her life in institutions. Bill and Ida met in a state hospital and liked each other, but Ida was transferred and it "broke" Bill's heart. By chance, the system reunited them fifteen years later when they both were assigned to the same day hospital. Now in their forties, Bill and Ida were engaged for two years. Bill had a vasectomy and then they were married. They lived in a small flat and traveled daily by bus to their jobs at a sheltered workshop. Ida did her best to keep Bill neat and he greatly improved in his hygiene. "There is a spring in his step, he looks up rather than down, his shoulders are erect; he is a man, and here is the woman to prove it" (Robinault, 1978, p. 55). They received support from community care agencies. Although Bill and Ida had friends, they took great pleasure in each other's company. When asked about their sex life, Bill and Ida looked at each other and smiled. "Bill took Ida's hand and said, 'It ought to be all right, we've been married so long'" (Robinault, 1978, p. 55).

The question of parenthood for exceptional individuals cannot be answered by examining the disability alone (Cornwell, 1977). Each couple must be assessed individually, and they must ask themselves whether they can meet the responsibilities for and the growth requirements of the child who must depend on them.

Having discussed some of the issues of marriage and child bearing, we now turn to the career development of exceptional learners.

Career Development

The term *vocational education* has traditionally been used in describing educational efforts to assist exceptional and nonexceptional learners prepare for a work life. However, the term is narrow, implying preparation for a specific occupation and neglecting the myriad of factors that are involved in our successful adjustment as adults. As a result, the term *career education* was introduced in 1971. It is defined by the Council for Exceptional Children (1977) as:

> The totality of experiences through which one learns to live a meaningful, satisfying work life . . . providing the opportunity for children to learn, in the least restricted environment possible, the academic, daily living, personal-social and occupational knowledge and skills necessary for attaining their highest levels of economic, and personal and social fulfillment. The individual can obtain this fulfillment through work (both paid and unpaid), and as citizen, volunteer, family member and participant in meaningful leisure-time activities.

This broader notion of preparation for adult life itself, rather than a single occupation, has received increased national recognition and support with various legislative actions at the federal level and cooperative agreements between vocational and rehabilitative organizations (Tesolowski, Rosenberg, & Hammond, 1980). Brolin and Kokaska (1979) have developed a curriculum model for career education that organizes learner competencies into three categories: (1) daily living skills, (2) personal-social skills, and (3) occupational guidance and preparation. Academic instruction is used across categories to help individuals acquire these competencies.

For example, the daily living skills curriculum includes the competencies of "managing family finances" and "buying and caring for clothing." In acquiring these competencies, the individual learns to "identify money and make correct change" and to "iron and store clothing." The personal-social skills curriculum includes such competencies as "achieving socially responsible behavior" and "achieving problem-solving skills." These are acquired as the individual learns "proper behavior in public places" and "anticipating consequences." Occupational guidance and preparation involves such competencies as "exhibiting appropriate work habits and behavior" and "seeking, securing, and maintaining employment." The curriculum teaches the individual to "accept supervision" and "how to interview for a job" in relation to these competencies.

People who have had serious emotional disorders have many employment barriers. The question of whether a former mental patient should reveal his or her illness to prospective employers is still being debated. The amount of pressure and interpersonal requirements are important considerations in job placement. Many individuals who have experienced emotional disorders will need continual or periodic follow-up services, including counseling, in order to maintain themselves in the community. The fear of failure and rejection by others will contribute to their feelings of inadequacy in the work situation (Brolin & Kokaska, 1979).

Assessment, evaluation, and long-range planning for the ultimate career or vocational development of exceptional individuals are still in rather formative stages (Brown et al., 1981; Lynch, Kiernan, and Stark, 1981; Sillington, 1981; Stodden & Lanocone, 1981). Part of the problem has been that, as with nonhandicapped learners, vocational education courses are often taught in isolation from the rest of the academic curriculum. There has, in fact, been very little systematic attempt to coordinate academic preparation, career or vocational education, and work experience in a comprehensive program for each handicapped student. Most authors agree that this planning should begin at the primary school level, or even before, so that plans to prepare a handicapped student for the world of work involve all of the child's teachers and touch each aspect of his or her total curriculum. Too often, vocational or career planning has been left until adolescence; thus, assessment of the student's readiness for work occurs when little time remains to prepare the student for the world of work.

Career education has vital significance for exceptional learners. Under Public Law 94–142, the school is responsible for providing an education for them until age twenty-one, and this type of curriculum can greatly increase the number who achieve a measure of independence and productivity in the community. Between 1973 and 1977, 2.5 million people in the general population left school. Clark (1980) has estimated that the following occurred:

1. 21 percent were either fully employed or enrolled in higher education

2. 40 percent were underemployed and at the poverty level

3. 8 percent were in their home community and idle much of the time

In the Soviet Union, all handicapped children are enrolled in twenty-four-hour residential schools. During a visit to Russia, one of the authors visited a school for elementary age, mildly retarded children. He was told that when each child turned eleven, a vocational planning council met to determine what his or her future vocation would be. Most of these vocations involved factory work, and once the selection had been made by the council, the child was sent several days a week to a factory for an apprenticeship. When the children reached seventeen, they undertook full-time employment in these jobs, left the special residential school, and were given apartments by the state. The pay scale for the job done was identical to that received by any nonhandicapped worker assigned the same job. This early preparation for an eventual vocation has many obvious advantages over waiting until age seventeen to begin such planning.

4. 26 percent were unemployed and on welfare

5. 3 percent were totally dependent and institutionalized

The 1980s is seen as a decade in which employment opportunities in certain occupations will increase; hopefully, the first figure cited by Clark will also increase with reference to exceptional learners. Job openings will occur in craft and mechanical occupations, farming, carpentry, and high-wage industries. Operative jobs, such as low-skilled clerical work, service occupations (e.g., hospital attendant), waiters, housekeepers, and laborers in industry should also become increasingly available. Finally, other hired labor jobs, such as those connected with laundry and dry cleaning operations, household help, cooking and kitchen work, and janitorial and cleaning work, will continue and require a larger working force. We have stressed many times in this text the

Figure 8–2.

The spirit of this call to service is vividly conveyed in the commencement address of an exceptional learner who was selected as a graduation speaker by his classmates. His parents and teachers tried to discourage him from attempting it. But the young man was determined to try and he worked for weeks on his speech, finally standing before his family, teachers, and friends and delivering it on graduation day.

> Mr. Reilly, honored guests, ladies and gentlemen and members of the graduating class of 1974. I want to take this opportunity to convey appreciation to you for allowing me to express my feelings this evening.
>
> Tonight represents a dream come true for my parents, friends and relatives. Tonight also represents the attainment of a goal for many interested and concerned teachers, counselors and staff. Tonight also represents the downfall of a diagnosis that was made over fifteen years ago. Let me explain.
>
> In 1958, a four-year-old boy was taken to the University Hospital at Ann Arbor for neurological examinations. After many hours of examinations, tests, x-rays, and waiting, a verdict and sentence was handed down by the University doctors. The parents were informed that their son was mentally handicapped and the best place for him was in an institution. "Your son, at best, may some day be able to sell papers on a street corner," the doctors informed the stunned couple. On the convictions of these parents, through the efforts of devoted teachers and the legislation of interested taxpayers like themselves, this would-be resident of Coldwater's Home for the Mentally Handicapped was placed in our local school system.
>
> This boy was loved and cared for not only at home, but also at school. Sure there were hard and rough times. It isn't easy competing with other kids, even when you are normal, much less handicapped. But, the love and the patience were there for nineteen long years. And, tonight I am proud to stand here and say that I am that boy—almost condemned to an institution. True, I am not an *A* student. But neither am I a dropout. I may never go to college, but I won't be on welfare rolls either. I may never be a great man in this world, but I will be a man in whatever way I am able to do it.
>
> For tonight, I say thanks to my parents who prayed and worked so hard. I say thanks to you, my instructors and the staff of Lakeshore High who had the patience and dedication to see me through. I say thanks to this audience for your work, your dollars, and your concern in providing me with an opportunity for my education. And, to you, my classmates, I also say thanks. I will always remember our years together and I hope that you will also.
>
> Remember me as you search for a place in life, for there will be youngsters needing your help as you select a vocation in life. Remember me as you become paying members of our communities because there will be children needing your financial support. And, remember me and others like me in your prayers because in some cases there are not always parents, teachers, and classmates like I have had at Lakeshore High School. Thank you.

He hesitated, lost his place, stuttered, but he went on. No senior in the assembly moved.*

---

*Brolin, D. E., and Kokaska, C. J., *Career Education for Handicapped Children and Youth* (3rd ed.). Columbus, Oh.: Charles E. Merrill Publishing Co., 1979, p. 86. Reprinted with permission.

impressive increase in services provided for exceptional learners over recent years. We should now stress the importance of exceptional learners learning to serve themselves, their families, and their community in as productive a manner as possible.

We turn now to a discussion of the adult functioning level of exceptional learners.

The visually handicapped individual faces certain unique problems as he or she matures. Three special preoccupations of the blind adolescent are found among most normal-seeing young men and women, but they are complicated by the fact of blindness (Cholden, 1958). One preoccupation is with the importance of bodily attractiveness to the female and masculine strength and independence to the male. The desire to impress the opposite sex and the anxiety surrounding sexual relationships are typical of adolescence but more difficult for the visually handicapped. The second preoccupation concerns independence and the dilemma of blind adolescents who cannot achieve a certain freedom from parents and others. The third common problem of all adolescents is to achieve a certain degree of exhibitionism while preserving the desire for anonymity, both of which are more difficult for the blind. In terms of sexual curiosity, dating, mobility, and concern for the future, Lowenfeld (1971) feels that the difficulties encountered by the blind adolescent can possibly affect his or her self-concept and attitudes toward interpersonal relationships, although he suggests that perhaps their adjustment is no more severe than that of all adolescents.

Limited vocational opportunities for visually impaired individuals, such as those provided by sheltered workshops, were more typical in the past than they are today. The influence of organizations for the blind, the expansion of the United States Office of Vocational Rehabilitation, and an increased emphasis on the integration of minorities and the handicapped in all walks of life have provided greater vocational and employment opportunities. Blind individuals can and do successfully undertake many types of jobs, such as farming, chemistry, teaching (at all levels), osteopathy, and law. They also can enter the fields of sales (including real estate and insurance), cooking (chef), nursing, television repair, medicine, court reporting, and clerical work.

But in what has sometimes been called an era of "the broadening vista of jobs for the blind," visually handicapped persons continue to have unsatisfactory vocational outcomes, despite their potential for vocational development (Davidson, 1975). A 1969 survey of 644 legally blind adults revealed their limited vocational success. Data from the survey indicated that more than one-half of the males were employed in thirteen occupations, and more than one-half of the females worked in only nine. Moreover, 87 percent of those interviewed earned less than $8,000 annually from their principal job, at a time when the median income in the United States was $8,400 annually. Surveys conducted between 1955 and 1973 have found far greater rates of unemployment for the visually impaired compared to the general population, with rates sometimes reported in the range of 40 to 50 percent.

These findings seem to support the widespread belief that visually handicapped adolescents are vocationally immature, more undecided, and less involved in career planning. However, visually impaired public and residential school adolescents have been found to be as involved in career planning as their sighted peers, to have a similar level of exploratory occupational experiences, and to show the same career maturity. Thus, the limited success in employment experienced by the visually impaired cannot be due solely to inadequate vocational development. Other problems include the lack of suitable training facilities, the failure of society to develop careers the visually handicapped can enter, and negative employer attitudes. In relation to the latter, Minnesota employers were asked whether or not they would consider blind persons for production, management, clerical, or sales jobs (Williams, 1972). Of the 108 respondents, 71.5, 58.5, 52.4, and 72.2 percent answered "never" with reference to the four occupations, respectively. Unfortunately, the image of the blind as individuals who are restricted to making brooms or cane chairs or selling pencils on the street has clearly not been eliminated (Nichols, 1970). Thus, the critical factor related to the vocational future for the blind seems to be society's acceptance of the blind in competitive employment.

The National Federation of the Blind has become increasingly vocal about creating a new image for the blind individual among both the blind and the general public. In a newspaper article reporting on some of the Federation's efforts, charges were leveled at society for overprotecting and babysitting the blind, thus preventing them from reaching full adulthood (*Los Angeles Times*, Dec. 25, 1975). The Mr. Magoo stereotype was particularly resented. Airline and railroad company policies restricting the travel of the blind have been challenged and, in some cases, such policies have been rescinded. For example, Amtrak once required blind passengers to be accompanied by a guide dog or sighted companion, but yielded to pressure from the Federation. Landlords are often accused of refusing to rent to the blind because of fears they will burn down the building or injure themselves.

Publications prepared to guide and teach the blind have been described as debasing and humiliating. One such publication gave instructions for drying oneself after a bath and concluded, "as towel gets damp, shift to a dry section." Another included a section on applauding; it read, "move each hand towards the other so they come in contact with one another towards the center of the body." The Federation believes such content reflects a public assumption that to be blind is to be mentally retarded, and that this attitude discourages the blind from rising above their handicap. This attitude is considered all the worse because it is not based on fear or anger, but on pity. The article concluded with the challenge that militancy among the blind may some day result in, among other changes, blind individuals having expanded and improved training opportunities, access to better occupations, the right to adopt children without a court fight, the right to serve on a jury, and the right to such a simple luxury as a safe deposit box.

There is some suggestion in the literature that hearing-handicapped individuals do not leave school with the same preparation for life as their normal-hearing counterparts (Altshuler, 1974). It has been found that the average individual in a special school for the deaf completes his or her education at age eighteen with a fourth- to fifth-grade proficiency in reading and arithmetic. Only one-quarter develop speech skills sufficient for effective communication with the hearing world. Deaf adolescents may continue to blame others for their problems longer than hearing children, and they may lack the camaraderie typically found among hearing adolescents. Because they learn by rote, even at older ages, the deaf may lack an awareness and understanding of dating and family roles, educational aspirations, or job responsibilities.

The New York State Deaf Population Research Program revealed that 99.2 percent of the deaf individuals surveyed had attended school at one time, 26 percent left school after age sixteen, and 3.7 percent attended or graduated from college (Altshuler & Baroff, 1969). Individuals who became deaf after age four had a greater chance of graduating from grade school or a school for the deaf. This fact has been attributed to the advantage of greater language development before the onset of deafness. Seventy-six percent of those in the study reported they liked school and their teachers.

In the vocational area, 87 percent of the deaf were performing some kind of manual labor, with one-half of this group falling in the skilled labor category. Deaf individuals appeared to be excellent employment risks, with 93 percent of the men and 69 percent of the women holding jobs for more than three years. Included in the study were a group of outstanding deaf achievers in the fields of art, architecture, engineering, chemistry, dentistry, and accounting (Jarvik, Salzberger, & Falek, 1969). It was concluded that unusual achievement is associated with factors that are similar for the deaf and the hearing. However, much more effort, endowment, and opportunity were required for equivalent accomplishments on the part of the deaf.

The increased ability in language and communication skills of the hard-of-hearing probably enables them to become absorbed in the hearing world. Also, some acquire their hearing impairment after establishing a vocational career. However, if hearing problems interfere with communication, language, and educational levels in childhood and adolescence, we can expect many of these individuals to fall short of their full adult potential (McConnell, 1973).

The individual who is orthopedically impaired often faces a difficult adjustment in approaching adult life. A study of cerebral-palsied students who entered college found that they generally experienced more academic difficulty than did nonimpaired students and that they required more time to complete undergraduate and graduate study (Muthard & Hutchison, 1969). A greater percentage of handicapped students chose counseling as a career than did nonhandicapped individuals. Only 4 percent of college graduates with cerebral palsy were unemployed, whereas about 70 percent of all cerebral-palsied adults are unemployed.

For the individual with cerebral palsy whose handicap is largely confined to the legs, a number of occupations are possible (Schonell, 1956). These include watch repairing, optical or dental mechanics, developing and printing film, clerical work, statistical and research work, assembling parts of small machinery or equipment, art, and pottery making. The chief obstacle in gaining employment may be getting to and from the job.

The major problems facing individuals with seizure disorders in later life relate to social adjustment and exclusion from employment. It has been estimated that 60 percent of all employers in the country will not hire individuals with epilepsy under any circumstances (Crowther, 1967). Despite improved drug therapy for seizure control and gradually changing attitudes toward epilepsy, there has been little change in the employment picture for the epileptic (Dennerll, Rodin, Gonzales, Schwartz, & Lin, 1966).

On the one hand, an individual with a seizure disorder wants a good job with a good salary and opportunity for advancement. He or she may live with the hope that the last seizure has occurred. On the other hand, the individual knows that a single seizure can bring about dismissal or exposure to embarrassment or danger. Once the disease is known and on his or her records, employment and insurance laws can block any future employment (Bridge, 1949). Undoubtedly, this kind of conflict and others experienced during earlier years in school place the individual with a seizure disorder under great stress and may largely account for the personality and social adjustment problems seen in adult life. Individuals with orthopedic impairments and other chronic health problems can enter occupations commensurate with their abilities. When adequate measures are taken to protect them and those with whom they work from possible hazards arising from their handicaps, they can contribute productively.

Gerri Jewell is a young woman who is a stand-up comedienne. Her act consists of one joke after another about cerebral palsy. What makes this more surprising is that she has cerebral palsy. Her head sways, her gait is awkward, and her speech is slurred. None of these problems, however, dim her determination and wit. In one joke she says, "I'm one of the few people who drives better than I walk. I've only been pulled over once for speeding but four times for walking." She has appeared in a number of television situation comedies, which pleased her immensely because most such shows employ nonhandicapped actors to portray the handicapped rather than let the handicapped portray themselves. In one show, she played a student who has an affair with a teacher, which also pleased her because she believes many handicapped individuals see themselves as asexual. A college drama instructor urged her to explore an acting and stand-up comedy career, refusing to baby or shelter her as most of her other teachers had done. Her accomplishments are an impressive example of individualization.

What happens to emotionally disturbed individuals as they mature and grow up? A long-range study by Robins examined the adult social and psychiatric outcomes of 524 child guidance clinic patients after a thirty-year interval and compared them with 100 normal school children of the same age, sex, neighborhood, race, and IQ (Robins, 1966). The patients were separated into "antisocial" and "neurotic" categories. Overall findings suggested that the antisocial group needed more help in adult life, whereas the neurotic group resembled the controls in later years.

The antisocial children had experienced more arrests and imprisonment; were more mobile geographically, and had more mental difficulties, poorer occupational and economic histories, impoverished social and organizational relationships, and poorer armed service records. They used alcohol in excess more frequently and in many respects were in poorer health. Antisocial behavior in childhood was not found to predict any specific deviance but rather a generalized inability to conform and perform in society in many areas.

The neurotic group did have more difficulty in several areas of adult life than did the antisocial group. For example, more men were deferred by draft boards for physical disability, more women earned less than eighty dollars per week, and more men and women reported nervous symptoms in one or more of their children. The group, however, was rated more favorably than the controls in some areas of later adjustment. There were fewer single women, and fewer women who sought medical help. Among the men, fewer received medical discharges in the armed services.

In selecting the control group for this study, three criteria were set: the control children (1) had not been referred to a psychiatric clinic, (2) had not repeated one full year of elementary school, and (3) had not left elementary school due to expulsion or transfer to a correctional institution. Only 2 percent of these children were ever seen by a juvenile court. The author reports that the control children from working-class backgrounds with predominantly average IQs actually achieved as good or better an adjustment as the gifted children from upper middle-class backgrounds in the Terman study discussed earlier.

Results of follow-up studies indicate a continuing poor prognosis for severely emotionally disturbed children (Hingtgen & Bryson, 1972). As such children mature, their psychotic behav-

The absence of serious problems in school is seen by Robins as an efficient predictor of successful adjustment in adult life. Whereas Terman's gifted children enjoyed spectacular school success and the control subjects in Robin's study experienced only a lack of serious school problems, there was virtually no difference between the two groups in rates of deviant behavior in adult life. Thus, a lack of problems in school appears correlated with adequacy of later adjustment. Only 15 percent of the highly antisocial children ever entered high school, whereas more than half the children in the study with little antisocial behavior went on to high school. More than two-thirds of the highly antisocial children did not even complete the eighth grade.

This study emphasizes the critical role of the school in relation to success in later life. Forces outside the control of the teacher and the school were probably primarily responsible for the poor performance by the antisocial group. However, if provisions had been made for early intervention in the school with regard to increasing the chances of success for these children, both school functioning and later adjustment might have been greatly improved. Whatever the limitations of our educational system, it exists as a miniature socialization arena within which many of society's demands for adjustment are made. Individuals who will eventually take their place in this society perhaps gain their most crucial training in school.

iors usually remain dominant, or evidence of organic damage or retardation increases. Complete remission has rarely been reported. Although behavior symptoms, such as rituals and resistance to change, may diminish with age, the child's social adjustment generally remains poor. One follow-up study of 3,370 children referred to a hospital psychiatry department in Melbourne found that 12 percent (406) were patients of the mental health department as adults (Mellsop, 1972). This represents a fourfold greater risk of becoming an adult psychiatric patient than would be found in the general population. When the mentally retarded were excluded, the rate was three-and-one-half times greater than expected for the general population. Results indicated that original symptoms had little predictive value.

Studies following autistic children from early childhood into adult life have shown that language abnormalities usually persist, interpersonal relationships improve but remain deficient, and obsessive-like rituals of behavior diminish but do not disappear (Rutter, 1972). Follow-up studies also demonstrate a major difference in outcome between autistic children of normal intelligence and those with mental retardation. The autistic child with a low IQ has a poor prognosis in all respects, and many develop a seizure disorder. Nearly all of those whose IQs are below 50 face long-term institutionalization. In contrast, the autistic child of normal intelligence has a better prognosis.

The relationship is less clear between childhood and adult schizophrenia. Evidence is accumulating that adults who develop schizophrenia often displayed emotional and behavioral problems of a nonpsychotic nature in childhood. Although studies indicate that schizophrenia often begins with prepsychotic characteristics in childhood, these traits do not form a sufficiently distinct pattern useful for prediction.

Speech-handicapped individuals have been found to have a tendency toward maladjustment that seems to increase as the speech defective grows older (Berry & Eisenson, 1956). The home adjustment of a group of college students with stuttering problems was studied and, as a group, they felt that they were misunderstood by their parents, that their maturity was underestimated, and that their parents were disappointed with them (Duncan, 1949). They also had strong desires to leave home. In his review of studies on the personality characteristics of stutterers, Sheehan found little evidence to suggest that stutterers "are different from anybody else," but did conclude that their levels of aspiration were lower (Sheehan, 1958).

Recovery rates for individuals with speech defects are not conclusively determined. The results of two studies on recovery from stuttering suggest that a significant proportion of children who stutter may outgrow their speech problem without therapeutic intervention. In a report of 5,138 college students examined as part of three general speech surveys, 147 claimed that they had at some time been definitely categorized as stutterers (Sheehan & Martyn, 1970). Spontaneous recovery was found in 80 percent of all stuttering cases. The investigators note, however, that because severity affects the probability of recovery, the 80-percent recovery possibility does not apply to every child who stutters. Of those whose stuttering was mild, 87 percent recovered. Seventy-five percent of the moderate stutterers recovered, whereas a severe stutterer's chances were only fifty-fifty. Familial incidence of stuttering did not distinguish those whose speech problems continued from those whose problems disappeared. With severity held constant, public school therapy had no effect on the probability of eventual recovery. Those who had received therapy described it as woefully inadequate.

In a replication of this study with a younger and more heterogeneous population—5,054 junior and senior high school students—119 active stutterers were found, as well as 68 students who reported recovery from stuttering. This 36-percent recovery rate for the total population of stutterers varied from less than 33 percent among the junior high students to 44 percent in the senior high group. As in the findings of the previous study, no relationship was found between recovery and participation in therapy when severity was controlled. It was concluded that a substantial proportion of stutterers may demonstrate spontaneous recovery.

In a critical review of research on prevalence, age of onset, and recovery from stuttering, however, it was concluded that the high rates of recovery reported in the above studies are overestimates (Young, 1975). Two major reasons are given for this conclusion. First, attempts to identify recovered stutterers based on self-reports of events that occurred in the remote past are not likely to yield accurate and verifiable data. Second, the onset of stuttering occurs in childhood, with essentailly no new onsets after age nine. And, since the prevalence of stuttering in both school-age and young adult populations is the same—0.7 percent—there is some doubt that substantial numbers of older individuals recover from stuttering. Thus, estimates of recovery rates for stuttering are at best tentative.

Little is known about recovery from such speech handicaps as delayed language (Weiner, 1974). Because delayed-language problems are not followed after the early school years, the actual level of language development, educational achievement, and social adjustment of language-delayed children approaching adulthood remains unknown.

The eventual individualization of disadvantaged individuals will reflect their motivation to succeed and their commitment to prepare themselves for the future. Marked differences have been found between lower- and middle-class children with respect to such motivation and

The media have reported on the National Stuttering Project, which is described as "the Alcoholics Anonymous for those who stutter." It was started by two adult stutterers who wanted to boost understanding of stuttering and eliminate its cartoon character, Porky Pig stereotype. At local chapters, stutterers join in group discussions and describe painful experiences they have had because of their speech problem. Such discussions are entered into with great enthusiasm because fearfulness and self-consciousness readily disappear.

commitment (Miller & Swanson, 1960). Middle-class children were found to believe that they could improve their economic position through effort and sacrifice. They expressed willingness to postpone immediate gratification for future rewards and saw a reputation for honesty, responsibility, and respectability as important. Individual advancement was seen as based on self-denial, competent performance, formal education, rationality, and hard work. Above all, mastery of self through a rational approach was viewed as a requirement for mastering the world.

Lower-class children tend to view success and security as uncertain and are more concerned with the present than the future. Formal education may be desirable but not essential for getting a job and holding it. Physical strength and manual skill are more highly valued. The lower-class child does not see self-control and responsibility as overly important and tends to seek pleasure now rather than to take a chance on an uncertain reward in the future.

Most American children, regardless of class, aspire to achieve a work career beyond the level of their parents. (Goldstein, 1967). Lower-class youth may be less likely to move toward higher education in order to attain professional status, and they may not be as optimistic as are higher-categorized youth. Most of them, however, are aware that "getting ahead" is expected of them.

A large-scale study was undertaken with 25,000 junior and senior high school students in North Carolina to determine (among other variables) the effect of social class, parent education, and parental pressure on achievement of adolescent motivation and achievement in school. (Elder, 1962). Among the findings were: (1) social class and parent education are positively related to academic motivation and achievement; (2) low achievers are more apt to report strong achievement demands from parents than are high achievers, middle- and lower-class parents being equally likely to put pressure on high achievers; and (3) middle-class parents are much more likely a determiner of student motivation and achievement than is social class status alone.

Descriptions in the literature of economically disadvantaged and/or culturally different individuals in later life suggest that some will encounter serious problems. A report based on 400 Plains Indian adolescents seen in a one-hundred-year-old Indian Boarding School in western Oklahoma describes dropout rates of up to 60 percent, educational achievement well below the national average, and high but undocumented incidences of glue-sniffing, alcoholism, and suicide attempts among the youth (Allen, 1973).

One study investigating the relationship between economic disadvantage and self-concept collected data on 600 urban, economically disadvantaged adults. (Miskimins & Baker, 1973). Results indicated that although the disadvantaged as a group did not differ greatly from the general population in self-esteem, they had "more than their share" of other problems, including higher levels of maladjustment, relationship problems, caution, and aloofness. Poverty affected women and men differently. Men were likely to show exaggerated self-esteem, extreme caution, suspicion, and aloofness in dealing with others. Women seemed to be more directly affected by economic disadvantage, indicating lower self-esteem and higher self-derogation.

In considering what happens to individuals with learning disabilities as they grow and mature, we are again faced with problems of definition. We have already discussed the dilemma of verifying the presence of neurological impairment and have admitted that many of the problems associated with learning disabilities, such as underachievement, hyperactivity, and distractibility, are commonly found among children with behavior disorders and children considered mentally retarded and disadvantaged. There is no universal agreement in special education as to when certainty of diagnosis allows us to exclude other primary causal factors and to settle on learning disability. Therefore, our discussion of individualization and the learning-disabled child will focus on the characteristic of hyperactivity and follow-up studies of hyperactive children. This focus is justifiable because the characteristic of hyperactivity has been reported as the single, most often observed characteristic of children with learning disabilities (Clements, 1966).

In general, the clinical literature suggests that hyperactivity diminishes with age (Bradley, 1957) and tends to disappear somewhere between the ages of twelve and eighteen (Laufer & Denhoff, 1957). However, serious educational and emotional problems have been found to persist (Laufer, 1962; Anderson & Plymate, 1962). In one follow-up study, forty-five teenagers (twelve to sixteen years of age), who had previously been seen in a clinic for hyperactivity, were interviewed, as were their mothers (Stewart, 1970). Data from the interviews with mothers indicated that these children had changed very little since they were first seen at the clinic. They still displayed restlessness, inability to concentrate or finish projects, overtalkativeness, and poor school performance. Many mothers described their youngsters as having low self-esteem. Increases were reported in impatience, resistance to discipline, irritability, and lying. Substantial proportions engaged in fighting, stealing, running away from home, and truancy. Drinking was not uncommon. Many of the teenagers themselves said that they had difficulty studying and were not interested in school. From these results and the findings of other studies, Stewart suggests that hyperactive children may "start life with a temperament that is distinctly abnormal" (p. 97). Here we see an overlap between children with behavior disorders and hyperactive children, the majority of whom may have serious learning problems in school and may be candidates for the label of learning disabled.

A five-year, follow-up study was done with sixty-four chronically and severely hyperactive children who were between the ages of six and thirteen at the initiation of the study and had an IQ above 84 (Weiss, Minde, Werry, Douglas, & Nemeth, 1971). At the time of the follow-up evaluation, they ranged in age from ten to eighteen. The most striking finding was that, whereas restlessness had been the main problem for each child five years before, it was no longer the chief complaint for any child. Classroom observations of the children revealed more restlessness than in normal children, but it was much more subdued and less disturbing (e.g., playing with a pencil) than it had been five years earlier (e.g., walking around the room). Distractibility was still evident but less so than at the onset of the study. A significant decrease was also seen in aggressiveness and excitability. The most common behavioral problem was emotional immaturity, which was

On the more positive side, there is some evidence that having a learning disability does not necessarily prohibit success in adult life. One follow-up study of twenty boys with serious reading problems found that all of them had gone to college and, except for two, had gained degrees, several of them beyond the bachelor's level (Rawson, 1968). All of the boys in this study had attended a private school, where they had received remedial reading instruction utilizing a multisensory approach. However, we should bear in mind that there is great variability among children considered learning disabled, and follow-up studies cited here cannot be considered to consist of matched populations of children. On a more optimistic note, evidence also has been collected that suggests that several men of eminence had specific language disabilities, particularly in reading and spelling (Thompson, 1971). Among them were Thomas Edison, Harvey Cushing, Woodrow Wilson, William James, Albert Einstein, Lawrence Lowell, George Patton, Auguste Rodin, and Paul Ehrlich.

reported by 70 percent of the parents. The second most common trait was described as a lack of ambition and a severe lack of ability to maintain goals. As in earlier studies, poor academic functioning most clearly distinguished the group as a whole. The authors concluded that although hyperactivity diminishes with age, other major handicaps such as underachievement and emotional immaturity persist.

Although these children had not reached adulthood, we can speculate, partly on the basis of the data on older individuals, that many would be poorly prepared for advanced schooling or vocational training due to academic deficiencies. As a result, they would have difficulty supporting themselves. Such traits as lack of ambition and inability to maintain goals may be strengthened in the adult years by continued failure and frustration, thus further diminishing the individual's chances for success. It may be that the minimal neurological impairment that was possibly present in some of these children and contributed to early childhood hyperactivity had been outgrown. However, what may really limit the learning-disabled child in pursuing a happy and successful adult life are the secondary problems of accumulated school failure and maladaptive behavior. Thus, capacity may be far less a determiner of individualization than is experience. Again, the importance of early intervention and the provision of education that helps children with learning disabilities to learn and succeed is vividly illustrated.

What happens to the mentally retarded individual when he or she reaches adult life? A longitudinal follow-up study (mentioned earlier) of persons who had been enrolled in public school classes for the mildly retarded in Lincoln, Nebraska, was begun in the 1930s and continued into the 1960s (Baller, 1936; Charles, 1953; Baller, Charles, & Miller, 1967). Of the 206 in the original sample, the death rate was slightly higher than that of the general population, but only a handful were in institutions. More than half of the males had been prosecuted for some violation of the law, but seldom for serious crimes and often for minor offenses such as traffic violations. Well over half had married, but roughly one-fifth of these were divorced—a rate equal at that time to the general population—although continuing follow-up showed a higher divorce rate in later years. The majority of their children were making satisfactory progress in school without evidence of retardation. A surprising number (55 percent) owned their own homes. Although these were often in poor condition, some were expensive, new houses. Over 80 percent had been self-supporting for some time, although their jobs were often in the semi-skilled and unskilled range. Favorable economic conditions were also a factor in these early studies. Two other studies (Fairbanks, 1935; Kennedy, 1966) of mildly retarded adults showed an even more favorable employment outlook than the first Nebraska study (Baller, 1936), which was conducted during the depression.

The average IQ of the Nebraska group on follow-up was 81, compared with a mean IQ of 58 when the group was originally tested. This and related research suggests that the mental age of mildly retarded persons continues to increase even into their late thirties (Fisher & Zeaman, 1970). It has been suggested that if mentally retarded individuals stayed in school until they were twenty-five or thirty, they might approach the educational accomplishments they fail to reach at the time of high school graduation (Holt, 1964). Special education does seem to make a difference. Comparative studies of mildly retarded graduates indicate that those who attended special classes made a better adjustment than those who had been in regular classrooms (Peck & Stephens, 1964; Porter & Milazzo, 1958).

Most studies reveal that mildly retarded individuals may progress in their level of adjustment as they move through adult life (Heber & Dever, 1970). Also, research findings have dispelled many myths regarding the tendency of retarded individuals to produce large families, including retarded offspring, or to become chronic law violators, moral deviates, or welfare-roll liabilities (Biklen, 1977; Browning, 1976). A study of adult male offenders in New England (MacEachron, 1979) suggested that prevalence rates of retarded offenders are only slightly higher than the prevalence rate of mental retardation itself and that social and legal factors are better predictors of criminality than is intelligence.

In fact, many workshop programs and vocational placement efforts have met with considerable success and have begun to establish the reputation of the retarded worker as a stable and dependable employee, but only if adequate preparation has been available prior to his or her entry into the job market (Forness, 1982b; Gold, 1973; Halpern, 1973). Retarded individuals often hold jobs that cluster in food services (waiter, kitchen helper), custodial and personal services (janitor, orderly, nurse's aide), industry (packaging, laundry, machine operator), and unskilled labor (Clark, Kivitz, & Rosen, 1968). Even severely retarded adults are capable of holding such jobs if systematic efforts are made to provide effective training and close supervision at the beginning of their career (Lynch, Kiernan, & Stark, 1982; Wehman, 1981, 1983).

Recent interest has also focused on agricultural job opportunities for retarded persons and on the less stressful demands afforded by rural living (Jacobs, 1978; Lynch, 1978). Several factors recently found to be good predictors of vocational adjustment in retarded adults include academic achievement (Quinones, 1978), adaptive behavior (Cunningham & Presnall, 1978), verbal manners and communication skills (Malgady, Barcher, Towner, & Davis, 1979), performance on vocational checklists (Walls & Werner, 1977), and actual samples of work behavior (Friedenberg & Martin, 1977; Schreiner, 1978; Stodden, Casale, & Schwartz, 1977). It is interesting to note that the issue of sex role stereotyping has lately been raised in some vocational preparation programs for retarded females (Danker-Brown, Sigelman, & Flexer, 1978; Sigelman, Ater, and Spanhel, 1978).

Retarded individuals who have been in institutions have less favorable prognoses, especially

Employment of retarded individuals does not *always* require specialized techniques or sheltered settings; rather, it requires an employer's willingness to take a business risk based on sound financial principles. This was demonstrated in a recent project in which McDonald's restaurants hired seventeen mentally retarded adults in a cooperative agreement with an Ohio county agency for the mentally retarded (Brickey & Campbell, 1981). The average IQ of these individuals was 57, and their ages ranged from twenty-one to fifty-two years. Without federal or state support and with relatively little assistance from county officials, McDonald's supervisory staff trained these new employees mainly for lot and lobby positions that involved cleaning grounds and tables. Several eventually moved up to more responsible positions working in the supply room, making french fries, and the like, although none were able to handle counter positions. After two years, the turnover rate of these employees was 42 percent compared to 175 percent turnover for nonhandicapped employees. When one considers that turnover costs (including advertising, interviewing, record keeping, orientation, training, etc.) range from $300 to $2,000 per person, McDonald's management appears to have made a sound fiscal investment in hiring these mentally retarded workers. It should also be noted that by working in private enterprise, these mentally retarded adults reduced their yearly dependence on county funds from nearly $5,000 per person to less than $2,300.

in the earlier studies (Channing, 1952), and nearly two-thirds of those with the most favorable predictions for community adjustment eventually have had to be reinstitutionalized (Windle, 1962). However, this is also usually the case with persons of normal intelligence who have disturbed personalities or histories of social maladjustment and who have been discharged from an institution. In both cases, the severity of the individual's problems determines his or her chances for success outside the institution (Crawford, Aiello, & Thompson, 1979; Sternlicht, 1978). In chapter 4, we discussed some problems of institutionalization. Recent studies of deinstitutionalized retarded adults have shown a slightly more favorable outcome because of increased vocational and social adjustment programs designed to prepare retarded persons to return to community settings (Birenbaum & Re, 1979; Gollay, 1977; McDevitt, Smith, Schmidt, & Rosen, 1978). The outlook for future planning seems even more positive in that fewer retarded persons may need to be in institutional settings (Roos, 1978; Sitkei, 1980; Tarjan, Wright, Eyman, & Keeran, 1973).

As expected, noninstitutionalized severely retarded adults, such as those who have attended classes for the trainable, fall somewhere between the mildly retarded and the institutionalized retarded in adult life adjustment. Although very few long-term studies have been done on this group, the results seem to indicate that about one-fourth will eventually be institutionalized (Kirk, 1964; Saenger, 1957). Also, those living at home will seldom hold meaningful employment. In a study of graduates of classes for the trainable mentally retarded in California, it was reported that less than one-half were working in sheltered workshops and none were self-supporting (Stanfield, 1973). Most had few social or leisure activities outside their immediate family. Sadly, the most pressing wish of these "graduates" and their parents was for them to achieve true adult status. For readers who are interested in what it is like to be retarded, an annotated bibliography of writings by retarded persons has been compiled (Stanovich & Stanovich, 1979).

The normative follow-up studies discussed previously may often mask the true picture of individualization. Edgerton has presented an informative and moving account of the day-to-day life of forty-eight retardates discharged from a state hospital for the retarded near Los Angeles (Edgerton, 1967; Edgerton, 1979; Edgerton & Bercovici, 1976). They had a mean IQ somewhat comparable to the initial IQ of the Nebraska subjects (Baller, Charles, & Miller, 1967). Few achieved an adjustment that could be called successful by middle-class standards, and many could not have achieved their present marginal adjustment without the help of a normal "benefactor" on whom they depended for assistance. The paucity of their leisure time activities was especially striking. Riding a city bus to the end of the line and a preoccupation with television were characteristic of how they spent their time. A more favorable outlook might have been expected had these retarded adults not been institutionalized at one time, though follow-up of adults from inner-city EMR classrooms reveals similar findings (Koegel & Edgerton, 1982). Edgerton describes the attempts of mildly retarded adults to pass as nonretarded or to weave for themselves a "cloak of competence." Tattered as these attempts may have been, they did enable them to achieve some level of individualization. It was hazardous to predict which persons would have difficulty; some retarded individuals who had serious problems in initial adjustment experienced success in later years. This is an important finding that must be stressed. The longer some retarded adults remained in the community, the better adjusted and happier their lives seemed to become. Learning to live in the world proved to be a rather painful process initially, but one that at least some retarded persons eventually were able to master.

Figure 8-3.

Normalization, helping the retarded to live their daily lives as normally as possible without being unnecessarily segregated from nonretarded persons, is now an accepted principle in planning services for the retarded (Flynn & Nitsch, 1980; Thurman & Fiorelli, 1979). Few retarded persons participate fully in adult life, however, and much remains to be done in the area of individualization (Bruininks, Meyers, Sigford, & Lakin, 1981; Reiter & Levi, 1981). Social activities are often confined to immediate communities (Corcoran & French, 1977; Edmondson, 1974; Marion, 1979a), but systematic travel training has been shown to increase this range (Hughes, Smith, & Benitz, 1977). Leisure-time activities for some severely and profoundly retarded persons seem to consist of toys or simple games (Day & Day, 1977; Favell & Cannon, 1976; Wehman, 1978), and mildly retarded adults seem to have difficulty in learning rules for competitive team sports (Levine & Langness, 1983). A leisure-time activities curriculum has been developed to assist parents and caretakers in planning for the developmental progress of retarded persons to more complex levels of play and socialization (Wehman, 1976).

Marriage often may be restricted to other retardates (Floor, Baxter, Rosen, & Zisfein, 1975). Sex education programs are frequently necessary (Edmondson, McCombs, & Wish, 1979) and are becoming more available for retarded individuals; but they continue to meet numerous objections, even from parents (Alcorn, 1974; Vockell & Mattick, 1972). Surgical contraception may be recommended in many cases (Bass, 1978). Although retarded persons are eligible to vote in most states, few ever exercise that option (Gerard, 1974; Olley & Ramey, 1978; Osborne, 1975). With the emphasis on normalization, law-related education on consumer and civic issues is now becoming an important part of the curriculum for retarded adolescents (Riekes, Spiegel, & Keilitz, 1977). The political knowledge of retarded adults has, in fact, been found to be at a level similar to that of normal fifth-grade children (Klein & Green, 1979). In this regard, police, lawyers, and judges have been found seriously lacking in knowledge of mental retardation (Reichard, Spencer, & Spooner, 1980; Schilit, 1979).

An increasingly popular living arrangement for retarded adults, rather than living with parents or in residential institutions, is the group home or apartment where several retarded persons share the duties and responsibilities of small-group communal living (Aninger & Bolinsky, 1977; Berdiansky & Parker, 1977; Crnic & Pym, 1979; Gardner, 1977; Gilbert & Hemming, 1979; Heal, Sigelman, & Switzkey, 1978; Janicki, Mayeda & Epple, 1983). Recently, this approach has encountered a number of problems, including housing discrimination toward mentally retarded persons (Meyers, 1980; Moen & Aanes, 1979; Trippi, Michael, Colao, & Alvarez, 1978); moreover, there is concern that community living arrangements may simply represent smaller versions of the large state institutions (Bercovici, 1977; Edgerton & Langness, 1978; Ellis et al., 1981; Landesman-Dwyer, 1981). Finally, the particularly troublesome issues of the aged retarded person (Kriger, 1975; Segal, 1977), passive euthanasia or withholding treatment from severely or profoundly retarded infants (Hardman & Drew, 1978), and indiscriminate therapeutic abortion of fetuses with conditions associated with mental retardation (Davis, 1981; Smith, 1981) must be addressed directly before practice outruns ethical guidelines.

It has long been considered that social incompetence, or the basic incapacity for self-management beyond a marginal level, is the only criterion that society can justly impose for mental retardation (Doll, 1941). This view regards the essential problem of the retarded as getting along in their environment, rather than adequacy in intelligence. Although opportunities for personal development and achievement in later life are certainly more limited for the retarded adult, current evidence reveals a more optimistic picture regarding individualization than might be assumed from the layman's traditional concept of mental retardation. Most incidence figures seem to show a marked decline of identified retarded persons after the formal school years. A careful study of the life histories of a large number of mildly retarded individuals (Richardson, 1978) seems to indicate that as many as 80 percent appeared to need no mental retardation services. Once the ordeal of school and its particular demands on the mentally retarded are over, many individuals considered retarded by the school seem to blend back into the fabric of society and achieve, however marginally, a measure of individualization.

In considering the eventual attainments of gifted individuals in adult life, the Terman study provides information on education, career achievement, and mental status. (Terman & Oden, 1959).

The individuals in the Terman study undertook most of their college work from 1930 to 1940, a period of widespread economic depression in which less than 8 percent of the general population of comparable age graduated from college. Within the Terman group, however, some 70 percent of the men and 67 percent of the women completed college. Of these, two-thirds of the men and almost three-fifths of the women entered graduate school; 56 percent of the men and 33 percent of the women completed one or more advanced degrees. Financial problems and lack of parental encouragement were frequently cited as reasons that approximately 30 percent of the group did not complete college. But the authors of the study conclude that the real cause usually was the failure of the high school to recognize the gifted individual's potential and give him or her the needed encouragement and stimulation.

More than 45 percent of the men in the Terman study entered the professional fields of law, university teaching, and engineering, in that order. An additional 40 percent entered managerial ranks in business and industry, public or private administration, or semiprofessional occupations. Among the women, one-half were housewives with no outside employment and 42 percent held full-time jobs. School teaching, including elementary and secondary administration and supervisory positions, was the most frequent occupation, accounting for almost one-fourth of the group. When career satisfaction and interest were examined, half of the men expressed "deep satisfaction" and another 37 percent stated they were "fairly content." Over 55 percent of the women expressed "deep satisfaction."

With respect to incidence of marriage, 93 percent of the men and almost 90 percent of the women were married by the time the average age of the subjects was forty-four. This was approximately the expected rate for the total national population of comparable age. Slightly more than one-fifth of these had a history of divorce. Although direct comparisons with the national population at large were not possible, the authors concluded that the longitudinal study of the group of gifted individuals over three and one-half decades has shown that, with few exceptions, the gifted child becomes the gifted adult who is superior in nearly every aspect.

Summary

To conclude this chapter on individualization, we review our discussion of the marriage and family life, career development, and adult functioning level of the exceptional learner.

Marriage and Family Life

All young people have questions and often profit from guidance regarding the physical changes and feelings they experience as they mature, including exceptional learners. Although some parents and others wish that sex would simply not be a part of the exceptional learners' life, it will be, just as it is part of a nonexceptional individual's life. Thus, it cannot be ignored. The exceptional learner should be prepared, by means of simple matter-of-fact statements, for the changes he or she will experience. In addition, some may need to be taught to distinguish between private and public situations with respect to engaging in sexual behavior.

It is difficult to rule out marriage for any exceptional learner, even for the severely retarded in some special cases. Blindness presents obvious inconveniences for child bearing and rearing, but these can be overcome. The same can be said for deafness and certain orthopedic impairments. When there is the possibility of an infant's being born with genetic defects or when exceptional individuals are likely to create a hazardous environment, child bearing must be carefully considered on an individual basis.

Career Development

The concept of career development and education in relation to exceptional learners is much broader than the traditional notion of vocational education. Career development includes preparation for successful, everyday living in addition to occupational skills. Unfortunately, occupational training often does not begin until the exceptional or nonexceptional individual is in late adolescence and potentially valuable training time during the childhood years is lost. Hopefully, the 1980s will see an increase in job opportunities that enable exceptional learners to attain a greater level of productivity and self-sufficiency.

Adult Functioning Level

Visually impaired individuals may encounter some difficulty and uncertainty in their relationships with members of the opposite sex, as may the hearing impaired whose difficulty in communication can delay adult social development. One problem faced by the blind, deaf, orthopedically impaired, chronically ill, and retarded is continued dependence on others. Some dependence may be necessary to insure safety and needed assistance, but some independence may be denied by societal attitudes and restrictive environments. Exceptional learners with visual, hearing, or orthopedic impairments are good employment risks, but opportunities are often limited by those same societal attitudes and restrictions.

Disturbed children with antisocial tendencies have been shown to make poorer adult adjustments than do those who are anxious and neurotic. Severe emotional disturbance seldom changes markedly in the adult years. Stuttering and hyperactivity seem to lessen in later adolescence and adulthood, but exceptional learners who have had these problems may reflect the effects of negative childhood experiences and manifest immaturity and lack of ambition. Socioeconomic class differences appear to separate middle- from lower-class individuals. Middle-class children and adolescents appear to view effort and sacrifice as essential for getting ahead in later life, whereas their lower-class counterparts are less likely to postpone immediate rewards for an uncertain future.

The individualization of the retarded has been studied more thoroughly than that of other exceptional learners. A long-term study of high school graduates enrolled in special classes revealed a striking degree of success. Some 80 percent were self-supporting, 50 percent were married and had nonretarded children, and their mean IQ increased from 58 at the time they left school to 81 in mid-adult life. More recent studies, however, reveal that many retarded people need supervised living arrangements in the community and assistance from a benefactor. This is particularly true of the retarded who have been institutionalized. The gifted have been found, in general, to enjoy a superior level of individualization.

Individualization, the eventual attainment of each adult, has only recently been focused on by society with respect to the exceptional learner. We are still a long way from understanding how, despite their limitations (in the case of the gifted, their outstanding abilities), exceptional learners can realize a sense of personal fulfillment and truly contribute to the welfare of society.

PART THREE

EDUCATIONAL DIMENSIONS

CHAPTER 9

The Learning Triangle

Up to this point in the text, we have been primarily concerned with introducing the exceptional learner and his or her unique characteristics. This chapter is concerned with approaches for dealing with these characteristics—ways of compensating for weaknesses and bolstering strengths. In other words, *special education*.

Only one kind of teaching really matters for all children—*good teaching*. Perhaps the major difference between teachers of nonexceptional learners and teachers of exceptional learners is that the latter have to worry more about the basic ingredients of good teaching—*curriculum, conditions*, and *consequences*.

Curriculum

Curriculum consists of any learning task, activity, or assignment that is directed toward increasing the child's knowledge or skill. It is the raw material of the learning situation. It is not restricted to basal reading or arithmetic texts or to the academic realm itself. For some autistic children, eye contact with the teacher is the initial curricular activity. Although social skills or language development may constitute long-term curricular goals, these goals cannot be attained without training sessions devoted to gaining the child's attention. Similarly, special educators working with children with behavior disorders often must concentrate on Seat-Sitting 1A, Waiting-Your-Turn 1A, or Rule-Following 1A, before getting on with Reading 1A. Curriculum for the exceptional learner involves "thinking small," "thinking basic," and "thinking sequentially."

In many instances, the exceptional learners's preacademic problems interfere with academic learning. Preacademic focus is important today because regular classroom teachers are assuming more responsibility for teaching the exceptional learners mainstreamed into their classrooms. Many such children must be helped to get ready to learn in a regular classroom while they are actually there.

Jack, who has a learning disability, may need help in establishing laterality (a consistent left-to-right orientation) in reading before he can become an efficient beginning reader. Certain educational tasks, such as focusing his attention on moving from left to right, may have to be introduced. Virgil, who is mildly mentally retarded, may need special help in understanding the directions associated with tasks in a beginning reading workbook, directions that are quickly understood by the nonexceptional child. Once Virgil understands the format and exactly what he is supposed to do, he will be more effective in working with the materials.

Disadvantaged Wayne may profit from beginning word-picture matching exercises that reflect elements of his environment. A neatly landscaped suburban home paired with the word *home* makes less sense than a two-story flat on a busy street. Shy, withdrawn Tommy may be excluded from active participation in an oral reading lesson and only expected to watch and listen until he seems ready to engage actively in verbal responding. The same may be true for Charles, who stutters. Oral reading may never be appropriate for him.

Perhaps a magazine on racing cars will gain Philip's attention. He is usually so fidgety and active that he disrupts the class. However, we can use Philip's interest in cars to encourage him to learn to read or to learn to spell words associated with racing. In the case of visually handicapped Bruce and hearing-handicapped Ann, the content and the level of the task may not be as important as the mode of presentation. For Bruce, tactual and auditory presentations will be necessary, and the visual mode will be emphasized for Ann. A teaching machine with a single button to push may be necessary for Mary, a cerebral palsied child who cannot write legibly.

The possibilities for varying educational tasks are almost endless. However, variation in content may be less significant in educating exceptional learners than variation in the conditions under which they must learn.

Conditions

Whatever the nature of the educational task, certain conditions and expectations must be met before the child can successfully undertake it. Consider this assignment. "Beverly, come to the front of the room and read to the class the sentence I have just written on the chalkboard." At first glance, this is a simple task; but on further analysis we are impressed with the conditions and expectations implied by the task.

When. The teacher has selected a given time for Beverly to be assigned this task. It may be 9:00 A.M. or 2:00 P.M. It may be following a playground fight Beverly had before coming into class. It may be the day after Beverly stayed up until 3:00 A.M. watching a late television movie. Nevertheless, Beverly is expected to respond *now*, and the condition of *when* must be met if she is to succeed.

Where. Beverly is expected to come to the front of the class, not remain at her desk or attempt the assignment privately in a study booth or with a small group of children seated around a worktable. At this moment, *where* she is to undertake the task is specifically defined.

How. Beverly also is expected to read out loud. She is not expected to point to a particular word, push the button on an automated teaching device, or circle the correct answer with her pencil on a worksheet. She is to walk to the front of the room, approach the chalkboard, and read orally what is written there.

How Much. If Beverly successfully meets the previous conditions associated with this task, there is still more to come. She is expected to read the entire sentence, not just the first word or two, to fulfill expectations.

How Long. Beverly will be expected to complete the task successfully within certain time limits. She cannot stand in front of the chalkboard and remain mute for ten minutes. She will be given only a certain number of trials before the teacher asks her to return to her seat and assigns another child in her place. In that event, Beverly will not succeed because she could not meet the condition of *how long*.

How Well. Even though she meets all of these conditons, Beverly's problems are not over. She will be expected to achieve a certain level of correctness in her reading in order to be considered successful. Stumbling on too many words, skipping over a word here and there, or totally mispronouncing a word will weigh against her as the teacher judges Beverly's competence in the assignment.

The world of school and learning is filled with expectations that must be met if the child is to be considered successful. More than the regular educator, the special educator has constantly had to exhibit flexibility in establishing conditions. However, times are changing, and regular teachers working with exceptional learners must be prepared to adjust classroom conditions to meet the needs of such children.

The selection of curricular tasks and the conditions of learning are controlled by the teacher. We are not responsible if children stay up all night watching television or are punished by their parents just before coming to school. But we are responsible for recognizing a poor child-task-condition match-up and for doing something about it. Besides assigning an alternate task, we can move the child from a group to an individual setting, modify the response mode of the task (e.g., "Johnny, you don't have to write your answers, just say them into the microphone of the tape recorder"), shorten the task or work period, or in some way communicate to the child that he or she is successful even though the work is not perfect. Selecting an appropriate task and anticipating the conditions under which it most likely can be done successfully is our major objective with each exceptional learner.

Finally, the consequences in learning are important to consider with respect to good teaching.

Consequences

Once the child completes a task, something usually happens. Perhaps the task itself has been rewarding because of the child's interest or sense of accomplishment. But it may also have been unpleasant and frustrating because of its level of difficulty. Perhaps a grade is given that determines the positive or negative consequences. Or the child's teacher may provide the consequences by smiling, frowning, or commenting, "Good work!" or "This is not acceptable." Consequences can also be delivered by classmates' looks of admiration or envy or ridiculing remarks and giggles.

In many regular classrooms, consequences may take care of themselves for a majority of children. That is, the interest level of the work or the desire to please the teacher may keep the class running smoothly. But for a few children in regular classrooms, we may have to pay special attention to consequences and make an extra effort to insure that something positive and rewarding occurs.

Certain positive consequences relied on by teachers of exceptional and nonexceptional learners are discussed in detail later in this chapter. They are:

- Joy

- Acquisition of knowledge and skill

- Knowledge of results

- Social approval

- Multisensory stimulation and activity

Figure 9–1.

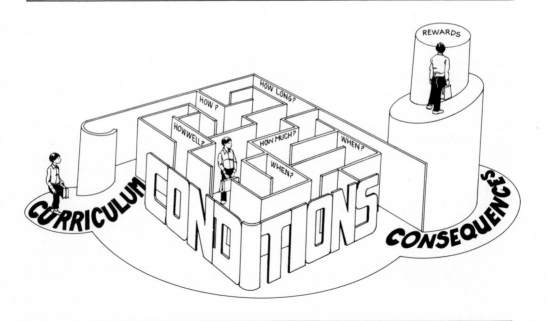

- Task completion

- Tangible rewards.

In addition to positive consequences, the use of negative consequences or punishment is of concern in both special and regular education. This issue is also discussed in a later section.

Curriculum, conditions, and consequences—they are the critical ingredients in all teaching and learning situations. We can conceive of these ingredients as the three sides of a learning triangle (see Figure 9–1).

When we have selected the appropriate curricular task, assigned it under appropriate conditions, and involved or followed it with consequences that satisfy the individual, we have maximized the chances for success. When children succeed, it is because the three sides are "working" for them. If they fail, it may be that one or more of the sides is "not working."

Mark is a good student most of the time. As long as the assignment (curriculum) we give him is at his level, conditions and consequences take care of themselves. But if the task is beyond him, he quickly becomes frustrated, sometimes breaking into tears or crumpling his paper. Thus, the curriculum side must get our special attention when we work with Mark. Betty is also a good student most of the time. As long as she is not sitting next to "chatterbox" Nancy, or not given assignments that take more than fifteen minutes to complete, she works hard and is motivated to succeed. But if distracted by her classmates or given half-hour or forty-minute tasks, she quickly becomes a troublemaker in class. The conditions side of the learning triangle is especially important for Betty. Then there is Bill, another good student most of the time. He has the skills to do all assigned class work and works well under all standard conditions. But Bill is bored. He seldom finishes a task and longs for recess, lunchtime, or the end of the school day. Bill's teacher has started to give him special privileges (e.g., hall monitor) following completion of his work.

Figure 9–2.

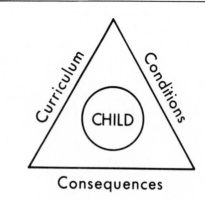

The Learning Triangle

Bill has really perked up, and the consequences side of the learning triangle has had a lot to do with it. When we consider the myriad of individual differences among exceptional learners, we can appreciate how many adjustments of one or more sides of the learning triangle might be necessary to insure their success.

A thorough presentation of even the highlights of effective teaching strategies for all types of exceptional learners would constitute a separate book or series of books. In this chapter, we briefly review some selected approaches for improving the competence of exceptional learners in preacademic areas—flexibility and sociality. Approaches for teaching language and academic subjects are beyond the scope of this text.

Flexibility Curriculum

In our discussion of flexibility curriculum, we are concerned with ways of helping the exceptional learner improve in attention, retention, perception, movement, and active participation.

Approaches and Activities Useful in Improving Attention and Retention   The listening attention of the visually handicapped child is crucially important in learning (Fitzhugh & Fitzhugh, 1966). This applies to both the partially seeing and to the blind. As these children progress through school, reading requirements constantly increase and the availability of materials in large type and Braille decreases. Therefore, it is essential that they derive maximum benefit from listening. These individuals frequently begin to depend on tape recordings, talking book records, and/or the help of sighted readers. Bishop (1971) has described a variety of activities that are useful in increasing the visually handicapped learner's listening skills. From simple sound-identification games, the child may be engaged in discriminating between tone and volume, reproducing sounds by imitation, and learning about the similarities between sounds through rhyming. To lengthen attention span, the teacher can repeat a sentence twice, changing a word or two during the second presentation. The child is asked to listen carefully and to note the exact changes that were made in the second sentence.

Auditory training for hard-of-hearing children attempts to develop systematically the child's discrimination of: (1) gross sounds, including environmental noises; (2) rhythm patterns of speech and music; (3) easy speech sounds in words, such as the vowels; (4) difficult speech sounds in works, such as the consonants; and (5) speech in noisy situations (Avery, 1967). Because the full use of residual hearing is critical in getting the child to pay attention and learn, a hearing aid is extremely important. Hearing-handicapped children's acceptance of a hearing aid will be determined partly by the increased listening skill it fosters and partly by the enthusiasm and support their families, teachers, and classmates show toward their wearing an aid.

Problems of distractibility often found in children with learning disabilities may hinder their acquisition of listening skills and hence their ability to follow directions. Listening exercises for such children are often helpful (Peterson, 1967). One exercise involves having someone who is out of sight produce various sounds for the children to identify, such as bouncing a ball, clapping, jumping, skipping, and shutting a door. When the group goes for a walk, the children can be instructed to listen for common sounds, including a car motor running, a train chugging, or a bird singing. To improve comprehension of spoken words in children with listening problems, the

In teaching children who have problems paying attention or retaining what they learn, increasing the vividness or impact of the task may be helpful. The work of Strauss and Lehtinen (1947) and Cruickshank (1967) has focused on the adaptation of curriculum materials for exceptional learners, particularly those with learning disabilities. For curriculum tasks, the authors emphasize increasing the stimulus value of the element to which the child's attention is to be directed. For example, a word-recognition lesson should not be prepared with black crayon on white paper, but rather with a bright color on colored paper. A different color can be used for each letter written on the paper, and each letter can be a different shape or size. As success is achieved in getting the child to attend to and learn under such conditions, more traditional approaches can be used.

teacher can give directions orally, beginning with short and simple ones ("Stand up") and increasing the difficulty as the child progresses ("Stand up, turn around, and then sit down"). Riddles also can be used to develop listening power and comprehension.

Studies of the retarded support an approach similar to that just described (Zeaman & House, 1963). These studies have investigated discrimination learning, since the ability to discriminate between two or more stimuli is basic to nearly every school learning task. Children, for example, must learn to discriminate one letter from another before they can begin to read, and they must be able to discern one number from another before they can learn to add. Discrimination learning has two components. First, the child must attend to the similarities or differences between two or more choices. Next, he or she must make the correct response, that is, choose the right one. Mentally retarded children tend to have considerable difficulty in the first area, called *attending*. But once they have learned to attend to relevant cues, they can acquire many responses almost as well as normal children (Zeaman & House, 1963).

Therefore, during the initial stages of a learning task, the teacher must increase the likelihood that the retarded child will attend to the relevant cues associated with each stimulus. In fostering the development of this discrimination, a teacher should use a variety of different cue dimensions, such as color, form, size, and texture. Once correct discriminations are established, the teacher can begin to reduce emphasis on these cues. This easy-to-hard sequencing ensures that the child moves gradually toward the final discrimination (such as between letters and words on a printed page) without undue failure or stress that might interfere with learning. The teacher also should try to help the retarded child develop an orientation for noticing the relevant cues and for paying attention to as many of the stimulus dimensions as possible before making a response. The work of Montessori (1964) supports the importance of increasing emphasis on relevant details and avoiding emphasis on irrelevant cues.

The Fernald Method (1943) has also been used with children with a variety of learning difficulties. It is directly concerned with focusing the child's attention on a task. In the beginning, words to be learned are written in large letters in crayon on newsprint paper. The child then traces the letters with his or her index finger, while saying the word aloud. Visual and auditory attention is thus heightened in relation to learning the word.

A considerable amount of research related to retention has been done with mentally retarded children because short-term memory problems are common among them. When information is presented and the retarded child is asked to retain it over a short period of time (less than one minute), he or she often does not retain the information as well as normal children do. Having the child rehearse or repeat aloud an item to be learned considerably enhances the ability to remember the item when called on. Practice in rehearsal strategies has been shown to improve retarded children's memory abilities, and this improvement appears to generalize to other areas (Turnbull, 1974). Other approaches are also helpful. For example, merely saying a vocabulary word may be enough for normal children; but, with the retarded, the teacher may have to show a child the printed word or show a picture illustrating the word, while saying it aloud and having the child repeat it. In effect, the retarded child needs to *overlearn* so that memory can be firmly established.

Intense drill in labeling every classroom object and its parts—every line, shape, color, and hue—may aid the retarded child. As the child practices labeling, he or she can be held accountable for greater accuracy and speed. Learning to invent labels for things that have no obvious names may also be helpful. The practice of grouping numbers, letters, and common classroom items increases short-term memory. Teachers also need to stress the perception and recognition of various aspects of objects, such as color, size, shape, composition, and use. Retarded children need practice in hearing a stimulus (e.g., teacher says "ball"), recognizing the stimulus symbolically (e.g., printed word "ball"), seeing an object (e.g., real ball), and then recognizing a stimulus by touch alone (e.g., holding ball while blindfolded).

Tasks and Activities That Help The Child to Improve in Visual and Auditory Perception   A number of authors have suggested tasks and activities for improving the visual perception of any child (Hammill, 1975; Smith, 1974; Passow, 1970; Barry, 1961). Some describe tasks for improving visual-motor skills, since visual perception is seldom a passive act. When we respond to a stimulus visually, we often move our eyes, head, or other parts of our body; hence, what is involved is both visual and motoric. Among the visual-perceptual and visual-motor training activities suggested are:

1. Visual tracking exercises to develop eye movements involve the child in watching lateral, vertical, diagonal, and rotary movements of a pencil, a moving penlight in a darkened room, or a headlight of an electric train moving in a darkened room.

2. Visual reception can be encouraged by having children identify common objects by name and tell both their proper use and to whom each object belongs. They can stand in front of a mirror each day and comment on what they see. Children can be given pictures to interpret in terms of objects seen, colors, sizes, motion, and details.

3. Visual form discrimination training may begin with children locating as many different shapes as possible in the classroom. They can examine objects and toys and report on the color, shape, size, texture, and materials used in their construction. The basic shapes can be taped on the classroom floor and used for follow-the-leader, hopping, and tag games. Copying, cutting, pasting, and drawing activities are also useful.

4. Visual memory can be developed by having children close their eyes and describe their clothing, a bulletin board in the room, or other children. Cards with geometric designs

can be briefly shown to the children, who can then replicate them on paper from memory.

5. Spatial training can be introduced by having the child find the top, bottom, sides, and back of an object. The concepts of up, down, over, under, in, bigger, heavier, et cetera, can be demonstrated. Puzzle making and form matching are also activities that help the child learn spatial relationships.

Problems in auditory perception may be linked to a particular exceptionality, or they may result from inattention or lack of motivation. Among the suggested activities designed to improve any child's auditory perception are the following (Hammill, 1975; Smith, 1974; Passow, 1970; Barry, 1961):

1. Auditory awareness can be encouraged by having children remember various types of sounds heard during a class walk. The children can identify the source of each sound and give it an appropriate label. The teacher can hold a wristwatch to a child's ear at varying distances and train the child to listen and to raise a hand when the ticking is no longer audible. Directions can be whispered to the child at varying distances from each ear. Quiet periods can be held, during which children are asked to listen for various sounds.

2. Auditory discrimination exercises can include hiding a ticking clock and asking a child to point to the direction of the clock. The teacher can tap several times on the desk and have children listen, count to themselves, and report the number of taps. While blindfolded, a child can identify a classmate by his or her voice. Children can be asked to distinguish between characteristics of sounds, such as loud-soft, high-low, pleasant-unpleasant, and happy-sad. Children can use a tape recorder to record their own different types of sounds.

3. Auditory memory and sequencing can be developed by asking children to repeat directions, phone numbers, and clapping patterns. They can listen to nursery rhymes and songs and pick out details (such as sounds and words) that they will be asked to repeat afterwards. Children can be given increasingly complex directions to follow. The teacher can tell simple jokes and have the children repeat them. A grocery list can be made using such props as an empty egg carton and tin cans. Each item is placed on a table as it is added to the list, and the children repeat the list. Children can also play with musical instruments and rhythm-band equipment.

Tasks That Help Improve Motoric Responding and Active Participation   Both the partially seeing and the blind tend to be deficient in physical skills and general coordination. This deficiency is not the direct result of visual impairment; it is due to limitations in range and nature of experience. Throughout childhood, special attention should be directed toward improving the motor abilities of the visually handicapped (Buell, 1973). In teaching motor skills to sightless children, vocal instruction is of limited value without kinesthetic cues. For example, blind children can "observe" the teacher perform by placing their fingers on the teacher's body. The teacher can bend large rubber dolls into desired positions so that blind children can examine

The Montessori training program is beneficial for mentally retarded children because it emphasizes visual, auditory, and tactile perception and requires attentiveness and orderliness (Goodman, 1974). All learning tasks are presented sequentially, from the simple to the complex, and precise directions and demonstrations are provided by the teacher.

Visual training tasks involve manipulation and sorting of objects of graded size, dimension, and color. One auditory training task has the child strike a bell from a series of thirteen different bells and then attempt to locate the same bell when the series of thirteen is sounded sequentially.

actions concretely with their fingers. Dolls can convey concepts basic to somersaults, flips, stunts, and other activities that cannot be discerned completely by touch. The teacher can also grasp the blind child's arms or legs and guide the child through the desired movements. A blind youngster can be taught to jump rope by standing behind the teacher and placing his or her hands on the teacher's hips. The partners practice jumping together before a rope is introduced.

When teaching a game, the teacher should give blind youngsters some idea of the whole activity first and then break the activity into its component parts. The teacher describes each part verbally and demonstrates it manually. Partially seeing children can observe demonstrations done in slow motion at close range, and some may benefit from having their limbs manipulated or from feeling a performer's movements.

It has been estimated that about two-thirds or 8,000 of the visually handicapped children attending public schools are excused from physical education or given watered-down courses (Buell, 1973). These conditions exist because many people feel that a blind child must be protected. In reality, however, the blind are capable of participating and succeeding in a variety of recreational activities, including sports.

Special equipment can help make ball games among blind and sighted children more meaningful and enjoyable. Associations for the blind and commercial sporting goods companies sell "audible balls," which contain bells or emit high-pitched beeps (battery operated), and battery-operated, audible goal locators for use on basketball backboards, swimming pools, playgrounds, and athletic fields. Sightless youngsters can also take part in relays when an easily identifiable turning point is provided, such as the edge of a grass surface or cement walk. Blind children can participate in tag games played on tennis courts surrounded by fences or plots of grass. Guide wires can be erected for track events and some running activities.

Active and independent participation for the child with cerebral palsy requires adapting furniture and equipment to the child's particular needs (Bowley & Gardner, 1972). The child may need a wheelchair for mobility. The play table may need to be raised so that the child can control and handle toys. Manipulation of materials is easier if a tray with a raised edge is fitted to the child's chair, especially if the child cannot sit in an ordinary chair at a table. The child can then use many of the usual nursery school educational tools (e.g., sorting and matching games, puzzles, beads, clay) and can paint or draw.

Smith (1974) has drawn from the work of Cratty (1974) and Kephart (1971) in specifying practical procedures for improving the motoric functioning of severely and profoundly retarded children. In developing gross motor skills, activities should be planned in which the children walk, run, slide, gallop, skip, and hop. They should run over uneven areas, dance freely and spontaneously, and practice walking like a cat, elephant, duck, crab, and worm. Balancing and walking on a fence or brick wall are also useful, as is crawling through large cylinders and other playground equipment. Songs that involve action and rhythm appeal to retarded children. Teachers initially should encourage the children to imitate them because such children often lack spontaneity.

Fine-muscle movement and eye-hand coordination can be developed by having children draw on a chalkboard or large piece of paper, do pegboard work, cut and paste, work on puzzles and Lotto games, manipulate toys, handle and sort small objects, throw balls, climb ropes, hang from playground equipment by their hands, copy patterns, color, trace, and work with buttons and zippers. When children draw on the chalkboard or paper, a left-right orientation should be encouraged because this relates to reading and writing. Vocal expression should be encouraged before, during, or immediately after the motor response in many activities (e.g., "I am going to jump over the box," "I am jumping," "I just jumped over the box").

As soon as gross and fine motor skills have developed, more complex activities can be introduced, such as batting a ball, kicking a can, and drawing a triangle. These activities involve a spatial and temporal understanding. For example, when batting a ball, the child must throw the ball into the air, estimate how rapidly it will fall in relation to his or her body position, and judge the speed at which to swing the bat.

Mobility Training   Mobility refers to the individual's ability to move through the environment with relative ease (Scholl, 1975). Four major travel possibilities are available to visually handicapped persons:

1. On their own, using their remaining vision

2. Reliance on a sighted guide

3. Use of a guide dog

4. Use of a cane.

Partially seeing children may need to be counseled by the teacher about the hazards involved in independent travel, such as fast-moving auto and pedestrian traffic. Since all visually handicapped individuals must at some time rely on a sighted guide, efficient methods of walking with a guide need to be taught. Taking the arm of the guide and walking slightly behind allows the blind person to react to changes in the terrain, such as a curb or step.

The use of guide dogs is normally restricted to adolescents and adults. In order for this to be an efficient method of travel, the individual must have good orientation, or awareness of his or her position in the environment, so that the dog can be instructed where to go. The dog and the blind person are normally trained together for at least a month. During that time, certain individuals who are not emotionally stable enough to work with a dog may be discouraged from selecting this travel possibility. It has been estimated that blind individuals with guide dogs actually travel more than those using sighted guides or canes (Finestone, Lukoff, & Whiteman, 1960).

The cane is a well-established device for helping the blind individual to move through the environment. Since World War II, the method of use has changed from tapping the cane to swinging it in front in an arc as wide as the body. The cane swings to the right just before the right foot takes a step, then to the left before the left foot moves forward. This technique can be taught as early as the fourth grade, but it requires the services of a skilled instructor (Scholl, 1967).

A program has been developed for teaching orientation and mobility skills to blind, retarded youth (Johnston & Corbett, 1973). The program emphasizes very basic pre-cane skills and introduces more intermediate steps into the standard teaching techniques. When they can use the cane, students "drive" toy plastic cars through a model of a two-street intersection, which is complete with sidewalks, center stripes, stop signs, and telephone poles, to develop an understanding of how traffic flows.

For almost fifty years, researchers have worked to devise sophisticated electronic devices to supplement or replace customary travel methods for the blind (Mims, 1973). More than twenty electronic guidance devices have been developed over the years, but only a handful remain. The devices use ultrasonic sound (radar-like or sonic devices) or invisible, infrared light to detect objects and to provide information about distance and the nature of the surface by giving different sound signals varying in intonation and amplitude. These devices can be built into a cane, spectacles, or wearing apparel.

Tasks and Activities That Aid in Acquiring Environmental Knowledge and Skill

Multisensory Experiences. To aid in the development of knowledge about the environment, blind children are often given small models of large-scale physical objects to examine by touch. A model of a house, a tree, a car, or an animal can be held and explored thoroughly by the blind individual as a step in learning the concepts of house, tree, car, or animal. Just how relevant such concrete exploration of specific models is to later acquisition of abstract concepts (e.g., all types of houses, trees, and animals) continues to be debated (Mandola, 1968). Lowenfeld (1971) thinks touching models is justified on a pragmatic basis until proof to the contrary is provided. However, teachers must be sure the child does not develop misconceptions about objects in the process.

Pictures in books and verbal descriptions have less impact in learning than does direct experience. This is particularly true with youngsters who cannot attach meaning to the pictures and words because they are not familiar with them. Although the disadvantaged child can see, he or she may share with the visually handicapped a need for direct multisensory experiences to compensate for limited opportunities for learning. For the disadvantaged, the problem is particularly related to the development of adequate language use and understanding. Teachers may use such words as *heavier, smoother,* or *uneven* with little awareness that some children do not understand what they mean. Linking the verbal label with the actual experience of looking, touching, and lifting may be essential for instilling an understanding of these concepts, in much the same way as suggested for other exceptional learners.

The mentally retarded child is a candidate for a wide range of experiences with the environment so that he or she can acquire a more extensive and complex repertoire of information for use in solving problems in school (Smith, 1968). Limited experience may actually account for some of the differences in abilities between retarded and normal children (Baumeister, 1967). The problems of retarded individuals in selecting relevant cues in learning tasks can be partially explained by restricted experience. With the severely retarded child, exploratory activities are particularly important since knowledge of the environment is essential for survival. Such children need to learn about their environment systematically so that problems of safety (e.g., touching something hot) and health (e.g., eating the wrong substances) are avoided (Johnson, 1975).

Discrimination exercises are helpful in developing the tactile-receptive skills of mentally retarded children. Placing objects (e.g., cloth scraps of different textures, familiar objects like a comb and ball) in a bag and asking the children to try to identify them by size, shape, texture, or name is both an instructive and motivating task. Activities derived from the Montessori approach are also useful for training other senses (Smith, 1974). The thermic sense can be developed by having the child feel the outside of metal bowls that contain water at different temperatures. The teacher can train the baric sense (sense of weight) by asking children to estimate the difference in weight between small blocks that are the same size and texture but made of different woods. To learn to discriminate taste, children's tongues are touched with solutions having different characteristics, such as salty, sweet, sour, bitter, acid, or neutral. The teacher can help the children learn to recognize various odors by first presenting the smell with the appropriate label and then asking them to discriminate among various odors while blindfolded.

For school-age disadvantaged children, "blindfold games" that eliminate the sense of sight and allow children to concentrate on discriminating via taste, touch, hearing, and smelling are successful (Schultz & Schroeder, 1971). In one exercise, the teacher plans a classroom party at which the children taste and describe several food treats while blindfolded, such as sour candies, peppermints, milk chocolate, and items with little or no taste, such as distilled water.

In learning, the ability to associate or organize concepts or facts is very important. We can help the retarded child to develop this ability in a number of ways (Smith, 1968). First, we can focus on the criterion of similarity or "likeness" among objects related to everyday life, such as things to ride in, eat for dinner, or wear to school. Next, we can emphasize the fact that some events naturally precede others. A story describing a boy arising in the morning, eating breakfast, walking to school, attending school, returning home, eating dinner, and going to bed might be pictorially presented out of sequence. Having the child reorder the events into a logical sequence is a useful association-training task. On a higher level, the relation between cause and effect can be stressed. Learning to cross the street by carefully watching the traffic lights avoids accidents. The frequent use of the word *why* in relation to rules and expected behavior also aids the child in learning the component aspects of cause-and-effect situations.

The meaningfulness of material to be learned is important for learning efficiency, as we have stressed several times (Baumeister, 1967). The retarded learner is more adversely affected by abstract, nonmeaningful material than is the nonexceptional individual; this is linked to the difficulty the retarded have in applying verbal labels to stimuli to be learned. In facilitating the transfer of response patterns from one problem situation to another, mildly retarded children profit most when the instructional presentation is concrete, the materials can be manipulated, and the tasks involved require little need for abstraction (Orton, McKay, & Rainy, 1964). This contrasts with practices suited for bright and gifted students, who often transfer response patterns best when they are first taught the use of rules, principles, and generalizations.

Also, improvement in learning, transfer of learning, and relearning are facilitated with the retarded if overlearning has taken place (Postman, 1962; Mandler & Heinemann, 1956).

Stressing accuracy in instructional approaches used with the retarded is critical because retarded individuals have a tendency to transfer negative rather than positive learning (Gilbert, 1957). Thus, when teaching a retarded child the skills to be applied in assembling a mechanical device, a trial-and-error approach should be avoided. In the final assembly stage, an accumulation of previous mistakes might be recalled more readily than the correct procedures.

Overlearning is achieved when the child practices a task well beyond the point of initial mastery. Such practice reduces the possibility of eliciting random responses at future times. A related instructional approach is to distribute the practice of tasks rather than to have the retarded child practice for a longer period during a single sitting. Spacing or sequencing practice sessions over time is considerably more beneficial to retarded children than to bright or average learners (Madsen, 1963).

An impressive and touching attempt to broaden the environmental experience of a group of profoundly retarded learners was made at Sonoma State Hospital in California. As in many state institutions, certain cottages or wards are set aside to house children who fall at the very low end of the adaptive continuum—who continuously depend on the care and attention of others for survival. These children are characteristically kept in crib-type beds for most of their lives, and the staff is primarily concerned with feeding, changing diapers, and maintaining hygienic standards. The profoundly retarded child may not be able to move or speak, and his or her life expectancy may be very limited. The child's world is confined to a small patch of bed linen and protective bed railing that shut off most outside visual stimulation. No one can deny that the situation is hopeless. Can anything be done to extend their range of environmental experience? The staff at Sonoma State decided something could be done. They introduced a more intensive program of physical rehabilitation with the assistance of trained specialists. The children's body positions were changed by propping them with pillows, slight movements of the fingers and toes were encouraged, and constant stimulation was provided.

As unlikely as it seems, chickens were let loose in the ward to perch on the bed railings and catch the children's eyes. Large, live, furry rabbits were placed in the cribs next to the children for tactual stimulation. Some of the children were carried from the ward to the grounds outside. They were put down in tall, wet grass, given flowers to touch, and placed in strollers and wagons for rides through the woods. No miracles occurred. The situation was still hopeless, but an important effort had been made to extend the children's exploratory experiences. This is only one example of a paradox often faced by the special educator: the situation is hopeless—but hopeful; we cannot do anything—but we can do something. Reflected in this paradox is much of the spirit and dedication on which the field was founded and greatly depends at the present time.

This text is written in the spirit of hopefulness. If we study each exceptional learner carefully, revise our conceptualization of curriculum to thimbleful levels, and use our creativity and imagination, we can teach every child something. A beautiful film, entitled *Somebody Waiting*, has been made of the Sonoma project.* In it, the "somethings" accomplished were readily

Somebody Waiting, 16 mm, color, 20 minutes. Available from Film Service, University of California Medical Center, 3rd and Parnassus, San Francisco, Calif. 94122.

apparent. Lethargy turned to alertness, eyes moved, fingers twitched, heads turned, and legs kicked. Although these are small somethings in the context of a seemingly hopeless situation, they are most important somethings.

Orientation Training. An outcome of multisensory experience is orientation, that is, the awareness an individual has about the environment and his or her position in it. Although used primarily to describe an important aspect of mobility for the visually handicapped, the broader concept of orientation has relevance for many exceptional learners.

The hands are often referred to as the eyes of the blind; however, many school-age blind children also have hands that are "blind" and so uncoordinated that they bring their owners little or no information (Fraiberg, 1971). This is the result of the child's failure to learn to use his or her hands as tools for acquiring knowledge about the environment. It can be prevented, however, by training during the first two years of life.

In one early training program, mothers and fathers are encouraged to engage the child in games and activities that involve bringing the hands together at the midline (the center) of the body—a prerequisite for coordinated use of the hands (Fraiberg, 1971). Mothers are instructed to place both the child's hands on the bottle during feeding and to play "patty-cake" and hand-clapping games with songs. Cradle games and dangling toys encourage hand use while the child is lying down. Presenting objects at midline while the child is sitting encourages bringing the hands together at this position. After training the child to bring the hands together at midline, exercises to encourage reaching and grasping are introduced. The parents use toys that combine tactile and sound qualities in order to teach sound-touch identity.

Special play tables and playpens are devised so that a sweep of the blind infant's hand guarantees an interesting discovery. After coordination of sound and grasping develops, the blind infant can track objects according to sound. More important, the infant now has the rudimentary conceptual equipment necessary for acquiring knowledge of the outside world.

In the course of acquiring an adequate orientation toward the environment, the blind individual must learn a number of important concepts (Hapeman, 1967). One has to do with the individual's own body image and an understanding of the nature of fixed, movable, and moving objects in the environment. The nature of the terrain, sounds, and odors must be understood. The blind person moving through the environment must determine the path of moving objects and the position of objects in space by an understanding of direction and sound localization.

Area maps that rely on nonvisual senses have been explored as an orientation aid (Blasch, Welsh, & Davidson, 1973). Auditory maps, recorded on cassette tapes, provide visually handicapped persons (fully trained in cane or guide dog mobility skills) with a verbal description to orient them to a specific travel area (e.g., downtown) or step-by-step instructions to guide them to a particular location (e.g., the capitol building). The verbal description points out landmarks of orientation, specific danger situations, traffic flow, distinctive smells to identify certain objects, and tactual differences in sidewalks. Tactual maps, which have raised impressions in plastic, may enhance a blind individual's knowledge of a particular environment. In a preliminary study on using a tactual map to describe a city environment, blind subjects were able to use a transport system without prior direct experience (James & Swain, 1975).

Field trips are extremely valuable for the visually handicapped, particularly if they are accompanied by a sighted companion who can describe activities in detail, answer questions, and share experiences (Pelone, 1957). The Los Angeles County Museum of Art offers special tours for the visually handicapped. Various sculptures from Africa, China, Egypt, Latin America, and Europe, made from such materials as wood, bronze, marble, and clay, are available for the tour participants to handle and tactually explore. The blind individual can learn more about form and texture through such exploration.

Because the ability to move about independently is basic to the life adjustment of the severely mentally retarded, orientation and mobility instruction techniques for the blind have been modified for use with them (Laus, 1974). In an experimental program with thirty-five, inner-city severely retarded youth, ages fourteen to twenty-one, orientation and mobility instruction began with training in basic skills required for outdoor travel: color and number recognition, personal grooming, verbal communication, basic sign reading, counting, and exchanging money. Once the students gained these skills, individual outdoor field experiences began. These experiences included instruction in crossing intersections and using public transportation to get to and from school.

Concrete landmarks were designated by the instructor as cues for ringing the bell to alert the bus driver to stop at the next intersection. The instructor remained physically close to the pupils during initial outdoor experiences but gradually withdrew, permitting the pupils to assert their newly developed skills and confidence. The average time period for learning to travel independently to and from school was two weeks of daily instruction.

In summary, here are twelve curricular considerations reflecting much of what is inherent in the principles, tasks, and activities discussed in this section.

1. Expect the Child to Learn. *Fundamental to the orientation of this text is allowing each exceptional child the dignity of being expected to learn. There is nothing more degrading or destructive than withholding such dignity or replacing it with pity or neglect.*

2. Take Nothing for Granted. *Be sure the child is ready for the level of the assigned task. Think small. Without the child's attention, we are locked out in our teaching efforts. Without understanding, we might as well be speaking to the child in a foreign tongue. Without motivation, we are fighting a losing battle.*

3. Bombard the Senses. *The world impinges on us through our senses. Some exceptional learners may need to develop intact senses to compensate for deficits in or the lack of one sense. But most can see and hear and touch. Combine these senses to involve the child more completely.*

4. Load Up the Cues. *Have the child label and describe what is happening. Use a variety of distinctive elements. Change colors, sizes, textures, sounds, smells, and taste experiences.*

5. Make it Vivid. *Increase the intensity of what is given to the child. Make it bigger, louder, more colorful, more imaginative, more exciting, more interesting. Be enthusiastic and animated.*

6. Repeat as Often as Necessary. *Be sure you have reached the child. Ask the child to tell you what has been presented. Repeat statements. Repeat directions. You do not have to be boring. Emphasize different elements of what you want the child to learn.*

7. Make It Relevant. *Enter the child's world. Give children content that is familiar and part of their out-of-school lives. Leave the classroom and physically enter the child's world. Teach children to recognize and better understand what they live with, rather than what the state department of education textbook committee decided they should learn.*

8. Make It Concrete. *Pictures and recordings and spoken words are fine, but do not stop there. Have the child become physically involved. No beautiful colored picture of an apple, described by the teacher as an "apple," ever made the impression that actually touching an apple, smelling it, biting into it, and savoring its flavor does.*

9. Surprise the Child. *Do the unexpected. Capitalize on the established principle that we all are excited by novelty. Have the room look different. Have the learning materials look different. Catch the child off guard.*

10. Accentuate the Positive. *Make a big deal about what was right, not wrong. When possible, ignore mistakes. When not possible, help the child to understand that if we did not make mistakes we would not know what we had to learn. Be aware that some children will remember what you said they did wrong better than what you said they did right. So, when appropriate, eliminate the negative.*

11. Move Sequentially. *When you leave the starting gate, move down the track in steps that are logical and that build on previous steps. Determine where you want the child to go; then, carefully think through the steps necessary to get the child there.*

12. Be Prepared to Back Up. *Fail gracefully. If the child is not successful, objectively review what is going on and whittle down expectations accordingly. But be ready to move ahead again as soon as possible.*

Social Curriculum

We will now consider tasks and activities for increasing social interaction and improving relationships and communication.

Tasks and Activities that Aid the Child in Establishing Active and Harmonious Relationships   Learning how to gain approval and avoid disapproval is more complex than learning how to pay attention, participate actively, or acquire knowledge and skill about the environment. The subtleties involved in interpersonal relationships, the vast individual differences among those with whom the exceptional learner comes in contact, and the relationship between the child's self-image and the way he or she perceives and interacts with others makes the building of social skills most difficult. Kirk (1972) calls attention to the "intangible" nature of social skill training with exceptional learners and concludes that such training cannot be taught like chemistry.

To improve social skills, the exceptional learner must understand the legal, moral, and social expectations of society and be sensitive to the feelings of others. Approaches used to improve

Modeling is effective in social skill training with the retarded partly because of their sensitivity to what others think of them and their strong desire to obtain social reinforcement. Placing a retarded child in close proximity to or in direct contact with a child whose behavior is exemplary, and who as a result receives positive reinforcement from the teacher, encourages the child to model the desired behavior in order to obtain similar rewards. This approach is more effective if the chosen model is a child of high prestige. The high-prestige child who begins to clean up the classroom may shortly have a number of helpers. These helpers may in turn serve as models for other classmates who consider them high-prestige individuals. The high-prestige model who also reinforces such helpers (e.g., "Thanks a lot for helping") increases the probability that new behavior patterns will be acquired.

social skills include modeling, role playing, coaching, shaping, and integrated group experiences with nonexceptional learners.

Modeling   More than the normal child, the retarded child needs particular help in understanding the reasons for laws and rules in our society and the complications and consequences involved in breaking these rules. The values of society, such as honesty, truthfulness, and respect for others, need to be stressed. Initially, training in these areas is best undertaken in small groups or on an individual basis in order to be certain that the retarded child has a clear idea of the principle involved. For example, it is much more reasonable to expect a child to understand and respect the feelings and attitudes of a classmate than to expect an awareness to generalize to many individuals in a large social context (Smith, 1974).

Although the retarded child's susceptibility to social praise, particularly from an adult, can be useful in encouraging the modeling of appropriate behavior, retarded children may be overly concerned with obtaining adult approval. As a result, they may rely too much on outside sources to solve their problems rather than on their own abilities. Their *outer-directedness* has been observed in a number of studies (Turnure, 1970; Turnure & Zigler, 1964). One found that retarded children involved in a learning task tended to glance more frequently at the adult experimenter than normals did. In another study, the retarded appeared more interested in watching an adult putting a puzzle together than they were in solving the puzzle that they had been assigned. Thus, they were less successful in solving this puzzle than were a group of normal children in the same situation. When the adult's puzzle was given to both groups, the retarded children did better than the normals because they had already observed the puzzle being solved. Mildly retarded children will more readily change their prediction of an event's outcome because of an adult's suggestion than will normal children (Carlson & MacMillan, 1970). This suggests that retarded children tend to trust an adult's judgment more than their own. When an adult models the correct solution of a puzzle for a retarded child, the child will acquire the concept much more readily, especially if the adult verbalizes the procedure as it is being carried out (Litrownik, Franzini, & Turner, 1976) and provides feedback in the form of praise (Filler & Bricker, 1976).

Although a degree of outer-directedness initially may be helpful in learning situations, it has been suggested that retarded children must become more inner-directed if they are to move to higher levels of cognitive development (Zigler, 1961). As the child grows older, independence training should be characterized by a continuous reduction in the cues provided by adults. This will help the child rely as much as possible on his or her own basic abilities. Thus, one task for the teacher in training social skills is to help retarded children become *less* social in certain situations and form their own judgments independently of what others say or do.

Multihandicapped, mentally retarded children may be confined to beds most of the time, and some are unable to see, much less interact with, other children around them. For these children, a mirror can be mounted over their beds so they can "socialize" by observing their neighbors frequently (Swartz & Cleland, 1973).

Just as watching a model engage in aggressive behavior causes some children to be more aggressive, models also serve more positive functions (Bandura, Ross, & Ross, 1961). One interesting approach used a twenty-three minute film that depicted eleven episodes of a child entering a group of other children (O'Connor, 1972). The film featured a narrator who called attention to what was happening and the relevant behavior involved. After a group of socially isolated preschool children viewed the film, they increased their interactions with other children; a control group that watched a film about dolphins did not. This increase was still evident during a follow-up assessment several weeks later. A related study found that social interaction was being maintained one month after exposure to the model in the training film (Evers & Schwarz, 1973).

The question of why socially isolated children learn better from film models than from real-life peer models is interesting to consider. Perhaps in the fast-moving pace of real world events, the child fails to attend to the significant and relevant elements of a socially well-adjusted child's behavior. The narrator in the films may serve the purpose of bringing these elements to the child's attention.

In one study, six behavior-disordered children were paired with six peers who were exemplary models of desirable social behavior (Csapo, 1972). The children with behavior disorders sat next to their classmate models and were told to do what the models were doing, so that they could learn how to get along better in class. This resulted in an increase in socially appropriate behavior on the part of the subjects that was maintained ten days after training had stopped. Being specifically directed to watch the classmates' model behavior and to emulate it may have served a purpose similar to that provided by the film narrators.

Role Playing. Role playing involves the dramatization of some social situation in which individuals assume the parts or roles of characters in that situation. In setting up a role-playing activity, teachers should identify a specific problem and situation to be enacted, specify the roles to be played and the participants to play each role, dramatize the problem, and finally discuss what happened and formulate alternative solutions, if necessary (Smith, 1974). Children with severe behavior disorders, including delinquents, have been helped in their social adjustment by role playing (Chandler, 1973; Chandler, Greenspan, & Barenboim, 1974). One training program engaged children in creating skits that were later videotaped, enabling the children to see themselves as others see them. There were two-to three-hour training sessions each week for ten weeks. The skits were brief and concerned individuals the same age as the subjects. The characters experienced problems familiar to the group, such as being "put down" by an authority figure. Each child took a part in the skit and each skit was rerun until everyone had a chance to play every part. Follow-up results indicated improvements in social adjustment among the participants, as rated by adults who worked with them.

Role-playing activites have been used to increase the amount of social play exhibited by severely retarded preschool children during free play periods (Strain, 1975). The subjects were eight four-year-old children, with IQs from 30 to 42, in a center for children with developmental disabilities. Social play was rare for each child. In the training program, the teacher read a familiar children's story, such as "The Three Bears," and prompted each child to assume the role of a character in the story by performing certain verbal or motor behaviors typical of the character; for example, the teacher would say "Lift your feet high, like you're climbing steps," or "Say 'soup'." Following these story-telling and role-playing sessions, there was a rapid acceleration in the amount of social play observed during free play time. When the story sessions were terminated, the amount of play immediately decreased but was quickly reinstated when the sessions resumed. The advantages of these techniques are their easy inclusion in the ongoing preschool routine and the limited teacher preparation and instruction time required.

A similar approach was used with behaviorally disordered preschool children who had extremely limited social and language development (Strain, Cooke, & Apolloni, 1976). The children were prompted to take roles during story sessions, and the amount of spontaneous play that occurred during a free period immediately following the story was measured. Results indicated that the amount of social play increased significantly following story sessions.

Coaching. In addition to modeling and role playing, social skills can be fostered by direct instruction, discussions, and coaching.

The blind child needs more social experience than does the sighted child in order to overcome the effects of environmental isolation. The child must be taught the give-and-take of social contacts and helped to avoid self-preoccupation or egocentricity. Facial expressions are important in social communication. Early in life, blind children must be encouraged to make faces depicting happiness, sadness, joy, and other emotions and to use facial expressions appropriate to their mood and conversation. The child should be instructed to look toward the person with whom he or she is speaking. Developing these habits early in life helps the blind child to appear more normal in later contacts.

One area of concern regarding the social competence of the blind is the development of peculiar mannerisms that may appear unpleasant or bizarre to others. These behaviors include body rocking, head rolling, waving the hands before the eyes, poking the fingers in the eyes, and fluttering the arms. Such mannerisms or stereotypic behaviors are not unique to blind children and can be seen in some mentally retarded and severely emotionally disturbed children. The cause appears related to a lack of environmental stimulation; the mannerisms may also represent an attempt on the child's part to cope with stress. Although stereotypic behaviors tend to disappear as the child grows older, they are best dealt with by parents and teachers on a preventive level. Providing constant activities of interest and increasing environmental stimulation will prevent boredom from occurring and lessen the chances of the child's seeking self-stimulation (Knight, 1972).

Chittenden (1974) trained preschool children with behavior disorders to behave coopera-tively by the ingenious use of dolls to illustrate peer conflict situations. High-dominating and low-cooperating children were encouraged to verbalize appropriate solutions to conflict. Each child was introduced to two dolls named Sandy and Mandy. In a series of situations, the dolls were shown trying to solve the problem of how to play with a single toy. Sometimes they were unsuccessful, and their interaction ended in a fight. At other times, they were successful, taking turns, sharing, or playing cooperatively. In eleven sessions, the purpose was to teach the children to discriminate happy outcomes, such as sharing and having a good time, and to resolve the conflicts the dolls faced. Later, the children were asked to verbalize to the dolls what they could do to play more successfully in a variety of situations with limited play resources. Observations in real-life play situations showed that the trained children had significantly decreased their amount of dominating behavior. They also increased in cooperative behavior, but the increase was not statistically significant. A control group that received no training showed little change in their behavior from pre- to posttest.

Most shaping and modeling studies use the frequency of interaction of subjects with peers as a measure of change. Although total frequency of interaction may not change, the nature of the interaction itself may change. One study attempted to train two third-grade children rated as low friendship choices by their peers; two similar children served as controls (Gottman, Gonso, & Rasmussen, 1975). Modeling and coaching began by showing the children a videotape of a child entering a group of peers. The videotape was discussed and the low-rated children role played situations in which they were new children in class who wanted to make friends. Results of the study indicated that the two children who were coached were later rated more highly by peers. Ratings given the two control children changed very little. Although observations in class revealed that none of the children increased their frequency of interaction, the two coached children selected different types of children for social interaction. One child sought out more popular children, and the other interacted more with other less popular children.

In another study, three children in each of eleven different third- and fourth-grade class-rooms were identified by sociometric measures as having few friends (Oden & Asher, 1975). One of the three in each room was coached. On five separate occasions, this child played a game with a different classmate. Before playing, the child was advised on how to have the most fun. The coach suggested such things as participating fully, cooperating, communicating, and showing interest in the classmate. The child was asked to think of specific examples to accomplish each of these suggestions. After playing the game, the child was asked by the coach "how it went," and the child discussed his or her experience. Another of the three low-rated children in each classroom participated in the same number of game-playing sessions but received no coaching. The remaining third child from each classroom was sent out of the room with a classmate, received no coaching, and played a game alone.

After five weeks of intervention training, children in the eleven classrooms were again asked to rate how much they liked to play with their classmates. Only the coached children received significantly higher ratings from their peers. Thus, it appears that coaching can improve children's social skills and lead to increased peer acceptance. However, the identified children did not change their actual behavior; for example, they did not begin to initiate interactions. Thus, as shown in the previous study, children may change their social behavior as a result of coaching, but this change may not involve increased contact with others.

With older retarded children, assistance with personal grooming is often very important because how one looks directly relates to how one is treated by others (Smith, 1968). The teacher should call the individual's attention to the possibility of offending others by not maintaining

A basic problem faced by many exceptional learners is learning to live with the stigma and labels associated with their handicaps and with the name calling, ridicule, and rejection often directed toward them by peers. In a study of this problem area, Jones (1972) reported on conclusions reached by teacher-led discussions with mildly retarded children that focused on negative peer experiences. In general, the retarded students concluded that they:

- Should accept themselves, do the best they can,

and develop a better outlook

- Should ignore or tolerate negative comments

- Should attempt to improve their own behavior and "act intelligent," as do regular students

- Actually have some advantages and skills themselves and can learn and excel in some areas

- Should consider other persons ignorant, immature, or inferior for calling them names.

appropriate grooming and the health reasons for cleanliness and good dress. This is particularly important because it is easier to detect and "size up" an untidy person at a glance than it is to identify an academic problem in the retarded.

Discussion groups composed of mildly retarded children in the upper-primary and intermediate grades can deal with such topics as "How should we act during our free time?" "What should I do when someone says that I am dumb or look funny?" and "Should I learn to smoke like my friends?" For older children and adolescents, topics of interest may include "What should I do when a boy makes advances toward me?" "How can I get my mother to allow me to wear cosmetics?" and "Why can't I quit school and get a job even though I don't know how to read?"

Smith (1974) has summarized a number of considerations he feels increase the effectiveness of instruction in social skills. Audiovisual aids, such as a videotape recorder, allow children to monitor and review their behavior in a social situation and to reflect on its appropriateness. When dealing with the retarded child's behavior, emphasis should be placed on what was done *correctly*, not incorrectly, because the retarded often remember their errors better than their correct responses. Older retarded persons should be constantly reminded of the relationship between their social and emotional behavior and their future vocational requirements. Professional consultation with school psychologists, guidance counselors, clergymen, local health officers, and other experts will help in planning social curriculums for exceptional learners. Opportunities to interact in real life situations with children and adults who are intellectually normal are also very helpful for retarded individuals and should be provided whenever possible. More mature retarded children can profit from experience with some level of self-government in the classroom to help them understand the complications and advantages of government and to encourage their participation in social and community affairs.

The severely mentally retarded often manifest serious social incompetence; therefore, training in personal and social skills may be the most critical curriculum area for them (Gearheart & Litton, 1975). These skills include developing a self-awareness, getting along with others, accepting and following directions, self-control, safety, manners (personal and table), use of leisure time, participation in group activities, recreation, hobbies, arts and crafts, and music appreciation.

Instruction related to these skills should be confined to specific activities that allow social interaction and establish classroom rules and boundaries. Global approaches in instructional environments are not generally effective with the severely retarded. Teachers need a great deal of patience and consistency. Repetition is important, but tension-producing situations should be avoided. Students should be taught to accept mistakes although errors should not receive primary emphasis. Teachers should accentuate the positive and, whenever possible, minimize or eliminate the negative.

In one study, the role of teacher of younger severely retarded children was assumed by older severely retarded adolescents and young adults in the same residential school (Wagner & Sternlicht, 1975). The tutors received thirty hours of training in teaching dressing techniques and thirty hours in teaching eating skills. Following their training, the tutors taught these skills to the younger children in eighteen and twenty hours, respectively. This program illustrated that the developmentally disabled can learn to dress and feed themselves and that older retarded persons can be trained as tutors. The tutors also benefited from the training; their own eating skills improved and their maladaptive behavior decreased.

Shaping. The individual application of behavior modification principles has been successful in increasing a child's social interaction. The principle of shaping was demonstrated effectively in an early study with an isolated four-year-old girl in a nursery school (Allen, Hart, Buell, Harris, & Wolf, 1964). The girl avoided contact with the other children in the school and sought continual attention from the teacher. During a five-day observation period, she interacted with peers 10 percent of the time and with the teacher 40 percent of the time. A training period was begun, during which the girl first was rewarded with teacher attention only when she was near another child. Later, she was only rewarded when she directly interacted with another child. These were the shaping stages. During these stages, the girl's time with peers increased to 60 percent and time with the teacher dropped to 20 percent. The experimenters found they could increase or decrease peer interaction time, depending on the behaviors they reinforced.

Unfortunately, from this and other studies, the social reinforcement provided by peer interaction does not appear to be strong enough to maintain social behavior when other reinforcers are abruptly withdrawn (O'Connor, 1972). Social reinforcement might be expected to develop over time as the nature of the social interactions become stimulating and rewarding to the child. An example of this occurred in one study in which the experimenter very gradually decreased the frequency of an adult's rewarding a child's social behavior. This study found that the social experience itself can become rewarding (Coats, 1967).

The principle of shaping is important to consider in helping exceptional learners improve their social behavior, but it deals with relatively simple behavior, such as being near other children. Efforts to develop complex social skills using shaping techniques are apt to be time-consuming and inefficient. Modeling and coaching may well be more direct and efficient and better able to provide the child with rules or general strategies to apply to social interactions.

Integrated Group Experiences. Mainstreaming, or the integration of exceptional learners into regular classrooms whenever possible and appropriate, is a key consideration of Public Law 94–142. The issue is examined in detail in the next chapter. Here, we review a number of studies that relate to peer acceptance of the exceptional learner.

With respect to the blind exceptional learner, it was found that seeing children who had known and attended school with the visually impaired were more positive in their appraisal of the abilities of the blind than those who lacked such experience (Bateman, 1962; Bateman, 1964; Steinzor, 1966). It was also found that personal contact with visually impaired persons failed to affect a sighted adult's perceptions of the abilities of the visually impaired. However, information-giving techniques increased the positiveness of these attituides. Thus, integration of visually impaired children can develop more positive attitudes among seeing children. Inservice programs designed to give information about the abilities of visually impaired children also are needed to develop more positive teacher attitudes in integrated schools.

The effects of integrated experience on peer acceptance of the physically handicapped have been studied (Rapier, Adelson, Carey, & Croke, 1972). A special unit for orthopedically handi- capped children was built on the grounds of a regular elementary school. Before it opened, the attitudes toward the physically handicapped of 152 nonhandicapped children in grades three through five were measured. The orthopedic unit opened, and during the first year of operation at least one physically handicapped child was integrated on a part-time basis into each of the classrooms of the selected nonhandicapped children. The nonhandicapped children also had contact with the handicapped children in the school auditorium and on the playground, where they watched some of them participate in a junior "wheelchair olympics." Following the opening of the unit and the integration of physically handicapped children into the regular classroom, the nonhandicapped children developed more positive attitudes toward them. Specifically, the handicapped children were viewed as less weak, less in need of attention, and better able to care for themselves than originally thought. Whereas boys and girls differed with respect to attitudes before integration, there were no such differences following integration; both boys and girls exhibited positive attitudes.

There has been some evidence that as physically handicapped children mature, an increase in unfavorable attitudes toward them occurs among nondisabled peers. Therefore, elementary-age handicapped individuals are subject to fewer negative attitudes than are disabled teenagers. Disabled college students encounter fewer negative attitudes than do graduates seeking employ- ment (Connor, Rusalem, & Cruickshank, 1971). According to this evidence, we might expect preschool, nondisabled children to be the most accepting of all in relation to the physically handicapped. This was found to be true with three-and four-year-olds (Connor, 1975). These children were less aware of developmental expectations than were school-age youngsters, more inclined to be helpful to a less capable child, and not repulsed by a handicap that to them did not yet carry a social stigma. It has also been found that frequency of speech and physical activity increases among handicapped preschoolers when they are in a group situation with nonhandi- capped children.

The likelihood of remaining in a regular classroom rather than being labeled "mentally retarded" and referred for special class placement has been found to be related to the child's social competence (Mercer, 1971). In investigating the differences between similar retardates, some of whom were functioning adequately in a regular class and some of whom were in special classes, it was found that the child who had a friend in the regular classroom was significantly less likely to be called retarded or to be assigned to a special class. Helping the retarded child to improve peer relationships, thus increasing chances for forming friendships, becomes particularly important in light of this finding.

In an effort to increase peer acceptance of exceptional learners, increased contact through integrated group experiences has been explored. In one study, 400 nonretarded, ninth-grade students from three suburban junior high schools were randomly assigned to experimental and control groups of equal size (Sheare, 1974). In the experimental condition, nonretarded and mildly retarded adolescents from the special classes in each school were integrated in nonacademic classes (shop, homemaking), clubs, and social and athletic activites. Control groups were not integrated. An Acceptance Scale was devised and administered to all subjects at midyear. Results revealed that the nonretarded subjects in the experiment consistently gave more positive ratings to their mildly retarded classmates than did control groups. Also, in all groups, female subjects were rated more positively than were males. It was concluded that the integration of the mildly retarded into regular classes and into social and recreational activities will result in more positive ratings of the retarded by nonretarded children.

Other research, however, does not support the contention that contact and integration are enough to increase peer acceptance of the mildly retarded (Iano, Ayers, Heller, McGettigan, & Walker, 1974). Forty mildly retarded children, who were previously placed in special classes, participated in a resource room program in which they were integrated part-time in regular classrooms. These retarded children were rated less favorably by the regular-class children than were other regular-class children or children in the class who were not retarded but who were referred for special education services to the resource room (e.g., children with learning disabilities).

The social acceptance of mildly retarded children, some of whom were segregated in special classes and some of whom were integrated full-time into a nongraded elementary school also has been examined (Goodman, Gottlieb, & Harrison, 1972). Although the teachers knew the identity of the retarded youngsters, it was presumed that the other children did not. Thirty-six nonretarded children (ages six to twelve) were administered sociometric questionnaires to determine their degree of social acceptance of other nonretarded children, mildly retarded children who were integrated with them in the nongraded program, and mildly retarded children who remained segregated in the school's only self-contained class.

The results indicated that both integrated and segregated mildly retarded children are rejected significantly more often than are nonretarded children; that younger subjects are more accepting than older subjects; that male subjects express more overt rejection than females; and that integrated mildly retarded children are rejected significantly more often than segregated ones by male subjects, but not by females. The authors suggest that one possible cause for the greater rejection of integrated mildly retarded children was that they were perceived by the other children as nonretarded and were expected to conform to the behavioral standards of normal children in the classroom. Failure to have done so may have resulted in their social rejection.

The social acceptability of integrated and segregated mildly retarded children attending a no-interior-wall, open-concept, nongraded school was compared with the acceptability of mildly retarded children in a traditional school building (Gottlieb & Budoff, 1973). A child in a no-interior-wall school is visually and physically accessible to all other children in the school. As a result, nonretarded children have more opportunities to become familiar with the mildly retarded. The architecture of the traditional school building containing separate classrooms tends to restrict the visual and physical access of a child to the children contained in other classrooms. Results indicated that the mildly retarded children in the unwalled school were known more often by their nonretarded peers, but they were rejected more frequently than were retarded children in the walled school. Also, integrated mildly retarded children were rejected more than were segregated retarded children. These two studies indicate that integration itself may not lead to increased acceptance of the retarded and that some specific procedures, such as modeling or coaching, may have to be instituted to improve the retarded child's social skills.

One approach to improving the attitudes of the nonexceptional toward the exceptional is to have the former role play being handicapped. In a study exploring the effects of role playing on nonhandicapped individuals' attitudes toward the physically handicapped, seventy-six college students were assigned to one of three groups—role playing, vicarious role playing, or control (Clore & Jeffrey, 1972). Subjects in the role-playing condition were asked to imagine that they had recently been involved in an auto accident that had left their legs permanently paralyzed. They were to pretend that it was the first day back on campus after the accident. Subjects in this condition then took a twenty-five minute wheelchair trip that involved traveling up an incline, four elevator rides, negotiating several ramps and doors, and a complicated procedure for getting coffee. Vicarious role players walked behind the role players at a distance of twenty feet and observed the role player's experiences. The control subjects spent an equivalent amount of time walking on campus and having coffee. Compared to the control group's experience, both direct and vicarious role playing led to more positive responses (1) to a specific disabled person, (2) to a series of issues concerning disabled students in general, and (3) to a disguised attitudinal measure obtained by telephone four months later. These results suggest that role playing a disabled person in a natural social environment has both immediate and long-term effects on interpersonal attitudes toward disabled students.

The most promising approach for improving the attitudes of others toward the disabled appears to be planned interaction between the two groups under favorable conditions. Such conditions would no doubt include opportunities for the disabled to enter into activities commensurate with their actual abilities in order to demonstrate to the nondisabled that they are not as restricted as others may think. Favorable interaction between the two groups would also help the disabled individual to develop interests, social skills, and a more realistic and positive self-concept. Although such group encounters under adult leadership may require social and psychological sophistication and educational engineering, the stakes are high enough for the adjustment of the handicapped child to warrant such careful planning (Connor, Rusalem, & Cruickshank, 1971).

A comprehensive attempt at devising a curriculum to help exceptional learners improve social skills is the Social Learning Curriculum (SLC) (Goldstein, 1974). The underlying goal of SLC is to build the child's potential for *critical thought* (i.e., drawing on stored and immediately available knowledge in making decisions) and for *independent action* (i.e., initiating, carrying out, and satisfactorily concluding activities). The theoretical foundations of the program are drawn from Gestalt psychology in which problem solving involves three stages: mass, differentiation, and integration. At the mass stage, the individual must separate the relevant from the irrelevant aspects of the problem situation. At the differentiation stage, the relevant elements are scrutinized individually and in association with one another. At the integration stage, the information and experience from the differentiation stage are integrated and become available for future problem solving.

The SLC program is designed to use Gestalt theory in learning. Nine of the curricular components or phases to the program are:

1. Perceiving individuality

2. Recognizing the environment

3. Recognizing interdependence

4. Recognizing the body

5. Recognizing and reacting to emotions

6. Recognizing what the senses do

7. Communicating with others

8. Identifying helpers

9. Maintaining body functions

The SLC has been published as a kit containing ten phase books. Each book details from fifteen to twenty lessons and describes instructional activities, games, and worksheet assignments related to the development of each phase. Seventy-two, eleven-by-fourteen photographs depicting events and problems associated with each phase accompany the phase books and are used to stimulate student involvement. The SLC also provides ideas for coordinating activities associated with the phases with science, mathematics, and physical education curricula.

Behavioral objectives are stated for each phase and for each lesson. For example, the major objective for Lesson 8 of Phase 2, "Recognizing the Environment," is: "The student should be able to explain the differences between borrowing and taking." In Phase 5, "Recognizing and Reacting to Emotions," the overall objective for all the lessons is: "The student should be able to identify specific emotions, causes of and changes in emotion, consequences of emotional reactions, degrees of emotions and moods created by emotions." The authors of SLC claim that it is appropriate for special children, developmentally disabled children, culturally deprived children, mildly retarded children, learning-disabled children, and children with special learning needs.

Although a wide variety of curricular approaches can be used to increase the exceptional learner's flexibility and social competence, we still must be concerned with the other two sides of the learning triangle—conditions and consequences—in our quest for success.

Conditions

Among the learning conditions that have been studied is the condition of *where* the exceptional individual is taught. Cruickshank (1967) has investigated the effects of stimulating versus nonstimulating classroom environments on brain-injured or (as they might be labeled today) learning-disabled children. According to Cruickshank, all visually and auditorily distracting stimuli in the classroom should be removed or reduced as much as possible. Walls, furniture, and woodwork should be painted the same color, bulletin boards removed, windows replaced with translucent glass, and cupboards equipped with solid wooden doors. Carpeting and acoustical ceiling treatment are suggested. Even the pencil sharpener should be removed from the room because of the extraneous auditory stimuli it produces.

The rationale for these adaptations is that children who are unable to refrain from reacting to stimuli must have extraneous stimuli removed so that they can direct their energies toward stimuli that are important to their learning and adjustment and through which they can achieve success. Reduction of space is also important; rooms smaller than the standardized classroom are specified. Within these rooms, small cubicles (each approximately 2-1/4 by 3-1/4 feet in size) with partitions between them are useful for individual children because they further limit visual distraction.

A study of hyperactive, distractible, brain-injured children over a two-year period investigated the effects of reducing classroom stimuli (Cruickshank, Bentzen, Ratzeberg, & Tannhauser, 1961). Four small classes of children were included. Two classes rigidly ahered to an experimental condition of reduced stimulation and space and to a carefully planned routine. The teachers in the other classes had knowledge of the experimental condition, but were free to maintain a more traditional program. At the end of the study, there were no significant differences between the experimental and control classrooms, but children in all four classes made significant gains in achievement, visual perception, and social behavior.

A similar study with emotionally disturbed children also included a behavioral approach that provided rewarding consequences for appropriate behavior and academic accomplishment (Haring & Phillips, 1962). When children taught by behavioral methods were compared with others taught in a less structured learning environment, the behavioral group showed better academic achievement.

Autistic children have been found to be particularly influenced by the condition of where instruction occurs. In one study, behaviors such as paying attention that were taught in a one-to-one setting were not performed consistently when the children (ages four to thirteen years) were placed in larger groups (even when only one child was added) (Koegel & Rincover, 1974). For example, two of the children had learned to imitate the teacher and follow simple directions so that in the one-to-one situation they were responding correctly almost 100 percent of the time. When one other child was added, the two children responded correctly only 70 percent and 65 percent, respectively. When placed in a group with eight other children, the correct responses of the two autistic children dropped to 45 percent and 20 percent, respectively.

In a second study, the same children were introduced to a larger group very gradually and at the same time had the individualized, one-to-one approach changed little by little. Under the gradual transition procedure, the children were found to learn quite effectively in a group situation.

A further investigation was concerned with determining why the children failed to maintain what they had learned in the one-to-one situation when they were placed in the larger group (Rincover & Koegel, 1975). It was found that the children were selectively responding to an incidental stimulus during the original training and were not responding solely to the specific

The effect of cubicles on the performace of brain-injured children on a reaction-time test also has been studied (Cruse, 1970). Results indicated that children working under stimulus-control conditions in a cubicle did not perform better than those working in cubicles with extraneous stimuli, such as toys, moving ballons, and mirrors. The efficacy of assigning emotionally disturbed children to cubicles was further investigated; significant increases in attention span as a result of working in cubicles were found (Shores & Haubrick, 1969). Academic progress in reading, however, was not significantly related to working in a cubicle.

In a later study by the same authors, these findings were replicated (Haubrick & Shores, 1976). Five emotionally disturbed children were involved. In addition to measuring attention and improvement in reading following placement in a study cubicle, the authors measured the same variables following use of rewards for correct answers on comprehension questions presented after the child's reading period. Both the cubicle and the reward system improved the children's attention, and the reward condition increased academic performance. Thus, systematic use of rewards was superior to cubicle placement for both increasing attention and facilitating reading improvement.

The issue of stimulus control has never been completely resolved by research. There is no question that many exceptional learners will profit from reduction of visual and auditory stimulation at certain times and with certain activities. The type of child originally considered in need of full-time placement in a study cubicle was the brain-injured, or hyperactive, distractible, learning-disabled child. Some of these children may learn more efficiently in a controlled environment, but in the author's experience stimulus control is a minor rather than a major consideration in most programs for exceptional learners.

cues provided by the teacher. For example, when the teacher said "Touch your chin" and the child touched his chin, it was assumed he was responding to the teacher's verbal command. But this was found to be incorrect. The child was actually responding to the hand-arm movement of the teacher toward the teacher's chin each time the command was given.

One boy was taught to respond to "Touch your nose" in a small room with a table and two chairs. When taken outside the room, the child never responded correctly. When the two chairs were taken outside and placed in the same position, no correct responding occurred. But when the chairs and the table were taken outside, the child exhibited 70 percent correct responding. The boy had learned to respond to the verbal command plus the presence of the table and chairs—not to the command alone, as might have been originally assumed by the teacher. On the basis of these findings, teachers working with autistic children need to determine exactly which stimuli the children are responding to before assuming that a lesson has been learned.

Some exceptional learners may learn effectively in a large group; for others, small-group or even individual instruction may be necessary. Hearing-impaired children may need intensive small-group and individual instruction to develop language skills. Children with visual impairment may spend long periods of time in a regular classroom but need individual instruction related to brailling skills. The orthopedically handicapped individual may participate full-time in a regular classroom if ready access is available (e.g., no stairs) and working space is accommodated to his or her handicap.

Some exceptional learners may learn better at certain times of the day; hence, the condition of *when* is important. For those who tire or become inattentive in the afternoon, morning instruction in subjects requiring alertness is desirable. The child who arrives in tears after a fight on the bus or who rushed in hot and sweaty after recess may not be the best candidate for a reading lesson. The period after lunch may be better suited to the teacher reading aloud than to arithmetic drill. Thus, an important determiner of whether a given child or group of children will be successful is when we choose to teach them.

The condition of *how* relates to the actual means the child uses to accomplish a task. Some exceptional learners are restricted in the use of ordinary pencils or pens and need larger writing implements. Some may need special teaching devices (e.g., teaching machines) where pushing a button or pulling a lever replaces handwriting. Stories can be written by some, but they can also be dictated to the teacher or into a tape recorder. Arithmetic problems are sometimes easier and more fun to do with poker chips, plastic soldiers, fingers, or flash cards rather than on worksheets. Braille will be a modality for some visually impaired individuals, large print for others.

A work period can be forty or fifty minutes in a regular classroom but may need to be much shorter for exceptional learners. Thus, *how long* we ask a child to work may be a key factor related to success. Some children work well for five minutes and start to drift. Others work for ten or fifteen minutes, some for longer. Sometimes a fifteen-minute work period can involve five minutes of academic and ten minutes of manipulative activities (e.g., making a peg board design) in order to promote success.

Related to this is *how much* we assign. The weekly spelling list of twenty words in a regular classroom may need to be reduced to three, four, or five for an exceptional learner. A page of ten arithmetic problems assigned in class may result in the completion of three and restless scribbling across the sheet. At moments like this, the condition of how much can be quickly altered by tearing the sheet in half, requiring only five problems. Any of these conditions can be altered over time or on-the-spot to achieve success with exceptional learners.

Perhaps the condition most likely to spell trouble for exceptional learners in the regular classroom is *how well*. This relates to accuracy and neatness. Some exceptional learners need to be praised and rewarded for trying, not necessarily for completing. Some need approval for completing rather than accuracy, some for a step in the right direction, and some for a thimbleful accomplishment. The criteria of being right in special education does not have to be related to letter grade standards. Being right more properly refers to "being right" for each child at his or her level. In discussing the condition of how well, we spoke of praise and rewards. The next section is related to these and other consequences—the third side of the learning triangle.

Consequences

Seven types of positive consequences that motivate both nonexceptional and exceptional learners are discussed first. Following this, we discuss the issue of negative consequences.

Positive Consequences

Joy.   At the Mount Everest level of positive consequences in education is the joy of learning, that is, a truly intrinsic satisfaction from involvement in a task. Although it exists in a somewhat rarified realm, it is the ultimate positive consequence. No one can deny that it exists, but to depend on its presence among the majority of learners is somewhat naïve.

Acquisition of Knowledge and Skill.   Coming down the slope from the pinnacle of joy, we encounter the consequence of acquiring knowledge and skill. Children who find themselves able to read the labels on boxes in the family pantry or the brand names in commericals on television are being positively reinforced for their reading efforts. Other examples are learning a new arithmetic skill that can facilitate such real world activity as figuring a favorite baseball player's batting average, or remembering the name of the state capital of Maine at just the right moment to impress the family at the dinner table. Of course, the latter example also contains elements of social approval, which we will discuss shortly.

Knowledge of Results.   At about the same level as acquiring knowledge, we find the positive consequence of knowing how you stand in relation to some criterion, such as grades. Some children work hard to receive a *B* rather than a *C*, 80 percent correct rather than 50 percent, to be on the dean's honor list, or to hold a high rank in their class. The American school has relied heavily on grading systems to reinforce children both positively and negatively, although the true value of such emphasis has been increasingly questioned.

An alternative to grades is a check-mark or point system. Children are given Work Record Cards with ruled squares on them. Every fifteen minutes, the teacher circulates and gives each child a possible ten check marks in the squares—five for the task undertaken during that time period and five for working under classroom rules or "being a student." An attempt is made to give the children as many check marks as possible, but when their accomplishments or behavior clearly fall below reasonable standards some check marks may be withheld to alert the children to the problem. In addition to check marks, alphabet letters can be given, with each letter standing for a particular behavior, for example:

- A—paying attention

- S—starting

- W—working

- T—taking part (oral participation or making a contribution to the class)

- F—following directions

- B—being a student

- D—doing what you are told

- G—getting along with others

- R—being right

- N—being next

Completed cards may be exchanged for periods of free time (e.g., twenty minutes to play a game with some friend) or the opportunity to "take a chance." This involves selecting a card from a deck on the teacher's desk. Each card has a class privilege on it (e.g., Be first in line for lunch for two days). The child gets the privilege on the selected card.

Recordings of the number of problems done correctly or incorrectly also can be made during academic work periods. It has been found that even children in the very early grades can take over the responsibility for counting their own correct and incorrect responses, if procedures are not too complicated. They can then make a chart or graph of the number of correct or incorrect things that they did over a period of time and compare their records each day. Teachers in this study reported that the children were often reinforced by plotting their response rates. In addition, as self-management skills increase and children become aware of their problem areas, they move toward re-entry into a regular class (Haring & Philips, 1972).

It has also been found that the correct academic response rate of children with behavior problems increased when children kept their own records and decided what criteria they would have to meet in order to obtain the privilege of free time (Lovitt & Curtis, 1969). Academic improvement was not determined by the extent of privileges available; it was determined by the opportunities for self-management that were provided. Thus, knowing where you stand and personally deciding on the value of your efforts can operate as rewarding consequences.

An after-school and Saturday morning remedial academic program was conducted for sixteen low achievers who attended regular classrooms during school hours (Wolf, Giles, & Hall, 1968). A point system was developed that first gave points for the correct completion of one problem and later required the correct completion of several problems before points were awarded. Points were redeemable for various consequences, such as field trips, daily snacks, money, and store items. To obtain each consequence, a child was required to gain a specific number of points. Points also were given for correct answers in remedial assignments and for homework completed. Finally, points were awarded for grades that were earned in the regular classroom during the day. An A earned 100 points; B, 75 points; C, 50 points; and D, 25 points. In addition to the points earned in the special program and during the school day, report card grades given by the regular teacher also were converted to points: an A earned 1,600 points; B, 800 points; C, 400 points; and D, 200 points. For several children who had serious records of academic failure, the teacher doubled their point totals for all letter grades associated with the regular classroom.

The results of the study indicate that the points were highly valued and definitely influenced the children's performances. The procedures followed (i.e., giving letter grades in regular classwork an exchange value) demonstrate how grades can be given concrete value and meaning. Such value and meaning can be extremely important for children who have little incentive to work for traditional letter grades.

Social Approval.   Social approval and disapproval may be the most frequently used consequences in the classroom. There are literally hundreds of social exchanges between teachers and children, children and children, and children and the principal, school clerks, librarian, custodian, playground coach, school bus driver, and crossing guards. Some of these exchanges are positive and some negative, but generally all are directed toward helping the child understand and learn the rules and expectations of the community setting of the school. This is not to say that there is always a constructive, fair, sensitive, and consistent pattern to social exchanges. The real world is a human world, the real people in it are human beings; as a result, children occasionally experience hard knocks at the hands of others. Most learn to adjust and to handle unfair, insensitive, and inconsistent social experiences. Exceptional learners, however, may be unusually vulnerable to these experiences.

The retarded child is particularly susceptible to social consequences. Some authors suggest that social consequences are much more powerful than are tangible or token consequences and that relying unnecessarily on tangibles may be an example of "reinforcement overkill" (Forness & MacMillan, 1972). The teacher should recognize the power of social attention, approval, and disapproval and use it carefully and wisely to improve the classroom performance of retarded children. The susceptibility of the retarded to social praise has been further illustrated (McManis, 1967). Mildly mentally retarded children who were seated next to another retarded child who was praised by the teacher, actually increased their performance, even though they themselves were not the targets of praise.

One study compared the effectiveness of food rewards, social praise, and food and social praise combined during a simple, marble-dropping task assigned to disturbed children (Levin & Simmons, 1962). The food rewards alone were more effective than were social praise or combined food and social praise. Some children with behavior disorders are not responsive to social approval given by the teacher, especially in the initial stages of a program. One boy with severe behavior problems, with whom the author worked, bit the teacher on the arm as she attempted to give him an approving pat on the shoulder. Another angrily shouted "shut up" when the teacher verbally praised him. An eleven-year-old boy with a behavior disorder would tear up his paper if the teacher made such comments as "Good work," and a withdrawn, anxious girl would run from the classroom if the teacher spoke to her in any way. The underlying reasons for these children's discomfort in such social situations were undoubtedly varied. However, the good intentions of the teacher did not make social contact or approval effective.

The use of check marks, previously discussed, can provide an effective shaping procedure for socially uncomfortable children. Initially, the check marks are administered as a reward for task completion or good behavior. The checks are given because "you earned them," or withheld because "you did not earn them." No mention is made of the teacher's pleasure or displeasure, approval or disapproval. However, since the teacher is the agent giving the check marks, his or her involvement and presence in the process is undeniable. A positive interaction is promoted between teacher and child by emphasizing the positive aspects of the child's behavior with the check marks; by clearly assigning tasks at the child's level so that he or she can readily succeed and earn check marks; and by having a completed card of check marks redeemable for a reward. The interaction can become increasingly more social as the teacher adds such comments as "I liked the way you raised your hand for help" or "This work is exactly as I wanted it" (when it appears the children can tolerate and profit from this social emphasis). Thus, the check-mark system can move from a more objective, neutral meeting ground for teacher and child to a highly social interaction. It is important that teachers initially respect some exceptional learners' preference for social distance and gradually move toward a positive, comfortable interaction when the children are ready for it.

A number of studies have investigated the effect of social consequences on the behavior of children with learning and behavior problems. Hall, Lund, and Jackson (1968) observed one first-grade student and five third-grade students who were given to disruptive, dawdling behavior. The teacher gave these children social attention for appropriate behavior and ignored them when they were inattentive or disruptive. The procedure sharply increased the study rates of the children. A reversal stage, during which the teacher paid attention to nonstudy behavior, produced low study rates. However, once the initial approach was reinstated, study rates again increased markedly and were maintained even after the experimental program ended.

An interesting aspect of controlling classroom behavior by social and verbal means was investigated (O'Leary, Kaufman, Kass, & Drabman, 1970). Initial observation of several regular classrooms that included a number of problem children revealed that most teacher reprimands for inappropriate behavior were loud in nature and could be heard by many children in the class. When the teachers were asked to speak privately, in a soft voice audible only to the child in question, the frequency of disruptive behavior declined in most of the children. A reversal of procedure produced an increase in disruptive behavior, whereas a return to the private, quiet reprimand caused such behavior to decline again.

A contrasting orientation that focuses on the inner life of the child and understanding his or her psychological conflicts is Life Space Interviewing (Redl, 1959; Morse & Small, 1959; Morse, 1976), which may be effective in dealing with more crisis-type behaviors than those of inattention, dawdling, or talking out in the classroom. The Life Space Interview technique gives therapeutic assistance by having the teacher and child discuss the events associated with a problem in school. If a child becomes so frustrated after an unsuccessful effort to complete an assignment that he or she tears up the worksheet, throws the book on the floor, and angrily strikes out at a classmate sitting nearby, the teacher might take the child aside, calm him or her, and engage in a therapeutic interview about what had happened. The teacher would focus on the actual environmental situation, what led up to the problem, and how such an upset might be avoided in the future. The psychodynamics of the child's problems over time are not dealt with, as they might be during a more formal therapy session with a psychiatrist or psychologist. Rather, an attempt is made to provide psychological "first aid" in the immediate setting in which a problem occurs.

The Life Space Interview technique aims at strengthening the child's coping skills so that he or she can deal with a wide variety of environmental demands. The concept of social consequences is broadened by this approach to include a therapeutic relationship between teacher and child and a more complex interaction than that involved when teacher-controlled attention, approval, or disapproval is used as a management technique.

In a national study that investigated school programs for emotionally disturbed children, the Life Space Interview or some form of counseling on an individual or group basis was one of three overall ways in which teachers attempted to manage classroom behavior (Morse, Cutler, & Fink, 1964). A second was indirect; it consisted of attempts to maintain a good program and reasonable routine in order to avoid management problems. A third stressed the student's individual responsibility for behavior by excluding the student from the classroom until he or she was ready to return. The use of exclusion or "time out" is considered as a negative consequence in a later section.

Multisensory Stimulation and Activity.   In our earlier discussion of flexibility curriculum, we found that active participation and acquisition of knowledge and skill can be enhanced for exceptional learners by enriching experiences, concrete involvement, and multisensory feedback. The rewarding consequences of multisensory stimulation and activity are directly built into each one of these considerations; hence, the pursuit of tasks related to them carries with it promise of its own reward. The materials that Itard used with Victor in the early 1800s and the training materials developed later by Seguin relied on such rewards to appeal to the learner (discussed in chapter 1). The carefully designed, intriguing, and colorful teaching materials in the Montessori classroom are other examples.

Special educators working with all types of exceptional learners have long recognized the value and importance of attractive curriculum materials that invite the child to look, listen, touch, and move. As a result, multisensory stimulation and activity are rewards associated with many types of specialized curriculum materials.

A systematic use of multisensory and activity rewards to improve social and academic behavior is illustrated in the application of the Premack principle (Premack, 1959). Essentially, the principle involves a well-known technique used by all parents and teachers to influence children's behavior. Two kinds of information are required:

1. Which behaviors *do not* occur with the frequency and ease that the parent or teacher considers desirable (e.g., taking out the garbage, completing an arithmetic assignment)?

2. Which behaviors *do* occur with predictable frequency and ease when the child is left to his own resources (e.g., watching television, browsing through the Exploratory Center in the classroom)?

The Premack principle simply states that low-frequency behaviors can be increased or accelerated if they are followed by high-frequency behaviors. The parent who says "Take the garbage out and then you may watch television" is applying this principle. We may expect the garbage-taking-out behavior to occur more frequently if television watching is contingent on its occurrence. In a like manner, the teacher who announces "Once your arithmetic assignment is complete, you may spend time at the game center," may expect assignments to be completed more frequently since time at the game center depends on it.

Whelan (1966) has discussed the use of the Premack principle in programs for exceptional learners. Initially, the teacher observes the child, noting both high- and low-frequency behaviors. Then task assignments, such as reading and arithmetic, are presented to the child and the how much condition specified (e.g., "Here is a page of six division problems"). When the six problems are done, the teacher specifies a how long condition for the high-interest activity (e.g., "You may now spend five minutes at the Exploratory Center"). Over time, the how much condition for the task assignment can be increased. Such assignments can be lengthened to eight, ten, twelve, or more problems, with each task assignment followed by a five-minute, free-time period. Care must be taken not to increase the task assignment too abruptly (e.g., from six problems to three pages of problems) or the approach will not work.

Activity rewards were given on a group basis with a fourth-grade class of twenty-four students (Barrish, Saunders, & Wolf, 1969). Seven students were identified who had problems of out-of-seat behavior, noisemaking, talking out, uncooperativeness, and general classroom disruption. The entire class was divided into two teams. Opportunities for privileges for each team, such as extra recess time, first in line for lunch, and time for special projects, were made contingent on the team's maintaining appropriate behavior. Whenever a child on either team behaved inappropriately, a mark was made on the chalkboard, and the team's chances for privileges were jeopardized. Thus, the entire team shared the loss of privileges when individual members demonstrated problem behavior. The approach significantly and reliably reduced the disruptive behavior of most of the problem students.

Task Completion.   Task completion is an important reward that largely involves guaranteeing success by reducing the criterion of how well the child must do in order to be rewarded. In general, task completion emphasizes starting, working, and finishing rather than quality of effort or correctness. Some may think it is wrong to reward a child when words in the lesson are misread or misspelled, or when arithmetic problems are incorrect. In so doing, we may be rewarding such errors and perhaps cause them to occur with increased frequency in subsequent lessons. Considering the tendency of retarded children to recall errors more frequently than do normals, we might be particularly concerned with allowing errors made by the retarded to go unchecked. Impulsive, uncritical children may race through a page of subtraction problems, add all the numbers, and hand in the assignment as completed. Should we reward this behavior? The answer is certainly not a clear-cut yes, however:

1. Task completion can best be used with tasks that do not require skills the child does not possess (e.g., reading).

2. Task completion can be used as a reward for tasks that the child has done incorrectly, if the teacher calls attention to some aspects of the task the child has done well. Even writing his or her name on the paper or making an effort to try can be acknowledged with positive consequences. The incorrect work can be (1) ignored (without telling the child he is right) *or* (2) examined, and a small portion pointed out as incorrect and discussed. Future assignments should be made in line with the child's functioning, and no child should be continuously given impossible work for the sake of task completion rewards.

A wholesale rejection of all the child's efforts should be avoided. The child should be made to feel good about responding and carefully led into a discussion of improving the quality of his or her work. These comments cannot be applied to every exceptional learner, however, since some are more than ready for imposition of the how well condition. But for those whose difficulties are so great that they are seldom candidates for positive classroom consequences, task completion can be a meaningful starting point for accentuating the positive.

Tangible Rewards.   We come at last to the bottom of our Mount Everest slope of reinforcement and enter the deep valley of M & M's! The use of candy, food, trinkets, and other tangible rewards to increase management and instructional effectiveness with various exceptional learners achieved increased respectability during the 1960s. Although they are unnecessary for most normal children, they are often ideal "launching fuel" for children who have known little joy in learning, acquired only limited knowledge and skill, received poor grades, experienced more social disapproval than approval in school, and found classrooms generally unstimulating and unrewarding.

Despite the reluctance of some educators to enter a realm that some consider one of compromise or bribery, studies have shown that so-called extrinsic rewards are usually only necessary on a temporary basis (Haring & Phillips, 1972; Forness, 1973). Once children begin to experience success in school, they become susceptible to other higher-level reinforcers. The logic behind their use is simple: the teacher who discovers that a child cannot add 2 + 2 because he or she does not understand their numerical value or the concept of addition, can quickly reduce the task to a concrete level and demonstrate with counters that two *things* added to two *things* equal four *things*. Similarly, when it is discovered that a child is not rewarded by grades, praise, or more symbolic and abstract rewards, the temporary use of concrete rewards makes good educational sense. Children given concrete arithmetic lessons will not have to carry around a large sack of counters to solve problems for the rest of their lives; they will soon learn to deal with numbers symbolically. The child given candy or tangible rewards will not become permanently dependent on them but will eventually respond to more traditional classroom incentives. As in our discussion of the selection and arrangement of conditions and expectations in learning, the flexible, open-minded extension of reinforcement practices is one of the distinguishing characteristics of the special educator and the regular-class teacher working with exceptional learners.

Negative Consequences

In addition to positive consequences, the real world of learning and school often involves negative consequences. Consider the following:

"Why do I always have to remind you several times to get out your reading book, Mark?"

"Kathy, you can just stay in your seat during recess because you haven't done anything I asked all morning."

"This arithmetic worksheet is simply unacceptable, Henry. The problems are all wrong, and you evidently weren't listening during yesterday's 'carrying' lesson."

Take a closer look at the examples of Mark, Kathy, and Henry and the possible effects of the teacher's negative remarks. When we criticize children or disapprove of their behavior in some way, our intentions may be positive. We hope that by alerting Mark to his slowness in getting ready that he will improve. Keeping Kathy in from recess might bring her in line the next day, and rejecting Henry's work could result in better attention during subsequent lessons. If these changes occurred, then the negative consequences given to the three would have had positive effects; that is, we would have diminished their problem behavior. Unfortunately, things are not always so predictable and simple with children who have behavior or learning problems. Besides the ideal of bringing about improved behavior through negative consequences, at least three other effects may occur.

First, the teacher may simply be tuned out and the child will not hear or understand the message implied by the consequences. Many exceptional learners have experienced so much verbal chastisement and lecturing in their interactions with the environment that the broken record quality of a lecture renders it totally ineffective. Examples of this are readily found with the disturbed, retarded, and disadvantaged. Also, words are abstract and may be essentially meaningless to many children. A more concrete means of feedback may be more effective, particularly in the initial stages of a program to help children with behavior and learning problems (e.g., a check-mark system).

Secondly, the teacher's remarks to Mark, Kathy, and Henry may only establish them more firmly as losers. Exceptional learners seldom need to be reminded that they do not measure up or that they are deficient. In and out of school, many of them have received more than their share of criticism, ridicule, rejection, and disapproval. As a result, they view themselves in an essentially negative light. They accept the role of clearly established losers and make little effort to try to win when the odds appear so overwhelming. Problem behavior should not always be overlooked. But in trying to help children with difficulties, we should be concerned that our efforts have a reasonable chance of accomplishing something positive and improving a situation—and do not merely contribute to an already existing problem or waste time.

Finally, it is possible that Mark, Kathy, and Henry will make no effort to change their behaviors; in fact, things may become worse. Even though the teacher's remarks were clearly negative (with a possible long-range positive effect expected), the remarks may actually have served to reward the problem behaviors on an immediate basis. Incongruous and illogical as this may seem, teacher attention to or verbal criticism of problem behavior often increases that behavior. Consider Mark. If he does little that results in positive consequences of any kind in the classroom, and if the teacher only pays attention to him when he is slow in getting ready or misbehaving, why not at least be noticed rather than ignored?

Targeting on misbehavior with children who are consistent losers may provide them with their only means of getting attention; as negative and critical as the teacher's remarks are, they may be better than no attention at all. Inadvertently strengthening problem behavior by rewarding it with teacher attention can thus establish the teacher as a loser. This possible effect is best handled by providing such attention when the child at least approximates desirable behavior. Catch John, who constantly leans back in his chair against classroom rules, when the four legs are momentarily on the floor ("I like the way your chair is in place, John"). Chatterbox Susan might be helped to lessen her talking by calling attention to her quiet working periods ("You are really working hard, Susan; keep it up"). These examples relate to our earlier remarks on thimbleful targeting.

What happens when none of the principles aimed at providing positive consequences or avoiding negative ones work? What happens when the child is out of control, refuses to work or cooperate, and causes a disturbance in the classroom? A period of exclusion or "time out" from the classroom may be useful. Technically, a child excluded by the teacher is removed from the physical and social environment of the classroom and hence from opportunities to obtain multisensory or social rewards. The act of exclusion itself, with the teacher leading the child to the door and saying, "You'll have to stay out in the hall until you can be good," is a negative social consequence—underscoring the teacher's disapproval of the child and his or her behavior and bolstered by the child's peers witnessing the whole scene. But some children, who are bored and miserable in the classroom, are only too glad to escape, and they may find the multisensory and social rewards of the hall or principal's office more exciting than those of the classroom.

However, a time-out period of isolation in a quiet, nonstimulating area or room may be effective in getting some children who are upset to settle down (Whelan & Haring, 1966). Removing them from the classroom also minimizes the effect of their disruptive behavior on other children.

From the authors' experience, a child's assignment to a time-out period should take into account the following considerations:

1. It should occur only after the child's behavior has exceeded limits that have been clearly stated previously.

2. It should occur with emotional control, not as a result of teacher exasperation.

3. It should be presented to the child as a constructive aid to learning, rather than as an arbitrary punishment. ("It seems as though you cannot function as a student right now in the classroom. I hope you will be able to after a time-out period.")

4. It should involve a specific period of time rather than an open-ended exclusion such as telling the child, "You may come back when you think you can behave."

5. It should place the child in the best available setting, where multisensory and social stimulation is limited.

6. Once the time-out period has passed, the child should immediately return to the class without any lecturing or attempts to get him or her to "promise to be good from now on."

What is implied is a systematic procedure, free from a punitive and arbitrary attitude on the teacher's part. The success of any time-out procedure hinges on a basic assumption that the positive aspects of the classroom program are so powerful that removal from the room is clearly a negative condition (Forness, 1978; Forness, Frankel, & Landman, 1976). Classroom learning environments must be so stimulating and rewarding that the child does not want to be away from class for any period of time. As idealistic as this may sound, it echoes the concern of many that education should take the offensive, rather than remain on the defensive, in reaching and teaching children. It is more desirable to have children actively seeking maximum time in the classroom because of the promise of stimulation and success than it is to rely on coercion to get them to school. The use of punishment in both special and regular education has received continued attention and never fails to generate controversy. Even a brief review of the issue and the literature related to it is beyond the scope of this text, and the reader is referred elsewhere (Wood & Lakin, 1978).

The outcome of a balanced learning triangle is success. Although it is a well-known and often repeated objective, success is truly central to educational efforts with all learners—exceptional and normal. Skinner has underscored the importance of success as a reinforcer in learning:

> The human organism fortunately for us all, is reinforced just by being successful. Consequently, if material is designed to facilitate correct responses, the resulting frequent success is enough reinforcement for most persons. Not only will the child's

behavior change as he learns to do things he could not do before, but he will become highly motivated, his morale will improve, and his attitude toward teachers will change. (Skinner, 1972, p. 11)

Motivation has special relevance to the learning and behavior problems of exceptional learners. Indeed, it is one of the most overworked terms that regular or special educators use to describe the problems they face in getting children to pay attention, respond, follow directions, improve their social relationships, and acquire knowledge and skill.

"Johnny is poorly motivated and could learn if he tried."

"I wish I could increase Diana's motivation to read at home. "

"Darryl's poor grades reflect his negative motivation toward school and not his real ability."

"Frank could be the real leader of the class but he simply isn't motivated to assume responsibility or cooperate."

What is being discussed in these examples? The children being described seem to lack a force or direction in their behavior that if present, would greatly improve their functioning level.

Human motivation has long been studied by psychologists who have pondered the variety of motives that exist, how they originate and develop, and how they determine behavior. For our purposes, we are interested in the motivation of exceptional learners to increase their flexibility, improve their social relationships, and master language, academic skills, and subject matter. When a child does not readily engage in activities designed to foster improvement in one or more of these areas, we say he or she is "poorly motivated." What we really mean is that the learning triangle has not been balanced properly so that the child actively participates, becomes involved, and learns. Therefore, the burden of responsibility for the existence of motivation in children in a learning situation rests with the environment. Instead of worrying about the internal readiness of the child to learn, we should worry more about the external readiness of the environment to teach.

Summary

In this chapter, we briefly reviewed the basic ingredients of all good teaching—curriculum, conditions, and consequences. Much of the curriculum provided the exceptional learner is pre-academic in nature. It is concerned with improving attention, retention, and visual and auditory perception. It also aims at enlisting the learner's active participation and improving motoric and verbal skills. Special education relies on multisensory experiences and emphasizes meaningfulness and motivation in improving flexibility competence. Building competence in social skills is an important goal of the special education curriculum. Modeling, role playing, coaching, shaping, and integrated group experiences with nonexceptional learners are useful techniques.

The conditions of learning may ultimately determine whether we are successful in teaching. When we teach, where we teach, how much we assign, and how long and how well we expect the child to work are among the concerns of the special educator. Finally, consequences—what happens after the exceptional learner undertakes the curriculum task under the conditions assigned—may be the particular ingredient to worry about with some exceptional learners. The good feeling from learning itself is always there as a possible consequence, and knowing where you stand in relation to a set criterion (e.g., grade) is basic to consequences provided in school. Social approval is a powerful reward, as are multisensory stimulation and activity and task completion. Tangible rewards may be useful with some on a temporary basis. Negative consequences are a part of the real world, including learning and the school. However, they may backfire with children who have experienced continual failure. The desired outcome of the curriculum, conditions, and consequences (i.e., the learning triangle) involved in any child's learning experience is success—a fundamental concern in all teaching.

CHAPTER 10

Making Special Education Work

In chapter 1, we considered the historical origins of special education that preceded Public Law 94–142, a landmark piece of federal legislation that has profoundly changed special education. In this final chapter, we discuss major aspects of this law and key issues that led to its implementation. In essence, we are making a "progress report" on the education of exceptional learners since the passage of the Education for All Handicapped Act. Although the law was passed in 1975, its full implementation has become uncertain due to the political and financial constraints of the early 1980s.

Public Law 94–142 was once described as the culmination of a revolution, embodying the hopes of all those concerned with special education that one day we would "be able to assure every child who has a handicap an opportunity for an education, that we would be free to advocate for appropriate educational services for these children, that we would be unfettered by inappropriate administrative constraints, and that we would not always have to temper critical decisions about children's lives by the inadequacy of public resources" (Weintraub, 1977, p. 114). Has this been the case?

There is no question that Public Law 94–142 changed special education and the roles of those associated with educating exceptional learners. Prior to its passage, the education of handicapped children was largely equated with a self-contained, special-class model of delivering services. Such a model essentially dictated a static role to most professionals involved in this enterprise. The role of school psychologists was basically to determine the eligibility of children for one of two or three types of special classes *after* these children had already been identified in regular classrooms. Systematic early identification programs in, or even substantially related to, the public schools were practically nonexistent, and preschool teachers for handicapped children were rare. The role of regular classroom teachers in reference to special education was primarily to refer children to special education classes. Special education teachers were as isolated from the mainstream of regular education as the children they taught. Their teaching function, in what were presumed to be homogeneous classes of special children, led to instructional approaches often as devoid of individual differences as those used in regular classrooms (Dunn, 1968; Forness, 1972). Terms such as *IEP, mainstreaming, least restrictive environment, noncategorical placement, pluralistic assessment,* and *child find* were not well known in the lexicon of special education. The same was true of such professionals as the resource teacher, the teacher consultant, the fair hearing officer, and the child advocate.

In addition to new roles and terminology, there have been substantial changes, many of which are now permanent features in education of the handicapped. In this chapter, therefore, we must consider the current status of special education practices and procedures. We do so by referring to major provisions of PL 94–142 that refer as well to long-standing issues in special education: (1) zero reject, (2) nondiscriminatory testing and classification, (3) individualized and appropriate education, (4) least restrictive placement, and (5) due process and parent participation. However, this is only a progress report; each of these concepts is still evolving on a yearly or, in some cases, even daily basis.

Zero Reject

In essence, the zero-reject provision of Public Law 94–142 means that no child between the ages of three and twenty-one can be denied a free, appropriate public education. The number of handicapped school children in the United States, at these ages, was estimated at 12 percent, based on U.S. Department of Education figures compiled from the best sources available at the time. The estimated percentages of children in each category of handicapping condition are presented in a table in chapter 2, the largest categories being the speech handicapped, learning disabled, mentally retarded, and emotionally disturbed, in that order. The combined remaining categories of sensory and physical handicaps accounted for only slightly more than 1 percent of all school-age children. Remember, however, that the gifted and the economically disadvantaged or culturally different were not included in the U.S. Department of Education estimates, nor are they mandated to be served as such under Public Law 94–142, unless they appear in other categories.

These were and largely remain the official *estimates* of handicapped children needing services; but, keeping in mind the zero-reject provision, how many children have actually been served? The answer to this question has generated major controversy.

The number of children receiving special education or related services is now obtained each year in a "child count," whereby each school district reports its census of handicapped pupils to its respective state department of education, which forwards the data to the Office of Special Education in the U.S. Department of Education.

The number of children served in the first full year of the law's implementation (the 1976–77 school year) was surprisingly reported as only slightly less than 8 percent of the school-age population, or approximately 3.7 million handicapped children. The U.S. Department of Education reports approximately 4.2 million children served in the 1981–82 school year, a figure approximately 10.5 percent instead of the estimated 12 percent. In other words, at this rate of increase, we might be tempted to conclude that approximately one-eighth of the children originally estimated still remain unserved.

Is this the case? Extremists might argue that either the original estimates were grossly inflated or the schools have indeed failed to find or refused to serve thousands of handicapped children. The truth no doubt lies somewhere between these two possibilities: original estimates were based on the best available data, but they were too generous; thus, some children (likely numbering in the hundreds or thousands) remain to be served or are actually now being served but are not known to school authorities. Table 10–1 illustrates the complexity of this problem.

These data suggest that in some categories of exceptional learners (such as the mentally retarded, learning disabled, and speech handicapped) more than four-fifths of the estimated number are being served. In other categories (such as emotionally disturbed), this number is about one-half. There is also much variability from state to state. Some states reported serving only 5 percent of their total school-age population as handicapped, whereas others reported nearly 12 percent. Of all handicapped children, very few were in the preschool (below age six) population, perhaps only 6 percent, with the same wide variability from state to state.

There is much speculation about the reasons for such uneven service to exceptional learners. Funding for Public Law 94–142 has been one problem. Although the federal government's share has been as high as one billion dollars, this represented only about 10 percent of the cost of educating every handicapped child, and future appropriations will be substantially less. Each state must pay the remainder. The law originally called for the federal share to be 40 percent. Variation from state to state in defining handicapping conditions has also been cited as a factor, and it has been suggested that these two problems, limited finances and definitions of handicap, are interrelated (Prehm & McDonald, 1979). Funding is tied to the child count, which in turn is based on categorical definitions for each handicap. Thus, much time is spent in determining the child's category of disability and in assigning separate specialists for each condition. Cross-categorical or noncategorical teaching, based on the children's needs and specific skill deficits, might allow funding to be tied to the number of teachers and support personnel rather than to the child count, thus leading to more flexibility and efficient programs (Dickie, 1982).

The problem of definitions also extends to specific categories of children. For example, it has

Table 10–1
Exceptional learners estimated to need services and those actually served

Category of Exceptional Learners	% of School-age Children Originally Estimated in 1975	% of School-age Children Reported as Served in 1981–1982*
Emotionally disturbed	2.0	0.9
Mentally retarded	2.3	2.0
Learning disabled	3.0	4.0
Speech handicapped	3.5	2.8
Children with physical and sensory handicaps	1.2	0.8
Total	12.0	10.5

*Represents data published by U.S. Department of Education (1982); data published in *Education of the Handicapped: The Independent Bi-Weekly News Service on Federal Legislation, Programs and Funding for Special Education*, Volume 9, 1983; and data published in Edgar, E., and Hayden, A., "Who are the children special education should serve and how many children are there?" Presented at American Association of Mental Deficiency, Boston, June 1982.

The problem of variability of handicaps from setting to setting may also be a factor in failing to count exceptional learners. Meyen and Moran (1979) suggest the case of a ninth grader with mild cerebral palsy who does well in his social studies class, where discussion and group projects are the norm, but whose English teacher may refer him for special education because his motor problems impair his ability to write compositions and finish essay exams in class. Such a student might reasonably be considered handicapped at nine o'clock but not at ten o'clock. Likewise, Algozzine and Ysseldyke (1981) reported a study in which school personnel were asked to decide if a variety of different children needed special education based on a large amount of assessment data on each child. They chose to label and place 51 percent of these children, *even though the data on each child was in the normal range*. Thus, the perspective of a child's handicaps may also vary from one school setting to another, depending on who is making the decision.

---

been pointed out that the category of "seriously emotionally disturbed" seems to exclude some children with only moderate or mild behavior disorders (Raiser & Van Nagel, 1980). A survey of behavior-disordered children in six states (Grosenick & Huntze, 1980) actually confirmed that the child count had missed large numbers in this category who should have been served. In other cases, the culturally or economically disadvantaged are sometimes precluded by definition from being diagnosed as learning disabled (Kavale, 1980).

There are other difficulties with the law that might preclude certain children from receiving needed services. Regulations around child-find programs and the child count have unfortunately led to a mere *inventory* of children already identified, rather than to true early prevention efforts (Cohen, Semmes, & Guralnick, 1979; Magliocca & Stephens, 1980). There have been few attempts to identify severely handicapped children *before* the mandatory school age of three years in order to prepare them for school entrance (Hayden, 1979). The majority of states, moreover, do not seem to have specific, well-defined criteria for what constitutes a preschool handicap (Lessen & Rose, 1980). Additionally, regular teachers may be reluctant to refer students for special education, since mainstreaming may require them to prepare an assessment report, attend an IEP meeting, and ultimately still be held accountable for the child's progress (Meyen & Moran, 1979).

At the other end of the developmental spectrum, there seem to be even more serious gaps in the quality and availability of certain educational services for handicapped adolescents or young adults (Boylan & Kaplan, 1980; Kahn, 1980; Wiederholt & McEntire, 1980). Shortcomings have been noted in such areas as physical education (Bird & Gansneder, 1979; Cratty, 1980), career education (Brolin & D'Alonzo, 1979; Clark, 1980; Mori, 1980), and vocational education (Forness 1982b; Razeghi & Davis, 1979) for handicapped adolescents. Finally, problems are evident with case finding or locating those to be served and with coordination of services for exceptional learners in nonpublic school settings, such as Headstart programs (Project Head Start, 1980), private schools (*Education of the Handicapped*, 1980), hospitals and clinics (Forness et al., 1980), and correctional facilities (Brown & Robbins, 1979; Johnson, 1979).

Despite these problems, we must conclude that the concept of zero reject is indeed a reality. Prior to Public Law 94–142, complete categories of exceptionality, such as the emotionally disturbed or the severely mentally retarded, and entire age ranges of children, from three to six and eighteen to twenty-one years, were routinely denied public school education in many states with no recourse. Such practices are now the rare exception rather than the rule.

Nondiscriminatory Testing and Classification

As mentioned in chapter 1, Public Law 94–142 directly addressed the problem of discrimination in both testing and classification. In evaluating a child for placement, tests must be selected and administered with due regard for a child's race and cultural background. Furthermore, no single test instrument may be the sole criterion for determining a child's functioning, and an interdisciplinary team including the child's teacher, parents, and a specialist must be involved in the final decision. In addition, this decision must give due consideration to all areas related to a child's suspected handicap, such as health, vision, hearing, motor abilities, language, social adaptation, and the like.

In large measure, these provisions of the law have been met, but some problems remain. One major concern is the assessment and placement of economically disadvantaged and culturally different children, who sometimes have been mislabeled or placed in special classes because of failure to take into account their differing backgrounds and experiences. Chan and Rueda (1979) have made the point that poverty and cultural background interact to affect a child's schooling. Poverty may adversely influence health and experience, leading to poor school performance in any culture. Cultural differences may compound the problem when they conflict with behaviors or standards expected in public schools. Failure to consider both may lead to inappropriate development of interventions. Sex bias is also a potential problem, particularly as programs are expanded for adolescents and young adults (Danker-Brown, Sigelman, & Flexer, 1978). The assessment of certain exceptional learners can be a problem, such as the multiply handicapped deaf whose testing and evaluation is a very complex matter (Flathouse, 1979). Related to this are the difficulties of coordinating a child's assessment with agencies outside the school setting (Bagnato, 1981; Sinclair, 1980; Sinclair & Kheifets, 1982).

Assessing the Economically Disadvantaged and/or Culturally Different Learner

Black, Hispanic, and Native American special educators have achieved significant changes in policy and practices relating to exceptional learners in such areas as intelligence testing, bilingual education, and culturally diverse curricula (Baca, 1980; Hilliard, 1980). Progress, however, is by no means complete or even agreed on. We discussed in chapter 7 how a federal judge in San Francisco recently banned the use of standard IQ tests in evaluating minority children for special classes whereas, a year later, a federal judge in Chicago upheld their use for such purposes. The point has also been made that the entire *system* of referral, evaluation, and placement is fraught with difficulty (Bailey & Harbin, 1980; Duffey, Salvia, Tucker, & Ysseldyke, 1981; MacMillan & Meyers, 1980; Meyers, MacMillan, & Yoshida, 1978) and that simply banning the use of IQ tests will not solve the problem of minority overrepresentation in special classes.

It was recently shown that the proportion of blacks in special classes for the mentally retarded has dropped significantly, perhaps because of legal rulings on such classes; but the number of blacks in learning disability programs has increased disproportionately (Tucker, 1980). Conservative and cautious approaches to diagnosing mild mental retardation have likewise meant that the children remaining in self-contained EMR classrooms are not at all like the previous mentally retarded children on whom much of our significant research was done in the past (MacMillan, Meyers, & Morrison, 1980). Instead, they tend to be children whose mild mental retardation, as discussed in chapter 4, is more likely to have been caused by subtle biomedical or neurological factors, who are generally functioning at lower levels, and who often have associated handicaps in physical or sensory areas.

Part of the reason for the change is the increased emphasis on measuring adaptive behavior. This measurement enables us to obtain information on a child's functioning in nonschool tasks and on the degree to which he or she meets culturally imposed demands for personal and social responsibility (Coulter & Morrow, 1978; Lambert & Nicholl, 1976; Windmiller, 1977). For a child with low academic performance, this becomes a check against incorrect classification (Argulewicz & Sanchez 1983; Knoff, 1983). Evaluating a child's response to a short course of intensive remedial instruction has likewise been suggested as a means of determining not only potential but educational needs as well (Meyen & Lehr, 1980). Also important is a heightened awareness in both regular and special educators to the special needs of economically disadvantaged and culturally different children. There are alternative ways of meeting their needs in the early school years, such as bilingual and multicultural programs, rather than treating such children as handicapped (Almanza & Mosley, 1980; Henderson, 1980). Exceptional learners from minority groups should also be given direct access to the least restrictive classroom environment and their progress monitored in such classes, before decisions are made to place them in special settings (Ysseldyke & Regan, 1980). The federal government's recent decision (February 1981) *not* to require bilingual education will unfortunately make it more difficult to use such regular classroom options.

There is another difficulty ahead that is not necessarily specific to economically disadvantaged or culturally different children; nonetheless, it may come under the provisions of nondiscriminatory testing. This is the movement toward certifying high school students for graduation or diplomas through tests measuring minimum competency in academic skills. For culturally diverse students, as well as for exceptional learners in a number of categories, passing a standard minimum competency test may be quite difficult. Yet the tendency is to require a high school diploma for entry into most occupations. Thus, even mainstreamed exceptional learners may be severely penalized (Safer, 1980). Lawsuits have already been brought to resolve certain issues, and it has been suggested that each child's IEP conference is the place to begin to determine modifications in minimum competency test procedures or variations in required skill levels (Pullin, 1980). Since only a few states seem to have addressed this issue directly (Smith & Jenkins, 1980), it remains to be seen whether professional standards for a high school diploma or the special needs of exceptional learners will prevail (McCarthy, 1980; Wiederholt, Cronin, & Stubbs, 1980).

The potential for tragic consequences resulting from misdiagnosis and mistaken placement of minority children in special classes for the mentally retarded was illustrated in the legal case of *Diana* v. *California State Board of Education*, decided in 1970. Possible long-term effects of special class placement in diminishing a child's ultimate educational attainment were at issue in that case. The following case also illustrates the stigma that often results from misdiagnosis.

In the UCLA Mental Retardation and Child Psychiatry Program, a monthly case conference or "clinical rounds" is held for all hospital and research faculty and their trainees. A few years ago, it was one author's responsibility, as a junior faculty member, to present a case to one clinical rounds devoted to the topic of assessing minority children. The invited faculty discussant was Dr. Jane Mercer, a distinguished sociologist from the Riverside campus of the University, whose work is discussed frequently in this text.

The author presented the case of a young black man in his early twenties who at one time had been referred by his primary teacher for evaluation of learning and behavior problems. Routine testing by a school psychologist suggested an IQ in the mildly mentally retarded range, and he was subsequently placed in an EMR classroom. No information was presented in the case history beyond that point. After presenting the case background, the author brought the young man into the room and interviewed him before the group. It emerged in the clinical interview that the young man's friendships had suffered and that he keenly felt the difference between his own academic progress and that of peers outside the special class. The author also allowed the audience to question the young man, with his permission, about his experience. He managed to respond with brief and direct answers, and it was clear from the level and phrasing of the

audience's solicitous questions that they were under the impression, given his case history, that the young man was indeed mentally retarded.

Since no one thought to ask this young man the outcome of his experience, the author concluded the interview by asking him about his current occupation. The young man responded that he was completing his master's degree at a nearby university with a combined emphasis in special education and black studies!

The author and the "patient" had colluded to save this information until the end, and thus managed to "illustrate" the problem of misdiagnosis. Disbelief was only partly diminished when the young man remained to engage Dr. Mercer in a lively discussion of the assumptions underlying her concept of pluralistic assessment. It is important to note that he did not purposely try to "act" mentally retarded in the interview. His case history, albeit incomplete, spoke for him.

This young man and the author had met several weeks before this incident when the author had lectured to his graduate class. Quite by accident, the young man's past experience in an EMR class had come to light in class discussion. As he neared his junior high years, he had noticed some of his neighborhood friends' textbooks and realized that he was not even remotely exposed to things they were learning. (The feelings he described in the clinical rounds interview concerning this problem were real.) He brought this to the attention of his mother, who had never been informed that he had been assigned to a special class, and was eventually returned to regular classes where, with considerable effort and study, he managed to make up for lost time. The willingness of the UCLA Mental Retardation and Child Psychiatry faculty to treat this young man as mentally retarded, based only on his case history, is but one illustration of the potential stigma that special class placement can involve.

Categorical Labels and Placement

The stigma from labeling children as mentally retarded, disabled, or otherwise handicapped has been discussed at several points in this text. It has been argued that a label's threat to our self-esteem is often related to how close the label comes to the core of our self-concept (Wright, 1960). Hence, mental retardation has been the label with the most pervasive stigma, since low intelligence is more difficult to accept without a major loss of self-esteem. In studying mentally retarded individuals, Edgerton (1967) found that not one used the term *mentally retarded* to explain why he or she had once been institutionalized. Most used terms like *alcoholic, delinquent,* or *nervous.* Jones (1972, 1974) found that adolescent mildly retarded students tried to avoid being identified as a member of the EMR class and reported that labeling or special class placement had hurt their friendships or made it more difficult to get a job. It has been claimed that *mentally retarded* and other such labels often act to diminish other people's expectations of a child, or even worse lead to discrimination and rejection (Mercer, 1973).

However, it has been pointed out that the label alone does not stigmatize the mentally retarded. MacMillan, Jones, and Aloia (1974), in a comprehensive review of labeling studies, have demonstrated that stigma is not just a function of the label but of the label *and* special class placement *and* special curriculum *and* a host of other variables that attach to a mentally retarded child. The contribution of each to stigmatization has proven difficult if not impossible to sort out (Guskin, Bartel, & MacMillan, 1975; Rowitz, 1981). Corman and Gottlieb (1978) have reviewed studies on mainstreaming that suggest that mentally retarded children integrated into regular

Figure 10–1.

classrooms are not necessarily socially accepted and that lack of acceptance does not seem to be related to their past EMR label. What seems to be at issue, as Gottlieb (1975) has shown, is that nonretarded peers may perceive bizarre behavior or academic incompetence exhibited by a retarded child differently from the same behavior or incompetence in a nonretarded child. In other words, if a child acts incompetently and is labeled retarded, normal classmates may excuse that behavior or even act in a protective way. In a nonlabeled child, the same incompetence might not be as readily excused or understood (Peck & Stephens, 1964).

Nonretarded peers' attitudes may also be influenced by their teachers. One of the first studies on negative teacher expectations of the retarded was done by Beez (1968), who had teachers tutor children on a list of words. One group of children were falsely presented as "slow learners," when in fact they were no different from the others. The "slow learners" did learn fewer words but, more significantly, the teachers attempted to teach them fewer words. Studies with disturbed and learning-disabled pupils have also demonstrated negative teacher expectations (Foster, Ysseldyke, & Reese, 1975; Ysseldyke & Foster, 1978). Observational studies of mentally retarded children in ongoing classrooms seem to suggest that their behavior is, for the most part, indistinguishable from that of nonretarded peers (Forness, Guthie & MacMillan, 1981; Gottlieb, Gampel, & Budoff, 1975). However, Brophy and Good (1974) have observed teacher interactions in the classroom with children whom the teachers identified as low achievers. Compared to other children in the class, these children were rejected more often in various ways by their teachers; and a recent study has demonstrated that teacher rejection affects how retarded children choose each other as friends (Morrison, Forness & MacMillan, 1983).

Yoshida and Meyers (1975) have argued that previous studies on labeling and teacher behavior, such as that by Beez, have shown expectancy effects only because the teachers were unfamiliar with the child and thus the label became more important in the situation. In actual practice, a teacher would probably determine his or her behavior towards a child only after extensive classroom experience with that child, as has been suggested by recent studies (Humphreys & Stubbs, 1977; Palmer, 1983; Reschly & Lamprecht, 1979). Teacher expectancy studies have been extensively criticized for other methodological problems as well (Elashoff & Snow, 1970). A recent study (Boucher & Deno, 1979) suggests that teachers may largely ignore labels when planning long-term classroom programs for exceptional learners.

There is no question that placement in special education and labeling may be problematic for some exceptional learners. However, recent studies have shown that full-time, special-class placement can be accompanied by *gains* in self-concept for handicapped children, as compared to being left in regular classes (Boersma, Chapman, & Battle, 1979; Ribner, 1978; Strang, Smith, & Rogers, 1978). Hobbs (1975) has suggested that there are pros and cons to any labeling and classification issue. Children may be stigmatized by labels, but labels can be used positively to influence public funding, conduct research, and open doors to needed classroom services. MacMillan (1977) concludes that available evidence on labeling, teacher expectancy, and self-concept fails to support the argument that devastating or long-lasting effects result from labeling a child and providing him or her help in special programs. Labels such as *blind* or *retarded* are harmful when they trigger off automatic expectations of dependency, helplessness, or hopelessness, but labels themselves may not be solely responsible. Rather, the child's classroom placement, simplified or adapted curriculum, and demonstrated level of competence may all conspire to produce the stigma that too often has been blamed on the label.

Ambivalence about the use of categorical and non-categorical labels continues to be evident. California has adopted a "master plan" for special education that is essentially intended to be noncategorical. The plan states that all handicapped children are henceforth given a *single* designation as "individuals with exceptional needs," and this designation "should have four subclassifications, which should be used *only* for data collection and reporting purposes" (*California Master Plan for Special Education*, 1974, p. 23).

One of these subclassifications, *Learning Handicapped* (LH), includes all behavior-disordered, learning-disabled, and EMR children. Although not expressly stated, it was originally hoped that LH classrooms might thus contain all three types

of children, grouped according to their common educational needs (Forness, 1974). For some, this would avoid the most stigmatizing label of mental retardation. The other three subclassifications are *Communicatively Handicapped* (including the deaf, aphasic, and speech handicapped), *Physically Handicapped* (blind, orthopedically handicapped, and health impaired), and *Severely Handicapped* (developmentally disturbed, TMR, autistic, and seriously emotionally disturbed). Autism later was reclassified as a physical handicap.

One school district, however, began informally to add *sub*designations to these categories, such as LH/EMR and LH/LD, suggesting to many observers that it might be difficult to part with the use of familiar categories.

It is possible, however, that Public Law 94–142 has fostered the practice of labeling, inasmuch as the law sets very strict definitions for each category of handicap and ties child counts and funding to these definitions (Sabatino, 1981). On the other hand, the law does provide for an *individualized* educational program and thus for individual consideration of each child's particular strengths and weaknesses in meeting his or her school needs.

Nationally, there seems to be no particular trend away from using categorical placements, and research findings are contradictory at best. Garrett and Brazil (1979) report a survey in which only a handful of states seem to be using noncategorical or more educationally relevant systems and conclude that there appears to be an *increase* in categories, with one state using as many as sixteen different labels. Recent federal laws on developmentally disabled persons, however, seem to be consolidating such categories (Ross, 1980); and, in fact, most special education resource room programs for mildly handicapped children are cross-categorical (Sparks & Richardson, 1981).

In studies of large numbers of EMR, LD, and ED children in special classes, Gajar (1979, 1980) used IQ, achievement tests, and behavior ratings to examine similarities and differences in these three groups. She found significant differences between the three groups, as we might predict, but also many similarities. LD and ED children were similar in IQ; EMR and ED children were both underachieving at similar levels in reading; and EMR and LD children did not seem to differ significantly in behavior ratings. Using five problem-solving tasks, Becker (1978) found differences generally favoring learning-and behavior-disordered students over EMR students. A recent comparison of mentally retarded and autistic children's cognitive functioning also seems to suggest significant differences, especially in the area of language (Sindelar, Meisel, Buy, & Klein, 1981). On the other hand, Forness, Guthrie, and MacMillan (1981) directly observed more than 900 children in TMR, EMR, and LH (the combined category for EMR, LD, and ED) classrooms, over several days. They found that total on-task behavior generally failed to distinguish among these groups and that variability *within* each category of children was far greater than that *between* categories. Other studies (Barnes & Forness, 1982; Forness and Cantwell, 1982) suggest that several different types of emotionally disturbed and mentally retarded children were actually recommended for placement in the same category of special education classrooms. Finally, Weener (1981) has re-examined a large number of studies comparing normal and learning-disabled children and has found that nearly one-fourth of the LD children scored higher than the average normal child on various measures. Thus, the differences between various types of handicapped children, as well as the differences between handicapped and normal, suggest that special education categories may in fact be quite arbitrary.

As a solution, several authors (Forness, 1983; Greenspan & Javel, 1982; Hallahan & Kauffman, 1977; Lilly, 1977) argue that children be considered candidates for special education on the basis of behavioral characteristics rather than traditional categories, a position generally favored in this text. The difficulty, as exemplified above and as these authors readily admit, is finding the *appropriate criteria* by which to group children. Forness (1981b) has summarized highlights of the research over the past decade and a half that has exponentially increased our knowledge of the complexity of educating exceptional learners. What emerges is the conclusion that even a momentary classroom transaction between an exceptional learner and his or her teacher is likely to represent a "minute-by-minute balancing of an array of social, attitudinal, temperamental, motivational, perceptual, linguistic, and cognitive variables" (Forness, 1981b, p. 60). Given so many possibilities, it may be quite difficult to categorize efficiently.

One right that Public Law 94–142 guarantees, through the mechanism of the IEP, is that the *appropriateness* of each child's assessment or program be determined on an individual basis. We can only hope that such individualization ultimately leads to the consideration of each child as his or her category.

Individualized and Appropriate Education

The individual educational plan (IEP) has been considered one of the most significant new developments in the education of handicapped children (Torres, 1977). It was clearly the cornerstone of Public Law 94–142. For most parents, teachers, administrators, and child care professionals, it has been a relatively new experience to meet together to design a year-long school program for a single child. It has been even more novel to put this plan in writing and to obtain agreement with all aspects of the plan. Much has been written about the IEP, and several informative reviews of IEP procedures are available (Arena, 1978; Golin & Ducanis, 1981; Hudson & Graham, 1978; Morgan, 1981; Poplin, 1979; Torres, 1977; Turnbull, Strickland, & Brantley, 1982; Turnbull, Strickland, & Hammer, 1978 a & b; Thies & Unrein, 1981; Turnbull & Turnbull, 1978).

The IEP is considered a significant advance in special education because it seems to have substantially modified the education of exceptional learners in several important ways (Forness, 1979a):

1. Each child's IEP is a document that, by its nature, draws together the efforts of several different professionals who work with the child. It has historically been the case that physicians, psychologists, counselors, teachers, and other professionals often work in isolation from one another and, on rare occasions, may even unwittingly work at cross purposes.

2. The IEP insures that parents are involved, not only as valuable sources of information on the child, but also as responsible members of the interdisciplinary team. Parents must not only be actively involved in the development of the written program but usually must also signify their agreement by signing the final draft.

3. The IEP forces professionals to consider systematically the prognosis for a child's education. This requires that goals and objectives be set for a child on a yearly basis, an exercise that compels professionals to make predictions about each child's progress and about the potential effectiveness of the school program.

4. The IEP often specifies who is responsible for various components of the child's program and thus places the burden for the child's progress on specific individuals. As mentioned earlier, not only does the IEP bring professionals from various disciplines together but it also specifies the responsibilities of each.

5. The IEP forces each professional to look at his or her own effectiveness. It is not enough to choose a classroom method, a treatment program, or a curriculum that research or experience has demonstrated as effective. It is now necessary to monitor the appropriateness and the effectiveness of a particular approach with each child.

6. As the name implies, an *individual* educational program insures that each child will be treated as unique. No longer will mildly retarded children, for example, be removed from the regular classroom just because they have been diagnosed or categorized as educable mentally retarded. No longer will all severely retarded children be assigned to special schools just because they have been diagnosed as trainable mentally retarded. Each child will be treated as a separate case and placed according to careful examination of his or her unique needs rather than according to his or her diagnosis. The IEP serves as a quasi-legal document around which the civil rights of the child and his family are monitored and protected in regard to school programs.

As mentioned earlier, the IEP is developed in a meeting in which the child's parents, teacher, and a special education teacher or supervisor must participate. Others may attend, including professionals or administrators who have either assessed the child or will be involved in his or her education. The child may even participate, when appropriate. As it has evolved over the past few years, the IEP must contain the following elements:

Level of Performance. The IEP must give some indication of the child's educational functioning level. This might include results of any or all of the following: health and physical examinations, screening tests in hearing and vision, the child's developmental history, psychological evaluation of intelligence or emotional functioning, perceptual or achievement testing, adaptive behavior ratings or other descriptions of the child's adjustment to home or neighborhood life, teacher rating scales or reports of direct observation of the child in the classroom or play situations, assessment of physical or motor dexterity, and vocational or career education evaluations. Note that all this information is not required in every case. Only two or three items may be sufficient in some cases.

Goals and Objectives. The IEP must contain the goals and short-term objectives for the child's school program, hopefully based on the assessments just described. Goals are referenced to expected progress for the child by the end of the school year. Separate goals may be written for each academic area (i.e., language, reading, mathematics, etc.) and for physical, social, emotional, or vocational skills. In some cases, goals need only be written for the one or two areas that are deficient. Objectives describe expected steps of progress for the child in reaching annual goals. For example, an objective in mathematics for a mildly retarded nine-year-old child might be, "He will be able to do simple two-place addition by the end of the semester."

Educational and Related Services. The IEP must specify the types of special education programs the child requires, any other services needed to support the child's educational progress, and, whenever applicable, the extent to which the child will participate in *regular* education programs. In simple cases, this may be a matter of specifying the type of special classroom the child will be placed in or the combination of resource room and regular classroom instruction the child will receive. In a more complex case, such as a severely retarded child with multiple handicaps, many services might need to be specified and coordinated.

Initiation and Duration of Services. The IEP must specify when the child will receive education or related services and how long these may be expected to continue. In some cases, such as speech therapy, the number and length of the sessions per week must be given; and some school districts include in their IEPs the names of various teachers or professionals responsible for each service provided.

Evaluation Criteria. The IEP must contain criteria and procedures for determining, at least on an annual basis, whether goals and objectives for the child are being achieved. For example, statements may be made about which techniques or tests will be used to measure the child's progress, which criteria will determine success in each area, and who will decide if each criterion has been met. Again, some cases may be simple. A child with a reading disability may only need to be tested by the teacher or school psychologist with a standard achievement test at the end of the year; if he scores at a certain level, he will have met the goal. The program of a mildly retarded child with an emotional problem, which affects his peer relations, might need to be evaluated through several means. His achievement may be tested with both standardized and criterion-referenced tests.

Achievement gains may be referenced to *expected* achievement for a mildly retarded child, using IQ or other means of determining expectations. Improvement in emotional problems may be measured *indirectly* by examining progress in peer relationships or observing behavior in classroom or playground situations, using specified criteria.

Some IEPs are exceedingly complex and thorough documents. The case of a severely mentally retarded child with a variety of associated speech and physical handicaps can result in an IEP of several pages. Assessments may need to be made in virtually *all* areas described in item 1. Parents and special teachers may be involved in the assessment as well as physicians, psychologists, school nurses, and a variety of other specialists. Goals and objectives may need to be specified in every academic and developmental area, and coordination of all services required to meet these goals and objectives may be extremely difficult. For example, this youngster may have to be placed in a special school, and justification statements should be made as to why and for how long. The child may need the ongoing services of a pediatrician for medication to control seizures or hyperactivity, and some statement may be needed about possible side effects of these drugs and how the special education teacher or parent should report these to the physician. If physical therapy or special physical education is needed, statements have to be made about how these will be coordinated with classroom activities. A speech articulation problem may require special sessions with the speech therapist, and a statement needed about how these will be coordinated with the special education teacher's language lessons. The family may require special assistance to support the child's schooling at home through language or play activities that complement those of the school; a statement may be needed about the role of the school social worker or counselor in instructing the family or in coordinating liaison between home and school. Long-term planning and coordination may be needed with other agency representatives for such things as vocational training and placement. The evaluation criteria and procedures may be extremely complex and involve year-end conferences with parents and all professionals involved to determine if goals and objectives have been met or what modifications may be needed in the overall plan.

Let us consider certain elements of the IEP and the impact they have had on educating exceptional learners. Bear in mind that the development of IEPs varies from state to state and even from one school district to another. The U.S. Office of Special Education and each state department of education publish guidelines to assist special educators and clarify certain points, but it is essentially each school district's responsibility to develop its own format for the IEP and related procedures.

Setting IEP Goals for Exceptional Learners

Although the field of special education is fairly sophisticated in assessing children's functioning (Wisland, 1977), the IEP calls for somewhat different types of assessment skills, which are only now beginning to be developed. Recent studies have shown that results of traditional psychoeducational evaluations often bear little if any relationship to the eventual goals or recommendations contained on individual educational plans (Schenck, 1980; Sinclair, 1980; Sinclair & Kheifets, 1982). A renewed emphasis on teacher-based assessment is obviously needed (Hawkins-Shepherd, 1978; Moran, 1979; Tymitz, 1981). It is also important to begin developing assessment instruments that measure *application* of skills learned in classroom settings, since long-term goals for exceptional learners must ultimately be concerned with career and vocational outcomes (Forness, Thornton, & Horton, 1981; Lynch, Kiernan, & Stark, 1981).

Although it has generally been the practice in special education for teachers to establish certain goals for their students, it is a relatively new exercise to put these goals in writing. Goal setting is a complex process, especially with handicapped children (Holland, 1980; Morgan, 1981). It involves making predictions about children who by definition do not progress in the normal manner and about whose progress we have very few research studies of a longitudinal nature to guide us (Prehm, 1976). Moreover, there is still no real agreement in the field of special education on such basic questions as whether we should teach to a child's strengths or to his weaknesses (Hammill, 1975; Payne, Polloway, Smith, & Payne, 1977) or what type of classroom placement is the most effective (as discussed earlier in this chapter).

How then should goals be set? It is clear that this has been and will continue to be a guessing game (Gallistel, 1978). Given the assessment of the child's strengths and weaknesses, the team must agree on which deficits are the most serious, whether they can in fact be remediated with reasonable effort, and how many skills should be targeted for development over the year. For some children, academic goals are primary; for others, social goals; for others, only the attainment of basic developmental skills may be possible. Although some learning-disabled children with normal potential can be expected to make reasonable academic progress with special instruction, some mildly retarded children may be expected to make far less progress even under the best of conditions. Measures of intelligence, despite their shortcomings, are sometimes helpful in setting goals because they can be thought of as a "rate" of expected progress over time (Zigler, 1969; Gallistel, 1978). Year-end goals can thus be referenced to *expected* progress.

In setting social or developmental goals, it is sometimes helpful to know both what normal children are capable of and the norms for groups of handicapped children (Gunzburg, 1973). Not knowing may create unnecessary pressure on the child and frustration for parents and teachers. Page (1980) has described in considerable detail the complexities of any decision made by an IEP team, and the necessity for team members to give cautious consideration to the validity and reliability of test norms and results before selecting goals and programs for each exceptional learner. He also suggests having "independent judges" assess the seriousness of problems in each social and academic area in relation to the child's total educational needs.

Selecting and Evaluating Programs

The types of programs for exceptional learners were once limited to two traditional models: special classes in public schools and special schools or institutions. Today, however, there is a bewildering array of options to choose from, and a continuum of possible services was introduced in chapter 2. Forness (1979a) has listed nearly twenty separate placement situations that would meet an exceptional learner's needs, and the list is by no means exhaustive. It is important to specify who is responsible for monitoring such programs and services so that these can be coordinated to insure effective progress for the child.

Selecting effective programs and services ultimately depends on an evaluation of each child's progress. An IEP team makes the initial placement decision, but it may not be clear until later in the year whether the decision was correct. For this reason, it is frequently recommended that the IEP be monitored twice during the first year and annually thereafter. Evaluation of children's programs can be an extremely complex enterprise involving many approaches and techniques (Dunst, 1979; Jenkins, Deno, & Mirkin, 1979; Maher & Barbrack, 1980; Peterson, Zabel, Smith &

White, 1983). When parents and regular teachers are involved, there is a particular need for direct and clear measurement of progress.

In its simplest form, evaluation can be observation. If an objective for a severely retarded youngster is for him to say five words at the end of the year, one simply observes if the child can do so. The problem then becomes one of objectivity (Lilly, 1977). Suppose that the child's articulation is so poor that only the parents and the teacher can understand him, or that the child can only repeat the words immediately after they are said by the teacher, or that he says them only when an actual representation of each word is physically present. One must assess the child carefully and objectively to specify the deficits in a clear manner, state goals (or at least objectives) in precise language, select procedures and programs so that their impact can be delineated, and specify in some detail what the outcome criteria will be. Evaluation is therefore a process that *permeates* the entire IEP. A more precise statement of the previous objective might not only specify the words the child will be taught but also give the conditions under which they will be elicited and perhaps specify a person, other than the teacher or parent, who will be present when the words are said to be sure that they are understandable.

Evaluation should be seen as a series of feedback points that determine the direction of each new step in the program, that is, movement to the next objective or level of placement, continuation of programs or services, or a change to a "branching" program that attempts to meet the same objective through different means. The ultimate standard for any evaluation is whether the entire interdisciplinary team, including the parents, understands and agrees on measures of progress. When the child meets the criteria, all members must be content that they as a team have made acceptable progress.

The IEP Team

The intent of Public Law 94-142 was clearly to involve teachers, parents, and administrators as equal partners in the interdisciplinary IEP process. It is not altogether clear that this has been accomplished. To begin with, a recent survey suggested that nearly two-thirds of IEP teams contacted had a significant number of members who were unaware of specific decisions they were enpowered to make (Fenton, Yoshida, Maxwell, & Kaufman, 1979). This lack of goal clarity might adversely effect the ability of team members to participate effectively. Participants in another study (Gilliam, 1979) were asked to rank the importance of each IEP team member in the planning process. Before the IEP meeting, parents, social workers, and principals were perceived as having considerable status in relation to the process; after the meeting, they were ranked low in terms of their contributions. Special education teachers and school psychologists, on the other hand, were generally ranked highest, both before and after the meeting. This is in spite of findings that suggest that no one group of professionals or parents has been found to be more "expert" in their judgements of various disabilities thought typical of exceptional learners (Alley, Deshler, & Mellard, 1979). Finally, in another study, Kehle and Guidubaldi (1980) found that complete IEP teams made no more effective special education decisions than did school psychologists who made such decisions alone, as they did under the traditional placement system.

Thus, it comes as no surprise in observation studies of several IEP meetings (Goldstein, Strickland, Turnbull, & Curry, 1980; Ysseldyke, Algozzine, & Thurlow, 1980) that such conferences typically involve special education resource teachers taking the initiative to review an already developed IEP with the parents, before obtaining their consent. These studies also suggest that regular classroom teachers are far more concerned with the behavior management of the child in the classroom than with curriculum or performance levels. Indeed, the concern of classroom teachers and their need for support in dealing with exceptional learners has been well documented (Hayes & Higgins, 1978; Safer, Morrissey, Kaufman, & Lewis, 1978). An overwhelming majority of IEPs studied tend to involve classroom teachers as the person responsible for implementing *and* evaluating IEP objectives (Andersen, Barner, & Larson, 1978). It is also interesting to note that a national survey of IEPs suggests that nearly half of them are only *three* pages or less in length (U.S. Department of Education, 1980).

In a comprehensive, year-long study of the daily logs of seventy-five special education teachers, Price and Godman (1980) found that an average of six and one-half hours was spent on developing each IEP. More than *two* of these hours were on the teacher's own time! Most of the total time was spent gathering diagnostic data and writing the IEP document; IEPs for the hearing impaired, emotionally disturbed, and physically handicapped seemed to require the most time and effort. It is not clear whether this trend will continue or whether the process will become easier and less time consuming as teachers become more experienced in developing IEPs or even in adapting microcomputers to the task (Budoff & Hutton, 1978). The provision of training in developing IEPs and feedback on the quality of each IEP was found to be necessary in helping teachers with the process (Maher, 1980).

The question of teacher "burnout" and stress in special education has arisen lately (Bensky et al., 1980; Weiskopf, 1980). The added time and effort involved in developing IEPs was mentioned as a factor. The wish for all concerned is that less time be spent on the IEP as a product (i.e., the final document) and more on improving the quality of instruction and interdisciplinary cooperation through the IEP *process* (Golin & Ducanis, 1981; Kaye & Aserlind, 1979; Thies & Unrein, 1981).

Least Restrictive Placement

The concept of the least restrictive environment was one of the most controversial aspects of Public Law 94–142. In a general sense, the concept has come to mean that handicapped children be provided services in as normal and integrated a fashion as possible (Thurman & Fiorelli, 1979). In a particular sense, the concept has become equated with mainstreaming children into regular classrooms. Although mainstreaming means different things to various professionals, there is some agreement that it is defined by the following four features (MacMillan, Jones, & Meyers, 1976):

1. The mainstreamed child must spend more than half the time in the regular classroom.

2. The regular classroom teacher must have *primary* responsibility for the child's progress.

3. No categorical labels (e.g., mentally retarded, emotionally disturbed) must be applied to the child.

4. The child's learning handicaps must not be so severe as to preclude their effective remediation in a regular classroom setting.

Controversy arose and continues because there is still no strong empirical evidence favoring either mainstreaming or special-class placement. With the mentally retarded, a number of studies on the effectiveness of special-class placement indicate that such children assigned to special classrooms have negligible or inferior academic performance when compared to retarded children left in regular classes (Guskin & Spiker, 1968; MacMillan, 1977). Nor is evidence clear in social functioning; some studies indicate that retarded children seem better adjusted and have better self-concepts after special-class placement, and others suggest that special-class placement has a harmful effect on the self-concept of retarded children and on their readiness to interact with neighborhood playmates (Lawrence & Winschel, 1973). The same conflicting results on these issues have been found in the few studies with emotionally disturbed (Quay, Glavin, Annesley, & Werry, 1972; Vacc, 1968, 1972) and learning-disabled children (Bersoff, Kabler, Fiscus, & Ankney, 1972; Macy & Carter, 1978; Sabatino, 1971). Carlberg and Kavale (1980) have

Figure 10-2.

recently done a meta-analysis of these studies in which results for fifty of the better designed studies were "pooled" in order to draw inferences from a total sample of 27,000 children. The results suggested a very slight *advantage*, in both achievement and social adjustment, for mentally retarded students left in regular classes and perhaps some *disadvantage* in leaving emotionally disturbed or learning-disabled students in the regular classrooms.

Another way this issue has been examined recently is to follow-up retarded children returned to regular classes after placement in special-class settings. These studies generally demonstrate that retarded children did not do very well on social and academic measures when compared to nonretarded peers in the same classrooms (Keogh & Levitt, 1976; Meyers, Sundstrom, & Yoshida, 1975; Semmel, Gottlieb, & Robinson, 1979). The points must be made, however, that these children were ordered to be mainstreamed because of court or legislative action; that many had already been in special classes for some time; that most were returned en masse to regular classes, often without full individual consideration of the particular benefits or disadvantages to each child; and that several were not systematically provided necessary services, such as resource teachers, to support them in the regular classroom.

Clearly, a fair test of either special-class placement or mainstreaming has not yet been made (Childs, 1979; Gottlieb, 1981; Jones, Gottlieb, Guskin, & Yoshida, 1978; MacMillan & Semmel, 1977; Zigler & Muenchow, 1979). The pendulum swing *toward* mainstreaming was doubtless premature and perhaps should have been arrested in mid-swing. A more balanced approach would be to determine which child, with what set of characteristics, is the best candidate for mainstreaming and which child should have special-class placement. Criteria for deciding whether to mainstream a particular child or to place that child in a special class relate to such factors as the age of the child, the pervasiveness and degree of handicap, the curriculum modifications needed, the child's peer relationships and social skills, the number of children in the regular classroom, the attitude and competence of the regular-class teacher, and the type of family support system the child has (Blacher-Dixon, Leonard, & Turnbull, 1981; Forness, 1979b; Gresham, 1982; Heron & Skinner, 1981; Hundert, 1982; Guralnick, 1981). A truly *individualized* educational program should account for each of these factors, both independently and cummulatively for each child, until research supplies a definitive answer.

Nevertheless the practice of mainstreaming appears to have fluctuated in recent years. On October 24, 1979, congressional testimony by the U.S. Office of Civil Rights, which monitors compliance with Public Law 94–142, indicated that the percentage of handicapped children in full-time special education programs dropped from 27 to 22 percent between 1976 and 1979. On August 10, 1982, congressional testimony by the Secretary of Education indicated that the percentage had risen to 32 percent. In other words, nearly two out of three exceptional learners are now mainstreamed, that is, they spend fewer than ten hours per week in special classrooms. This survey did not count handicapped children in private schools at public expense, many of whom could doubtless be considered in full-time special education. These figures are also somewhat misleading because children in the two largest categories, learning disabled and speech handicapped, have traditionally been mainstreamed. As shown in Table 10–1, these two categories together account for more than 60 percent of all *handicapped* children. The mentally retarded, physically handicapped, and hearing impaired are placed quite frequently in *full-time special education*; but together, these groups account for only a relatively small proportion of all exceptional learners. Recent figures suggest that well over 90 percent of all handicapped school children are now educated in regular schools, even though many attend special classes in these schools (U.S. Department of Education, 1982).

Concerns of Regular Educators about Mainstreaming

Major resistance to mainstreaming has come from regular classroom teachers, and with some justification. It is they who bear the primary burden of mainstreaming. The National Education Association, representing regular educators, has generally not disputed the *rationale* behind mainstreaming. As a matter of fact, it supported passage of Public Law 94–142. However, its membership expressed several misgivings about the *fact* of mainstreaming, in terms of increased inservice needs, unavailability of support services, demands on teacher time, and additional administrative responsibilities for IEPs (Ryor, 1978). Results of questionnaires continue to suggest that regular-class teachers feel that special-class placement is a better option (Hudson, Graham, & Warner, 1979; Stephens & Braun, 1980). As we examine attitudes of regular educators more closely, we find that those apt to be more directly involved in mainstreaming (e.g., teachers rather than administrators) hold more ambivalent attitudes (Glicking & Theobald, 1975; Keogh & Levitt, 1976); that actual experience with mainstreaming is likely to produce either positive (Harasymiw & Horne, 1975; Smart, Wilton, & Keeling, 1980) or negative attitudes (Palmer, 1979; Shotel, Iano, & McGettigan, 1972); and that teachers who feel some degree of confidence in their own ability and training are more inclined to accept a mainstreamed child into their classrooms (Larrivee, 1981; Larrivee & Cook, 1979; Stephens & Braun, 1980). In regard to this last point, Ringlaben and Price (1981) found that more than half of the regular-class teachers they surveyed had never received any inservice training in special education and more than 80 percent had never had a course in dealing with mainstreamed children. Robson (1981) likewise found that school principals often see a special education staff member as encroaching on their "turf" and thus may make it more difficult for their teachers to receive the special education consultation they need.

The implications of these findings have led to continued emphasis on university instruction of regular classroom teachers in special education techniques and methods (Miller, Sabatino, & Larsen, 1980; Naor & Milgram, 1980). Increased emphasis has also been placed on a variety of inservice programs to train and prepare regular classroom teachers on the job. These programs seem to be most effective if teachers are given actual "hands-on" experience with exceptional learners in addition to standard lectures and presentations (Johnson & Cartwright, 1979; Neilsen, 1979; Soloway, 1974). School principals are often a key in facilitating the work of regular classroom teachers and in seeing they receive the support they need to deal with mainstreamed children (Raske, 1979). It has even been suggested that school administrators use a "teacher effort index" (Ryor, 1978) in which the type or degree of handicapping condition the child has is counted toward the total number of children assigned to any one classroom teacher (e.g., a slow learner counts as 1.5 regular pupils, an emotionally disturbed child counts as 2.5, and so forth). Recent analysis of studies on class size suggests that the *smaller* the number of children in the classroom, the better the achievement and social adjustment of *all* the children in the class (Glass & Smith, 1979; Smith & Glass, 1980).

Teachers and even parents were initially quite concerned that mainstreaming would mean wholesale "dumping" of severely and profoundly handicapped children into regular classrooms. Although this has not generally been the case, the debate continues over exactly how the concept of least restrictive environment will be interpreted in regard to this population (Burton & Hirshoren, 1979; Sontag, Certo, & Button, 1979). The issue seems to come down to whether placing severely or profoundly handicapped children in regular schools might unfairly raise their parents' expectations, decentralize or render ineffective the impact of resources and trained personnel, and subject such children to further rejection and social isolation. The point must be made (as it has been several times in this text) that there is a considerable range of abilities in any given category of exceptional learners, even the severely and profoundly handicapped (Guess & Horner, 1978), and that *individual* consideration of each case is essential. Programs have been developed that suggest that "dispersing" severely handicapped children in special classes in regular schools, throughout each school district, can effectively provide at least some contact with nonhandicapped children along with needed services (Thomason & Arkell, 1980; Zeigler & Hambleton, 1976). Related to this is the largely unresolved issue of whether severely handicapped children should receive year-round schooling so that they will not regress over the summer months (Leonard, 1981; McMahon, 1983). The level of the debate on these issues has improved compared to twenty years ago, when the discussion centered on whether or not TMR children should even be considered a public school responsibility (Goldberg & Cruickshank, 1958).

Misgivings of both professionals and parents about mainstreaming also have to do, at least in part, with the potential adverse effect the presence of a handicapped child might have on the learning of other youngsters in a regular classroom. Social interaction between handicapped and nonhandicapped pupils is sometimes considered a source of potential discipline or management problems for regular teachers (Dunlop, Stoneman, & Cantrell, 1980; Johnson & Johnson, 1980; Schopler & Bristol, 1980). Some of these issues were discussed in chapter 6. Concerns have also been expressed about the extra time and effort that an exceptional learner might require from the teacher, thus taking teaching time away from other children, and about the fact that instruction in regular classrooms is often based on standard progress of normal children, and a handicapped child might slow up the entire group (Bullock & Rigg, 1980; Diamond, 1979; Miller & Switzky, 1978; Rauth, 1981; Richey, Miller, & Lessman, 1981).

There is little empirical evidence to suggest that the presence of mainstreamed exceptional learners actually has an adverse effect on the academic progress of children in regular classrooms. Such evidence is difficult to obtain because it usually requires testing of large numbers of classrooms of normal children to see if their performance actually suffers when a mainstreamed child is assigned. What little research exists does not suggest a detrimental effect (Bradfield, Brown, Kaplan, Rickert, & Stannard, 1973; Cantrell & Cantrell, 1976). A recent study in southern California by Johnson (1980) involved more than 5,000 children in more than 200 elementary school classrooms. Some 400 exceptional learners were mainstreamed into these classrooms, and all the students were tested at the beginning and end of the year, both before and after mainstreamed children were integrated. A number of variables were examined, including the amount of time the mainstreamed child was integrated, the total number of pupils per classroom, and the number of exceptional learners integrated per classroom. No significant adverse effects were obtained. In fact, there was a slight *advantage* found for some classrooms containing children from mainly lower socioeconomic neighborhoods. Academic progress of the nonhandicapped children in these classrooms tended to be better when handicapped children were mainstreamed. There was speculation that teachers in these classrooms benefited from having to individualize or adapt instruction to the mainstreamed child and that this skill "spilled over" to the instruction of other children.

The difficulties of exceptional learners in social adjustment and peer acceptance in the regular classroom were discussed earlier in this chapter and presented in some detail in chapter 6. Several approaches have been suggested for modifying the attitudes of regular-class students toward the handicapped (Gottlieb & Leyser, 1981; Guralnick, 1981; Keogh, 1981; Simpson, 1980; Woodward, 1980). Many nonhandicapped children tend to recognize deviant behavior, whether or not the child exhibiting the behavior has been labeled handicapped. Often, these perceptions are affected, for better or worse, by the attitudes and behavior of teachers or other adults toward such a child. In general, normal children with more positive self-concepts tend to be more accepting, as do females and younger children. One of the first steps toward positive acceptance is to establish a positive and close working relationship between special and regular education at all levels within a school setting. It is also essential to review several concepts with nonhandicapped children to prepare them beforehand for the experience of having handicapped children in their classes. These concepts include the notion of individual differences being on a continuum from exceptional to normal, ways in which a given child might be handicapped and yet still be normal in other respects, special curriculum modifications or classroom approaches that might be needed in specific cases, and historical figures who had handicaps. Care should be taken to structure initial positive interactions or experiences between handicapped and normal children. Parents of both handicapped and nonhandicapped children should be the focus of specific programs designed to familiarize them with the realities of mainstreaming and to respond to their worries and concerns. Although these approaches cannot guarantee that a mainstreamed exceptional learner will be accepted completely by classmates, they may at least minimize the rejection and social difficulty that such a child would ordinarily experience.

The Resource Room and the Special Education Teacher Consultant

Mainstreaming has proven to be a complex procedure that often taxes the flexibility of regular school programs (Heron, 1978). There have generally been two types of support systems for mainstreamed exceptional learners: the resource room and the teacher consultant. Neither is a new concept in the field of special education (Hammill & Wiederholt, 1972; McKenzie, 1972); both, however, are still in the process of being refined and studied. The resource room is essentially a special setting in either an elementary or secondary school to which mainstreamed exceptional learners can be referred for brief periods of specialized instruction, which they might not be able to receive in the regular classroom. The special education teacher consultant is a person prepared to provide support or consultation in such areas as curriculum, instruction, and child management to regular classroom teachers who have exceptional learners mainstreamed in their classrooms. Neither of these systems is necessarily separate or mutually exclusive, and it is common practice for resource room teachers to spend part of their day consulting with regular classroom teachers (Brown, Kiraly, & McKinnon, 1979; McLoughlin & Kass, 1978; Wiederholt, Hammill, & Brown, 1978).

Conflict may sometimes occur between these two roles, leading to some confusion in the expectations of both resource and regular classroom teachers. Resource teachers generally prefer to be involved in the total school program for mainstreamed exceptional learners (D'Alonzo & Wiseman, 1978), but often report spending less time in actual consultation than in any other role (Evans, 1980). Sargent (1981) found that about half of the resource teacher's time was spent instructing children and less than 10 percent was spent consulting with regular teachers. Glicking, Murphy, and Mallory (1979) asked both regular teachers and resource specialists to specify their ideal expectations, and results suggested that both were in almost unanimous agreement that the resource teacher's caseload approximate that of a regular classroom teacher's. Their preference was for twenty children served directly and ten children served through teacher consultation, suggesting that the more important role for the resource specialist was direct instruction, a finding similar to that of Evans (1981).

How effective are resource programs? Sindelar and Deno (1978) examined some seventeen studies in this area. Their survey suggested that a number of studies suffer from the same methodological flaws and inconclusive results that characterize special-class efficacy studies, referred to earlier in this chapter. There seemed to be a slight advantage in academic progress for children served in resource programs, but personal-social gains were not always predictable. A recent study by O'Connor, Stuck, and Wynne (1979) demonstrated higher gains in both academic achievement and task attention for elementary-age children with learning and behavior problems who participated in an eight-week resource room program in the morning hours. Compared to similar children who remained full-time in regular classrooms, the resource room participants more than doubled their task attention and gained more than twice the academic achievement of the control children. These gains were maintained over a four-month period after intervention. Other studies by Ito (1980) and Reich, Hambleton, and Houldin (1977) found, however, that gains made by resource room participants or those taught by itinerant teachers tend to disappear even after extended intervention.

Miller and Sabatino (1978) compared the resource room and teacher consultant models and found that academic and performance gains were similar for both approaches and that both approaches were significantly better than no service at all. Observed behaviors of regular classroom teachers seemed to improve slightly under the teacher consultant model, suggesting an advantage to increased instruction in the regular classroom. Effective resource programs at the preschool or kindergarten level have also been developed for early identification and remediation of learning disabilities (Peterson & Haralick, 1977; Rothenberg, Lehman, & Hackman, 1979). There has been concern that learning disability specialists have not been included on school evaluation teams, as originally envisioned under Public Law 94–142; thus, early detection of learning disabilities may therefore be more difficult (Larsen & Deshler, 1978; Poplin & Larsen, 1979).

It is important to note that alternative models to using highly trained resource specialists are also being explored. One such program, developed by Chalfant, Pysh, and Moultrie (1979), brings together a team of three regular classroom teachers who meet with the referring teacher and the child's parents to form a "teacher assistance team," which serves as a first-line problem-solving and special education service system. The three regular teachers are chosen by their colleagues. Such informal teams were able to handle the problems of nearly two-thirds of the children referred; the remainder were then passed along to those trained in special education. Another program described by Haisley, Tell, and Andrews (1981) used trained adolescents to tutor other children with learning problems, thus relieving the resource teacher of having to deal directly with each child in his or her caseload. The use of classmates as tutors, however, is a complex issue, and such approaches should be employed cautiously (Krouse, Gerber, & Kaufman, 1981).

It has also been suggested that the role of at least some regular classroom teachers needs to be upgraded (Forness, 1981b). Even though most regular teachers are usually required to have at least one course in special education, it would seem necessary to have *one* regular teacher at every grade level in a school who is certified as a regular classroom special educator. This person would likely have a few courses in special education but considerably less preparation than a special education teacher or resource specialist. The regular classroom special educator would nonetheless be able to guarantee that a child receives all the advantages of a normalized classroom experience without diminishing that child's opportunity for special individual instruction. Only a few classrooms in each school would have to be designated for mainstreaming. Since the difference between exceptional and normal is often only a point on a continuum, it would seem logical to have a differentiated continuum of services, with more gradations from self-contained to completely mainstreamed teaching situations. Having a resource room as the only recourse between special- and regular-class placement, as is frequently the case, may not be sufficient.

Despite the possibility of new approaches, it is not clear how much the practice of mainstreaming can be expected to increase in the future. MacMillan and Borthwick (1980) have demonstrated that the types of children currently remaining in self-contained EMR classes, for example, are a much more disabled group than those characteristically placed in such classrooms in the past. In effect, we may have mainstreamed as many of these children as is possible. The task now seems to be one of systematically mainstreaming most exceptional learners with moderate and mild handicaps early in their school years, before resorting to special classroom placement. Only *after* resource room programs and special education teacher consultants fail to provide appropriate education to a handicapped child, should special class placement be considered. This may require some modification of existing state and federal laws requiring official identification of a child as handicapped. Unfortunately, such laws seem based on mistrust and suspicion of special education funding on a "per child" basis (Kaufman, 1980; Magliocca & Stephens, 1980). At the same time, it has been suggested that we not forget "exit criteria," (Algozzine, Whorton, & Reid, 1979) so that individual and timely decisions can be made to take exceptional learners *out* of special classrooms when they are ready.

Due Process and Parent Participation

As indicated in chapter 1, Public Law 94–142 was basically a civil rights act for handicapped children and their families, in relation to public schooling. In the past, parents typically were told that their child had been evaluated, found to be retarded, and was being placed in a special class. Parents were not given access to the tests or in many cases told their child's IQ score. School professionals justified this on the basis that parents would not understand the meaning of test scores or other data. Teachers or others in the school often made subjective or anecdotal notes in the child's school records, since parents were generally denied access to these records. Thus, a number of what we now consider basic rights were violated, and parents were rarely involved in significant decisions concerning their child's schooling (Turnbull, 1981).

As a result of Public Law 94–142, parents have become more integrally involved in the planning of their handicapped child's schooling, and several protections guarantee this involvement (Turnbull, Strickland, & Brantley, 1982; Turnbull, Strickland, & Goldstein, 1978; Turnbull & Turnbull, 1978; Yoshida, Fenton, Kaufman, & Maxwell, 1978; Yoshida & Gottlieb, 1977). Parents must give permission for their child to be tested or evaluated for special education. Written notice must be given of the proposed evaluation, and this and other such notices from the school must be in language the parents understand. Parents must approve the evaluation plan and be allowed to examine or have explained to them the evaluation methods and results. Independent evaluations by outside experts may, in some cases, be provided at the school's expense. Notice must likewise be given as to the time and place of the IEP meeting. The school must document attempts to contact parents, and appoint an advocate for the child when parents are unavailable or unable to participate.

Figure 10–3.

At nearly every point in the process, parents have the right to challenge the school's procedures and decisions. If such challenges cannot be resolved by negotiation or mediation, parents and school personnel have the right to settle such issues before a due process hearing. Such proceedings are conducted by an impartial hearing officer who is not employed by the school district; and both parties have the right to be represented by counsel, present evidence and testimony, cross examine witnesses, examine school records, and receive a written transcript and statements of the decisions reached. Furthermore, written school records and other information on each child are protected in terms of their confidentiality; and parents must be informed of the methods for safeguarding or releasing such information. Parents also have the right to examine their child's school record, have its contents explained, and challenge statements that they consider inaccurate or unfair. An example of the timelines for the entire IEP procedure, as recently revised and developed in one state (California Senate Bill 1870), is provided in Figure 10-4.

Has this process of parental involvement and legal guarantees worked as intended? Tremendous advances have been made, and it is now relatively unusual for parents *not* to be involved in or at least informed of school decisions regarding their child. The process nonetheless has its problems. For example, informing parents of their rights and obligations has been somewhat difficult. A recent survey suggested that, whereas school administrators and teachers are relatively aware of the law, parents report being considerably less knowledgeable and often dependent on their child's teacher or a local parent group for information (Carpenter & Robson, 1977; Joiner & Sabatino, 1981). It has been shown, moreover, that even school professionals are not as thoroughly familiar with the law as perhaps they should be (Saunders & Sultana, 1980). Two recent private foundation reports (Gliedman & Roth, 1980; Salett & Henderson, 1980) call for amendments to Public Law 94-142 to make it easier for parents to be knowledgeable and to "hold their own" in disputes wtih schools. Both reports suggest such things as making public funds available for legal fees, outside evaluations, and expert witnesses, and call for better monitoring of the extent of parent participation by state and federal agencies.

Figure 10-4.
Timeline for an IEP procedure.

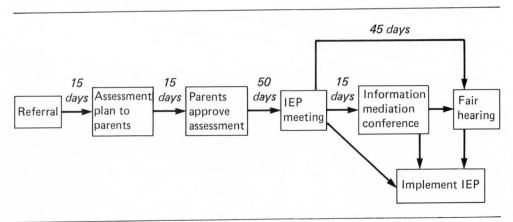

The problem of advocacy continues to be a critical one, and it is common for individuals, parent groups, or outside agencies to have to serve as advocates to see that parental rights are protected. The suggestion has been made that school personnel themselves become active advocates for parents (McLoughlin, McLoughlin, & Stewart, 1979). Though teachers or administrators sometimes feel uncomfortable with increased parent participation, it is ultimately in the school's best interest to insure that parents are totally involved from the very beginning. Parents may find it unnerving to attend a conference with four or five highly trained professionals, an experience for which they are rarely prepared in advance. They may not feel that their attempts to participate are encouraged or taken seriously. School professionals should therefore view parents as valuable partners in both the evaluation and planning process. To encourage parental participation, professionals should reduce their reliance on professional jargon, communicate with parents on a regular basis, prepare them for their involvement, and encourage or support their efforts at every stage of the IEP process. Otherwise, the process may evolve into one in which parents and school personnel become antagonists; and, at that point, outside advocates may have to be called in or time-consuming due process procedures invoked (Budoff & Orenstein, 1981; Smith, 1981; Yoshida, 1979).

Parents and the Diagnostic Process

We discussed problems faced by parents and families of exceptional learners in chapter 6. Public Law 94–142 involves such parents at every stage of the identification and evaluation process. Assessment procedures not only call for new sensitivity to cultural issues in testing but also for simple, direct explanations of test results. Parents want the right to know why certain tests are being used and to question professional assumptions regarding the significance of diagnostic findings (Dembinski & Mauser, 1977; Turnbull & Turnbull, 1978). Even parents of normal children have difficulty understanding their child's test results (Hopper, 1979). It is also becoming evident to professionals that commonly used tests of academic achievement do not always reflect what a handicapped child has actually learned (Jenkins & Pany, 1978), and that new approaches to interpreting or reporting test results are often necessary.

Parents themselves may not always perceive their child's behavior accurately, or at least not view their child's behavior as the school does; and school professionals may lack experience in dealing with such disagreements or misperceptions (Litcher, 1976; Mealor & Richmond, 1980). It has been shown that parents may often suspect a developmental delay early in their child's life but needlessly wait for the school to confirm it (Neyhus & Neyhus, 1979). Teachers, unaware of the child's early history, might initially assume the child is only slow or immature and thus not refer him or her for evaluation until considerable time passes. More attention is now being paid to assessing parents' views of their children and in using such information to plan more carefully for intervention (Gilliam & Coleman, 1981; Lusthaus, Lusthaus, & Gibbs, 1981; Shapero & Forbes, 1981; Sloman & Webster, 1978; Stevens, 1980). Goldstein and Turnbull (1982) have found that sending questions to parents before the IEP meeting, as cues to what will be discussed, tended to increase attendance; unfortunately, recent surveys suggest that many parents do not attend the IEP meeting despite the schools' efforts (U.S. Department of Education, 1980; Scanlon, Arick, & Phelps, 1981; Schenk, 1981).

A number of excellent texts are available to train teachers and other personnel to listen

Unless handled correctly, the fair hearing process can be a complex and difficult experience for all concerned. One author recalls his first experience, in 1977, as a fair hearing officer in a large suburban school in Los Angeles. The case involved the issue of appropriateness of funding private school placement for a seriously handicapped youngster. The school district maintained that its own programs were appropriate; the parents contended that the school district must fund a comprehensive private, residential treatment program, as the only way their child could make acceptable school progress. The outcome of this case was ultimately decided in a civil court and is not essential to our discussion here. What is important is the time and effort required of all parties.

The hearing began at noon in a small conference room in the school district office. On one side of the table were both parents, a private educational psychologist who had evaluated the child, the parents' lawyer, and two legal interns who had gathered affidavits and other material on the parents' behalf. On the other side were the special education director of the school district, the school district psychologist, the child's teacher, and a lawyer for the school district. The official hearing panel consisted of three officers, as per California law at that time. The author had been chosen by both sides and the other two officers were each chosen by one of the parties. In this case, an administrator from another school district and a counselor from a local regional developmental disability center had been chosen.

Lawyers for both sides did most of the talking, despite the panel's insistence that parents and teachers be allowed to speak for themselves. Each side also had tape recorders operating, even though the district was responsible for the official transcript of record. The entire proceeding lasted for seven hours, with only two short breaks. The hearing officers then left the room at 7 P.M. to convene privately and reach a decision. They returned an hour later to present their decision to both parties and arrange for the "official statement of fact" and

"final decision" to be typed the following day, subsequently proofread, signed by all three hearing officers, and forwarded in copies to all concerned.

During the proceedings, the hearing officers were asked to decide several *procedural* issues, in addition to reaching a final decision. These issues included whether to "swear in" witnesses so the transcript could be presented as evidence in case of appeal to a civil court, whether private school funding regulations in effect at the time of referral would prevail over more recent regulations, whether a document could be introduced as evidence if both parties had not had a chance to examine it previously, and whether all aspects of residential treatment could be considered for funding or just educational services. All members of the hearing panel, including the author, felt as though nothing had really prepared them to exercise such judicial powers. A recent survey of hearing officers confirms that they feel the need for a great deal of additional training in this area (Turnbull, Strickland, and Turnbull, 1981).

The mood of both parties was unfortunately rather combative, and a long history of troublesome relationships between these parents and the school district was apparent. It was clear that fault could be found on both sides for misperception and miscommunication. The hearing was unhappily an object lesson in how *not* to rely on conciliation and negotiation to achieve equitable and cooperative agreement on a child's educational program. Although hearing panel officers all volunteered to serve without salary or expenses, the total estimated cost of conducting this proceeding, considering only each person's salary for eight or nine hours, was easily in the neighborhood of two to three thousand dollars. Such a sum would have been better spent on improving the child's education. Although most due process proceedings are likely to be briefer and less expensive, the point is that even due process should occur in a more informal and conciliatory atmosphere, with the needs of the child uppermost in the minds of all concerned.

effectively to what parents are saying and to use these data in planning a comprehensive program of education or remediation (Chinn, Winn, & Walters, 1978; Losen & Diament, 1978; Kroth, 1975; Paul, 1981; Stewart, 1978; Turnbull & Turnbull, 1978). It has been suggested that parent conferences also be part of an active strategy in sensitively instructing parents about the nature and extent of their child's problems and their role in the educational process (Cooper & Edge, 1978; Kroth & Simpson, 1978; Michaelis, 1980; Swick, Flake-Hobson, & Raymond, 1980; Tymchuk, 1979).

Finally, a number of authors have given specific and detailed suggestions on the strategies needed for effective communication of evaluation results and proposed educational plans (Bromwich, 1981; Deno & Mirkin, 1980; McLoughlin, Edge, & Strenecky, 1978 a and b; Rockowitz & Davidson, 1979; Turnbull & Strickland, 1981). School personnel should review evaluation procedures carefully with parents so that they understand how the assessment results were achieved. They also need to insure that parents have ample opportunity to express their own assessment of the child's functioning. The formal assessment findings should then be presented in clear, direct fashion and summarized regarding the child's strengths and deficits. Parents should be given a chance to react at each stage of the presentation, and their views should be restated to make certain there are no misunderstandings. Only after time has been allowed for reaction and discussion should recommendations be made, one at a time, with further opportunity for reaction. A final summary of findings and recommendations, amended by parental input, should then be reviewed. Plans for future contact with parents may be necessary when they clearly need more time to digest findings or reconsider their agreement with the recommendations. Economically disadvantaged or culturally different parents may require additional or alternative means of support to insure their full participation in and understanding of such proceedings (Marion, 1979, 1980).

Parents and the Intervention Process

Parental involvement obviously does not end after they sign their child's IEP. The importance of involving parents of handicapped children in the ongoing educational process was stressed in a recent report by the Ford Foundation (1980). The report indicated that Public Law 94–142 has helped to repair broken or mistrustful relationships between parents and educators. Teachers must continue to encourage parents to share responsibility for their children's schooling, rather than to use the familiar excuses for not involving parents, for example, parents are not objective, are unreliable, or lack the necessary skills. The trend is decidedly toward increasing parental participation (Feldman, Byalick, & Rosedale, 1975).

The particular importance of parents in early intervention was discussed in chapter 7. Those programs that tended to be home-based or to train and involve parents seemed much more effective than those that brought children to school or clinic settings for intervention. Parents of older and less severely handicapped children may sometimes be more resistant to the school's efforts because they tend to see normalization or mainstreaming less positively (Ferrara, 1979). They may favor it as a general concept, but not for their child; thus, particular effort may be necessary to support them in whatever decision is appropriate for their child's educational progress. Yoshida et al. (1978) have shown that most school personnel feel that reviewing the appropriateness of a child's ongoing school program is an important activity for parents.

Berger (1981) has suggested several helpful ways to implement programs to be carried out on a cooperative basis between home and school, including tips on using reinforcement principles at home to support the work of the teacher and on materials or methods that parents can use to supplement teaching programs. It has been shown that having parents systematically deliver praise and support for their child's daily school progress increases the child's classroom performance over and above that achieved by teacher praise alone (Hickey, Imber, & Ruggiero, 1979). Winton and Turnbull (1981) have found that parents value most the continuing informal contact with their child's teacher as a way to maintain their involvement with their child's school program. It has also been suggested, however, that some parents may choose *not* to become involved in their child's program and may welcome the opportunity to trust school personnel to care for their child during the school day, a right that should be equally respected (MacMillan & Turnbull, 1983).

Before leaving the topic of parental involvement, we should mention a special group of parents who may need particular help and support. Public Law 94–142 provided for parent counseling and assistance in a variety of ways; yet, the possibility that certain parents *themselves* may be developmentally disabled or otherwise handicapped has not been widely considered. Some attention has been paid to the problems of teachers in working directly with exceptional adults as pupils (Boylan & Kaplan, 1980) or in extending services for exceptional learners beyond high school (Jones & Moe, 1980). Ironically, Public Law 94–142 may in effect increase the number of handicapped individuals who become responsible citizens and, ultimately, parents. Some handicapped parents may have difficulty understanding the public school system, and this is critical if they have a handicapped child. The increased sophistication needed to understand the complexity of school learning and behavior problems may leave the developmentally disabled parent, especially those who are mentally retarded, at a particular disadvantage. Evidence suggests that even nonhandicapped parents frequently turn to printed literature or parent groups for guidance and direction (Cain, 1976; Clarke-Stewart, 1978; Lloyd-Bostock, 1976), which may pose a particular problem for parents who are mentally retarded or otherwise handicapped. It has been suggested that systematic training in the use of community resources is critical for such parents (Madsen, 1979). Public school would seem to be among the most important of these resources.

Model for Implementing Public Law 94–142

Total adherence to all aspects of Public Law 94–142 has frequently been difficult for public schools. Serving all handicapped children in a manner that is individualized and nondiscriminatory, providing a system for functional IEPs, arranging for gradation of services from most to least restrictive, and involving parents as partners in the educational enterprise is a tall order. No one school program or district will probably ever exemplify all that needs to be done. However, let us at least attempt to illustrate these concepts more realistically.

Both authors of this text have been involved in developing cross-categorical educational programs for exceptional learners, both in the public schools (Hewett & Taylor, 1980; Taylor, Hewett, Artuso, Soloway, Quay, & Stillwell, 1972) and in a psychiatric hospital setting (Forness, 1976, 1977, 1983; Forness & Langdon, 1974). Both programs have similarities and were developed in a rather parallel fashion. The public school program, known as the Madison School Plan, is summarized here as one approach that addresses certain issues and concepts presented in this text. Other equally deserving and effective school programs across the country could certainly be presented as models, but the cross-categorical nature of the Madison School Plan fits more closely the general approach of this text.

Madison School Plan

The Madison School Plan (Taylor, Hewett, Artuso, Quay, Soloway, & Stillwell, 1972) was an extension and elaboration of the engineered classroom design developed earlier in the Santa Monica, California, public schools (Hewett, 1968). It was based on two assumptions. The *first* was that all exceptional children are first and foremost learners, and many can be combined into a single special education program. Thus, it combined children traditionally categorized as behavior disordered, learning disabled, and educable mentally retarded into a single program. Blind, partially seeing children, and partially hearing children also were included from time to time, as were speech-handicapped, disadvantaged, and gifted children. The *second* assumption was that most exceptional children can profit from some integration in a regular-class program, provided they are properly scheduled and provided with appropriate supportive services. A major focus of the approach therefore was to prepare exceptional learners for integration and participation in the regular classroom by means of a special education program.

When developing a program to foster integration of exceptional learners in the regular classroom, one must first conceptualize the primary requisites for survival and success in such a classroom. Using the major components of any interaction between a teacher and a child—curriculum, conditions, and consequences—we can describe exceptional learners with respect to their competence and readiness in these three areas. In terms of curriculum, children may be described by their level of developmental or academic competence. In other words, they may have primary problems in preacademic skills, such as paying attention or perceptual-motor adequacy; or they may have primarily academic curriculum problems, ready for work in remedial or grade-level texts. Regarding conditions of learning, some children may work better in a one-to-one relationship with the teacher and others may need experience in a highly interactional, small-group setting. Conditions refer to how, or in what situation, learning can best take place. Consequences simply mean that some children may be particularly motivated by a check-mark system, backed up by tangible rewards or consequences, and others may be quite susceptible to social attention and praise.

The Madison Plan conceptualizes exceptional learners in terms of their strengths and weaknesses in relation to curriculum, conditions, and consequences. It provides a four-level administrative and instructional framework for increasing their competence in these three areas.

The four levels have been termed *Preacademic I, Preacademic II, Academic I,* and *Academic II.* The emphasis is on academic readiness rather than on diagnostic category. These four levels are on a continuum of readiness for classroom functioning. Children functioning at Preacademic I are least ready for regular classrooms; Academic II children are almost completely able to function in a regular class. Table 10–2 summarizes the levels of readiness for each group.

In any innovative approach designed for implementation in the public school, careful attention must be paid to the requirements for facilities, staff, equipment, and teaching materials. Should these requirements greatly exceed those available to the existing program, the innovative efforts may be dismissed as impractical and unrealistic. For this reason, the Madison School Plan used resources that were already in existence in the district's traditional special-class programs for children with behavior disorders, children with learning disabilities, and mildly retarded children. The typical school program for these exceptional children included two classrooms, two teachers, and two aides. Children with behavior disorders and those with learning disabilities were combined under the category *educationally handicapped*, and the mildly retarded were considered a separate group. Thus, these self-contained facilities became the basis for the Madison School Plan. Although the plan is presented here in its original form, it is flexible and can be adapted to a variety of administrative requirements.

Program and Facilities

The Madison School Plan is essentially a Learning Center, located in a regular elementary school, in which mildly retarded, emotionally disturbed, learning-disabled, hearing-handicapped, and speech-handicapped children have all been grouped together. Placement at each level of the Learning Center is based on a child's readiness for *regular* classroom functioning. In fact, each child is assigned a place in one of the regular classrooms in the school and spends as much time in that classroom's daily routine as possible. The Learning Center itself is composed of four classroom areas based on the children's preacademic and academic skills, their ability to learn in traditional classroom settings, and their response to incentives normally available in the classroom.

Preacademic I is a classroom of eight to ten pupils who work with a teacher and aide at individual desks. Much of the emphasis in this class is on learning to pay attention and on following directions. There is no group instruction and children receive check marks at regular intervals. *Preacademic II* is a classroom of six to eight pupils who can begin to handle the more formal demands of the classroom. Here the program shifts to remedial academic work with emphasis on group participation under a teacher or an aide. There are still check marks, but these are now exchanged for free-choice activities instead of candy or trinkets. *Academic I* provides a simulated regular classroom experience with the teacher in front of the class directing sixteen to eighteen pupils seated at desks like a regular class. Pupils are usually capable of regular academic work and may use many of the same curricular materials found in the regular class. A grading system replaces the check marks, but grades are assigned hourly to give more immediate feedback. *Academic II* is the regular classroom in which all Preacademic II and Academic I children spend as much time as possible. Teachers in the regular grades who have children assigned part-time to the Learning Center give them daily ratings similar to those in Academic I.

Figure 10–5 illustrates the floorplan of a typical Learning Center. PAI has been arranged

Table 10-2
Summary of curriculum, conditions, and consequences on four levels of the
Madison School Plan

	Preacademic I	Preacademic II	Academic I	Academic II (the regular classroom)
Curriculum	Emphasis on pre-academic skills of paying attention, actively participating, following directions, and exploring. De-emphasis on social and academic levels.	Emphasis on pre-academic skills of verbal participation and sociality. Emphasis on academic level with intensive remedial work.	Emphasis on academic skills. Regular-class curriculum content with remedial work as necessary.	Emphasis on grade-level curriculum and academic work.
Conditions	Primary use of teacher-child instructional setting with de-emphasis on group instruction. Interest and activity centers utilized.	Primary instructional setting is teacher-small group with provision of one-to-one instruction as needed.	Simulated regular classroom teacher-large group setting. Small group and individual instruction available as needed.	Teacher-large group setting with alternative settings as indicated or as possible.
Consequences	Check-mark system administered every 20 minutes, backed up by tangible and free-choice time exchange. Task-completion and activity rewards as appropriate.	Check-mark system administered every 20 minutes and backed up by free-choice time exchange only. Social praise also emphasized as appropriate.	Numerical grading system for work accomplishment and behavior administered hourly. Social praise, grades, acquisition of knowledge and skill emphasized.	Regular school grading system with acquisition of knowledge and skill, social praise, and activity as available rewards.

with twelve double desks in the central area of the room. These are two-by-four-foot tables that provide a large working area for each student and allow the teacher to work one-to-one with the child. Three screened-off study cubicles are also available for children who need a reduction of visual distraction. Four centers surround the room, providing science, art, communication, and order activities. The connecting open doorway to PAII and AI allows easy access to the transitional settings that move toward the regular classroom. The PAII setting is located in the adjoining classroom and may occupy one-fourth to one-third of the floorspace. The desk arrangement supports the type of instructional setting at this level. Several tables are clustered around a teacher's station, where group lessons are provided. Individual and shared desk space is provided nearby where independent and child-with-child assignments can be undertaken. The AI setting may in some situations take up the major floorspace in the room. The desks are arranged to simulate a regular classroom. Bulletin boards and activity centers common to regular class-rooms are also established here.

As stated earlier, the Madison School Plan used facilities and staff already available in the special-class program. The staff consisted of two teachers and two teacher aides. Because of the

Figure 10–5.
Learning Center Floorplan.

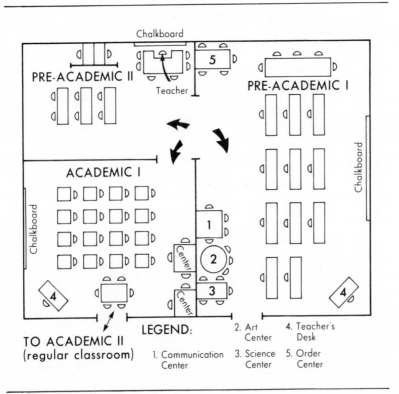

highly individualized nature of the PAI setting, one teacher and one aide were assigned to work with the twelve children in that setting. Next door, PAII and AI used the services of the other teacher and aide. For academic instruction, the teacher alternates between the PAII and AI settings; the aide works in these settings for follow-up and drill-type assignments. Six to eight children are assigned to the PAII group and twelve to sixteen students work in the AI setting.

The teachers in the program are certified elementary teachers who may also hold special education teaching credentials. The teacher aides are usually individuals with bachelor degrees who have not had special education training. The ability to work with children with learning and behavior problems and to form an effective working partnership with the teacher appear to be the most important requisites for the teacher-aide role. When visually handicapped or hearing-handicapped children participate in the Madison School Plan, their special instructional needs in Braille and language training are handled by certified teachers of the blind and deaf who function as itinerant teachers.

Placement Procedures

Prior to the Madison Plan, the process of identifying a child for participation in the special education program was usually initiated by a regular classroom teacher who called the principal's attention to a pupil who was having learning or behavior problems and appeared to require some special help. The principal in turn called on the district department of special services for assistance, and the child was ultimately evaluated and placed in a special classroom.

Under the Madison Plan, exceptional learners are identified and assigned to special education in a different fashion. Rather than set up a special education program for identified children that starts the first day of the fall semester, as many such children as possible are assigned full-time to regular classrooms for a two-week period of evaluation. This assignment is made by the school principal, who attempts to provide the best match-up of child, class, and teacher within the existing possibilities of the school. The purpose of this regular class placement at the start of the year is:

> To establish the children as members of existing regular classes from the beginning of the year and the regular-class teachers as their "real" teachers in the school.

> To establish desks or working areas specifically for these children, to which they may return over the year during periods designed to lead to eventual integration. A desk is permanently assigned to each child.

> To allow the regular-class teacher to become familiar with the children and their problems, which will help in eventually placing them in one of the settings in the Learning Center.

> To allow the regular-class teacher to assess the children's readiness for continued participation in various scheduled activities in the regular-class program.

Within any group of children who have serious learning and behavior problems, there are some who will become automatic losers if full-time placement in a regular class is attempted at the start of the school year. But over a number of years, the Santa Monica School District has found the number of such youngsters to be small; perhaps no more than three or four of the thirty identified exceptional learners in a given school fall into this category. These children would not start school until the third week or until the Learning Center program was underway. Undoubtedly, they would be assigned to the Preacademic I setting, which provides a full-time, special-class placement for such children.

The initial evaluation made when the exceptional learner participates for two weeks in a regular classroom provides information about the child's readiness to profit from such participation in a way that can never be matched by psychological testing or other evaluative procedures. The child is not abandoned in the regular class. At any time during the two-week period or thereafter, if the teacher does not feel the child can participate in all or even part of the regular class day, he or she is referred out to the Learning Center.

After the two-week period of regular class integration and the assignment of children to particular settings, the Learning Center program begins. The following considerations determine each child's placement:

1. If children cannot participate during any regular classroom activity, they will be assigned full time to PAI, which will function as a self-contained class for them. However, as soon as it appears they can be successfully integrated for even brief periods of time, they will be assigned to a regular classroom.

2. Children assigned to the AI or PAII settings, as well as any child assigned to the PAI setting who is ready for some integration, will continue on an assigned basis in the regular classroom. This time may be only for opening exercises in the morning or for physical education, art, or music activities, but may also include an academic period during the day.

3. Although children initially start work at the Learning Center in a particular setting, they may be included for certain activities in other settings. Thus, children may be assigned to PAI for the major part of the day but join the PAII group for an arithmetic lesson, if they are ready to profit from group-oriented instruction in that subject.

4. Changes in setting and program assignment are made during frequent meetings of the two teachers and aides. No type of formal evaluation or recordkeeping has been found effective as a basis for making such changes.

5. Changes in the scheduled time for the child in the regular classroom are based on informal contacts between the Learning Center staff and the regular classroom teachers. Again, no simple evaluation or recordkeeping system has proven effective in this regard. The school principal maintains close contact with all faculty concerned with an individual child and participates in any decision making.

6. While the child is integrated in the regular classroom, the management procedures used with all the children are followed for discipline problems. If behavior problems are typically handled by sending the child to the principal's office, then this is done for the exceptional learner as well. Under no circumstances does the teacher send the child back to the Learning Center because "he can't behave in this class."

The actual Learning Center program operates on a regular daily schedule, offering instruction in basic skills and subject areas, according to the curriculum, conditions, and consequences emphasis presented earlier. Concern arises here over the grade-level range that should be included. Since children from grades one to six may be assigned to the Learning Center, it is difficult to imagine a meaningful curriculum and class grouping at the AI level that covers such a span. In practice, children who are assigned to the AI level are largely from grades four to six. Younger children may be returned to regular primary-level classrooms for combined AI- and AII-level work, because the class groupings and range of academic material provided offer more opportunities for individualization and flexibility than in the upper grades.

Extension of the Learning Center program to include gifted children, as well as the program's ability to provide remedial offerings for unclassified regular-class children, allows it to play more of a total school resource role than the traditional self-contained special class. This can be a vital component in building a bridge between special and regular education. All children in the school population are conceived of as individuals who are functioning at varying levels of learning competence. What is "special" about special educational approaches is that they encompass the entire range of the differing levels of competence and offer assistance to everyone needing it. This concept is more oriented to the total educational field than is the idea of considering special education solely as an aid to the retarded, disturbed, or handicapped.

How does the Madison School Plan help to resolve the labeling dilemma in special education? Beginning with the global notions that every child is a learner and that some regular classroom integration is a positive goal for most, the Madison School Plan describes exceptional learners in terms of their competence in relation to curriculum, conditions, and consequences and assigns them to an educational program that meets their immediate needs. Karen, the mildly retarded child, becomes Karen, the learner who needs help in building the preacademic skills of responding and following directions and the academic skills of reading and written language. She works best on a one-to-one basis and is highly susceptible to social attention and teacher praise.

Michael, the child with a behavior disorder, becomes Michael, the learner who must learn to work cooperatively with other children and to improve his oral participation and language skills. He is ready to work in a small-group instructional setting but is most effectively reached by an objective check-mark system, rather than by social or verbal reinforcement from the teacher. The hypothetical combinations of learning characteristics are almost endless. No lockstep program or rigid formula for providing special educational services for all of them can be conceived. But we can broadly define program parameters and service guidelines that hopefully will allow us to individualize our efforts to a considerable degree. This is the goal of the Madison School Plan.

The Madison School Plan confronts the special- versus regular-class issue directly by attempting to offer the best of both worlds—full-time, special-class placement if necessary and limited, part-time resource help if appropriate. This "swinging door" idea has been literally applied to all components of the program. Placement in PAI, which for some may be a full-time setting, does not mean placement behind closed doors. The option always exists for the child to move on to PAII or to the regular classroom. The regular classroom door, which in the past was closed to exceptional learners, has also been replaced by a swinging door. Children with learning and behavior problems who are ready to profit from some experiences in the regular classroom can enter on a part-time basis and freely move out again for special educational help in the

Learning Center. Regular classroom children who are never classified as exceptional may also move out for part-time assistance in the Learning Center. As it becomes apparent that a child can profit from longer periods in the regular classroom, he or she can increase time there. Conversely, if circumstances indicate that the child should be removed from scheduled participation, time in the Learning Center program can be increased. The extended resource program of the Madison School Plan with its self-contained placement options has proven effective as a viable option to traditional either-or approaches.

However well conceived and organized a viable option may be, it eventually depends on a regular classroom door that swings in a free and easy manner because of the teacher's willingness to participate. This brings us to a third and final issue—the merging of special and regular education. As barriers between special and regular education have begun to disappear and mainstreaming has increased, the problem arises of just how realistic this increased acceptance of children with learning and behavior problems into the regular classroom is. Many regular teachers already feel they are overburdened and do not need more pupils with learning and behavior problems. Thus, any merging of special and regular programs must contain more for regular teachers than an opportunity to express their altruism or dedication to children.

The Madison School Plan builds in teacher incentives by offering them assistance with unclassified children during those times the Learning Center children are integrated. In addition, materials and approaches used in the Learning Center are shared with the regular classroom teacher. These benefits have proven reasonably effective, but more are needed. Toward that end, an inservice training program for regular school faculty, "Train and Trade," was developed to support the Madison School Plan. This program is aimed at increasing the regular staff's knowledge about exceptional learners and introducing them to the philosophy and strategies of working with such children. The program covers six weeks and involves two components. In the first, a weekly forty-five-minute session is held with all regular staff after school. This session includes teachers, principals, school nurses, coaches, and any other personnel likely to be involved with children. A brief filmstrip is shown each week illustrating certain issues, concepts, or strategies concerning exceptional learners, and a discussion follows. The second component involves each staff member's working as a teacher in the Learning Center for one full day. As an added incentive, staff are given university extension credit for the course. In a study of the "Train and Trade" program (Solloway, 1974), participating teachers significantly increased their positive attitudes about the handicapped, as compared to a control group of teachers who were not involved. Perhaps more significantly, these teachers also seemed more able and willing to maintain exceptional learners in their classrooms and referred significantly fewer children back to the Learning Center the following year.

A final word should be mentioned about the Santa Monica Schools' approach to developing IEPs. Termed the "ABCs of the IEP" (Hewett & Taylor, 1980), the approach provides a framework for selecting appropriate goals and objectives for each child on an individual basis. The six levels of learning competence described in chapter 9 are used as organizers, that is, Attention, Response, Order, Exploratory, Social, and Mastery. Each level is subdivided into a few *A* headings that broadly define general areas of skill. For example, the Mastery Level is divided into the six areas of self-help, health and hygiene, reading, written language, computation, and vocational or career development. The *B* headings then define specific skills under each of these areas; for example, vocational or career development is divided into preparation, seeking employment, and conduct on the job. Finally, the *C* headings list specific objectives for each skill area. The first objective under seeking employment in the vocational and career development area is "reads newspaper to locate jobs or training."

Thus, the ABCs provide a catalogue of appropriate objectives for each child's IEP and help to insure that no skill area is overlooked. It provides teachers a beginning curriculum for each exceptional learner and reduces the time needed to prepare an IEP. It allows parents to examine the range of skills, along with the progression of learning in each skill area, to which their child's individual educational program should be addressed. Thus, the Madison School Plan effectively addresses several of the issues and dilemmas concerning education of exceptional learners that were discussed in this chapter and elsewhere in the text.

Summary and Conclusion

Since Public Law 94–142 was passed in the middle 1970s, there has been a profound change in the way special education works. All handicapped children must now be provided a free, appropriate education at public expense. Federal monies are used to assist states in this regard, and some four million children are now receiving services. There are still problems in this zero-reject concept; a small percentage of children may not receive adequate services depending on varying definitions of what constitutes a handicapping condition for school purposes or on early identification of such problems. An important advance is that children's educational needs are now established using techniques and procedures that take into account cultural or language differences of children and their families. IQ testing has come under particular scrutiny, as has the practice of labeling children by their category of handicaps.

Much of the key to special education practices and safeguards is the individual educational plan. The IEP must generally specify the child's level of functioning, educational goals, school programs needed, responsibilities for delivering these services, and means to evaluate the child's progress. It is developed in a meeting with parents, teachers, and specialists; and specific timelines are provided to make sure that appropriate educational services are delivered within a reasonable time. Review of these procedures suggests that parents and regular teachers probably have less influence on IEP decisions than was originally intended. In cases where parents or others disagree with the IEP, there are due process procedures, including a fair hearing, to resolve these differences. Unfortunately, such protection procedures are among the most vulnerable to funding cuts. In fact, the content and extent of written IEPs, the procedures to involve parents in IEP meetings, and the scope of fair hearings were all to have been reduced in recent federally proposed amendments to Public Law 94–142; but these amendments were not passed by Congress.

Another trend is toward mainstreaming children into regular classes, whenever possible, or at least into educational settings that do not restrict the child from more normal social and educational opportunities. There is still disagreement as to how effective either regular- or special-class placement actually is, and recent federal proposals have even sought to diminish mandatory mainstreaming policies. There has nonetheless been much progress in establishing resource rooms and/or special consultants to provide individual instruction for mainstreamed children and to assist regular-class teachers with handicapped children placed in their classrooms. To illustrate how some of these concepts of mainstreaming, noncategorical education, individual instruction, flexibility in classroom placement, nondiscriminatory assessment, and the like have actually been implemented, the Madison School Plan for the Santa Monica Public Schools was described in some detail.

This discussion of the real world issues confronting education—special and regular—fittingly brings the third edition of this text to a close. We have chronicled the past and present of special education and have tried to anticipate future directions in the field. No final destination was reached with Public Law 94–142. As in any period in history, the pendulum swing of public opinion regarding the handicapped is difficult to gauge. In 1981, the Supreme Court ruled that a recently enacted "bill of rights" for the disabled was not to be taken literally by the states. In 1982, the Supreme Court ruled that schools did not have to provide a sign language interpreter for deaf children. Thus, the pendulum that was swinging in favor of the handicapped now seems to be swinging in the opposite direction. A range of possibilities exists for the next few years. On the one hand, a political climate of reduced federal intervention in education could lead to proposals to eliminate IEP meetings, reduce parental input, diminish emphasis on mainstreaming, and eliminate some funding for less obvious handicapping conditions, such as learning disabilities. On the other hand, the families of handicapped children will not easily surrender their hard-won gains. It is clear that school programs for most handicapped children will not be allowed to disappear, that a new climate of acceptance for the handicapped child as a learner will continue to prevail, and that continued attention to individualized instruction of all children with handicaps will still be the norm.

Attempts to return control of handicapped education to state governments have been partially successful. The *spirit* of the Education for All Handicapped Act is perhaps more important in the long run, however, than the law itself. Thus, the field of special education is still on the move. Its diversity and complexity preclude anticipating the future with any degree of certainty. But, if we have facilitated the movement of the field from its deficit-oriented, categorically bound past and achieved some measure of unification, the purpose of this text will have largely been fulfilled.

References

AAHPER. A resource guide in sex education for the mentally retarded. *Booklet by American Association for Health, Physical Education and Recreation in collaboration with SEICUS*. Washington, D.C.: AAPHER Publications, 1971.

ABEL, G. L. The blind adolescent and his needs. *Exceptional Children*, 1961, 27, 309–310; 331–334.

ABRAMOWICZ, H. K., & RICHARDSON, S. A. Epidemiology of severe mental retardation in children. *American Journal of Mental Deficiency*, 1975, 80, 18–39.

ABROMS, K. I., & BENNETT, J. W. Current findings in Down's Syndrome. *Exceptional Children*, 1983, 49, 449–450.

ACHENBACH, T. M. *Developmental psychopathology*. New York: Ronald Press Co., 1974.

ACKERMAN, P. T., PETERS, J. E., & DYKMAN, R. A. Children with specific learning disabilities: WISC profiles. *Journal of Learning Disabilities*, 1971, 4, 150–166.

ADELMAN, H. S. An interactional view of causality. In D. Hammill & N. Bartel (Eds.), *Educational perspectives in learning disabilities*. New York: John Wiley & Sons, 1971.

ADELMAN, H. S. Diagnostic classification of LD: Research and ethical perspectives as related to practice. *Learning Disability Quarterly*, 1979, 2, 5–15.

ADELSON, E., & FRAIBERG, S. Gross motor development in infants blind from birth. *Child Development*, 1974, 45, 114–126.

AIKEN, L. R. *Psychological testing and assessment* (2nd ed.). Boston: Allyn & Bacon, 1976.

AISENBERG, R. B., WOLFF, P. H., ROSENTHAL, A., & NADAS, A. S. Psychological impact of cardiac catheterization. *Pediatrics*, 1973, 51, 1051–1059.

ALATIS, J. E., & TWADELL, K. (Eds.). *English as a second language in bilingual education*. Washington, D.C.: TESOL, 1976.

ALCOHOLIC BABIES. Column, *U.S. News & World Report*, May 17, 1976.

ALCORN, D. Parental views of sexual development and education of the retarded. *Journal of Special Education*, 1974, 8, 119–130.

ALEXANDER, C., & STRAIN, P. S. A review of educator's attitudes toward handicapped children and the concept of mainstreaming. *Psychology in the Schools*, 1978, 15, 390–396.

ALEXANDER, G. Doctor, 83, grows up with practice. *Los Angeles Times*, August 25, 1980.

ALGOZZINE, B., WHORTON, J. E., & REID, W. R. Special class exit criteria: A modest beginning. *Journal of Special Education*, 1979, 13, 131–136.

ALGOZZINE, B., & YSSELDYKE, J. E. Special education services for normal children: Better safe than sorry? *Exceptional Children*, 1981, 48, 238–243.

ALLEN, J. R. The Indian adolescent: Psychological tasks of the Plains Indians of Western Oklahoma. *American Journal of Orthopsychiatry*, 1973, 43, 368–375.

ALLEN, K. E., HART, B. M., BUELL, J. S., HARRIS, F. R., & WOLF, M. M. Effects of social reinforcement on isolate behavior of a nursery school child. *Child Development*, 1964, 35, 511–518.

ALLEN, M. K. Persistent factors leading to application for admission to a residential institution. *Mental Retardation*, 1972, 10, 25–28.

ALLEN, R. M., CORTAZZO, A. D., & ADAMS, C. Factors in an adaptive behavior checklist for use with retardates. *Training School Bulletin*, 1970, 67, 144–157.

ALLEN, V. L. Personality correlates of poverty. In V. L. Allen (Ed.), *Psychological factors in poverty*. Chicago: Markham Publishing Co., 1970.

ALLEY, G. R., & DESHLER, D. D. *Teaching the learning disabled adolescent: Strategies and methods*. Denver: Love Publishing Co., 1979.

ALLEY, G. R., DESHLER, D. D., & MELLARD, D. Identification decisions: Who is the most consistent? *Learning Disability Quarterly*, 1979, *2*, 99–103.

ALMANZA, H. P., & MOSLEY, W. J. Curriculum adaptations and modifications for culturally diverse handicapped children. *Exceptional Children*, 1980, *46*, 608–614.

ALOIA, G. F. Effects of physical stigmata and labels. *Mental Retardation*, 1975, *13*, 17–21.

ALOIA, G. F., BEAVER, R. J., & PETTUS, W. F. Increasing initial interactions among integrated EMR students and their nonretarded peers in a gameplaying situation. *American Journal of Mental Deficiency*, 1978, *82*, 573–579.

ALOIA, G. F., MAXWELL, J. A., & ALOIA, S. D. Influence of a child's race and the EMR label on initial impressions of regular-classroom teachers. *American Journal of Mental Deficiency*, 1981, *85*, 619–623.

ALTSHULER, K. Z. Theoretical considerations in development and psychopathology of the deaf. In J. D. Ranier & K. Z. Altshuler (Eds.), *Psychiatry and the deaf*, (Social and Rehabilitation Service #URA 67–32). Washington, D.C., 1967.

ALTSHULER, K. Z. The social and psychological development of the deaf child: Problems, treatment, and prevention. *American Annals of the Deaf*, 1974, *119*, 365–376.

ALTSHULER, K. Z., & BAROFF, G. S. Educational background and vocational adjustment. In J. D. Ranier, K. Z. Altshuler, & F. J. Kallman (Eds.), *Family and mental health problems in a deaf population*. Springfield, Ill.: Charles C. Thomas, 1969.

AMOSS, H. *Ontario School Ability Examinations: A performance test prepared more especially for use among children who are deaf, whose native tongue is other than English, or who for any reason are lacking in language facility*. Toronto, Canada: Ryerson Press, 1936.

ANASTASI, A. *Differential psychology* (3rd ed.). New York: Macmillan Publishing Co., 1958.

ANASTASIOW, N. J. (Ed.). *Preventing tomorrow's handicapped child today: A middle school child development curriculum*. Bloomington, Ind.: Institute for Child Study, 1977.

ANASTASIOW, N. J. Early childhood education for the handicapped in the 1980's: Recommendations. *Exceptional Children*, 1981, *47*, 276–282.

ANDERSEN, L. H., BARNER, S. L., & LARSON, H. J. Evaluation of written individualized education programs. *Exceptional Children*, 1978, *45*, 207–208.

ANDERSON, C. M., & PLYMATE, H. B. Management of the brain damaged adolescent. *American Journal of Orthopsychiatry*, 1962, *32*, 492–500.

ANINGER, M., & BOLINSKY, K. Levels of independent functioning of retarded adults in apartments. *Mental Retardation*, 1977, *15*, 12–13.

APGAR, V., & JAMES, L. S. Further observations on the newborn scoring system. *American Journal of Diseases of Children*, 1962, *104*, 419–428.

ARENA, J. *How to write an IEP*. Novato, Calif.: Academic Therapy Publications, 1978.

ARGULEWICZ, E. N., & SANCHEZ, D. The special education evaluation as a moderator of false positives. *Exceptional Children*, 1983, *49*, 452–454.

ARNOFF, F. N. Social consequences of policy toward mental illness. *Science*, 1975, *188*, 1277–1281.

ARTHUR, G. Arthur Point Scale of Performance Tests. Form I. Chicago: C. H. Stoelting Co., 1943. Revised Form II. New York: Psychological Corporation, 1947.

ASHURST, D. I., & MEYERS, C. E. Social system and clinical model in school identification of the educable retarded. In R. K. Eymans, C. E. Meyers, & G. Tarjan (Eds.), Sociobehavioral studies in mental retardation, *Monographs of the American Association on Mental Deficiency*, 1973, No. 1, 150–163.

AVERY, C. B. The education of children with impaired hearing. In W. M. Cruickshank & G. O. Johnson (Eds.), *Education of exceptional children and youth* (2nd ed.). Englewood Cliffs, N.J.: Prentice-Hall, 1967.

AVERY, C. B. The education of children with impaired hearing. In W. M. Cruickshank & G. O. Johnson

(Eds.), *Education of exceptional children and youth* (3rd ed.). Englewood Cliffs, N.J.: Prentice-Hall, 1975.

BACA, L. Issues in the education of culturally diverse exceptional children. *Exceptional Children*, 1980, *46*, 583.

BAGLEY, C. R. The educational performance of children with epilepsy. *The British Journal of Educational Psychology*, 1970, *40*, 82–83.

BAGNATO, S. J. Developmental diagnostic reports: Reliable and effective alternatives to guide individualized intervention. *Journal of Special Education*, 1981, *15*, 65–76.

BAILEY, D. B., JR., & HARBIN, G. L. Nondiscriminatory evaluation. *Exceptional Children*, 1980, *46*, 590–596.

BAILEY, K. G., TIPTON, R. M., & TAYLOR, P. F. The threatening stare: Differential response latencies in mild and profoundly retarded adults. *American Journal of Mental Deficiency*, 1977, *81*, 599–602.

BAILEY, L. J. *Career and vocational education in the 1980's: Toward a process approach.* Carbondale, Ill.: Southern Illinois University, 1976.

BAKER, A. M. Cognitive functioning of psychotic children: A reappraisal. *Exceptional Children*, 1979, *45*, 344–348.

BAKER, B. L., SELTZER, G. B., & SELTZER, M. M. *As close as possible: Community residences for retarded adults.* Boston: Little, Brown and Co., 1979.

BALLA, D. A. Relationship of institution size to quality of care: A review of the literature. *American Journal of Mental Deficiency*, 1976, *81*, 117–124.

BALLA, D., & ZIGLER, E. Personality development in retarded persons. In N. Ellis (Ed.), *Handbook of mental deficiency, psychological theory, and research* (2nd ed.). Hillsdale, N.J.: Lawrence Erlbaum Assoc., 1979.

BALLER, W. R. A study of the present social status of a group of adults who, when they were in elementary schools were classified as mentally deficient. *Genetic Psychology Monographs*, 1936, *18*, 165–244.

BALLER, W. R., CHARLES, D., & MILLER, E. Midlife attainment of the mentally retarded: A longitudinal study. *Genetic Psychology Monographs*, 1967, *75*, 235–329.

BALTAXE, C. Pragmatic deficits in autistic adolescents. *Journal of Pediatric Psychology* (Autism Issue), 1977, *2*, 176–180.

BALTAXE, C., & SIMMONS, J. Q. Language in childhood psychosis. *Journal of Speech and Hearing Disorders*, 1975, *40*, 439–458.

BALTAXE, C., & SIMMONS, J. Q. Speech characteristics in childhood psychosis. In J. Darby (Ed.), *Speech evaluation in psychiatry and medicine.* New York: Grune and Stratton, 1980.

BALTHAZAR, E. *Behavior scales of adaptive behavior.* Champaign, Ill.: Research Press, 1971.

BALTHAZAR, E. *Training the retarded at home or in school.* Palo Alto, Calif.: Psychologists Press, 1976.

BANDURA, A., ROSS, D., & ROSS, S. A. Transmission of aggression through imitation of aggressive models. *Journal of Abnormal and Social Psychology*, 1961, *63*, 575–582.

BARAN, S. J., & MEYER, T. P. Retarded children's perceptions of favorite television characters as behavioral models. *Mental Retardation*, 1975, *13*, 28–31.

BARBE, W. B., & RENZULLI, J. D. (Eds.). *Psychology and education of the gifted* (2nd ed.,). New York: John Wiley & Sons, 1975.

BARCLAY, W. *Train up a child.* Philadelphia: Westminster, 1959.

BAREN, M., LIEBEL, R., & SMITH, L. *Overcoming learning disabilities: A team approach (Parent-Teacher-Physician-Child).* Reston, Va.: Reston Publishing Company, 1978.

BARNARD, K. E., & POWELL, M. L. *Teaching the mentally retarded child: A family care approach.* St. Louis: C. V. Mosby Co., 1972.

BARNES, T., & FORNESS, S. R. Learning Characteristics of children and adolescents with various psychiatric diagnoses. In R. Rutherford & A. Prieto (Eds.), *Severe behavior disorders of children and youth* (Vol. 5). Reston, Va.: Council for Children with Behavior Disorders, 1982.

BAROFF, G. S. Patterns of socialization and community integration. In J. D. Ranier, K. Z. Altshuler, & F. J. Kallman (Eds.), *Family and mental health problems in a deaf population*. Springfield, Ill.: Charles C. Thomas, 1969.

BAROFF, G. S. *Mental retardation: Nature, cause, and management*. New York: John Wiley & Sons, 1974.

BARRISH, H. H., SAUNDERS, M., & WOLF, M. M. Good behavior game: Effects of individual contingencies for group consequences on disruptive behavior in a classroom. *Journal of Applied Behavior Analysis*, 1969, *2*, 119–124.

BARRY, H. *The young aphasic child, evaluation and training*. Washington, D.C.: Alexander Graham Bell Association for the Deaf, 1961.

BARSCH, R. H. *A movigenic curriculum*. Madison, Wis.: Bureau of Handicapped Children, 1965.

BARSCH, R. H. Counseling the parents of the brain-damaged child. In E. Firerson & W. Barbe (Eds.), *Education of children with learning disabilities*. New York: Appleton-Century-Crofts, 1967.

BARSCH, R. H. *The parent of the handicapped child: The study of child-rearing practices*. Springfield, Ill.: Charles C. Thomas, 1968.

BARTAK, L., RUTTER, M. & COX, A. A comparative study of infantile autism and specific developmental receptive language disorder. I. The children. *British Journal of Psychiatry*, 1975, *126*, 127–145.

BASS, M. Sex education for the handicapped. *The Family Coordinator*, 1974, *16*, 27–33.

BASS, M. Surgical contraception: A key to normalization and prevention. *Mental Retardation*, 1978, *16*, 399–404.

BATEMAN, B. D. Sighted children's perceptions of blind children's abilities. *Exceptional Children*, 1962, *29*, 42–46.

BATEMAN, B. D. *Reading and psycholinguistic processes of partially seeing children*. Arlington, Va.: The Council for Exceptional Children, 1963.

BATEMAN, B. D. The modifiability of sighted adults' perceptions of blind children's abilities. *New Outlook for the Blind*, 1964, *58*, 133–135.

BATEMEN, B. D. Visually handicapped children. In N.C. Haring & R. I, Schiefelbush (Eds.), *Methods in special education*. New York: McGraw-Hill, 1967.

BAUMEISTER, A. A. Learning abilities of the mentally retarded. In A. A. Baumeister (Ed.), *Mental retardation: Appraisal, education, and rehabilitation*. Chicago: Aldine, 1967.

BAUMEISTER, A. A. Mental retardation policy and research: The unfulfilled promise. *American Journal of Mental Deficiency*, 1981, *85*, 449–456.

BAUMEISTER, A. A., & MacLEAN, W. E. Brain damage and mental retardation. In N. Ellis (Ed.), *Handbook of mental deficiency, psychological theory, and research* (2nd ed.). Hillsdale, N.J.: Lawrence Erlbaum Assoc. 1979.

BAUMEISTER, A. A., & MUMA, J. On defining mental retardation. *Journal of Special Education*, 1975, *9*, 293–306.

BAYLEY, N. *Bayley Scales of Infant Development*. New York: Psychological Corp., 1969.

BEATTIE, A. D., MOORE, M. R., & GOLDBERG, A. Role of chronic low level head exposure in the aetiology of mental retardation. *Lancet*, 1975, *1*, 589–592.

BEATTIE v. STATE BOARD OF EDUCATION, 169 Wis. 231, 127 N. W. 153 (1919).

BECKER, L. D. Learning characteristics of educationally handicapped and retarded children. *Exceptional Children*, 1978, *44*, 502–511.

BECKER, S., & GLIDDEN, L. M. Imitation in EMR boys: Model competency and age. *American Journal of Mental Deficiency*, 1979, *83*, 360–366.

BECKER, W. C., & ENGLEMAN, S. *The Oregon Direct Instruction Model: Comparative results in project Follow Through, a summary of nine years work*. Eugene, Oreg.: University of Oregon, 1977.

BEEZ, W. V. *Influence of biased psychological reports on teacher behavior*. Unpublished doctoral dissertation, Indiana University, 1968.

BEGAB, M. J. The major dilemma of mental retardation: Shall we prevent it? (Some social implications of research in mental retardation). *American Journal of Mental Deficiency*, 1974, 78, 519–529.

BEGAB, M. J., HAYWOOD, H. C., & GARBER, H. (Eds.), *Psychosocial influences in retarded performance. Volume 1: Issues and theory in development.* Baltimore: University Park Press, 1981.

BELL, N. IQ as a factor in community life style of previously institutionalized retardates. *Mental Retardation*, 1976, 14, 29–33.

BELMONT, I., FLEGENHEIMER, H., & BIRCH, H. G. Comparison of perceptual training and remedial instruction for poor beginning readers. *Journal of Learning Disabilities*, 1973, 6, 230–235.

BELMONT, J. M. Long-term memory in mental retardation. In N. R. Ellis (Ed.), *Research in mental retardation.* New York: Academic Press, 1966.

BELMONT, J. M., & BUTTERFIELD, E. C. The instructional approach to developmental cognitive research. In R. V. Kail, & J. W. Hagen (Eds.), *Perspectives on the development of memory and cognition.* Hillsdale, N.J.: Lawrence Erlbaum Assoc. 1977.

BELMONT, J. M., FERRETTI, R. & MITCHELL, D. Memorizing: A test of untrained mildly retarded children's problem solving. *American Journal of Mental Deficiency*, 1982, 87, 197–210.

BELTO, E. W. A comparative study of certain physical abilities of children with speech defects and children with normal speech. *Journal of Speech Disorders*, 1941, 6, 187–203.

BENDER, L. Child schizophrenia: A review. *International Journal of Psychiatry*, 1968, 5, 211–220.

BENDER, M., & VALLETUTTI, P. J. *Teaching the moderately and severely handicapped: Curriculum objectives, strategies and activities* (Vols. 1–3). Baltimore: University Park Press, 1976.

BENDER, N. N. Verbal mediation as an instructional technique with young trainable mentally retarded children. *Journal of Special Education*, 1977, 4, 449–455.

BENNETT, F., HUGHES, A., & HUGHES, H. Assessment techniques for deaf-blind children. *Exceptional Children*, 1979, 45, 287–289.

BENSKY, J. M., SHAW, S. F., GOUSE, A. S., BATES, H., DIXON, B., & BEANE, W. E. Public Law 94–142 and stress: A problem for educators. *Exceptional Children*, 1980, 47, 24–29.

BENSON, H. A Epilepsy and employment: Placement problems and techniques. *American Rehabilitation*, 1978, 3, 3–8; 32.

BENTON, A. L. Some conclusions about dyslexia. In A. L. Benton & D. Pearl (Eds.), *Dyslexia: An appraisal of current knowledge.* New York: Oxford University Press, 1978.

BERCOVICI, S. M. *Applied research and program development for the retarded adult in the community.* Presented at the annual meeting of the American Association on Mental Deficiency, New Orleans, May, 1977.

BERDIANSKY, H. A., & PARKER, R. Establishing a group home for the adult mentally retarded in North Carolina. *Mental Retardation*, 1977, 15, 8–11.

BEREITER, C., & ENGLEMANN, S. *Teaching disadvantaged children in the preschool.* Englewood Cliffs, N.J.: Prentice-Hall, 1966.

BERGER, E. H. *Parents as partners: The school and home working together.* St. Louis: C. V. Mosby Co., 1981.

BERKOVITZ, I. H. School interventions: Case management and school mental health consultation. In P. Sholevar, R. Benson, and B. J. Blinders (Eds.), *Emotional disorders in children and adolescents; Medical and psychological approaches to treatment.* New York: Spectrum Publications, 1980.

BERKSON, G., & LANDESMAN-DWYER, A. Behavioral research on severe and profound mental retardation (1955–1974). *American Journal of Mental Deficiency*, 1977, 81, 428–454.

BERRY, M. F., & EISENSON, J. *Speech disorders.* New York: Appleton-Century-Crofts, 1956.

BERRY, P., & MARSHALL, B. Social interactions and communication patterns in mentally retarded children. *American Journal of Mental Deficiency.* 1978, 83, 44–51.

BERSOFF, D. N., KABLER, M., FISCUS, E., & ANKNEY, R. Effectiveness of special class placement for children labeled neurologically handicapped. *Journal of School Psychology*, 1972, *10*, 157–163.

BETTELHEIM, B. *The empty fortress*. New York: Free Press, 1967.

BIALER, I. Relationship of mental retardation to emotional disturbance and physical disability. In H. C. Haywood (Ed.), *Sociocultural aspects of mental retardation*. New York: Appleton-Century-Crofts, 1970.

BIDGOOD, F. E. A study of sex education programs for visually handicapped persons. *New Outlook for the Blind*, 1971, *65*, 318–323.

BIKLEN, D. Myths, mistreatment, and pitfalls: Mental retardation and criminal justice. *Mental Retardation*, 1977, *15*, 51–56.

BINET, A., & SIMON, T. New methods for the diagnosis of the intellectual level of subnormals. *L'Annee Psychologique*, 1905. Translated and reprinted in A. Binet & T. Simon, *The development of intelligence in children*. Baltimore: Williams & Wilkins, 1916.

BINGHAM, G. Career attitudes among boys with and without specific learning disabilities. *Exceptional Children*, 1978, *44*, 341–342.

BIRCH, H. G. Malnutrition, learning, and intelligence. *American Journal of Public Health*, 1972, *62*(6), 773–784.

BIRCH, H. G., & GUSSOW, J. D. *Disadvantaged children; health, nutrition, and school failure*. New York: Harcourt Brace Jovanovich, 1970.

BIRD, P. J., & GANSNEDER, B. M. Preparation of physical education teachers as required under Public Law 94-142. *Exceptional Children*, 1979, *45*, 464–466.

BIRENBAUM, A., & RE, M. A. Resettling mentally retarded adults in the community almost 4 years later. *American Journal of Mental Deficiency*, 1979, *83*, 323–329.

BISHOP, V. E. *Teaching the visually limited child*. Springfield, Ill.: Charles C. Thomas, 1971.

BLACHER-DIXON, J., LEONARD, J., & TURNBULL, A. P. Mainstreaming at the early childhood level: Current and future perspectives. *Mental Retardation*, 1981, *19*, 235–241.

BLACHER-DIXON, J., & SIMEONSSON, R. J. Effect of shared experience on role-taking performance of retarded children. *American Journal of Mental Deficiency*, 1978, *83*, 21–28.

BLACK, F. W. Self-concept as related to achievement and age in learning-disabled children. *Child Development*, 1974, *45*, 1137–1140.

BLACKMAN, L. S., BILSKY, L. H., BURGER, A. I., & MOR, H. Cognitive processes and academic achievement in EMR adolescents. *American Journal of Mental Deficiency*, 1976, *81*, 125–134.

BLACKMAN, S. & GOLDSTEIN, K. Cognitive styles and learning disabilities. *Journal of Learning Disabilities*, 1982, *15*, 106–115.

BLAHA, J., & VANCE, B. The hierarchial factor structure of the WISC-R for learning disabled children. *Learning Disability Quarterly*, 1979, *2*, 71–75.

BLANK, H. R. Dreams of the blind. *The Psychoanalytic Quarterly*, 1958, *27*, 158–161.

BLANK, M. Review of "Toward an understanding of dyslexia": Psychological factors in specific reading disability. In A. L. Benton and D. Pearl (Eds.), *Dyslexia: An appraisal of current knowledge*. New York: Oxford University Press, 1978.

BLASCH, B. B., WELSH, R. L., & DAVIDSON, T. Auditory maps; An orientation aid for visually handicapped persons. *New Outlook for the Blind*, 1973, *67*, 145–158.

BLATT, B., WINSCHEL, J. F., & ENSHER, G. L. Institutions for the mentally retarded: A war disguised as debate. *The Journal of Special Education*, 1977, *11*, 267–273.

BLOCH, E. L., & GOLDSTEIN, L. D. Functional speech disorders and personality: A decade of research. *Journal of Speech and Hearing Disorders*, 1971, *36*, 295–314.

BLOOM, B. S. *Stability and change in human characteristics*. New York: John Wiley and Sons, 1964.

BLOOM, B. S. The role of gifts and markers in the development of talent. *Exceptional Children*, 1982, *48*, 510–522.

BLOOM, L., & LAHEY, M. *Language development and language disorders.* New York: John Wiley and Sons, 1978.

BOBATH, B., & BOBATH, K. *Motor development in the different types of cerebral palsy.* London: Heinemann Medical Books, 1975.

BOE, R. B. Economical procedures for the reduction of aggression in a residential setting. *Mental Retardation*, 1977, *15*, 25–28.

BOERSMA, F., CHAPMAN, J. W., & BATTLE, J. Academic self-concept change in special education students: Some suggestions for interpreting self-concept scores. *Journal of Special Education*, 1979, *13*, 433–442.

BOGER, R. P. & AMBRON, S. R. Subpopulational profiling of the psychoeducational dimensions of disadvantaged preschool children. In E. Grotberg (Ed.), *Critical issues in research related to disadvantaged children.* Princeton, N.J.: Educational Testing Service, 1969.

BORKOWSKI, J. G., & CAVANAUGH, J. C. Maintenance and generalization of skills and strategies by the retarded. In N. Ellis (Ed.), *Handbook of mental deficiency, psychological therapy and research* (2nd ed.). Hillsdale, N.J.: Lawrence Erlbaum Assoc., 1979.

BORKOWSKI, J. G., & KONARSKI, E. A. Educational implications of efforts to train intelligence. *Journal of Special Education*, 1981, 15, 289–305.

BORTNER, M., & BIRCH, H. G. Cognitive capacity and cognitive competence. *American Journal of Mental Deficiency*, 1970, 74, 735–744.

BOUCHER, C. R., & DENO, S. L. Learning disabled and emotionally disturbed: Will the labels affect teacher planning. *Psychology in the Schools*, 1979, *16*, 395–402.

BOWER, E. M. *Early identification of emotionally handicapped children in school.* Springfield, Ill.: Charles C. Thomas, 1960.

BOWER, E. M. Primary prevention in a school setting. In G. Caplan (Ed.)., *Mental disorders in children.* New York: Basic Books, 1961.

BOWER, E. M. The emotionally handicapped child and the school. In H. W. Harshman (Ed.), *Educating the emotionally disturbed.* New York: Thomas Y. Crowell Co.,, 1969.

BOWLEY, A. H., & GARDNER, L. *The handicapped child* (3rd ed.). Edinburgh and London: Churchill Livingston, 1972.

BOYER, E. L., & HUMPHREYS, R. R. *Memorandum calling for the development of formal cooperative agreements between special education, vocational rehabilitation, and vocational education programs to maximize services to handicapped individuals.* Washington, D.C.: U.S. Department of Health, Education, and Welfare, November 21, 1978.

BOYLAN, C., & KAPLAN, P. Preparing teachers to work with exceptional adults. *Exceptional Children*, 1980, 46, 557–559.

BRADFIELD, R. H., BROWN, J., KAPLAN P., RICKERT, E., & STANNARD, R. The special child in the regular classroom. *Exceptional Children*, 1973, 39, 384–390.

BRADLEY, C. Characteristics and management of children with behavior problems associated with brain damage. *Pediatric Clinics of North America*, 1957, 4, 1049–1060.

BRAGA, J. L. Early admission: Opinion verses evidence. *Elementary School Journal*, 1969, 72, 35–46.

BRAGINSKY, D., & BRAGINSKY, B. *Hansels and Gretels: Studies of children in institutions for the mentally retarded.* New York: Holt, Rinehart and Winston, 1971.

BREWER, N. Motor components in the choice reaction time of mildly retarded adults. *American Journal of Mental Deficiency*, 1978, 82, 565–572.

BREWER, N., & NETTLEBECK, L. Influence of contextual cues on the choice reaction time of mildly retarded adults. *American Journal of Mental Deficiency*, 1977, *82*, 37–43.

BRICKER, D. D., & BRICKER, W. A. Psychological issues in language development in the mentally retarded child. In I. Bialer & M. Sternlicht (Eds.), *The psychology of mental retardation: Issues and ap-*

proaches. New York: Psychological Dimensions, 1977.

BRICKER, W. A., MACKE, P. R., LEVIN, J. A., & CAMPBELL, P. H. The modifiability of intelligent behavior. *Journal of Special Education*, 1981, *15*, 145–163.

BRICKEY, M., & CAMPBELL, K. Fast food employment for moderately and mildly mentally retarded adults: The McDonald's Project. *Mental Retardation*, 1981, *19*, 113–116.

BRIDGE, E. M. *Epilepsy and convulsive disorders in children*. New York: McGraw-Hill, 1949.

BRILL, R. G. Hereditary aspects of deafness. *Volta Review*, 1961, *63*, 168–175.

BROLIN, D. E. *Vocational preparation of retarded citizens*. Columbus, Ohio: Charles E. Merrill Publishing Co., 1976.

BROLIN, D. E., & KOKASKA, C. J. *Career education for handicapped children and youth*. Columbus, Ohio: Charles E. Merrill Publishing Co., 1979.

BROLIN, E. E., & D'ALONZO, B. J. Critical issues in career education for handicapped students. *Exceptional Children*, 1979, *45*, 246–253.

BROMWICH, R. *Working with parents and infants: An interactional approach*. Baltimore: University Park Press, 1981.

BRONFENBRENNER, U. A report on longitudinal evaluations of preschool programs (Vol. 2). *Is early intervention effective?* Washington, D.C.: DHEW Publication No. OLD 74-25, 1974.

BROOKS, C. R., & RIGGS, S. WISC-R, WISC and reading achievement relationships among hearing impaired children attending public schools. *Volta Review*, 1980, *82*, 96–102.

BROOKS, P. H., & BAUMEISTER, A. A. A plea for consideration of ecological validity in the experimental psychology of mental retardation: A guest editorial. *American Journal of Mental Deficiency*, 1977, *81*, 407–416.

BROPHY, J. E., & GOOD, T. L. *Teacher-student relationships: Causes and consequences*. New York: Holt, Rinehart and Winston, 1974.

BROWN, L. F., KIRALY, J., & McKINNON, A. Resource rooms: Some aspects for special educators to ponder. *Journal of Learning Disabilities*, 1979, *12*, 480–482.

BROWN, L., PUMPIAN, I., BAUMGART, D., VANDEVENTER, P. FORD, A., NISBET, J., SCHROEDER, J., & GRUENWALD, L. Longitudinal transition plans in programs for severely handicapped students. *Exceptional Children*, 1981, *47*, 624–630.

BROWN, S. M., & ROBBINS, M. J. Serving the special education needs of students in correctional facilities. *Exceptional Children*, 1979, *45*, 574–79.

BROWN v. *BOARD OF EDUCATION*, 347 U.S. 483, 74 S. Ct. 686 (1954).

BROWNE, E. G. *Arabian medicine*. New York: Macmillan Publishing Co., 1921.

BROWNING, P. L. *Rehabilitation and the retarded offender*. Springfield, Ill.: Charles C. Thomas, 1976.

BRUININKS, R., MEYERS, C., SIGFORD, B., & LAKIN, K. C. (Eds.). *Deinstitutionalization and community adjustment of mentally retarded people*. Washington, D.C.: American Association on Mental Deficiency, 1981.

BRUININKS, R. H., RYNDERS, J. E., & GROSS, J. C. Social acceptance of mildly retarded pupils in resource rooms and special classes. *American Journal of Mental Deficiency*, 1974, *78*, 377–383.

BRUNO, R. Interpretation of pictorially presented social situations by learning disabled and normal children. *Journal of Learning Disabilities*, 1981, *14*, 350–352.

BRYAN, T. H. An observational analysis of classroom behaviors of children with learning disabilities. *Journal of Learning Disabilities*, 1974, *7*, 26–34. (a)

BRYAN, T. H. Peer popularity of learning disabled children. *Journal of Learning Disabilities*, 1974, *7*, 261–268. (b)

BRYAN, T. H. Social skills of learning disabled children and youth: An overview. *Learning Disability Quarterly*, 1982, *5*, 332–333.

BRYAN, T. H., & BRYAN, J. H. *Understanding learning disabilities* (2nd ed.). Sherman Oaks, Calif.: Alfred Publishing Co., 1978.

BRYAN, T., & McGRADY, H. J. Use of a teacher rating scale. *Journal of Learning Disabilities*, 1972, *5*, 199–206.

BRYAN, T., & WHEELER, R. Perception of learning disabled children: The eye of the observer. *Journal of Learning Disabilities*, 1972, *5*, 484–488.

BRYAN, T., WHEELER, R., FELCAN, J., & HENEK, T. Come on dummy: Children's comprehension of nonverbal communication. *Journal of Learning Disabilities*, 1976, *10*, 661–699.

BRYANT, J. E. Parent-child relationships: Their effect on rehabilitation. *Journal of Learning Disabilities*, 1971, *4*, 325–329.

BUCKHALT, J. A., RUTHERFORD, R. B., & GOLDBERG, K. F. Verbal and nonverbal interaction of mothers with their Down Syndrome and nonretarded infants. *American Journal of Mental Deficiency*, 1978, *82*, 337–343.

BUDOFF, M., & GOTTLIEB, J. Special class EMR children mainstreamed: A study of an aptitude (learning potential) and treatment interaction. *American Journal of Mental Deficiency*, 1976, *81*, 1–11.

BUDOFF, M., & HUTTON, L. Microcomputers in special education: Promises and pitfalls. *Exceptional Children*, 1982, *49*, 123–128.

BUDOFF, M., & ORENSTEIN, A. Special education appeals hearings: Are they fair and are they helping? *Exceptional Education Quarterly*, 1981, *2*, 37–48.

BUDOFF, M., & SIPERSTEIN, G. N. Low-income children's attitudes toward mentally retarded children: Effects of labeling and academic behavior. *American Journal of Mental Deficiency*, 1978, *82*, 474–479.

BUDOFF, M., & SIPERSTEIN, G. N. Judgements of EMR students toward their peers: Effects of label and academic competence. *American Journal of Mental Deficiency*, 1982, *86*, 367–371.

BUELL, C. E. Motor performances of visually handicapped children. *Exceptional Children*, 1950, *17*, 69–72.

BUELL, C. E. *Physical education and recreation for the visually handicapped*. Washington, D.C.: American Association for Health, Physical Education, and Recreation, 1973.

BULLOCK, L. M., & RIGG, W. C., Jr. Relationship of individualized instruction to placement of exceptional children. *Exceptional Children*, 1980, *47*, 224–225.

BURKE, A. A. Placement of black and white children in educable mentally handicapped classes and learning disability classes. *Exceptional Children*, 1975, *41*, 438–440.

BURTON, J. L. Intelligence and intelligence testing. In M. Cowles (Ed.), *Perspectives in the education of disadvantaged children*. Cleveland: The World Publishing Co., 1967.

BURTON, T. A. *The trainable mentally retarded*. Columbus, Ohio: Charles E. Merrill Publishing Co., 1976.

BURTON, T. A., BURTON, S. F., & HIRSHOREN, A. For sale: The state of Alabama (a commentary on litigation and the institutionalized retarded). *The Journal of Special Education*, 1977, *11*, 59–72.

BURTON, T. A., & HIRSHOREN, A. The Education of severely and profoundly retarded children: Are we sacrificing the child to the concept? *Exceptional Children*, 1979, *45*, 598–602.

BUSS, A. H. *Psychopathology*. New York: John Wiley and Sons, 1966.

BUTTERFIELD, E. C., & BELMONT, J. Assessing and improving the executive and cognitive functions of mentally retarded people. In I. Bialer & M. Steinlicht (Eds.), *Psychological issues in mental retardation*. New York: Psychological Dimensions, 1977.

CAIN, L. F. Parents' groups: Their role in a better life for the handicapped. *Exceptional Children*, 1976, *42*, 432–438.

CAIN, L. F., LEVINE, S., & ELZEY, F. F. *Manual for the Cain-Levine Social Competency Scale*. Palo Alto, Calif.: Consulting Psychologists Press, 1963.

CALDWELL, M., & STEDMAN, J. *Infant education: A guide for helping handicapped children in the first three years*. New York: Walker and Co., 1977.

CALIFORNIA MASTER PLAN FOR SPECIAL EDUCATION. Sacramento: Bureau of Publications, California State Department of Education, 1974.

CAMPBELL, J., MOFFAT, K., & BRACKETT, L. The effect of language instruction on the math skills of retarded children. *Mental Retardation*, 1978, *17*, 167–169.

CAMPIONE, J. C., & BROWN, A. L. Memory and metamemory development in educable retarded children. In R. J. Kail and J. W. Hagen (Eds.), *Perspective on the development of memory and cognition*. New York: John Wiley and Sons, 1977.

CANTRELL, R. P., & CANTRELL, M. L. Preventative mainstreaming: Impact of a supportive services program on pupils. *Exceptional Children*, 1976, *42*, 381–386.

CANTWELL, D. P., BAKER, L., & MATTISON, R. The prevalence of psychiatric disorders in children with speech and language disorders. *Journal of American Academy of Child Psychiatry*, 1979, *20*, 450–461.

CAPLAN, P. J. Helping parents help their children. *Bulletin of the Orton Society*, 1976, *26*, 108–123.

CARLBERG, C., & KAVALE, K. The efficacy of special versus regular class placement for exceptional children: A meta-analysis. *Journal of Special Education*, 1980, *14*, 296–309.

CARLSON, J., & MACMILLAN, D. Comparison of probability judgements between EMR and nonretarded. *American Journal of Mental Deficiency*, 1970, *74*, 697–700.

CARLSON, J. S., & MICHAELSON, L. H. Methodological study of conservation in retarded adolescents. *American Journal of Mental Deficiency*, 1973, *78*, 348–353.

CARPENTER, R. L., & ROBSON, D. L. P.L. 94–142: Perceived knowledge, expectations, and early implementation. *Journal of Special Education*, 1977, *13*, 307–314.

CARTER, D., & CLARK, L. MA intellectual assessment by operant conditioning of Down's Syndrome children. *Mental Retardation*, 1973, *11*, 39–41.

CASTIGLIONI, A. *Adventures of the mind*. New York: Alfred A. Knopf, 1946.

CATTELL, P. *Cattell infant intelligence scale*. New York: Psychological Corporation, 1976.

CAVENESS, W. F., & MERRITT, H. H. A survey of public attitudes toward epilepsy in 1964. *Epilepsia*, 1965, *6*, 75–86.

CHALFANT, J. C., PYSH, M. V., & MOULTRIE, R. Teacher assistance teams: A model for within-building problem solving. *Learning Disability Quarterly*, 1979, *2*, 85–96.

CHAN, K. S. *The economically disadvantaged: Learning disabilities or learning differences*. Paper presented at the Learning Disabilities in Children Seminar, Monterey, California, May 1975.

CHAN, K. S., & KEOGH, B. K. Interpretation of task interruption and feelings of responsibility for failure. *Journal of Special Education*, 1974, *8*, 175–178.

CHAN, K. S., & RUEDA, R. Poverty and culture in education: Separate but equal. *Exceptional Children*, 1979, *45*, 422–428.

CHANDLER, M. J. Egocentrism and antisocial behavior: The assessment and training of social perspective-talking skills. *Developmental Psychology*, 1973, *9*, 326–332.

CHANDLER, M. J., GREENSPAN, S., & BARENBOIM, C. Assessment and training of role-taking and referential communication skills in institutionalized emotionally disturbed children. *Developmental Psychology*, 1974, *10*, 546–553.

CHANNING, A. *Employment of mentally deficient boys and girls*. Washington, D.C.: U.S. Department of Labor, Children's Bureau Publication No. 210, 1952.

CHARLES, D. C. Ability and accomplishment of persons earlier judged mentally deficient. *Genetic Psychology Monographs*, 1953, *47*, 3–71.

CHESELDINE, S., & McCONKEY, R. Parental speech to young Down's Syndrome children: An intervention study. *American Journal of Mental Deficiency*, 1979, *83*, 612–620.

CHESS, S. The influence of defect on development in children with congenital rubella. *Merrill-Palmer Quarterly*, 1974, *20*, 255–274.

CHILDS, R. E. A drastic change in curriculum for the educable mentally retarded child. *Mental Retardation*, 1979, *17*, 299–301.

CHILDS, R. E. A study of the adaptive behavior of retarded children and the resultant effects of this use in the diagnosis of mental retardation. *Education and Training of the Mentally Retarded*, 1982, *17*, 109–113.

CHINN, P. C., WINN, J., & WALTERS, R. H. *Two-way talking with parents of special children*. St. Louis: C. V.

Mosby Co., 1978.

CHITTENDEN, G. F. An experimental study in measuring and modifying assertive behavior in young children. *Monographs of the Society of Research in Child Development*, 1942, *7(1)*.

CHOLDEN, L. S. *A psychiatrist works with blindness.* New York: American Foundation for the Blind, 1958.

CHRISTIE, L. S., McKENZIE, H. S., & BURDETT, C. S. The consulting teacher approach to special education: Inservice training for regular classroom teachers. *Focus on Exceptional Children*, October 1972, 1–9.

CIHA, T. E., HARRIS, R., HOFFMAN, C., & POTTER, M. W. Parents as identifiers of giftedness, ignored but accurate. *Gifted Child Quarterly*, 1974, *18*, 191–195.

CLARK, G. M. Career preparation for handicapped adolescents: A matter of appropriate education. *Exceptional Education Quarterly*, 1980, *1*, 11–17.

CLARK, G. R., KIVITZ, M. S., & ROSEN, M. A. *A transitional program for institutionalized adult retarded.* Elwyn, Pa.: Elwyn Institute, 1968.

CLARKE, A. D. B., & CLARKE, A. M. Prospects for prevention and amelioration of mental retardation: A guest editorial. *American Journal of Mental Deficiency*, 1977, *81*, 523–533.

CLARKE-STEWART, K. Popular primers for parents. *American Psychologist*, 1978, *33*, 359–369.

CLELAND, C. C. Possibilities for social research among profoundly retarded? *American Association on Mental Deficiency, Monograph No. 1*, 1973, 134–149.

CLELAND, C. C. *Mental retardation: A developmental approach.* Englewood Cliffs, N.J.: Prentice-Hall, 1978.

CLELAND, C. C. *The profoundly mentally retarded.* Englewood Cliffs, N.J.: Prentice-Hall, 1979.

CLEMENTS, S. D. Minimal brain dysfunction in children. *NINDB Monograph No. 3.* Public Health Service Bulletin No. 1415. Washington, D.C.: U.S. Department of Health, Education, and Welfare, 1966.

CLEMENTS, S., & PETERS, J. Minimal brain dysfunction in the school age child. *Archives of General Psychiatry*, 1962, *6*, 185–197.

CLEVELAND, D. W., & MILLER, N. Attitudes and life commitments of older siblings of mentally retarded adults: An exploratory study. *Mental Retardation*, 1977, *15*, 38–41.

CLORE, G. L., & JEFFREY, K. M. Emotional role playing, attitude change, and attraction toward a disabled person. *Journal of Personality and Social Psychology*, 1972, *23(1)*, 105–111.

CLOSE, D. W., IRVIN, L. K., TAYLOR, V., & AGOSTA, J. Community living skills instruction for mildly retarded persons. *Exceptional Education Quarterly*, 1981, *2*, 75–85.

COATS (1967), reported in BAER, D. M., & WOLF, M. M. Recent examples of behavior modification in preschool settings. In C. Neuringer & J. L. Michael (Eds.), *Behavior modification in clinical psychology.* New York: Appleton-Century-Crofts, 1970.

COHEN, A., FATHMAN, A., & MERINO, B. The Redwood City bilingual education project, 1971–1974: Spanish and English proficiency, mathematics and language use over time. *Working Papers on Bilingualism*, 1976, *8*, 1–29.

COHEN, A. D., & SWAIN, M. Bilingual education: The "immersion" model in the North American context. *TESOL Quarterly*, 1976, *10*, 45–63.

COHEN, S. Teacher receptivity to the concept of parent participation in the education of handicapped children: Some preliminary findings. *Rehabilitation Literature*, 1977, *38*, 151–153.

COHEN, S., SEMMES, M., GURALNICK, M. J. Public Law 94–142 and the education of preschool handicapped children. *Exceptional Children*, 1979, *45*, 279–285.

COLE, M., & BRUNER, J. S. Preliminaries to a theory of cultural differences. In I. J. Gordon (Ed.), *Early childhood education: The 71st Yearbook of the National Society for the Study of Education. Part II.* Chicago: University of Chicago Press, 1972.

COLEMAN, J. C. *Abnormal psychology and modern life* (4th ed.). Glenview, Ill.: Scott, Foresman and Co., 1972.

COLEMAN, J. S., CAMPBELL, E. Q., HOBSON, C. J., McPARTLAND, J., MOOD, A. M., WEINFELD, F. D., & YORK, R. L. *Equality of educational opportunity.* Washington, D.C.: U.S. Government Printing Office, 1966.

COLES, G. S. The learning-disabilities test battery: Empirical and social issues. *Harvard Educational Review*, 1978, *48*, 313–340.

COLLINGS, G. D. Case review: Rights of the retarded. *Journal of Special Education*, 1973, *7*, 27–37.

CONNOLLY, J. A. Intelligence levels of Down's Syndrome children. *American Journal of Mental Deficiency*, 1978, *83*, 193–196.

CONNOR, F. P. The education of children with crippling and chronic medical conditions. In W. M. Cruickshank & G. O. Johnson (Eds.), *Education of exceptional children and youth* (3rd ed.). Englewood Cliffs, N.J.: Prentice-Hall, 1975.

CONNOR, F. P., RUSALEM, H., & CRUICKSHANK, W. M. Psychological considerations of crippled children. In W. Cruickshank (Ed.), *Psychology of exceptional children and youth*. Englewood Cliffs, N.J.: Prentice-Hall, 1971.

CONNOR, F. P., WILLIAMSON, G. G., & SIEPP, J. M. (Eds.). *Program guide for infants and toddlers with neuromotor and other developmental disabilities*. New York: Teachers College Press, 1978.

CONNOR, G. B., & MULDOON, J. F. A statement of the needs of blind and visually impaired individuals. *New Outlook for the Blind*, 1973, *67*, 352–362.

CONROY, J. W. Trends in deinstitutionalization of the mentally retarded. *Mental Retardation*, 1977, *15*, 44–46.

CONSORTIUM FOR LONGITUDINAL STUDIES. *Lasting effects after preschool*. Washington, D.C.: U.S. Department of Health, Education, and Welfare, Office of Human Development Services Administration for Children, Youth and Families, September 1979. DHEW Pub. No. (OHDS) 79-30179.

COOKE, G., COOKE, T. P., & APOLLONI, T. Generalization of language training with the mentally retarded. *The Journal of Special Education*, 1976, *10*, 299–304.

COOPER, J. V., & EDGE, D. *Parenting: Strategies and educational methods*. Columbus, Ohio: Charles E. Merrill Publishing Co., 1978.

CORAH, N. L., ANTHONY, E. J., PAINTER, P., STERN, J. A., & THURSTON, D. L. Effects of perinatal anoxia after seven years. *Psychological Monographs*, 1965, *79*, (3, Whole No. 596).

CORCORAN, E. L., & FRENCH, R. W. Leisure activity for the retarded adult in the community. *Mental Retardation*, 1977, *15*, 21–23.

CORMAN, L., & GOTTLIEB, J. Mainstreaming mentally retarded children: A review of research. In N. R. Ellis (Ed.), *International review of research in mental retardation* (Vol. 9). New York: Academic Press, 1978.

CORNWELL, M. *Early Years*. London: Disabled Living Foundation, 1975. (Reviewed in *Rehabilitation World*, 1977, Spring, 42).

CORRIGAN, D. M. The challenge of the resource center. In J. E. Jan, R. D. Freeman, & E. P. Scott (Eds.), *Visual impairment in children and adolescents*. New York: Grune and Stratton, 1977.

COTT, A. Orthomolecular medicine. In *Selected papers on learning disabilities, Association for children with learning disabilities, Ninth Annual Conference*. Pittsburgh: Association for Children with Learning Disabilities, 1975, pp. 17–22.

COULTER, W. A., & MORROW, H. W. (Eds.). *Adaptive behavior: Concepts and managements*. Austin, Tex.: Texas Regional Resource Center, 1978. (a)

COULTER, W. A., & MORROW, H. W. Requiring adaptive behavior management. *Exceptional Children*, 1978, *45*, 133–135. (b)

COUNCIL FOR EXCEPTIONAL CHILDREN. U.S. commissioners pursue systems linkage. *Insight*, 1977, *12*, 1.

COUNCIL FOR EXCEPTIONAL CHILDREN. *Position paper on career education*. Reston, Va.: Council for Exceptional Children, 1978.

COWEN, E. L. The Primary Mental Health Project: Yesterday, today, and tomorrow. *Journal of Special Education*, 1980, *14*, 134–154.

COWEN, E. L., UNDERBERG, R., VERILLO, R. T., & BENHAM, F. G. *Adjustment to visual disability in adolescence.* New York: American Foundation for the Blind, 1961.

CRAFT, M., & CRAFT, A. *Sex and the mentally handicapped.* London: Routledge and Kegan Paul, 1978.

CRANDALL, B. F. Genetic disorders and mental retardation. *Journal of the American Academy of Child Psychiatry.* 1977, *16,* 88–108.

CRATTY, B. J. *Motor activity and the education of retardates* (2nd ed.). Philadelphia: Lea and Febiger, 1974.

CRATTY, B. J. Motor development for special populations: Issues, problems, and operations. *Focus on Exceptional Children* 1980, *13,* 1–11.

CRAVIOTO, J., & DeLICARDIE, E. Environmental and nutritional deprivation in children with learning disabilities. In W. M. Cruickshank and D. P. Hallahan (Eds.), *Psychoeducational practices. Perceptual and learning disabilities in children* (Vol. 1). Syracuse, N.Y.: Syracuse University Press, 1975.

CRAWFORD, J. L., AIELLO, J. R., & THOMPSON, D. E. Deinstitutionalization and community placement: Clinical environmental factors. *Mental Retardation,* 1979, *17,* 59–62.

CRNIC, K. A., & PYM, H. A. Training mentally retarded adults in independent living skills. *Mental Retardation,* 1979, *17,* 13–16.

CROMER, R. F. Conservation by the congenitally blind. *British Journal of Psychology,* 1973, *64,* 241–250.

CROMWELL, R. L. Personality evaluation. In A. A. Baumeister (Ed.), *Mental retardation.* Chicago: Aldine Publishing Co., 1967.

CRONBACH, L. J. *Essentials of psychological testing* (2nd ed.). New York: Harper and Row, 1960.

CROSS, L. Identification of young children with handicaps: An overview. In N. Ellis and L. Cross (Eds.), *Planning programs for early identification of the handicapped.* New York: Walker and Co., 1977.

CROW, L. D., MURRAY, W. I., & SMYTHE, H. H. *Educating the culturally disadvantaged child.* New York: David McKay Co., 1966.

CROWTHER, D. L. Psychosocial aspects of epilepsy. *Pediatric Clinics of North America,* 1967, *14,* 921–932.

CRUICKSHANK, W. M. The development of education for exceptional children. In W. M. Cruickshank & G. O. Johnson (Eds.), *Education of exceptional children and youth.* Englewood Cliffs, N.J.: Prentice-Hall, 1967.

CRUICKSHANK, W. M. A new perspective in teacher education: The neuro-educator. *Journal of Learning Disabilities,* 1981, *14,* 337–341.

CRUICKSHANK, W. M., BENTZEN, F., RATZEBERG, F., & TANNHAUSER, M A. *Teaching method for brain-injured and hyperactive children.* Syracuse, N.Y.: Syracuse University Press, 1961.

CRUICKSHANK, W. M., & HALLAHAN, D. P. *Psychoeducational foundations of learning disabilities.* Englewood Cliffs, N.J.: Prentice-Hall, 1973.

CRUICKSHANK, W. M., & PAUL, J. L. The psychological characteristics of children with learning disabilities. In W. M. Cruickshank (Ed.), *Psychology of exceptional children and youth* (4th ed.). Englewood Cliffs, N.J.: Prentice-Hall, 1980, pp. 497–541.

CRUSE, D. The effect of distraction upon the performance of brain-injured and familial retarded children. In E. Trapp & P. Himmelstein (Eds.), *Readings on the exceptional child.* New York: The Free Press, 1970.

CSAPO, M. Peer models reverse the "one bad apple spoils the barrel" theory. *Teaching Exceptional Children,* 1972, *5,* 20–24.

CUBAN, L. *To make a difference: Teaching in the inner city.* New York: The Free Press, 1970.

CUMMINGS, S. T. The impact of the child's deficiency on the father: A study of fathers of mentally retarded and of chronically ill children. *American Journal of Orthopsychiatry,* 1976, *46,* 246–255.

CUMMINGS, S. T., BAYLEY, H. C., & RIE, H. E. Effects of the child's deficiency on the mother: A study of mothers of mentally retarded, chronically ill and neurotic children. *American Journal of Orthopsychiatry,* 1966, *36,* 595–608.

CUNNINGHAM, T., & PRESNALL, D. Relationship between dimension of adoptive behavior and sheltered workshop productivity. *American Journal of Mental Deficiency*, 1978, *83*, 386-393.

CUTSFORTH, T. D. *The blind in school and society* (Rev. ed.). New York: American Foundation for the Blind, 1951.

DALBY, J. T. Deficit or delay: Neuropsychological models of developmental dyslexia. *Journal of Special Education*, 1979, *13*, 239-264.

D'ALONZO, B. J., & WISEMAN, D. E. Actual and desired roles of the high school learning disability resource teacher. *Journal of Learning Disabilities*, 1978, *11*, 390-397.

DANKER-BROWN, P., SIGELMAN, C. K., & FLEXER, R. W. Sex bias in vocational programming for handicapped students. *Journal of Special Education*, 1978, *12, 451*-458.

DARLINGTON, R. B., ROYCE, J., SNIPPER, A., MURRAY, H., & LAZAR, I. Preschool programs and later school competence of children from low-income families. *Science*, 1980, *208*, 202-204.

DAS, J. P., & CUMMINS, J. Academic performance and cognitive processes in EMR children. *American Journal of Mental Deficiency*, 1978, *83*, 197-199.

DAS, J. P., & PRIVATO, E. Malnutrition and cognitive functioning. In N. R. Ellis (Ed.), *International review of research in mental retardation* (Vol. 8). New York: Academic Press, 1977.

DAVID, H. P., SMITH, J. D., & FRIEDMAN, E. Family planning services for persons handicapped by mental retardation. *American Journal of Public Health*, 1976, 66, 1053-1057.

DAVIDSON, T. M. The vocational development and success of visually impaired adolescents. *New Outlook for the Blind*, 1975, *69*, 314-316.

DAVIES, S. P., & ECOB, K. G. *The mentally retarded in society*. New York: Columbia University Press, 1959.

DAVIS, H. Audiometry: Pure tone and simple speech tests. In H. Davis & S. R. Silberman (Eds.), *Hearing and deafness* (3rd ed.). New York: Holt, Rinehart and Winston, 1970.

DAVIS, H., & SILBERMAN, S. R. *Hearing and deafness*. New York: Holt, Rinehart and Winston, 1978.

DAVIS, J. G. Ethical issues arising from parental diagnosis. *Mental Retardation*, 1981, *19*, 12-15.

DAY, R. M., & DAY, H. M. Leisure skills instruction for the moderately and severely retarded: A demonstration program. *Education and Training of the Mentally Retarded*, 1977, *12*, 128-131.

DEMAINE, G. C., & SILVERSTEIN, A. B. MA changes in institutionalized Down's Syndrome persons: A semi-longitudinal approach. *American Journal of Mental Deficiency*, 1978, *82*, 429-432.

DEMBINSKI, R. J., & MAUSER, A. J. What parents of the learning disabled really want from professionals. *Journal of Learning Disabilities*, 1977, *10*, 578-584.

DeMYER, M. K., BARTON, S., DeMYER, W. E., NORTON, J. A., ALLEN, J., & STEELE, R. Prognosis in autism: A follow-up study. *Journal of Autism and Childhood Schizophrenia*, 1973, *3*, 199-246.

DeMYER, M. K., BARTON, S., KIMBERLIN, C., ALLEN, J., YANG, E., & STEELE, R. The measured intelligence of autistic children. *Journal of Autism and Childhood Schizophrenia*, 1974, *4*, 42-60.

DeMYER, M. K., BARTON, S., & NORTON, J. A. A comparison of adaptive verbal, and motor profiles of psychotic and nonpsychotic children. *Journal of Autism and Childhood Schizophrenia*, 1972, *2*, 359-377.

DENCKLA, M. B., & RUDEL, R. Rapid 'automatized' naming (R.A.N.): Dyslexia differentiated from other learning disabilities. *Neuro-psychologia*, 1976, *14*, 471-479.

DENNERLL, R. D., RODIN, E. A., GONZALES, S., SCHWARTZ, M. L., & LIN, Y. Neurological and psychological factors related to employability of persons with epilepsy. *Epilspsia*, 1966, *1*, 318-329.

DENNIS, W. A further analysis of reports of wild children. *Child Development*, 1951, *22*, 153-158.

DENNY, M. R. Research in learning and performance. In H. A. Stevens & R. Heber (Eds.), *Mental retardation: A review of research*. Chicago: University of Chicago Press, 1964.

DENNY, M. R. A theoretical analysis and its application to training the mentally retarded. In N. R. Ellis (Ed.), *International review of research in mental retardation* (Vol. 2). New York: Academic Press, 1966.

DENO, E. Special education or developmental capital. *Exceptional Children*, 1970, *37*, 229-237.

DENO, S. L., & MIRKIN, P. K. Data-based IEP development: An approach to substantive compliance. *Teaching Exceptional Children*, 1980, *12*, 92–97.

DEUTSCH, C. P. Social class and child development. In B. M. Caldwell & H. N. Ricciuti (Eds.), *Review of child development research* (Vol. III). Chicago: University of Chicago Press, 1973.

DEWART, M. H. Language comprehension processes of mentally retarded children. *American Journal of Mental Deficiency*, 1979, *84*, 177–183.

DIAMOND, B. Myths of mainstreaming. *Journal of Learning Disabilities*, 1979, *12*, 246–250.

DIAMOND, M. Sexuality and the handicapped. *Rehabilitation Literature*, 1974, *35*, 34.

DICKIE, R. F. Categorical vs. non-categorical conceptions of children: An issue revisited. *Education and Treatment of Children*, 1982, *5*, 355–363.

DIEBOLD, M. H., CURTIS, W. S., & DuBOSE, R. Developmental scales versus observational measures for deaf-blind children. *Exceptional Children*, 1978, *44*, 275–278.

DINGMAN, H. F., & TARJAN, G. Mental retardation and the normal distribution curve. *American Journal of Mental Retardation*, 1960, *64*, 991–994.

DODGE, P. R. Neurological disorders of school-age children. *Journal of School Health*, 1976, *46*, 338–343.

DOEHRING, D. G. The tangled web of behavioral research on developmental dyslexia. In A. L. Benton and D. Pearl (Eds.), *Dyslexia: An appraisal of current knowledge*. New York: Oxford University Press, 1978, pp. 123–138.

DOLL, E. A. The essentials of an inclusive concept of mental deficiency. *American Journal of Mental Deficiency*, 1941, *46*, 214–219.

DOLL, E. A. *Vineland social maturity scale: Manual of directions*. Minneapolis: Educational Test Bureau, 1947.

DOLL, E. A. *Vineland school maturity scale*. Minneapolis: Educational Test Bureau, 1953.

DOLL, E. E. A historical survey of research and management of mental retardation in the United States. In E. P. Trapp & P. Himmelstein (Eds.), *Readings on the exceptional child: Research and theory*. New York: Appleton-Century-Crofts, 1962.

DOLLAR, S. J., & BROOKS, C. Assessment of severely and profoundly handicapped persons. *Exceptional Education Quarterly*, 1980, *1*, 87–101.

DONALDSON, J., & MARTINSON, M. C. Modifying attitudes toward physically disabled persons. *Exceptional Children*, 1977, *43*, 337–341.

DOUGLAS, V. I. Stop, look, and listen: The problems of sustained attention and impulse control in hyperactive and normal children. *Canadian Journal of Behavioral Science*, 1972, *4*, 259–282.

DREWS, E., & TEAHAN, J. Parental attitudes and academic achievement. *Journal of Clinical Psychology*, 1957, *13*, 328–332.

DRILLIEN, C. *The growth and development of the prematurely born infant*. Baltimore: Williams and Wilkins, 1964.

DROTAR, D., BASKIEWICZ, A., IRVIN, N., KENNELL, J. H., & KLAUS, M. H. The adaptation of parents to the birth of an infant with a congenital malformation: A hypothetical model. *Pediatrics*, 1975, *56*, 710–717.

DUFFEY, J. B., SALVIA, J., TUCKER, J., & YSSELDYKE, J. Nonbiased assessment: A need for operationalism. *Exceptional Children*, 1981, *47*, 427–434.

DUGDALE, R. L. *The Jukes* (4th ed.). New York: Putnam, 1910.

DUNCAN, M. H. Home adjustment of stutterers and non-stutterers. *Journal of Speech and Hearing Disorders*, 1949, *14*, 255–259.

DUNLAP, J. M. The education of children with high mental ability. In W. M. Cruickshank & G. O. Johnson (Eds.), *Education of exceptional children and youth*. Englewood Cliffs, N.J.: Prentice-Hall, 1967.

DUNLAP, W. R., & HOLLINSWORTH, J. S. How does a handicapped child affect the family? Implications for practitioners. *Family Coordinator*, 1977, *26*, 286–293.

DUNLOP, K. H., STONEMAN, Z., & CANTRELL, M. L. Social interaction of exceptional and other children in a mainstreamed preschool classroom. *Exceptional Children*, 1980, 47, 132–141.

DUNN, L. M. Special education for the mildly retarded: Is much of it justifiable? *Exceptional Children*, 1968, 35, 5–22.

DUNN, L. M. An overview. In L. Dunn (Ed.), *Exceptional children in the schools* (2nd ed.). New York: Holt, Rinehart and Winston, 1973. (a)

DUNN, L. M. Children with moderate and severe general learning disabilities. In L. M. Dunn (Ed.), *Exceptional children in the schools* (2nd ed.). New York: Holt, Rinehart and Winston, 1973. (b)

DUNST, C. J. Program evaluation and the Education for All Handicapped Children Act. *Exceptional Children*, 1979, 46, 24–31.

DURANT, W. *Caesar and Christ*. New York: Simon and Schuster, 1944.

DURANT, W. *The age of faith*. New York: Simon and Schuster, 1950.

DURANT, W. *Our Oriental heritage*. New York: Simon and Schuster, 1954.

DURANT, W. *The life of Greece*. New York: Simon and Schuster, 1966.

DURANT, W., & DURANT, A. *The age of Voltaire*. New York: Simon and Schuster, 1965.

EDGERTON, R. B. *The cloak of competence: Stigma in the lives of the mentally retarded*. Berkeley: University of California Press, 1967.

EDGERTON, R. B. *Mental retardation*. Cambridge: Howard University Press, 1979.

EDGERTON, R. B., & BERCOVICI, S. The cloak of competence: Years later. *American Journal of Mental Deficiency*, 1976, 80, 485–497.

EDGERTON, R. B., & LANGNESS, L. L. Observing mentally retarded persons in community settings: An anthropological perspective. In G. D. Sackett (Ed.), *Observing behavior, Volume I: Theory and applications in mental retardation*. Baltimore: University Park Press, 1978.

EDLUND, C. The effect on the test behavior of children, as reflected in IQ scores, when reinforced after each correct response. *Journal of Applied Behavioral Analysis*, 1972, 5, 317–319.

EDMONDSON, B. Measurement of social participation of retarded adults. *American Journal of Mental Deficiency*, 1974, 78, 494–501.

EDMONDSON, B., McCOMBS, K., & WISH, J. What retarded adults believe about sex. *American Journal of Mental Deficiency*, 1979, 84, 11–18.

EDUCATION OF THE HANDICAPPED: BEH clears up private school provisions of P.L. 94–142. *Education of the Handicapped*, 1979, 5, 1.

EISENBERG, L. Strengths of the inner city child. *Baltimore Bulletin of Education*, 1963-1964, 41, 10–16.

EISENBERG, L., & KANNER, L. Childhood schizophrenia. *American Journal of Orthopsychiatry*, 1956, 26, 556–565.

EISENSON, J. Speech defects: Nature, causes, and psychological concomitants. In W. M. Cruickshank (Ed.), *Psychology of exceptional children and youth* (4th ed.). Englewood Cliffs, N.J.: Prentice-Hall, 1980.

EISENSON, J., & OGILVIE, M. *Speech correction in the schools* (4th ed.). New York: Macmillan Publishing Co., 1977.

EISMAN, B. S. L. Paired associate learning, generalization, and retention as a function of intelligence. *American Journal of Mental Deficiency*, 1958, 63, 451–489.

ELASHOFF, J. D., & SNOW, R. E. *A case study in statistical inference: Reconsideration of the Rosenthal-Jacobson data on teacher expectancy*. (Technical Report No. 15). Stanford, Calif.: Stanford University, Stanford Center for Research and Development, 1970.

ELDER, G. H., Jr. *Adolescent achievement and mobility aspirations*. Chapel Hill, N.C.: University of North Carolina, Institute for Research in Social Science, 1962.

ELLIOTT, M. Quantitative evaluation procedures for learning disabilities. *Journal of Learning Disabilities*, 1981, 14, 84–87.

ELLIS, D. Visual handicaps of mentally handicapped people. *American Journal of Mental Deficiency*, 1979, 83, 497–511.

ELLIS, N. R. The stimulus trace and behavioral inadequacy. In N. R. Ellis (Ed.), *Handbook of mental deficiency*. New York: McGraw-Hill, 1963.

ELLIS, N. R. A behavioral research strategy in mental retardation: Defense and critique. *American Journal of Mental Deficiency*, 1969, *73*, 557–566.

ELLIS, N. R. Memory processes in retardates and normals. In N. R. Ellis (Ed.), *International review of research in mental retardation* (Vol. 4). New York: Academic Press, 1970.

ELLIS, N. R., BALLA, D., ESTES, O., WARREN, S. A., MEYERS, C. E., HOLLIS, J., ISAACSON, R. L., PALK, B. E., & SIEGEL, P. S. Common sense in the habilitation of mentally retarded persons: A reply to Menolascino and McGee. *Mental Retardation*, 1981, *19*, 221–225.

ELLIS, N. R., DEACON, J., HARRIS, L., POOR, A., ANGERS, D., DIORIO, M., WATKINS, R., BOYD, B., & CAVALIER, A. Learning, memory and transfer in profoundly, severely and moderately mentally retarded persons. *American Journal of Mental Deficiency*, 1982, *87*, 186–196.

ENGEL, E. One hundred years of cytogenetic studies in health and disease. *American Journal of Mental Deficiency*, 1977, *83*, 109–116.

ENIS, C. A., & CATARIZOLO, M. Sex education in the residential school for the blind. *Education of the Visually Handicapped*, 1972, *4*(2), 61–64.

ERIKSON, E. H. *Childhood and society* (2nd ed.). New York: W. W. Norton, 1963.

ESCALONA, S. K. Socio/emotional. In background papers of the Boston Conference on Screening and Assessment of Young Children at Developmental Risk. *DHEW Publication*, 1972 (OS), 73–91.

ESVELDT, K., DAWSON, P., & FORNESS, S. Effect of video feedback on children's classroom performance. *Journal of Educational Research*, 1974, *67*, 453–456.

EVANS, S. The consultant role of the resource teacher. *Exceptional Children*, 1980, *46*, 402–404.

EVANS, S. Perceptions of classroom teachers, principals, and resource room teachers of the actual and desired roles of the resource teacher. *Journal of Learning Disabilities*, 1981, *14*, 600–603.

EVERHART, R. W. The relationship between articulation and other developmental factors in children. *Journal of Speech and Hearing Disorders*, 1953, *18*, 332–338.

EVERS, W. L., & SCHWARZ, J. C. Modifying social withdrawal in preschoolers: The effects of filmed modeling and teacher praise. *Journal of Abnormal Child Psychology*, 1973, *1*, 248–256.

EYDE, D. R., & ALTMAN, R. *An exploration of metamemory processes in mildly and moderately retarded children*. (U.S. Office of Education Project Report No. 443AH60046). University of Missouri Department of Special Education, 1978.

EYMAN, R. K., O'CONNOR, G., TARJAN, G., & JUSTICE, R. Factors determining residential placement of mentally retarded children. *American Journal of Mental Deficiency*, 1974, *76*, 692–698.

EYMAN, R. K., SILVERSTEIN, A. B., McLAIN, R. E., & MILLER, C. R. Effects of residential settings on development. In P. Mittler & J. deJong (Eds.), *Research to practice in mental retardation: Care and intervention* (Vol. 1). Baltimore: University Park Press, 1977.

EYSENCK, H. J. *The measurement of intelligence*. Baltimore: Williams and Wilkins Co., 1973.

FAIR, G. W. Employment opportunities in the 80's for special needs students. *Journal for Vocational Special Needs Education*, 1980, *3*, 18–20.

FAIRBANKS, R. The subnormal child seventeen years after. *Mental Hygiene*, 1933, *17*, 177–208.

FARBER, B. Effects of a severely mentally retarded child on family integration. *Monographs of the Society for Research on Child Development*, 1959, *24* (2, Series No. 71).

FARBER, B. *Mental retardation: Its social context and social consequences*. Boston: Houghton Mifflin Co., 1968.

FARBER, B. Family adaptations to severely mentally retarded children. In M. J. Begab & S. A. Richardson (Eds.), *The mentally retarded and society: A social science perspective*. Baltimore: University Park Press, 1975.

FAVELL, J. E., & CANNON, P. R. Evaluation of entertainment materials for severely retarded persons. *American Journal of Mental Deficiency*, 1976, *81*, 357–361.

FAVELL, J. E., FAVELL, M., & RISLEY, T. A quality-assurance system for ensuring client rights in mental retardation facilities. In G. T. Hannah, W. Christian, & H. Clark (Eds.). *Preservation of client rights: A handbook for practitioners providing therapeutic, educational, and rehabilitative services.* New York: The Free Press, 1981.

FEDERAL REGISTER. *Procedures for evaluating specific learning disabilities.* 42(250) (December 29): Section 121a.541. Department of Health, Education and Welfare, Office of Education, 1977.

FEINGOLD, B. F. Hyperkinesis and learning disabilities linked to the ingestion of artificial food colors and flavors. *Journal of Learning Disabilities,* 1976, 9, 551–559.

FEINGOLD, B. F., & BANK, C. J. *Developmental disabilities of early childhood.* Springfield, Ill.: Charles C. Thomas, 1978.

FELDHUSEN, J. F., ROESER, T. D., & THURSTON, J. R. Prediction of social adjustment over a period of 6 or 9 years. *Journal of Special Education,* 1977, 11, 30–36.

FELDMAN, M., BYALICK, R., & ROSEDALE, M. Parent involvement programs—a growing trend in special education. *Exceptional Children,* 1975, 41, 291–304.

FENTON, K. S., YOSHIDA, R. K., MAXWELL, J. P., & KAUFMAN, M. J. Recognition of team goals: An essential step toward rational decision making. *Exceptional Children,* 1979, 45, 638–644.

FERNALD, G. M. *Remedial techniques in basic school subjects.* New York: McGraw-Hill, 1943.

FERNALD, W. E. Care of the feeble-minded. *Conference of Charities and Corrections, National Proceedings,* 1904, 3–390.

FERRARA, D. M. Attitudes of parents of MR children toward normalization activities. *American Journal of Mental Deficiency,* 1979, 84, 145–151.

FEURSTEIN, R., MILLER, R., HOFFMAN, M. B., RAND, Y., MINTZKER, Y., & JENSEN, M. R. Cognitive modifiability in adolescence: Cognitive Structure and the effects of intervention. *Journal of Special Education,* 1981, 15, 269–287.

FEURSTEIN, R., MILLER, R., RAND, Y., & JENSEN, M. R. Can evolving techniques better measure cognitive change? Journal of Special Education, 1981, 15, 201–219.

FEURSTEIN, R., RAND, Y., HOFFMAN, M., & MILLER, R. *Instrumental enrichment.* Baltimore: University Park Press, 1980.

FILLER, J., & BRICKER, W. Teaching styles of mothers and the match-to-sample performance of their retarded preschool age children. *American Journal of Mental Deficiency,* 1976, 80, 504–511.

FINESTONE, S., LUKOFF, I., & WHITEMAN, M. *The demand for dog guides and travel adjustment of blind persons.* New York: Research Center, Columbia University, 1960.

FISHER, M. A., & ZEAMAN, D. Growth and decline of retardate intelligence. In N. R. Ellis (Ed.), *International review of research in mental retardation* (Vol. 4). New York: Academic Press, 1970.

FISHER, M. A., & ZEAMAN, D. An attention-retention theory of retardate discrimination. In N. Ellis (Ed.), *International review of research on mental retardation.* New York: Academic Press, 1973.

FITZHUGH, K., & FITZHUGH, L. *The Fitzhugh plus program.* Galien, Mich.: Allied Education Council, 1966.

FLANAGEN, J. C., DAILEY, J. T., SHAYCOFT, M. F., GORHAM, W. A., ORR, D. B., & GOLDBERG, I. *Design for a Study of American Youth.* Boston: Houghton Mifflin Co., 1962.

FLATHOUSE, V. Multiply handicapped deaf children and Public Law 94–142. *Exceptional Children,* 1979, 45, 560–565.

FLOOR, L., BAXTER, D., ROSEN, M., & ZISFEIN, L. A survey of marriage among previously institutionalized retardates. *Mental Retardation,* 1975, 13, 33–37.

FLOOR, L., & ROSEN, M. Investigating the phenomenon of helplessness in mentally retarded adults. *American Journal of Mental Deficiency,* 1975, 79, 565–572.

FLOWER, R. M., LEACH, E., STONE, C. R., & YODER, D. E. Case selection. *Journal of Speech and Hearing Disorders,* 1967, 32, 65–70.

FLYNN, R. J., & NITSCH, K. E. (Eds.). *Normalization, social integration, and community services.* Baltimore: University Park Press, 1980.

FORD FOUNDATION. *Exceptional teaching for exceptional learning.* Ford Foundation Report, P.O. Box 559, Naugatuck, Conn., 1980.

FORNESS, S. R. The mildly retarded as casualties of the educational system. *Journal of School Psychology,* 1972, *10,* 117–126.

FORNESS, S. R. The reinforcement hierarchy. *Psychology in the Schools,* 1973, *10,* 168–177.

FORNESS, S. R. Educational approaches to autism. *Training School Bulletin,* 1974, *71,* 167–173. (a)

FORNESS, S. R. Implications of recent trends in educational labeling. *Journal of Learning Disabilities,* 1974, *7,* 445–449. (b)

FORNESS, S. R. Educational approaches to hyperactive children. In D. Cantwell (Ed.), *The hyperactive child: Diagnosis, management, and current research.* New York: Spectrum Publications, 1975.

FORNESS, S. R. Behavioristic orientation to categorical labels. *Journal of School Psychology,* 1976, *14,* 90–96.

FORNESS, S. R. A transition model for placement of handicapped children in regular and special classes. *Contemporary Educational Psychology,* 1977, *2,* 37–49.

FORNESS, S. R. Developmental programming for the use of aversive procedures in a hospital school. In F. H. Wood & K. C. Lakin (Eds.), *Punishment and aversion stimulation in special education.* Minneapolis: Minnesota University Advanced Training Institute Monograph, 1978.

FORNESS, S. R. Developing the individual educational plan: Process and perspectives. *Education and Treatment of Children,* 1979, *2,* 43–55. (a)

FORNESS, S. R. Clinical criteria for mainstreaming mildly handicapped children. *Psychology in the School,* 1979, *16,* 508–514. (b)

FORNESS, S. R. *Recent concepts in dyslexia: Implications for diagnosis and remediation.* Reston, Va.: Council for Exceptional Children Reports, 1981. (a)

FORNESS, S. R. Concepts of school learning and behavior disorders: Implications for research and practice. *Exceptional Children,* 1981, *48,* 56–64. (b)

FORNESS, S. R. Diagnosing dyslexia: A note on the need for ecologic assessment. *American Journal of Diseases of Children,* 1982, *134,* 237–242. (a)

FORNESS, S. R. Prevocational academic assessment of children and youth with learning and behavior problems: The bridge between the school classroom and vocational training. In K. Lynch, W. Kiernan, & J. Stark (Eds.), *Prevocational and vocational education for special needs youth.* Baltimore: Paul Brookes Publishing, 1982. (b)

FORNESS, S. R. Diagnostic schooling for children or adolescents with behavior disorders. *Behavioral Disorders,* 1983, *8,* 176–190.

FORNESS, S. R., BENNETT, L., & TOSE, J. Academic deficits in emotionally disturbed children revisited. *Journal of Child Psychiatry,* 1983, *22,* 140–144.

FORNESS, S. R., & CANTWELL, D. DSM III psychiatric diagnoses and special education categories. *Journal of Special Education,* 1982, *6,* 49–63.

FORNESS, S. R., & DVORAK, R. Effects of test time limits on achievement scores of behavior disordered adolescents. *Behavioral Disorders,* 1982, *7,* 207–212.

FORNESS, S., & ESVELDT, K. Classroom observation of learning and behavior-problem children. *Journal of Learning Disabilities,* 1975, *8,* 382–385.

FORNESS, S. R., FRANKEL, F., & LANDMAN, R. Use of different types of classroom punishment by preschool teachers. *Psychological Record,* 1976, *26,* 263–268.

FORNESS, S. R., GUTHRIE, D., & HALL, R. Follow-up of high risk children identified in kindergarten through direct classroom observations. *Psychology in the Schools,* 1976, *13,* 45–49.

FORNESS, S. R., GUTHRIE, D., & MacMILLAN, D. L. Classroom behavior of mentally retarded children across different classroom settings. *Journal of Special Education,* 1981, *15,* 497–509.

FORNESS, S. R., GUTHRIE, D., & MacMILLAN, D. Classroom environments as they relate to retarded children's observable behavior. *American Journal of Mental Deficiency*, 1982, 87, 259–265.

FORNESS, S. R., HALL, R., & GUTHRIE, D. Eventual school placement of kindergartners observed as high risk in the classroom. *Psychology in the Schools*, 1977, 14, 315–317.

FORNESS, S., & KAVALE, K. Remediation of reading disabilities: Current issues and approaches. *Learning Disabilities: An International Journal*, in press.

FORNESS, S. R., & LANGDON, F. School in a psychiatric hospital. *Journal of Child Psychiatry*, 1974, 13, 562–575.

FORNESS, S. R. & MacMILLAN, D. Reinforcement overkill: Implications for education of the retarded. *Journal of Special Education*, 1972, 6, 220–230.

FORNESS, S. R., SILVERSTEIN, A., & GUTHRIE, D. Relationship between classroom behavior and psychometric achievement in mildly retarded children. *American Journal of Mental Deficiency*, 1979, 84, 260–265.

FORNESS, S. R., SINCLAIR, E., & GUTHRIE, D. Learning disability discrepancy formulas: Their use in actual practice. *Learning Disability Quarterly*, 1983, 6, 107–114.

FORNESS, S. R., THORNTON, R. L., & HORTON, A. A. Assessment of applied academic and social skills. *Education and Training of the Mentally Retarded*, 1981, 16, 104–109.

FORNESS, S. R., URBANO, R., ROTBERG, J., BENDER, M., GARDNER, T. P., LYNCH, E. W., & ZEMANEK, D. H. Identifying children with learning and behavior problems served by interdisciplinary clinics and hospitals. *Child Psychiatry and Human Development*, 1980, 11, 67–78.

FOSTER, G. G., YSSELDYKE, J. E., & REESE, J. H. "I wouldn't have seen it if I hadn't believed it." *Exceptional Children*, 1975, 41, 469–473.

FRAIBERG, S. Intervention in infancy: A program for blind infants. *Journal of the American Academy of Child Psychiatry*, 1971, 10, 381–405.

FRAIBERG, S. *Insights from the blind: Comparative studies of blind and sighted infants.* New York: Basic Books, 1977.

FRANKEL, F., FORNESS, S., ROWE, S., & WESTLAKE, J. Individualizing schedules of instruction for handicapped children. *Psychology in the Schools*, 1979, 16, 270–278.

FRANKENBURG, W. K., & DOBBS, J. B. Denver developmental screening test. *Journal of Pediatrics*, 1971, 71, 171–191.

FREEMAN, R. D., MALKIN, S. F., & HASTINGS, J. O. Psychosocial problems of deaf children and their families: A comparative study. *American Annals of the Deaf*, 1975, 120, 391–405.

FRIEDENBERG, W. P., & MARTIN, A. S. Prevocational training of the severely retarded using task analysis. *Mental Retardation*, 1977, 15, 16–20.

FRIEDLANDER, B. Z., STERRITT, G. M., & KIRK, G. E. *Exceptional infant:* (Vol. 3), *Assessment and intervention.* New York: Brunner/Mazel, 1975.

FRIEDMAN, M., KRUPSKI, A., DAWSON, E., & ROSENBERG, P. Metamemory and mental retardation: Implications for research and practice. In P. Mittler (Ed.), *Research to practice in mental retardation: Education and training* (Vol. II). Baltimore: University Park Press, 1977.

FRIEDMAN, S., & SIGMAN, M. *Preterm birth and psychological development.* San Francisco: Academic Press, 1981.

FRIERSON, E. C. Upper and lower status gifted children: A study of differences. *Exceptional Children*, 1965, 32, 83–90.

FRISTOE, M. Communication assessment in the mentally retarded. In P. Mittler (Ed.), *Research to practice in mental retardation: Education and training* (Vol. II). Baltimore: University Park Press, 1977.

FRISTOE, M., & LLOYD, L. Nonspeech communication. In N. Ellis (Ed.), *Handbook of mental deficiency, psychological theory and research* (2nd ed.). Hillsdale, N.J.: Lawrence Erlbaum Assoc., 1979.

FRITH, G. H. "Advocate" vs. "Professional employee": A question of priorities for special educators. *Exceptional Children*, 1981, 47, 486–495.

FROST, J. L., & HAWKES, G. R. (Eds.). *The disadvantaged child*. Boston: Houghton Mifflin Co., 1966.

FROSTIG, M., & HORNE, D. *The Frostig program for the development of visual perception*. Chicago: Follett Publishing Co., 1964.

FURTH, H. G. Linguistic deficiency and thinking: Research with deaf subjects, 1964–1969. *Psychological Bulletin*, 1971, 76, 58–72.

FURTH, H. G., & YOUNISS, J. Formal operations and language: A comparison of deaf and hearing adolescents. *International Journal of Psychology*, 1971, 6, 49–64.

GAJAR, A. H. Educable mentally retarded, learning disabled and emotionally disturbed: Similarities and differences. *Exceptional Children*, 1979, 45, 470–472.

GAJAR, A. H. Characteristics across exceptional categories: EMR, LD, and ED. *Journal of Special Education*, 1980, 14, 166–173.

GALLAGHER, J. J. *The gifted child in the elementary school: What research says to the teacher*, No. 17 (1st ed.). Washington, D.C.: American Educational Research Association, N.E.A., Department of Classroom Teachers, 1959.

GALLAGHER, J. J. *Teaching the gifted child* (2nd ed.). Boston: Allyn and Bacon, 1975.

GALLIMORE, R., BOGGS, J. W., & JORDAN, C. *Culture, behavior, and education: A study of Hawaiian-Americans*. Beverly Hills, Calif.: Sage Publications, 1974.

GALLISTEL, E. Setting goals and objectives for LD children—process and problems. *Journal of Learning Disabilities*, 1978, 11, 177–184.

GAMPEL, D. H., GOTTLIEB, J., & HARRISON, R. N. Comparison of classroom behavior of special class EMR, integrated EMR, low IQ, and nonretarded children. *American Journal of Mental Deficiency*, 1974, 79, 16–21.

GAN, J., TYMCHUK, A. J., & NISHIHARA, A. Mildly retarded adults: Their attitudes toward retardation. *Mental Retardation*, 1977, 15, 5–9.

GARBER, H. "Milwaukee" kids revisited. *RT II: Research and Training Center in Mental Retardation*, 1980, 2, 1–12.

GARBER, H., & HEBER, F. R. The Milwaukee Project: Indications of the effectiveness of early intervention in preventing mental retardation. In P. Mittler (Ed.), *Research to practice in mental retardation: Care and intervention* (Vol. 1). Baltimore: University Park Press, 1977.

GARDNER, J. M. *The comprehensive behavior check list: Manual*. Columbus, Ohio: Columbus State Institute, 1970.

GARDNER, J. M. Community residential alternatives for the developmentally disabled. *Mental Retardation*, 1977, 15, 3–8.

GARRETT, J. E., & BRAZIL, N. Categories used for identification and education of exceptional children. *Exceptional Children*, 1979, 45, 291–292.

GARRISON, M., & HAMMILL, D. Who are the retarded? Multiple criteria applied to children in educable classes. *Exceptional Children*, 1971, 38, 13–20.

GEARHEART, B. R., & LITTON, F. W. *The trainable retarded: A foundations approach*. St. Louis: C. V. Mosby Co., 1975.

GEIGER, W. L., BROWNSMITH, K., & FORGNONE, C. Differential importance of skills for TMR student as perceived by teachers. *Education and Training of the Mentally Retarded*, 1978, 13, 259–264.

GELB, A., & GOLDSTEIN, K. M. *Psychologishe Analysen Hirpathologisher Feele*. Leipzig: Ambr. Barth, 1920. (Partially translated in *Sourcebook of Gestalt Psychology*. New York: Harcourt, Brace and World, 1938.)

GERARD, E. O. Exercise of voting rights by the retarded. *Mental Retardation*, 1974, 12, 45–47.

GESELL, A., et al. *Gesell developmental schedules*. New York: Psychological Corporation, 1940.

GESELL, A., & ILG, F. L. *Infant and child in the culture of today*. New York: Harper and Row, 1943.

GETMAN, G. N. The visuomotor complex in the acquisition of learning skills. In J. Hellmuth (Ed.), *Learning Disorders*, Vol. I. Seattle: Special Child Publications, 1965.

GETMAN, G. H., DANE, E., HALGREN, M., & McKEE, G. *Developing learning readiness*. Manchester, Mo.: Webster Division, McGraw-Hill, 1968.

GETZELS, J. W., & DILLON, J. The nature of giftedness and the education of the gifted. In R. Travers (Ed.), *Second handbook of research on teaching*. Chicago: Rand McNally and Co., 1973.

GETZELS, J. W., & JACKSON, P. W. *Creativity and intelligence*. New York: John Wiley and Sons, 1962.

GEZI, K. Bilingual-bicultural education: A review of relevant research. *California Journal of Educational Research*, 1975, *25*, 223–239.

GILBERT, K. A., & HEMMING, H. Evironmental change and psycholinguistic ability of mentally retarded adults. *American Journal of Mental Deficiency*, 1979, *83*, 453–459.

GILBERT, T. R. Overlearning and the retention of meaningful prose. *Journal of General Psychology*, 1957, *56*, 281–289.

GILHOOL, T. K. The uses of litigation: The right of retarded children to a free public education. *Peabody Journal of Education*, 1973, *50*, 120–217.

GILLIAM, J. E. Contributions and status rankings of educational planning committee participants. *Exceptional Children*, 1979, *45*, 466–468.

GILLIAM, J. E., & COLEMAN, M. C. Who influences IEP committee decisions? *Exceptional Children*, 1981, *47*, 642–644.

GILLINGHAM, A., & STILLMAN, B. *Remedial training for children with specific disability in reading, spelling, and penmanship*. Cambridge, Mass.: Education Publishing Service, 1960.

GINSBERG, G., & HARRISON, C. H. *How to help your gifted child: A handbook for parents and teachers*. New York: Monarch Press, 1977.

GLASS, G. V., & SMITH, M. L. Meta-analysis of the research on class size and achievement. *Educational Evaluation and Policy Analysis*, 1979, *1*, 2–16.

GLAZZARD, P. Simulation of handicaps as a teaching strategy for preservice and inservice training. *Teaching Exceptional Children*, 1979, *11*, 101–104.

GLICKING, E. E., MURPHY, L. C., & MALLORY, D. W. Teachers' preferences for resource services. *Exceptional Children*, 1979, *45*, 442–449.

GLICKING, E. E., & THEOBALD, J. T. Mainstreaming: Affect or effect. *Journal of Special Education*, 1975, *9*, 317–328.

GLIDDEN, L. M. Training of learning and memory in retarded persons: Strategies, techniques, and teaching tools. In N. Ellis (Ed.), *Handbook of mental deficiency, psychological theory and research* (2nd ed.). Hillsdale, N.J.: Lawrence Erlbaum Assoc., 1979.

GLIEDMAN, J., & ROTH, W. *The unexpected minority: Handicapped children in America*. New York: Harcourt Brace Jovanovich, 1980.

GODDARD, H. H. *The Kallakak Family: A study in the heredity of feeble-mindedness*. New York: Macmillan Publishing Co., 1912.

GOERTZEL, V., & GOERTZEL, M. *Cradles of eminence*. Boston: Little, Brown and Co., 1962.

GOLD, M. W. Research on the vocational habilitation of the retarded: The present, the future. In N. R. Ellis (Ed.), *International review of research on mental retardation* (Vol. 6). New York: Academic Press, 1973.

GOLDBERG, B., & SOPER, J. Childhood psychosis or mental retardation: A diagnostic dilemma. *Canadian Medical Association Journal*, 1963, *89*, 1015–1019.

GOLDBERG, I. I., & CRUICKSHANK, W. M. Trainable but noneducable. *National Educational Association Journal*, 1958, *47*, 622–623.

GOLDBERG, M. L. Factors affecting educational attainment in depressed urban areas. In A. H. Passow (Ed.), *Education in depressed areas*. New York: Teachers College Press, 1963.

GOLDBERG, M. L. Methods and materials for educationally disadvantaged youth. In A. H. Passow, M. Goldberg, & A. J. Tannenbaum (Eds.), *Education of the disadvantaged*. New York: Holt, Rinehart and Winston, 1967.

GOLDSTEIN, B. *Low income youth in urban areas*. New York: Holt, Rinehart and Winston, 1967.

GOLDSTEIN, H. *Social aspects of mental deficiency* (unpublished Ed. D. Dissertation, University of Illinois, 1957).

GOLDSTEIN, H. Incidence, prevalence and causes of blindness in selected countries. *Public Health Review*, 1972, *1*, 42–69.

GOLDSTEIN, H. *The social learning curriculum*. Columbus, Ohio: Charles E. Merrill Publishing Co., 1974.

GOLDSTEIN, H., & GOLDSTEIN, M. *Reasoning ability of mildly retarded learners*. Reston, Va.: Council for Exceptional Children, 1980.

GOLDSTEIN, S., STRICKLAND, B., TURNBULL, A. P., & CURRY, L. An observational analysis of the IEP conference. *Exceptional Children*, 1980, *46*, 278–286.

GOLDSTEIN, S., & TURNBULL, A. Strategies to increase parent participation in IEP conferences. *Exceptional Children*, 1982, *48*, 360–361.

GOLIN, A. K., & DUCANIS, A. *The interdisciplinary team: A handbook for the education of exceptional children*. Rockville, Md.: Aspen, 1981.

GOLLAY, E. Deinstitutionalized mentally retarded people: A closer look. *Education and Training of the Mentally Retarded*, 1977, *12*, 137–144.

GOODENOUGH, F. L., & HARRIS, D. B. *Goodenough-Harris Drawing Test*. New York: Harcourt Brace Jovanovich, 1963.

GOODMAN, H., GOTTLIEB, J., & HARRISON, R. H. Social acceptance of EMRs integrated into a nongraded elementary school. *American Journal of Mental Deficiency*, 1972, *76*, 412–417.

GOODMAN, L. Montessori education for the handicapped: The methods—The Research. In L. Mann & D. A. Sabatino (Eds.), *The second review of special education*. Philadelphia: JSE Press, 1974.

GORDON, S. *Facts about sex for exceptional youth*. New York: Charles Brown, 1969.

GORHAM, K. A., DES JARDINS, C., PAGE, R., PETTIS, E., & SCHEIBER, B. Effects on parents. In N. Hobbs (Ed.), *Issues in the classification of children*. San Francisco: Jossey-Bass, 1975.

GOTTLIEB, J. Attitudes toward retarded children: Effects of labeling and behavioral aggressiveness. *Journal of Educational Psychology*, 1975, *67*, 581–585.

GOTTLIEB, J. Mainstreaming: Fulfilling the promise? *American Journal of Mental Deficiency*, 1981, *86*, 115–126.

GOTTLIEB, J., & BUDOFF, M. Social acceptability of retarded children in nongraded schools differing in architecture. *American Journal of Mental Deficiency*, 1973, *78*, 15–19.

GOTTLIEB, J., & DAVIS, J. E. *Social acceptance of EMR's during overt behavior interaction*. Cambridge, Mass.: Studies in learning potential, Research Institute for Education Problems, Vol. 2, 1971.

GOTTLIEB, J., GAMPEL, D. H., & BUDOFF, M. Classroom behavior of retarded children before and after reintegration into classes. *Journal of Special Education*, 1975, *9*, 307–315.

GOTTLIEB, J., & GOTTLIEB, B. W. Stereotypic attitudes and behavior intentions toward handicapped children. *American Journal of Mental Deficiency*, 1977, *82*, 65–71.

GOTTLIEB, J., & LEYSER, H. Facilitating the social mainstreaming of retarded children. *Exceptional Education Quarterly*, 1981, *1*, 57–69.

GOTTLIEB, J., & SWITZKY, H. N. Development of school-age children's stereotypic attitudes toward mentally retarded children. *American Journal of Mental Deficiency*, 1982, *86*, 596–600.

GOTTMAN, J., GONSO, J., & RASMUSSEN, B. Social interaction, social competence, and friendship in children. *Child Development*, 1975, *46*, 709–718.

GOTTS, E. E. The training of intelligence as a component of early intervention: Past, present, and future. *Journal of Special Education*, 1981, *15*, 257–268.

GOWMAN, A. G. *The war blind in American social structure*. New York: American Foundation for the Blind, 1957.

GRACE, H. A., & BOOTH, N. L. Is the gifted child a social isolate? *Peabody Journal of Education*, 1958, *35*, 195–196.

GRAY, S. W., KLAUS, R. A., MILLER, J. O., & FORRESTER, B. J. *Before first grade*. New York: Teachers College Press, 1966.

GREEN, C., & ZIGLER, E. Social deprivation and the performance of retarded and normal children on a satiation-type task. *Child Development*, 1962, *33*, 499–508.

GREENSPAN, S. Social intelligence in the retarded. In N. Ellis (Ed.), *Handbook of mental deficiency, psychological theory and research* (2nd ed.). Hillsdale, N.J.: Lawrence Erlbaum Assoc., 1979.

GREENSPAN, S. I. Clinical developmental approaches to infants and their families: Theoretical perspectives and a research agenda. *Zero to Three*, 1980, *1*, 3–11.

GREENSPAN, S. Defining childhood social competence: A proposed working model. In B. K. Keogh (Ed.), *Advances in special education* (Vol. 3). Greenwich, Conn.: JAI Press, 1981.

GREENSPAN, S., & JAVEL, M. E. Personal competence profiling of exceptional children: Proposed alternative to traditional categorization. In T. R. Kratochwill (Ed.), *Advances in school psychology* (Vol. 4). Hillsdale, N.J.: Lawrence Erlbaum Assoc., 1982.

GRESHAM, F. M. Misguided mainstreaming: The case for social skills training with handicapped children. *Exceptional Children*, 1982, *48*, 422–433.

GRESHAM, F. M. Social skills assessment as a component of mainstreaming placement decisions. *Exceptional Children*, 1983, *49*, 331–336.

GRINSPOON, L., & SINGER, S. B. Amphetamines in the treatment of hyperkinetic children. *Harvard Educational Review*, 1973, *43*, 515–555.

GROSENICK, J. K., & HUNTZE, S. L. *National needs analysis in behavior disorders*. Columbia, Mo.: University of Missouri, Department of Special Education, 1980.

GROSSMAN, F. K. *Brothers and sisters of retarded children: An exploratory study*. Syracuse, N.Y.: Syracuse University Press, 1972.

GROSSMAN, H. J. (Ed.). *Manual on terminology and classification in mental retardation*. Washington, D.C.: American Association on Mental Deficiency, Special Publications, No. 2, 1973.

GROSSMAN, H. J. (Ed.). *Classification in mental retardation*. Washington, D.C.: American Association on Mental Deficiency, 1983.

GRUEN, G. E., OTTINGER, D. R., & OLLENDICK, T. H. Probability learning in retarded children with differing histories of success and failure in school. *American Journal of Mental Deficiency*, 1974, *79*, 417–423.

GRUENBERG, E. Epidemiology. In H. Stevens & R. Heber (Eds.), *Mental retardation: A review of research*. Chicago: University of Chicago Press, 1964.

GUERIN, G. R. School achievement and behavior of children with mild or moderate health conditions. *Journal of Special Education*, 1979, *13*, 179–186.

GUESS, D., & HORNER, R. The severely and profoundly handicapped. In E. Meyen (Ed.), *Exceptional children and youth: An introduction*. Denver: Love Publishing Co., 1978.

GUESS, D., & NOONAN, M. J. Curricula and instructional procedures for severely handicapped students. *Focus on Exceptional Children*, 1982, *14*, 1–12.

GUILFORD, J. P. Traits of creativity. In H. Anderson (Ed.), *Creativity and its cultivation*. New York: Harper and Row, 1959.

GUILFORD, J. P. *The nature of human intelligence*. New York: McGraw-Hill, 1967.

GUNZBURG, H. *Social competence and mental handicap*. Baltimore: Williams and Wilkins Co., 1973.

GURALNICK, M. V. Programmatic factors affecting child-child social interactions in mainstreamed preschool programs. *Exceptional Education Quarterly*, 1981, *1*, 71–91.

GUSKIN, S. L. Research on labeling retarded persons: Where do we go from here? (A reaction to MacMillan, Jones, & Aloia). *American Journal of Mental Deficiency*, 1974, *79*, 262–264.

GUSKIN, S. L. Theoretical and empirical strategies for the study of the labeling of mentally retarded persons. In N. R. Ellis (Ed.), *International review of research in mental retardation* (Vol. 9). New York: Academic Press, 1978.

GUSKIN, S. L., BARTEL, N. R., & MacMILLAN, D. L. The perspective of the labeled child. In N. Hobbs (Ed.), *Issues in the classification of exceptional children* (Vol. 2). San Francisco: Jossey-Bass, 1975.

GUSKIN, S. L., & SPICKER, H. H. Educational research in mental retardation. In N. R. Ellis (Ed.), *International review of research in mental retardation* (Vol. 3). New York: Academic Press, 1968.

GUTTMAN, A. J., & RONDAL, J. A. Verbal operants in mothers' speech to nonretarded and Down's syndrome children matched for linguistic level. *American Journal of Mental Deficiency*, 1979, *83*, 446–452.

HAGBERG, B. Epidemiological and preventive aspects of cerebral palsy and severe mental retardation in Sweden. *European Journal of Pediatrics*, 1979, *130*, 71–78.

HAISLEY, F. B., TELL, C., & ANDREWS, J. Peers as tutors in the mainstream: Trained teachers of handicapped adolescents. *Journal of Learning Disabilities*, 1981, *14*, 224–226.

HALL, R. V., LUND, D., & JACKSON, D. Effects of teacher attention on study behavior. *Journal of Applied Behavior Analysis*, 1968, *1*, 1–2.

HALLAHAN, D. P., & KAUFFMAN, J. M. Labels, categories, behaviors: ED, LD and EMR reconsidered. *The Journal of Special Education*, 1977, *11*, 139–149.

HALLAHAN, D. P., KAUFFMAN, J. M., KNEEDLER, R. D., SNELL, M. E., & RICHARDS, H. C. Being initiated by an adult and the subsequent imitative behavior of retarded children. *American Journal of Mental Deficiency*, 1977, *81*, 556–560.

HALPERN, A. S. General unemployment and vocational opportunities for EMR individuals. *American Journal of Mental Deficiency*, 1973, *78*, 123–127.

HAMILTON, J. L., & BUDOFF, M. Learning potential among the moderately and severely retarded. *Mental Retardation*, 1974, *12*, 33–36.

HAMMILL, D. D. Assessing and training perceptual-motor processes. In D. D. Hammill & N. R. Bartel (Eds.), *Teaching children with learning and behavior problems*. Boston: Allyn and Bacon, 1975.

HAMMILL, D., & WIEDERHOLT, J. L. *The resource room: Rationale and implementation*. Philadelphia: Buttonwood Press, 1972.

HANNAFORD, A. E., SIMON, J., & ELLIS, D. Criteria for special class placement of mildly retarded: Multidisciplinary comparisons. *Mental Retardation*, 1975, *13*, 7–10.

HAPEMAN, L. B. Developmental concepts of blind children between ages of three and six as they relate to orientation and mobility. *International Journal of the Education of the Blind*, 1967, *17*, 41–48.

HARASYMIW, W. J., & HORNE, M. D. Integration of handicapped children: Its effect on teacher attitudes. *Education*, 1975, *96*, 153–158.

HARASYMIW, W. J., & HORNE, M. D. Teacher attitudes toward handicapped children and regular class integration. *Journal of Special Education*, 1976, *10*, 393–400.

HARBER, J. Issues in the assessment of language and reading disorders in learning disabled children. *Learning Disability Quarterly*, 1980, *3*, 20–29.

HARDMAN, M. L., & DREW, C. J. The physically handicapped retarded individual: A review. *Mental Retardation*, 1977, *15*, 43–48.

HARDMAN, M. L., & DREW, C. J. Life management practices with the profoundly retarded: Issues of euthanasia and withholding treatment. *Mental Retardation*, 1978, *16*, 390–396.

HARE, B. A., HAMMILL, D. D., & CRANDELL, J. M. Auditory discrimination ability of visually limited children. *The New Outlook for the Blind*, 1970, *64*, 287–292.

HARING, N. G., & BROWN, L. J. (Eds.). *Teaching the severely handicapped*. New York: Grune and Stratton, 1977.

HARING, N. G., & PHILLIPS, E. L. *Educating emotionally disturbed children*. New York: McGraw-Hill, 1962.

HARING, N. G., & PHILLIPS, E. L. *Analysis and modification of classroom behavior*. Englewood Cliffs, N.J.: Prentice-Hall, 1972.

HARRELL, R. F., CAPP, R. H., DAVIS, D. R., PEERLESS, J., & RAVITZ, L. R. Can nutritional supplements help mentally retarded children? An exploratory study. *Proceedings of the National Academy of Science*, 1981, *78*, 574–578.

HARRIS, R. A protocol for rubella vaccine. *The Female Patient*, 1979, *60*, 56–57.

HARTER, S. Mental age, IQ, and motivational factors in the discrimination learning set performance of normal and retarded children. *Journal of Experimental Child Psychology*, 1967, *5*, 123–141.

HARTH, R., & GLAVIN, J. Validity of teacher rating as a subtest for screening. *Exceptional Children*, 1971, *37*, 605–606.

HASKETT, J., & HOLLAR, W. D. Sensory refinement and contingency awareness of profoundly retarded children. *American Journal of Mental Deficiency*, 1978, *83*, 60–68.

HASKINS, R., FINKELSTEIN N., & STEDMAN, D. Effects of infant and preschool stimulation programs on high risk children: Intelligence, social behavior, and health. *Pediatric Annuals*, 1978, *7*, 123–144.

HAUBRICK, P. A., & SHORES, R. Attending behavior and academic performance of emotionally disturbed children. *Exceptional Children*, 1976, *42*, 337–338.

HAWKINS-SHEPARD, C. Working with the IEP: Some early reports. *Teaching Exceptional Children*, 1978, *10*, 95–97.

HAYDEN, A. H. Handicapped children, birth to age 3. *Exceptional Children*, 1979, *45*, 510–516.

HAYES, J., & HIGGINS, S. T. Issues regarding the IEP: Teachers on the front line. *Exceptional Children*, 1978, *44*, 267–273.

HAYES, S. P. *Contributions to a psychology of blindness*. New York: American Foundation for the Blind, 1941.

HAYES, S. P. *First regional conference on mental measurement of the blind*. Watertown, Mass.: Perkins Institute for the Blind, 1952.

HAYWOOD, H. C. (Ed.). *Sociocultural aspects of mental retardation*. New York: Appleton-Century-Crofts, 1970.

HAYWOOD, H. C. What happened to mild and moderate mental retardation? *American Journal of Mental Deficiency*, 1979, *83*, 429–431.

HEAL, L. W., SIGELMAN, C. K., & SWITZKEY, H. N. Research on community residential alternatives for the mentally retarded. In N. R. Ellis (Ed.), *International review of research on the mentally retarded* (Vol. 9). New York: Academic Press, 1978.

HEBER, R. F. *Epidemiology of mental retardation*. Springfield, Ill.: Charles C. Thomas, 1970.

HEBER, R. F., & DEVER, R. Research on education and habilitation of the mentally retarded. In H. C. Haywood (Ed.), *Socio-cultural aspects of mental retardation*. New York: Appleton-Century-Crofts, 1970.

HEBER, R., & GARBER, H. The Milwaukee project: A study of the use of family intervention to prevent cultural-familial mental retardation. In B. Friedlander, G. Sterritt, & G. Kirk (Eds.), *Exceptional infant*. New York: Brunner/Mazel, 1975.

HEFFERNAN, M., & FORNESS, S. Effects of social modeling on classroom performance. *Florida Journal of Educational Research*, 1972, *14*, 3–9.

HEIDER, G. M. Adjustment problems of the deaf child. *Nervous Child*, 1948, 7, 1.

HEKKEMA, N., & FREEDMAN, P. E. Effects of imitation training on immediate and delayed imitation by severely retarded children. *American Journal of Mental Deficiency*, 1978, 83, 129–134.

HENDERSON, R. W. Social and emotional needs of culturally diverse children. *Exceptional Children*, 1980, 46, 598–605.

HENDRIX, D. H. Evaluation of learning disabilities. Who should test what? *Journal of Learning Disabilities*, 1981, 14, 82–83.

HERMELIN, B., & O'CONNOR, N. *Speech and thought in severe subnormality*. New York: Macmillan Publishing Co., 1963.

HERON, T. E. Maintaining the mainstreamed child in the regular classroom: The decision-making process. *Journal of Learning Disabilities*, 1978, 11, 210–216.

HERON, T. E., & SKINNER, M. E. Criteria for defining the regular classroom as the least restrictive environment for LD students. *Learning Disability Quarterly*, 1981, 4, 115–120.

HESS, R. D. The transmission of cognitive strategies in poor families: The socialization of apathy and underachievement. In V. L. Allen (Ed.), *Psychological factors in poverty*. Chicago: Markham Publishing Co., 1970.

HESS, R. D., & SHIPMAN, V. Maternal influences upon early learning: The cognitive environments of urban pre-school children. In R. C. Hess & R. M. Bear (Eds.), *Early education*. Chicago: Aldine, 1968.

HESSLER, G. L., & KITCHEN, D. W. Language characteristics of a purposive sample of early elementary learning disabled students. *Learning Disability Quarterly*, 1980, 3, 36–41.

HETHERINGTON, E. M., & PARKE, R. D. *Child psychology: A contemporary viewpoint*. New York: McGraw-Hill, 1979.

HEWETT, F. M. *The emotionally disturbed child in the classroom*. Boston: Allyn and Bacon, 1968.

HEWETT, F. M. Strategies of special education. *Pediatric Clinics of North America*, 1973, 20, 695–704.

HEWETT, F. M., & BLAKE, P. R. Teaching the emotionally disturbed. In R. W. Travers (Ed.), *Second handbook of research on teaching*. Chicago: Rand McNally and Co., 1973.

HEWETT, F. M., & TAYLOR, F. D. *The emotionally disturbed child in the classroom* (2nd ed.). Boston: Allyn and Bacon, 1980.

HEWETT, F. M., & WILDERSON, F. B. Developmentally backward and emotionally disturbed children. In J. J. Gallagher (Ed.), *Windows on Russia* (DHEW Publication #CE 74–0500 1). Washington, D.C., 1974.

HICKEY, K. A., IMBER, S. C., & RUGGIERO, E. A. Modifying reading behavior of elementary special needs children: A cooperative resource-parent program. *Journal of Learning Disabilities*, 1979, 12, 444–449.

HILL, D. S. A comparison of the performance of normal, learning disabled, and educable mentally retarded children on Cattell's ability constructs. *Journal of Learning Disabilities*, 1980, 13, 38–41.

HILLIARD, A. G., III. Cultural diversity and special education. *Exceptional Children*, 1980, 46, 584–588.

HILLIARD, L. T. *Mental Deficiency*. Boston: Little, Brown and Co., 1965.

HILTENBRAND, D., & NEWTON, S. Future progress—present changes: Work placement for the handicapped worker in the 1980s. *Journal for Vocational Special Needs Education*, 1980, 3, 9–11.

HINGTGEN, J. N., & BRYSON, C. Q. Recent developments in the study of early childhood psychoses: Infantile autism, childhood schizophrenia, and related disorders. *Schizophrenia Bulletin*, 1972, 5, 8–53.

HINSHELWOOD, J. *Congenital word blindness*. London: H. K. Lewis, 1917.

HIRSHOREN, A., & KAVALE, K., HURLEY, O. L., & HUNT, J. T. The reliability of the WISC-R performance scale with deaf children. *Psychology in the Schools*, 1977, 14, 412–415.

HOBBS, N. *The futures of children*. San Francisco: Jossey-Bass, 1975.

HOBSON, P. A., & DUNCAN, P. Sign learning and profoundly retarded people. *Mental Retardation*, 1979, 17, 33–37.

HODGES, W., & COOPER, M. Head start and follow through: Influences on intellectual development. *Journal of Special Education*, 1981, *15*, 221–238.

HOFFMAN, J. V. The disabled reader: Forgive us our regressions and lead us not into expectations. *Journal of Learning Disabilities*, 1980, *13*, 2–6.

HOFFMAN, S. P., ENGELHARDT, D. M., MARGOLIS, R. A., POLIZOS, P., WAIZER, J., & ROSENFELD, R. Responses to methylphenidate in low socioeconomic hyperactive children. *Archives of General Psychiatry*, 1974, *30*, 354–359.

HOFFNUNG, A. Judging cognition during language assessment. *Topics in Language Disorders*, 1981, *1*, 3.

HOLDEN, R. H. Prediction of mental retardation in infancy. *Mental Retardation*, 1972, *10*, 28–30.

HOLLAND, R. P. An analysis of the decision-making processes in special education. *Exceptional Children*, 1980, *46*, 551–554.

HOLLINGWORTH, L. S. *Children above 180 IQ, Stanford-Binet*. New York: World Book, 1942.

HOLT, J. *How children fail*. New York: Ditman Publishing, 1964.

HONZIK, M. P. Value and limitations of infant tests: An overview. In M. Lewis (Ed.), *Origins of intelligence: Infancy and early childhood*. New York: Plenum Publishing, 1976.

HOPPER, C., & WAMBOLD, C. Improving the independent play of severely mentally retarded children. *Education and Training of the Mentally Retarded*, 1978, *13*, 42–46.

HOPPER, G. Parental understanding of their child's test results as interpreted by elementary teachers. In I. J. Lehmann and W. Mehrene (Eds.), *Educational research: Reading in focus*. New York: Holt, Rinehart and Winston, 1979.

HOROWITZ, F., & PADEN, L. Effectiveness of environmental intervention programs. In B. Caldwell & H. Riciutti (Eds.), *Child development research (Vol. 3): Child development and social policy*. Chicago: University of Chicago Press, 1973.

HOWELL, K. W., KAPLAN, J. S., & O'CONNELL, C. *Evaluating exceptional children: A task analysis approach*. Columbus, Ohio: Charles E. Merrill Publishing Co., 1979.

HUBERTY, T. J., KROLLER, J. R., & TEN BRINK, T. D. Adaptive behavior in the definition of the mentally retarded. *Exceptional Children*, 1980, *46*, 256–261.

HUDSON, F. G., & GRAHAM, S. An approach to operationalizing the I.E.P. *Learning Disability Quarterly*, 1978, *1*, 13–32.

HUDSON, F., GRAHAM, S., & WARNER, M. Mainstreaming: An examination of the attitudes and needs of regular classroom teachers. *Learning Disability Quarterly*, 1979, *2*(3), 58–62.

HUDSON, M. Lesson areas for the trainable child. *Exceptional Children*, 1960, *27*, 224–229.

HUGHES, M. C., SMITH, R. B., & BENITZ, F. Travel training for exceptional children. *Teaching Exceptional Children*, 1977, *9*, 90–91.

HUMPHREYS, L., & STUBBS, J. Longitudinal analysis of teacher expectation, student expectation, and student achievement. *Journal of Educational Measurement*, 1977, *14*, 261–270.

HUNDERT, J. Some considerations of planning the integration of handicapped children into the mainstream. *Journal of Learning Disabilities*, 1982, *15*, 73–80.

HUNT, J. McV. *Intelligence and experience*. New York: Ronald Press, 1961.

HUNT, T. D. Early number "conservation" and experimenter expectancy. *Child Development*, 1975, *46*, 984–987.

HURLEY, R. *Poverty and mental retardation: A causal relationship*. New York: Vintage Books, 1969.

HUTT, M. L., & GIBBY, R. G. *The mentally retarded child development, education, and treatment* (3rd ed.). Boston: Allyn and Bacon, 1976.

HUTTON, W. O., TALKINGTON, L. W., & ALTMAN, R. Concomitants of multiple sensory defect. *Perceptual and Motor Skills*, 1973, *37*, 740–742.

IANO, R., AYERS, D., HELLER, H., McGETTIGAN, J., & WALKER, V. Sociometric status of retarded children in an integrative program. *Exceptional Children*, 1974, *40*, 267–271.

IDOL-MAESTAS, L., LLOYD, S., & LILLY, M. S. A noncategorical approach to direct service and teacher education. *Exceptional Children*, 1981, *48*, 213–220.

ILLINOIS BUREAU OF EMPLOYMENT SECURITY. *Illinois handicapped workers 1980*. Chicago: Publications and Project Development Section, March, 1980.

INHELDER, B., & PIAGET, J. *The early growth of logic in the child*. New York: Harper and Row, 1964.

ITO, H. R. Long-term effects of resource room programs on learning disabled children's reading. *Journal of Learning Disability*, 1980, *13*, 322–326.

JACKSON, A. M., FARLEY, G. K., ZIMET, S. G., & GOTTMAN, J. M. Optimizing the WISC-R test performance of low- and high-impulsive emotionally disturbed children. *Journal of Learning Disabilities*, 1979, *12*, 622–625.

JACOB, T. Family interaction in disturbed and normal families: A methodological and substantive review. *Psychological Bulletin*, 1975, *82*, 33–65.

JACOBS, J. W. Gleaning: Sheltered employment for retarded adults in rural areas. *Mental Retardation*, 1978, *16*, 118–122.

JAMES, G., & SWAIN, R. Learning bus routes using a tactual map. *New Outlook for the Blind*, 1975, *69*, 212–217.

JAN, J. E., FREEMAN, R. D., & SCOTT, E. P. *Visual impairment in children and adolescents*. New York: Grune and Stratton, 1977.

JANICKI, M. P., MAYECLA, T., & EPPLE, W. Availability of group homes for persons with mental retardation in the United States. *Mental Retardation*, 1983, *21*, 45–51.

JARVIK, L. F., SALZBERGER, R. M., & FALEK, A. Deaf persons of outstanding achievement. In J. D. Rainer, K. Z. Altschulter, & F. J. Kallmann (Eds.), *Family and mental health problems in a deaf population*. Springfield, Ill.: Charles C. Thomas, 1969.

JENKINS, E., & LOHR, F. E. Severe articulation disorders and motor ability. *Journal of Speech and Hearing Disorders*, 1964, *29*, 286–292.

JENKINS, J. R., DENO, S. L., & MIRKIN, P. K. Measuring pupil progress toward the least restrictive alternative. *Learning Disability Quarterly*, 1979, *2*, 81–91.

JENKINS, J. R., & PANY, D. Standardized achievement tests: How useful for special education? *Exceptional Children*, 1978, *44*, 448–453.

JENSEMA, C. J. A note on the achievement test scores of multiply handicapped hearing impaired children. *American Annals of the Deaf*, 1975, *120*, 37–39.

JENSEN, A. R. How much can we boost IQ and scholastic achievement? *Harvard Educational Review*, 1969, *39*, 1–123.

JENSEN, A. R. A theory of primary and secondary familial mental retardation. In N. R. Ellis (Ed.), *International review of research in mental retardation* (Vol. IV). New York: Academic Press, 1970.

JENSEN, A. R. *Genetics and education*. New York: Harper and Row, 1972.

JENSEN, A. R. *Bias in mental testing*. New York: The Free Press, 1980.

JOHNSON, A. B., & CARTWRIGHT, C. A. The roles of information and experience in improving teachers' knowledge and attitudes about mainstreaming. *Journal of Special Education*, 1979, *13*, 453–462.

JOHNSON, A. F. Retrospective study of the relationship between regular class integration of learning handicapped students and academic achievement of their nonhandicapped classmates. Los Angeles: UCLA Doctoral Dissertation, 1980.

JOHNSON, C. F., KOCH, R., PETERSON, R. M., & FRIEDMAN, E. G. Congenital and neurological abnormalities in infants with phyenylketonuria. *American Journal of Mental Deficiency*, 1978, *83*, 375–379.

JOHNSON, C. M. *Preparing handicapped students for work: Alternatives for secondary programming.* Reston, Va.: Council for Exceptional Children, 1980.

JOHNSON, D. W., & JOHNSON, R. T Integrating handicapped students into the mainstream. *Exceptional Children*, 1980, *47*, 90–98.

JOHNSON, J. L. An essay on incarcerated youth: An oppressed group. *Exceptional Children*, 1979, *45*, 566–571.

JOHNSON, K. L., & KOPP, C. B. *An analysis of tests for infants.* Los Angeles: UCLA Project for Research on Early Abilities of Children with Handicaps (REACH), 1981.

JOHNSON, O., & MYKLEBUST, H. R. *Learning disabilities: Educational principles and practices.* New York: Grune and Stratton, 1967.

JOHNSON, R. A. Models for alternative programming: A new perspective. In E. Meyers and G. Vergason (Eds.), *Alternatives for teaching exceptional children.* Denver: Love Publishing Co., 1975.

JOHNSON, R. K. The deaf. In R. E. Hardy & J. G. Cull (Eds.), *Severe disabilities: Social and rehabilitation approaches.* Springfield, Ill.: Charles C. Thomas, 1974.

JOHNSTON, B. C., & CORBETT, M. C. Orientation and mobility instruction for blind individuals functioning on a retarded level. *New Outlook for the Blind*, 1973, *67*, 27–31.

JOHNSTON, R. B., & MAGRAB, P. R. *Developmental disorders: Assessment, treatment, education.* Baltimore: University Park Press, 1976.

JOINER, L. M., & SABATINO, D. A. A policy study of P.L. 94–142. *Exceptional Children*, 1981, *48*, 24–33.

JONES, K. L., SMITH, D. W., ULLELAND, C. N., & STREISSGUTH, A. P. Patterns of malformation in offspring of chronic alcoholic mothers. *Lancet*, 1973, *2*, 1267–1271.

JONES, L. A., & MOE, R. College education for mentally retarded adults. *Mental retardation*, 1980, *18*, 59–62.

JONES, R. C., GOTTFRIED, N. W., & OWENS, A. The social distance of the exceptional: A study of the high school level. *Exceptional Children*, 1966, *32*, 551–556.

JONES, R. L. Labels and stigma in special education. *Exceptional Children*, 1972, *38*, 553–564.

JONES, R. L. Student views of special placement and their own special classes: A clarification. *Exceptional Children*, 1974, *41*, 22–29.

JONES, R. L., GOTTLIEB, J., GUSKIN, S., & YOSHIDA, R. K. Evaluating mainstreaming programs: Models, caveats, considerations, and guidelines. *Exceptional Children*, 1978, *44*, 518–601.

JONES, R. L. LAVINE, K., & SHELL, J. Blind children integrated in classrooms with sighted children: A sociometric study. *New Outlook for the Blind*, 1972, *66*, 75–80.

KAGAN, S., & CARLSON, H. Development of adaptive assertiveness in Mexican and United States children. *Developmental Psychology*, 1975, *11*, 71–78.

KAGAN, S., & ENDER, P. B. Maternal response to success and failure of Anglo-American, Mexican-American, and Mexican children. *Child Development*, 1975, *46*, 452–458.

KAHN, J. V. Moral and cognitive development of moderately retarded, mildly retarded, and nonretarded individuals. *American Journal of Mental Deficiency*, 1976, *81*, 209–214.

KAHN, J. V. Piaget's theory of cognitive development and its relationship to severely and profoundly retarded persons. In P. Mittler (Ed.), *Research to practice in mental retardation: Education and training* (Vol. II). Baltimore: University Park Press, 1977.

KAHN, M. S. Learning problems of the secondary and junior college learning disabled student: Suggested remedies. *Journal of Learning Disabilities*, 1980, *13*, 445–449.

KAMHI, A. G. Developmental vs. difference theories of mental retardation: A new look. *American Journal of Mental Deficiency*, 1981, *86*, 1–7.

KANNER, L. Itard, Seguin, Howe: Three pioneers in the education of retarded children. *American Journal of Mental Deficiency*, 1960, *65*, 2–10.

KANNER, L. Emotionally disturbed children: A historical review. *Child Development*, 1962, *33*, 97–102.

KANNER, L. *A history of the care and study of the mentally retarded*. Springfield, Ill.: Charles C. Thomas, 1964.

KARNES, M., & TESKA, J. Children's response to intervention programs. In J. Gallagher (Ed.), *The application of child development research to exceptional children*. Reston, Va.: Council for Exceptional Children, 1975.

KARNES, M., ZEHRBACK, R. R., STUDLEY, W. M., & WRIGHT, W. R. *Culturally disadvantaged children of higher potential: Intellectual functioning and educational implications*. Champaign, Ill.: Champaign Community Unit 4 Schools, 1965.

KARRER, R. (Ed.). *Developmental psychophysiology of mental retardation*. Springfield, Ill.: Charles C. Thomas, 1976.

KAUFFMAN, J. M. *Characteristics of children's behavior disorders*. Columbus, Ohio: Charles E. Merrill, 1977.

KAUFFMAN, J. M. Where special education for disturbed children is going: A personal view. *Exceptional Children*, 1980, *46*, 522–527.

KAUFMAN, A. S. The WISC-R and learning disabilities assessment: State of the art. *Journal of Learning Disabilities*, 1981, *14*, 520–526.

KAUFMAN, A. S., & KAUFMAN, N. *Kaufman assessment battery for children*. Circle Pines, Minnesota: American Guidance Service, 1983.

KAUFMAN, M. E., & ALBERTO, P. A. Research on efficacy of special education for the mentally retarded. In N. R. Ellis (Ed.), *International review of research in mental retardation* (Vol. 8). New York: Academic Press, 1977.

KAVALE, K. A. Learning disability and cultural-economic disadvantage: The case for relationship. *Learning Disability Quarterly*, 1980, *3*, 97–112.

KAVALE, K. Functions of the Illinois Test of Psycholinguistic Abilities (ITPA): Are they trainable? *Exceptional Children*, 1981, *47*, 496–510.

KAVALE, K. The efficacy of stimulant drug treatment for hyperactivity: A meta-analysis. *Journal of Learning Disabilities*, 1982a, *15*, 280–289.

KAVALE, K. Meta-analysis of the relationship between visual perceptual skills and reading achievement. *Journal of Learning Disabilities*, 1982b, *15*, 42–51.

KAVALE, K., & ANDREASSEN, E. Factors in diagnosing the learning disabled: Analysis of judgmental policies. *Journal of Learning Disabilities*, in press.

KAVALE, K., & FORNESS, S. Hyperactivity and diet treatment: A meta-analysis of the Feingold hypothesis. *Journal of Learning Disabilities*, 1983, *16*, 324–330.

KAVALE, K., & FORNESS, S. A meta-analysis assessing the validity of Wechsler Scale profiles and recategorizations: Patterns or parodies? *Learning Disability Quarterly*, in press.

KAVALE, K., & FORNESS, S. Learning disability: A victim of its own history. *Journal of Special Education*, in press.

KAVALE, K., & GLASS, G. Meta-analysis and the integration of research in special education. *Journal of Learning Disabilities*, 1981, *14*, 531–538.

KAVALE, K., & GLASS, G. The efficacy of special education interventions and practices: A compendium of meta-analysis findings. *Focus on Exceptional Children*, 1982, *15*, 1–14.

KAVALE, K., & MATTSON, P. "One jumped off the balance beam:" Meta-analysis of perceptual-motor training, *Journal of Learning Disabilities*, 1983, *16*, 165–173.

KAYE, N. L., & ASERLIND, R. The IEP: The ultimate process. *Journal of Special Education*, 1979, *13*, 137–143.

KAZIMOUR, K. K., & RESCHLY, D. J. Investigation of the norms and concurrent validity for the adaptive behavior inventory for children (ABIC). *American Journal of Mental Deficiency*, 1981, *85*, 512–520.

KEATING, L. E. Epilepsy and behavior disorder in school children. *Journal of Mental Science*, 1961, *107*, 161–180.

KEHLE, T. J., & GUIDUBALDI, J. Do too many cooks spoil the broth? Evaluation of team placement and individual educational plans on enhancing the social competence of handicapped students. *Journal of Learning Disabilities*, 1980, 13, 552–556.

KEISER, H., MONTAGUE, J., WOLD, D., MAUNE, S., & PATTISON, D. Hearing loss of Down Syndrome adults. *American Journal of Mental Deficiency*, 1981, 85, 467–472.

KELLER, H. A. *Teacher: Anne Sullivan Macy: A tribute by the foster-child of her mind.* Garden City, N.Y.: Doubleday and Co., 1955.

KENNEDY, R. J. R. The social adjustment of morons in a Connecticut city: Summary and conclusions, and abstract of a Connecticut community revisited: A study of social adjustment of a group of mental deficient adults in 1948 and 1960. In T. E. Jordan (Ed.), *Perspectives in mental retardation.* Carbondale, Ill.: Southern Illinois University Press, 1966.

KEOGH, B. K. Overview. In B. K. Keogh (Ed.), *Advances in special education*, Vol. 3: *Socialization influences on exceptionality.* Greenwich, Ct.: JAI Press, 1981.

KEOGH, B. K., & BECKER, L. D. Early detection of learning problems: Questions, cautions, and guidelines. *Exceptional Children*, 1973, *40*, 5–11.

KEOGH, B. K., & HALL, R. Wisc subtest patterns of educationally handicapped and educable mentally retarded pupils. *Psychology in the Schools*, 1974, *9*, 296–300.

KEOGH. B. K., & KOPP, C. B. From assessment to intervention: An elusive bridge. In F. Minafee and L. Lloyd (Eds.), *Communication and cognitive abilities: Early childhood assessment.* Baltimore: University Park Press, 1978.

KEOGH, B. K., & LEVITT, M. L. Special education in the mainstream: A confrontation of limitations? *Focus on Exceptional Children*, 1976, *8*, 1–11.

KEOGH, B. K., MAJOR, S. M., REID, H. P., GANDARA, P., & OMORI, H. Marker variables: A search for comparability and generalizability in the field of learning disabilities. *Learning Disability Quarterly*, 1978, *1*, 5–11.

KEOGH, B. K., & MARGOLIS, J. Learn to labor and to wait: Attentional problems of children with learning disabilities. *Journal of Learning Disabilities*, 1976, *9*, 276–286.

KEOGH, B. K., & PULLIS, M. Temperament influences on exceptionality: Basic constructs and theoretical orientations. In B. Keogh (Ed.), *Advances in special education* (Vol. I). Greenwich, Conn.: JAI Press, 1980.

KEOGH, B. K., TCHIR, C., & WINDEGUTH-BEHN, A. Teachers' perceptions of educationally high risk children. *Journal of Learning Disabilities*, 1974, *7*, 367–374.

KEPHART, J. G., KEPHART, C. P., & SCHWARTZ, G. C. A journey into the world of the blind child. *Exceptional Children*, 1974, *40*, 421–427.

KEPHART, N. C. *The slow learner in the classroom* (2nd ed.). Columbus, Ohio: Charles E. Merrill Publishing Co., 1971.

KIRK, D. A community prevalence study of mental retardation in New York state. *The Journal of Special Education*, 1978, *12*, 83–88.

KIRK, S. A. *Early education of the mentally retarded.* Urbana, Ill.: University of Illinois Press, 1958.

KIRK, S. A. *Educating exceptional children* (1st ed.). Boston: Houghton Mifflin, 1962.

KIRK, S. A. Research in education. In H. Stevens and R. Heber (Eds.), *Mental retardation: A review of research.* Chicago: University of Chicago Press, 1964.

KIRK, S. A. *Educating exceptional children* (2nd ed.). Boston: Houghton Mifflin Co., 1972.

KIRK, S. A., & GALLAGHER, J. J. *Educating exceptional children* (3rd ed.). Boston: Houghton Mifflin Co., 1979.

KIRK, S. A., & KIRK, W. D. *Psycholinguistic learning disabilities: Diagnosis and remediaton*. Urbana, Ill.: University of Illinois Press, 1971.

KIRK, S., McCARTHY, J., & KIRK, W. *Illinois Test of Psycholinguistic Abilities (rev. ed.), Examiners manual*. Urbana, Ill.: University of Illinois Press, 1968.

KIRTLEY, D. D. *The psychology of blindness*. Chicago: Nelson-Hall, 1975.

KITANO, M., & CHAN, K. S. Taking the role of retarded children: Effects of familiarity and similarity. *American Journal of Mental Deficiency*, 1978, *83*, 37–39.

KLEIN, N. K., & GREEN, B. B. Levels of political knowledge of mildly mentally retarded adults. *American Journal of Mental Deficiency*, 1979, *84*, 159–164.

KLEIN, N. K., & SAFFORD, P. L. Application or Piaget's theory to the study of thinking of the mentally retarded: A review of research. *Journal of Special Education*, 1977, *11*, 201–216.

KNIGHT, J. J. Building self-confidence in the multiply handicapped blind child. *New Outlook for the Blind*, 1971, *65*, 152–154.

KNIGHT, J. J. Mannerisms in the congenitally blind child. *New Outlook for the Blind*, 1972, *66*, 297–302.

KNOBLOCK, P. Psychological considerations of emotionally disturbed children. In W. M. Cruickshank (Ed.), *Psychology of exceptional children and youth* (4th ed.). Englewood Cliffs, N.J.: Prentice-Hall, 1980.

KNOFF, H. M. Effect of diagnostic information on special education placement decisions. *Exceptional Children*, 1983, *49*, 440–444.

KOCHANEK, T. T. Early detection programs for preschool handicapped children: Some procedural recommendations. *Journal of Special Education*, 1980, *14*, 347–353.

KOEGEL, P., & EDGERTON, R. B. Labeling and the perception of handicap among Black mildly mentally retarded adults. *American Journal of Mental Deficiency*, 1982, *87*, 266–276.

KOEGEL, R. L., & RINCOVER, A. Treatment of psychotic children in a classroom environment: 1. Learning in a large group. *Journal of Applied Behavior Analysis*, 1974, *7*, 45–49.

KOUNIN, J. S. Experimental studies of rigidity, I. The measurement of rigidity in normal and feeble-minded persons. *Character and Personality*, 1941a, *9*, 251–273.

KOUNIN, J. S. Experimental studies of rigidity. II. The explanatory power of the concept of rigidity as applied to feeblemindedness. *Character and Personality*, 1941b, *9*, 273–282. (b)

KRAGER, J. M., & SAFER, D. J. Type and prevalence of medication used in the treatment of hyperactive children. *New England Journal of Medicine*, 1974, *291*, 1118–1120.

KRASHEN, S. Formal and informal linguistic environments in language acquisition and language learning. *TESOL Quarterly*, 1976, *10*, 157–168.

KRIGER, S. F. *Life styles of aging retardates living in community settings in Ohio*. Columbus, Ohio: Psychologia Metrika, 1975.

KROTH, R. C. *Communicating with parents of exceptional children*. Denver: Love Publishing Co., 1975.

KROTH, R. C., & SIMPSON, R. L. *Parent conferences as a teaching strategy*. Denver: Love Publishing Co., 1977.

KROUSE, J., GERBER, M. M., & KAUFMAN, J. Peer tutoring: Procedures, promises, and unresolved issues. *Exceptional Education Quarterly*, 1981, *1*, 107–115.

KRUPSKI, A. Are retarded children more distractible? Observational analysis of retarded and nonretarded children's classroom behavior. *American Journal of Mental Deficiency*, 1979, *84*, 1–10.

KRUPSKI, A. An interactional approach to the study of attention problems in children with learning handicaps. *Exceptional Education Quarterly*, 1981, *2*, 1–11.

KUTNER, B., WILKINS, C., & YARROW, P. R. Verbal attitudes and overt behavior involving racial prejudice. *Journal of Abnormal and Social Psychology*, 1952, *47*, 649–652.

LACOSTE, R. Early intervention: Can it hurt? *Mental Retardation*, 1978, *16*, 266–268.

LAMBERT, N. M. Psychological evidence in Larry P. v. Wilson Riles. *American Psychologist*, 1981, *36*, 937–952.

LAMBERT, N. M., & NICHOLL, R. C. Dimensions of adaptive behavior of retarded and nonretarded public-school children. *American Journal of Mental Deficiency*, 1976, *81*, 135–146.

LANDAU, E. D., EPSTEIN, S. L., & STONE, A. P. *The exceptional child through literature*. Englewood Cliffs, N.J.: Prentice-Hall, 1978.

LANDESMAN-DWYER, S. Living in the community. *American Journal of Mental Deficiency*, 1981, *86*, 223–234.

LANDESMAN-DWYER, S., BERKSON, G., & ROMER, D. Affiliation and friendship of mentally retarded residents in group homes. *American Journal of Mental Deficiency*, 1979, *83*, 571–580.

LANGLEY, M. B. *The teachable moment and the handicapped infant*. Reston, Va.: Council for Exceptional Children ERIC Monograph, 1980.

LaPIERE, R. T. Attitudes versus actions. *Social Forces*, 1934, *14*, 230–237.

LARRIVEE, B. Effect of inservice training intensity on teacher's attitudes toward mainstreaming. *Exceptional Children*, 1981, *48*, 34–39.

LARRIVEE, B., & COOK, L. Mainstreaming: A study of the variables affecting teacher attitude. *Journal of Special Education*, 1979, *13*, 315–324.

LARSEN, S. C., & DESHLER, D. D. Limited role for learning disability specialist. *Learning Disability Quarterly*, 1978, *1*, 2–5.

LATHAM, G., & HOFMEISTER, A. A mediated training program for parents of the preschool mentally retarded. *Exceptional Children*, 1973, *39*, 472–473.

LATHAM, L. L. Construct and ecological validity of short-term memory measures in retarded persons. *American Journal of Mental Deficiency*, 1978, *83*, 145–155.

LATHEY, J. W. Assessing classroom environments and prioritizing goals for the severely retarded. *Exceptional Children*, 1978, *11*, 190–195.

LAUFER, M. W. Cerebral dysfunction and behavior disorders of adolescents. *American Journal of Orthopsychiatry*, 1962, *32*, 501–506.

LAUFER, M. W., & DENHOFF, E. Hyperkinetic behavior syndrome in children. *Journal of Pediatrics*, 1957, *50*, 463–474.

LAUS, M. D. Orientation and mobility instruction for the sighted trainable mentally retarded. *Education and Training of the Mentally Retarded*, 1974, *9*, 70–72.

LaVECK, B., & BREHM, S. S. Individual variability among children with Down's Syndrome. *Mental Retardation*, 1978, *16*, 135–137.

LAWRENCE, E. A., & WINSCHEL, J. F. Self-concept and the retarded: Research and issues. *Exceptional Children*, 1973, *39*, 310–319.

LAWRENCE, E. A., & WINSCHEL, J. F. Locus of control: Implications for special education. *Exceptional Children*, 1975, *41*, 483–490.

LAYCOCK, F. *Gifted children*. Glenview, Ill.: Scott, Foresman and Co., 1979.

LAYTON, L. L., & SHARIFI, H. Meaning and structure of Down's syndrome and nonretarded children's spontaneous speech. *American Journal of Mental Deficiency*, 1978, *83*, 439–445.

LEI, T. J., BUTLER, E. W., ROWITZ, L., & McALLISTER, R. J. Agency-labeled mentally retarded persons in a metropolitan area: An ecological study. *American Journal of Mental Deficiency*, 1974, *79*, 22–31.

LENNOX, W. G., & LENNOX, M. A. *Epilepsy and related disorders*. Boston: Little, Brown and Co., 1960.

LEONARD, J. 180 Day Barrier: Issues and concerns. *Exceptional Children*, 1981, *47*, 246–253.

LESSEN, E. I., & ROSE, T. L. State definitions of preschool handicapped populations. *Exceptional Children*, 1980, *46*, 467–469.

LEVIN, G., & SIMMONS, J. Response to praise by emotionally disturbed boys. *Psychological Reports*, 1962, *11*, 10.

LEVINE, E. S. Mental health clinic in New York. *Silent Worker*, 1956, *9*, 7.

LEVINE, H. G., & LANGNESS, L. Context ability, performance: Comparison of competitive athletics among mildly retarded and non-retarded adults. *American Journal of Mental Deficiency*, 1983, *87*, 528–538.

LEVISON, B. Understanding the child with school phobia. *Exceptional Children*, 1962, *38*, 393–397.

LEVITT, E., & COHEN, S. An analysis of selected parent-intervention programs for severely handicapped and disadvantaged children. *Journal of Special Education*, 1975, *9*, 345–365.

LEWANDOWSKI, L. J., & CRUICKSHANK, W. M. Psychological development of crippled children and youth. In W. M. Cruickshank (Ed.), *Psychology of exceptional children and youth* (4th ed.). Englewood Cliffs, N.J.: Prentice-Hall, 1980.

LEWIN, K. *A dynamic theory of personality: Selected papers*. Translated by A. K. Adams & K. E. Zener. New York: McGraw-Hill, 1936.

LEWIS, M. *Origins of intelligence: Infancy and early childhood*. New York: Plenum Publishing, 1976.

LEWIS, W. Continuity and interventions in emotional disturbance: A review. *Exceptional Children*, 1965, *31*, 465–475.

LEWITTER, F. I. *A genetic analysis of specific reading disability*. Master's thesis. University of Colorado, Department of Anthropology, Boulder, Colorado, 1975.

LI, A. K. Play and the mentally retarded child. *Mental Retardation*, 1981, *19*, 121–126.

LIBBEY, S. S., & PRONOVOST, W. Communication practices of mainstreamed hearing-impaired adolescents. *Volta Review*, 1980, *82*, 197–213.

LILLY, M. S. Evaluating individual educational programs. In S. Torres (Ed.), *A primer on individualized educational programs for handicapped children*. Reston, Va.: Foundation for Exceptional Children, 1977a.

LILLY, M. S. The merger of categories: Are we finally ready? *Journal of Learning Disabilities*, 1977b, *10*, 115–121.

LIPSCOMB, D. M. Ear damage from exposure to rock and roll music. *Archives of Otolaryngology*, 1969, *90*, 545–555.

LIPTON, H. L., & SVARSTAD, B. Sources of variation in clinicians' communication to parents about mental retardation. *American Journal of Mental Deficiency*, 1977, *82*, 155–161.

LITCHER, P. Communicating with parents: It begins with listening. *Teaching Exceptional Children*, 1976, *8*, 66–75.

LITROWNIK, A. J., FRANZINI, L. R., LIVINGSTON, M. K., & HARVEY, S. Development priority of identity conservation: Acceleration of identity and equivalence in normal and moderately retarded children. *Child Development*, 1978, *49*, 201–208.

LITROWNIK, A., FRANZINI, L., & TURNER, G. Acquisition of concepts by TMR children as a function of type of modeling, rule verbalization, and observer gender. *American Journal of Mental Deficiency*, 1976, *80*, 620–628.

LIVINGSTON, S. What the teacher can do for the student with epilepsy. *National Educational Association Journal*, 1966, *55*, 24–26.

LLOYD, L. L. Audiologic aspects of mental retardation. In N. R. Ellis (Ed.), *International review of research in mental retardation*. New York: Academic Press, 1970.

LLOYD, L. L. (Ed.). *Communication assessment and intervention strategies*. Baltimore: University Park Press, 1976.

LLOYD-BOSTOCK, S. Parents' experiences of official help and guidance in caring for a mentally handicapped child. *Child: Care, Health and Development*, 1976, *2*, 325–338.

LOMBARDI, T. Identifying children's abilities in classes for the mentally retarded. *Mental Retardation*, 1975, *13*, 3–6.

LOS ANGELES TIMES, Vol. XCV, December 25, 1975.

LOSEN, S. M., & DIAMENT, B. *Parent conferences in the schools*. Boston: Allyn and Bacon, 1978.

LOVAAS, O. I., & SIMMONS, J. Q. Manipulation of self-destruction in children. *Journal of Applied Behavior Analysis*, 1969, *2*, 143–157.

LOVITT, T. C., & CURTIS, K. A. Academic response rate as a function of teacher and self-imposed contingencies. *Journal of Applied Behavior Analysis*, 1969, *2*, 49–53.

LOWELL, E. L. *Personal communication*, 1981.

LOWENFELD, B. Meeting the needs of visually handicapped preschool children. *Sight-Saving Review*, 1950, *20*, 145–150.

LOWENFELD, B. Psychological problems of children with impaired vision. In W. M. Cruickshank (Ed.), *Psychology of exceptional children and youth*. Englewood Cliffs, N.J.: Prentice-Hall, 1971.

LOWENFELD, B. (Ed.). *The visually handicapped child in school*. New York: John Day Co., 1973.

LOWENFELD, B. Psychological problems of children with severely impaired vision. W. M. Cruickshank (Ed.), *Psychology of exceptional children and youth* (4th ed.). Englewood Cliffs, N.J.: Prentice-Hall, 1980.

LUBIN, R., JACOBSON, J. W., & KIELY, M. Projected impact of the functional definition of developmental disabilities: The categorically disabled population and service eligibility. *American Journal of Mental Deficiency*, 1982, *87*, 73–79.

LUETKE, B. Questionnaire results from Mexican-American parents of hearing impaired children in the United States. *American Annals of the Deaf*, 1976, *121*, 565–568.

LURIA, A. R. Psychological studies of mental deficiency in the Soviet Union. In N. Ellis (Ed.), *Handbook of mental deficiency*. New York: McGraw-Hill, 1963.

LUSTHAUS, C. S., LUSTHAUS, E. W., & GIBBS, H. Parents' role in the decision process. *Exceptional Children*, 1981, *48*, 256–257.

LUSTMAN, N., & ZIGLER, E. Imitation by institutionalized and noninstitutionalized mentally retarded and nonretarded children. *American Journal of Mental Deficiency*, 1982, *87*, 252–258.

LUSZKI, W. A. Intellectual functioning of spastic cerebral palsied. *Cerebral Palsy Journal*, 1966, *27*, 7–9.

LYNCH, K. Severely retarded master complex jobs. *Los Angeles Times*, October 22, 1978 (page 10).

LYNCH, K., KIERNAN, W. E., & STARK, J. A. (Eds.). *Prevocational and vocational education for special needs youth: A blueprint for the 1980's*. Baltimore: Paul Brookes Publishing, 1982.

LYON, H. Education of the gifted and talented. *Exceptional Children*, 1976, *43*, 166–168.

MacANDREW, C., & EDGERTON, R. On the possibility of friendship. *American Journal of Mental Deficiency*, 1966, *70*, 612–621.

McCARTHY, M. M. Minimum competency testing and handicapped students. *Exceptional Children*, 1980, *47*, 166–173.

McCARTY, B. M., & WORCHEL, P. Rate of motion and object perception in the blind. *New Outlook for the Blind*, 1954, *48*, 316–322.

McCARVER, R., & CRAIG, E. Placement of the retarded in the community: Prognosis and outcome. In N. Ellis (Ed.), *International review of research in mental retardation*. New York: Academic Press, 1974.

McCONNELL, F. Children with hearing disabilities. In L. M. Dunn (Ed.), *Exceptional children in the schools* (2nd ed.). New York: Holt, Rinehart and Winston, 1973.

McDEVITT, S. C., SMITH, P. M., SCHMIDT, D. W., & ROSEN, M. The deinstitutionalized citizen: Adjustment and quality of life. *Mental Retardation*, 1978, *16*, 22–24.

MacEACHRON, A. E. Mentally retarded offenders: Prevalence and characteristics. *American Journal of Mental Deficiency*, 1979, *84*, 165–176.

MacFARLANE, J., ALLEN. L., & HONZIK, M. *A developmental study of the behavior problems of normal children between 21 months and 14 years*. Berkeley: University of California Press, 1955.

McGHIE, A., & CHAPMAN, J. Disorders of attention and perception in early schizophrenia. *British Journal of Medical Psychology*, 1961, *34*, 103–116.

McGILLIVRAY, R. H. Differences in home backgrounds between high achieving and low achieving gifted children. A study of one hundred grade eight pupils in the City of Toronto Public School. *Ontario Journal of Educational Research*, 1964, *6*, 99–106.

McGUIRE, L. L., & MEYERS, C. E. Early personality in the congenitally blind child. *The New Outlook for the Blind*, 1971, *65*, 137–143.

McINNES, J. M., & TREFFREY, J. A. The deaf-blind child. In J. E. Jan, R. D. Freeman, & E. P. Scott (Eds.), *Visual impairment in children and adolescents*. New York: Grune and Stratton, 1977.

McKAY, H., SINISTERRA, L., McKAY, A., GOMEZ, H., & LLOREDA, P. Improving cognitive ability in chronically deprived children. *Science*, 1978, *200*, 270-278.

McKENZIE, H. S. Special education and consulting teachers. In F. Clark, D. Evans, & L. Hammerlynk (Eds.), *Implementing behavioral programs for schools*. Champaign, Ill.: Research Press Co., 1972.

McLEOD, J. Educational underachievement: Toward a defensible psychometric definition. *Journal of Learning Disabilities*, 1979, *12*, 322-330.

McLOUGHLIN, J. A., EDGE, D., & STRENECKY, B. Parent involvement: A consumer perspective—In the clinic. *Education and Training of the Mentally Retarded*, 1978, *13*, 427-429. (a)

McLOUGHLIN, J. A., EDGE, D., & STRENECKY, B. Perspective of parent involvement in the diagnosis and treatment of learning disabled children. *Journal of Learning Disabilities*, 1978, *11*, 291-296. (b)

McLOUGHLIN, J. A., & KASS, C. Resource teachers: Their role. *Learning Disability Quarterly*, 1978, *1*, 56-62.

McLOUGHLIN, J. A., McLOUGHLIN, R., & STEWART, W. Advocacy for parents of the handicapped: A professional responsibility and challenge. *Learning Disability Quarterly*, 1979, *2*, 51-57.

McMAHON, J. Extended school year programs. *Exceptional Children*, 1983, *46*, 457-460.

McMANIS, E. Marble sorting persistence in mixed verbal incentive and performance level pairings. *American Journal of Mental Deficiency*, 1967, *71*, 811-817.

MacMILLAN, D. L. Special education for the mentally retarded: Servant or Savant? *Focus on Exceptional Children*, 1971, *2*, 1-11. (a)

MacMILLAN, D. L. The problem of motivation in the education of the mentally retarded. *Exceptional Children*, 1971, *37*, 579-586. (b)

MacMILLAN, D. L. *Mental retardation in school and society*. (2nd ed.). Boston: Little, Brown and Co., 1983.

MacMILLAN, D. L., & BORTHWICK, S. The new educable mentally retarded population: Can they be mainstreamed? *Mental Retardation*, 1980, *18*, 155-158.

MacMILLAN, D. L., FORNESS, S., & TRUMBULL, B. The role of punishment in the classroom: Review and speculation. *Exceptional Children*, 1973, *40*, 85-96.

MacMILLAN, D. L., JONES, R., & ALOIA, G. The mentally retarded label: A theoretical analysis and review of research. *American Journal of Mental Deficiency*, 1974, *79*, 241-261.

MacMILLAN, D., JONES, R., & MEYERS, C. E. Mainstreaming the mentally retarded: Questions, cautions and guidelines. *Mental Retardation*, 1976, *14*, 3-10.

MacMILLAN, D. L., & KEOGH, B. K. Normal and retarded children's expectancy for failure. *Developmental Psychology*, 1971, *4*, 343-348.

MacMILLAN, D. L., & MEYERS, C. E. Larry P: An educational interpretation. *School Psychology Review*, 1980, *9*, 136-148.

MacMILLAN, D. L., MEYERS, C. E., & MORRISON, G. System identification of mildly mentally retarded children: Implications for interpreting and conducting research. *American Journal of Mental Deficiency*, 1980, *85*, 108-115.

MacMILLAN, D. L., & SEMMEL, M. I. Evaluation of mainstreaming programs. *Exceptional Children*, 1977, *9*, 1-14.

MacMILLAN, D. L., & TURNBULL, A. Parent involvement with special education: Respecting individual preferences. *Education and Training of the Mentally Retarded*, 1983, *18*, 4-9.

MACY, D. J., & CARTER, J. L. Comparison of a mainstream and self-contained special education program. *The Journal of Special Education*, 1978, *12*, 303-313.

MADSEN, M. C. Distribution of practice and level of intelligence. *Psychological Reports*, 1963, *13*, 39-42.

MADSEN, M. K. Parenting classes for the mentally retarded. *Mental Retardation*, 1979, *17*, 195-196.

MAGLIOCCA, L. A., & STEPHENS, T. M. Child identification or child inventory? A critique of the federal design of child-identification systems implemented under P.L. 94-142. *Journal of Special Education*, 1980, *14*, 23-36.

MAGUIRE, M. Failure effects on outerdirectedness: A failure to replicate. *American Journal of Mental Deficiency*, 1976, *81*, 256–259.

MAHER, C. A. Training special service teams to develop IEP's. *Exceptional Children*, 1980, *47*, 206–211.

MAHER, C. A., & BARBRACK, C. R. A framework for comprehensive evaluation of the Individualized Education Program (IEP). *Learning Disability Quarterly*, 1980, *3*, 49–55.

MAHONEY, G. J., & SEELY, P. The role of social agent on language acquisition: Implications for language intervention. In N. R. Ellis (Ed.), *International review of research in mental retardation* (Vol. 8). New York: Academic Press, 1976.

MAJOR, I. How do we accept the handicapped? *Elementary School Journal*, 1961, *61*, 328–330.

MALGADY, R. B., BARCHER, P. R., TOWNER, G., & DAVIS, J. Language factors in vocational evaluation of mentally retarded workers. *American Journal of Mental Deficiency*, 1979, *83*, 432–438.

MALONE, D. R., & CHRISTIAN, W. P., Jr. Adaptive behavior scale as a screening measure for special education placement. *American Journal of Mental Deficiency*, 1975, *79*, 367–371.

MANDLER, G., & HEINEMANN, S. H. Effect of overlearning of a verbal response on transfer of training. *Journal of Experimental Psychology*, 1956, *52*, 39–46.

MANDOLA, J. A theoretical approach to graphic aids for the blind. *International Journal for the Blind*, 1968, *18*, 22–24.

MANSFIELD, R. S., & BUSSE, T. *The psychology of creativity and discovery*. Chicago: Nelson-Hall, 1981.

MARDELL-CZUDNOWSKI, C. D. The four Ws of current testing practices: Who; what; why; and to whom—An exploratory survey. *Learning Disability Quarterly*, 1980, *3*, 73–83.

MARION, R. L. Leisure time activities for trainable mentally retarded adolescents. *Teaching Exceptional Children*, 1979, *11*, 158–160. (a)

MARION, R. L. Minority parent involvement in the IEP process: A systematic model approach. *Focus on Exceptional Children*, 1979, *10*, 1–15. (b)

MARION, R. L. Communicating with parents of culturally diverse exceptional children. *Exceptional Children*, 1980, *46*, 616–623.

MARLAND, S. *Education of the gifted and talented*. Reports to the subcommittee on Education, Committee on Labor and Public Welfare, U.S. Senate, Washington, D.C., 1972.

MARTIN, F. Is it necessary to retest children in special education classes? *Journal of Learning Disabilities*, 1979, *12*, 388–392.

MARTIN, J. E., RUSCH, F. R., & HEAL, L. W. Teaching community survival skills to mentally retarded adults: A review and analysis. *The Journal of Special Education*, 1982, *16*, 243–267.

MARTIN, P. Marital breakdown in families of patients with *spina bifida cystica*. *Developmental Medicine and Child Neurology*, 1975, *17*, 757–764.

MARTIN, R. Legal issues in assessment in special education. *Exceptional Education Quarterly*, 1980, *1*, 13–19.

MARTIN, W. E., & STENDLER, C. B. *Child behavior and development*. New York: Harcourt, Brace, and World, 1959.

MASLOW, A. H. Creativity in self-actualizing people. In H. Anderson (Ed.), *Creativity and its cultivation*. New York: Harper and Row, 1959.

MASON, J. M. Role of strategy in reading by mentally retarded persons. *American Journal of Mental Deficiency*, 1978, *82*, 467–473.

MEALOR, D. J., & RICHMOND, B. O. Adaptive behavior: Teachers and parents disagree. *Exceptional Children*, 1980, *46*, 386–393.

MEDNICK, B. R. Intellectual and behavioral functioning of ten-to-twelve-year-old children who showed certain transient symptoms in the neonatal period. *Child Development*, 1977, *48*, 844–853.

MEEHL, P. Schizotaxia, schizotypy, schizophrenia. In A. Buss (Ed.), *Theories of Schizophrenia*. New York: Atherton Press, 1969.

MEHLER, J., & BEVER, T. G. Cognitive capacity of very young children. *Science*, 1967, *158*, 141–142.

MEICHENBAUM, D., & ASARNOW, J. Cognitive-behavior modification and metacognitive development: Implications for the classroom. In P. Kendall & S. Hollon (Eds.), *Cognitive-behavioral interventions: Theory, research, and procedure*. New York: Academic Press, 1978.

MELINSKY, A. (Ed.). *Genetic disorders and the fetus*. New York: Plenum Publishing, 1979.

MELISH, M. E., & HANSHAW, J. B. Congenital cytomegalovirus infection: Developmental progress of infants detected by routine screening. *American Journal of Diseases of Children*, 1973, *126*, 190–194.

MELLSOP, G. W. Psychiatric patients seen as children and adults: Childhood predictors of adult illness. *Journal of Child Psychology and Psychiatry*, 1972, *13*, 91–101.

MENOLASCINO, F. J., & EGGER, M. L. *Medical dimensions of mental retardation*. Lincoln, Neb.: University of Nebraska Press, 1978.

MERCER, C. D., ALGOZZINE, B., & TRIFILETTI, J. Early identification—An analysis of the research. *Learning Disability Quarterly*, 1979, *2*, 12–24. (a)

MERCER, C. D., ALGOZZINE, B., & TRIFILETTI, J. Early identification: Issues and considerations. *Exceptional Children*, 1979, *46*, 52–54. (b)

MERCER, C. D., & SNELL, M. E. *Learning theory research in mental retardation: Implications for teaching*. Columbus, Ohio: Charles E. Merrill Publishing Co., 1977.

MERCER, J. The meaning of mental retardation. In R. Koch & J. Dobson (Eds.), *The mentally retarded child and his family*. New York: Brunner/Mazel, 1971.

MERCER, J. R. *Labeling the mentally retarded*. Berkeley: University of California Press, 1973. (a)

MERCER, J. R. The myth of 3% prevalence. *American Association on Mental Deficiency Monograph*, No. 1, 1973, 1–18. (b)

MERCER, J. R., & LEWIS, J. P. System of multicultural pluralistic assessment: Technical manual. Unpublished manuscript. University of California at Riverside, 1975.

MESSNER, S. A., & HAYNES, U. Cerebral palsy. In J. F. Garrett & E. S. Levine (Eds.), *Rehabilitation practices with the physically disabled*. New York: Columbia University Press, 1973.

MEYEN, E. L., & ALTMAN, R. Public school programming for the severely/profoundly handicapped: Some researchable problems. *Education and Training of the Mentally Retarded*, 1976, *11*, 40–45.

MEYEN, E. L., & CARR, D. L. A social attitude approach in sex education for educable mentally retarded. *Inservice Training Materials for Teachers of Educable Mentally Retarded*, Session III. Iowa State Department of Public Instruction, Special Ed Curriculum, 1967.

MEYEN, E. L., & LEHR, D. H. Evolving practices in assessment and intervention for mildly handicapped adolescents: The case for intensive instruction. *Exceptional Education Quarterly*, 1980, *1*, 19–26.

MEYEN, E. L., & MORAN, M. R. A perspective on the unserved mildly handicapped. *Exceptional Children*, 1979, *45*, 526–530.

MEYEROWITZ, J. H. Peer groups and special classes. *Mental Retardation*, 1967, *5*, 23–26.

MEYERS, C. E. *Quality of life in severely and profoundly mentally retarded people: Research foundation for improvement*. Washington, D.C.: American Association on Mental Deficiency Monograph, 1978.

MEYERS, C. E., MacMILLAN, D. L., & YOSHIDA, R. K. Validity of psychologists' identification of EMR students in the perspective of the California decertification experience. *Journal of School Psychology*, 1978, *16*, 3–15.

MEYERS, C. E., NIHIRA, K., & ZETLIN, A. The measurement of adaptive behavior. In N. R. Ellis, (Ed.), *Handbook of mental deficiency*. Lawrence Erlbaum Assoc., 1979.

MEYERS, C. E., SUNDSTROM, P. E., & YOSHIDA, R. K. The school psychologist and assessment in special education. *School Psychology Monographs*, 1974, *2*, 3–57.

MEYERS, C. E., SUNDSTROM, P. E., & YOSHIDA, R. K. Correlates of success in transition of MR to regular class (Final Report for U.S. Office of Education Grant –73–5263). Pomona, Calif.: Pacific State Hospital Research Group, 1975.

MEYERS, R. Retarded newlyweds seek new life. *The Washington Post*, No. 259, Section A, pp. 1 & 16, Sunday, August 21, 1977.

MEYERS, R. Attitudes of parents of institutionalized mentally retarded individuals towards deinstitutionalization. *American Journal of Mental Deficiency*, 1980, *85*, 184–187.

MICHAELIS, C. T. *Home and school partnerships in exceptional education.* Rockville, Md.: Aspen Publications, 1980.

MILISEN, R. Methods of evaluation and diagnosis of speech disorders. In L. E. Travis (Ed.), *Handbook of speech pathology.* New York: Appleton-Century-Crofts, 1957.

MILLER, D. R., & SWANSON, G. E. *Inner conflict and defense.* New York: Holt, Rinehart and Winston, 1960.

MILLER, L. B., & DYER, J. L. Four preschool programs: Their dimensions and effects. *Monographs of the Society for Research in Child Development*, 1975, *40*, (5–6, Serial No. 162).

MILLER, M. On the attempt to find WISC-R profiles for learning and reading disabilities (A response to Vance, Wallbrown, and Blaha). *Journal of Learning Disabilities*, 1980, *13*, 338–340.

MILLER, R. V. Social status and socio-empathic differences among mentally retarded children. *Exceptional Children*, 1956, *23*, 114–119.

MILLER, S. R., SABATINO, D. A., & LARSEN, R. P. Issues in the professional preparation of secondary school special educators. *Exceptional Children*, 1980, *46*, 344–350.

MILLER, T. L., & DAVIS, E. E. Can change in intelligence be measured by contemporary techniques. *Journal of Special Education*, 1981, *15*, 185–200.

MILLER, T. L., & SABATINO, D. A. An evaluation of the teacher consultant model as an approach to mainstreaming. *Exceptional Children*, 1978, *45*, 86–91.

MILLER, T. L., & SWITZKY, H. N. The least restrictive alternative: Implications for service providers. *Journal of Special Education*, 1978, *12*, 123–131.

MIMS, F. M. Sensory aids for blind persons. *New Outlook for the Blind*, 1973, *67*, 407–414.

MISKIMINS, R. W., & BAKER, B. R. Self-concept and the disadvantaged. *Journal of Community Psychology*, 1973, *1*, 347–361.

MOEN, M. G., & AANES, D. Eclipse of the family group home concept. *Mental Retardation*, 1979, *17*, 17–19.

MOLNAR, G. E. Analysis of motor disorder in retarded infants and young children. *American Journal of Mental Deficiency*, 1978, *83*, 213–222.

MONEY, J., & EHBARAT, A. A. *Man and woman, boy and girl.* Baltimore: Johns Hopkins University Press, 1972.

MONNIN, L. M., & HUNTINGTON, D. A. Relationship of articulatory defects to speech-sound identification. *Journal of Speech and Hearing Research*, 1974, *17*, 352–366.

MONSON, L. B., GREENSPAN, S., & SIMEONSSON, R. J. Correlates of social competence in retarded children. *American Journal of Mental Deficiency*, 1979, *83*, 627–630.

MONTESSORI, M. *The Montessori method.* New York: Schocken, 1964.

MONTGOMERY, J. R. Congenital Rubella—Baylor Study. Forty-ninth Biennial Conference, Association for Education of the Visually Handicapped. Pp. 1–7, 1979.

MOON, M. S., & RENZAGLIA, A. Physical fitness and the mentally retarded: A critical review of the literature. *The Journal of Special Education*, 1982, *16*, 269–287.

MOORE, B. C., & MOORE, S. M. *Mental retardation: Causes and prevention.* Columbus, Ohio: Charles E. Merrill Publishing Co., 1977.

MOORE, W. D., HAHN, W. G., & BRENTNALL, L. C. Academic achievement of gifted children: A comparative approach. *Exceptional Children*, 1978, *44*, 618–619.

MOORES, D. F. *Educating the deaf: Principles and practices.* Boston: Houghton Mifflin Co., 1978.

MORAN, M. R. *Assessment of the exceptional learner in the regular classroom*. Denver: Love Publishing, 1979.

MORGAN, D. P. *A primer on individualized education programs for exceptional children: Preferred strategies and practices* (2nd ed.). Reston, Va.: Foundation for Exceptional Children, 1981.

MORGAN, W. A case of congenital word-blindness. *British Medical Journal*, 1896, *2*, 1378-1379.

MORI, A. A. Career education for the learning disabled—Where are we now? Learning Disability Quarterly, 1980, *3*, 91-101.

MORRIS, G. A stimulating seminar for rural youth. *Journal of the National Association of Women Deans and Counselors*, 1957, *21*, 31-34.

MORRISON, F. J., GIORDANI, B., & NAGY, I. Reading disability: An information processing analysis. *Science*, 1977, *196*, 77-79.

MORRISON, G. M., Perspectives of social status of learning handicapped and nonhandicapped students. *American Journal of Mental Deficiency*, 1981, 86, 243-251.

MORRISON, G. M., FORNESS, S., & MacMILLAN, D. Influences on the sociometric ratings of mildly handicapped children: A path analysis. *Journal of Educational Psychology*, 1983, 75, 63-74.

MORSE, W. C. The crisis teacher. In N. Long, W. Morse, & R. Newman (Eds.), *Conflict in the classroom: The education of emotionally disturbed children* (2nd ed.). Belmont, Cal.: Wadsworth, 1976.

MORSE, W. C., CUTLER, R. L., & FINK, A. H. *Public school classes for the emotionally handicapped: A research analysis*. Washington, D.C.: The Council for Exceptional Children, 1964.

MORSE, W. C., & SMALL, E. Group life space interviewing in a therapeutic camp. *American Journal of Orthopsychiatry*, 1959, *29*, 27-44.

MULHERN, T., & BULLARD, K. In order to pass as mentally retarded: Behavioral features associated with mental retardation. *Mental Retardation*, 1978, *17*, 171-173.

MURPHY, A. T. Attitudes of education toward the visually handicapped. *The Sight-Saving Review*, 1960, *30*, 156-161.

MUTHARD, J. E., & HUTCHISON, J. H. Cerebral palsied college students. *Journal of School Health*, 1969, *39*, 317-321.

MYERS, P. I., & HAMMILL, D. D. *Learning Disabilities: Basic concepts, assessment practices, and instructional strategies*. Austin, Tex.: PRO-ED, 1982.

MYKLEBUST, H. R. Psychological and psychiatric implications of deafness. *Archives of Otolaryngology*, 1963, 78, 790-793.

MYKLEBUST, H. R. *The psychology of deafness*. New York: Grune and Stratton, 1964.

NAIMAN, N., FROHLICH, M., STERN, H. H., & TODESCO, A. *The good language learner* (Research in Education Series No. 7). Toronto: Modern Language Center, Ontario Institute for Studies in Education, 1978.

NAOR, M., & MILGRAM, R. M. Two preservice strategies for preparing regular class teachers for mainstreaming. *Exceptional Children*, 1980, 47, 126-129.

NASH, B. C., & McQUISTEN, J. Self-concepts of senior TMR students at a semi-integrated setting. *Mental Retardation*, 1977, *15*, 16-18.

NATIONAL ADVISORY COMMITTEE ON THE HANDICAPPED. *The unfinished revolution, education for the handicapped*. Washington, D.C.: U.S. Government Printing Office, 1976.

NATIONAL ADVISORY COUNCIL ON THE EDUCATION OF DISADVANTAGED CHILDREN. *Title I: Expanding Educational Growth*. Annual Report to the President and the Congress, 1975. Washington, D.C.: U.S. Government Printing Office, 1976.

NATIONAL INSTITUTE OF CHILD HEALTH AND HUMAN DEVELOPMENT. *Malnutrition, learning, and behavior*. Bethesda, Md.: Department of Health, Education and Welfare Publication No. (NIH) 76-1036, 1976.

NATIONAL SOCIETY FOR THE PREVENTION OF BLINDNESS. *Helping the partially seeing child in the regular classroom.* Publication No. P-3000. New York: National Society for the Prevention of Blindness, 1965.

NATIONAL/STATE LEADERSHIP TRAINING INSTITUTE ON THE GIFTED AND TALENTED. *Fact sheet.* Los Angeles: 316 West Second Street, October 1979.

NEER, W., FOSTER, D., JONES, J., & REYNOLDS, D. Sociometric bias in the diagnosis of mental retardation. *Exceptional Children*, 1973, *40*, 38–39.

NEIL, S. B. Clearing the air in career education. *American Education*, 1977, *13*, 6–9, 13.

NEILSEN, L. An in-service program for secondary learning disabilities teachers. *Journal of Learning Disabilities*, 1979, *12*, 423–427.

NEISWORTH, J. T., WILLOUGHBY-HERB, S. J., BAGNATO, S. J., CARTWRIGHT, C. A., & LAUB, K. W. *Individualized education for preschool exceptional children.* Gaithersburgh, Md.: Aspen, 1980.

NELSON, C. M. Personal communication, 1978.

NETTELBECK, T., & LALLY, M. Age, intelligence, and inspection time. *American Journal of Mental Deficiency*, 1979, *83*, 398–401.

NEUFELD, G. G. The bilingual's lexical store. *IRAL*, 1976, *14*, 15–35.

NEUGARTEN, B. L. Social class and friendship among school children. *American Journal of Sociology*, 1946, *51*, 305–313.

NEWLAND, T. E. *The gifted in socioeducational perspective.* Englewood Cliffs, N.J.: Prentice-Hall, 1976.

NEWLAND, T. E. Psychological assessment of exceptional children and youth. In W. M. Cruickshank (Ed.), *Psychology of exceptional children and youth* (4th ed.). Englewood Cliffs, N.J.: Prentice-Hall, 1980.

NEWMAN, J. Psychological problems of children and youth with chronic medical disorders. In W. M. Cruickshank (Ed.), *Psychology of exceptional children and youth* (3rd ed.). Englewood Cliffs, N.J.: Prentice-Hall, 1971.

NEWMAN, J. Faculty attitudes toward handicapped students. *Rehabilitation Literature*, 1976, *37*, 194–197.

NEWMAN, J. Psychological problems of children and youth with chronic medical disorders. In W. M. Cruickshank (Ed.), *Psychology of exceptional children and youth* (4th ed.). Englewood Cliffs, N.J.: Prentice-Hall, 1980.

NEYHUS, A. I., & NEYHUS, M. Relationship of parents and teachers in the identification of children with suspected learning disabilities. *Journal of Learning Disabilities*, 1979, *12*, 379–383.

NICHOLS, W. H. Blind persons in data processing: The attitude of industry. *The New Outlook for the Blind*, 1970, *64*, 293–296.

NIETUPSKI, J., WILLIAMS, W., & YORK, R. Teaching selected phonic word analysis reading skills to TMR labeled students. *Teaching Exceptional Children*, 1979, *11*, 140–143.

NIHIRA, K. Dimensions of adaptive behavior in institutionalized mentally retarded children and adults: Developmental perspective. *American Journal of Mental Deficiency*, 1976, *81*, 215–226.

NIHIRA, K. Development of adaptive behavior in the mentally retarded. In P. Mittlen (Ed.), *Research to practice in mental retardation education and training* (Vol. II). Baltimore: University Park Press, 1977.

NIHIRA, K., FOSTER, R., SHELLHAAS, M., & LELAND, H. *Adaptive behavior scale manual.* Washington, D.C.: American Association on Mental Deficiency, 1969.

NIHIRA, K., FOSTER, R., SHELLHAAS, M., & LELAND, H. *AAMD adaptive behavior scale, 1974 revision.* Washington, D.C.: American Association of Mental Deficiency, 1974.

NIHIRA, K., MINK, I. T., & MEYERS, C. E. Relationship between home environment and school adjustment of TMR children. *American Journal of Mental Deficiency*, 1981, *86*, 7–15.

OAKLAND, T. Nonbiased assessment of minority group children. *Exceptional Education Quarterly*, 1980, *1*, 31–46.

O'CONNER, W. A., & STACHOWIAK, J. G. Patterns of interaction in families with low adjusted, high adjusted and mentally retarded members. *Family Process*, 1971, *10*, 229–241.

O'CONNOR, P. D., STUCK, G. B., & WYNNE, M. D. Effects of a short-term intervention resource-room program on task orientation and achievement. *Journal of Special Education*, 1979, *13*, 375–385.

O'CONNOR, R. D. Relative efficacy of modeling, shaping, and the combined procedures for modification of social withdrawal. *Journal of Abnormal Psychology*, 1972, *79*, 327–334.

ODEN, S. L., & ASHER, S. R. *Coaching children in social skills for friendship-making*. Paper presented at the biennial meeting of the Society for Research in Children Development at Denver, Colorado, 1975.

ODOM, S. L., JENKINS, J. R., SPEITZ, M. L., & DeKLYEN, M. Promoting social integration of young children at risk for learning disabilities. *Learning Disability Quarterly*, 1982, *5*, 379–387.

O'LEARY, R. D., & DRABMAN, R. Token reinforcement programs in the classroom: A review. *Psychological Bulletin*, 1971, *75*, 379–398.

O'LEARY, R. D., KAUFMAN, K. F., KASS, R. E., & DRABMAN, R. S. Effects of loud and soft reprimands on the behavior of disruptive students. *Exceptional Children*, 1970, *37*, 145–155.

OLLEY, J. G., & RAMEY, G. Voter participation of retarded citizens in the 1976 presidential election. *Mental Retardation*, 1978, *16*, 255–258.

O'MALLEY, J. E., & EISENBERG, L. The hyperkinetic syndrome. *Seminars in Psychiatry*, 1973, *5*, 95–103.

OPPENHEIM, A. N. *Questionnaire design and attitude measurement*. New York: Basic Books, 1966.

ORNITZ, E. M., & RITVO, D. Perceptual inconstancy in early infantile autism. *Archives of General Psychiatry*, 1968, *18*, 76–98.

ORTON, L. D., McKAY, E., & RAINY, D. The effect of method of instruction on retention and transfer for different levels of ability. *School Review*, 1964, *72*, 451–461.

OSBORNE, A. G., Jr. Voting practices of the mentally retarded. *Mental Retardation*, 1975, *13*, 15–17.

PAGE, E. B. Tests and decisions for the handicapped: A guide to evaluation under the new laws. *Journal of Special Education*, 1980, *14*, 423–483.

PAGE, E. B., & GRANDON, G. M. Massive intervention and child intelligence: The Milwaukee Project in critical perspective. *Journal of Special Education*, 1981, *15*, 239–256.

PALMER, D. J. Regular-classroom teachers' attributions and instructional prescriptions for handicapped and nonhandicapped pupils. *Journal of Special Education*, 1979, *13*, 324–337.

PALMER, D. J. An attributional perspective on labeling. *Exceptional Children*, 1983, *49*, 423–429.

PARMELEE, A. H., & HABER, A. Who is the "risk infant?" *Clinical Obstetrics and Gynecology*, 1973, *16*, 376–387.

PARMELEE, A. H., KOPP, C., & SIGMAN, M. Selection of developmental assessment techniques for infants at risk. *Merrill-Palmer Quarterly*, 1976, *22*, 178–199.

PASSOW, A. H. Early childhood and compensatory education. In A. H. Passow (Ed.), *Reaching the disadvantaged learners*. New York: Teachers College Press, 1970.

PASSOW, A. H. Urban education in the 1970s. In A. H. Passow (Ed.), *Opening opportunities for disadvantaged learners*. New York: Teachers College Press, 1972.

PASSOW, A. H. The nature of giftedness and talent. *Gifted Child Quarterly*, 1981, *19*, 5–10.

PATRICK, J. L., & RESCHLY, D. J. Relationship of state educational criteria and demographic variables to school-system prevalence of mental retardation. *American Journal of Mental Deficiency*, 1982, *86*, 351–360.

PAUL, J. L. (Ed.). *Understanding and working with parents of children with special needs*. New York: Holt, Rinehart and Winston, 1981.

PAULSTON, C. B. (Ed.). Research. In Center for Applied Linguistics, *Bilingual education: Current perspectives* (Vol. 2: Linguistics). Arlington, Va.: Center for Applied Linguistics, 1977.

PAYNE, J. S. The gifted. In N.H. Haring (Ed.), *Behavior of exceptional children: An introduction to special education*. Columbus, Ohio: Charles E. Merrill Publishing Co., 1974.

PAYNE, J. S., KAUFFMAN, J. M., BROWN, G. B., & DeMOTT, R. M. *Exceptional children in focus*. Columbus, Ohio: Charles E. Merrill Publishing Co., 1974.

PAYNE, J. S., POLLOWAY, E. A., SMITH, J. E., Jr., & PAYNE, R. A. *Strategies for teaching the mentally retarded.* Columbus, Ohio: Charles E. Merrill Publishing Co., 1977.

PECK, C. A., APPOLONI, T., COOKE, T. P., & RAVER, S. A. Teaching retarded preschoolers to imitate the free-play behavior of nonretarded classmates: trained and generalized effects. *Journal of Special Education*, 1978, *12*, 195-207.

PECK, J. R., & STEPHENS, W. B. *Success of young adult male retardates.* (Cooperative Research Project 1533). Austin: University of Texas, 1964.

PEGNATO, C. W., & BIRCH, J. W. Locating gifted children in junior high school. *Exceptional Children*, 1959, *25*, 300-304.

PELONE, A. J. *Helping the visually handicapped child in a regular class.* New York: Bureau of Publications, Teachers College Press, 1957.

PERKINS, S. A. Malnutrition and mental development. *Exceptional Children*, 1977, *43*, 214-220.

PERKINS, W. N. *Speech pathology* (2nd ed.). St. Louis: C. V. Mosby Co., 1977.

PERSKE, R., & PERSKE, M. Sexual development. In R. Perske & M. Perske (Eds.), *New directions for parents of persons who are retarded.* Nashville: Abington Press, 1973.

PETERSON, C. P. Retention of MR children in a community school program: Behaviors and teacher ratings as predictors. *Mental Retardation*, 1977, *15*, 46-49.

PETERSON, D. R. Behavior problems of middle childhood. *Journal of Consulting Psychology*, 1961, *25*, 205-209.

PETERSON, G. Factors related to the attitudes of nonretarded children toward their EMR peers. *American Journal of Mental Deficiency*, 1974, *79*, 412-416.

PETERSON, N., & HARALICK, J. Integration of handicapped and nonhandicapped preschoolers: An analysis of play and social interaction. *Education and Training of the Mentally Retarded*, 1977, *12*, 235-245.

PETERSON, R. L., ZABEL, R., SMITH, C., & WHITE, M. Cascade of services model and emotionally disturbed student. *Exceptional Children*, 1983, *49*, 404-408.

PETERSON, W. Children with specific learning disabilities. In N. G. Haring & R. L. Schiefelbusch (Eds.), *Methods in special education.* New York: McGraw-Hill, 1967.

PHILIPS, I., & WILLIAMS, N. Psychopathology and mental retardation: A study of 100 mentally retarded children. *American Journal of Psychiatry*, 1975, *132*, 1265-1271.

PIERCE, J. W., & BOWMAN, P. Motivation patterns of superior high school students. In *The gifted student*, (Cooperative Research Monograph No. 2). Washington, D.C.: U.S. Office of Education, Government Printing Office, 1960.

PINTNER, E. M., EISENSON, J., & STANTON, M. *The psychology of the physically handicapped.* New York: Appleton-Century-Crofts, 1945.

PLESS, I. B., & DOUGLAS, J. W. Chronic illness in childhood. I. Epidemiological and clinical characteristics. *Pediatrics*, 1971, *47*, 405-414.

PLESS, I. B., & ROGHMANN, K. J. Chronic illness and its consequences: Observations based on three epidemiologic surveys. *The Journal of Pediatrics*, 1971, *79*, 351-359.

PLOWMAN, P., & RICE, J. *California Project Talent.* Final Report. Sacramento: California State Department of Education, 1967.

POLIFKA, J. C. Compliance with Public Law 94-142 and consumer satisfaction. *Exceptional Children*, 1981, *48*, 250-253.

POPLIN, M. J. The science of curriculum development applied to special education and the IEP. *Focus on Exceptional Children*, 1979, *12*, 1-16.

POPLIN, M., & GRAY, R. A conceptual framework for assessment of curriculum and student progress. *Exceptional Education Quarterly*, 1980, *1*, 75-86.

POPLIN, M. S., & LARSEN, S. C. Current status of learning disability specialists. *Learning Disability Quarterly*, 1979, *2*, 2-7.

PORGES, S. W., & HUMPHREY, M. M. Cardiac and respiratory responses during visual search in nonretarded children and retarded adolescents. *American Journal of Mental Deficiency*, 1977, *82*, 162-169.

PORTER, R. B., & MILAZZO, T. C. A comparison of mentally retarded adults who attended a special class with those who attended regular school classes. *Exceptional Children*, 1958, *24*, 410–412.

PORTEUS, S. D. *Porteus Maze Test: Fifty years' application*. Palo Alto, Calif.: Pacific Books, 1965.

POSTMAN, L. Retention as a function of degree of overlearning. *Science*, 1962, *135*, 666–667.

PREHM, H. Special education research: Retrospect and prospect. *Exceptional Children*, 1976, *43*, 10–19.

PREHM, H. J., & McDONALD, J. E. The yet to be served—A perspective. *Exceptional Children*, 1979, *45*, 502–507.

PREMACK, D. Toward empirical behavior laws: Position reinforcement. *Psychological Review*, 1959, *66*, 219–233.

PRESIDENT'S COMMITTEE ON MENTAL RETARDATION. *Report to the president: A proposed program for national action to combat mental retardation*. Washington, D.C.: U.S. Government Printing Office, October 1962.

PRESIDENT'S COMMITTEE ON MENTAL RETARDATION. *The six-hour retarded child*. Washington, D.C.: U.S. Government Printing Office, 1970.

PRESIDENT'S COMMITTEE ON MENTAL RETARDATION. *Changing patterns in residential services for the mentally retarded*. Washington, D.C.: U.S. Government Printing Office, 1976.

PRESIDENT'S COMMITTEE ON MENTAL RETARDATION. *Mental retardation, the leading edge: Service programs that work*. Washington, D.C.: U.S. Government Printing Office, 1978.

PRICE, M., & GOODMAN, L. Individualized education programs: A cost study. *Exceptional Children*, 1980, *46*, 446–454.

PRILLAMAN, D. Acceptance of learning disabled students in the mainstream environment: A failure to replicate. *Journal of Learning Disabilities*, 1981, *14*, 344–346.

PRINGLE, M. L. *Able misfits: A study of educational and behavior difficulties of 103 very intelligent children (IQs 120–200)*. London: Longmans, 1970.

PRINS, D. Personality, stuttering severity, and age. *Journal of Speech and Hearing Research*, 1972, *15*, 148–154.

PRIOR, M. R., & CHEN, C. C. Learning set acquisition in autistic children. *Journal of Abnormal Psychology*, 1975, *84*, 701–708.

PRITCHARD, D. G. *Education and the handicapped: 1760–1960*. London: Routledge and Kegan Paul, 1963.

PROJECT HEAD START. *The status of handicapped children in Head Start Programs*. Washington, D.C.: Administration for Children, Youth and Families, HEW, 1980.

PRONOVOST, W., BATES, J., CLASBY, E., MILLER, N. E., MILLER, N. J., & THOMPSON, R. Hearing impaired children with associated disabilities. *Exceptional Children*, 1976, *42*, 439–443.

PUESCHEL, S. M., & MURPHY, A. Assessment of counseling practices at the birth of a child with Down's syndrome. *American Journal of Mental Deficiency*, 1976, *81*, 325–330.

PULLIAM, J. D. *History of Education in America*. Columbus, Ohio: Charles E. Merrill, 1968.

PULLIN, D. Mandated minimum competency testing: Its impact on handicapped adolescents. *Exceptional Education Quarterly*, 1980, *1*, 107–115.

QUAY, H. C. Some basic considerations in the education of emotionally disturbed children. *Exceptional Children*, 1963, *30*, 27–31.

QUAY, H. C. Dimensions of problem behavior and educational programming. In P. S. Graubard (Ed.), *Children against schools*. Chicago: Follett Publishing, 1969.

QUAY, H. C., GLAVIN, J. P., ANNESLEY, F. R., & WERRY, J. S. The modification of problem behavior and academic achievement in a resource room. *Journal of School Psychology*, 1972, *10*, 187–197.

QUAY, H. C., MORSE, W. C., & CUTLER, R. L. Personality patterns of pupils in special classes for the emotionally disturbed. *Exceptional Children*, 1966, *33*, 297–301.

QUAY, H. C., & PETERSON, D. R. Manual for the behavior problem checklist. Unpublished manuscript, 1975.

QUINN, J. M. Do animals have belly buttons? *Child Today*, 1976, *5*, 2–9.

QUINONES, W. A. A test battery for assessing the vocational competency of moderately mentally retarded persons. *Mental Retardation*, 1978, *16*, 412–415.

RAGO, W. V., Jr. Eye gaze and dominance hierarchy in profoundly mentally retarded males. *American Journal of Mental Deficiency*, 1977, *82*, 145–148. (a)

RAGO, W. V., Jr. Identifying profoundly mentally retarded subtypes as a means of institutional grouping. *American Journal of Mental Deficiency*, 1977, *81*, 470–473. (b)

RAGO, W. V., Jr., & CLELAND, C. C. Future directions in the education of the profoundly retarded. *Education and Training of the Mentally Retarded*, 1978, *13*, 184–186.

RAGO, W. V., Jr., PARKER, R. M., & CLELAND, C. C. Effect of increased space on the social behavior of institutionalized profoundly retarded male adults. *American Journal of Mental Deficiency*, 1978, *82*, 554–558.

RAISER, L., & VAN NAGEL, C. The loophole in Public Law 94–142. *Exceptional Children*, 1980, *46*, 516–520.

RAMEY, C., & CAMPBELL, F. Compensatory education for disadvantaged children. *School Review*, 1979, *87*, 171–189. (a)

RAMEY, C., & CAMPBELL, F. Early childhood education for psychosocially disadvantaged children. *American Journal of Mental Deficiency*, 1979, *83*, 645–648. (b)

RAMEY, C. T., STEDMAN, D. J., BORDERS-PATTERSON, A., & MENGEL, W. Predicting school failure from information available at birth. *American Journal of Mental Deficiency*, 1978, *82*, 525–534.

RAPIER, J., ADELSON, R., CAREY, R., & CROKE, K. Changes in children's attitudes toward the physically handicapped. *Exceptional Children*, 1972, *39*, 219–223.

RAPPAPORT, S. R. In *Proceedings of the 1965 Pathway School Institute*. Narberth, Pa.: Livingston Publishing Co., 1966.

RARICK, G. L., DOBBINS, D. A., & BRODHEAD, G. D. *The motor domain and its correlates in educationally handicapped children*. Englewood Cliffs, N.J.: Prentice-Hall, 1976.

RASKE, D. E. The role of general school administrators responsible for special education programs. *Exceptional Children*, 1979, *45*, 645–646.

RAUTH, M. What can be expected of the regular education teacher? Ideals and realities. *Exceptional Education Quarterly*, 1981, *2*, 27–36.

RAWSON, M. B. *Developmental language disability: Adult accomplishments of dyslexic boys*. Baltimore: Johns Hopkins University Press, 1968.

RAZEGHI, J. A., & DAVIS, S. Federal mandates for the handicapped: Vocational education opportunity and employment. *Exceptional Children*, 1979, *45*, 353–359.

REDL, F. Strategy and techniques of the life space interview. *American Journal of Orthopsychiatry*, 1959, *29*, 1–8.

REDNER, R. Others' perceptions of mothers of handicapped children. *American Journal of Mental Deficiency*, 1980, *85*, 176–183.

REICH, C., HAMBLETON, D., & HOULDIN, J. The integration of hearing impaired children in regular classrooms. *American Annals of the Deaf*, 1977, *122*, 534–543.

REICHARD, C. L., SPENCER, J., & SPOONER, F. The mentally retarded defendant-offender. *Journal of Special Education*, 1980, *14*, 113–119.

REID, D. K., & HRESKO, W. P. Thinking about thinking about it in that way: Test data and instruction. *Exceptional Education Quarterly*, 1980, *1*, 47–57.

REIRICH, S. R., & ROTHROCK, I. A. Behavior problems of deaf children and adolescents: A factor-analytic study. *Journal of Speech and Hearing Research*, 1972, *15*, 93–100.

REITER, S., & LEVI, A. M. Leisure activities of mentally retarded adults. *American Journal of Mental Deficiency*, 1981, *86*, 201–203.

RENZULLI, J. S. Will the gifted child movement be alive and well in 1990? *Gifted Child Quarterly*, 1980, *24*, 3–9.

RENZULLI, J. S., & SMITH, L. H. The approaches to identification of gifted students. *Exceptional Children*, 1977, *43*, 512–518.

RESCHLY, D. J. Evaluation of the effects of SOMPA measures on classification of students as mildly mentally retarded. *American Journal of Mental Deficiency*, 1981, 86, 16–30.

RESCHLY, D. J., & LAMPRECHT, M. J. Expectancy effects of labels: Fact or artifact? *Exceptional Children*, 1979, *46*, 55–58.

RESEARCH FOR BETTER SCHOOLS. *Clarification of PL 94–142 for the classroom teacher.* Philadelphia, Pa.: Research for Better Schools, 1978.

RESNICK, R. Creative movement classes for visually handicapped children in a public school setting. *New Outlook for the Blind*, 1973, *67*, 442–447.

REYNOLDS, W. M., & REYNOLDS, S. Prevalence of speech and hearing impairments of noninstitutionalized mentally retarded adults. *American Journal of Mental Deficiency*, 1979, *84*, 62–66.

RIBNER, S. The effects of special class placement on the self-concept of exceptional children. *Journal of Learning Disabilities*, 1978, *11*, 319–323.

RICH, J. Teacher expectations and pupil performance: A review of research on the Pygmalion effect (Manuscript 1491). *Catalog of Selected Documents in Psychology*, May 1977, 7, 52–53.

RICHARDSON, S. A. Careers of mentally retarded young persons: Services, jobs, and interpersonal relations. *American Journal of Mental Deficiency*, 1978, *82*, 349–358.

RICHARDSON, S. A., KOLLER, H., KATZ, M., & McLAREN, J. A functional classification of seizures and its distribution in a mentally retarded population. *American Journal of Mental Deficiency*, 1981, 85, 457–466.

RICHEY, D. D., MILLER, M., & LESSMAN, J. Resource and regular classroom behavior of learning disabled students. *Journal of Learning Disabilities*, 1981, *14*, 163–166.

RICHMAN, C. L., ADAMS, K. A., NIDA, S. A., & RICHMAN, J. Performance of mix-matched nonretarded and retarded children on discrimination learning and transfer-shift tasks. *American Journal of Mental Deficiency*, 1978, *83*, 262–269.

RIE, H. E., RIE, E. D., STEWART, S., & AMBUEL, J. P. Effects of Ritalin on underachieving children: A replication. *American Journal of Orthopsychiatry*, 1976, *46*, 313–322.

RIEKES, L., SPIEGEL, S., & KEILITZ, I. Law-related education for mentally retarded students. *Mental Retardation*, 1977, *15*, 7–9.

RIES, P. *Additional handicapping conditions among hearing impaired students; United States: 1971.* Annual Survey of Hearing Impaired Children and Youth. Washington, D.C.: Gallaudet College Office of Demographic Studies, Ser. D., No. 14, 1973.

RIMLAND, B. Psychogenesis versus biogenesis: The issues and the evidence. In S. Plot & R. Edgerton (Eds.), *Changing perspectives in mental illness.* New York: Holt, Rinehart and Winston, 1969.

RINCOVER, A., & KOEGEL, R. L. Setting generality and stimulus control in autistic children. *Journal of Applied Behavior Analysis*, 1975, *8*, 235–246.

RINGLABEN, R. P., & PRICE, J. R. Regular classroom teachers' perceptions of mainstreaming effects. *Exceptional Children*, 1981, *47*, 302–304.

RITVO, E. R., ORNITZ, E. M., TANGUAY, P., & LEE, J. C. *Neurophysiologic and biochemical abnormalities in infantile autism and childhood schizophrenia.* Paper presented at the meeting of the American Orthopsychiatric Association, San Francisco, March 1970.

RIVERS, L. W., HENDERSON, D. M., JONES, R. L., LADNER, J. A., & WILLIAMS, R. L. Mosaic of labels for black children. In N. Hobbs (Ed.), *Issues in the classification of children* (Vol. 2). San Francisco: Jossey-Bass, 1975.

ROBINAULT, I. P. *Sex, society, and the disabled: A developmental inquiry into roles, reactions, and responsibilities.* New York: Harper and Row, 1978.

ROBINS, L. N. *Deviant children grow up.* Baltimore: The Williams and Wilkens Co., 1966.

ROBINSON, H. B., & ROBINSON, N. M. *The mentally retarded child* (2nd ed.). New York: McGraw-Hill, 1976.

ROBISON, H. F. Early childhood education for the disadvantaged: What research says. In A. H. Passow (Ed.), *Opening opportunities for disadvantaged learners*. New York: Teachers College Press, 1972.

ROBSON, D. L. Administering educational services for the handicapped: Role expectations and perceptions. *Exceptional Children*, 1981, *47*, 377–378.

ROCKOWITZ, R. J., & DAVIDSON, P. W. Discussing diagnostic findings with parents. *Journal of Learning Disabilities*, 1979, *12*, 2–7.

ROGERS, C. R. Toward a theory of creativity. In H. Anderson (Ed.), *Creativity and its cultivation*. New York: Harper and Row, 1959.

ROGOW, S. Perceptual organization in blind children. *New Outlook for the Blind*, 1975, *69*, 226–233.

ROHR, A., & BURR, D. B. Etiological differences in patterns of psycholinguistic development of children of IQ of 30 to 60. *American Journal of Mental Deficiency*, 1978, *6*, 549–553.

ROLF, J. E., & HARIG, P. T. Etiological research in schizophrenia and the rationale for primary intervention. *American Journal of Orthopsychiatry*, 1974, *44*, 538–554.

ROOS, S. The future of residential services for the mentally retarded in the United States: A Delphi study. *Mental Retardation*, 1978, *16*, 355–356.

ROSENBLITH, J. F. Prognostic value of neonatal behavior tests. In B. Z. Friedlander, G. M. Sterritt, & G. F. Kirk (Eds.), *Exceptional infant*. New York: Brunner/Mazel, 1975.

ROSENTHAL, D. (Ed.). *The Genain quadruplets: A case study and theoretical analysis of heredity and environment in schizophrenia*. New York: Basic Books, 1963.

ROSENTHAL, R., & JACOBSON, L. *Pygmalion in the classroom: Teacher expectations and pupils' intellectual development*. New York: Holt, Rinehart and Winston, 1968.

ROSENZWEIG, M. R. Neural bases of intelligence and training. *Journal of Special Education*, 1981, *15*, 105–123.

ROSS, A. O. Family problems. In R. M. Smith & J. T. Neisworth (Eds.), *The exceptional child: A functional approach*. New York: McGraw-Hill, 1975.

ROSS, D. M., & ROSS, S. A. Cognitive training for the EMR child: Language skills prerequisite to relevant-irrelevant discrimination tasks. *Mental Retardation*, 1979, *17*, 3–7.

ROSS, E. C. Developing public policy for persons with disabilities: The case for a categorical approach. *Mental Retardation*, 1980, *18*, 159–163.

ROSS, R. T., & BOROSKIN, A. Are IQ's below 30 meaningful? *Mental Retardation*, 1972, *10*, 24–25.

ROTHENBERG, J. J., LEHMAN, L. B., & HACKMAN, J. D. An individualized learning disabilities program in the regular classroom. *Journal of Learning Disabilities*, 1979, *12*, 496–499.

ROTTER, J. B. Some problems and misconceptions related to the construct of internal versus external control of reinforcement. *Journal of Consulting and Clinical Psychology*, 1975, *43*, 56–67.

ROWITZ, L. A sociological perspective on labeling in mental retardation. *Mental Retardation*, 1981, *19*, 47–51.

RUBIN, E. Z., SIMSON, C. B., & BETWEE, M. C. *Emotionally handicapped children and the elementary school*. Detroit: Wayne State University Press, 1966.

RUBIN, R. A., KRUS, R., & BALOW, B. Factors in special class placement. *Exceptional Children*, 1973, *39*, 452–457.

RUSSELL, A., & FORNESS, S. Behavioral disturbance in mentally retarded children in TMR and EMR classrooms. *American Journal of Mental Deficiency*, in press.

RUSSELL, A. T., & TANGUAY, P. E. Mental illness and mental retardation: Cause or coincidence? *American Journal of Mental Deficiency*, 1981, *85*, 570–574.

RUSSELL, W. K., QUIGLEY, S., & POWER, D. Linguistics and deaf children. *Transformational syntax and its applications*. Washington, D.C.: Volta Bureau, 1976.

RUTTER, M. Psychiatry. In J. Wortis (Ed.), *Mental retardation: An annual Review* (Vol. 3). New York: Grune and Stratton, 1970.

RUTTER, M. Normal psychosexual development. In S. Chess & A. Thomas (Eds.), *Annual progress in child psychiatry and child development*. New York: Brunner/Mazel, 1972.

RUTTER, M. Prevalence and types of dyslexia. In A. L. Benton & D. Pearl (Eds.), *Dyslexia: An appraisal of current knowledge*. New York: Oxford University Press, 1978.

RUTTER, M. Maternal deprivation, 1972–1978: New findings, new concepts, new approaches. *Child Development*, 1979, *50*, 283–305.

RUTTER, M., MAUGHAM, B., MORTIMORE, P., OUSTON, J., & SMITH, A. *Fifteen thousand hours: Secondary schools and their effects on children*. Cambridge, Mass.: Harvard University Press, 1979.

RYDER, V. A decent program in science for gifted elementary pupils. *Exceptional Children*, 1972, *38*, 629–631.

RYNDERS, J., & HORROBIN, J. Project EDGE: University of Minnesota's communication stimulation program for Down's syndrome infants. In B. Friedlander (Ed.), *Exceptional infant* (Vol. 3). New York: Brunner/Mazel, 1975.

RYNDERS, J. E., SPIKER, D., & HORROBIN, J. M. Underestimating the educability of Down's syndrome children: Examination of methodological problems in recent literature. *American Journal of Mental Deficiency*, 1978, *82*, 440–448.

RYOR, J. PL 94–142—The perspective of regular education. *Learning Disability Quarterly*, 1978, *1*, 6–14.

SABATINO, D. A. An evaluation of resource rooms for children with learning disabilities. *Journal of Learning Disabilities*, 1971, *4*, 27–35.

SABATINO, D. A. Are appropriate educational programs operationally achievable under mandated promises of PL 94–142? *Journal of Special Education*, 1981, *51*, 9–23.

SABATINO, D. A., & MILLER, T. L. (Eds.). *Describing learner characteristics of handicapped children and youth*. New York: Grune and Stratton, 1979.

SABATINO, D. A., MILLER, P. F., & SCHMIDT, C. Can intelligence be altered through cognitive training? *Journal of Special Education*, 1981, *15*, 125–144.

SACHS, B. B. Psychological assessment of the deaf person. *Mental Health in Deafness*, 1977, *1*, 93–95.

SAENGER, G. *The adjustment of severely retarded adults in the community*. Albany, N.Y.: Interdepartmental Health Resources Board, 1957.

SAFER, D. J., & ALLEN, R. P. *Hyperactive children: Diagnosis and management*. Baltimore: University Park Press, 1976.

SAFER, D. J., ALLEN, R., & BARR, E. Depression of growth in hyperactive children on stimulant drugs. *New England Journal of Medicine*, 1972, *287*, 217–220.

SAFER, N. D. Implications of minimum competency standards and testing for handicapped students. *Exceptional Children*, 1980, *46*, 288–290.

SAFER, N. D., MORRISSEY, P. A., KAUFMAN, M. J., & LEWIS, L. Implementation of IEPs: New teacher roles and requisite support systems. *Focus on Exceptional Children*, 1978, *10*, 1–20.

SAILOR, W., & WILCOX, B. (Eds.). *Methods of instructions for serving handicapped students*. Baltimore: Paul Brookes, 1981.

SALETT, S., & HENDERSON, A. *The education for all handicapped children act: Are parents involved?* Columbia, Md.: National Committee for Citizens in Education, 1980.

SALISBURY, L. H. Cross-cultural communication and dramatic ritual. In L. Thayer (Ed.), *Communication: Concepts and Perspectives*. Washington, D.C.: Spartan-Macmillan, 1967.

SALKEVER, D. Children's health problems: Implications for parental labor supply and earnings. In V. Fuchs (Ed.), *Economic Aspects of Health*. Chicago: University of Chicago Press, 1982.

SAMEROFF, A. J., & CHANDLER, J. J. Reproductive risk and the continuum of care-taking casualty. In F. D. Horowitz, M. Hetherington, S. Scarr-Salapatek, & G. Siegel (Eds.), *Review of child development research* (Vol. 4). Chicago: University Press, 1975.

SAMUELS, S. J., & EDWALL, G. The role of attention in reading with implications for the learning disabled student. *Journal of Learning Disabilities*, 1981, *14*, 353–361.

SANDERS, D. A. Psychological implications of hearing impairment. In W. M. Cruickshank (Ed.), *Psychology of exceptional children and youth* (4th ed.). Englewood Cliffs, N.J.: Prentice-Hall, 1980.

SARASON, S. B., & DORIS, J. *Psychological problems in mental deficiency* (4th ed.). New York: Harper & Row, 1969.

SARGENT, L. R. Resource teacher time utilization: An observational study. *Exceptional Children*, 1981, *47*, 420–425.

SATTLER, J. M. *Assessment of children's intelligence*. Philadelphia: W. B. Saunders, 1974.

SAUNDERS, M. K., & SULTANA, Q. Professionals' knowledge of educational due process rights. *Exceptional Children*, 1980, *46*, 559–561.

SCANLON, C. A., ARICK, J., & PHELPS, N. Participant in the development of the IEP: Parents perspective. *Exceptional Children*, 1981, *47*, 373–374.

SCARR-SALAPATEK, S., & WILLIAMS, M. L. The effects of early stimulation on low-birth-weight infants. *Child Development*, 1973, *44*, 99–101.

SCHACHTER, M., RICE, J. A., CORMIER, H. G., CHRISTENSEN, P. M., & JAMES, N. J. A process for individual program planning based on the adaptive behavior scale. *Mental Retardation*, 1978, *16*, 259–263.

SCHAIN, R. J., & REYNARD, C. L. Observations on effects of a central stimulant drug (methylphenidate) in children with hyperactive behavior. *Pediatrics*, 1975, *55*, 709–716.

SCHEERENBERGER, R. C. Public residential services, 1981: Status and trends. *Mental Retardation*, 1982, *20*, 210–215.

SCHEERENBERGER, R. C. *A history of mental retardation*. Baltimore, Md.: Paul H. Brookes Publishing Co., 1983.

SCHEERENBERGER, R. C., & FELSENTHAL, D. Community settings for MR persons: Satisfaction and activities. *Mental Retardation*, 1977, *15*, 3–7.

SCHENCK, S. J. The diagnostic/instructional link in Individualized Education Programs. *Journal of Special Education*, 1980, *14*, 337–345.

SCHENCK, S. J. Analysis of IEP's for LD youngsters. *Journal of Learning Disabilities*, 1981, *14*, 221–223.

SCHILIT, J. The mentally retarded offender and criminal justice personnel. *Exceptional Children*, 1979, *46*, 16–23.

SCHLAEGEL, T. F. The dominant method of imagery in blind as compared to sighted adolescents. *Journal of Genetic Psychology*, 1953, *83*, 265–277.

SCHLESINGER, H. S., & MEADOW, K. P. Development of maturity in deaf children. *Exceptional Children*, 1972, *38*, 461–467.

SCHOENBAUM, R. M., & ZINOBER, J. W. Learning and memory in mental retardation: The defect-developmental distinction re-evaluation. In I. Bialer & M. Sternlicht (Eds.), *The psychology of mental retardation: Issues and approaches*. New York: Psychological Dimensions, 1977.

SCHOLL, G. T. The education of children with visual impairments. In W. M. Cruickshank & G. O. Johnson (Eds.), *Education of exceptional children and youth*. Englewood Cliffs, N.J.: Prentice-Hall, 1956.

SCHOLL, G. T. The education of children with visual impairments. In W. M. Cruickshank & G. O. Johnson (Eds.), *Education of exceptional children and youth*. Englewood Cliffs, N.J.: Prentice-Hall, 1967.

SCHOLL, G. T. The education of children with visual impairments. In W. M. Cruickshank & G. O. Johnson (Eds.), *Education of exceptional children and youth* (3rd ed.). Englewood Cliffs, N.J.: Prentice-Hall, 1975.

SCHONELL, F. E. *Educating spastic children*. London: Oliver and Boyd, 1956.

SCHONELL, F. J., & WATTS, B. H. A first survey of the effects of a subnormal child on the family unit. *American Journal of Mental Deficiency*, 1956, *61*, 210–219.

SCHOPLER, E., & BRISTOL, M. M. *Autistic children in public school*. Reston, Va.: Council for Exceptional Children ERIC Monograph, 1980.

SCHREINER, J. Prediction of retarded adults' work performance through components of general ability. *American Journal of Mental Deficiency*, 1978, *83*, 77–79.

SCHULTZ, B., & SCHROEDER, E. N. Outdoor laboratory experiences for older children. In J. B. Bergeson & G. S. Miller (Eds.), *Learning activities for disadvantaged children*. New York: Macmillan, 1971.

SCHWIRIAN, P. M. Effects of the presence of a hearing-impaired preschool child in the family on behavior patterns of older "normal" siblings. *American Annals of the Deaf*, 1976, *121*, 373–380.

SCHWORM, R. W. Hyperkinesis: Myth, mystery, and matter. *The Journal of Special Education*, 1982, *16*, 129–148.

SCOTT, K. G. Learning theory, intelligence, and mental development. *American Journal of Mental Deficiency*, 1978, *82*, 325–336.

SEAGOE, M. V. *Terman and the gifted*. Los Altos, Calif.: W. Kaufman, 1975.

SEARS, P. S., & BARBEE, A. H. Career and life satisfactions among Terman's gifted women. In J. Stanley, W. George, & C. Solano (Eds.), *The gifted and the creative*. Baltimore: Johns Hopkins University Press, 1977.

SEARS, R. R. Sources of life satisfactions of the Terman gifted men. *American Psychologist*, 1977, *32*(2), 119–128.

SEGAL, R. Trends in services for the aged mentally retarded. *Mental Retardation*, 1977, *15*, 25–27.

SELLIN, D. F. *Mental retardation nature, needs, and advocacy*. Boston: Allyn and Bacon, 1979.

SELLS, C. J., & BENNETT, F. C. Prevention of mental retardation: The role of medicine. *American Journal of Mental Deficiency*, 1977, *82*, 117–129.

SEMMEL, M., GOTTLIEB, J., & ROBINSON, N. Mainstreaming: Perspectives on educating handicapped children in the public school. In D. Berliner (Ed.), *Review of research in education* (Vol. 7). Washington, D.C.: American Educational Research Association, 1979.

SENF, G. M. Future research needs in learning disabilities. In R. P. Anderson & C. G. Halcomb (Eds.), *Learning disabilities/minimal brain dysfunction syndrome: Research perspectives and application*. Springfield, Ill.: Charles C. Thomas, 1976.

SERVICE, J. Glamour on wheels. *Rehabilitation Gazette*, 1971, *14*, 9–10.

SHAPERO, S., & FORBES, C. B. A review of involvement programs for parents of learning disabled children. *Journal of Learning Disabilities*, 1981, *14*, 499–504.

SHATTUCK, R. *The forbidden experiment: The story of the wild boy of Aveyron*. New York: McGraw-Hill, 1980.

SHEARE, J. B. Social acceptance of EMR adolescents in integrated programs. *American Journal of Mental Deficiency*, 1974, *78*(6), 678–682.

SHEEHAN, J. G. Conflict theory of stuttering. In J. Eisenson (Ed.), *Stuttering: A symposium*. New York: Harper and Row, 1958.

SHEEHAN, J. G., & MARTYN, M. M. Stuttering and its disappearance. *Journal of Speech and Hearing Research*, 1970, *13*, 279–289.

SHEPARD, L. An evaluation of the regression discrepancy method for identifying children with learning disabilities. *Journal of Special Education*, 1980, *14*, 79–91.

SHERE, M. O. Socio-emotional factors in families of the twin with cerebral palsy. *Exceptional Children*, 1956, *22*, 197–199, 206–208.

SHORES, R. E., & HAUBRICH, P. A. Effect of cubicles in educating emotionally disturbed children. *Exceptional Children*, 1969, *36*, 31–34

SHOTEL, J. R., IANO, R. P., & McGETTIGAN, J. F. Teacher attitudes associated with the integration of handicapped children. *Exceptional Children*, 1972, *38*, 677–683.

SHUEY, A. M. *The testing of Negro intelligence* (2nd ed.). New York: Social Science Press, 1966.

SHUSHAN, R. D. *Assessment and reduction of deficits in the physical appearance of mentally retarded people*. Doctoral dissertation, University of California, Los Angeles, 1974. University Microfilm, Library Services, Xerox Corp., Ann Arbor, Michigan 48106.

SIGELMAN, C., ATER, C., & SPANHEL, C. Sex-role stereotypes and the homemaking participation of mentally retarded people. *Mental Retardation*, 1978, *16*, 357–358.

SIGELMAN, C., BUDD, E., SPANHEL, C., & SCHOENROCK, C. When in doubt, say yes: Acquiescence in interviews with mentally retarded persons. *Mental Retardation*, 1981, *19*, 53–58.

SIGMAN, M., COHEN, S., & FORSYTHE, A. The relation of early infant measures to later development. In S. Friedman & M. Sigman (Eds.), *Preterm birth and psychological development*. San Francisco: Academic Press, 1981.

SIGMAN, M., & PARMELEE, A. Longitudinal evaluation of the high-risk infant. In T. Field, S. Sostak, S. Goldberg, & H. Shuman (Eds.), *Infants born at risk*. New York: Spectrum, 1979.

SILBERBERG, N. E., IVERSEN, I. A., & GOINS, J. T. Which remedial method works best? *Journal of Learning Disabilities*, 1973, *6*, 547–555.

SILVA, R. M., & FAFLAK, P. From institution to community—A new process? *Mental Retardation*, 1976, *14*, 25–28.

SILVERMAN, S. R., & LANE, H. S. Deaf children. In H. Davis & S. R. Silverman (Eds.), *Hearing and deafness* (3rd ed.). New York: Holt, Rinehart and Winston, 1970.

SIMMONS, J. Q., & BALTAXE, C. Language patterns of adolescent autistics. *Journal of Autism and Childhood Schizophrenia*, 1975, *5*, 333–351.

SIMON, E. P., & GILLMAN, A. E. Mainstreaming visually handicapped preschoolers. *Exceptional Children*, 1979, *45*, 463–464.

SIMPSON, G. G. *The meaning of evolution*. New Haven, Conn.: Yale University Press, 1950.

SIMPSON, H. M., & MEANEY, C. Effects of learning to ski on the self concept of mentally retarded children. *American Journal of Mental Deficiency*, 1979, *84*, 25–29.

SIMPSON, R. L. Modifying the attitudes of regular class students toward the handicapped. *Focus on Exceptional Children*, 1980, *13*, 1–11.

SINCLAIR, E. Relationship of psychoeducational diagnosis to educational placement. *Journal of School Psychology*, 1980, *18*, 349–353.

SINCLAIR, E., & KHEIFETS, L. Use of clustering techniques in deriving psycho-educational profiles. *Contemporary Educational Psychology*, 1982, *7*, 81–89.

SINDELAR, P. T., & DENO, S. L. The effectiveness of resource programming. *Journal of Special Education*, 1978, *12*, 17–28.

SINDELAR, P. T., MEISEL, C. J., BUY, M. J., & KLEIN, E. S. Differences in cognitive functioning of retarded children and retarded autistic children: A response to Ahmad Baker. *Exceptional Children*, 1981, *47*, 406–411.

SINGER, J. H. Evaluating program placement in an institution for the mentally retarded: A multivariate approach. *Journal of Special Education*, 1978, *12*, 133–142.

SINGER, J. L., & STEINER, B. F. Imaginative content in the dreams and fantasy play of blind and sighted children. *Perceptual and Motor Skills*, 1966, *22*, 475–482.

SIPERSTEIN, G. N., BUDOFF, M., & BAK, J. Effects of the labels "mentally retarded" and "retard" on the social acceptability of mentally retarded children. *American Journal of Mental Deficiency*, 1980, *84*, 596–601.

SIPERSTEIN, G. N., & GOTTLIEB, J. Physical stigma and academic performance as factors affecting first impressions of handicapped children. *American Journal of Mental Deficiency*, 1977, *81*, 455–462.

SISK, D. Issues and future directions in gifted education. *Gifted Childs Quarterly*, 1980, *1*, 29–32.

SITKEI, E. G. After group home living—what alternatives? Results of a two-year mobility follow-up study. *Mental Retardation*, 1980, *18*, 9–13.

SITLINGTON, P. L. Vocational and special education in career programming for the mildly handicapped adolescent. *Exceptional Children*, 1981, *47*, 592–598.

SKEELS, H. H. Adult status of individuals who experienced early intervention: A follow-up report. *Monographs of the Society for Research in Child Development*, 1966, *31*, (Serial No. 105).

SKINNER, B. F. Teaching: The arrangement of contingencies under which something is taught. In N. G. Haring & H. Hayden (Eds.), *Improvement of instruction*. Seattle, WA.: Special Child Publications, 1972.

SKLARSKY, S., & BAXTER, M. R. Science study with a community accent. *Elementary School Journal*, 1961, *61*, 301–307.

SKUTNABB-KANGAS, T., & TUOKOMAA, P. *Teaching migrant children's mother-tongue and learning the language of the host country in the context of the sociocultural situation of the migrant family.* Helsinki: The Finnish National Commission for UNESCO, 1976.

SLINGERLAND, B. H. *Preventive teaching programs in the classroom: A general educational responsibility* (Bulletin, Reprint #50). Towson, Md.: Orton Society, 1972.

SLOMAN, L., & WEBSTER, C. D. Assessing the parents of the learning disabled child: A semistructured interview procedure. *Journal of Learning Disabilities*, 1978, *11*, 73–79.

SMART, R., WILTON, K., & KEELING, B. Teacher factors and special class placement. *Journal of Special Education*, 1980, *14*, 217–229.

SMITH, C. R., & KNOFF, H. M. School psychology and special education students' placement decisions: IQ still tips the scale. *Journal of Special Education*, 1981, *15*, 55–64.

SMITH, D. W., & WILSON, A. A. *The child with Down's syndrome (Mongolism)*. Philadelphia: W. B. Saunders, 1973.

SMITH, I. L. Statistical realities of special class distributions. *American Journal of Mental Deficiency*, 1974, *78*, 740–447.

SMITH, I. L., & GREENBERG, S. Teacher attitudes and the labeling process. *Exceptional Children*, 1975, *41*, 319–324.

SMITH, J. D. Down's syndrome, amniocentesis, and abortion: Prevention or elimination? *Mental Retardation*, 1981, *19*, 8–11.

SMITH, J. D., & JENKINS, D. S. Minimum competency testing and handicapped students. *Exceptional Children*, 1980, *46*, 441–443.

SMITH, M. D., COLEMAN, J. M., DOKECKI, P. R., & DAVIS, E. E. Intellectual characteristics of school-labeled learning disabled children. *Exceptional Children*, 1977, *43*, 352–357. (a)

SMITH, M. D., COLEMAN, J. M., DOKECKI, P. R., & DAVIS, E. E. Recategorizing WISC-R scores of learning disabled children. *Journal of Learning Disabilities*, 1977, *10*, 437–443. (b)

SMITH, M. L., & GLASS, G. V. Meta-analysis of research on class size and its relationship to attitudes and instruction. *American Educational Research Journal*, 1980, *17*, 419–433.

SMITH, R. M. *Clinical teaching: Methods of instruction for the retarded*. New York: McGraw-Hill, 1968.

SMITH, R. M. *Clinical teaching: Methods of instruction for the retarded* (2nd ed.). New York: McGraw-Hill, 1974.

SMITH, T. E. C. Status of due process hearings. *Exceptional Children*, 1981, *48*, 232–236.

SNELL, M. E. (Ed.). *Systematic instruction of the moderately and severely handicapped*. Columbus, Ohio: Charles E. Merrill Publishing Co., 1978.

SOEFFING, M. Y. New assessment techniques for mentally retarded and culturally different children: A conversation with Jane R. Mercer. *Education and Training of the Mentally Retarded*, 1975, *10*, 110–116.

SOLOWAY, M. M. *Development and evaluation of a special education inservice training program for regular classroom teachers* (Tech. Rep. SERP 1974-A8). Los Angeles: University of California, 1974.

SOMMERS, D., McGREGOR, G., LESH, E., & REED, S. A rapid method for describing the efficacy of early intervention programs for developmentally disabled children. *Mental Retardation*, 1980, *18*, 275–378.

SOMMERS, V. S. *The influence of parental attitudes and social environment on the personality development of adolescent blind.* New York: American Foundation for the Blind, 1944.

SONTAG, E. (Ed.). *Educational programming for the severely and profoundly handicapped.* Reston, Va.: Council for Exceptional Children, 1977.

SONTAG, E., CERTO, N., & BUTTON, J. E. On a distinction between the education of the severely and profoundly handicapped and a doctrine of limitations. *Exceptional Children*, 1979, *45*, 604–616.

SONTAG, E., SMITH, J., & SAILOR, W. The severely/profoundly handicapped: Who are they? Where are they? *Journal of Special Education*, 1977, *11*, 5–11.

SONTAG, L. W., BAKER, C. T., & NELSON, V. L. *Mental growth and personality development: A longitudinal study* (Society for Research in Child Development, Inc., Vol. 23, Serial No. 68, No. 2). Lafayette, Ind.: Purdue University Press, 1958.

SPACHE, G. D. *Diagnosing and correcting reading disabilities.* Boston: Allyn and Bacon, 1981.

SPARKS, R., & RICHARDSON, S. O. Multicategorical/cross categorical classrooms for learning disabled students. *Journal of Learning Disabilities*, 1981, *14*, 60–61.

SPEARMAN, C. *The abilities of man.* New York: Macmillan, 1927.

SPICKER, H. M. Intellectual development through early childhood intervention. *Exceptional Children*, 1971, *37*, 629–640.

SPITALNIK, D. M., & ROSENSTEIN, I. (Eds.). *All children grow and learn.* Philadelphia, Pa.: Temple University Developmental Disabilities Center, 1976.

SPITZ, H. H. The role of input organization in the learning and memory of mental retardates. In N. Ellis (Ed.), *International review of research in mental retardation* (Vol. 2). New York: Academic Press, 1966.

SPITZ, H. H. Consolidating facts into the schematized learning and memory system of educable retardates. In N. Ellis (Ed.), *International review of research in mental retardation* (Vol. 6). New York: Academic Press, 1973.

SPITZ, H. H. Beyond field theory in the study of mental deficiency. In N. Ellis (Ed.), *Handbook of mental deficiency, psychological theory and research* (2nd ed.). Hillsdale, N.J.: Lawrence Erlbaum Assoc., 1979.

SPRAGUE, R., & SLEATOR, E. Methylphenidate in hyperkinetic children: Differences in dose effects on learning and social behavior. *Science*, 1977, *198*, 1274–1276.

STAGER, S. F., & YOUNG, R. D. Intergroup contact and social outcomes for mainstreamed EMR adolescents. *American Journal of Mental Deficiency*, 1981, *85*, 497–503.

STANFIELD, J. Graduation: What happens to the retarded child when he grows up? *Exceptional Children*, 1973, *39*, 548–552.

STANHOPE, L., & BELL, R. Parents and families, in Kaufman, J. M., and D. P. Hallahan (Eds.), *Handbook of special education.* Englewood Cliffs, N.J.: Prentice-Hall, Inc., 1981.

STANOVICH, K. E., & STANOVICH, P. J. Speaking for themselves: A biography of writings by mentally handicapped individuals. *Mental Retardation*, 1979, *17*, 83–86.

STEDMAN, D. J., & WIEGERINK, R. Futures of service delivery systems for handicapped individuals. *DD Themes and Issues*, 1978, *12*, 1–12.

STEINZOR, L. V. School peers of visually handicapped children. *New Outlook for the Blind*, 1966, *60*, 312–314.

STEPHEN, E., & HAWKS, G. Cerebral palsy and mental subnormality. In A. Clarke & D. Clarke (Eds.), *Mental deficiency: The changing outlook* (3rd ed.). New York: The Free Press, 1974.

STEPHENS, B. Symposium: Developmental gains in the reasoning, moral judgment, and moral conduct of retarded and non-retarded persons. *American Journal of Mental Deficiency*, 1974, *79*, 113–161.

STEPHENS, T. M., & BRAUN, B. L. Measures of regular classroom teachers' attitudes toward handicapped children. *Exceptional Children*, 1980, 46, 292-294.

STERNBERG, R. J. Cognitive behavioral approaches to the training of intelligence in the retarded. *Journal of Special Education*, 1981, 15, 165-183.

STERNBERG, R. J., & DETTERMAN, D. K. *Human intelligence: Perspectives on its theory and measurement.* Norwood, N.J.: Ablex Publishing, 1979.

STERNLICHT, M. Variables affecting foster care placement of institutionalized retarded residents. *Mental Retardation*, 1978, 16, 25-28.

STEVENS, G. D., & BIRCH, J. W. A proposal for clarification of the terminology used to describe brain-injured children. *Exceptional Children*, 1957, 23, 346-349.

STEVENS, S. H. *The learning disabled child: Ways that parents can help.* Winston-Salem, N.C.: John F. Blair, 1980.

STEVENS, T. M. *Activity level: A comparison between objective and subjective measures and a classroom management approach.* Unpublished doctoral dissertation, Northwestern University, Chicago, Illinois, 1977.

STEVENSON, L. P. WISC-R analysis: Implications for diagnosis and intervention. *Journal of Learning Disabilities*, 1980, 13, 346-349.

STEWART, J. C. *Counseling parents of exceptional children.* Columbus, Ohio: Charles E. Merrill Publishing Co., 1978.

STEWART, M. A. Hyperactive children. *Scientific American*, 1970, 222, 94-99.

STEWART, W. A. Toward a history of American Negro dialect. In F. Williams (Ed.), *Language and poverty.* Chicago: Markham Publishing Co., 1970.

STODDEN, R. A., CASALE, J., & SCHWARTZ, S. E. Work evaluation and the mentally retarded: Review and recommendations. *Mental Retardation*, 1977, 15, 25-27.

STODDEN, R. A., & IANACONE, R. N. Career/vocational assessment of the special needs individual: A conceptual model. *Exceptional Children*, 1981, 47, 600-608.

STONE, N., & CHESNEY, B. Attachment behaviors in handicapped infants. *Mental Retardation*, 1978, 16, 8-12.

STORM, R. H., & WILLIS, J. H. Small-group training as an alternative to individual programs for profoundly retarded persons. *American Journal of Mental Deficiency*, 1978, 83, 283-288.

STOUFFER, S. A., & SHEA, P. D. *Your educational plans.* Chicago: Science Research Associates, 1959.

STRAIN, P. S. Increasing social play of severely retarded preschoolers with socio-dramatic activities. *Mental Retardation*, 1975, 13, 7-9.

STRAIN, P. S., COOKE, T. P., & APOLLONI, T. *Teaching exceptional children: assessing and modifying social behavior.* New York: Academic Press, 1976.

STRANG, R. Psychology of gifted children and youth. In W. Cruickshank (Ed.), *Psychology of exceptional children and youth.* Englewood Cliffs, N.J.: Prentice-Hall, 1963.

STRANG, L., SMITH, M. D., & ROGERS, C. M. Social composition, multiple reference groups, and the self concepts of academically handicapped children before and after mainstreaming. *Journal of Educational Psychology*, 1978, 70, 487-497.

STRAUSS, A. A., & LEHTINEN, L. *Psychopathology and education of the brain-injured child.* New York: Grune and Stratton, 1947.

SUMPTION, M. R., & LUECKING, E. M. *Education of the gifted.* New York: Ronald Press Co., 1960.

SUPER, D. E. Career education and the meanings of work. *Monographs on Career Education.* Washington, D.C.: U.S. Office of Education, U.S. Department of Health, Education and Welfare, June 1976.

SWAN, W. W. The handicapped children's early education program. *Exceptional Children*, 1980, 47, 12-16.

SWANSON, H. L. Response strategies and stimulus salience with learning disabled and mentally retarded children on a short-term memory task. *Journal of Learning Disabilities*, 1977, 10, 635-642.

SWARTZ, J. D., & CLELAND, C. C. *Multihandicapped mentally retarded: Training and enrichment strategies.* Austin, Tex.: The Hogg Foundation for Mental Health, University of Texas, Austin, 1973.

SWERDLIK, M. E., & WILSON, F. R. A comparison of WISC and WISC-R subtest scatter. *Journal of Learning Disabilities*, 1979, *12*, 105–107.

SWICK, K., FLAKE-HOBSON, C., & RAYMOND, G. The first step—establishing parent teacher communication in the IEP conference. *Teaching Exceptional Children*, 1980, *12*, 144–145.

SWITZKY, H. N., HAYWOOD, H. C., & ROSTATORI, A. F. Who are the severely and profoundly mentally retarded? *Education and Training of the Mentally Retarded*, 1982, *17*, 268–272.

SWITZKY, H. N., LUDWIG, L., & HAYWOOD, H. C. Exploration and play in retarded and nonretarded preschool children: Effects of object complexity and age. *American Journal of Mental Deficiency*, 1979, *83*, 637–644.

SYKES, D., DOUGLAS, V., & MORGANSTERN, G. The effect of methylphenidate (Ritalin) on sustained attention of hyperactive children. *Psychopharmacologia*, 1972, *25*, 262–274.

SYKES, D. H., DOUGLAS, V. I., WEISS, G., & MIND, K. K. Attention in hyperactive children and the effect of methylphenidate (Ritalin). *Journal of Child Psychology and Psychiatry*, 1971, *12*, 129–139.

SYKES, K. Print reading for visually handicapped children. *Education of the Visually Handicapped*, 1972, *4*, 71–75.

SZYMANSKI, L. S., & TANGUAY, P. E. (Eds.). *Emotional disorders of mentally retarded persons: Assessment, treatment, and consultation.* Baltimore: University Press, 1980.

TARJAN, G., DINGMAN, H., & MILLER, C. Statistical expectations of selected handicaps in the mentally retarded. *American Journal of Mental Deficiency*, 1960, *65*, 335–341.

TARJAN, G., & FORNESS, S. Disturbances of intellectual functioning. In G. Usdin & J. Lewis (Eds.), *Psychiatry in general practice.* New York: McGraw-Hill, 1979.

TARJAN, G., WRIGHT, S. W., EYMAN, R. K., & KEERAN, C. V. Natural history of mental retardation: Some aspects of epidemiology. *American Journal of Mental Retardation*, 1973, *77*, 369–579.

TARVER, S. G., & HALLAHAN, D. P. Attention deficits in children with learning disabilities: A review. *Journal of Learning Disabilities*, 1974, *7*, 560–569.

TAYLOR, A. M., THURLOW, M. L., & TURNURE, J. E. Vocabulary development of educable retarded children. *Exceptional Children*, 1977, *10*, 444–449.

TAYLOR, A. M., & TURNURE, J. E. Imagery and verbal elaboration with retarded children: Effects of learning and memory. In N. Ellis (Ed.), *Handbook of mental deficiency, psychological theory and research* (2nd ed.). Hillsdale, N.J.: Lawrence Erlbaum Assoc., 1979.

TAYLOR, F. D., HEWETT, F. M., ARTUSO, A. A., QUAY, H. C., SOLOWAY, M. M., & STILLWELL, R. J. A learning center plan for special education. *Focus on Exceptional Children*, 1972, *4*, 1–7.

TELFORD, C. W., & SAWREY, J. M. The *exceptional individual.* Englewood Cliffs, N.J.: Prentice-Hall, 1967.

TERMAN, L. M., & MERRILL, M. A. *Stanford-Binet Intelligence Scale: Manual for the third revision, forms L-M.* Boston: Houghton Mifflin Co., 1973.

TERMAN, L. M., & ODEN, M. H. *The gifted child grows up.* Stanford, Calif.: Stanford University Press, 1947.

TERMAN, L. M., & ODEN, M. H. *The gifted group at mid-life.* Stanford, Calif.: Stanford University Press, 1959.

TESOLOWSKI, D. G., ROSENBERG, H., & HAMMOND, M. V. Interagency cooperation through organizational advocacy. *Journal for Vocational Special Needs Education*, 1980, *3*, 12–14, 17, 23.

THIES, A. P., & UNREIN, J. Preserving education: IEP policies and procedures. *Journal of Learning Disabilities*, 1981, *14*, 335–336.

THOMAS, A., CHESS, S., & BIRCH, H. *Temperament and behavior disorders in children.* New York: New York University Press, 1969.

THOMASON, J., & ARKELL, C. Educating the severely/profoundly handicapped to the public schools: A side-by-side approach. *Exceptional Children*, 1980, *47*, 114–122.

THOMPSON, L. J. Language disabilities in men of eminence. *Journal of Learning Disabilities*, 1971, *4*, 34–35.

THRONE, J. M. Increasing intelligence through training: A future role for school and residential facilities for the retarded? *Mental Retardation*, 1977, *15*, 25–27.

THRONE, J. M. Deinstitutionalization: Too wide a swath. *Mental Retardation*, 1979, *17*, 171–176.

THURMAN, S. K., & FIORELLI, J. S. Perspectives on normalization. *Journal of Special Education*, 1979, *13*, 339–346.

TJOSSEM, T. D. *Intervention strategies for high risk infants and young children*. Baltimore: Park Press, 1976.

TORBETT, D. S. A humanistic and futurist approach to sex education for blind children. *New Outlook for the Blind*, 1974, *68*, 210–215.

TORGESEN, J. K. The role of non-specific factors in the task performance of learning disabled children: A theoretical assessment. *Journal of Learning Disabilities*, 1979, *10*, 33–40.

TORRANCE, E. P. *Guiding creative talent*. Englewood Cliffs, N.J.: Prentice-Hall, 1962.

TORRANCE, E. P. *Creativity*. Belmont, Calif.: Dimensions Publishing Co., 1969.

TORRANCE, E. P. Psychology of gifted children and youth. In W. M. Cruickshank (Ed.), *Psychology of exceptional children and youth* (4th ed.). Englewood Cliffs, N.J.: Prentice-Hall, 1980.

TORRES, S. (Ed.). *A primer on individualized educational programs for handicapped children*. Reston, Va.: Foundation for Exceptional Children, 1977.

TOWNSEND, P. W., & FLANAGAN, J. Experimental preadmission program to encourage home care for severely and profoundly retarded children. *American Journal of Mental Deficiency*, 1976, *80*, 562–569.

TRAVIS, L. E. The unspeakable feelings of people in reference to stuttering. In L. E. Travis (Ed.), *Handbook of speech pathology and audiology*, Englewood Cliffs, N.J.: Prentice-Hall, 1971.

TRIPPI, J. Special class placement and suggestibility of mentally retarded children. *American Journal of Mental Deficiency*, 1973, *78*, 220–222.

TRIPPI, J., MICHAEL, R., COLAO, A., & ALVAREZ, A. Housing discrimination toward mentally retarded persons. *Exceptional Children*, 1978, *11*, 430–433.

TRYBUS, R. J., & KARCHMER, M. A. School achievement scores of hearing impaired children: National data on achievement status and growth patterns. *American Annals of the Deaf*, 1977, *122*, 62–69.

TUCKER, G. E. The linguistic perspective. In Center for Applied Linguistics (Ed.), *Bilingual education: Current perspectives* (Vol. 2: Linguistics). Arlington, Va.: Center for Applied Linguistics, 1977.

TUCKER, J. A. Ethnic proportions in classes for the learning disabled: Issues in nonbiased assessment. *Journal of Special Education*, 1980, *14*(1), 93–105.

TURNBULL, A.P. Teaching retarded persons to rehearse through cumulative overt labeling. *American Journal of Mental Deficiency*, 1974, *79*, 331–337.

TURNBULL, A. P., & SCHULTZ, J. *Mainstreaming handicapped students: A guide for the classroom teacher*. Boston, Allyn & Bacon, 1979.

TURNBULL, A. P., & STRICKLAND, B. Parents and the educational system. In J. L. Paul (Ed.), *Understanding and working with parents of children with special needs*. New York: Holt, Rinehart and Winston, 1982.

TURNBULL, A. P., STRICKLAND, B., & BRANTLEY, J. C. *Developing and implementing individualized education programs* (2nd ed.). Columbus, Ohio: Charles E. Merrill Publishing Co., 1982.

TURNBULL, A. P., STRICKLAND, B., & GOLDSTEIN, S. Parental involvement in developing and implementing the IEP: Training professionals and parents. *Education and Training of the Mentally Retarded*, 1978, *13*, 414–423.

TURNBULL, A. P., STRICKLAND, B., & HAMMER, S. E. The individualized education program—Part I: Procedural guidelines. *Journal of Learning Disabilities*, 1978, *11*, 40–46. (a)

TURNBULL, A. P., STRICKLAND, B., & HAMMER, S. E. The individualized education program—Part 2: Translating law into practice. *Journal of Learning Disabilities*, 1978, *11*, 67–72. (b)

TURNBULL, A. P., STRICKLAND, B., & TURNBULL, H. R. Due process hearing officers: Characteristics, needs, and appointment criteria. *Exceptional Children*, 1981, *48*, 48–54.

TURNBULL, A. P., & TURNBULL, H. R. *Parents speak out*. Columbus, Ohio: Charles E. Merrill Publishing Co., 1978.

TURNBULL, A. P., & TURNBULL, H. Parent participation in the education of exceptional children (special issue). *Exceptional Education Quarterly*, 1982, *3*, 1–88.

TURNBULL, H. R. Legal precedent and the individual case: How much can be generalized from court findings? *Exceptional Education Quarterly*, 1981, *2*, 81–90.

TURNBULL, H. R., & TURNBULL, A. P. Deinstitutionalization and the law. *Mental Retardation*, 1975, *13*, 14–20.

TURNBULL, H. R., & TURNBULL, A. P. *Free appropriate public education: Law and implementation*. Denver: Love Publishing, 1978.

TURNURE, J. E. Distractibility in the mentally retarded: Negative evidence for an orienting inadequacy. *Exceptional Children*, 1970, *37*, 181–186.

TURNURE, J. E., & THURLOW, M. L. Effects of structural variations in elaboration on learning by EMR and nonretarded children. *American Journal of Mental Deficiency*, 1975, *79*, 632–639.

TURNURE, J. E., & ZIGLER, E. Outer directedness in the problem solving of normal and retarded children. *Journal of Abnormal and Social Psychology*, 1964, *69*, 427–436.

TURTON, L. J. Education of children with communication disorders. In W. M. Cruickshank & G. O. Johnson (Eds.), *Education of exceptional children and youth* (3rd ed.). Englewood Cliffs, N.J.: Prentice-Hall, 1975.

TYMCHUK, A. J. Personality and sociocultural retardation. *Exceptional Children*, 1972, *38*, 721–728.

TYMCHUK, A. J. *Parent and family therapy: An integrative approach to family intervention*. New York: Spectrum Publications, 1979.

TYMITZ, B. L. Teacher performance on IEP instructional planning tasks. *Exceptional Children*, 1981, *48*, 258–260.

ULLMAN, D. G., & KAUSCH, D. F. Early identification of developmental strengths and weaknesses in preschool children. *Exceptional Children*, 1979, *46*, 8–15.

U.S. COMMISSION ON CIVIL RIGHTS. *Mexican-American educational series, Report II, The unfinished education: Outcomes for minorities in the five southwestern states*. Washington, D.C.: U.S. Government Printing Office, 1971.

U.S. DEPARTMENT OF EDUCATION. *Individualized education programs (IEPs)*. Washington, D.C.: Office of Special Education Policy Paper, May 23, 1980.

U.S. DEPARTMENT OF EDUCATION. *Fifth annual report to Congress on the implementation of Public Law 94-142*. Washington, D.C.: U.S. Government Printing Office, 1983.

UZGIRIS, I. C., & HUNT, J. M. *Assessment in infancy*. Urbana, Ill.: University of Illinois Press, 1975.

VACC, N. A. A study of emotionally disturbed children in regular and special classes. *Exceptional Children*, 1968, *35*, 197–204.

VACC, N. Long-term effects of special class intervention on emotionally disturbed children. *Exceptional Children*, 1972, *39*, 15–22.

VANCE, H. B., & SINGER, M. G. Recategorization of the WISC-R subtest scaled scores for learning disabled children. *Journal of Learning Disabilities*, 1979, *12*, 487–491.

VANCE, H. B., WALLBROWN, F. H., & BLAHA, J. Determining WISC-R profiles for reading disabled children. *Journal of Learning Disabilities*, 1978, *11*, 657–661.

VANDERVEER, B., & SCHWEID, E. Infant assessment: Stability of mental functioning in young retarded children. *American Journal of Mental Deficiency*, 1974, *79*, 1–4.

VANE, J., WEITZMAN, J., & APPLEBAUM, A. P. Performance of negro and white children and problem and nonproblem children on the Stanford-Binet Scale. *Journal of Clinical Psychology*, 1966, *22*, 431–435.

VAN ETTEN, C., & WATSON, B. Career education materials for the learning disabled. *Journal of Learning Disabilities*, 1977, *10*, 10–16.

VAN RIPER, C. G., & IRWIN, J. V. *Voice and articulation*. Englewood Cliffs, N.J.: Prentice-Hall, 1958.

VELLUTINO, F. R. Toward an understanding of dyslexia: Psychological factors in specific reading disability. In A. L. Benton & D. Pearl (Eds.), *Dyslexia: An appraisal of current knowledge*. New York: Oxford University Press, 1978.

VELLUTINO, F. R. *Dyslexia: Theory and Research*. Cambridge, Mass.: MIT Press, 1979.

VERNON, M. Fifty years of research on the intelligence of deaf and hard-of-hearing children: A review of literature and discussion of implications. *Journal of Rehabilitation of the Deaf*, 1968, *2*, 1–12.

VERNON, M., & BROWN, D. W. A guide to psychological tests and testing procedures in the evaluation of deaf and hard-of-hearing children. *Journal of Speech and Hearing Disorders*, 1964, *29*, 414–423.

VERNON, M., & RABUSH, D. Major developments and trends in deafness. *Exceptional Children*, 1981, *48*, 254–255.

VERNON, P. E., ADAMSON, G., & VERNON, D. F. *The psychology and education of gifted children*. London: Methuen, 1977.

VITELLO, S. J. Quantitative abilities of mentally retarded children. *Education and Training of the Mentally Retarded*, 1976, *11*, 125–129.

VOCKELL, E. L., & MATTICK, P. Sex education for the mentally retarded: An analysis of problems, programs, and research. *Education and Training of the Mentally Retarded*, 1972, *7*, 129–134.

VOELLER, K. K. S., & ROTHENBERG, M. B. Psychosocial aspects of the management of seizures in children. *Pediatrics*, 1973, *51*, 1072–1082.

VON ISSER, A. Psycholinguistic abilities in children with epilepsy. *Exceptional Children*, 1977, *43*, 270–275.

WAGNER, P., & STERNLICHT, M. Retarded persons as "teachers": Retarded adolescents tutoring retarded children. *American Journal of Mental Deficiency*, 1975, *79*, 674–679.

WALKER, J. H., TOMAS, M., & RUSSELL, I. T. *Spina bifida*—and the parents. *Developmental Medicine and Child Neurology*, 1971, *13*, 462–476.

WALLACE, G., & LARSEN, S. C. *Educational assessment of learning problems: Testing for teaching*. Boston: Allyn and Bacon, 1978.

WALLBROWN, F. H., BLAHA, J., & VANCE, H. B. A reply to Miller's concerns about WISC-R profile analysis. *Journal of Learning Disabilities*, 1980, *13*, 340–345.

WALLBROWN, F. H., VANCE, H. B., & BLAHA, J. Developing remedial hypotheses from ability profiles. *Journal of Learning Disabilities*, 1979, *12*, 557–561.

WALLIN, J. E. *Education of mentally handicapped children*. New York: Harper and Row, 1955.

WALLS, R., TSENG, M., & ZARIN, H. Time and money for vocational rehabilitation of clients with mild, moderate, and severe mental retardation. *American Journal of Mental Deficiency*, 1976, *80*, 595–601.

WALLS, R. T., & WERNER, T. J. Vocational behavior checklists. *Mental Retardation*, 1977, *15*, 30–35.

WALSH, B. F., & LAMBERTS, F. Errorless discrimination and picture fading as techniques for teaching sight words to TMR students. *American Journal of Mental Deficiency*, 1979, *83*, 473–479.

WARDEN, S. A. *The leftouts*. New York: Holt, Rinehart and Winston, 1968.

WARE, M. A., & SCHWAB, L. O. The blind mother providing care for an infant. *The New Outlook for the Blind*, 1971, *65*, 169–174.

WATSON, J. B. *Behaviorism*. New York: Norton, 1924.

WEAVER, C. H., FURBEE, C., & EVERHART, R. Articulatory competency and reading readiness. *Journal of Speech and Hearing*, 1960, *3*, 174–180.

WEBB, C. E., & KINDE, S. Speech, language, and hearing of the mentally retarded. In A. Baumeister (Ed.), *Mental retardation: Appraisal, education, and rehabilitation*. Chicago: Aldine, 1967.

WEBB, R. C., & KELLER, J. R. Effects of sensorimotor training on intellectual and adaptive skills of profoundly retarded adults. *American Journal of Mental Deficiency*, 1979, *83*, 490–496.

WECHSLER, D. *The measurement and appraisal of adult intelligence*. Baltimore: Williams and Wilkins Co., 1958.

WECHSLER, D. *Manual for the Wechsler Intelligence Scale for Children* (rev. ed.). New York: Psychological Corp., 1974.

WEENER, P. On comparing learning disabled and regular classroom children. *Journal of Learning Disabilities*, 1981, *14*, 227–232.

WEHMAN, P. H. A leisure time activities curriculum for the developmentally disabled. *Education and Training of the Mentally Retarded*, 1976, *11*, 309–313.

WEHMAN, P. *Helping the mentally retarded acquire play skills*. Springfield, Ill.: Charles C. Thomas, 1977.

WEHMAN, P. Effects of different environmental conditions on leisure time activity of the severely and profoundly handicapped. *Journal of Special Education*, 1978, *12*, 183–193.

WEHMAN, P. *Competitive employment: New horizons for the severely disabled*. Baltimore: Paul Brookes Publishing, 1981.

WEHMAN, P. Toward the employability of severely handicapped children and youth. *Teaching Exceptional Children*, 1983, *15*, 220–225.

WEHMAN, P., & HILL, J. W. Competitive employment for moderately and severely handicapped individuals. *Exceptional Children*, 1981, *47*, 338–345.

WEHMAN, P., & McLAUGHLIN, P. J. Teachers' perceptions of behavior problems with severely and profoundly handicapped students. *Mental Retardation*, 1979, *17*, 20–21.

WEINER, P. S. A language-delayed child at adolescence. *Journal of Speech and Hearing Disorders*, 1974, *39*, 202–212.

WEINROTT, M. R. A training program in behavior modification for siblings of the retarded. *American Journal of Orthopsychiatry*, 1974, *44*, 362–375.

WEINTRAUB, F. J. The end of the quiet revolution: The Education for All Handicapped Children Act of 1975. *Exceptional Children*, 1977, *44*, 114–128.

WEISKOPF, P. E. Burnout among teachers of exceptional children. *Exceptional Children*, 1980, *47*, 18–23.

WEISS, D. A. *Cluttering*. Englewood Cliffs, N.J.: Prentice-Hall, 1964.

WEISS, G., MINDE, K., WERRY, J. S., DOUGLAS, V., & NEMETH, E. Studies on the hyperactive child: Five-year follow-up. *Archives of General Psychiatry*, 1971, *24*, 409–414.

WENDER, E. H. Food additives and hyperkinesis. *American Journal of Disease of Children*, 1977, *131*, 1204–1206.

WEPMAN, J. *Auditory discrimination test*. Chicago: Language Research Associates, 1958.

WERRY, J. S. The diagnosis, etiology, and treatment of hyperactivity in children. In J. Hellmuth (Ed.), *Learning disorders* (Vol. 3). Seattle: Special Child Publications, 1968.

WERRY, J. S. Psychosomatic disorders, psychogenic symptoms, and hospitalization. In H. C. Quay and J. S. Werry (Eds.), *Psychopathological disorders of childhood* (2nd ed.). New York: John Wiley & Sons, 1979.

WESTLING, D. L., & MURDEN, L. Self-help skills training: A review of operant studies. *Journal of Special Education*, 1978, *12*, 253–283.

WHALEN, C., & HENKER, B. Psychostimulants and children: A review and analysis. *Psychological Bulletin*, 1976, *83*, 1113–1130.

WHELAN, R. F. The relevance of behavior modification procedures for teachers of emotionally disturbed children. In P. Knoblock (Ed.), *Intervention approaches in educating emotionally disturbed children*. Syracuse, N.Y.: Syracuse University Press, 1966.

WHELAN, R. F., & HARING, N. G. Modification and maintenance of behavior through systematic application of consequence. *Exceptional Children*, 1966, *32*, 281–189.

WHITMAN, T. L., & SCIBAK, J. W. Behavior modification research with the severely and profoundly retarded.

In N. Ellis (Ed.), *Handbook of mental deficiency, psychological theory, and research* (2nd ed.). Hillsdale, N.J.: Lawrence Erlbaum Assoc., 1979.

WHITMORE, J. R. *Giftedness, conflict, and underachievement*. Boston: Allyn and Bacon, 1980.

WIEDERHOLT, J. L., CRONIN, M. E., & STUBBS, V. Measurement of functional competencies of the handicapped: Constructs, assessments, and recommendations. *Exceptional Education Quarterly*, 1980, *1*, 59-73.

WIEDERHOLT, J. L., HAMMILL, D. D., & BROWN, V. *The resource teacher*. Boston: Allyn and Bacon, 1978.

WIEDERHOLT, J. L., & McENTIRE, B. Educational options for handicapped adolescents. *Exceptional Education Quarterly*, 1980, *1*, 1-10.

WILDER, B. J., KING, R. L., & SCHMIDT, R. P. Comparative study of secondary epileptogenesis. *Epilepsia*, 1968, *9*, 275-289.

WILLEY, N. R., & McCANDLESS, B. R. Social stereotypes for normal, educable mentally retarded, and orthopedically handicapped children. *Journal of Special Education*, 1973, *7*, 283-288.

WILLIAMS, C. A. Is hiring the handicapped good business? *Journal of Rehabilitation*, 1972, *38*, 30-34.

WINDLE, C. Prognosis of mental subnormals. *American Journal of Mental Deficiency*, 1962, *66*, (Monograph Supplement).

WINDMILLER, M. An effective use of the public school version of the AAMD adaptive behavior scale. *Mental Retardation*, 1977, *15*, 42-45.

WING, J. Review of *The empty fortress* by B. Bettelheim. *British Journal of Psychiatry*, 1968, *114*, 788-791.

WINNICK, M. *Malnutrition and brain development*. New York: Oxford University Press, 1976.

WINTHROW, F. B. Learning technology and the hearing impaired (Special Issue). *Volta Review*, 1981, *83*, 263-358.

WINTON, P., & TURNBULL, A. Parent involvement as viewed by parents of preschool handicapped children. *Topics in Early Childhood Special Education*, 1981, *1*, 11-19.

WISCONSIN V. *Constantineau*, 39 U.S.L.W. 4128 (Jan. 19, 1971).

WISLAND, M. *Psychoeducational diagnosis of exceptional children*. Springfield, Ill.: Charles C. Thomas, 1977.

WOLF, M. M., GILES, D. K., & HALL, R. V. Experiments with token reinforcement in a remedial classroom. *Behavior Research and Therapy*, 1968, *6*, 51-64.

WOLFENSBERGER, W. Counseling parents of the retarded. In A. A. Baumeister (Ed.), *Mental retardation: Appraisal, education, and rehabilitation*. Chicago: Aldine, 1967.

WOLFENSBERGER, W. *The principle of normalization in human services*. Toronto: National Institute on Mental Retardation, 1972.

WOLFENSBERGER, W., & KURTZ, R. A. (Eds.). *Management of the family of mentally retarded: A book of readings*. Chicago: Follett Publishing, 1969.

WONG, B. The role of theory in learning disability research. Part II. A selective review of current theories of learning and reading disabilities. *Journal of Learning Disabilities*, 1979, *12*, 649-658.

WOOD, F. H., & LAKIN, K. C. (Eds.). *Punishment and aversive stimulation in special education*. Minneapolis: University of Minnesota Press, 1978.

WOOD, F. H. Affective education and social skills training: A consumer's guide. *Teaching Exceptional Children*, 1983, *15*, 212-216.

WOOD, H. *The labor supply for lower level occupations* (R & D Monograph No. 42, U.S. Department of Labor Employment and Training Administration Publication). Washington, D.C.: U.S. Government Printing Office, 1976.

WOODEN, H. Z. Deaf and hard-of-hearing children. In L. M. Dunn (Ed.), *Exceptional Children in the Schools*. New York: Holt, Rinehart and Winston, 1963.

WOODS, C. L. Social position and speaking competence of stuttering and normally fluent boys. *Journal of Speech and Hearing Research*, 1974, *17*, 740-747.

WOODS, C. L., & WILLIAMS, D. E. Speech clinicians' conceptions of boys and men who stutter. *Journal of Speech and Hearing Disorders*, 1971, *36*, 225–234.

WOODS, F. J., & CARROW, M. A. The voice-rejection status of speech defective children. *Exceptional Children*, 1959, *25*, 279–283.

WOODWARD, D. M. *Mainstreaming the learning disabled adolescent*. Rockville, Md.: Aspen Suskins Corp., 1980.

WOODWARD, W. M. Piaget's theory and the study of mental retardation. In N. Ellis (Ed.), *Handbook of mental deficiency: Psychological theory and research* (2nd ed.). Hillsdale, N.J.: Lawrence Erlbaum Assoc., 1979.

WOODY, G. E. A lowered incidence of infantile cerebral palsy. *Developmental Medical Child Neurology*, 1963, *5*, 449–450.

WOODY, R. H. *The use of electroencephalography and mental abilities test in the diagnosis of behavioral problem males*. Unpublished doctoral dissertation, Michigan State University, 1964.

WOODY, R. H. Diagnosis of behavioral problem children: Mental abilities and achievement tests. *Journal of School Psychology*, 1968, *6*, 111–116.

WOODY, R. H. *Behavioral problem children in the schools*. New York: Appleton-Century-Crofts, 1969.

WORCHEL, P., & ANDIES, J. C. The perception of obstacles by the blind. *Journal of Experimental Psychology*, 1950, *40*, 170–176.

WORCHEL, P., & DALLENBACH, K. M. Facial vision: Perception of obstacles by the deaf-blind. *American Journal of Psychology*, 1947, *60*, 502–553.

WORCHEL, P., & MAUNEY, J. The effect of practice on the perception of obstacles by the blind. *Journal of Experimental Psychology*, 1951, *60*, 746–751.

WRIGHT, B. A. *Physical disability: A psychological approach*. New York: Harper and Row, 1960.

WRIGHTSTONE, J. W., JUSTMAN, J., & MOSKOWITZ, S. *Studies of children with cardiac limitations*. New York: Board of Education of the City of New York, 1953.

WRIGHTSTONE, J. W., JUSTMAN, J., & MOSKOWITZ, S. *Studies of children with physical handicaps II: The child with orthopedic limitations*. New York: Board of Education of the City of New York, Bureau of Education Research, 1954.

WYNE, M. D., & O'CONNOR, P. D. *Exceptional children: A developmental view*. Lexington, Ky.: D. C. Heath and Co., 1979.

YAIRI, E., & WILLIAMS, D. E. Reports of parental attitudes by stuttering and by nonstuttering children. *Journal of Speech and Hearing Research*, 1971, *14*, 596–604.

YALE LAW SCHOOL. Father and mother know best: Defining the liability of physicians for inadequate genetic counseling. *Yale Law Journal*, 1978, *87*, 1488–1515.

YOSHIDA, R. *Developing assistance linkages for parents of handicapped children*. Washington, D.C.: Bureau of Education for the Handicapped, 1979.

YOSHIDA, R., FENTON, K., KAUFMAN, M., & MAXWELL, J. Parental involvement in the special education pupil planning process: The school's perspective. *Exceptional Children*, 1978, *44*, 531–534.

YOSHIDA, R., & GOTTLIEB, J. Model of parental participation in the pupil planning process. *Mental Retardation*, 1977, *15*, 17–20.

YOSHIDA, R. R., & MEYERS, C. E. Effects of labeling as EMR on teachers' expectancies for change in a student's performance. *Journal of Educational Psychology*, 1975, *67*, 521–527.

YOUNG, M. A. Onset, prevalence, and recovery from stuttering. *Journal of Speech and Hearing Research*, 1975, *40*, 49–58.

YOUNISS, J. Operational development in deaf Costa Rican subjects. *Child Development*, 1974, *45*, 212–216.

YSSELDYKE, J. E., & ALGOZZINE, B. Perspectives on assessment of learning disabled students. *Learning Disability Quarterly*, 1979, *2*, 3–12.

YSSELDYKE, J. E., ALGOZZINE, B., RICHEY, L., & GRADEN, J. Declaring students eligible for learning disability services: Why bother with the data? *Learning Disability Quarterly*, 1982, *5*, 37–44.

YSSELDYKE, J. E., ALGOZZINE, B., & THURLOW, M. (Eds.). *A naturalistic investigation of special education team meetings.* Minneapolis: University of Minnesota Institute of Research on Learning Disabilities, 1980.

YSSELDYKE, J. E., & FOSTER, G. G. Bias in teachers' observations of emotionally disturbed and learning disabled children. *Exceptional Children*, 1978, *44*, 613–615.

YSSELDYKE, J. E., & REGAN, R. R. Nondiscriminatory assessment: A formative model. *Exceptional Children*, 1980, *46*, 465–466.

ZACHOFSKY, T., REARDON, D., & O'CONNER, G. Response of institutionalized retarded adults to social pressure in small group. *American Journal of Mental Deficiency*, 1974, *79*, 10–15.

ZARFAS, D. E., & WOLF, L. C. Maternal age patterns and the incidence of Down's syndrome. *American Journal of Mental Deficiency*, 1979, *83*, 353–359.

ZASLOW, R. W., & BREGER, L. A theory and treatment of autism. In L. Breger (Ed.), *Clinical-cognitive psychology: Models and integrations.* Englewood Cliffs, N.J.: Prentice-Hall, 1969.

ZEAMAN, D., & HOUSE, B. The role of attention in retardate discrimination learning. In N. Ellis (Ed.), *Handbook of mental deficiency.* New York: McGraw-Hill, 1963.

ZEAMAN, D., & HOUSE, B. A review of attention theory. In N. Ellis (Ed.), *Handbook of mental deficiency, psychological theory, and research* (2nd ed.). Hillsdale, N.J.: Lawrence Erlbaum Assoc., 1979.

ZEIGLER, S., & HAMBLETON, D. Integration of young TMR children into a regular elementary school. *Exceptional Children*, 1976, *42*, 459–461.

ZESKIND, P. S., & RAMEY, C. T. Fetal malnutrition: An experimental study of its consequences on infant development in two caregiving environments. *Child Development*, 1978, *49*, 1155–1162.

ZETLIN, A .G., & GALLIMORE, R. A cognition skills training program for moderately retarded learners. *Education and Training of the Mentally Retarded*, 1980, *15*, 121–131.

ZETTEL, J., & BALLARD, J. A need for increased federal effort for the gifted and talented. *Exceptional Children*, 1979, *44*, 261–267.

ZIGLER, E. F. Social deprivation and rigidity in the performance of feebleminded children. *Journal of Abnormal and Social Psychology*, 1961, *62*, 413–421.

ZIGLER, E. F. Rigidity and social reinforcement effects in the performance of institutionalized and noninstitutionalized normal and retarded children. *Journal of Personality*, 1963, *31*, 258–269.

ZIGLER, E. F. Research on personality structure of the retardate. In N. Ellis (Ed.), *International review of research in mental retardation* (Vol. 1). New York: Academic Press, 1966.

ZIGLER, E. F. Developmental vs. difference theories of mental retardation and the problems of motivation. *American Journal of Mental Deficiency*, 1969, *73* 536–556.

ZIGLER, E. Social class and the socialization process. *Review of Educational Research*, 1970, *40*, 87–110.

ZIGLER, E. National crisis in mental retardation research. *American Journal of Mental Deficiency*, 1978, *83*, 1–8.

ZIGLER, E. *Early intervention: Where we've been and where we're going.* Paper presented at UCLA Department of Psychology, February 1981.

ZIGLER, E., ABELSON, W., & SEITZ, V. Motivational factors in the performance of economically disadvantaged children on the Peabody Picture Vocabulary Test. *Child Development*, 1973, *44*, 294–303.

ZIGLER, E., & BALLA, D. A. Impact of institutional experience on the behavior and development of retarded persons. *American Journal of Mental Deficiency*, 1977, *82*, 1–11.

ZIGLER, E. F., & BUTTERFIELD, E. C. Motivational aspects of changes in IQ test performance of culturally deprived nursery school children. *Child Development*, 1968, *39*, 1–14.

ZIGLER, E., & MUENCHOW, S. Mainstreaming: The proof is in the implementation. *American Psychologist*, 1979, *34*, 993–996.

ZIGLER, E., & TRICKETT, P. IQ, social competence, and evaluation of ending childhood intervention programs. *American Psychologist*, 1978, *33*, 789–798.

ZILBOORG, G., & HENRY, G. W. *A history of medical psychology.* New York: W. W. Norton, 1941.

ZINTZ, M. V. Problems of classroom adjustment of Indian children in public elementary schools in the southwest. *Science Education*, 1962, *46*, 261–269.

ZLOTNICK, P. Chrome-plated femininity. *Accent on Living*, 1974, *19*, 42–45.

ZUCKER, S. H. Sensitivity of retarded children's classroom performance to school psychological influences. *Education and Training of Mentally Retarded*, 1978, *13*, 189–194.

Author Index

AAHPER, 232
Aanes, D., 251
Abelson, W., 212
Abramowicz, H. K., 131, 132
Abroms, K. I., 130
Achenbach, T. M., 199, 201
Ackerman, P. T., 213
Adamson, G., 142
Adelman, H. S., 115, 213
Adelson, E., 151
Adelson, R., 280
Aiello, J. R., 249
Aisenberg, R. B., 176
Alberto, P. A., 129
Alcorn, D., 251
Alexander, G., 11
Algozzine, B., 117, 129, 213, 219, 226, 302, 314, 332
Allen, J. R., 138, 180, 245
Allen, K. E., 279
Allen, L., 87
Allen, R., 117, 118
Allen, R. P., 93
Allen, V. L., 102
Alley, G. R., 113, 314
Almanza, H. P., 304
Aloia, G. F., 183, 186, 306
Altman, R., 136, 188, 215
Altshuler, K. Z., 174, 208, 240
Alvarez, A., 251
Ambron, S. R., 100
Ambuel, J. P., 118
Anastasi, A., 140
Anastasiow, N. J., 227
Anderson, C. M., 246
Anderson, L. H., 315
Andies, J. C., 153
Andrews, J., 322
Angers, D., 213
Aninger, M., 251
Annesley, F. R., 316
Anthony, E. J., 164
Apgar, V., 135
Apolloni, T., 186, 188, 276
Applebaum, A. P., 209
Arena, J., 309
Arick, J., 325
Arkell, C., 319
Arthur, G., 207
Artuso, A. A., 329
Aserlind, R., 315

Asher, S. R., 277
Ashurst, D. I., 127, 204
Ater, C., 248
Avery, C. B., 72, 206, 262
Ayers, D., 281
Azarnow, J., 119

Baca, L., 303
Bagley, C. R., 210
Bagnatto, S. J., 303
Bailey, D. B., Jr., 202, 304
Bailey, K. G., 188
Baker, A. M., 211
Baker, B. L., 138
Baker, B. R., 245
Baker, L., 178
Balla, D. A., 138, 187
Ballard, J., 218
Baller, W. R., 234, 247, 248, 250
Balow, B., 204
Baltaxe, C., 210
Balthazar, E., 136
Bandura, A., 275
Bank, C. J., 138
Baran, S. J., 187
Barbee, A. H., 140, 218
Barbrack, C. R., 313
Barcher, P. R., 248
Barclay, W., 4
Baren, M., 112, 114
Barenboim, C., 177, 275
Barnard, K. E., 136
Barner, S. L., 315
Barnes, T., 309
Baroff, G. S., 126, 174, 240
Barr, E., 117
Barrish, H. H., 292
Barry, H., 264, 265
Barsch, R. H., 113, 192
Bartel, N. R., 306
Barton, S., 209
Baskiewicz, A., 191
Bass, M., 233, 251
Bateman, B. D., 172, 206, 280
Battle, J., 307
Baumeister, A. A., 123, 160, 213, 214, 216, 217, 269
Baxter, D., 251
Baxter, M. R., 144
Bayley, H. C., 192
Bayley, N., 135

Beattie, A. D., 127
Beaver, R. J., 186
Becker, L. D., 220, 308
Becker, S., 186
Becker, W. C., 225, 228
Beez, W. Z., 307
Begab, M. J., 127, 185
Bell, N., 122
Bell, R., 193
Belmont, I., 119
Belmont, J., 214, 215, 217
Belto, E. W., 156
Bender, L., 92
Bender, M., 137
Bender, N. N., 214
Benham, F. G., 174
Benitz, F., 251
Bennett, F., 134, 208
Bennett, J. W., 130
Bennett, L., 210
Bensky, J. M., 315
Benton, A. L., 212
Bentzen, F., 119, 284
Bercovici, S., 187, 250, 251
Berdiansky, H. A., 251
Bereiter, C., 224
Berger, E. H., 328
Berkovitz, I. H., 210
Berkson, G., 130, 186
Berry, M. F., 243
Berry, P., 187
Bettelheim, B., 94
Betwee, M. C., 176
Bever, T. G., 215
Bialer, I., 160
Biklen, D., 248
Bilsky, L. A., 215
Binet, A., 9-10, 28, 30
Birch, H., 50-52
Birch, H. G., 101, 104, 119, 216
Birch, J. W., 112, 141
Bird, P. J., 302
Birenbaum, A., 249
Bishop, V. E., 262
Blacher-Dixon, J., 186, 317
Black, F. W., 183
Blackman, L. S., 215
Blackman, S., 119
Blaha, J., 212, 213
Blake, P. R., 91
Blank, H. R., 150

Blank, M., 212
Blasch, B. B., 271
Blatt, B., 138
Bloch, E. L., 178
Bloom, B. S., 203
Bloom, L., 211
Bobath, B., 79
Bobath, K., 79
Boe, R. B., 188
Boersma, F., 307
Boger, R. P., 100
Boggs, J. W., 179
Bolinsky, K., 251
Booth, N. L., 188
Borders-Patterson, A., 127
Borkowski, J. G., 215
Boroskin, A., 135
Borthwick, S., 322
Bortner, M., 216
Bower, E. M., 91, 176, 209, 210
Bowman, P., 218
Boucher, C. R., 307
Bowley, A. H., 266
Boyd, B., 213
Boylan, C., 302, 328
Brackett, L., 188
Bradfield, R. H., 319
Bradley, C., 246
Braga, J. L., 143
Braginsky, B., 203
Braginsky, D., 203
Brantley, J. C., 309, 323
Braun, B. L., 318
Brazil, N., 308
Brehm, S. S., 216
Brentnall, L. C., 217
Brewer, N., 160
Bricker, D. D., 187, 211
Bricker, W. A., 187, 211, 214, 274
Brickley, M., 249
Bridge, E. M., 241
Brill, R. G., 233
Bristol, M. M., 319
Brodhead, G. D., 160
Brolin, D. E., 236, 238
Brolin, E. E., 302
Bromwich, R., 327
Bronfenbrenner, U., 104, 225
Brooks, C. R., 207, 209
Brooks, P. H., 217
Brophy, J. E., 307
Brown, A. L., 215
Brown, D. W., 208
Brown, G. B., 139
Brown, J., 319
Brown, L., 236
Brown, L. F., 321
Brown, L. J., 137
Brown, S. M., 302

Brown, V., 321
Browne, E. G., 12
Browning, P. L., 248
Brownsmith, K., 136
Bruininks, R. H., 185, 251
Bruner, J. S., 101
Bryan, J. H., 115, 119, 158, 182, 183
Bryan, T. H., 115, 119, 158, 182, 183
Bryant, J. E., 178
Bryson, C. Q., 156, 177, 211, 242
Buckhalt, J. A., 187
Budd, E., 187
Budoff, M., 217, 281, 307, 315, 325
Buell, C. E., 152, 265, 266
Buell, J. S., 279
Bullard, K., 184
Bullock, L. M., 319
Burger, A. I., 215
Burke, A. A., 127
Burr, D. B., 187
Burton, J. L., 200
Burton, S. F., 138
Burton, T. A., 136, 138, 319
Buss, A. H., 92
Butler, E. W., 126
Butterfield, E. C., 186, 214, 215, 217
Button, J. E., 136, 137
Buy, M. J., 308
Byalick, R., 327

Cain, L. F., 135, 328
Caldwell, M., 227
California Master Plan for Special
    Education, 308
Campbell, F., 128, 226
Campbell, J., 188
Campbell, K., 249
Campione, J. C., 215
Cannon, P. R., 251
Cantrell, M. L., 319
Cantrell, R. P., 319
Cantwell, D., 112, 178, 309
Caplan, P. J., 192
Capp, R. H., 134
Carey, R., 280
Carlberg, C., 316
Carlson, H., 179
Carlson, J., 187, 215, 274
Carpenter, R. L., 324
Carr, D. L., 234
Carrow, M. A., 177
Carter, D., 135
Carter, J. L., 316
Cartwright, C. A., 318
Casale, J., 248
Castiglioni, A., 8
Cattell, P., 135
Cavalier, A., 213
Cavanaugh, J. C., 215

Caveness, W. F., 176
Certo, N., 136, 137, 319
Chalfant, J. C., 321
Chan, K. S., 100, 186, 216
Chandler, J. J., 164, 220, 222
Chandler, M. J., 177, 275
Channing, A., 249
Chapman, J., 155, 307
Charles, D., 234, 247, 250
Chen, C. C., 211
Chesaldine, S., 187
Chesney, B., 136, 222
Chess, S., 50–52, 164
Childs, R. E., 126
Chinn, P. C., 327
Chittenden, G. F., 276
Cholden, L. S., 239
Christensen, P. M., 135
Ciha, T. E., 193
Clark, G. M., 236, 302
Clark, G. R., 248
Clark, L., 135
Clarke, A. D. B., 127, 134, 225
Clarke, A. M., 127, 134, 225
Clarke-Stewart, K., 328
Cleland, C. C., 137, 162, 188, 275
Clements, S. D., 112, 115, 160, 246
Cleveland, D. W., 186
Clore, G. L., 282
Coats, N., 279
Cohen, S., 221, 222, 225, 227, 302
Colao, A., 251
Cole, M., 101
Coleman, J. C., 6, 9, 13, 17
Coleman, J. M., 212
Coleman, M. C., 325
Coles, G. S., 212
Collings, G. D., 136
Connolly, J. A., 216
Connor, F. P., 136, 280, 282
Connor, G. B., 172
Conroy, J. W., 138
Consortium for Longitudinal Studies,
    225
Cook, L., 318
Cooke, G., 188
Cooke, T. P., 186, 188
Cooke, T. T., 276
Cooper, J. V., 327
Cooper, M., 225
Corah, N. L., 164
Corbett, M. C., 268
Corcoran, E. L., 251
Corman, L., 306
Cormier, H. G., 135
Cornwell, M., 235
Corrigan, D. M., 70
Cott, A., 118
Coulter, W. A., 304

Council for Exceptional Children, 235
Cowen, E. L., 174, 210
Craft, A., 232, 233
Craft, M., 232, 233
Craig, E., 122
Crandall, B. F., 134
Crandell, J. M., 150
Cratty, B. J., 160, 266, 302
Cravioto, J., 115
Crawford, J. L., 249
Crnic, K. A., 251
Croke, K., 280
Cromer, R. F., 206
Cromwell, R. L., 161
Cronbach, L. J., 200, 211
Cronin, M. E., 304
Cross, L., 219
Crow, L. D., 179
Crowther, D. L., 241
Cruickshank, W. M., 24, 115, 118, 119, 159, 175, 209, 213, 263, 280, 282, 283, 284
Cruse, D., 285
Csapo, M., 275
Cuban, L., 157
Cummings, S. T., 192
Cummins, J., 215
Cunningham, T., 248
Curry, L., 314
Curtis, K. A., 288
Curtis, W. S., 208
Cutler, R. L., 156, 290
Cutsforth, T. D., 173

Dailey, J. T., 139
Dalby, J. T., 211
Dallenbach, K. M., 153
D'Alonzo, B. J., 302, 321
Danker-Brown, P., 248, 303
Darlington, R. B., 225
Das, J. B., 215
David, H. P., 234
Davidson, P. W., 327
Davidson, T., 239, 271
Davies, S. P., 21
Davis, D. R., 134
Davis, E. E., 205
Davis, H., 72, 206
Davis, J., 248
Davis, J. E., 184
Davis, J. G., 251
Dawson, E., 215
Day, H. M., 251
Day, R. M., 251
Deacon, J., 213
Deklyen, 183
DeLicardie, E., 115
Demaine, G. C., 216

Dembinski, R. J., 325
DeMott, R. M., 139
DeMyer, M. K., 209, 211
Denhoff, E., 246
Dennerll, R. D., 241
Dennis, W., 18
Denny, M. R., 214
Deno, E., 54
Deno, S. L., 307, 313, 321, 327
Deshler, D. D., 113, 314, 321
Detterman, D. K., 203
Deutsch, C. P., 100, 101
Dever, R., 248
Dewart, M. H., 187
Diament, B., 327
Diamond, B., 319
Diamond, M., 232
Dickie, R. F., 301
Diebold, M. H., 208
Dillon, J., 139
Dingman, H., 131, 187
Diorio, M., 213
Dobbins, D. A., 160
Dobbs, J. B., 135
Dokecki, P. R., 212
Doll, E. A., 22, 23, 122, 123, 251
Dollar, S. J., 209
Douglas, J. W., 78
Douglas, V., 113, 246
Drabman, R. S., 94, 290
Drew, C. J., 160, 251
Drews, E., 218
Drillien, C., 126
Drotar, D., 191
DuBose, R. S., 208
Ducanis, A., 309, 315
Duffey, J. B., 304
Dugdale, R. L., 10
Duncan, H., 244
Duncan, P., 162
Dunlap, J. M., 162
Dunlap, W. R., 192
Dunlop, K. H., 139
Dunn, L. M., 22, 54, 299
Dunst, C. J., 313
Durant, A., 14
Durant, W., 4, 5, 14
Dvorak, R., 210
Dyer, J. L., 223, 224, 225
Dykman, R. A., 213

Ecob, K. G., 21
Edgar, E., 53, 301n.
Edge, D., 327
Edgerton, R. B., 186, 187, 189, 250, 251, 306
Edlund, C., 203
Edmondson, B., 251

Education of the Handicapped, 221, 302
Edwell, G., 113
Egger, M. L., 134
Eisenberg, L., 91, 118, 157, 178, 179
Eisenson, J., 96, 97, 207, 211, 243
Eisman, B. S. L., 215
Elashoff, J. D., 307
Elder, G. H., Jr., 245
Elliott, M., 212
Ellis, D., 160, 204
Ellis, N. R., 213, 215, 217, 251
Elzey, F. F., 135
Ender, P. B., 179
Engel, E., 130
Engelmann, S., 224, 225, 228
Englehardt, D. M., 118
Ensher, G. L., 138
Epple, W., 251
Erikson, E. H., 93, 180
Escalona, S. K., 220
Esveldt, K., 183
Evans, S., 321
Everhart, R. W., 211
Evers, W. L., 275
Eyde, D. R., 215
Eyman, R. K., 131, 138, 160, 249
Eysenck, H. J., 200

Faflak, P., 138
Fairbanks, R., 248
Falek, A., 241
Farber, B., 24, 138, 186
Farley, G. K., 210
Favell, J. E., 251
Federal Register, 110
Feingold, B. F., 112, 118, 138
Felcan, J., 183
Feldhusen, J. F., 209
Feldman, M., 327
Felsenthal, D., 138
Fenton, K. S., 314, 323
Fernald, G. M., 119, 263
Fernald, W. E., 10
Ferrara, D. M., 327
Ferretti, R., 215
Feuerstein, R., 119, 205, 215
Filler, J., 274
Finestone, S., 267
Fink, A. H., 290
Finklestein, N., 225
Fiorelli, J. S., 251, 315
Fisher, M. A., 214, 248
Fitzhugh, K., 262
Fitzhugh, L., 262
Flake-Hobson, C., 327
Flanagan, J., 136, 139
Flathouse, V., 209, 303
Flegenheimer, H., 119

Flexer, R. W., 248, 303
Floor, L., 161, 251
Flower, R. M., 98
Flynn, R. J., 251
Forbes, C. B., 325
Ford Foundation, 327
Forgnone, C., 136
Forness, S. R., 109, 112, 113, 114,
    117, 118, 119, 120, 128, 136,
    160, 183, 185, 186, 205, 211,
    215, 248, 289, 295, 299, 302,
    307, 308, 312, 313, 317, 323,
    329
Forrester, B. J., 223
Forsythe, A., 221
Foster, D., 127
Foster, G. G., 307
Foster, R., 122, 135
Fraiberg, S., 151, 206, 227, 271
Frankel, F., 136, 295
Frankenburg, W. K., 135
Franzini, L. R., 215, 274
Freedman, P. E., 186
Freeman, R. D., 67, 69, 192, 193
French, R. W., 251
Freud, S., 11
Friedenberg, W. P., 248
Friedlander, B. Z., 163
Friedman, E., 133, 234
Friedman, M., 215
Friedman, S., 222
Frierson, E. C., 190
Fristoe, M., 135, 137
Frost, J. L., 102
Frostig, M., 113, 117, 119
Furbee, C., 211
Furth, H. G., 208

Gajar, A. H., 209, 210, 308
Gallagher, J. J., 125, 131, 139, 141,
    143, 188, 189, 190, 217, 218,
    219
Gallimore, R., 137, 179
Gallistel, E., 313
Gampel, D. H., 307
Gan, J., 185
Gansneder, B. M., 302
Garber, H., 120, 185, 226
Gardner, J. M., 251
Gardner, L., 266
Garrett, J. E., 308
Garrison, M., 129, 204
Gearheart, B. R., 278
Geiger, W. L., 136
Gelb, A., 111
Gerard, E. O., 251
Gerber, M. M., 322
Gesell, A., 114–115, 135
Getman, G. H., 113

Getzels, J. W., 139
Gibbs, H., 325
Gibby, R. G., 136
Gilbert, K. A., 251
Gilbert, T. R., 270
Giles, D. K., 288
Gilham, J. E., 314, 325
Gillingham, A., 119
Ginsberg, G., 193
Giordani, B., 213
Glass, G., 119, 318
Glavin, J., 90, 316
Glicking, E. E., 318, 321
Glidden, L. M., 186, 215
Gliedman, J., 324
Goddard, H. H., 10
Goertzel, M., 219
Goertzel, V., 219
Goins, J. T., 119
Gold, M. W., 248
Goldberg, A., 172
Goldberg, B., 211
Goldberg, I., 139
Goldberg, K. F., 187
Goldberg, M. L., 158, 180
Goldstein, B., 130, 245
Goldstein, H., 24, 214, 282
Goldstein, K., 111, 119
Goldstein, M., 214
Goldstein, S., 314, 323, 325
Golin, A. K., 309, 315
Gollay, E., 249
Gonso, J., 277
Gonzales, S., 241
Good, T. L., 307
Goodenough, F. L., 207
Goodman, H., 281
Goodman, L., 266, 315
Goodstein, L. D., 97, 178
Gordon, S., 233
Gorham, W. A., 139
Gottfried, N. W., 184
Gottlieb, B. W., 184
Gottlieb, J., 183, 184, 217, 281, 306,
    307, 317, 320, 323
Gottman, J., 210, 277
Gotts, E. E., 225
Gowman, A. G., 172
Grace, H. A., 188
Graden, J., 117
Graham, S., 309, 318
Grandon, G. M., 227
Gray, R., 205
Gray, S. W., 223
Green, B. B., 251
Green, C., 161
Greenberg, S., 127
Greenspan, S., 122, 177, 222, 275, 309

Gresham, F. M., 186, 317
Grinspoon, L., 117
Grosenick, J. K., 302
Gross, J. C., 185
Grossman, H. J., 121, 132, 192
Gruen, G. E., 216
Gruenberg, E., 123
Guerin, G. R., 209
Guess, D., 136, 319
Guidubaldi, J., 314
Guilford, J. P., 200
Gunzburg, H., 122, 313
Guralnick, M. J., 221, 227, 302
Guralnick, M. V., 317, 320
Guskin, S. L., 306, 316, 317
Gussow, J. D., 101, 104
Guthrie, D., 160, 185, 205, 212, 307,
    308
Guttman, A. J., 187

Haber, A., 164
Hackman, J. D., 321
Hagberg, B., 132
Hahn, W. G., 217
Haisley, F. B., 322
Hall, R., 205, 212
Hall, R. V., 288, 290
Hallahan, D. P., 115, 158, 159, 187,
    309
Halpern, A. S., 248
Hambleton, D., 136, 319, 321
Hamilton, J. L., 217
Hammer, S. E., 309
Hammill, D. D., 112, 129, 150, 204,
    264, 265, 313, 320, 321
Hammond, M. V., 236
Hannaford, A. E., 204
Hanshaw, J. B., 133
Hapeman, L. B., 271
Haralick, J., 321
Harasymiw, W. J., 184, 318
Harber, J., 212
Harbin, G. L., 202, 304
Hardman, M. L., 160, 251
Hare, B. A., 150
Harig, P. T., 164
Haring, N. G., 137, 284, 288, 293,
    295
Harrell, R. F., 134
Harris, D. B., 207
Harris, F. R., 279
Harris, L., 213
Harris, R., 73, 193
Harrison, C. H., 193
Harrison, R. H., 281
Hart, B. M., 279
Harter, S., 186
Harth, R., 90
Harvey, S., 215